W9-AZD-896

ON THE ROAD

YOUR COMPLETE DESTINATION GUIDE
In-depth reviews, detailed listings
and insider tips

San Andrés
& Providencia
p168

Caribbean Coast
p115

Pacific Coast p249

Boyacá, Santander &
Norte de Santander p79

Medellín &
Zona Cafetera
p182

Bogotá p38

Cali &
Southwest
Colombia
p218

Amazon Basin p262

SURVIVAL GUIDE

VITAL PRACTICAL INFORMATION TO
HELP YOU HAVE A SMOOTH TRIP

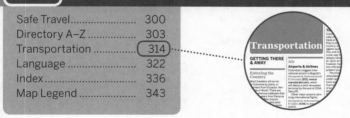

THIS EDITION WRITTEN AND RESEARCHED BY

**Kevin Raub,
Alex Egerton, Mike Power**

welcome to Colombia

Diverse Landscapes

Colombia's equatorial position affords it a diversity of landscapes matched by few countries. A slight tinkering in altitude takes you from sun-toasted Caribbean sands to coffee-strewn, emerald-green hilltops in the Zona Cafetera. Continue to climb and there's Bogotá, the bustling cradle of Colombia and the third-highest capital city in the world. Throw in another few thousand meters and you'll find snow-capped peaks, high-altitude lakes and the eerie, unique vegetation of the *páramo* (high-mountain plains). Then the bottom drops out as the Andes give way to Los Llanos, a 550,000-sq-km swath of tropical grasslands shared with Venezuela and of-

ten called the Serengeti of South America. From the towering dune desertscapes of Punta Gallinas to the Amazon jungle, Colombia's kaleidoscopic range of color and landscape has few rivals.

Outdoor Adventures

The country's varied terrain is fertile ground for outdoor adventure and Colombia dives, climbs, rafts, treks and soars with reckless abandon. The undisputed adventure capital is San Gil, but the country boasts alfresco pleasures in all corners. Two of the continent's iconic treks are here, both dramatically different: Ciudad Perdida is a five-/six-day jungle walk to the ancient ruins of the Tayrona civiliza-

File under Colombia: soaring Andean summits, unspoiled Caribbean coast, enigmatic Amazon jungle, cryptic archaeological ruins, and cobbled colonial communities. Colombia boasts all of South America's allure and more.

(left) Waterfront and village, Taganga (p146)
(below) Plaza San Pedro Claver (p123), Cartagena

tion, while the weeklong Güicán–El Cocuy trek places intrepid hikers on the highest reaches of the country's Andean mountaintops. Providencia's world-class reef spells aquatic heaven for scuba divers, while whale-watchers journey to Colombia's Pacific coast to see majestic humpbacks in the wild.

Extraordinary Culture

A wealth of ancient civilizations left behind a fascinating spread of archaeological and cultural sites throughout Colombia. The one-time Tayrona capital, Ciudad Perdida, built between the 11th and 14th centuries, is one of the continent's most mysterious and lovingly preserved ancient cities, arguably second only to Machu Picchu. Even more shrouded in mystery is San Agustín, where more than 500 life-sized, ancient, sculpted statues of enigmatic origin dot the surrounding countryside. And then there's Tierradentro, where elaborate underground tombs scooped out by an unknown people add even more mystique to Colombia's past. Mix in the influences of Spanish colonizers, African slaves, 20th-century European and Middle Eastern immigrants and large, intact indigenous groups like La Guajira Peninsula's Wayuu, and you get a rich recipe complex in both form and function. This intoxicating cocktail unravels in the food, music, architecture and lifestyles that shake and stir the melting pot of contemporary Colombia.

Colombia

Providencia
Crystal-azure waters, diving, Raizal culture (p176)

PNN Tayrona
Boulder-strewn bays, white-sand beaches (p150)

Ciudad Perdida
Scenic trek to ancient ruins (p153)

Cartagena
Beautifully preserved colonial old town (p117)

Baríchara
Cinematic colonial village, fried ants (p102)

Medellín
Stylish restaurants, legendary nightlife (p183)

San Gil
High-adrenaline capital of Colombia (p99)

PNN El Cocuy
Pristine trekking through majestic mountains (p96)

NETHERLANDS ANTILLES (NETHERLANDS)
Aruba Curaçao Bonaire

CARIBBEAN SEA

La Guajira Peninsula

VENEZUELA

PANAMA

CARACAS
VALENCIA
SAN CARLOS
GUANARE
BARQUISIMETO
TRUJILLO
BARINAS
MÉRIDA
CORO
MARACAIBO
Lago de Maracaibo
SAN CRISTÓBAL
CÚCUTA
ARAUCA
Arauca
Río Arauca
Río Casanare
Río Casanare
Casanare
YOPAL
PUERTO CARREÑO
PUERTO AYACUCHO

RIOHACHA
Guajira
VALLEDUPAR
Cesar
SANTA MARTA
Parque Nacional Natural Tayrona
Ciudad Perdida
Magdalena
Atlántico
BARRANQUILLA
CARTAGENA
Bolívar
Sucre
SINCELEJO
MONTERÍA
Córdoba
Mompox
El Banco
Río Magdalena
Río Nechí
Río Cauca
Parque Nacional Natural El Cocuy
Norte de Santander
BUCARAMANGA
Santander
Baríchara
San Gil
Boyacá
TUNJA
Villa de Leyva
Fundi...
Cundinamarca

Turbo
Capurganá
Sapzurro
Río Atrato
Antioquia
MEDELLÍN
Santa Fe de Antioquia
QUIBDÓ
Chocó
Caldas
Guachalito

PANAMA CITY
COLÓN

San Andrés (Colombia)
Providencia (Colombia)

80°W 78°W 76°W 74°W 72°W 70°W 68°W
14°N 12°N 10°N 8°N 6°N

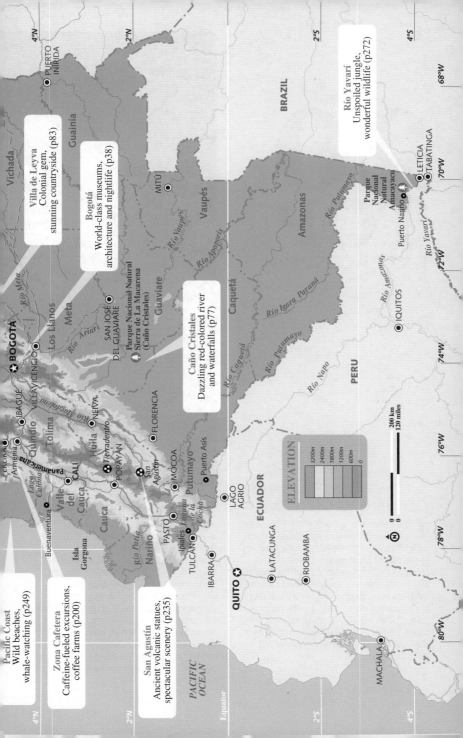

Villa de Leyva
Colonial gem, stunning countryside (p83)

Bogotá
World-class museums, architecture and nightlife (p38)

Río Yavarí
Unspoiled jungle, wonderful wildlife (p272)

Caño Cristales
Dazzling red-colored river and waterfalls (p77)

Pacific Coast
Wild beaches, whale-watching (p249)

Zona Cafetera
Caffeine-fueled excursions, coffee farms (p200)

San Agustín
Ancient volcanic statues, spectacular scenery (p235)

Parque Nacional Natural Sierra de La Macarena (Caño Cristales)

ELEVATION
3200m
2400m
1800m
1200m
600m
0

200 km
120 miles

PACIFIC OCEAN

ECUADOR
★ QUITO
IBARRA
TULCÁN
LATACUNGA
RIOBAMBA
MACHALA

PERU
IQUITOS

BRAZIL
LETICIA
TABATINGA

Parque Nacional Natural Amacayacu
Puerto Nariño

COLOMBIA
★ BOGOTÁ
VILLAVICENCIO
IBAGUÉ
Armenia
CALI
NEIVA
FLORENCIA
POPAYÁN
MOCOA
PASTO
Ipiales
Tierradentro
San Agustín
SAN JOSÉ DEL GUAVIARE
MITÚ
PUERTO INÍRIDA

Vichada
Guainía
Meta
Los Llanos
Vaupés
Amazonas
Caquetá
Guaviare
Putumayo
Nariño
Cauca
Huila
Tolima
Quindío
Valle del Cauca

Río Meta
Río Ariari
Río Vaupés
Río Apaporis
Río Putumayo
Río Igara Paraná
Río Caquetá
Río Putumayo
Río Napo
Río Amazonas
Río Yavarí
Río Caguán
Río Magdalena
Río Patía
Río Cauca
Laguna de la Cocha
Laguna Catima

Buenaventura
Isla Gorgona
Panamericana

LAGO AGRIO
Puerto Asís

Equator

4°N
2°N
2°S
4°S
2°N
4°S

80°W
78°W
76°W
74°W
72°W
70°W
68°W

20 TOP EXPERIENCES

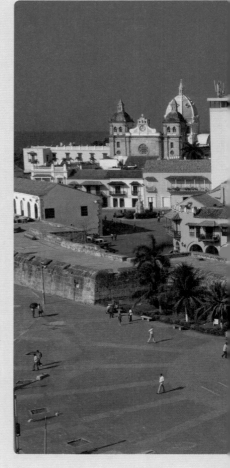

Cartagena's Old Town

1 The hands of the clock of the Puerta del Reloj wind back 400 years in an instant as visitors enter Cartagena's walled old town (p120). Strolling the streets here is to step into the pages of a novel by Gabriel García Márquez. The pastel-toned balconies overflow with bougainvillea and the streets are abuzz with food stalls around magnificent, Spanish-built churches, squares and historic sites. This is a living, working town that just happens to look a lot like it did centuries ago.

Trekking in El Cocuy

2 The weeklong Güicán–El Cocuy trek in Parque Nacional Natural (PNN) El Cocuy (p96) is one of Colombia's most coveted – and for good reason. In season (December to February), everything throughout the Sierra Nevada del Cocuy region is characterized by burnt-auburn sunrises that bounce off craggy peaks, and the *páramo* ecosystem of glacial valleys, mountain plains and high-altitude lakes. On clear days, the entire swath of Los Llanos can be seen before you from the surrounding 4650m-high peak viewpoints.
Valle de los Cojines (p98)

Coffee Fincas in the Zona Cafetera

3 Jump in a classic WWII jeep and go on a caffeine-fueled, coffee-tasting adventure. Many of Zona Cafetera's (p200) best coffee farms have thrown open their gates and embraced tourism – eager to show visitors what sets Colombian coffee apart and share a little of their hardworking culture. Strap on a basket and head into the plantation to pick your own beans before heading back to the traditional farmhouse to enjoy the end product, accompanied by the sounds of flowing rivers and birdsong. Hacienda Guayabal (p204)

Bogotá's Museo del Oro

4 There are few places in the world where one can get a sense of what finding a long-lost buried treasure might be like, but Bogotá's Museo del Oro (p48) – one of South America's most astonishing museums – will floor you with a sensation of Indiana Jones proportions. Over 55,000 pieces of spit-shined gold and other materials from all the major pre-Hispanic cultures in Colombia are exhibited thematically over three floors, culminating in the astonishing and intricate Balsa Muisca, found in 1969.

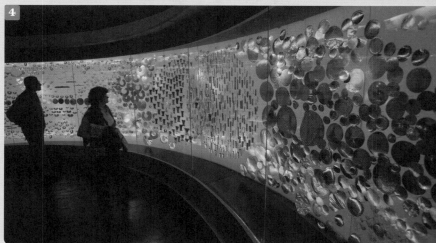

Wildlife Lodges on the Río Yavarí

5 The sheer size of the Amazon is nearly incalculable to the average person (Colombia's portion alone is bigger than Germany), so it goes without saying there are many places to bed down on a once-in-a-lifetime trip. But the protected Río Yavarí (p272), which forms the border between Brazil and Peru for over 800km, is one of the only spots to access all three Amazonian ecosystems: *terra firme* (dry), *várzea* (semi-flooded) and *igapó* (flooded). A mob of wildlife awaits.
Pygmy Marmoset

Beaches of PNN Tayrona

6 The beaches at Parque Nacional Natural (PNN) Tayrona (p150) near Santa Marta on the Caribbean coast are among the country's most beautiful. Tayrona's limpid waters heave against a backdrop of jungle that sweeps like a leafy avalanche down from the soaring Sierra Nevada de Santa Marta, the world's highest coastal mountain range. The picturesque white-sand beaches are lined with palm trees and strewn with vast boulders, some cleaved in half, looking as if a giant has had a geological temper tantrum.

Ancient Statues of San Agustín

7 Scattered throughout rolling green hills, the statues of San Agustín (p235) are a magnificent window into pre-Columbian culture and one of the most important archaeological sights on the continent. More than 500 of the monuments, carved from volcanic rock and depicting sacred animals and anthropomorphic figures, have been unearthed. Many statues are grouped together in an archaeological park, but many more are in situ, and can be explored on foot or by horseback along trails through countryside full of waterfalls, rivers and canyons.

ILDI_PAPP/ISTOCKPHOTO ©

Trek to Ciudad Perdida

8 The trip to Ciudad Perdida (p153) is a thrilling jungle walk through some of the country's most majestic tropical scenery and has become renowned as one of Colombia's best multiday hikes. Surging rivers pump faster than your pulse can keep pace as you ford them, waist deep, and balance the quiet beauty of the Sierra Nevada. Your destination – an ancient lost city 'discovered' by graverobbers and gold-digging bandits deep in the mountains, laid out in mysterious, silent terraces – is awe-inspiring and will stun even the most jaded visitor.

Whale-Watching on the Pacific Coast

9 There are few sights in nature as impressive as watching a 20-ton whale launch itself through the air against a backdrop of lush forest-covered mountains. Every year, hundreds of humpback whales make a phenomenal 8000km-plus journey from the Antarctic to give birth and raise young in Colombia's Pacific waters. These spectacular mammals come so close to shore in Parque Nacional Natural (PNN) Ensenada de Utría (p254) that you can watch them cavorting in the shallow waters from the breakfast table. To get even closer, sign up for a boat tour.

Colonial Barichara

10 There is something immediately transcendent about stepping foot in stunning Barichara (p102), arguably Colombia's most picturesque and pristinely preserved colonial village: its rust-orange rooftops, large, symmetrically cobbled streets, whitewashed walls and potted-plant balconies all contrast against a backdrop of postcard-perfect Andean green. Barichara is a slow-paced marvel – its name means 'place of relaxation' in the regional Guane dialect – and finding oneself wandering its streets in a sleepwalker's daze, blindsided by its beauty, wouldn't be unusual.

Caño Cristales

11 Held hostage by guerrillas for two decades, Caño Cristales (p77) is once again open for business. One of Colombia's most fascinating natural wonders, this gorgeous river canyon, flanked by the verdant jungle and mountainous terrain that forms the transition to the Colombian Amazon, explodes into an astonishing sea of red for a couple of months between July and November, when a unique phenomenon causes an eruption of kaleidoscopic algae along the riverbed. Trekking from one waterfall and natural swimming pool to another is a fabulous experience.

Salsa in Cali

12 Cali (p220) might not have invented salsa, but this hardworking city has taken the genre to its heart and made it its own. Going out in Cali is going out to dance salsa – it's how *caleños* express themselves. From the tiny barrio bars with oversized sound systems to the mega *salsatecas* (salsa dance clubs) of Juanchito, salsa helps to break down social barriers and unites this sprawling city. If you know how to dance, this is the place to show off your moves and, if not, there is nowhere better to learn.

KEVIN RAUB/LONELY PLANET IMAGES ©

AFP/GETTY IMAGES ©

MARGIE POLITZER/LONELY PLANET IMAGES ©

Cañon de Río Claro

13 A majestic canyon carved in marble, the Reserva Natural Cañon de Río Claro (p199) is one of Colombia's top natural destinations and it lies just 2km off the main Bogotá–Medellín highway. Through the middle of the reserve runs a crystal-clear river, which forms numerous swimming holes with impressive rock formations. Fly along a zipline over the river, explore bat-filled caves or go rafting. In the evening, as the setting sun paints the rocks in warm tones, flocks of birds spring to life and the canyon fills with the sounds of the jungle.

Carnaval de Barranquilla

14 Hold tight as the continent's second-biggest Mardi Gras celebrations (p139) kick off into a four-day, flour-dusted, rum-drenched, sun-seared orgy of masquerade, booming mobile sound systems and spontaneous outbreaks of dancing in the streets. There's salsa, merengue, bachata, reggaeton, cumbia, and dozens more styles and many live bands. Dress to distress and get involved – this isn't a party for lollygaggers or wallflowers. The Carnaval concludes on Tuesday with a symbolic burial of festival icon, Joselito Carnaval – and a brutal, hundred-block hangover for the ages.

Desierto de la Tatacoa

15 An other-worldly anomaly, the Desierto de la Tatacoa (p241) is a striking landscape of ocher and gray sands, sculptured cliffs and clumps of cactus. Surrounded by mountains, the semi-arid landscape sits in a rain shadow formed by the towering Nevado de Huila and is a silent, spiritual place with an ecosystem unlike any other in Colombia. The lack of cloud cover and light pollution make it the best place in the country for stargazing, either with the naked eye or at the local observatory.

Outdoor Adventures in San Gil

16 As far as Colombian cities go, San Gil (p99) isn't much to look at, but what it lacks in natural beauty, it more than makes up in high-octane amusements. Peddle, paddle, rappel, spelunk, bungee or paraglide – whatever your poison – San Gil is Colombia's go-to outdoor adventure playground, most famous for heart-stopping Classes IV and V rapids on the Río Suárez, but boasting a résumé far beyond whitewater rafting. Get wet, get airborne, get your courage boots on – San Gil is not for the faint of heart. Abseiling

Medellín After Dark

17 After sunset, Medellín (p183) really comes into its own, with stylish restaurants and buzzing nightlife that goes on until the early hours. El Poblado in particular is crammed with classy eateries, many of which turn into lively bars when the plates are cleared away. Later on, attention turns to the sweaty discos of Barrio Colombia, and later still to the neon-lit mega clubs of Autopista Sur. And don't leave town without visiting the elite bars of La Strada, which offer great people-watching among the city's rich and surgically enhanced.

Scuba Diving in Providencia

18 This tranquil, culturally rich archipelago (p176) is just a 1½-hour flight from the mainland coast (Cartagena). The 35km coral reef offers guaranteed views of astounding wildlife (visibility here is often a superb 40m), which include sting rays and eels, making this area a diver's paradise. The reef was declared a Marine Protected Area in 2005 – so it's no surprise that the island offers some of the best sub-aqua experiences in South America. Cayo Cangrejo (p177)

Colonial Villa de Leyva

19 Big, wide-eyed blue skies hover over the high-altitude valley that forms the backdrop of the impressive Villa de Leyva (p83). Just 165km north of Bogotá, Villa is a sleepy, colonial village, with one of the largest and prettiest main squares in the Americas, Plaza Major. Lazy Villa and its picturesque center are flush with international gastronomic pleasures, rich history, ancient churches, interesting museums and artisan shopping. You'll also find a wealth of low-key outdoor adventures in the surrounding countryside.

Hiking in PNN Los Nevados

20 The snow-covered peaks of Parque Nacional Natural (PNN) Los Nevados (p205), which soar above 5000m, have long been revered by indigenous cultures and visitors alike. Covering a total of 583 sq km, the reserve is home to some of the most breathtaking stretches of the Colombian Andes. It offers fantastic multiday trekking opportunities through diverse ecosystems ranging from humid cloud forests to rare high-altitude *páramo*. The pristine lakes and canyons of the southern portion especially attract adventurous hikers.

need to know

Currency
» Colombian peso (COP$)

Language
» Spanish (+ English in San Andrés & Providencia only)

When to Go

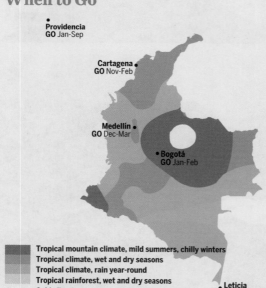

Providencia
GO Jan-Sep

Cartagena
GO Nov-Feb

Medellín
GO Dec-Mar

Bogotá
GO Jan-Feb

Leticia
GO Mar-Nov

- Tropical mountain climate, mild summers, chilly winters
- Tropical climate, wet and dry seasons
- Tropical climate, rain year-round
- Tropical rainforest, wet and dry seasons
- Cold climate

High Season
(Dec-Feb)

» Sunny skies and warmish days throughout the Andes

» Stay dry everywhere but the Amazon

» San Andrés and Providencia are gorgeous, as usual

Shoulder
(Mar-Sep)

» Bogotá, Medellín and Cali suffer a secondary rainy season in April/May

» Best whale-watching is July to October on the Pacific coast

» Cartagena shines through April, hard rains begin in May

Low Season
(Oct-Nov)

» Flash floods often wash out roads in the Andean region

» Cartagena is disproportionally wet in October

» A glimmer of hope in the Amazon: low water levels mean excellent hiking and white-sand beaches

Your Daily Budget

Budget less than
COP$ 50,000

» Dorm bed COP$15,000-30,000

» *Comida corriente* (set meal) COP$5000-7000; self-catering in supermarkets

Midrange
COP$ 50,000-175,000

» Doubles in midrange hotel COP$80,000–130,000

» Mains in decent local restaurant COP$15,000-25,000

Top End over
COP$ 175,000

» Double room in a top-end hotel from COP$160,000

» Multicourse meal with wine from COP$40,000

» One-way flight to the Caribbean coast or Amazon COP$80,000-250,000

Money

» ATMs (cajeros) are widely available in cities. Credit cards widely accepted in urban areas.

Visas

» Not required for stays up to 90 days for citizens of the Americas, Australia, New Zealand, Japan, South Africa and most of Western Europe.

Cell Phones

» Colombia uses the GSM 850/1900 network. Most cell phones will work with a local SIM card.

Transportation

» Vehicle rental is expensive. Most travelers utilize the country's extensive bus and domestic air network.

Websites

» **Lonely Planet** (www.lonelyplanet.com/Colombia) Information, forums, hotel bookings, shop.

» **Proexport Colombia** (www.colombia.travel) Official government tourism portal.

» **Colombia Reports** (www.colombiareports.com) Top English-language news source.

» **BBC News** (bbc.co.uk/news) The Beeb has excellent South American coverage.

» **Parques Nacionales Naturales de Colombia** (www.parquesnacionales.gov.co, in Spanish) Detailed parks information

Exchange Rates

Australia	A$1	COP$1896
Brazil	R$1	COP$1025
Canada	C$1	COP$1797
Eurozone	€1	COP$2330
Japan	¥100	COP$2388
New Zealand	NZ$1	COP$1459
UK	£1	COP$2815
USA	US$1	COP$1838

For current exchange rates see www.xe.com

Important Numbers

Country code	☎+57
International access code	☎00
Directory assistance	☎113
Ambulance	☎125
Fire & police	☎123

Arriving in Colombia

» **Bogotá** Aeropuerto Internacional El Dorado Bus (COP$1400); every 15 min, 6am to 9pm Taxi (COP$22,000); 30 min to the center

» **Medellín** Aeropuerto Internacional José María Córdoba Bus (COP$7000); every 15 min, 5am to 9pm Taxi (COP$54,000); 45 min to the city

» **Cartagena** Aeropuerto Internacional Rafael Núñez Bus (COP$1800), every 15 min, 6:50am to 11:45pm; taxi (COP$12,000-15,000), 15 min to old town

Is Colombia Safe?

The short answer? Yes!

Fine print: anything can happen, but compared with neighboring countries, Colombia is much safer, though the country has seen a slight lapse in security since hardline President Álvaro Uribe left office in 2010. That said, it's infinitely safer than it once was and the average traveler visiting the destinations included in this book will run little risk. A street-savvy traveler who keeps their wits about them is unlikely to be mugged, and if they are, coughing up as little as COP$50,000 should avoid any further confrontation.

The risk of kidnapping or guerrilla-inspired violence is negligible, though remote pockets of the country, especially the high mountains and the deep jungle, continue to be controlled by the Fuerzas Armadas Revolucionarias de Colombia (FARC) and/or paramilitaries. For more information on safe travel in Colombia, see p300.

if you like...

National Parks

Colombia has carved out 12% of its national territory for its Natural National Park (Parques Nacionales Naturales; PNN) system, which includes nearly 60 protected areas culling cool Caribbean waters, soaring Andean peaks, tropical grasslands and expansive Amazon jungle.

PNN Tayrona One of Colombia's most popular parks; palm-packed white-sand beaches at the foot of the Sierra Nevada de Santa Marta mountains (p150)

PNN El Cocuy A *páramo* ecosystem of glacial valleys, high-mountain plains, lakes and craggy peaks highlight Colombia's most picturesque park (p96)

PNN Sierra de La Macarena A former guerilla stronghold, now-accessible PNN Sierra de La Macarena is home to the unique Caño Cristales (p77)

Santuario de Iguaque Steeped in Muisca legend, this 67.5-sq-km national park is easily reached from Villa de Leyva and offers beautiful *páramo* landscapes (p91)

PNN El Tuparro Off the beaten path in the Los Llanos nature reserve, boasting sandy river beaches, green grasslands and some 320 species of birds, plus jaguars, tapirs and otters (p76)

Museums

A fascinating clash of indigenous culture, colonization and conflict means Colombia has a wealth of history to cull for its plethora of museums. Bogotá is Colombia's museum epicenter with more than 60 venues.

Museo del Oro One of South America's most extraordinary museums; home to the biggest collection of pre-Hispanic goldwork in the world (p48)

Museo de Antioquia Along with Bogotá's Museo Botero, this is one of Colombia's best museums to admire the portly works of native *paisa* son Fernando Botero (p183)

Museo Nacional A building in the shape of a Greek cross building designed as a prison by an English architect, Colombia's national museum is an exhaustive look at the nation's heritage (p50)

Museo de Caribe This modern museum utilizes multimedia to chronicle the culture and history of the people of Colombia's Caribbean coast (p138)

Palacio de la Inquisición Call it macabre, but the frightening instruments of torture on display at this 1776 Cartagena palace will have little trouble commanding your attention (p120)

Hiking

Colombia's varied terrain has some of the world's most stunning hikes. You'll find jungle terrain, sky-high mountains and snowcapped Andean peaks, including the abundant *páramo* (high-mountain plains), a rarity found in just a handful of countries.

PNN El Cocuy Commanding peaks, mountain lakes, icy glaciers and views to Venezuela highlight this weeklong, high-altitude jaunt (p96)

Ciudad Perdida A chance to make a multiday jungle trek across surging rivers to one of the largest pre-Columbian cities discovered in the Americas (p153)

PNN Los Nevados Crest over 5000m on this one-day trek to the snowline of the imposing Nevado del Ruiz volcano (p205)

Valle de Cocora Gawk at giant wax palms (Colombia's national tree) strewn about verdant valleys and misty green hills through the heart of coffee country on this half-day hike (p216)

Tierradentro Take in all of Tierradentro's pre-Columbian underground tombs on this four- to six-hour hike surrounded by gorgeous surrounding hillsides (p239)

» Playa Blanca, Isla de Baru (p134)

Memorable Food

Colombian gastronomy won't satiate foodies like Peru's famed cuisine, Brazil's multicultural fare or Argentina's gaucho grill culture, but there is amazingly fresh seafood, succulent steaks and no shortage of unique culinary curiosities.

Rafael Peruvian heaven; widely regarded by chefs as Bogotá's finest (p60)

Punta Gallinas No restaurants, but how does fresh lobster grilled by the Wayuu people sound? (p159)

Color de Hormiga Santander is famous for its crunchy, earthy, salty, *hormiga culonas* (fat-bottomed ants). Try them here where they are made more palatable by a gourmet chef (p105)

Central Cevicheria This Bogotá hipster hangout serves some of the most innovative ceviche in Colombia (p60)

Asadero de Cuyes Pinzón Throw yourself mouth-first into Pasto culture by dining on the local delicacy: grilled guinea pig (p244)

Mercagán Some say it's the nation's best steak (p107)

La Cevicheria This is Cartagena's tiny, hidden gem serving world-renowned ceviche and seafood (p129)

Beaches

Colombia is more famous for mountains than beaches, but seeing that the country is blessed with both Caribbean and Pacific coasts, sun-toasted stretches of floury sands are never more than an overnight bus or quick flight away.

Playa Taroa Slide down a towering sand dune onto Colombia's most beautiful – and emptiest – beach in Punta Gallinas (p159)

Capurganá & Sapzurro La Miel, on the Panamanian side, and Colombia's Playa Soledad, are both palm-strewn patches of paradise straddling the border (p164)

Playa Morromico Flanked by waterfalls crashing down from jungle-covered mountains, this secluded private beach is one of Chocó's most romantic destinations (p256)

PNN Tayrona Preserved and very popular, this national park has serene bays and cerulean waters (p150)

Playa Guachalito This is one of the Pacific coast's most idyllic beaches, flush with orchids, heliconias and wild jungle encroaching its gray sands (p256)

Playa Blanca A novel, 3015m-high white-sand lakeside beach deep in the Andes (p84)

Wildlife

Pristine Amazon jungle accounts for more than a third of Colombia's total area – it's the best spot to observe wildlife in its natural habitat. But along with the jungle, there are many interesting opportunities throughout Colombia, one of the world's most biodiverse nations.

Río Yavarí Technically straddling Brazil and Peru, the lodges along this Amazon tributary, reached from Leticia, are surrounded by abundant fauna (p272)

PNN Amacayacu Home to 500 bird species and 150 mammals – including a brilliant outpost of rehabilitating monkeys – deep in the Amazon rainforest (p270)

PNN Ensenada de Utría This is whale-watching central on Colombia's Pacific coast, a preserved inlet teeming with humpbacks from July to October (p254)

Reserva Ecológica Río Blanco You'll find 13 of Colombia's endemic bird species in this undeveloped bird-watchers' paradise near Manizales – and 362 other species to boot (p203)

Santuario de Flora y Fauna Los Flamencos A vibrant colony of pink flamingos descends on this 700-hectare nature reserve in La Guajira Peninsula – some 10,000 in the wet season (p157)

month by month

January

Colombia's equatorial position means temperatures fluctuate by altitude, not season, making almost anytime a good time to visit. But January could be considered ideal for dissipating holiday crowds coupled with lingering festivals and parties.

⭐ Carnaval de Blancos y Negros

Pasto's uproarious post-Christmas bash (p245), originating during slavery times, sees drunken crowds throwing grease, talcum powder, flour and chalk on each other until everyone is coughing up powdery mucus and doused in gunk. Leave the *haute couture* at the hotel.

⭐ Feria de Manizales

The highlight of Manizales' annual festival (p201) is the bullfighting – the feria (fair) attracts some of the world's best bullfighters and Colombia's feistiest bulls. There's also the usual assortment of parades and craft fairs and, of course, a beauty pageant.

February

The Andean region remains pleasant and Cartagena almost drought-stricken, making February a great time to beach hop along the Caribbean coast. With kids back in school and domestic merrymakers returned to the grind, Colombia is *tranquilo*.

⭐ Fiesta de Nuestra Señora de la Candelaria

A solemn procession is held in Cartagena (p126) to honor the town's patron saint at the Convento de la Popa, during which the faithful carry lit candles. Celebrations begin nine days earlier, the so-called Novenas, when pilgrims flock to the convent.

⭐ Carnaval de Barranquilla

Held 40 days before Easter, Barranquilla's Carnaval (p139) is the continent's second-biggest after Rio de Janeiro. A spectacular four-day bash of drinking, dancing, parades, costumes and Colombian music concludes on Fat Tuesday with the symbolic burial of 'festival icon' Joselito Carnaval.

March

As with most Catholic countries, Easter is big business. Whether it falls in March or April, the country is seriously tuned in. Expect crowds, high prices and weather taking a turn for the worse.

⭐ Semana Santa in Popayán

The most famous Semana Santa (Holy Week) celebration is held in Popayán (p231), with nighttime processions on Maundy Thursday and Good Friday. Thousands of the faithful and tourists take part in this religious ceremony and the accompanying festival of religious music.

⭐ Semana Santa in Mompox

Colombia's second-most important Semana Santa celebration is in the sleepy river town of Mompox (p137), near the Caribbean coast.

⭐ Festival Iberoamericano de Teatro

Held during Semana Santa, this biennial festival of Latin American theater

(Above) Carnaval de Barranquilla (p139)
(Below) Catagena's Reinado Nacional de Belleza (p126)

(p53) takes place every even-numbered year, and ends with a fireworks spectacular in Bogotá's football stadium. Check out www. festivaldeteatro.com.co for more information.

June

After a respite in April and May, storm clouds once again loom. Bogotá is at its driest, though, and humpback whales begin arriving on the Pacific coast in earnest. Prices rise for summer school vacations.

⊙ A Whalin' Good Time

June marks the beginning of the spectacular whale-watching season on Colombia's Pacific coast (p254), when hundreds of humpback whales arrive from Antarctica with up to 8500km in their rearview mirrors to give birth and raise their young in Colombia's tropical waters.

August

Relatively mild August can be drizzly, but excellent festivals more than make up for impending rains. Bogotá, Cali and Medellín all soak up the end-of-summer atmosphere with a bonanza of music and culture.

☆ Festival de Música del Pacífico Petronio Álvarez

This Cali festival (p221) celebrates the music of the Pacific coast, heavily influenced by African rhythms introduced to Colombia by the slaves that originally populated the region. For more information, see www.festivalpetronioalvarez.com.

Feria de las Flores

This weeklong feria is Medellín's most spectacular event. The highlight is the Desfile de Silleteros (p189), when up to 400 *campesinos* (peasants) come down from the mountains and parade along the streets carrying flowers on their backs.

September

Showers berate most of the country, but Amazonian river levels are low, making it an excellent time for wildlife viewing, hiking or just kicking back on a sandy river beach.

Festival Mundial de Salsa

Don't miss this classic Cali festival (p221). It's not really a worldwide festival, but you'll still see some amazing dancers, and there are often free salsa shows at the outdoor amphitheater, Teatro al Aire Libre Los Cristales.

Eat Your Heart Out

Every year top chefs from different countries are invited to cook up a storm in tiny colonial Popayán for the gastro-fueled Congreso Nacional Gastronómico (p231). Visit www.gastronomicopopayan.org to see what's on the menu.

Get Jazzed!

Jazz aficionados get psyched for the annual Festival Internacional Medellín de Jazz y Músicas del Mundo (p189), often featuring prominent musicians from

North America, Europe and Cuba. Concerts usually take place at Teatro Universidad and El Tesoro shopping mall, some of which are free.

Festival Internacional de Teatro

Held since 1968, Manizales' theater festival (p201) is Colombia's second-most important theater festival (after Bogotá's Festival Iberoamericano de Teatro). It features free shows in Plaza de Bolívar.

October

On average, this is one of Colombia's two rainiest months (the other is November). Bogotá, Cali, Medellín and Cartagena are all at the mercy of the weather.

Festival de Cine de Bogotá

With a 20-year history, the city's film festival (p53) attracts films from all around the world, including a usually strong Latin American selection. Check out www.bogocine.com for info and year-by-year selections.

Rock al Parque

Three days of rock/metal/pop/funk/reggae bands rocking out at Parque Simón Bolívar in Bogotá (p53). It's free and swarming with fans – some 400,000 attended in 2004 for the fest's 10th anniversary. Did we mention it's *free*?

November

Like October, November is wet, wet, wet throughout Colombia. Your best

refuge from the deluge is in Bogotá, but you'll still be breaking out umbrellas on a regular basis.

Reinado Nacional de Belleza

Also known as the Carnaval de Cartagena or Fiestas del 11 de Noviembre, this beauty pageant and festival (p126), Cartagena's most important annual bash, celebrates the city's independence day and the crowning of Miss Colombia with street dancing, music and fancy-dress parades.

December

The rains begin to recede and the country is awash instead in holiday festivals, spectacular light displays and spur-of-the-moment partying. Expect crowds and cries of joy throughout Colombia.

Let There Be Light!

Every Christmas, Colombian cities compete in the annual Alumbrado Navideño (Christmas Lighting) to see who can put up the most elaborate lighting display along their respective rivers – Medellín's (p189) colorful display often wins and is well worth a detour.

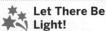

Feria de Cali

Commerce pretty much grinds to a halt during Cali's annual bash (p221). Instead, parties spill into the streets, food and beer pavilions magically appear, spontaneous dancing in the streets commences, and the Río Cali is illuminated in a spectacular display of lights.

itineraries

Whether you've got six days or 60, these itineraries provide a starting point for the trip of a lifetime. Want more inspiration? Head online to lonelyplanet. com/thorntree to chat with other travelers.

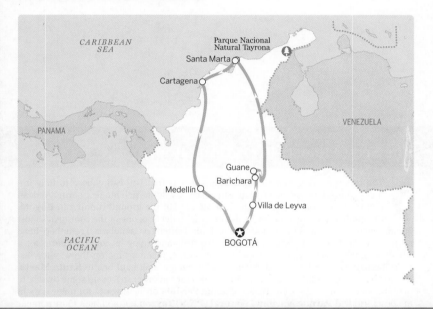

Two Weeks
Bogotá to Bogotá

> Welcome to Colombia! Cosmopolitan cities, looming mountains, colonial villages, verdant jungles and Caribbean beaches await. Pulling off this itinerary requires 5th gear and copious amounts of caffeine – good thing you're in the land of coffee! Take a day or two in **Bogotá**, admiring La Candelaria (its colonial center), the best of myriad museums and world-class food and nightlife. Shake off the hangover a few hours north in the calming colonial villages of **Villa de Leyva** and **Barichara**, both miraculously preserved and picturesque. Take a day to walk the historic El Camino Real to **Guane**. Grab the long bus ride from San Gil to Santa Marta, from where you can access **Parque Nacional Natural (PNN) Tayrona** – linger on the park's otherworldly beaches for a few days. Continue southwest along the Caribbean coast to **Cartagena**, Colombia's crown jewel – a postcard-perfect old city chock full of colonial romance. It's another long bus (or consider flying) to **Medellín**, where again you're faced with Colombia on overdrive: culture, cuisine and Club Colombia, *paisa*-style. Raise a toast to El Dorado and exit via Bogotá, bowled-over by Colombia's hospitality.

The See-(Almost)-Everything Route

The beauty of Colombia's diverse landscapes is that you can choose to fully immerse yourself in just one (Caribbean beaches, wildlife-rich jungle, soaring Andean highlands) or you can go for the Full Monty! Hit the ground running in **Bogotá**, Colombia's Gotham, and don't miss the Museo del Oro, one of the continent's most fascinating museums, and the atmospheric colonial center, La Candelaria. From there head north to **Villa de Leyva**. Explore its cobbled streets and enjoy its colonial charm for a day or two, then visit **San Gil** for hiking and rafting, making time on the way for historic **Barichara**. Pass through Bucaramanga to catch a long-haul bus to **Santa Marta**. It's worth moving quicker than normal up to this point in order to free up some time here to do the sweaty, five- to six-day trek to **Ciudad Perdida** or blissing-out for a few days in the beach-riddled **Parque Nacional Natural (PNN) Tayrona**, Colombia's most popular national park. Next stop, **Cartagena** – you'll need a few days to fully indulge this exquisite colonial city.

From the Caribbean, take a bus or fly south to **Medellín**, and on to the Zona Cafetera and enjoy some time in the nature reserves around **Manizales** and the **Valle de Cocora** outside Salento. Want to take a piece of Colombia home with you? Visit a coffee *finca* (farm) near Armenia and stock up on single-origin coffee beans direct from the source.

Further south is **Cali** and the city's sweaty, hopping salsa joints. Travel down through **Popayán** to the archaeological ruins at **Tierradentro** and **San Agustín**, the two most important pre-Columbian sites in Colombia after Ciudad Perdida. Return to Bogotá via the startling **Desierto de la Tatacoa** and catch a flight to **Leticia**, where a wildly different Colombia exists. Spend a few days exploring the three Amazonian ecosystems: *terra firme* (dry), *várzea* (semiflooded) and *igapó* (flooded) along the **Río Yavarí**, the best spot in Amazonia to observe wildlife undisturbed in its natural habitat. Fly back to Bogotá, or, from Tabatinga across the Brazilian border from Leticia, head deeper into the Amazon via adventurous river-boat rides to Manaus (Brazil) or Iquitos (Peru).

» (above) Las Bóvedas (p124),
  Cartagena
» (left) Parque El Gallineral (p100),
  San Gil

One Month
A Tale of Two Coasts

This is the ultimate beach junkie journey. Colombia's contrasting coasts offer a little bit of everything to lovers of the sea, from translucent Caribbean waters to Pacific black-sand beaches – both against a backdrop of Crayola-green jungle. Start out east of Santa Marta at **Cabo de la Vela** on La Guajira Peninsula, a striking landscape where the desert meets the sea at the top of the continent. Don't skip South America's northernmost tip, **Punta Gallinas**, where you can sleep in a hammock and feast on local lobster near towering dunes somersaulting into remote beaches.

Heading southwest, make your way to **Parque Nacional Natural (PNN) Tayrona**, very popular among aspiring beach bums, and consider stopping a day or two near wonderful Palomino on the way, where you'll find the paradisiacal **Reserva Natural El Matuy**, a small bird sanctuary and beach offering way more palm trees than people.

Head west to explore **Cartagena**, then make the arduous journey southwest to tiny **Capurganá** and **Sapzurro**, two cute beachside neighbors set right on the border with Panama. La Miel, easily reached on foot across the border in Panama (bring your ID), offers idyllic sands.

From here fly via Medellín to Bahía Solano on the **Pacific coast**, great during whale-watching season, and spend a few days on the spectacular rainy, gray beaches along this coastline, sandwiched between jungle and sea. There are fine, midrange ecolodges where you can surf and go diving near **Bahía Solano**, **El Valle** and **Guachalito**. A 45-minute boat ride from **Nuquí** brings you to multi-hued **Jurubidá**, where it's a quick boat-hop to **Morromico** – couples might consider losing themselves on this ecoresort's magnificent and romantic beach.

Suitably pampered, head back to Nuquí and travel via overnight cargo boat to Buenaventura, the jumping-off point for **Isla Malpelo**, where advanced divers can mingle with huge schools of sharks. It's a minimum eight-day live-aboard dive cruise (reservations essential). For a less challenging taste of the Pacific coast's diving, head on to **Guapi** and catch a weekend dive cruise to **Isla Gorgona**, and visit the ruins of the island's former penal colony. Once you return to Buenaventura, catch a bus back to mainstream Colombia via the Buenaventura-Cali highway.

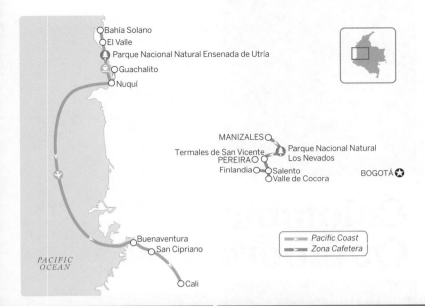

Two Weeks
Zona Cafetera

In this arabica-fueled region, hearts are pumped by caffeine as much as blood. It's serious business. Visiting coffee farms will keep you hyped for exploring the region's highlights, starting with the nature parks around **Manizales** – Los Yarumos, Recinto del Pensamiento and Reserva Ecológica Río Blanco, the latter a bird-watching favorite. Indulge in the coffee tour just outside town at Hacienda Venecia, with great views and an excellent overview of all things cafe. Spend a day or two hiking among snow-covered volcanic peaks in **Parque Nacional Natural (PNN) Los Nevados** and sleep in the *páramo* (high-mountain plains) at the 4180m-high cabins at El Cisne, accessed from Las Brisas. Return to Manizales and head toward Pereira, where you can arrange an aching-muscle treatment at **Termales de San Vicente**, 36km east of town. Next stop: coffee-crazy **Salento** south of Pereira, full of quaint charm and typical *bahareque* (adobe and reed) architecture. Detour just east to the numerous small production *fincas* (farms) around slow-paced **Finlandia** – and the expansive views from its *mirador* (lookout) – before toasting your tour in the impressive **Valle de Cocora**, one of Colombia's most beautiful half-day hikes.

10 Days
Pacific Coast

Long off-limits due to Colombia's civil war, the exotic Pacific coast has reopened for tourism but remains undervisited. Colombia's ultimate off-the-beaten-path destination boasts tropical jungle, diving, whale-watching, world-class sportfishing and black-sand beaches. It isn't cheap – all transportation is by small plane and boat – but it's worth it. Start in **Bahía Solano**. Numerous nearby beach resorts can organize activities, including jungle walks. From Bahía Solano, head south to **El Valle**. During turtle season you can spot turtles laying eggs on the beach, and visit a biological research station. Hike south to the northern end of **Parque Nacional Natural Ensenada de Utría** and take a boat across to the national park's visitor center, where you can spend the night. During whale season you can watch playful whales as they enter the narrow bay just offshore. Take a boat to **Nuquí** and visit nearby **Guachalito**, a beautiful beach with well-tended tropical gardens. From Nuquí, try your luck with irregular overnight cargo boats heading south to **Buenaventura**; or catch a quick flight. Return to Cali via **San Cipriano**, deep in the tropical forest and only accessible by a unique moto-propelled rail cart.

Colombia Outdoors

Best Treks

Ciudad Perdida The most popular trek: a five-/six-day, 44km-long walk through jungle mountains to the remarkably preserved ruins of the lost city of Tayrona

Parque Nacional Natural (PNN) El Cocuy The best long trek: this weeklong Güicán-El Cocuy trek has it all: soaring mountaintops, miraculous sunrises, glacial lakes, *páramo* (high-mountain plains) landscapes – and views your camera will never do justice to

Valle de Cocora The best half-day trek: the towering wax palm (the world's largest palm, and Colombia's national tree), juts through misty green hills on this half-day hike in caffeine country

Best Diving

San Andrés & Providencia A 35km reef through warm Caribbean waters is home to spectacular colored corals, large pelagic fish, portly eels and long-lost shipwrecks

Best White-Water Rafting

Río Suárez Near San Gil, Classes IV and V rapids await on the country's wildest river

Exploring the dramatic variety of landscapes is a highlight for visitors – from the *páramo* (high-mountain plains) to the jungles of the Pacific coast, the stunning green lushness of the Zona Cafetera to the dry, Hades-like heat of the Caribbean coast, both the outdoor dabbler and the hard-core trekking guru will find something to fascinate them.

Strap yourself in. There's high-mountain trekking and mountaineering in Parque Nacional Natural (PNN) El Cocuy and Parque Nacional Natural (PNN) Los Nevados, white-water rafting and paragliding in San Gil, kitesurfing and windsurfing at Lago Calima and the Caribbean coast, world-class scuba diving near San Andrés, Capurganá and Islas Malpelo and Gorgona, whale-watching up and down the Pacific coast and bird-watching pretty much everywhere.

For decades the countryside held great danger, and Colombians were trapped in their cities. No longer. To encourage adventure tourism, the Colombian government has deployed the army to many of the most popular outdoor spots to make them safe for foreign tourists. Now that relative calm has come to Colombia, locals and foreigners alike are taking advantage of the chance to get out and see what this amazing country has to offer.

Hiking & Trekking

Colombia has some of South America's best hiking opportunities. The casual hiker looking for good one-day walks also has many options to choose from and most, like Guane or Valle de Cocora, can be done independently without a guide. On guided day hikes, prices are between around COP$30,000 to COP$50,000, increasing to COP$80,000 to COP$110,000 per day for more significant multiday hikes depending on difficulty. The best times of year for a walk include February, on the coast, and December to February in the mountains.

Where to Go

There are some short walks near Manizales, such as in Recinto del Pensamiento, Río Blanco, Los Yarumos and Guane, which are also worth the trip. Those wanting a taste of the jungle have several options on the Pacific coast. Some main areas:

Ciudad Perdida (p153) On the Caribbean coast; this long trek can only be reached by a sweaty, five-/six-day hike through the jungle and across waist-high rivers. At the end you arrive at the long-forgotten ruins of the Tayrona civilization.

Güicán-El Cocuy (p94) A high-mountain long-haul trek that rarely drops below 4000m and offers some of the country's most miraculous landscapes along the way. Those with the lungs for it should not miss it.

Valle de Cocora (p216) Near Salento; the country's best half-day hike takes you up into the national park amid wax palms.

El Valle to Lachunga (p253) A recommended walk at the northern end of the Parque Nacional Natural (PNN) Ensenada de Utría on the Pacific coast. You can visit and stay the night in the national park.

Capurganá (p164) Walk across the frontier to visit beautiful La Miel, a beach just north of the Panamanian border.

Tierradentro (p239) A spectacular one-day walk in the south that traverses a triangular ridgeline and visits all of the nearby tombs.

Volcán Puracé (p235) Near Popayán; can be summited in one day (weather permitting).

Farallones de Cali (p227) Near Cali; offers several day-long, and longer, walks.

Diving & Snorkeling

Colombia's Caribbean coast offers scuba diving at budget prices. Two-tank dives along the coast average between COP$150,000 and COP$225,000.

Where to Go

The Caribbean coast has real jewels for diving, but the Pacific coast offers a completely different diving experience. There is slightly less visibility, but the quantity and size of the marine life is jaw-dropping.

San Andrés (p172) **& Providencia** (p177) Offer classic Caribbean diving, with excellent visibility, fine coral reefs and a variety of marine life. There are even two sunken ships you can visit.

Taganga (p146) On the Caribbean coast itself, offers some of the cheapest diving courses on the planet. Here you can get your PADI or NAUI certification from around COP$580,000 for a four-day course. (The diving itself is second-rate, but at these prices, it's hard to complain.)

Cartagena (p117) Boasts good diving nearby.

Islas de Rosario (p134) Is famous for its diving, although warm-water currents have damaged the reef somewhat, and the diving is no longer as good as it once was.

Capurganá & Sapzurro (p164) These small Pacific coast towns are just minutes from the Panamanian border. Once too dangerous to visit, they are now slowly attracting adventurous travelers seeking the best beaches and reefs. The tricky bit is getting here – you'll either need to endure a long boat journey from Turbo, or fly from Medellín.

Isla Malpelo (p261) A small Pacific island 500km west of the continent that's home to schools of more than a thousand sharks. It can only be reached by joining a minimum eight-day live-aboard dive cruise from Buenaventura on Colombia's Pacific coast or Puerto David, Panama.

Isla Gorgona (p260) A larger island near the Pacific coast, also offers fine diving, and in whale-watching season you can observe whales from below the waves.

Playa Huína (p252) There are also some diving opportunities near Bahía Solano, where a warship that survived Pearl Harbor has been sunk to create an artificial reef.

Hyperbaric Chambers

There are numerous hyperbaric chambers, should you find yourself with a case of decompression sickness (ie 'the bends').

Base Naval Bahía Málaga Hospital (☎2 246 0624, emergency 2 246 0872) The only one on the Pacific coast is located near Buenaventura.

Hospital Departamental Amor de Patria (☎8 512 0753) On San Andrés.

Hospital Naval de Cartagena (☎5 665 3987) In Cartagena, on the Caribbean coast.

BIRD-WATCHING IN COLOMBIA

Clocking in at 1876 bird species (so far recorded; new species are still being discovered), Colombia is the world's number one country in bird diversity and easily holds its own against Peru and Brazil in endemic species. The Andean mountains are full of hummingbirds (more than 160 species), the Amazonian jungle is full of toucans, parrots and macaws, and Parque Nacional Natural (PNN) Puracé, near Popayán, is home to condors, which the wardens will tempt down with food so you can see them up close. The Pacific coast is flooded with swarms of pelicans, herons and other water birds.

Some 70% of the country's birds live in the Andean cloud forest, one of the world's most endangered ecosystems. The single best bird-watching spot in the country is Montezuma Peak, located inside Parque Nacional Natural (PNN) Tatamá in the Cordillera Occidental between the departments of Chocó, Valle del Cauca and Risaralda. Here you'll find the best mix of Chocó and Andean birds in the country – packed with endemics, regional specialties and mega-rare birds. Other great bets include Río Blanco (p203) near Manizales, and Km18 (p221) near Cali. The Amazon basin near Leticia (p263) is also an excellent spot for jungle birds; as is the Chocó (p251). Colombia also features the western third of the Los Llanos area (p76), shared by Venezuela, a fine spot to see the birds this region attracts.

For a countrywide overview of the Important Bird Areas (IBAs), an invaluable resource is **Humboldt Institute** (http://aicas.humboldt.org.co), which breaks the country down by department. The **Red Nacional de Observadores de Aves** (Colombian Bird Watchers Network, RNOA; www.rnoa.org) is also a good place to start. For Andean bird-watching, you may be able to find a guide through one of the many local operators (see www.mapalina.com).

Finding bird-watching guides in Colombia can be difficult. In many remote areas, locals can take you where they know birds are, but it'll be up to you to find them. One reputable bird-watching tour company is **Colombia Birding** (www.colombiabirding.com), run by a bilingual Colombian whose network of local guides can show you around many of the country's most popular bird-watching areas. It charges US$100 per day plus expenses. Its website has information on birds by region.

Robin Restall's *Birds of Northern South America* (2007) is the essential bird-watcher's field guide to Colombian birds, with full-color plates for every bird you're likely to see here. *A Guide to the Birds of Colombia* (1986), by Steven L Hilty and William L Brown, is a must for Amazon-bird viewers.

For comprehensive internet information on bird-watching in Colombia, see www.proaves.org as well as Colombia's official tourism portal, www.colombia.travel, which does a surprisingly good job with bird-watching.

White-Water Rafting, Canoeing & Kayaking

Rafting trips average between COP$30,000 and COP$125,000 depending on length and adrenaline-level.

Canoeing and kayaking aren't especially popular in Colombia, but opportunities are growing. You can rent kayaks in both San Gil and San Agustín. You can also rent sea kayaks in Ladrilleros (p258) for a paddle around Bahía Malága. **Bicivan** (www.bicivan.com.co; ☏312 296 1584) offers adventure kayaking trips in the Sabaletas and Anchicaya rivers as well as multiday trips in Bahía Malága. For some high-altitude paddling, you can rent kayaks in Guatapé (p196) to explore its extensive artificial lake.

Where to Go

Some options for white-water rafting:

San Gil (p100) This is the white-water rafting capital. The rapids are spectacular Classes IV and V; you're in for some serious thrills (and spills).

San Agustín (p237) A close second to San Gil. Here you can go white-water rafting on the Río Magdalena, one of Colombia's most important rivers. There are easy Classes II and III trips, and longer, more difficult trips for the experienced rafter.

Río Claro (p199) Offers a quiet paddle through the jungle, roughly halfway between Medellín and

Bogotá, and smooth Class I trips along the nearby river. It's a fine spot to admire the flora and fauna instead of obsessing about falling out of the raft.

Rock Climbing & Abseiling

The birthplace of Colombian rock climbing is Suesca (p74), a quick day trip from Bogotá, where you'll find 4km-long sandstone Guadalupe formations and more than 400 climbing routes, both traditional and bolted. Suesca-based Dealturas offers five-day climbing courses for COP$500,000; or day climbing (including equipment) for COP$120,000. In Medellín, Psiconautica (p188) runs a rock-climbing/abseiling/canyoning school as well.

If you want to test your skills before committing to a full-on rock-climbing adventure, Gran Pared (p51), in Bogotá, offers a well-organized and challenging climbing wall where you can get a feel for the sport.

Kitesurfing & Windsurfing

Colombia is one of the cheapest places in the world to go kitesurfing (kiteboarding) and windsurfing.

The casual traveler will find the learning curve for windsurfing much shorter than for kitesurfing; it's also a fair bit cheaper. Prices vary considerably. Expect to pay roughly COP$50,000 to COP$60,000 per hour for

A WHALE OF A VIEW

Every year whales living near Chile's Antarctic waters make the 8000km-plus journey to Colombia's Pacific coast to give birth and raise their young. These are humpback whales (yubartas, sometimes called jorobadas), and more than 800 have been recorded off the Colombian coast. They grow to 18m long and weigh up to 25 tons; there are few things cuter than spotting a ballenato (baby whale) already the size of a small truck, nosing its way through the surface.

The best whale-watching is from July through October, though arrivals begin in June. Whales can be seen all along the Pacific coast, and there are comfortable resorts where you can relax before and after a boat tour. Sometimes whales come so close to shore they can be seen from the beach, or from lookouts in the hills. Most whale-watching tours last 1½ to two hours and cost around COP$30,000 to COP$60,000 per person (although these prices can vary widely depending on the operator).

Where to Go

Humpback whales can be seen all along Colombia's Pacific coast but are not always easy to spot from the beach. Check out our list of the best places to observe these magnificent mammals:

» **Bahía Solano** (p251) & **El Valle** (p253) Offers resort accommodation with a lookout point from where you can spot whales playing just off the coast. Whale-watching packages include a boat trip and a number of other adventure activities; packages start from COP$875,000 per person.

» **Guachilito** (p256) Luxury accommodation near Nuquí available with hilltop perches to spot whales in season. Whale-watching packages include two boat trips and start from COP$790,000 person.

» **Parque Nacional Natural (PNN) Ensenada de Utría** (p254) This narrow inlet of water, in the Chocó, is one of the best places to see whales up close while staying on dry land. During the calving season the whales enter the *ensenada* (inlet) and play just a few hundred meters from shore. The visitors center on the eastern shore of the *ensenada* has recently refurbished cabins designed to accommodate up to 30 people. Whale-watching tours begin in Bahía Solano and end in Nuquí or vice versa, and include a whale-spotting boat trip. These are the most scientific of the tour packages in the area. Whale-watching packages start from COP$932,000 per person.

» **Ladrilleros** (p258) Great for budget whale-watching tours.

» **Isla Gorgona** (p260) Southwest of Buenaventura; it's also possible to go scuba diving with the whales.

windsurfing instruction and COP$80,000 to COP$100,000 per hour for individual kite-surf instruction (prices are lower in groups). Rentals go for around COP$150,000 per day. If you've got your own gear, you'll pay COP$20,000 to COP$30,000 for each water entrance.

The most comprehensive guide to kite-surfing in Colombia can be found at www.colombiakite.com.

Where to Go

There's also good kitesurfing on the Caribbean coast, where the winds are best from January to April. Good spots:

Lago Calima (p228) The star kitesurfing spot is not where you might think: Lago Calima is an artificial reservoir (elevation 1800m) 86km north of Cali. The appeal is year-round 18 to 25 knot winds, which attract world champions to its competitions held every August and September. There's no beach here; access to the water is via the grassy slopes along the lake.

La Boquilla (p135) Just near Cartagena.

Cabo de la Vela (p158) Terrific remote beaches; stunning backdrops.

San Andrés (p172) You can rent boards here.

Paragliding

Colombia's varied mountain terrain means there are lots of great thermals to ride if you want to go *parapente* (paragliding). Tandem flights in Bucaramanga are cheap – a mere COP$50,000 – which elsewhere in the country go for up to COP$100,000. You can also enroll in a 10-day paragliding course for COP$1,900,000 and become an internationally accredited paragliding pilot.

Where to Go

Popular spots:

Bucaramanga (p107) Arguably the country's paragliding capital, which attracts paragliders from around the world.

San Gil (p100) Near Bucaramanga.

Parque Nacional del Chicamocha (p106) One of the most spectacular spots, where rides run from 30 to 45 minutes and are priced accordingly at COP$170,000.

Medellín (p188) Urban paragliders can test their wings on Medellín's outskirts, where a number of schools offer tandem flights and instruction.

Canopying

Sometimes called 'zip lines' in North America, canopying involves strapping yourself into a harness and zipping around the forest canopy on cables. You use a heavy leather glove on top of the cable to brake. The last several years have seen an explosion in popularity of this sport in Colombia, particularly in the mountain regions.

Where to Go

One of the best is in Río Claro, halfway between Medellín and Bogotá, where a series of canopy lines zigzags across the river. It's a hoot in its own right, and it also provides a great vantage point from which to spot the local birds.

Other spots where you can go canopying include Los Yarumos (p203) near Manizales, the shores of Embalse Guatapé (p196), near Medellín, Termales San Vicente (p210) near Pereira and Jardín Botánico del Pacífico (p253) in the Chocó. There are also several canopy lines near Villa de Leyva (p86).

Mountain Biking

Bicycling is very popular in Colombia, although most of it is road cycling. Prices for bike rental vary across regions, depending on bike quality – expect to pay anywhere from COP$10,000 to COP$50,000 per half-day bike rental.

Where to Go

There's something about mountains that makes bicyclists want to conquer them. Mountain biking per se is most popular in San Gil (p100) and Villa de Leyva (p86) where several bike rental shops can facilitate your adrenaline fix. Popular short mountain bike adventures include the downhill runs from the thermal springs in Coconuco (p234) to Popayán (p229) and from El Rocio to Salento (p214).

For a longer, more challenging ride, Kumanday Adventures (p200), in Manizales, offers four-day bike trips through the high-mountain *páramo* of Parque Nacional Natural (PNN) Los Nevados. Because of the remoteness and altitude (over 4000m), a guide and support vehicle are mandatory. This tour doesn't run often, and isn't cheap. You'll need to contact Kumanday for its latest prices, which vary depending on the size of your group.

regions at a glance

Bogotá

Architecture ✓✓✓
Museums ✓✓✓
Wining & Dining ✓✓✓

Colonial Epicenter

Flanked by magnificent mountains to the east, Colombia's bustling high-altitude capital grew from the inside north, jutting out from the historic colonial center of 300-year-old homes, churches and buildings known as La Candelaria. A preserved mix of Spanish and baroque architecture styles pervade here, mixed among palatial government seats and the occasional modern eyesore. It all commences in the grand and magnificent Plaza de Bolívar, a picture-perfect living museum for Colombia's Andean showpiece.

p38

World-Class Museums

Anchored by one of South America's most brilliantly curated and designed museums, the fascinating Museo del Oro, Bogotá boasts more than 60 museums, many of which hold rank among Latin America's best. Everything from top-draw artists (Fernando Botero) to independence heroes (Simón Bolívar) to polarizing drug barons (Pablo Escobar) is idolized here in a gluttony of must-see museums.

Wining & Dining

Eating well in Bogotá is as a distinguished pursuit as anywhere. You'll find sweet street eats, regional specialties like *ajiaco* (an Andean chicken stew with corn), dressed up Colombian classics and no shortage of modern takes on high-end international fare highlighted by Peruvian, Mexican and Italian. But mostly, it's fuel for the city's raging nightlife, which carries on until daybreak in a number of rumba-run districts like Zona T and Parque 93. *Then* there's Andrés Carne de Res.

Boyacá, Santander & Norte de Santander

Villages ✓✓✓
Adventure ✓✓✓
Nature ✓✓

Colonial Villages

This region has three of Colombia's most striking colonial villages: Barichara and Villa de Leyva, both well-established tourist haunts preserved with precision; and sleepier Monguí, which rarely receives tourists and remains unspoiled.

Thrilling Adventures

Whether seeking a challenging high-altitude trek or white-knuckle adventure, Boyacá and Santander deliver. The weeklong Güicán-El Cocuy trek around Parque Nacional Natural (PNN) El Cocuy is one of Colombia's most rewarding, while the small town of San Gil is ground zero for outdoor adventure and extreme sport options.

Great Outdoors

Nature enthusiasts should flock to Villa de Leyva and Barichara with their excellent natural surroundings. Lago de Tota (Colombia's largest lake) ups the ante with *páramo* (high-mountain plains) trekking and a sky-high beach.

p79

Caribbean Coast

Beaches ✓✓✓
Architecture ✓✓✓
Trekking ✓✓

Beaches
The idyllic beaches of Colombia's Caribbean coast and islands are Colombia's best – and offer much more variety than the classic coconut-strewn clichés. Here, white sands are fringed with seething jungle or dramatic deserts or – for the purists – plenty of palm trees. Whatever your poison, there's sun and sand for all.

Colonial Architecture
The walled city of Cartagena offers ornate churches and romantic, shaded squares, while Mompox and Santa Marta's faded grandeur kindle a half-forgotten memory of an imperial dream.

Trekking
The five-/six-day trek to Ciudad Perdida (the Lost City) is one of the continent's classic hikes – six days in the jungle, fording rivers and creeping through the canopy; the destination is a mysterious ancient city belonging to a disappeared culture.

p115

San Andrés & Providencia

Diving ✓✓✓
Beaches ✓✓✓
Hiking ✓✓

Diving
Both islands have extensive coral reefs totaling 50km with a biodiversity that equals any in the region. Sponges are the standout, but there's a swarm of lobsters, turtles, barracudas, sting rays, manta rays and eagle rays just offshore.

Beaches
Indulge your Robinson Crusoe fantasies for a day and lay your head on the snow-white sand of the Johnny Cay Natural Regional Park, a coral islet 1.5km offshore from San Andrés that's home to around 500 iguanas.

Hiking
San Andrés and Providencia don't just cater for beach bums and divers: the island's interior is mountainous, and El Pico Natural Regional Park on Providencia offers walkers a breathtaking, crow's nest 360-degree view of the Caribbean.

p168

Medellín & Zona Cafetera

Coffee ✓✓✓
Nightlife ✓✓
Hiking ✓✓

Coffee Fincas
Throughout Caldas, Risaralda and Quindío departments, some of Colombia's best coffee *fincas* (farms) welcome visitors onto their plantations to learn all about the growing process and the rich culture that has developed around it.

Nightlife
Going out in Medellín is all about seeing and being seen. *Paisas* (inhabitants of Antioquia) love to dress up and go out, and from the open-air bars of Parque Lleras to the timeless tango clubs downtown, you can pretty much find a party for all tastes any day of the week.

Hiking
From high-altitude treks to more sedate strolls through municipal nature reserves, the Zona Cafetera offers hikes to match all energy levels. Don't miss the Valle de Cocora, near Salento, with its towering wax palms.

p182

Cali & Southwest Colombia

Archaeology ✓✓✓
Salsa ✓✓
Architecture ✓✓

Pre-Columbian Ruins
Less than 100km apart amid stunning Andean panoramas sit Colombia's two most important archaeological sites. More than 500 large statues carved out of volcanic rock are scattered in the hills around San Agustín. At Tierradentro, archaeologists have unearthed more than 100 underground tombs.

Salsa
From small barrio bars to the elegant *salsatecas* (salsa dance clubs), Cali is the place to dance salsa. It's also one of the continent's best places to learn – or let the pros show you how it's done at the World Salsa Championships.

Architecture
Boasting grandiose white-washed mansions and splendid churches, Popayán is an enchanting example of Spanish-colonial architecture. Continue the colonial theme in Cali's Barrio San Antonio or head to Santuario de Las Lajas to check out its immense neo-Gothic church.

p218

Pacific Coast

Marine Life ✓✓✓
Beaches ✓✓
Nature ✓✓

Marine Life
Get close to massive humpback whales at Parque Nacional Natural (PNN) Ensenada de Utría or head out at night to watch nesting sea turtles lay their eggs near El Valle. Divers can swim among hundreds of sharks at Islas Malpelo and Gorgona.

Beaches
Framed by jungle-covered mountains, the rugged gray beaches of the region are breathtaking and mostly deserted. Guachalito and Playa Almejal both have fine resorts wedged between the jungle and the sea. Surfers will find excellent breaks around El Terquito and Ladrilleros.

Nature
Often overlooked by hikers, the Chocó offers challenging off-the-beaten-track treks to waterfalls deep in the jungle. Or check out the region's amazing biodiversity while paddling up the Río Jobí or Río Juribidá in a dugout canoe.

p249

Amazon Basin

Wildlife ✓✓✓
Jungle ✓✓✓
Ecovillages ✓✓✓

Wild Kingdom
While human encroachment, both legal and otherwise, have pushed the Amazon's wildlife population in the wrong direction, it remains an incomprehensibly gigantic hotbed of biodiversity, the world's largest collection of living plants and animal species.

Jungle
The mother of all jungles, no word conjures up a more alluring mix of enigmatic rainforest, enormous rivers, indigenous folklore and tropical wildlife than the Amazon. You won't find Tarzan here, but if there ever was a place where imagination meets reality, it's in this endless sea of green.

Ecovillages
The ecological village of Puerto Nariño – a living model for sustainable living in the middle of the world's largest jungle – is a charming, architecturally interesting, damn near perfect place to chill out in the rainforest.

p262

> Every listing is recommended by our authors, and their favorite places are listed first

> Look out for these icons:

 Our author's top recommendation

 A green or sustainable option

 No payment required

On the Road

Bogotá

Best Places to Eat

» Andrés Carne de Res (p62)

» Rafael (p60)

» Central Cevicheria (p60)

» Abasto (p61)

» Agave Azul (p59)

Best Places to Stay

» Casa Deco (p53)

» Casa Platypus (p54)

» Usaquén Art Suites (p58)

» La Pinta (p55)

» Cranky Croc (p54)

Why Go?

Bogotá is Colombia's beating heart, an engaging and vibrant capital cradled by chilly Andean peaks and steeped in sophisticated urban cool. The city's cultural epicenter is La Candelaria, the cobbled historic downtown where most travelers gravitate. Here, a potpourri of preciously preserved colonial buildings house museums, restaurants, hotels and bars peppered amid 300-year-old homes, churches and convents. Nearly all of Bogotá's traditional attractions are here – radiating out from Plaza de Bolívar – and gorgeous Cerro de Monserrate is just east.

The city's grittier sides sit south and southwest, where working-class barrios continue to battle well-earned reputations of drugs and crime. In the ritzier north, you'll find boutique hotels and well-heeled locals piling into chic entertainment districts such as the Zona Rosa and Zona G. Here, rust-tinted sunsets dramatically bounce off the bricks of upper-class Bogotá's Andes-hugging residential buildings – a cinematic ceremony that begins the city's uproarious evenings.

When to Go
Bogotá

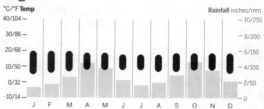

Jun & Jul Temperatures aren't as high as May, but rainfall drops dramatically in the capital.

Aug Fiesta free-for-all: Salsa al Parque and the Festival de Verano get the city's hips shaking.

Dec *Bogotanos* fall hard for Christmas, when the city sparkles in a festival of lights.

A Bite of Bogotá

Compared to other South American metroplexes like Lima or São Paulo, Bogotá has traditionally lagged behind in gastronomic terms, but don't think for a minute there isn't plenty to sooth your inner foodie. Bogotá is generally chilly, so it's no surprise that two of the most *Bogotano* contributions to Colombia's culinary landscape are warm and soothing. In the city and the Andean region, *ajiaco* is a homey soup made of chicken, corn, many different types of potatoes, avocado and a local herb known as *guasca*. For *onces* (midafternoon tea), there is nothing more inviting than *chocolate completo* (hot chocolate with cheese, buttered bread and a biscuit) – you'll find dozens of quaint cafes offering their take on this cold-weather warm-up. On the street, Bogotá is sweet: *obleas con arequipe* are thin wafers doused in milk caramel; and *coajada con melao* is fresh cheese with melted jaggery. Traditions aside, Bogotá is an international city, with no shortage of excellent eats and fine dining, from coastal Caribbean cevicherias to life-changing Peruvian, Bogotá has it all.

DON'T MISS

There is plenty to see and do in Bogotá proper, but a visit to Colombia's capital cannot exclude the Salt Cathedral of Zipaquirá (p73), 50km north of Bogotá, one of only three such structures in the world (the other two are in Poland). Around 250,000 tons of salt was cleared away to carve out the moody, ethereal underground sanctuary, heralded as one of Colombia's greatest architectural achievements. As you descend to 180m below ground through 14 small chapels representing the Stations of the Cross – Jesus' last journey – each a maudlin-lit triumph of both symbolism and mining, nothing prepares you for the trail's culmination in the main nave, where a mammoth cross (the world's largest in an underground church) is illuminated from the base up like heaven itself.

Bogotá's Top Museums

» Museo del Oro (p48)
» Museo Botero (p43)
» Museo Nacional (p50)
» Casa de Moneda (p47)
» Iglesia Museo de Santa Clara (p43)

ARRIVING IN BOGOTÁ

International and domestic flights arrive at Bogotá's Aeropuerto Internacional El Dorado, while buses call at La Terminal, the city's extraordinarily efficient bus terminal.

Fast Facts

» Population: 7.4 million
» Area: 1587 sq km
» Telephone area code: ✆1
» Elevation: 2625m

Top Tip

» After calling a taxi, you'll need to give the driver a password (clave), which is normally the last two digits of the phone you called from. Without it, he cannot begin his meter.

Resources

» Bogota Turismó (www.bogotaturismo.gov.co/en) Official tourism site.
» Lonely Planet (www.lonelyplanet.com/colombia/bogota) Destination information, hotel bookings, traveler forum and more.

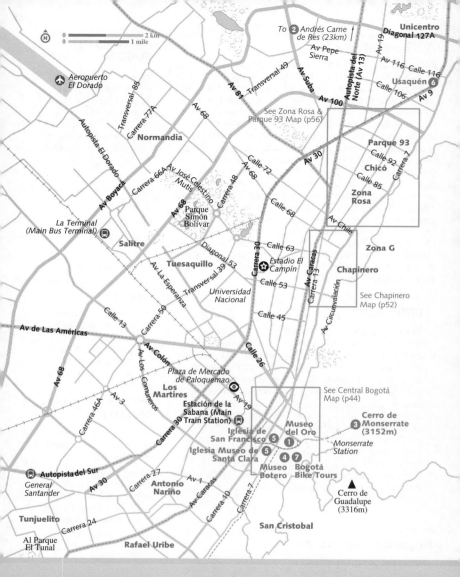

Bogotá Highlights

1 Ponder Colombia's El Dorado myths throughout the glittering displays at one of the continent's top museums, **Museo del Oro** (p48)

2 Step through the looking glass into the surreal nightlife world of the indescribable **Andrés Carne de Res** (p62) in Chía

3 Take a Sunday trek, among the pilgrims, up the towering **Cerro de Monserrate** (p49) for a sweeping view of the capital

4 Ponder all things plump at the (free!) **Museo Botero** (p43)

5 Worship the striking interiors of **Iglesia Museo de**

Santa Clara (p43) and **Iglesia de San Francisco** (p49)

6 Soak up the village colonial feel of food-centric **Usaquén** (p50)

7 Attack Bogotá by bike on a fascinating two-wheel tour with **Bogotá Bike Tours** (p51)

History

Long before the Spanish Conquest, the Sabana de Bogotá, a fertile highland basin which today has been almost entirely taken over by the city, was inhabited by one of the most advanced pre-Columbian indigenous groups, the Muisca. The Spanish era began when Gonzalo Jiménez de Quesada and his expedition arrived at the Sabana, founding the town on August 6, 1538 near the Muisca capital, Bacatá.

The town was named Santa Fe de Bogotá, a combination of the traditional name, Bacatá, and Quesada's hometown in Spain, Santa Fe. Nonetheless, throughout the colonial period the town was simply referred to as Santa Fe.

At the time of its foundation Santa Fe consisted of 12 huts and a chapel where a Mass was held to celebrate the town's birth. The Muisca religious sites were destroyed and replaced by churches.

During the early years Santa Fe was governed from Santo Domingo (on the island of Hispaniola, the present-day Dominican Republic), but in 1550 it fell under the rule of Lima, the capital of the Viceroyalty of Peru and the seat of Spain's power for the conquered territories of South America. In 1717 Santa Fe was made the capital of the Virreynato de la Nueva Granada, the newly created viceroyalty comprising the territories of present-day Colombia, Panama, Venezuela and Ecuador.

Despite the town's political importance, its development was hindered by the area's earthquakes, and also by the smallpox and typhoid epidemics that plagued the region throughout the 17th and 18th centuries.

After independence the Congress of Cúcuta in 1821 shortened the town's name to Bogotá and decreed it the capital of Gran Colombia. The town developed steadily and by the middle of the 19th century it had 30,000 inhabitants and 30 churches. In 1884 the first tramway began to operate in the city and, soon after, railway lines were constructed to La Dorada and Girardot, giving Bogotá access to the ports on the Río Magdalena.

Rapid progress came only in the 1940s with industrialization and the consequent peasant migrations from the countryside. On April 9, 1948 the popular leader Jorge Eliécer Gaitán was assassinated, sparking the uprising known as El Bogotazo. The city was partially destroyed; 136 buildings were burnt to the ground and 2500 people died.

Tranquil life in Bogotá was rocked again on November 6, 1985 when guerrillas of the M-19 revolutionary movement invaded the Palace of Justice in Bogotá and made hostages of the 300-plus civilians in the building. By the next day, 115 people were dead, including 11 supreme court judges.

In the '90s and '00s, Bogotá has made many surprising advances – an 8% year-on-year drop in murder rates as of late 2011, a host of progressive projects under successive mayors (eg the 350km of CicloRuta bike lanes) and major strides toward positioning itself as a cultural capital.

BOGOTÁ IN...

Two Days

Start in La Candelaria, with a snack at **La Puerta Falsa**, a look at **Plaza de Bolívar**, then see sculptures of chubby bodies at the **Museo Botero**. Lunch at **Quinua y Amaranto**, then walk over to take in Colombia's golden past at **Museo del Oro**, and grab dinner in **Zona G**, **Zona Rosa** or **Parque 93**, where you can eat and drink until your heart's content.

On your second day, you'll want to ride up **Monserrate** for massive capital views, then grab a nap: at night, enter the surreal bizarro world of **Andrés Carne de Res**, a 23km taxi ride north in Chía.

Four Days

Follow the two-day itinerary, then take a day trip to the salt cathedral at **Zipaquirá** – easily reached by public transportation. On your last day, start out with a brunch and stroll through the lively market in **Usaquén**, before heading to the city for a tour on two wheels to otherwise no-go neighborhoods with **Bogotá Bike Tours**. Afterward grab a hot cup of *canelazo* (made with aguardiente, sugarcane, cinnamon and lime) in a cafe in **La Candelaria**, and have a lovely farewell meal in the bohemian foodie neighborhood of **Macarena**.

ℹ️ LAY OF THE LAND

Sprawling Bogotá stretches mostly north–south (and west in recent years) with the towering peaks of Monserrate and Guadalupe providing an easterly wall.

Locating an address in the city is generally a breeze…after getting your head around the mathematical precision of it all. Calles run east–west, rising in number as you go north, while Carreras go north–south, increasing in number as they go west (away from the mountains). Handily, any street address also indicates the nearest cross streets; Calle 15 No 4-56, for example, is on 15th St between Carreras 4 and 5.

Central Bogotá has four main parts: the partially preserved colonial sector La Candelaria (south of Av Jiménez and between Carreras 1 and 10), with lots of students, bars and hostels; the aged business district 'city center' (focused on Carrera 7 and Calle 19, between Av Jiménez and Calle 26); the highrise-central of Centro Internacional (based on Carreras 7, 10 and 13, roughly between Calles 26 and 30); and, just east toward the hills, the bohemian eatery district Macarena.

Northern Bogotá is known as the wealthiest part of the city. The north, more or less, begins 2km north of Centro Internacional. A scene of theaters, antique shops and many gay bars, the sprawling Chapinero (roughly between Carrera 7 and Av Caracas, from Calle 40 to Calle 67 or so) is scruffier than areas further north, beginning with Zona G, a pint-sized strip of high-end eateries (east of Carrera 7 and Calle 80). Chapinero Alto is an artsy, up-and-coming mini-enclave in Chapinero between Carrera 7a and Av Circunvalar from Calles 53 to 65.

Ten blocks north, lively Zona Rosa (or Zona T; stemming from the 'T-shaped' pedestrian mall between Carreras 12 and 13, at Calle 82A) is a zone of clubs, malls and hotels. A more sedate version – with many restaurants – rims the ritzier Parque 93 (Calle 93 between Carreras 11A & 13), part of the Chicó neighborhood, and the one-time pueblo plaza at Usaquén (corner Carrera 6 and Calle 119). The rather unappealing modern buildings of the so-called 'financial district' line Calle 100 between Av 7 and Carrera 11.

The most popular links between the center and north are Carrera Séptima (Carrera 7; 'La Séptima') and Carrera Décima (Carrera 10), crowded with many *busetas* (small buses). Another, Av Caracas (which follows Carrera 14, then Av 13 north of Calle 63) is the major north–south route for the TransMilenio bus system. Calle 26 (or Av El Dorado) leads west to the airport.

◉ Sights

Most attractions are in historic La Candelaria, where Bogotá was born, and you'll probably want more than a day to look around the area.

If you're thinking of going to a museum on a Sunday, think twice – Bogotá has half-a-hundred options, and most get crammed with locals, particularly on free day (the last Sunday of the month); we've seen 45-minute lines outside a modest museum or two not even listed here! It's quieter during the week.

When walking about, pop into random churches too. Most are beauties, often dating from the 17th and 18th centuries – often with more elaborate decoration than the exterior would suggest. Some show off a distinctive Spanish-Moorish style called Mudejar (mainly noticeable in the ceiling ornamentation) as well as paintings of Colombia's best-known colonial-era artist, Gregorio Vásquez de Arce y Ceballos.

CENTRAL BOGOTÁ

LA CANDELARIA

Blissfully alive and chock full of key things to see, La Candelaria is Bogotá's colonial barrio, with a mix of carefully restored 300-year-old houses, some rather dilapidated ones, and still more marking more modern eras.

The usual place to start discovering Bogotá is **Plaza de Bolívar** (Map p44), marked by a bronze statue of Simón Bolívar (cast in 1846 by Italian artist, Pietro Tenerani). It was the first public monument in the city.

The square has changed considerably over the centuries and is no longer lined by colonial buildings; only the Capilla del Sagrario dates from the Spanish era. Other buildings are more recent and flaunt different architectural styles.

Some of La Candelaria's most popular sights, as well as the new Centro Cultural Gabriel García Márquez, are within a couple of blocks east of the plaza. The slightly confusing web of museums run by the Banco de la Republicano, including Museo Botero and Casa de Moneda, is easily one of Bogotá's top attractions.

It's best to avoid walking alone here after dark.

TOP CHOICE **Museo Botero**   MUSEUM
(Map p44; www.banrepcultural.org/museo-del-oro; Calle 11 No 4-41; admission free; ⊙9am-7pm Mon-Sat, 10am-5pm Sun) Set over two floors past a fountain-filled courtyard and small store of Botero-themed wares you'll find the location's highlight. At the front of the building there are several halls dedicated to all things chubby: hands, oranges, women, mustached men, children, birds, violins, Fuerzas Armadas Revolucionarias de Colombia (FARC) leaders – all, of course, the robust paintings and sculptures of Colombia's most famous artist, Fernando Botero. (Botero himself donated these works.) The collection also includes several works by Picasso, Chagall, Renoir, Monet, Pissarro and Miró, and hilarious sculptures by Dalí and Max Ernst.

TOP CHOICE **Iglesia Museo de Santa Clara**   CHURCH
(Map p44; www.museoiglesiasantaclara.gov.co; Carrera 8 No 8-91; adult/student/child COP$3000/2000/500; ⊙9am-5pm Tue-Fri, 10am-4pm Sat & Sun) This church facing the palace from the west (on Carrera 8) is one of Bogotá's most richly decorated (and one of the city's oldest, along with Iglesia de San Francisco) and is now run by the government as a museum. Considering all the other same-era churches that can be seen for free, many visitors pass on this one, but it is a stunner. Built between 1629 and 1674, the single-nave construction features a barrel vault coated in golden floral motifs looking down over walls entirely covered in paintings (98 not including the closed-off loft, by our count) and statues of saints.

FREE **Catedral Primada**   CHURCH
(Map p44; www.catedraldebogota.org; Plaza de Bolívar; ⊙9am-5pm Tue-Sun) The main plaza's dominating building, facing from the northeast corner, is this neoclassical cathedral which stands on the site where the first Mass *may* have been celebrated after Bogotá had been founded in 1538 (some historians argue it happened at Plazoleta del Chorro de Quevedo, just east). Either way, it's Bogotá's largest. The original simple thatched chapel was replaced by a more substantial building in 1556–65, which later collapsed due to poor foundations. In 1572 the third church went up, but the earthquake of 1785 reduced it to ruins. Only in 1807 was the massive building – that stands to this day – initiated and it was successfully completed by 1823. It was partially damaged during the Bogotazo riots in 1948. Unlike many Bogotá churches, the spacious interiors have relatively little ornamentation. The tomb of Jiménez de Quesada, the founder of Bogotá, is in the largest chapel off the right-hand aisle.

Capitolio Nacional   HISTORIC BUILDING
(Map p44; closed to the public) On the southern side of the plaza stands this neoclassical seat of Congress. It was begun in 1847 (its square-facing facade was built by English architect Thomas Reed), but due to numerous political uprisings was not completed until 1926. To visit, call **Citizen Services** (☑382 6129).

Palacio de Justicia   HISTORIC BUILDING
(Map p44; closed to the public) On the northern side of the plaza, this massive, rather styleless edifice serves as the seat of the Supreme Court. It's seen its troubles. The first court building, erected in 1921 on the corner of Calle 11 and Carrera 6, was burnt down by a mob during El Bogotazo. A modern building was then constructed here, but in 1985 it was taken by M-19 guerrillas and gutted by fire in a fierce 28-hour offensive by the army in an attempt to reclaim it. The new building was designed in a completely different style.

GREEN PEOPLE WATCHING FROM ABOVE

While walking around La Candelaria, try keeping one eye down for fresh dog feces and missing pothole covers, *and* another one up for a unique art project peering down from rooftops, window ledges and balconies. Made in the past decade, the artworks – green figures made from recycled materials representing local *comuneros* (commoners) – come from local artist Jorge Olavé.

Note the guy watching over Plaza de Bolívar from atop the **Casa de Comuneros** (Map p44) at the southwest corner – best seat in town.

Central Bogotá

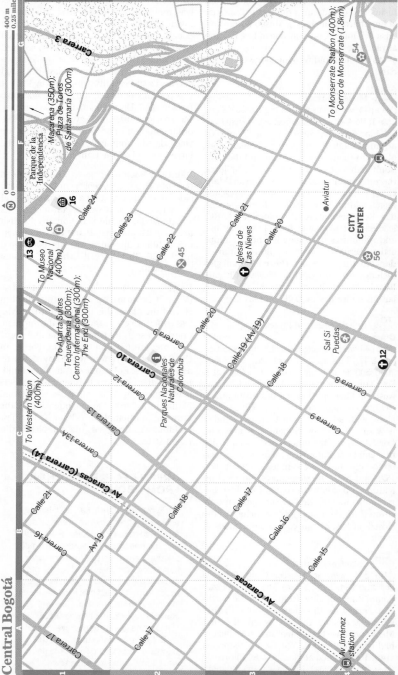

400 m
0.25 miles

Parque de la
Independencia

Macarena (350m);
Plaza de Toros
de Santamaría (300m)

Carrera 3

To Monserrate Station (400m);
Cerro de Monserrate (1.8km)

To Museo
Nacional
(400m)

To Aparta Suites
Tequendema (300m);
Centro Internacional (300m);
The End (300m)

To Western Union
(400m)

Calle 24

Calle 23

Calle 22

Calle 21

Calle 20

Iglesia de
Las Nieves

Aviatur

CITY
CENTER

Calle 20

Carrera 9

Calle 19 (Av 19)

Calle 18

Carrera 8

Sal Si
Puedas

Carrera 10

Parques Nacionales
Naturales de
Colombia

Carrera 12

Carrera 13

Carrera 13A

Av Caracas (Carrera 14)

Calle 21

Carrera 16

Av 19

Calle 18

Calle 17

Calle 17

Calle 16

Calle 15

Av Caracas

Carrera 17

Calle 17

Av Jiménez
station

Carrera 6

Calle 16

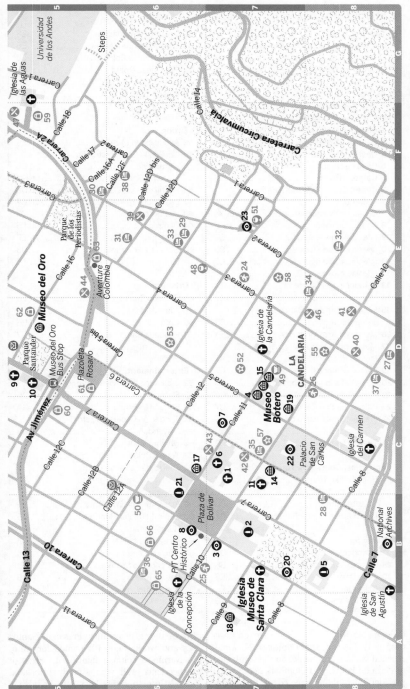

Central Bogotá

Casa de Nariño　　　　　　HISTORIC BUILDING
(Map p44) Beyond the Capitolio Nacional, reached via Carreras 8 or 7, on the south side of Plaza de Bolívar, is Colombia's neoclassical presidential building erected at the begin-ning of the 20th century. President Santos lives and works here. It's named for Anto-nio Nariño, a colonial figure with ideas of independence and who secretly translated France's human rights laws into Spanish –

and went to jail for it, a couple of times. In 1948 the building was damaged during El Bogotazo riots and only restored in 1979. To visit, you'll need to log on www.presidencia. gov.co and scroll down to the link 'Visitas guiadas a la Casa de Nariño,' under Servicios al Ciudadano, or contact visitas@presidencia. gov.co.

You don't need permission to watch the changing of the presidential guard – best seen from the east side – which is held at 4pm on Wednesday, Friday and Sunday.

Note: guards around the president's palace stand at barriers on Carreras 7 and 8. It's OK to pass them, just show the contents of your bag and stay clear of the fence-side sidewalks.

FREE Casa de Moneda   MUSEUM
(Mint; Map p44; www.banrepcultural.org/museos -y-colecciones/casa-de-la-moneda; Calle 11 No 4-93; ⊙9am-7pm Mon-Sat, 10am-5pm Sun) At the west end of the block, you'll find this historic museum, which now houses the Colección Numismática in most of its front two floors. The exhibits (with a bit of English) start with pre-Columbian exchanges of pots and lead chronologically to misshapen coins, the introduction of a centralized bank in 1880 and how the cute tree art on the current 500 peso coin was made in the late 1990s. Behind the coins are the 10 halls of the Arte Colección, reached by overly elaborate ramps. Most of it sticks with modern splashes of oils by Colombian artists; the best, perhaps, are the giant figurative paintings by Luis Caballero (1943–95) on the 1st floor. A bit at odds with the rest are the two 1st-floor halls toward the east, focusing on 17th- and 18th-century religious objects, including two extraordinary *custodias* (monstrances). The largest was made of 4902g of pure gold encrusted with 1485 emeralds, one sapphire, 13 rubies, 28 diamonds, 168 amethysts, one topaz and 62 pearls. But who's counting?

FREE Museo Histórico Policía   MUSEUM
(Museum of Police History; Map p44; ☎233 5911; Calle 9 No 9-27; ⊙8am-5pm Tue-Sun) This surprisingly worthwhile museum not only gets you inside the lovely ex-HQ (built in 1923) of Bogotá's police force, but gives you 45 minutes or so of contact time with 18-year-old, English-speaking local guides who are serving a one-year compulsory service with the police (interesting tales to be heard). The best parts otherwise follow cocaine-kingpin

Pablo Escobar's demise in 1993 – with a model dummy of his bullet-ridden corpse, his Harley Davidson (a gift to a cousin) and his personal Bernadelli pocket pistol, otherwise known as his 'second wife.'

Museo del 20 de Julio   MUSEUM
(Casa del Florero; Map p44; www.mincultura.gov.co; Calle 11 No 6-94; adult/student COP$3000/2000; ⊙9am-5pm Tue-Fri, 10am-4pm Sat & Sun) The late-16th-century home that houses this museum marks the spot where a 'broken vase was heard around the world.' Apparently. Just after Napoleon overcame Spain in 1810, a local Creole Antonio Morales came here, according to the story, and demanded an ornate vase from its Spanish owner José González Llorentes, which led to a fistfight on the street (plus one shattered vase, and some hurt feelings) – eventually spurring a rebellion. In these hallowed halls you can see the broken vase in question.

FREE Museo de Arte del Banco de la República   MUSEUM
(Map p44; www.banrepcultural.org/museodearte. htm; Calle 11 No 4-21; ⊙9am-7pm Mon & Wed-Sat, 10am-5pm Sun) Past a wall fountain and cafe. It shows changing exhibits, and its auditorium hosts many free events.

Museo de Arte Colonial   MUSEUM
(Museum of Colonial Art; Map p44; Carrera 6 No 9-77; adult/student COP$3000/2000; ⊙9am-5pm Tue-Fri, 10am-4pm Sat & Sun) Occupies a one-time Jesuit college and does a nice job of tracing the evolution of how religious and portrait art pieces are made, particularly by Colombia's favorite baroque artist, Gregorio Vásquez de Arce y Ceballos (1638–1711). Its upstairs exhibits begin with a messy gallery space (eg trial sketches on walls) and lead into a hall with sketch pieces and a couple of dozen (finished) Vásquez works from the museum's collection of nearly 200 by the artist. Downstairs exhibits focus on religious artifacts.

FREE Capilla del Sagrario   CHURCH
(Sagrario Chapel; Map p44; Plaza de Bolívar, Carrera 7 No 10-40; ⊙7am-noon & 1-5:30pm Mon-Fri, 3-5:30pm Sun) This smaller, baroque cathedral has more to see than its bigger brother next door, the Catedral Primada, including six large paintings by Gregorio Vásquez.

Plazoleta del Chorro de Quevedo   PLAZA
(Map p44; cnr Carrera 2 & Calle 12B) No one agrees exactly where Bogotá was originally

founded – some say by the Catedral Primada on the Plaza de Bolívar, others say here, in this wee plaza lined with cafes, a small white church and many boho street vendors (or hacky-sack players). It's a cute spot at any time of day, but particularly as dark comes – and students pour onto the scene – in the narrow funnel-like alley leading past pocket-sized bars just north.

Iglesia de San Ignacio   CHURCH
(Map p44; Calle 10 No 6-35) The Jesuits began this iconic church in 1610 and, although opened for worship in 1635, it was not completed until their expulsion in 1767. It was the largest church during colonial times and perhaps the most magnificent. It's undergoing a long-winded renovation. Hopefully when it reopens visitors should be able to see one of the city's most richly decorated churches.

Teatro Colón   THEATER
(Map p44; ☑284 7420; www.bogota-dc.com/eventos/teatro/colon.html; Calle 10 No 5-32) With its adorable Italian-style facade, which has had various names since its birth in 1792, this latest version you see opened as Teatro Nacional in 1892 and was designed by Italian architect Pietro Cantini. Its lavish interiors are undergoing a long renovation that – apparently – could go five more years. Normally, concerts, opera and ballet are performed here, and day-time tours are on offer.

FREE Museo Militar   MUSEUM
(Military Museum; Map p44; ☑281 2548; Calle 10 No 4-92; ⊗9am-4pm Tue-Sun) This two-floor museum is run by military guys in fatigues, and may be interesting to some for its playful models sporting the history of military uniforms (note the 'antiterrorist' outfit), a Korean War room, a video of the operation that rescued Ingrid Betancourt, and a courtyard of artillery and aircraft including a presidential helicopter. ID required.

Edificio Liévano   HISTORIC BUILDING
(Map p44; closed to the public) On the western side of the plaza, this French-style building is now home to the *alcaldía* (mayor's office). The building was erected between 1902 and 1905.

Palacio de San Carlos   PALACE
(Map p44; Calle 10 No 5-51) This massive edifice has seen a few lives, notably as the presiden-

tial HQ of Simón Bolívar, who narrowly escaped an assassination attempt here in 1828 when his friend-with-privileges Manuelita Sáenz tipped him off and became known in Bogotá circles as 'the liberator of the liberator.' A (dramatically worded) sign in Latin under his window (to the right) retells it.

Centro Cultural Gabriel García Márquez   CULTURAL CENTER
(Map p44; ☑283 2200; www.fce.com.co; Calle 11 No 5-60) Opened in 2008 and a modern addition to La Candelaria, this expansive new complex pays homage to Colombia's most famous author in name, but its events span the cultural spectrum way past literature. There's also a giant bookstore (with a few English titles), a great hamburger restaurant and a Juan Valdéz cafe.

FREE Observatorio Astronómico   OBSERVATORY
(Map p44) Conceptualized by celebrated Colombian botanist José Celestino Mutis, the 1803 tower is reputedly the first astronomical observatory built on the continent. It's possible to visit Monday to Friday at 11am and 1pm, but you must reserve a week ahead. Email your name, nationality and passport number to museos@unal.edu.co to reserve a spot.

CITY CENTER
Not a heartbreaker, Bogotá's scrappy business center – busiest along Calle 19 and Carrera 7 – is easiest to deal with on Sunday, when Ciclovía shuts down Carrera 7, and the Mercado de San Alejo flea market (p68) is in force. Some of its most-visited parts (notably the Museo del Oro) cluster near La Candelaria by Av Jiménez.

TOP CHOICE Museo del Oro   MUSEUM
(Map p44; ☑343 2222; www.banrepcultural.org/museo-del-oro; Carrera 6 No 15-88; admission free Sun, COP$3000 Mon-Sat, audioguide COP$6000; ⊗9am-6pm Tue-Sat, 10am-4pm Sun) Bogotá's most famous museum and one of the most fascinating in all of South America, the recently renovated Gold Museum contains more than 55,000 pieces of gold and other materials from all the major pre-Hispanic cultures in Colombia. All is laid out in logical, thematic rooms over three floors – with descriptions in Spanish and English.

Second-floor exhibits break down findings by region, with descriptions of how pieces were used. There are lots of mixed

CERRO DE MONSERRATE

Bogotá's proud symbol – and convenient point of reference – is the white-church-topped 3152m **Monserrate peak** (Map p40) flanking the city's east, about 1.5km from La Candelaria and visible from most parts across Sabana de Bogotá (Bogotá savannah; sometimes called the valley). The top has gorgeous views of the 1700-sq-km capital sprawl. On a clear day you can even spot the symmetrical cone of Nevado del Tolima, part of Los Nevados volcanic range in the Cordillera Central, 135km west.

The **church** up top is a major mecca for pilgrims, due to its altar statue of the Señor Caído (Fallen Christ), dating from the 1650s, to which many miracles have been attributed. The church was erected after the original chapel was destroyed by an earthquake in 1917.

At the time of writing the trail had been closed for maintenance for two years with plans to open soon. When it does, on Saturday or Sunday morning, consider following the hordes up a steep **1500-step hike** – past snack stands – to the top (60 to 90 minutes' walk up); on other days it can be dangerous, as thefts occur, so take the regular *teleférico* (cable car) or funicular, which alternate schedules up the mountain from **Monserrate station** (Map p40; www.cerromonserrate.com; round trip COP$14,400 7:45am-5:30pm Mon-Fri, COP$17,000 5:30-11pm Mon-Fri, COP$8200 Sun; ⊙7:45am-midnight Mon-Sat, 6:30am-6:30pm Sun). Generally the funicular goes before noon (3pm on Saturday), the cable car after.

The funicular is a 20-minute walk up from the Iglesia de las Aguas (along the brick walkways with the fountains – up past the Universidad de los Andes), at the northeast edge of La Candelaria – but you're best off doing it on weekends, particularly in the morning, when many pilgrims are about. During the week the trail and the short walk between Quinta de Bolívar and Monserrate occasionally see robberies. You're best off taking a taxi or the bus that reads 'Funicular' up to the station.

animals in gold (eg jaguar/frog, man/eagle); and note how women figurines indicate how women of the Zenú in the pre-Columbian north surprisingly played more important roles in worship.

The 3rd-floor 'Offering' room exhibits explain how gold was used in rituals, such as ornate *tunjos* (gold offerings, usually figurines depicting a warrior) thrown into the Laguna de Guatavita (p74); the most famous one, actually found near the town of Pasca in 1969, is the unlabeled gold boat, called the Balsa Muisca. It's uncertain how old it is, as generally only gold pieces that include other materials can be carbon dated.

There's more to understanding the stories than the descriptions tell, so try taking a free one-hour tour Tuesday through Saturday (in Spanish and English; 11am and 4pm), which varies the part of the museum to be highlighted. Audioguides are available in Spanish, English and French.

Iglesia de San Francisco　　　CHURCH
(Map p44; www.templodesanfrancisco.com; cnr Av Jiménez & Carrera 7; ⊙7am-7pm Mon-Fri, 7am-2pm & 4:30-7:30pm Sat & Sun) Built between 1557 and 1621, the Church of San Francisco, just

west of the Gold Museum, is Bogotá's oldest surviving church. Of particular interest is the extraordinary 17th-century gilded main altarpiece, which is Bogotá's largest and most elaborate piece of art of its kind. It's hard to get a close look, as Masses run nearly hourly all day. It's less intrusive to look up at the green-and-gold Mudejar ornamentation of the ceiling under the organ loft.

Quinta de Bolívar　　　MUSEUM
(off Map p44; www.quintadebolivar.gov.co; Calle 20 No 2-91 Este; adult/child COP$3000/1000; ⊙9am-5pm Tue-Fri, 11am-4pm Sat & Sun) About 250m downhill to the west from Monserrate station, this lovely historic home museum is set in a garden at the foot of the Cerro de Monserrate. The mansion was built in 1800 and donated to Simón Bolívar in 1820 in gratitude for his liberating services. Bolívar spent 423 days here over nine years. Its rooms are filled with period pieces, including Bolívar's sword. Less is said about its later days as a mental institution.

There's an English- and French-language brochure available for COP$2500, or a Spanish-language audioguide for COP$1000.

Mirador Torre Colpatria   VIEWPOINT

(Map p44; Carrera 7 No 24-89; admission COP$3500; ◷6-9pm Fri, 11am-5pm Sat, Sun & holidays) Monserrate offers superb views, but only from the 48th-floor outside deck of the Colpatria Tower can you catch a superb view of the bullring, backed by office buildings and the mountains – there are also fine 360-degree vistas across the city. The 162m-high skyscraper – Colombia's tallest – was finished in 1979.

Museo de Arte Moderno   MUSEUM

(MAMBO; Map p44; www.mambobogota.com; Calle 24 No 6-00; adult/student COP$4000/2000; ◷10am-6pm Tue-Sat, noon-5pm Sun) Opened in the mid-1980s in a spacious hall designed by revered local architect Rogelio Salmona, the Museum of Modern Art focuses on various forms of visual arts (painting, sculpture, photography, video) from the beginning of the 20th century to the present. Exhibits change frequently, often highlighting Latin America artists. The cinema here screens films on weekends at 3pm and 5pm (COP$4000).

Iglesia de la Veracruz   CHURCH

(Map p44; Calle 16 No 7-19; ◷4:30-7:30pm Mon-Fri, Mass 8am, 11am, noon & 6pm Mon-Fri, noon & 6pm Sat, 11am, noon & 5pm Sun) Iglesia de la Veracruz is known as the National Pantheon because many of the heroes of the struggle for independence have been buried here.

Iglesia La Tercera   CHURCH

(Map p44; Calle 16 No 7-54; ◷7am-6pm Mon-Fri, Mass 11am Sat, noon & 1pm Sun) Boasts a fine stone facade and lovely wood-carved altars in walnut and cedar set on white walls below a wood-carved ceiling.

CENTRO INTERNACIONAL

Business offices look over the Carrera 7 in this busy pocket of the city, where you'll find a few attractions and lots of business meetings. In January and February, the Plaza de Toros de Santamaría (p66) gets crammed with bullfighting fans.

TOP CHOICE **Museo Nacional**   MUSEUM

(National Museum; off Map p44; www.museona cional.gov.co; Carrera 7 No 28-66; admission free Sun, Mon-Sat adult/student COP$2000/500; ◷10am-6pm Tue-Sat, to 5pm Sun) Housed in the expansive, Greek cross-shaped building called El Panóptico and designed as a prison by English architect Thomas Reed in 1874. Walking through the (more or less) chronological display of Colombia's past, you pass iron-bar doors into white-walled halls. Signage is Spanish only, but each floor offers a few handy English placards you can take along with you for the highlights.

The ground floor looks at pre-Columbian history, with rather oblique references to past groups and some gripping Muisca mummies that may date as far back as 1500 years. On the 3rd floor, room 16 gives the best sense of old prison life – with old cells now done up in various exhibits. The first on the right regards Jorge Gaitán, the populist leader whose 1948 assassination set off the Bogotazo violence – and coincidentally delayed the opening of this museum!

Afterward, the lovely gardens have a nice glass Juan Valdéz cafe, and there are many good eating options on nearby Calle 29.

NORTHERN BOGOTÁ

Museo El Chicó   MUSEUM

(Map p56; ☎623 1066; www.museodelchico.com; Mercedes Sierra de Pérez, Carrera 7A No 93-01; adult/student COP$3500/2500; ◷10am-1pm & 2-5pm Mon-Fri, 8am-noon Sat) Housed in a fine 18th-century *casona* (large, rambling house) surrounded by what was once a vast hacienda. It features a collection of historic objects of decorative art mostly from Europe – the exquisitely tiled bathroom is worth a visit alone – plus a picnic-perfect park.

Plaza Central de Usaquén   PLAZA

(Los Toldos de San Pelayo; Carrera 6A btwn Calles 119 & 119A) It's best coming on the weekend for its flea market, which is at its most vibrant on Sunday.

WESTERN BOGOTÁ

Parque Simón Bolívar   PARK

(Map p40; Calle 63 & 53 btwn Carreras 48 & 68; ◷6am-6pm) At 360 hectares, it's slightly larger than New York's Central Park, something that more than a few of the weekend draw of 200,000 local park goers like to point out. It's a nice spot, with lakes, bike paths and walkways, public libraries, stadiums and many events including the beloved Rock al Parque in October or November. The 'Simón Bolívar' stop on TransMilenio's E line reaches the east end of the park (at Av Ciudad de Quito and Calle 64).

🏃 Activities

If you're looking for a place to kick around a football or go for a jog, try the Parque Simón Bolívar, or just go for a climb up Monserrate (p49) on weekend mornings. To get out on two wheels, nothing beats Bogotá's incredible 350km network of **CicloRuta** – separate bike lanes that cross the city. Or **Ciclovía** (www.idrd.gov.co), when 120km or so of roads open for bikes and pedestrians only on Sundays and holidays from 7am to 2pm.

 Bogotá Bike Tours   CYCLING
(Map p44; ☏312 502 0554; www.bogotabiketours. com; rentals half-/full day COP$15,000/30,000) Run by California bike enthusiast Mike Caesar, this is a fascinating way to see Bogotá, especially in the neighborhoods that would be otherwise no-go for anyone other than crazies. Tours leave daily at 10:30am and 1:30pm (COP$30,000) from the La Candelaria office. Typical highlights include La Candelaria, a fruit market – watch those spice vendors! – the Plaza de Toros de Santamaría, the Central Cemetery and the Red Light district. Mike also rents bikes.

Gran Pared   ROCK CLIMBING
(Map p52; www.granpared.com; Carrera 7 No 50-02; per hr with equipment & instructor COP$19,000, without instructor COP$14,000; ◷10am-10pm Mon-Sat, to 6pm Sun) Bogotá rock climbers head off to nearby Suesca (p74), but if you want to hone your skills in town, this towering climbing wall is challenging and well-organized.

Courses

Spanish in Colombia comes with a clearer pronunciation than some Latin American destinations.

International House Bogotá   LANGUAGE
(Map p44; ☏336 4747; www.ihbogota.com; Calle 10 No 4-09; ◷closed Sun) Offers group Spanish-language courses in La Candelaria (US$220 per week for five four-hour mornings) or private tutors (US$30 per hour).

Escuela de Artes y Oficios Santo Domingo   HANDICRAFTS
(Map p44; ☏282 0534; www.eaosd.org; Calle 10 No 8-65) This donation-sustained organization offers one- and two-month (and beyond) courses in woodworking, leather, silver and embroidery from COP$150,000 in a gorgeous restored building in La Candelaria. And, though technically not a store, its shop is the best spot in town for well-made, gorgeous handicrafts.

Nueva Lengua   LANGUAGE
(☏861 5555; www.nuevalengua.com/spanish; Calle 69 No 11A-09, Quinta Camacho) This language school offers a number of study programs – also at its branches in Medellín and Cartagena. A 25-hour week with a private teacher costs US$610, a 20-hour week in a small class is US$180 and a four-week (minimum) study-and-volunteer program, including work at an orphanage or hospital, is US$720.

Universidad Javeriana's Centro Latinoamericano   LANGUAGE
(☏320 8320, ext 4620; www.javeriana.edu.co/centrolatino; Transversal 4 No 42-00, piso 6) Bogotá's best-known school of the Spanish language offers private lessons (COP$91,000 per hour) or 80-hour courses (COP$1,952,000 per person).

Tours

Destino Bogotá offers a host of unusual city tours and small-scale day trips, while Sal Si Puedes runs weekend walking trips around the Bogotá area; see p69. Also, some of the Puntos de Información Turística (PIT) information centers offer free walking tours daily; see p68. A great new (nearly free) option is the **Bogotá Graffiti Tour** (☏321 297 4075; www.bogotagraffiti.com), a three-hour walking tour (COP$4000) through Bogotá's considerable and impressive urban art every Tuesday, Thursday and Saturday at 1pm starting from Parque de los Periodistas.

Festivals & Events

A mix of local and national festivals takes place constantly throughout the year. The following is a selection of the best. Also ask around as smaller festivals are held each month.

BOGOTÁ FOR CHILDREN

Some Bogotá attractions are particularly kid-friendly. **Maloka** (www.maloka. org; Carrera 68D No 51; museum/cinema/ both COP$10000/10,500/17,000; ◷8am-5pm Mon-Fri, 10am-7pm Sat, 11am-7pm Sun) is a children-oriented science museum with a dome cinema, and Museo El Chicó (p50) has a kid's park and library. In the Museo Nacional (p50) you can see mummies and old jail cells. Vendors sell bird seed for the (many) pigeons in Plaza de Bolívar (p42). And you can marvel at the funny hats of the changing of the presidential guard nearby (p46).

Chapinero

N
0 _____ 400 m
0 _____ 0.2 miles

To Zona Rosa (1km);
Parque 93 (2.1km)

To Post Office
(500m)

Calle 73

Calle 68

Calle 70

Av Chile (Calle 72)

12 Calle 71

Calle 70A

Flores

Carrera 11

Calle 68

Calle 69

Carrera 9

Carrera 8

Calle 70

Calle 67

Carrera 7A

2

Carrera 7A

Calle 66

Calle 70

Calle 69A 5

Av Caracas (Carrera 14)

Calle 68

Calle 69

Carrera 13

Calle 64

Carrera 7

Calle 63

Calle 63

11

Carrera 4

10

Carrera 11

Calle 62

3

Carrera 9A

Calle 65

Carrera 5

Calle 61

Calle 62

Carrera 9

13

Calle 58 bis

Calle 59

CHAPINERO
ALTO

8

7

Calle 57

Calle 59

Carrera 4

Calle 57

Carrera 13

14

Carrera 8

6

9

4

Carrera 3A

Calle 56

Av Circunvalación

Calle 55

Carrera 7

Calle 54A

Calle 53

Calle 54

Transversal 3

Calle 51

Calle 51A

1

C 51

Chapinero

Feria Taurina   BULLFIGHTING
(Jan & Feb) Bogotá has its bullfighting season when the major corridas take place, with bullfights held on most Sundays. Famous international matadors are invited, mostly from Spain and Mexico.

Festival Iberoamericano de Teatro THEATER
(Mar & Apr) A theater festival featuring groups from all of Latin America and beyond; takes place in every evenly numbered year.

Salsa al Parque   SALSA
(Aug) A salsa extravaganza in Parque Simón Bolívar.

Festival de Verano   CULTURAL
(Aug) Ten days of free music and culture in Parque Simón Bolívar.

Festival de Jazz   JAZZ
(Sep) Organized by the Teatro Libre, this festival features local and national Latin jazz artists, plus an occasional US or European star.

Festival de Cine de Bogotá   CINEMA
(Oct) With a 20-year history, the city's film festival attracts films from all around the world, including a usually strong Latin American selection.

Hip Hop al Parque   HIP-HOP
(Oct) Two days of hip-hop taking over Parque Simón Bolívar.

Rock al Parque   ROCK
(Oct & Nov) Three days of (mostly South American) rock/metal/pop/funk/reggae bands at Parque Simón Bolívar. It's free and swarming with fans.

Expoartesanías   ARTS & CRAFTS
(Dec) This crafts fair gathers together artisans and their products from all around the country. Crafts are for sale and it's an excellent place to buy them.

🛏 Sleeping

Bogotá is experiencing a hotel boom, with new big business-oriented chains like Hilton and Marriott now firmly planted in – particularly along Av El Dorado in (remote) Salitre, a few kilometers east of the airport. Many other high-end choices loom way north. It's fine to be up there if you want more security for 10pm walks, or to be near malls and dress-up bars. If travel's your game and time's short, La Candelaria is where most of Bogotá's attractions are located.

CENTRAL BOGOTÁ

LA CANDELARIA
In the past couple of years, the historic suburb of La Candelaria has seen an explosion in hostels. Generally private rooms in hostels are better than cheapie rooms in the several dated, grubby hotels around here. Higher-end travelers have a couple of fine locales with more colonial spirit than you'll find anywhere else in the capital.

Casa Deco   BOUTIQUE HOTEL $$$
TOP CHOICE
(Map p44; ☎282 8640; www.hotelcasadeco.com; Calle 12C No 2-30; s/d incl breakfast from COP$184,000/218,000; @🖥) A 21-room gem run by an Italian emerald dealer (no pun intended), this discerning option is a serious step up from the sea of hostels surrounding it. Rooms come in seven bright colors and are laced with bespoke hardwood art deco–style furniture, desks and futon beds. There's a guitarist at breakfast, lovely staff, and a mesmerizing terrace with Monserrate and Cerro de Guadalupe views.

Hotel de la Ópera   BOUTIQUE HOTEL $$$
(Map p44; ☎336 2066; www.hotelopera.com.co; Calle 10 No 5-72; r incl breakfast COP$378,000-

407,000, ste incl breakfast COP$546,000-554,800; (@🌐🛜🏊) La Candelaria's poshest hotel – named for the leotard shows at Teatro Colón next door – features gracefully restored rooms of two historic Spanish-colonial townhouses enveloping two courtyards (it's 'totally colonial!' to quote insistent staff). Book standard rooms 710–712 in the new art deco annex for superb views.

Casa Platypus
GUESTHOUSE $$

(Map p44; 📞281 1801; www.casaplatypus.com; Carrera 3 No 12F-28; s/d/tr incl breakfast COP$130,000/150,000/170,000; @🛜) This newer 'boutique' branch to the Platypus hostel nearby goes for the private-bathroom crowd, with great rooms with masculine hardwoods, a narrow terrace perfect for watching the 5pm weekday university fashion show in the street below, and a wonderful rooftop terrace.

Cranky Croc
HOSTEL $$

(Map p44; 📞342 2438; www.crankycroc.com; Calle 12D No 3-46; dm COP$20,000, s/d/tr COP$65,000/70,000/105,000, s/d/tr without bathroom COP$46,000/60,000/90,000; @🛜) Our favorite hostel in town. It's run by a friendly Aussie and offers five dorms and eight rooms around several communal areas, including a chef-driven kitchen with made-to-order breakfasts and excellent coffee. Dorm beds get lockers and reading lamps. It all combines together with some great tunes.

Platypus
HOSTEL $

(Map p44; 📞352 0127; www.platypusbogota.com; Calle 12F No 2-43; dm COP$20,000, s/d without bathroom COP$36,000/44,000, r COP$55,000; @🛜) Run by a Bogotá legend, Germán Escobar, a friendly world-traveler who opened a hostel in La Candelaria when no one dared. The hostel fills three homes with simple, clean rooms. There's a cozy kitchen area, and friendly staff (including Germán) offer great travel info. Reserve ahead, and if possible, stick to the main building rather than some 14 annexed beds nearby.

Anandamayi Hostel
HOSTEL $$

(Map p44; 📞341 7208; www.amandamayihostel.com; Calle 9 No 2-81; dm/s/d without bathroom COP$30,000/90,000/120,000; @🛜) South of most of the hostel zone, this lovely white-washed colonial home has small but well-furnished rooms with wood-beam ceilings, plenty of wool blankets and colonial furniture. A few rooms have private bathrooms

but it's potluck and the same price. Rooms and the 14-bed dorm surround a few semi-leafy central courtyards with hammocks. For La Candelaria, it's noticeably chill and rates include breakfast.

Hotel Abadia Colonial
HOTEL $$$

(Map p44; 📞341 1884; www.abadiacolonial.com; Calle 11 No 2-32; s/d incl breakfast COP$155,000/220,000; @🛜) More intimate than other higher-priced hotels in La Candelaria, this pleasant 12-room hotel has tidy white-walled rooms with colorful blankets, wall safes and a sense of colonial style, while adding floor heaters and TV. Breakfast is served in one of the pleasant courtyard seating areas.

🌿 Musicology
HOSTEL $

(Map p44; 📞286 9093; www.musicologyhostel.com; Calle 9 No 3-15; dm COP$18,000-26,000; @🛜) This French-managed, Israeli-owned all-dorm hostel has the eco-edge in La Candelaria, with all beds and chairs throughout fashioned from demolition wood, a paper-free check-in and no plastic waste. It's musically themed (named after a Prince track), with 13 security cameras insuring the record never screeches with a theft or otherwise. Rates include breakfast *and* dinner.

Destino Nómada
HOSTEL $$

(Map p44; 📞352 0932; www.dnhostels.com; Calle 11 No 00-38; dm COP$21,000-27,000, s/d COP$62,000/72,000, without bathroom COP$37,000/43,000; @🛜) Travelers have been raving about this newcomer where camaraderie is high among guests due to *mucho* barbecues and themed nights. Rooms are actually dead simple, but it's nicely located a few blocks from Museo Botero.

Casa de la Botica
BOUTIQUE HOTEL $$$

(Map p44; 📞281 0811; www.hotelcasadelabotica.com; Carrera 6 No 8-77; s/d/ste incl breakfast COP$237,500/300,000/360,000; @🛜) Near Congress commuters on a central lane dominated by the Colegio Mayor de San Bartolomé, this tranquil, 21-room hotel pairs colonial style with a modern feel in its older carpeted rooms (the new wing offers a contemporary upgrade). Opt up for the bigger suite – with fireplace and full windows overlooking a tiny rock garden.

Hostal Sue Candelaria
HOSTEL $

(Map p44; 📞344 2647; www.suecandelaria.com; Carrera 3 No 12C-18; dm COP$20,000, s/d without bathroom COP$36,000/50,000, r COP$55,000;

@🛜) The friendly and bright Sue Candelaria, the newer of the two Sue's in La Candelaria, wins the most festive bedspreads competition in a fine string of rooms in a smaller, colonial-style layout. Free coffee all day and breakfast is included. The bar at this location gives it a leg up over the original location next to Platypus.

Hotel Lido
HOTEL $

(Map p44; 📞341 2582; www.hotellidoplaza.com; Calle 11 No 9-45; s/d/tr COP$70,000/94,000/147,000; @🛜) On a block of tailors, a block-and-a-half south of the main plaza, this neat 20-room job has compact carpeted rooms, with TV, telephone and private bathrooms. Super friendly.

CENTRO INTERNACIONAL

The center's grubby loud blocks have several hotels – some pleasant enough – but we've focused on the nicer areas to the north in the Centro Internacional.

Aparta Suites Tequendama
APARTMENT, HOTEL $$$

(off Map p44; 📞381 3705; www.apartasuitestequendama.com; Carrera 10 No 27-51; apt incl breakfast from COP$424,000; @🛜🏊) The newly remodeled apartments in the towering Residencias' building (soon to be a Crowne Plaza) get our nod over its more famous cousin Tequendama next door, with spacious, contemporary apartments with lovely hardwood floors, plasma flat-screens and modern kitchenettes.

NORTHERN BOGOTÁ

If you are here on business or are used to the high life, you may be best served by the hotels scattered north of Calle 65, many of which are within walking distance of the lively scene of Zona G, Zona Rosa or Parque 93.

CHAPINERO

TOP CHOICE La Pinta
HOSTEL $$

(Map p52; 📞211 9526; www.lapinta.com.co; Calle 65 No 5-67; dm COP$22,000, s/d from COP$55,000/66,000, all incl breakfast; @🛜) In an unmarked residential home in a great Chapinero location just steps from La Septima, this spotless little secret offers a fantastic back garden; big, modern bathrooms and colorful down comforters in hardwood-floored rooms that approach boutique-hotel levels. There's a large, communal kitchen and a whacky, lovable dog. Room 304 is the best double with a garden view.

ZONA G

La Casona del Patio
GUESTHOUSE $$$

(Map p52; 📞212 8805; www.lacasonadelpatio.net; Carrera 8 No 69-24; s/d incl breakfast COP$127,000/170,000; @🛜) This newly renovated guesthouse in an historical home has grown to 24 rooms and feels a bit like an adult hostel. Old rooms surrounding a small courtyard now boast LCD TVs in addition to faux wood floors and are picture-themed for area attractions. Newer rooms in a second, attached home are more modern but maintain the simple vibe of this friendly spot in a quiet part of Zona G.

ZONA ROSA & PARQUE 93

TOP CHOICE Cité
BOUTIQUE HOTEL $$$

(Map p56; 📞646 7777; www.citehotel.com; Carrera 15 No 88-10; s/d incl breakfast from COP$500,000/560,000; ❄@🛜🏊) Between Zona Rosa and Parque 93 and part of a small Bogotá chain, this business-hip boutique hotel is new and novel, with rarely seen advantages like a heated rooftop pool, extra large rooms with lots of natural light and even some with bathtubs, a true rarity. Perhaps coolest of all is that there are bicycles for guests to use for free – handy as you are on a CicloRuta path.

Chapinorte Bogotá
HOSTEL $

(Map p56; 📞256 2152; www.chapinortehostelbogota.com; Calle 79 No 14-59; dm COP$30,000, s/d COP$70,000/95,000, without bathroom COP$70,000/80,000, all incl breakfast; @🛜) In a nondescript residential building just beyond the northern edges of the Chapinero, this 10-room hostel is a great anti-Candelaria choice. Run by a friendly Spaniard, some stylish rooms have monstrous bathrooms and cable TV. Rates drop between COP$5000 and COP$10,000 on weekdays.

Sofitel
HOTEL $$$

(Map p56; 📞621 2666; www.sofitel.com; Carrera 13 No 85-80; r from COP$986,000; ❄@🛜) One of Zona Rosa's best-run hotels, the Sofitel was recently gutted and reshined, with rooms now brimming in soothing Cabernet color schemes localized by tasteful replica items from the Museo del Oro. They're soundproof, too, but its location on a tranquil street with several excellent restaurants means it's not that vital.

Hotel Virrey Park
HOTEL $$$

(Map p56; 📞218 1625; www.hotelvirreypark.com; Carrera 15 No 87-94; s/d/tr incl breakfast COP$197,000/227,371/287,371; ❄@🛜) Just

Zona Rosa & Parque 93

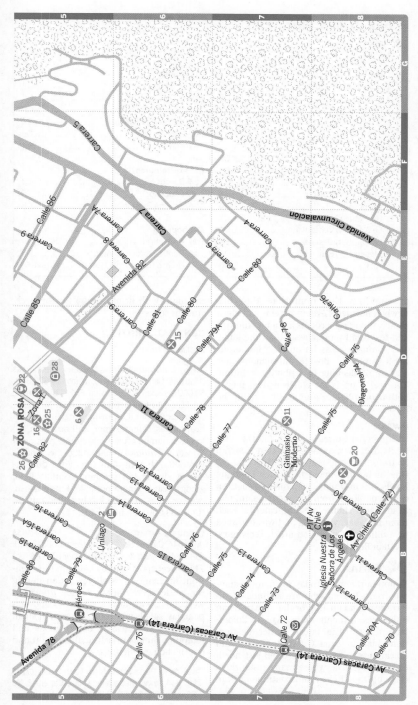

Carrera 5

Calle 86

Calle 85

Carrera 7A

Carrera 7

Carrera 8

Avenida 82

Carrera 9

Calle 81

Calle 80

Carrera 6

Calle 80

Avenida Circunvalación

Carrera 4

Calle 79A

Calle 78

Calle 76

Diagonal 74

Calle 75

Carrera 11

Calle 78

Calle 77

Gimnasio Moderno

Calle 75

ZONA ROSA

Calle 82

Carrera 13

Carrera 12A

Carrera 14

Uniilago

Carrera 16

Carrera 16A

Carrera 18

Calle 80

Calle 79

Héroes

Avenida 78

Carrera 15

Calle 76

Calle 76

Calle 75

Calle 74

Carrera 13

Calle 73

Carrera 12

Calle 72

Calle 70A

Calle 70

PIT Av Chile

Iglesia Nuestra Señora de Los Ángeles

Av Chile (Calle 72)

Carrera 11

Carrera 10

Av Caracas (Carrera 14)

Av Caracas (Carrera 14)

26 16 25 6 22 27 28 15 11 2 20 9

Zona Rosa & Parque 93

across Virrey Park from Hotel Cité, this newly renovated 47-room hotel is a modern choice, though the rooms are a bit cramped and feel a tad more classic than the lobby and common areas let on. The numerous photographs of Bogotá throughout give a sense of sleeping in a photo exhibition. The real coup is for coffee fiends: there's both a Juan Valdéz *and* an Illy cafe in the lobby.

USAQUÉN

Usaquén Art Suites BOUTIQUE HOTEL **$$$**
(☑214 2029; www.usaquenartsuites.com; Carrera 5 No 117-07; r incl breakfast from COP$250,000; 🛜)
One of Bogotá's most boutiquey boutique hotels, this new nine-room modern spot is a couple of blocks from Usaquén's quaint plaza and area shops, bars and eateries. Each room has shaggy carpets and was designed by a different Colombian artist. Feels more LA than Bogotá.

Eating

Fusion is the word today for many restaurateurs in Bogotá who are running Mediterranean, Italian, Californian or pan-Asian influences through many typical Colombian dishes. The latest dinner destinations include Zona G's chic eateries and Macarena's slightly boho scene, just north of La Candelaria, where many restaurants close up the kitchen and continue on into

the night with drinks (only) for the lively student scene.

CENTRAL BOGOTÁ

LA CANDELARIA

TOP CHOICE **La Condesa Irina Lazaar** AMERICAN **$$$**
(Map p44; Carrera 6 No 10-19; mains COP$20,000-30,000; ⊙noon-3:30pm Mon Fri) This small, unsigned 10-table eatery run by a Mexican-American from California catering to bohos, judges, Congressmen and others in the know is named after a forgettable American Western, *Shalako*. Thankfully, the food is way better than the film. Chef Edgardo dishes out simple but soothing comfort food, going organic where possible. Line-cut fish, organic chicken and a lovely grilled salmon (COP$33,000) are highlights.

Quinua y Amaranto VEGETARIAN **$$**
(Map p44; Calle 11 No 2-95; set lunch COP$12,000; ⊙8am-4pm Mon & Sat, 8am-7:30pm Tue-Fri; 🖉) This sweet spot – run by ladies in the open-front kitchen – goes all vegetarian during the week (there's often chicken *ajiaco* on weekends), with tasty set lunches and empanadas, salads and coffee later on. A small section of coco leaves, baked goods and tempting chunks of artisanal cheese round out the homey offerings.

Café de la Peña Pastelería Francesa CAFE **$**
(Map p44; www.cafepasteleria.com; Carrera 3 No 9-66; items COP$5000-12,800) Colombians run

this fabulous French-style bakery, with local art adorning the walls of a garden and a couple of seating areas, but you'd never know it. They make some of the nicest sweets and *pan de chocolate* in the area; and roast their own excellent coffee.

La Puerta Falsa   FAST FOOD $
(Map p44; Calle 11 No 6-50; candies COP$1500, meals COP$3500-5000) This is Bogotá's most famous snack shop – with displayed multicolored candies beckoning you into this tiny spot that's been in business since 1816. Some complain it's nothing but foreigners with their Lonely Planet guides these days, but don't buy it – there were no other gringos on a Saturday morning in September. The moist tamales and *chocolate completo* (hot chocolate with cheese, buttered bread and a biscuit; COP$5000) remain a Bogotá snack of lore.

Enchiladas   MEXICAN $$
(Map p44; Calle 10 No 2-12; dishes COP$13,000-27,000; ◷noon-5pm Sun-Mon, to 10pm Tue-Sat) You'll either be mildly satisfied (if you're American or Mexican) or head over heels (if you're from somewhere with a distinct lack of Mexican cuisine) at this festive spot, with Mayan reliefs, a toasty fireplace and old Mexican film photos on the walls.

Asociación Futuro   BREAKFAST $
(Map p44; Calle 12D No 2-21; set meals from COP$4900) Splitting its breakfast trade evenly between locals and backpackers, this cute, community-run corner pad churns out great set breakfasts and Colombian dishes later on.

CITY CENTER

Pastelería Florida   COLOMBIAN $
(Map p44; Carrera 7 No 21-46; snacks COP$900-15,000, chocolate completo COP$7300) Those needing a bit of pomp or history with their *chocolate santafereño* (hot chocolate served with cheese) should make the hike to this classic snack shop–restaurant (a legendary spot for hot chocolate since 1936), with uniformed waiters serving up a variety of cakes.

Restaurante La Pola   COLOMBIAN $$
(Map p44; Calle 19 No 1-85; set lunch COP$8500; ◷11am-5pm Mon-Sat) This rambling classic on the road to Monserrate has a mix of old-style rooms and a small courtyard, and offers some great lunch grills or order à la carte for some of the city's best *ajiaco*.

Olimpica   SUPERMARKET $
(Map p44; Av Jiménez No 4-70; ◷7am-9pm Mon-Sat, 9am-4pm Sun) About a five-minute walk from most hostels.

MACARENA

A dozen blocks north of La Candelaria (or a couple uphill from Centro Internacional), Macarena is an up-and-coming dining district – with a stream of excellent, stylish choices – holding true to its local roots, with passersby likely to pop in and chat with diners.

There are also many worthy choices on Calle 29, just northeast of the Museo Nacional, in Centro Internacional.

TOP
CHOICE **Agave Azul**   MEXICAN $$$
(☑315 277 0329; www.restaurantagaveazul.blog spot.com; Carrera 4A No 26B-22; average meal COP$60,000-70,000; ◷noon-3pm & 6-10pm Tue-Fri, 1-4pm & 7-10:30pm Sat) This expanding five-table restaurant is a trip, both literally and figuratively, through truly authentic Mexican cuisine by way of Chicago, New York and Oaxaca. Chef Tatiana Navarro has no menu – just a daily open-ended tasting menu (you just call, 'Uncle!'). Possibilities include a ridiculous salmon ceviche in a habanero and passionfruit sauce, adobo prawn tacos or *huitlacoche* (corn fungus) and cheese dumplings, usually served alongside vibrant small-town salsas. Chase it with an outstanding chipotle margarita and you have reached *nirvana cocina Mexicana*. Reservations essential.

La Tapería   TAPAS $$
(Carrera 4A No 26B-12; tapas COP$8900-15,900) The urbanite sophisticate doppelgänger to Tapas Macarena nearby, both run by a Dutch/Colombian couple, who churn out delectable tapas like *lomo* with blue cheese or mussels in whiskey sauce in a cool, loft-aesthetic lounge. There's live flamenco on Thursdays and a DJ on weekends.

NORTHERN BOGOTÁ

For shoppers, high-class foodies, or the boutique-hotel and club crowd, Bogotá's north offers endless options.

CHAPINERO

The burgeoning Chapinero Alto is a close-knit artistic community with all kinds of quaint neighborhood cafes and shops.

Dulce Mini-Mál

SWEETS $

(Map p52; www.mini-mal.org; Calle 57 No 4-09; set meals from COP$4900; ⊙closed Sun) This tiny corner bakery in Chapinero Alto run by an adorable gastro-alchemist specializes in sweets and cakes with Colombian ingredients used in wildly unexpected ways. There's a *chontaduro* crème brûlée, for example, made with a palm from the Valle del Cauca; and the *coup de maître*: a sinister-good brownie lollipop made with smoked Amazon peppers. Delish!

Salvo Patria

CAFE $

(Map p52; www.salvopatria.com; Carrera 4A No 57-28; mains COP$16,000-21,000; ⊙closed Mon) This quaint cafe is the epitome of the Chapinero Alto scene, set in a historical corner building overlooking Parque Portugal. It's one part very serious coffeehouse that serves single-origin coffee prepared in rare ways like the siphon and Chemex methods (the *bogotano* owner honed his barista skills in Australia); and also an eatery with a casual menu of reasonably priced Mediterranean-French bistro fare that changes often.

ZONA G

Bogotá's primo dining area fills a couple of blocks of converted brick houses into a mix of excellent eateries (Argentine steaks, Italian, French), about 10 blocks south of Zona Rosa.

TOP CHOICE ⟩ Rafael

PERUVIAN $$$

(Map p52; 📞255 4138; www.rafaelosterling.com; Calle 70 No 4-63/65; mains COP$39,800-59,500; ⊙closed Sun) *Bogotano* foodies and chefs are nearly unanimous in calling Peruvian Chef Rafael Osterling's creative homegrown cuisine the city's most consistently innovative. The contemporary space melds cold aesthetics like concrete ceilings with a warm and intimate garden; and the food leaves no man unsatisfied. Favorites like sticky duck rice braised in black beer or a crunchy *cochinillo* (suckling pig) in *mikakami* juice confit are staples on the ever-changing menu, but leave room for dessert. The trio of *limón suspiros* (layered merengue and *dulce de leche;* traditional, *lúcuma* and *chirimoya*) and the plantain cheesecake under a swath of Nutella are both fitting ends to a dazzling travel meal.

ZONA ROSA & PARQUE 93

Within the Zona Rosa, the 'Zona T' – named for its T-shaped pedestrian zone filled with bars, restaurants and a few chains – also has oodles more options on surrounding blocks. If you need a peso break, nearby Carrera 15 is lined with places selling cheap empanadas and pizza-and-soda deals. Ten blocks north, the more-sedate Parque 93 and Calle 94 have even classier spots.

TOP CHOICE ⟩ Central Cevicheria

COLOMBIAN/SEAFOOD $$

(Map p56; www.centralcevicheria.com; Carrera 13 No 85-14; ceviche COP$14,800-16,800) This good-time, high-concept cevicheria is the real deal: Bogotá's high and mighty ogle over each other as well as the superb ceviches, split into spicy and non-spicy categories, of which there are a dozen inventive offerings. We opted for the kick-laced *picoso,* swimming in three peppers, cilantro and fresh corn. But it doesn't stop there: there are numerous *tiraditos* (long-cut ceviches without onions), tartares and higher-priced fresh seafood main dishes. It's Colombian coastal cuisine on overdrive.

Di Lucca

ITALIAN $$

(Map p56; Carrera 13 No 85-32; pizza COP$19,900-29,000) Locals unanimously gush over this smart trattoria and its soothing prices. Pizza, pasta and risottos rule. Solo travelers could do much worse than bellying up to the hardwood bar and ordering a perfectly executed off-menu *medium* prosciutto pizza (COP$14,000 – that's right, around $8!). Great food. Low bills.

Harry Sasson

FUSION $$$

(Map p56; 📞347 7155; www.harrysasson.com; Carrera 9 No 75-70; mains COP$30,000-56,000) Bogotá's most famous chef has opened his new namesake restaurant in a gorgeous remodeled 1934 mansion. The stunning bar, an ode to the Bird's Nest architecture of Beijing's National Stadium, is all glass, girders and sexiness. And the food: a fused mix of Asian influences and Colombian foundations. Highlights include a smoky, wood-fired tomato soup (COP$16,600) that will make your knees buckle and a perfect shrimp and chicken fried rice doused in sesame oil (COP$32,900). Reservations essential.

Nick's

SANDWICHES $$

(Map p56; www.nicks-café.com; Carrera 9 No 79A-28; sandwiches COP$14,900-16,900; ⊙closed Sun) Nick honed his deli skills in Boston and recognized a niche in his hometown, and now his killer deli sandwiches are all the rage in El Nogal, a quiet neighborhood just east of Zona Rosa. Some 20 sandwiches are churned out on soft ciabatta, feeding a frenzy that turns the narrow space into a full-on bar at night. Discounts to bike arrivals!

Museo del Tequila MEXICAN **$$**
(Map p56; Carrera 13A No 86A-18; mains COP$9900-32,999) Trouble finds you in the form of over 3000 tequila bottles decorating this festive, fun-time Mexican, but the food – with specialties from all over Mexico – is the real draw.

La Areparia Venzolana AREPAS, FAST FOOD **$**
(Map p56; Calle 85 No 13-36; arepas COP$8500-11,500; ⊗to 4am Mon-Sat) Firmly rooted late-night hotspot for drunken munchies right off Zona Rosa. Venezuelan-style *arepas* (corn cakes; better than Colombian) are stuffed with all manner of fillings.

Once a village to the north, Usaquén has been overtaken by Bogotá – but still lives at its own quiet pace. You'll find snazzy Chinese, Mediterranean or burger joints within a block of the main plaza.

TOP CHOICE Abasto BREAKFAST **$$**
(Carrera 6 No 119B-52; breakfast COP$5500-10,500, mains COP$18,900-36,900) A weekend pilgrimage north to Usaquén is in order to indulge in the creative breakfasts at this rustic-trendy restaurant and gourmet food shop. Inventive *arepas* and fantastic eggs dishes like *migas* (scrambled with bits of *arepas* and *hogao,* a concoction of onion, tomatoes, cumin and garlic) are washed down with organic coffee by true morning sustenance connoisseurs.

BOGOTÁ CHAINS

We're not accustomed to touting chains, but Bogotá has some surprisingly worthy ones you'll find in most neighborhoods, particularly in the north.

Wok ASIAN **$$$**
(www.wok.com.co) Centro Internacional (Map p56; Carrera 6 No 29-07); Parque 93 (Map p56; Calle 93B No 12-28; mains COP$10,900-28,900); Zona Rosa (Map p56; Carrera 13 No 82-74) Choosing at this hip chain with a social/environmental bent is as agonizing as deciding which of your children to throw to the wolves: excellent Chinese, Vietnamese, Indonesian and Cambodian dishes abound (including line-caught sushi), attracting a steady stream of cool locals. Other convenient locations are in Zona Rosa and next door to Museo Nacional.

La Hamburgueseria BURGERS **$$**
(www.lahamburgueseria.com) Macarena (Carrera 4A No 27-27; burgers COP$11,500-21,300; ⊗to 11pm); Parque 93 (Map p56; Calle 93B No 11A-34); Usaquén (Calle 118 No 6A-40) The city's best burgers are to be found in this trendy, Macarena-born joint: thick patties in gourmet versions with an international flare (Thai, Italian, Greek, Arab etc) and served alongside five housemade relishes and sauces. There are additional locations in Parque 93 and Usaquén, which both feature live music. You will also see the chain El Corral and El Corral Gourmet everywhere – the former is probably the best fast-food burger you'll ever have.

Bogotá Beer Company BAR **$$**
(www.bogotabeercompany.com) Usaquén (Carrera 6 No 119-24; pints COP$9500, burgers COP$19,900-21,900; ⊗to 2am); Zona Rosa (Map p56; Carrera 12 No 83-33) These pubby-style, upscale beer joints are a Godsend for beer lovers, with some 14 seasonal microbrews on tap. The Usaquén and Macarena locales are a bit more laid-back than the other half-a-dozen.

Crepes & Waffles CAFE **$$**
(Map p56; Carrera 9 No 73-33; crepes COP$9600-31,900) One of 35 Bogotá locations of this ever-busy chain – which employs women in need – we like this one best: a two-story brick home with sidewalk seats between Zona G and Zona Rosa. Like the others, it serves up veggie, meat and seafood crepes, plus irresistible ice cream–topped waffles (COP$5000).

🍷 Drinking

Some of the city's most atmospheric bars – that is, if you're into 300-year-old homes with corner fireplaces and old tile floors – are in La Candelaria, a great spot to try a hot mug of *canelazo* (a drink made with aguardiente, sugarcane, cinnamon and lime), while watering holes get more Euro-styled and upscale around Zona Rosa or Parque 93.

CENTRAL BOGOTÁ

LA CANDELARIA

Considering the student scene in the area, La Candelaria cafes focus on drinks alone after hours. You can find plenty of life around the corner of Calle 15 and Carrera 4 – with reggae, rock and tango bars – or along Calle 11 by Universidad de la Salle (cnr Calle 11 and Carrera 2), but our favorite is Callejón del Embudo ('Funnel') – the tiny alley north of Plazoleta del Chorro de Quevedo, lined with sit-and-chat cafes and bars selling *chicha* (an indigenous corn beer).

Pequeña Santa Fe   BAR
(Map p44; Carrera 2 No 12B-14) A cozy, historic two-story home with a fireplace by the bar and soft-lit loft upstairs sits next to the evocative Plazoleta del Chorro de Quevedo. It's one of a few great spots here to sample a hot mug of '*canelazo* Santa Fe' (a yerba-buena tea with aguardiente), or a beer.

Casa de Citas   CAFE
(Map p44; Carrera 3 No 12B-35; admission COP$10,000-15,000; ⊙noon-5pm Mon, to 4pm & 6-10pm Tue-Thu, to 4am Fri & Sat, to 5pm Sun) Named for an earlier incarnation – when prostitutes advertised themselves from the balcony above – the saloon-styled Citas is now an atmospheric cafe, adorned with Castro photos, that hosts live rumba, jazz or salsa shows Thursday through to Saturday. Weekends are lovely.

CENTRO INTERNACIONAL

The business district tends to clear out after dark. You can find a few bars up the hill in Macarena, which draws a more sophisticated, thirtysomething crowd of newlyweds, latent singles and those looking for more of a lounge experience than a club.

TOP CHOICE **El Bembe**   SALSA BAR
(Calle 27B No 6-73; cover Fri & Sat COP$15,000-20,000) Head up the Cuban-colored stairs to this little piece of *tropacalia* on a magical cobbled street in the Macarena, where an actual living and breathing Cuban co-runs the show (and the kitchen). It's what Havana would be like if there were no US embargo: bright colors; breezy, beautiful balconies; and outstanding salsa. On Fridays, the bolero lunch morphs into an all-out salsa *revolución* that carries into the wee hours.

DON'T MISS

ANDRÉS CARNE DE RES

You cannot describe the indescribable but here goes: the legendary **Andrés Carne de Res** (✆863 7880; www.andrescarnederes.com; Calle 3 No 11A-56, Chía; mains COP$16,202-65,405, cover Fri & Sat COP$15,000; ⊙11am-3am Thu-Sat, till midnight Sun) is an otherworldly entertainment cocktail that's equal parts Tim Burton, Disneyland and Willy Wonka – with a dash of junkyard kitsch and funhouse extravaganza. No, wait. A Swedish tourist said it better: 'It's like eating dinner in a washing machine.' *Whatever*. Andrés blows everyone away – even repeat visitors – for its all-out-fun atmosphere with awesome steaks – the menu is a 62-page magazine! – and all sorts of surreal decor. For most, it's more than a meal, but an up-all-night, damn-the-torpedoes spectacular. The catch is that it's out of town – in Chía, 23km north toward Zipaquirá. A taxi from Bogotá costs about COP$60,000, or COP$180,000 round-trip including wait time. Many Candelaria hostels also operate a party bus to Andrés on Saturday nights for COP$50,000 (includes admission and booze on the bus). If it's not the most insane night you have ever had, you've done too many drugs.

A more sedate location closer to town, **Andrés DC** (Map p56; ✆863 7880; Centro Comercial El Retiro, Calle 82 No 12-21; ⊙noon-3am), has opened – it lacks that certain indescribable something, but is fun, too.

CHAPINERO

This edgy, sprawling bohemian district with many gay bars and theaters sits south of the high-end eateries of the more polite northern neighbor Zona G. Start on Calle 60, between Carreras 8 and 9, and head south on Carrera 9. Further south, Calle 51 between Carrera 7 and 8 is something of a 'student street' with half a dozen flirt-all-day, glassed-in bars and a couple of dance clubs. This is where the urbanites and teenage anarchists go to party.

Treffen BAR

(Map p52; Carrera 7 No 56-17) Meaning 'encounter' in German, but no words describe this quirky bar's cartoon nightmare mood, with nooks and crannies filled with stuffed animals, colorful tables and games menus. It probably exists due to Andrés Carne de Res, but that doesn't mean you won't trip the light fantastic here.

Invitro BAR

(Map p52; www.invitrobar.com; Calle 59 No 6-38, piso 2; cover COP$10,000-15,000) This gritty 2nd-floor Chapinero Tuesday-night staple got its start showing independent films (still going at 8pm Tuesday and Wednesday) but morphed into streetwise urban club drawing an eclectic mix of artsy cool kids, most from upper-class families dressing down to shake the stigma. Funk, house, electrocumbia and drum 'n' bass rule the decks, giving the space a bit of an underground London feel.

Taller de Té CAFE

(Map p52; www.tallerdete.com; Calle 60A No 3A-38; ⊗closed Sun; ⊛) Run by a lovely defected Colombia tourism official turned tea hippie (compliment), this is one of the only places to buy and drink serious tea in Bogotá. Owner Laura sources her teas from plantations around the world and blends with Colombian teas. There's a small garden to sip the day away.

NORTHERN BOGOTÁ

Though the area's more famous for its clubs (and malls!), you'll have no problem finding a place for a cocktail, beer or coffee around Zona Rosa or Parque 93. In the former, start in the pedestrian mall (Zona T), where you'll find an endlessly entertaining choice of nocturnal diversion and pub crawl out in all directions.

COFFEE CULTURE

Coffee's huge in Bogotá – supposedly nine in 10 households brew a pot daily – but much of it isn't very good. That's a pity considering the quality of the bean Colombia produces. The two big chains here – Juan Valdéz and Oma – are Starbucks-styled, but do as reliable a job with a *tinto* (black coffee), cappuccino or *cafe americano* as anyone in town. You'll find them all over town (particularly the mustached icon of Juan Valdéz); the north has the most, so here are a couple of central locales:

Juan Valdéz CAFE

(www.juanvaldezcafe.com; ⊛) Museo Botero (Map p44; Museo Botero, Calle 11 No 4-41); Zona Rosa (Map p56; cnr Calle 73 & Carrera 9)

Oma CAFE

(Map p44; www.cafeoma.com; cnr Carrera 8 & Calle 12; ⊗closed Sun; ⊛) Also has sandwiches (COP$7700 to COP$9500).

Armando Records BAR

(Map p56; www.armandorecords.org; Calle 85 No 14-46, piso 4; cover Thu-Sat COP$15,000-20,000; ⊗to 3am Wed-Sat) This 4th-floor retro rooftop bar is all the rage in Bogotá and rightfully so. It's the kind of place where the tunes guide your evening – think LCD Soundsystem and Empire of the Sun. Alterna-hipsters pack the leafy, lowlit space, mulling the next spin over fabulous *lulo* (fruit) mojitos (COP$18,000) and wondering how they will cope when this hip spot falls out of favor.

El Coq BAR

(Map p56; Calle 84 No 14-02, piso 2; cover Fri & Sat COP$20,000; ⊗to late Wed-Sat) Battling head-to-head with Armando Records for hipper-than-thou rights in the city, this see-and-be-seen spot evokes a French countryhouse/greenhouse, complete with farmhouse basketball goals and Spanish moss strewn across the retractable ceilings. The electro/indie soundtrack skips happily between Phoenix and Friendly Fires, then throws you for a loop with '80s hip-hop. Andrés Juan, a Colombian actor who isn't afraid to throw down with the cool kids, runs the show.

La Puerta Grande   TAPAS, CLUB
(Map p56; ☎636 3425; www.lapuertagrande.net; Carrera 12 No 93-64; cover Fri & Sat COP$15,000; ⏱noon-3am Mon-Sat, to 5pm Sun) This Spanish-run spot is a doozy: wander through six Spain-themed environments (Gaudí-evoking Barcelona is our favorite), split between the restaurant areas and the DJ/live music areas. There's an open jam session on Monday, live flamenco on Wednesday and live rock on Thursday, with DJs spinning house, pop and electrocumbia in between. The food excels: traditional tapas like the *jamón serrano* croquettes (Serrano ham; COP$18,999) and the *tortilla de patatas* (Spanish potato omelette; COP$7999) will transport you, as if you weren't already there.

Yumi Yumi   COCKTAILS
La Candelaria (Map p44; Carrera 3 No 16-40; ⏱closed Sun); Zona Rosa (Map p56; Carrera 13 No 83-83; ⏱3pm-1am Mon-Thu, 3pm-3am Fri & Sat) Students, passersby and hostel guests cram into the minuscule Candelaria space for excellent, experimental cocktails (try the sour *lulita*, with tequila, shaved cinnamon and *lulo* fruit) and a great Thai curry special on Tuesday and Wednesday (COP$10,400). In the Zona Rosa branch, you'll find double the prices but double the space and fun: two-for-one cocktails as a general rule and three-for-one on Wednesday. Cheers!

Pub   PUB
(www.thepub.com.co) Zona Rosa (Map p56; Carrera 12A No 83-48); Usaquén (Carrera 6A No 117-45) This large, enduringly popular Irish-style pub draws beer hounds aching for a proper pint. There's Murphy's on tap and fish and chips. There's also a branch in Usaquén.

☆ Entertainment

Bogotá has far more cultural activities than any other city in Colombia. Check out *Qué Hacer* section of local paper *El Tiempo,* a what's-on section listing events. Other listings you'll find around town include **Plan B** (www.planb.com.co) and **Vivo.In** (www.bogota.vive.in). For cultural events and commentary in English, pick up the free monthly *City Paper* (www.thecitypaperbogota.com).

For schedules and tickets to many events (theater, rock concerts, football games), check **Tu Boleta** (www.tuboleta.com).

Nightclubs

Strap yourself in: Bogotá boogies. There's all sort of ambience and musical rhythm on offer – from rock, techno and metal to salsa, vallenato and samba. If you don't know how to dance, be prepared to prove it. Strangers frequently ask each other to dance and everyone seems to know the words to every song played.

The relatively laid-back club scene of La Candelaria caters to local students, who don't always care what they're wearing. Up north, particularly the chic scene around the sparkling, vibrant (if pretentious) *salsatecas* (salsa dance clubs) and clubs of Zona Rosa and Parque 93, you may be turned away for not being dressed up to the part.

Cover charges vary from free to COP$50,000.

CENTRAL BOGOTÁ

El Candelario   BAR, CLUB
(Map p44; www.elcandelario.net; Carrera 5 No 13-14; ⏱9:30pm-3am Fri & Sat) Open for six years – an eternity in Bogotá – this quintessential Latin hotspot hovers in delicate nightlife purgatory between bar and disco. It's all exposed brick, large antique mirrors and upside-down restored rocking chairs hanging from the ceiling, all of which help defer the vibrations of all that cumbia (a popular musical rhythm and corresponding dance of the Caribbean coast; African in origin), reggaeton, tropicalia and electronica. It draws a fun, mixed crowd not looking for trouble, and is walkable from La Candelaria lodgings.

The End   CLUB
(off Map p44; ☎341 7903; Aparta Suites Tequendema, Carrera 10 No 27-51; ⏱8pm-late Fri & Sat) After Bogotá shuts down, a kaleidoscopic cross-section of *bogotano* life turns up at this 30th-floor hot spot guarded by the military – so the police can't enforce the city's standard last-call laws! There are insane 360-degree views and the diverse crowd (who would have never hung out together otherwise) keep the good times rollin' past sunrise.

Quiebra Canto   SALSA
(Map p44; www.quiebracanto.com; Carrera 5 No 17-76; ⏱6:30pm-2:30am Thu-Sat) Name-dropped first – for years now – by salsa-seekers across town, the Canto is a double-level disco a short walk from La Candelaria. Wednesday is big with expats for electronica DJs, but weekends go for live salsa.

El Goce Pagano   SALSA, REGGAE
(Map p44; www.elgocepagano.com; Carrera 1 No 20-04; ⏱7pm-3am Fri & Sat) Nearing 40, the divey salsa/reggae bar near Los Andes university

GAY & LESBIAN BOGOTÁ

Bogotá has a large, frequently changing gay scene, mostly centered in Chapinero, nicknamed 'Chapi Gay' between Carrera 7 and 13 from Calle 58 to Calle 63. Browse www. guiagaycolombia.com/bogota for more details on dozens of varied clubs and bars, or check online listings from **Colombia Diversa** (www.colombiadiversa.org), a not-for-profit organization promoting gay and lesbian rights in Colombia.

On a small road (between Carreras 9 and 13) in the heart of Chapinero, the classic **Theatron** (Map p52; ☏235 6879; www.theatrondepelicula.com; Calle 58 No 10-32; ☺9pm-late Thu-Sat), carved from a huge converted film house, draws gays and straights – some 3000 on weekends! – among its eight different environments, though some areas are men only.

There are dozens of bars in the area. Glamy **Romeo* Disco Club** (Map p52; Calle 62 No 11-49, piso 2; ☺10pm-3am Thu-Sat) is where uptown boys go to take the edge on. It hosts Julieta by Romero on the last Friday of each month – Bogotá's best lesbian party. In Parque 93, the stylish Bardot (p65) hosts gay night on Sundays.

is a smoky place with DJs and sweat-soaked bodies from all over Colombia, moving to ethnic rhythms.

NORTHERN BOGOTÁ

Cachao
SALSA

(Map p56; Carrera 13 No 82-52; ☺to 3am Mon-Sat) This excellent salsa bar is inspired by the artistic life of Cuban mambo musician Israel 'Cachao' López. Crowds pile onto bar stools fashioned from congos or congregate on the breezy outdoor patio – either way, they have the city's best mojitos in hand (COP$18,000 to COP$29,700), rhythm serum to accompany the outstanding nightly salsa.

Bardot
CLUB

(Map p56; ☏616 0036; www.bardotbar.com; Calle 93B No 11A-14, piso 2; ☺10:15pm-3am Fri & Sat) Bardot is Bogotá's hot spot of the moment, where celebs and A-listers gather to show off their wealth and beauty in a space that one local described as 'dark and Elton John-style.' It's true. Velvet-lined Louis XV violet and black chairs and Rococo-style lamps dominate the decor; house, techno, reggae and reggaeton dominate the soundtrack. We're warning you: there's no chance in hell you are getting in if your name is not on that list. Prepare for a fight at the door.

Gaira Café
LIVE MUSIC

(☏636 2696; Carrera 13 No 96-11) Vallenato legend Carlos Vives' ultrafun dancehall-restaurant for live vallenato – or modern takes on it. Locals pack in for food and rum drinks, and dance in the tight spaces around tables to an 11-piece band. Cocktails cost COP$20,000 to COP$25,000, sandwiches and salads from COP$13,900. To reach here from Parque 93, head north three blocks on

Carrera 13, west one block on Calle 95, north one block on Carrera 14 and east two blocks on Calle 96.

Salomé Pagana
SALSA

(Map p56; www.salomepaganaclubsocial.com; Carrera 14A No 82-16; ☺to 3am Tue-Sat) A little less shiny than most of trendy Zona Rosa, this intimate, red-walled *salsateca* is run by the gray-haired collector César Pagano, who hits the black-and-white checkered dance floor most weekend nights.

Cinemas

Bogotá has dozens of cinemas offering the usual Hollywood fare. Major universities have *cineclubes* (film clubs) showing films on campus or using commercial cinemas or the auditoriums of other institutions – accessible to all. Tickets run up to COP$9000 after 3pm, COP$6000 before 3pm.

Cine Colombia Andino
CINEMA

(Map p56; www.cinecolombia.com; Centro Comercial Andino, Carrera 12 No 82-01, piso 3) Multiplex cinema in Zona Rosa's Andino mall.

Cinemateca Distrital
CINEMA

(Map p44; www.cinematecadistrital.gov.co; Carrera 7 No 22-79) Art-house cinema hosts frequent film festivals.

Multiplex Cine Colombia
CINEMA

(Map p44; www.cinecolombia.com; Calle 24 No 6-01) A six-screen multiplex in the city center.

Theater

Bogotá is big on theater with more than a dozen options. Many lefty, politicized troupes dominate La Candelaria, while more mainstream options linger 'uptown' in the north.

Teatro Colón
TRADITIONAL THEATER

(Map p44; www.bogota-dc.com/eventos/teatro/colon.html; Calle 10 No 5-32) La Candelaria's most famous – and the city's loveliest – stage is undergoing a long renovation that could last another few years. When it reopens, it'll resume its repertoire of large-scale opera and the occasional drama for a dress-up, high-end crowd.

Teatro Nacional
TRADITIONAL THEATER

(Map p52; ☑217 4577; www.teatronacional.com.co; Calle 71 No 10-25; tickets COP$45,000) Stand-up comedy and similar program to Teatro Colón.

Teatro de La Candelaria
ALTERNATIVE THEATER

(Map p44; Calle 12 No 2-59; tickets adult/student COP$20,000/10,000) One of the edgiest theaters in the city center, with a mix of political shows (often lefty, sometimes covering women's-rights issues) that always know when to put in a joke to diffuse any tension.

Fundación Gilberto Alzate Avendaño
CULTURAL INSTITUTE

(Map p44; www.fgaa.gov.co; Calle 10 No 3-16) This cultural institute in La Candelaria hosts many events (including dance and theater, and also some concerts). In 2008 a Goya painting was stolen during an art exhibit here.

Teatro Experimental La Mama
ALTERNATIVE THEATER

(Map p52; ☑211 2709; www.teatrolamama.com; Calle 63 No 9-60; admission COP$20,000) Now in its fifth decade, this alternative, 'experimental' theater in Chapinero stages various performances by amateur groups not shy to provoke.

Live Music

Clubs across town stage live music nightly in Bogotá (see p64), and outdoor events like Rock al Parque (p53) are huge festivals that attract fans from all over the continent. Posters around town tout big-name acts, who play at Estadio El Campín, Parque Simón Bolívar or Parque Jaime Duque (on the way to Zipaquirá, north of the city).

Biblioteca Luis Ángel Arango
LIVE MUSIC

(Map p44; www.banrepcultural.org; Calle 11 No 4-14) This huge La Candelaria library hosts a selection of instrumental and vocal concerts per month; Wednesday events are more expensive (from COP$21,000) than other days (COP$3000 to COP$6000).

Sports

Many outsiders equate Colombia's national sport – football (soccer) – with the shooting of Andrés Escobar after his own goal eliminated Colombia from the 1994 World Cup, but seeing games here is generally a calm affair (perhaps wearing neutral colors isn't a bad idea though). The two big rivals here are the (blue-and-white) **Los Millonarios** (Map p52; www.millonarios.com.co; Carrera 9 No 70-09) and (red-and-white) **Santa Fe** (www.independientesantafe.com; Calle 64A No 38-08).

The principal venue is the **Estadio El Campín** (Map p40; ☑315 8726; Carrera 30 No 57-60). Games are played on Wednesday night and Sunday afternoon. Tickets can be bought at the stadium before the matches (from COP$14,000). For international matches, check with **Federación Colombiana de Fútbol** (www.colfutbol.org) for locations that sell tickets.

Bullfighting is invariably popular, with fights held at the Plaza de Toros de Santamaría on most Sundays in January and February. The events bring the area to a standstill, while the bullring itself (a 1931 red-brick ring) often fills to capacity (14,500) or beyond.

🔒 Shopping

Locals are in love with the malls, but Sunday flea markets and the crusty Plaza de Mercado de Paloquemao are more inviting attractions. Also, look along Carrera 9, south of Calle 60, for Chapinero's antique shops.

If you're looking for cutting-edge Colombian fashions, there's a small cluster of boutiques in the Chapinero on Carrera 7 between Calles 54 and 55.

🎁 Mambe
HANDICRAFTS

(www.mambe.org; Carrera 5 No 117-25) A limited but extremely well-done selection of weekly rotating Fair Trade handicrafts from 40 artisan-driven communities around Colombia.

🎁 Artesanías de Colombia
HANDICRAFTS

(Map p44; www.artesaniasdecolombia.com.co; Carrera 2 No 18A-58; ⊙closed Sun) In a hacienda next to the Iglesia de las Aguas, this classy shop has higher-end crafts (lots of home accessories, plus purses, toys, hammocks and some clothing), with 70% of the profits going directly back to the village artisans.

Brincabrinca CLOTHING
(Map p56; www.brincabrinca.com; Carrera 14 No 85-26; ⊙10:30am-2pm Mon-Sat) Designer T-shirt addicts should head straight here for some of Bogotá's most stylish tees (COP$60,000), designed by a bastion of Colombian and international contest winners.

La Casona del Museo HANDICRAFTS
(Map p44; Calle 16 No 5-22/24) By the Gold Museum, this old building houses a convenient, cheerful collection of nice souvenir stands (the best for handicrafts being Colombia es Bella on the 2nd floor – says so right on the sign) and a nice cafe.

Plaza Central de Usaquén MARKET
(Los Toldos de San Pelayo; Carrera 6A btwn Calles 119 & 119A; ⊙8am-6pm Sat & Sun) Just north of the main square in the village-like Usaquén, you'll find stallholders selling food, colorful purses, assorted handicrafts and bamboo saxophones – there's a satellite area a couple of blocks east too.

Pasaje Rivas HANDICRAFTS
(Map p44; cnr Carrera 10 & Calle 10) A couple of blocks west of Plaza de Bolívar, this craft market is a good spot for cheap nontouristy buys, including lots of straw hats, T-shirts, toy figurines, baskets and *ruanas* (Colombian ponchos). The entrance next to Iglesia de la Concepción reads 'Pasaje Paul.'

HOW TO BUY EMERALDS

Some of the world's highest quality emeralds are mined chiefly in the Muzo area of Boyacá and Colombia is the world's largest exporter of emeralds, making these precious stones a coveted notch on tourists' 'To Buy' lists when visiting Bogotá and the surrounding regions.

In years past the beauty of Colombia's emeralds had been overshadowed by the dangerous conditions in which they were mined. Some locals compared Colombia's emerald market with the diamond industry in Africa. In 2005 the government abolished tariffs and taxes associated with mining, effectively ending the power of the black market and associated elements.

Travelers can now buy emeralds in good conscience, but visiting emerald mines is still not possible without an invitation. In the capital, emeralds are sold in the flourishing **Emerald Dealers Market** (Map p44; cnr Av Jiménez & Carrera 7) and nearby Plazoleta Rosario, where dozens of *negociantes* (traders) buy and sell stones – sometimes on the sidewalks. You will also be offered emeralds on the street. Don't do it – glass imitations these days look a lot like emeralds!

Here are a few tips to keep in mind while shopping for emeralds:

» When looking at emeralds, you have to inspect the person selling you the emerald as closely as the emerald itself. Find a seller that you feel comfortable with. You will be surprised at how obvious it is to either run away or relax when you just give some well-placed attention on the seller.

» Gems and jewelry are very subjective and often when looking at emeralds in the shops or from dealers your first impression is the best and most reliable impression. Don't be in a hurry when buying a gem or jewelry piece. The quality of the gem in any Colombian shop is regulated by the tourist industry and there are never disputes as to quality, so just concentrate on the price. Don't be afraid to walk away if you feel the price is too high.

» When looking at a stone, you have to assess the harmony between the color, clarity, brightness and the size.

» Colombians are convivial and often comical. If you find a jeweler or dealer you like, invite him for tea or a *tinto* (black coffee). You will hear good stories and will have an ally in the emerald business.

One reliable emerald dealer in Bogotá is **Gems Metal** (Map p44; ☎311 493 1602; Carrera 7 No 14-28, oficina 707). Dealer Oscar Baquero has over 30 years' experience in the emerald industry. English is spoken.

Authors BOOKSTORE
(Calle 70 No 5-23) An all-English bookstore filling two floors along with a nice cafe.

Librería Lerner BOOKSTORE
(Map p44; www.librerialerner.com.co; Av Jiménez 4-35; ⊘closed Sun) Stocks many Spanish-language guidebooks on Colombia, as well as the full gamut of maps, including the *AutoGuía Turística de Colombia* (a color, spiral-bound map/guide; COP$19,900), and the 12-map series of national routes *Mapas de Ruta* (sold individually for COP$1300, or as a packet for COP$13,500).

Plaza de Mercado de Paloquemao MARKET
(Map p40; cnr Av 19 & Carrera 25; ⊘8am-1pm) A real-deal, messy Colombian market. Go early on Tuesday or Friday – flower days!

Mercado de San Alejo FLEA MARKET
(Map p44; Carrera 7 btwn Calles 24 & 26; ⊘9am-5:30pm Sun) This city-center classic fills a parking lot with a host of yesteryear items (posters, books, knickknacks) that are fun to sift through.

Camping Amarelo CAMPING GEAR
(Map p52; ☑211 8082; www.campingamarelo.com; Calle 57 No 9-29, oficina 301; ⊘9am-12:30pm & 1-5:30pm Mon-Fri, 9am-noon Sat) This small shop sells and rents all the camping gear you'll need (eg tents start at COP$35,000 per day) and takes bookings for rooms in its bungalow at Suesca. Sells boots too.

San Miguel MILLINER
(Map p44; Calle 11 No 8-88; ⊘closed Sun) Open more than 70 years, this classic milliner is the best of the bunch on the block. Mostly felt fedoras or cowboy hats pressed before your eyes.

Centro de Alta Technología ELECTRONICS
(Map p56; Carrera 15 No 77-05; ⊘closed Sun) Packed with digital camera and computer accessories, as is the adjoining Unilago Mall.

Hacienda Santa Bárbara SHOPPING MALL
(www.haciendasantabarbara.com.co; Carrera 7 No 115-60) Built around a colonial *casona* (large, old house; 1847), making the place a fine combination of historic and modern architecture, and it's quieter than the Zona Rosa scene.

Centro Comercial El Retiro SHOPPING MALL
(Map p56; www.elretirobogota.com; Calle 81 No 11-84) Zona Rosa's fanciest, with an entire food court run by Andrés Carne de Res (p62).

Centro Comercial Andino SHOPPING MALL
(Map p56; www.centroandino.com.co; Carrera 11 No 82-71) Most popular Zona Rosa mall.

ℹ Information

Dangers & Annoyances
Despite great progress over the course of two decades, security in Bogotá has taken a step backwards since the early 2010s, though the city is still infinitely safer than it once was. La Candelaria (near some poorer areas like Egipto, just southeast) is generally safe, but has a more questionable reputation after 9pm or so when an increase in robberies and attacks has been seen after the very-evident police presence from the day packs it in. In 2010 a wave of hostel robberies plagued this backpacker haven – including one very serious sexual assault – so choose accommodations here not only based on your general criteria but security as well.

At its north end, Parque de los Periodistas (Av Jiménez and Carrera 4) has seen muggings after dark – as well as some drug sales. La Perseverancia barrio, just north of Macarena, has a dodgy rep too.

One notorious area for knife-point muggings is along the seemingly innocent walk up to Cerro de Monserrate – either on the mountainside trails, or the short walk between the cable-car station and Quinta de Bolívar just below; the same area on busy weekends is generally quite safe. A general rule of thumb is never wander east of the main Av Caracas TransMilenio line unless you are with someone who knows what they are doing.

Overcrowding and a snarling expansion project has seen a dramatic increase in crime on the TransMilenio public transit system – 350 additional police officers were assigned to the TransMilenio beat in 2011 to combat a surge in pickpockets and robberies.

The north is, on the whole, a different story. Many locals walk well after dark between, say, Zona Rosa and Parque 93's club/restaurant scene. That said, the area has seen a few isolated bombings.

Obviously, don't fight back if you've been targeted – hand over your money and move on. Meanwhile, avoid deserted streets and take taxis after hours.

Despite the downturn, Bogotá generally feels safer than its continental brethren, Río de Janeiro, São Paulo, Quito and Lima among them.

Emergency
Ambulance ☑125
Fire ☑123
Police ☑123
Tourist police ☑280 9900

Internet Access

It's not difficult finding internet access. Nearly all accommodations listed have wi-fi access and/or computers to use. There are also many cafes, most of which have telephone booths for making long-distance or international calls. PIT information centers offer visitors 15 minutes' free internet. Wi-fi is common at many cafes, bars and restaurants.

A few convenient choices, most with telephone service, include the following:

AC&C Internet (Carrera 15 No 94-80; per hr COP$1600)

ETB (Carrera 7 No 19-65; per hr COP$2000; ☺closed Sun)

Skape Internet (Carrera 3 No 10-24; per hr COP$1200) Note the Green Guy (see the boxed text, p43) above.

Medical Services

It's preferable to use private clinics rather than government-owned institutions, which are cheaper but may not be as well equipped.

Clínica de Marly (www.marly.com.co; Calle 50 No 9-67) A recommended clinic with doctors covering most specialties; sometimes handles vaccinations.

Dr Paul Vaillancourt (☑635 6312; Carrera 11 No 94A-25, oficina 401; ☺closed Sun) A recommended English-speaking, half-French-Canadian doctor, who charges COP$120,000 per consultation (no medical insurance accepted). If you're heading to Brazil (or any area requiring immunization against yellow fever), this is the easiest place to get your vaccination (COP$54,000). Note that you must have the vaccination 10 days prior to arriving in Brazil.

Fundación Santa Fe (www.fsfb.org.co; Av 9 No 116-20) Very professional private hospital.

Money

Banks in Bogotá tend to open 9am to 3pm or 3:30pm Monday to Friday. The banks listed here also change cash, but check the *casas de cambio* (currency exchanges) beforehand, which may offer the same rates and do things much more quickly. Money changers at the airport have slightly worse exchange rates – and require a thumb print to cash in your pesos!

The following banks give cash advances on Visa and/or MasterCard. Most banks have ATMs.

Bancolombia (Carrera 8 No 12B-17) Changes traveler's checks. There is another branch on Carrera 3 No 18-19.

Citibank (cnr Carrera 12A & Av 82, Zona Rosa)

Edificio Emerald Trade Center (Av Jiménez No 5-43) There are four exchange offices here.

Titán Intercontinental (www.titan.com.co; Carrera 7 No 18-42) A *casa de cambio;* can also receive money from overseas.

Western Union (Calle 28 No 13-22, local 28) Can wire money.

Post

Courier Box (Map p44; Carrera 7 No 16-50) FedEx, DHL, TNT and UPS rep.

Post office Centro Internacional (off Map p44; Carrera 7 No 27-54); Chapinero (off Map p56; cnr Av Chile & Carrera 15); La Candelaria (Map p44; cnr Calle 12A & Carrera 8) Branches of 4-72, Colombia's postal service.

Tourist Information

Colombia's energetic **Instituto Distrital de Turismo** (www.bogotaturismo.gov.co) is making visitors feel very welcome, with a series of Puntos de Información Turística (PIT) branches opening at key locations around Bogotá operated by very friendly English-speaking staff. A couple of PIT locations offer free walking tours (scheduled separately in English or Spanish). In addition to the listings following, there are PITs at each of the airport terminals.

Parques Nacionales Naturales (PNN) de Colombia (Ecoturismo; Map p44; ☑353 2400, ext 138; www.parquesnacionales.gov.co; Carrera 10 No 20-34) This central office has information on Colombia's national parks and can help arrange accommodations at some. Also see p44.

PIT Av Chile (Map p56; ☑248 0181; cnr Carrera 11 & Calle 72) In the outdoor square at Centro Commercial Av Chile.

PIT Centro Histórico (Map p44; ☑283 7115; cnr Carrera 8 & Calle 10) Facing Plaza de Bolívar, this location has walking tours in English at 2pm Tuesday and Thursday.

PIT Terminal de Transporte (☑295 4460; La Terminal, Transversal 66 No 35-11, módulo 5) At the arrival hall of the main bus terminal.

Travel Agencies

Aventure Colombia (Map p44; ☑702 7069; www.aventurecolombia.com; Av Jiménez No 4-49, oficina 204) A good-time agency run by a charming French expat. It specializes in off the beaten path destinations nationwide like Punta Galinas (p159), indigenous Wiwa homestays in the Cerro de Santa Nevada and the fascinating Caño Cristales (July to November) in Meta (p77).

Destino Bogotá (☑753 4887; www.destinobogota.com; Calle 110 No 9-25) Offers many playful city and area tours. Coffee Plantation Tour? Party bus club-hopping? Salsa lesson and club debut? Check. Plus more standard fare like a worthy Guatavita/Zipaquirá Salt Cathedral day trip. Most trips require a minimum of two or four people; city tours/day trips start at COP$60,000/115,000 per person.

Ecoguías (☑347 5736; info@ecoguias.com) This well-run adventure-travel company run by a Brit who's lived in Colombia for over a decade offers countrywide itineraries with an emphasis on ecotourism to the coffee region, Choco, Villa de Leyva, Cartagena, Santa Marta and environs and Amazonas, as well as river trips on the Río Magdalena, taking in the colonial towns of Honda and Mompox.

Sal Si Puedes (Map p44; ☑283 3765; www. salsipuedes.org; Carrera 7 No 17-01, oficina 640; ☺8am-3pm Mon-Thu, to 2pm Fri) This is an association of outdoor-minded people who organize weekend walks in the countryside (COP\$37,000 to COP\$40,000 per person, including transportation and Spanish-speaking guides). Most last nine or 10 hours. Drop by for a schedule.

Visa Information

Shortly after research, Colombia's intelligent agency, DAS, who also handled visa extensions, was dissolved. At the time of writing, foreign visa formalities were to carry on status quo in former DAS offices by the **Ministerio de Relaciones Exteriores** (off Map p56; www. cancilleria.gov.co; ☑595 3525; Calle 100 No 11B-27; ☺7:30am-4:30pm Mon-Fri) but that situation was extremely fluid. Check ahead before visiting the address indicated here and taking the info following as gospel: a 30-, 60- or 90-day visa extension can be obtained here, up to the complete discretion of the officer. Your passport, two photocopies of your passport (picture page and arrival stamp) and two passport-sized photos are required, and you'll need to show an air ticket out of the country in most cases. Show up first to fill out forms, then you'll be directed to a nearby Davivienda (subject to change) to pay the COP\$72,350 fee. You get the extension on the spot.

🔾 Getting There & Away

Air

Bogotá's aged airport, **Aeropuerto Internacional El Dorado** (Map p40; www.elnuevodorado. com; Av El Dorado), which handles nearly all domestic and international flights, was undergoing a massive US\$350 million facelift at the time of research. The new airport, in the same location 13km northwest of the city center, was scheduled to debut by the end of 2014. Meanwhile, there are two terminals: the principal one (El Dorado) is 1km west of **Puente Aéreo** (☑413 9511; Av El Dorado), principally used for some of Avianca's international and domestic flights.

At El Dorado you'll find money-exchange services at the arrivals gate; when entering the departures hall, head to the left and to reach arrivals. Rates are generally a bit worse than at banks in the city center. ATMs and internet access points are only found upstairs in the

departures hall – up the stairs from the check-in counter (accessible to all).

Most airline offices in Bogotá are in the north; some have more than one office. For details on international airlines serving Colombia's capital, see p314. There are also plenty of domestic flights to destinations all over the country. Some of the major routes are given on p317. Major domestic airlines serving Bogotá:

Avianca (www.avianca.com)

Copa/AeroRepública (www.copaair.com)

EasyFly (www.easyfly.com.co)

Lan (www.lan.com)

Satena (www.satena.com)

Bus

Bogotá's main bus terminal, **La Terminal** (Map p40; La Terminal; ☑423 3600; www.terminal detransporte.gov.co; Diagonal 23 No 69-60, off Av de La Constitución), about 5km west of the city center in the squeaky-clean planned neighborhood of La Salitre, is one of South America's best, most efficient and shockingly unsketchy. It's housed in a huge, arched red-brick building divided into five *módulos* (units). Southbound buses leave at the west end from No 1 (color-coded yellow); east- and westbound from No 2 (blue); and northbound from No 3 (red). *Colectivo* vans leave for some nearby towns like Villavicencio from No 4, while all arrivals come into No 5 (at the station's eastern end).

There are plenty of food options, ATMs, left-luggage rooms, (clean) bathrooms and even showers (COP\$6500), and a PIT information center in *módulo* No 5, which will help you track down bus times or call for accommodations.

Each *módulo* has a number of side-by-side ticket vendors from various companies, sometimes trying to hassle you for their buses. For some long-distance destinations – particularly to the Caribbean coast – you can sometimes haggle in low season. The usual type of bus is the *climatizado*, which is air-conditioned.

DOMESTIC BUSES

For all domestic destinations listed in the Domestic Bus Routes table (p71) there are frequent departures during the day (for destinations like Medellín, Cali or Bucaramanga usually half-hourly) by a few different companies (at least). Shop around for prices and departure times.

Expreso Bolivariano (☑800 011 9292; www. bolivariano.com.co) is Colombia's nicest national bus company.

INTERNATIONAL BUSES

Buses for cities around South America depart from *módulo* 2 (blue) in the bus terminal. **Expreso Ormeño** (☑428 9210; www.grupo -ormeno.com.pe) sells tickets for most destina-

DOMESTIC BUS ROUTES

DESTINATION	PRICE (COP$)	DURATION	MÓDULO (NO)
Armenia	30,000-40,000	7hr	yellow (1)
Barranquilla	90,000-130,000	17-20hr	red (3) & blue (2)
Bucaramanga	45,000-77,000	8-9hr	red (3)
Cali	40,000-55,000	8-10hr	yellow (1) & blue (2)
Cartagena	138,000-160,000	12-20hr	blue (2) & red (3)
Cúcuta	77,000-100,000	15-16hr	red (3)
Ipiales	84,000-104,000	22hr	yellow (1)
Manizales	35,000-40,000	8-9hr	blue (2)
Medellín	35,000-60,000	8-9hr	yellow (1) & blue (2)
Neiva	26,000-39,000	5hr	yellow (1) & blue (2)
Pasto	74,000-100,000	18-20hr	yellow (1)
Pereira	30,000-43,000	7-9hr	yellow (1)
Popayán	65,000-75,000	12-16hr	yellow (1) & blue (2)
Ráquira	16,000-22,000	3-4hr	red (3)
Riohacha	95,000-130,000	23hr	red (3) & blue (2)
San Agustín	42,000-52,000	9-10hr	yellow (1)
San Gil	30,000-60,000	6-7hr	red (3)
Santa Marta	80,000-120,000	16-18hr	blue (2) & red (3)
Tunja	12,000-18,000	3hr	red (3)
Villavicencio	20,000	3hr	blue (2)
Villa de Leyva	20,000	4hr	red (3)
Zipaquirá	3700	1½hr	red (3)

tions. See the International Bus Routes table (p72) for details.

❶ Getting Around

Rush hour in the morning and afternoon can really clog roads – and space on the buses.

To/From the Airport

Both El Dorado and Puente Aéreo terminals are accessible from the city center by *busetas* and *colectivos* marked 'Aeropuerto.' In the city center you catch them on Calle 19 or Carrera 10. They all pass Puente Aéreo en route. From El Dorado terminal, black 'Germania – Carrera 4' buses depart from Av El Dorado (Calle 26), a five-minute walk outside arrivals. Urban transportation to the airport stops at about 9pm.

If going by taxi (about COP$18,000), you pay a *sobrecargo* (surcharge) of COP$3300.

Both terminals have a special taxi service aimed at protecting passengers from overcharging by taxi drivers. At the exit from the baggage-claim area there's a taxi booth where you get a computer printout indicating the expected fare to your destination. You then take the taxi, which waits at the door, and show the printout to the driver. The fare on the receipt is paid upon arrival at your destination, regardless of what the meter says.

The TransMilenio expansion to the airport was set to open by the time you read this, though Portal El Dorado stops a few kilometers short of the terminal. A shuttle scheme was expected to be launched upon its opening.

To/From the Bus Terminal

During rush hour the bus trip between the bus terminal and the city center may take up to an hour. To the terminal, take a northbound *colectivo* marked 'Terminal' from Carrera 10 anywhere between Calles 17 and 26. From the terminal, the black *colectivo* 'Ruta C-23' (COP$1400) stops right outside the PIT information center every 30 minutes or so between 6am and 9:30pm Monday to Saturday (until 6pm Sunday). It can drop you along Carrera 4 through the heart of La Candelaria.

The best and fastest way is to take a taxi (around COP$11,000 from La Candelaria). In

INTERNATIONAL BUS ROUTES

DESTINATION	PRICE (COP$)	DURATION	DEPARTURE
Buenos Aires	779,000	6 days	Tue & Sun
Caracas	174,000	34hr	Thu
Guayaquil	174,000	36hr	Tue & Sun
Lima	389,000	2½ days	Tue & Sun
Mendoza	759,000	5½ days	Tue & Sun
Quito	174,000	28hr	Tue & Sun
Santiago	603,000	5½ days	Tue & Sun

módulo 5, the bus terminal has an organized taxi service like the one at the airport. Rates are around COP$10,400 to La Candelaria, COP$10,600 to Chapinero and COP$8100 to the Zona Rosa.

By the time you read this the new TransMileno stop near Carrera 68 just outside La Salitre will open, making a short taxi/TransMilenio combo the fastest and most convenient way to reach La Terminal.

Bicycle

Bogotá has one of the world's most extensive bike-route networks, with over 350km of separated, clearly marked bike paths called CicloRuta. Free Bogotá maps from PIT information centers show the CicloRuta paths.

In addition, on Sunday and holidays about 120km of city roads are closed to traffic from 7am to 2pm for a citywide Ciclovía, a well-run event to get Bogotá out on two wheels. Fruit juice and street food vendors, performers and bike repair stands line the cross-town event, which is a good-time street party with or without a bike. You can rent a bike at Bogotá Bike Tours (p51). Ciclovía runs along Carrera 7 all the way from La Candelaria to Usaquén – it's worth witnessing even if on foot.

Bus & Buseta

Apart from TransMilenio, Bogotá's public transportation is operated by buses and *busetas* (small buses). They all run the length and breadth of the city, usually at full speed if traffic allows.

Except on a few streets, there are no bus stops – just wave down the bus or *buseta*. Board via the front door and pay the driver or the assistant; you won't get a ticket. In buses you get off through the back door, where there's a bell to ring to let the driver know to stop. In *busetas* there's usually only a front door through which all passengers get on and off. When you want to get off tell the driver *'por acá, por favor'* (here, please).

Each bus and *buseta* displays a board on the windscreen indicating the route and number. For locals they are easily recognizable from a distance, but for newcomers it can be difficult to decipher the route description quickly enough to wave down the right bus.

Flat fares, regardless of distance traveled, are posted, and are generally around COP$1300 to COP$1400. It's sometimes slightly higher at night (after 8pm) and on Sunday and holidays.

There are also minibuses called *colectivos*, which operate on major routes. They are faster and cost about COP$1200.

Taxi

Bogotá's impressive fleet of Korean-made yellow taxis are a safe, reliable and relatively inexpensive way of getting around. They all have meters and drivers almost always use them. When you enter a taxi, the meter should read '25,' which relates to a coded pricing scheme (a laminated card should be hanging on the front passenger seat to see). The minimum unit fare is '50,' which equates to COP$3300. The meter should change every 100m. Taxi trips on Sundays and holidays, or after dark, include a COP$1600 surcharge; trips to the airport have a COP$3300 surcharge. There is a COP$600 surcharge for called taxis.

A 10km ride (eg from Plaza de Bolívar to Calle 100 in northern Bogotá) shouldn't cost more than COP$17,000. If you're going to make a couple of trips to distant places, it may be cheaper to hire a taxi by the hour for about COP$16,000 per hour.

Don't even think about waving down a taxi in the street unless you are with a local. When you do so, you're not registered and forfeit all the security measures put in place to protect you, increasing your chances of robbery exponentially. Request one by phone from numerous companies that provide radio service instead; try **Taxis Libres** (☎311 1111), **Taxi Express** (☎411 1111), **Radio Taxi** (☎288 8888) or **Taxi Real** (☎333 3333). Plan ahead on Friday night –

after 4pm, it's impossible even to get a call through.

Naturally don't ride with a driver that refuses to use a meter. Most drivers are honest, but it's worth confirming the final fare with the price card. Some drivers, particularly in late hours, will round fares up a bit. Drivers don't often get tips.

TransMilenio

The ambitiously named **TransMilenio** (www.transmilenio.gov.co) has revolutionized Bogotá's public transportation. After numerous plans and studies drawn up over 30 years to build a metro, the project was eventually buried and a decision to introduce a fast urban bus service called TransMilenio was taken instead.

It is, in essence, a bus system masquerading as a subway. Covering 84km with a fleet of 1100 buses, TransMilenio has 114 of its own self-contained stations (keeping things orderly and safe). Buses have their own lanes, which keeps them free from auto traffic. The service is cheap (COP$1700), frequent and operates from 5am to 11pm Monday to Saturday, 6am to 10pm Sunday. Tickets are bought at the entrance of any TransMilenio station. You can load up to 50 rides on a card to avoid waiting in line every time. TransMilenio serves up to 1.7 million people daily –
500,000 over its capacity – so buses get *very* crowded at rush hour; transfers at Av Jiménez resemble punk-rock mosh pits.

On posted maps in stations, routes are color coded, with different numbered buses corresponding to various stops. The main Trans-Milenio line runs along Av Caracas north–south of town. There are also lines on Carrera 30, Av 81, Av de Las Américas and a short spur on Av Jiménez to Carrera 3. There are plans to build more lines, including one to the airport. There are three terminuses, but the only one of real use to travelers is the **northern terminus** (Portal del Norte; Calle 170).

It takes practice to understand which bus to take. 'Ruta Facil' routes, for example, stop at every station on a line, while others zip along some sort of express route – leapfrogging, in confusing patterns, several stations at a time.

You can also preplan your routes online at www.surumbo.com; click on your departure and destination station for options. Most key north-central routes change in Calle 22, while Av Jiménez has many more transfers (sometimes meaning an underground walk between neighboring stations).

Key routes:

La Candelaria to Portal del Norte (for Zipaquirá buses) Take B74 direct to 'Portal del Norte' (last stop).

La Candelaria to Zona G From 'Las Aguas' or 'Museo del Oro' stations, take D70 to Calle 22, switch to B13 to 'Flores.'

La Candelaria to Zona Rosa From 'Las Aguas' or 'Museo del Oro,' take D70 to Calle 22, switch to B13 to Calle 85.

Portal del Norte to La Candelaria Take J72 from 'Portal del Norte' direct to 'Museo del Oro' or 'Las Aguas.'

Zona G to La Candelaria From 'Flores' take H13 to 'Calle 22,' switch to J24 to 'Museo del Oro' or 'Las Aguas.'

Zona G to Zona Rosa From 'Flores' take B1 or B13 to 'Calle 85.'

Zona Rosa to La Candelaria From 'Calle 85' take H13 to Calle 22, switch to J24 to 'Museo del Oro' or 'Las Aguas.'

AROUND BOGOTÁ

Most *bogotanos* looking for a break from the city also look for warmth. Some towns within a couple of hours – like Villavicencio – rest way below Bogotá's elevation, with rising temperatures. There are also significant changes in landscape outside the capital, where you can find lakes, waterfalls, cloud forests, mountains and a maze of small towns and villages, many of them holding onto their colonial fabric.

North of Bogotá

Many day-trippers out of the capital head this way. It's possible to combine a trip to Zipaquirá and Guatavita in a day – a taxi to both, with a couple hours at each, runs about COP$180,000 depending on your negotiation skills. Agencies like Destino Bogotá (p68) offer combo day trips to Zipaquirá and Guatavita.

ZIPAQUIRÁ

1 / POP 101,000 / ELEV 2650M

The most popular day trip from Bogotá, 50km north, Zipaquirá is a cute historic town noted for its salt mines, particularly the one fashioned as a surreal walk following Jesus' last steps and finishing in a stunning three-part cavernous cathedral 190m below the ground, highlighted by the largest cross ever built in an underground church; see also the boxed text, p39. Salt was a major resource in this area before the Spanish showed up in those metal hats, and local mines still churn out 40% of Colombia's salt resources.

Zipaquirá's main plaza is lined with cafes and ATMs and has a lovely church to peek into.

In the mountains about 500m southwest are two underground cathedrals carved out of salt. The first opened in 1954, then was closed in 1992 for safety reasons. You can visit its stunning replacement **salt cathedral** (www.catedraldesal.gov.co; adult/child COP$20,000/14,000). It was built between 1991 and 1995 (a total of 250,000 tons of salt were removed).

All visitors must join regularly departing groups on hour-long tours – you can leave them once you're inside if you want. The walk leads past 13 stages of Jesus' fateful day, with hollowed-out crosses symbolizing nakedness or death (sadly the view of No 11 – of the crucifixion – is now somewhat marred by the unfortunate placement of the souvenir shop just behind). The tradition of mixing religion with salt has logical roots: work in the mines was dangerous so altars were made. The 75m-long mine can accommodate 8400 people and holds services on (very busy) Sundays.

About 15km northeast, the town of **Nemocón** is home to a smaller (and less touristy) salt mine that can be visited daily. This one has been in use for 400 years, once serving as the town hall.

❶ Getting There & Away

One way to Zipaquirá is hopping on a frequent bus from the Portal del Norte TransMilenio station at Calle 170, about a 45-minute ride from the city center. From here, buses to Zipaquirá (COP$3600, 1½ to 2½ hours) leave every 10 minutes or so until 8pm from the Flota lane on the east side of the Portal in front of the Éxito supermarket. From Zipaquirá it's possible to catch a few daily buses on to Villa de Leyva.

The alternative is to take the **Turistren** (www.turistren.com.co), which runs Saturday and Sunday from Bogotá to Zipaquirá (round trip adult/child COP$38,000/23,000). The train departs Bogotá's main train station **Estación de la Sabana** (Map p40; Calle 13 No 18-24) at 8:30am, stops briefly at **Usaquén Station** (Calle 100 & Carrera 9A) at 9:20am and reaches Zipaquirá at 11:30am. (At research time, curiously, it returned from nearby Cajicá, 15km south!)

A round-trip taxi from Bogotá should run about COP$180,000 including time to see the mine.

SUESCA
☑1 / POP 14,000 / ELEV 2584M

One of Colombia's most popular rock-climbing destinations lurks just south of this colonial town, 65km north of Bogotá. Arriving by car or bus, you'll pass the 4km-long sandstone Guadalupe formations standing up to 370m high along the Río Bogotá, and home to 400 (and counting) routes.

Many visitors come for day trips from Bogotá, particularly on weekends, when the half a dozen (or so) outfitters open their doors to greet a couple of hundred climbers daily. There are also rafting options, but the water is much warmer in Tobía.

Two Spanish-language guides for up to four for Suesca climbs runs COP$95,000 per person and can be arranged at Gran Pared in Bogotá (p51).

English-speaking guide **Hugo Rocha** (☑315 826 2051; contacto@dealturas.com) has been here for over a decade, offering day/overnight trips and lessons. Hugo works with **Dealturas** (www.dealturas.com), a climbing school, which offers a five-day course for COP$500,000 and a day climb (including equipment) for COP$120,000, as well as accommodations for COP$25,000 in a private room. **El Vivac Hostel** (☑311 480 5034; www.elvivachostal.com; tent/dm/r COP$20,000/25,000/65,000) is a farm-turned-hostel run by a local woman climber pioneer who arranges climbs and rents bikes (from COP$10,000).

There are also many camping options, or you can rent a full cabaña from **Camping Amarelo** (☑in Bogotá 1 217 8082) for COP$45,000 per person.

To get to Suesca, take the TransMilenio to its northern terminus at Portal del Norte, and catch a frequent direct 'Alianza' or 'Ayacucho' bus (COP$4500, 40 minutes).

LAGUNA DE GUATAVITA
ELEV 3000M

Many hopes of finding El Dorado, it was once believed, converged on this small, circular lake about 50km northeast of Bogotá. Rimmed by mountains, lovely Guatavita was the sacred lake and ritual center of the Muisca people, where – half a millennium ago – the gold-dust-coated Zipa, the Muisca *cacique* (indigenous tribal head), would throw precious offerings into the lake from his ceremonial raft and then plunge into the waters to obtain godlike power.

Today you can't follow the Zipa's lead (no swimming), but there are several lookouts on a trail above the water. The area is higher up than Bogotá – and you'll feel the difference on the 15-minute hike up to the lakeside hilltops from the **site entrance** (Colombian/foreigner COP$8800/13,200; ☺closed Mon).

The town of Guatavita, 18km southwest, is the chief gateway. On weekends you're likely to find transportation to the lake, but it's not guaranteed. The town was created in the mid-1960s – for locals displaced by the nearby reservoir Embalse de Tominé – and does a fine job of re-creating the white-washed Spanish colonial template, with a bullring, and a pedestrian mall center with souvenir shops, restaurants, a museum and a hotel or two. It's dead quiet during the week, but avoid both on Sundays if possible, when everyone and their mother goes.

❶ Getting There & Away

Laguna de Guatavita isn't the most convenient to reach by public transportation. From the TransMilenio northern terminus (Portal del Norte) in northern Bogotá, buses leave every 20 minutes or so from inside the Portal's Inter-muncipales platform (COP$7000) to the town of Guatavita, via Sesquilé. About 11km north of town, the bus passes the 7km uphill road to the lake – no public transportation. Ask to get out, and walk or hitch (follow the signs to the right near the Escuela Tierra Negra), or go on to Guatavita, where on Sundays *colectivos* go directly from the central plaza to the lake. Taxis are scarce here.

A round-trip taxi from Bogotá costs about COP$120,000.

West of Bogotá

Those heading to the beach, Medellín or coffee country head west from Bogotá. Many don't stop, but there are a few places that qualify as destinations. If you're coming that way by your own means, note that two highways head out of Bogotá – take the northerly route via La Vega (west on Calle 80), a nicer drive than the southern route via Facatativa, which hooks up with the La Vega route (after many suburbs and truck jams) at Villeta, about 65km west.

Cloud forest *(bosque de niebla)* hikes await only 20km west of Bogotá in the gorgeous privately owned **Parque Natural Chicaque** (☑in Bogotá 1 368 3114; www.chicaque.com; admission COP$11,000). The 3-sq-km area features half a dozen walks (about 8km altogether), which are among the nation's best marked. During rainy season, walks lead to waterfalls. On weekends you can hire a horse to ride back up the steep hill paths.

You arrive above the trails, and below – a steep hike down – you'll find various **accommodations** (campsite/dm/bungalow incl all meals COP$51,000/62,000/268,000), including a nice bungalow for two. You can also camp up at the entrance for COP$8500 (no meals).

BOGOTÁ WEST OF BOGOTÁ

LAKE OF (FOOLS') GOLD

Traditionally, the Muisca felt that Laguna de Guatavita – once set in a perfectly round crater rimmed by green mountains – was created by a crashing meteor that transported a golden god who resided in the lake's floor. (Turns out, it's now believed, boring ol' volcanoes may be more likely the lake's creator.) The Muisca paid tribute to the god by crafting elaborate *tunjos* (ornate gold pendants and figurines), inscribed with wishes, and tossing them into the lake. (You can see many such pieces at Bogotá's Museo del Oro; see p48).

This led to a frenzy for gold for the Spaniards, and many other outsiders, who naturally felt they reached a watery El Dorado. Over the years many painstaking, fruitless efforts were made to uncover the treasures lurking below.

In the 1560s a wealthy merchant Antonio de Sepúlveda cut a gap on one side – still visible today – to drain the lake, yielding a mere 232 pesos of gold. Sepúlveda died bankrupt. By the late 19th century an English company managed to drain the lagoon, finding only 20-odd objects – not nearly enough to pay off the UK£40,000 or eight years invested in the project.

In the 1940s US divers with metal detectors searched out treasures, and the Colombian authorities – finally – banned such activities in 1965. Not to say that all treasure seekers obeyed. In the 1990s access to the lake required a permit to keep track of visitors (illegally coming with scuba gear to search out fortunes).

Despite its fame, Guatavita never yielded much gold. Colombia's best-known piece – the Balsa Muisca (also at the Museo del Oro) – was actually found in a cave near the village of Pasca.

The golden god must be enjoying a chuckle over all this.

The reserve is a few kilometers off the Soacha–La Mesa road. To get there from Bogotá's center, take the TransMilenio to Portal del Sur, where buses leave for the park at 9am, noon, 3pm and 5pm (COP$6000), returning at 8am, 10am, 1:30pm and 4pm.

South of Bogotá

The unique climate conditions of the Andean highlands have been conducive to the preservation of mummies across parts of Colombia – some of which have been relocated as far away as the British Museum in London. One place you can see some is the 'mummy town' of San Bernardo, about 87km southeast of Bogotá. A century ago, several dozen bodies were unearthed from the cemetery after interment fees were not paid and diggers, surprisingly, found mummies – a product of the unique soil and the local diet of *guatila* fruit. Some are on view in glass cases in the cemetery crypt in town. You're best off having your own transportation to get here.

LOS LLANOS

As you head southeast away from Bogotá, the jagged, Andean terrain soon drops and flattens out as if a giant guillotine dropped havoc across the mountains, revealing an endless sea of green grasslands. This is Los Llanos (The Plains).

Sometimes called the Serengeti of South America, Los Llanos is teeming with wildlife. It harbors more than 100 species of mammals and more than 700 species of birds, about the same number of birds as found in the entire USA. According to the Nature Conservancy, Los Llanos is also home to some of the most endangered species on Earth, including the Orinoco crocodile, the Orinoco turtle, giant armadillo, giant otter, black-and-chestnut eagle and several species of catfish.

The flat, grassy plains make this region ideal for cattle grazing. *Llaneros* (Colombian

DON'T WANDER OFF...

It is important to note that in all of Los Llanos, you cannot wander off on your own. The security situation in Colombia is very fluid and can change very quickly – always check current situations with authorities and/or travel agencies before embarking anywhere in this region.

cowboys) spend long hours herding cattle in grueling conditions on mega ranches, some of which are thousands of hectares in size. Their hard, isolated life inspired a unique culture very different from 'mainstream' Colombia. *Llaneros* are associated with their distinctive straw hats, *coleo* rodeos, the *joropo* dance and their bluegrass-like genre of folk music known as *música llanera*.

Los Llanos occupies the Colombian departments of Arauca, Casanare, Guainía, Meta and Vichada. As recently as 2003, much of this area was off-limits to foreigners. Today many of the bigger cities are safe and open for business, including Villavicencio, Puerto López and (to a lesser extent) Puerto Gaitán.

Unfortunately, despite many recent Colombian military victories, FARC rebels and other guerrilla groups still control swaths of Los Llanos. At the time of writing, independent travel was slightly dicey but relatively fine if you stick to the towns of Yopal, Inirida and San José del Guaviare; the area south of San José del Guaviare remains very dangerous. The road from Puerto López to Puerto Carreño on the Venezuelan border remains problematic as well.

Parque Nacional Natural (PNN) Sierra de La Macarena (www.parquesnacionales.gov.co), home to the marvelous Caño Cristales (p77), was the most tourist-friendly attraction in Los Llanos at the time of research, reopened in 2009 to authorized agencies after the army regained control of the region. Parque Nacional Natural (PNN) El Tuparro (www.parquesnacionales.gov.co), a 548,000-hectare nature reserve on the Venezuelan border, is a biosphere of sandy river beaches and green grasslands and home to some 320 species of birds plus jaguars, tapirs and otters. De Una Colombia Tours (☎1 368 1915; www.deunacolombia.com; Carrera 26A No 40-18, Apt 202, La Soledad, Bogotá) organizes guided tours to Tuparro.

VILLAVICENCIO

8 / POP 385,000 / ELEV 467M

The heavily militarized highway heading south from Bogotá leads to Villavicencio, 'La Puerta al Llano' – the gateway to the Llanos – a bustling though not particularly interesting city 75km to the southeast with a serious penchant for nightlife and grilled meat.

The main attractions are its green spaces, such as the downtown Parque de los Fundadores and Bioparque Los Ocarros (a zoo 3km north of town, which houses crocodiles and capybaras) and *asaderos* (restaurants serving roasted or grilled meats) offering the regional specialty, *mamona* (baby beef). The city is a good base for exploring the plains and the jumping-off point for trips to Caño Cristales.

Turismo Villavicencio (www.turismovillavicencio.gov.co) operates four tourist information points: at the airport during flights, at the bus station, and in Centro Comerciales La Sabana and Llano Centro.

Gringos are still a novelty in Villavo – you'll likely catch an occasional, usually harmless glare.

🛏 Sleeping & Eating

Hotel Serranía Real   HOTEL $
(☏662 0250; hotelserraniareal@gmail.com; Calle 37A No 29-63; s/d/tr COP$39,950/59,000/70,500; 🛜) Budget hotels are a dime a dozen in central Villavicencio, but this one wins praise for its super-friendly and helpful owners, who speak a tad of English and French. On offer are basic, clean rooms on a bustling street across from an Éxito supermarket and steps from a (mediocre) 24-hour bakery.

Hotel Sol Dorado   HOTEL $$
(☏670 1717; hotelsoldorado@hotmail.com; Calle 37 No 29-66; s/d incl breakfast from COP$78,000/112,000; 🛜❄) A more upscale choice, this sparkling new hotel teeters on boutique, though its 31 rooms could do with a new decorator (some gaudy furnishings and grandmotherly bedspread styles here). But it's comfortable, with a clean restaurant.

El Ranchón del Maporal   COLOMBIAN $$
(Km1 via a Restrepo; mains COP$12,000-26,500) This trendy restaurant on the edge of town does solid steaks and seafood under an open-air atmosphere. It swarms with beautiful people as the night wears on and it morphs into a bar, with DJs on weekends.

Dulima   COLOMBIAN $
(Carrera 30A No 38-46; set meals COP$9000-10,000) A *comida corriente* (set menu of the day) staple since 1967, this always-packed choice dishes up traditional set lunch plates served by friendly waitresses in cowgirl outfits. They do a great breakfast as well from 7am.

☆ Entertainment

Los Capachos   CLUB
(www.loscapachos.com; Km4 via Acacias; cover COP$5000-25,000; ⏱to late Fri-Sun) Villavo holds nothing back at night and this mas-

---

WORTH A TRIP

HOT, HOT HONDA

About 132km west of Bogotá – and at the crossroads for Medellín, Cartagena and Cali – Honda is an historic river town that is starting to draw some attention for its atmospheric old center of cobblestone streets and elegantly preserved colonial mansions. Ecoguías (p68) in Bogotá can arrange overnight stays here as well as boat trips on the Río Magdalena and visits to nearby Río Claro (p199).

A great overnight option is **Casa Belle Epoque** (☏312 478 0173; www.casabelleepoque.com; Calle 12 No 12A-21; s/d incl breakfast COP$75,000/120,000; 🛜❄), with 10 rooms, a Jacuzzi, and terraces with tropical flowers and hammocks.

---

sive, multi-environment nightclub is one of Colombia's most famous, a real doozy featuring DJs in solid brick booths, painted milk jugs hanging from ceilings and a wild crowd that ain't going home until forced. If you are having a bad time here, just change rooms!

❶ Getting There & Away

Numerous daily buses serve Villavicencio from Bogotá (COP$20,000, three hours). **Aires** (☏664 8550) and **Satena** (☏662 1260) offer daily flights, but all said and done, it's not much faster than the bus. Charter flights to La Macarena (COP$200,000 to COP$400,000), for Caño Cristales, leave from here, sometimes in a six-seat Cessna, sometimes in a 1940s-era DC-3!

CAÑO CRISTALES

It's been a long time since anyone visited one of Colombia's most impressive ecological wonders on a regular basis – guerrilla, paramilitary and army activity in the department of Meta over the last few decades has meant that **Parque Nacional Natural (PNN) Sierra de La Macarena**, better known as **Caño Cristales**, has been closed to tourism since 1989. And, officially, it still is. But some pioneering tour agencies with an eye on preservation have secured authorization to visit the site and began offering carefully crafted tours to the area in 2009, despite continued FARC presence in the greater surrounding areas.

Caño Cristales, located in the Macarena Mountains, has been called everything from 'The River of Five Colors' to the 'The

A GREEN SUCCESS STORY

Off the beaten path, **Gaviotas** (www.friendsofgaviotas.org), about 100km southeast of Villavicencio, is a 'green' success story. The UN called the village a model of sustainable development, and Gabriel García Márquez called founder Paolo Lugari the 'inventor of the world.' The village of 200 people is operated on wind and solar power. Residents farm organically and have planted millions of trees. The town has become a world-class research and development center for green technologies and the commune-like society has no police, no mayor and no weapons. The village was profiled in journalist Alan Weisman's book, *Gaviotas: A Village to Reinvent the World.*

Liquid Rainbow.' Why all the superlatives? Well, for most of the year, you'd be right to inquire, but for a couple of months some time between July and November, water levels are just so for a unique biological phenomenon: an eruption of algae produced by a unique species of plant called *Macarenia Clavigera* forms an underwater blanket of bright red, transforming the crystal-clear water into a river of Cabernet that contrasts with the lunarscape of ancient, hollowed-out riverbed rock and surrounding savannah-meets-jungle landscape, dramatically altering the whole area into a thousand shades of awe.

Not only that, but there are numerous swimmable waterfalls and natural pools along the river, and the 10-minute ride from La Macarena along the Río Guayabero yields impressive wildlife, from sizable turtles and iguanas to macaws and *aguilas* (Colombia's national bird, not the beer) to Hoatzins, fascinating tropical pheasants with sinister faces!

You cannot yet visit Caño Cristales on your own – you are obligated to go with an agency or guide. Aventure Colombia (p68) and De Una Colombia Tours (p76) both offer fascinating three-day tours to the region from COP$950,000; but it's also feasible to go independently: get yourself to Villavicencio (easy bus ride from Bogotá; COP$20,000, three hours) and contact **Ecoturismo Sierra de La Macarena** (☑8 664 2691; www.ecoturismosierradelamacarena.com; Aeropuerto) at the airport, which can arrange your charter flight to the small, otherwise inaccessible base town of La Macarena and a guide.

Caño Cristales is no secret – Colombians swarm to it on weekends and holidays, but a maximum daily visitor count of 160 keeps crowds at bay, though this can still seem like a lot if everyone is in the same area of the park.

Boyacá, Santander & Norte de Santander

Best Places to Eat

» La Bonita (p88)
» Color de Hormiga (p105)
» Gringo Mike's (p101)

Best Places to Stay

» Renacer Guesthouse (p87)
» Finca San Pedro (see the boxed text, p84)

Why Go?

Boyacá, Santander and Norte de Santander together form one of the first areas settled by Spanish conquistadores, many of whose colonial towns still stand today, and its calling as Colombia's heartland cannot be understated. It's here that the seeds of revolution were sowed, culminating in victory at Puente de Boyacá that ultimately led to Colombia's independence.

Amid its deep gorges, fast-flowing rivers and soaring, snowcapped mountains, adventurers can choose between white-water rafting and paragliding in San Gil, mountain biking and horseback riding in Villa de Leyva, or trekking through the glacial peaks of Parque Nacional Natural (PNN) El Cocuy. Those less audacious can bliss out around Lago de Tota, Colombia's largest lake, shop for pottery in Ráquira or hit the fashionable clubs of Bucaramanga.

It all culminates in the perfectly preserved town of Barichara, a cinematic, cobblestoned village of stone churches and uniform architecture that evokes life inside a painting.

When to Go

Bucaramanga

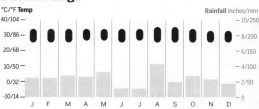

Jan The driest, clearest days on El Cocuy, one of Colombia's coveted trekking peaks.

Feb & Mar The pre-Semana Santa (Holy Week) season has less crowds and full-bloom parks.

Dec Like elsewhere in Colombia, a festival of lights illuminates the region's charming villages.

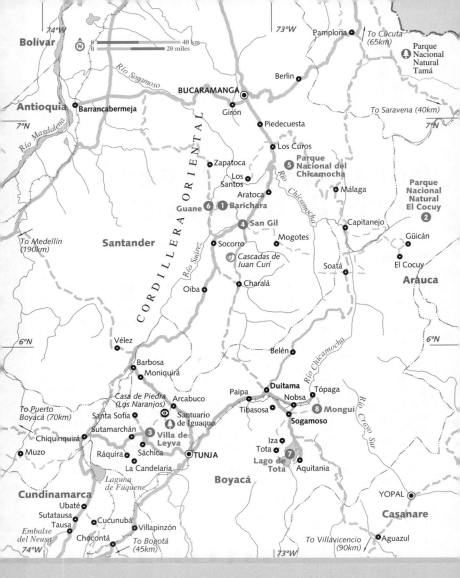

Boyacá, Santander & Norte de Santander Highlights

1. Wander a living museum in the cobbled colonial village of **Barichara** (p102)

2. Ogle all of Los Llanos during one of South America's most spectacular treks in **Parque Nacional Natural (PNN) El Cocuy** (p96)

3. Tour the lovely countryside surrounding the charming colonial village of **Villa de Leyva** (p83) on bicycle or horseback

4. Rappel, paddle, mountain bike or spelunk your way around **San Gil** (p99)

5. Ride the wind in a 2000m-high paragliding flight over **Parque Nacional del Chicamocha** (p106)

6. Hike along the ancient road from Barichara to the tiny hamlet of **Guane** (p104)

7. Catch some Andean rays at the 3015m-high white-sand Playa Blanca on **Lago de Tota** (p84)

8. Mosey the color-coordinated, stuck-in-time village of **Monguí** (p84)

History

The Muiscas (Boyacá) and the Guane people (Santander) once occupied the regions north of what is now Bogotá. Highly developed in agriculture and mining, the Muisca traded with their neighbors and came into frequent contact with Spanish conquistadores. It was their stories of gold and emeralds that helped fuel the myth of El Dorado. The conquistadores' search for the famed city also sparked settlements and the Spanish founded several cities, including Tunja in 1539.

Several generations later, Colombian nationalists first stood up to Spanish rule in Socorro (Santander), stoking the flames of independence for other towns and regions. It was also here that Simón Bolívar and his upstart army took on Spanish infantry, winning decisive battles at Pantano de Vargas and Puente de Boyacá. Colombia's first constitution was drawn up soon after in Villa del Rosario, between the Venezuelan border and Cúcuta.

❶ Getting There & Around

The region is easily accessible by public transportation. Most of its cities are located along the safe and modern highway that stretches from Bogotá in the south to the Caribbean coast. Buses are frequent, comfortable and economical. There are regular buses along the main highway from Bogotá to Bucaramanga and beyond. Cúcuta is a major entry point for travelers coming from Venezuela.

Within the region intercity buses and minivans depart frequently, so you never have to wait long. But in smaller towns buses may only run once or twice a day. Taxis are plentiful but can be pricey. In Villa de Leyva, a bike or horse might be a more suitable and fun way to explore the countryside.

By plane, many cities, including Bucaramanga and Cúcuta, are increasingly served by low-cost airlines.

BOYACÁ

The department of Boyacá evokes a sense of patriotism among Colombians; it was here that Colombian troops won their independence from Spain at the Battle of Boyacá. The department is dotted with quaint colonial towns; you could easily spend a few days bouncing between them. Boyacá's crown jewel is the spectacular Parque Nacional Natural (PNN) El Cocuy, located 249km northeast of the department capital, Tunja.

Tunja

📍 8 / POP 171,000 / ELEV 2820M

Often ballyhooed by Colombians and overlooked by travelers rushing on to Villa de Leyva, Tunja, the capital of Boyacá and a bustling student center, can't compete with Boyacá's big guns, but it does offer an imposing central square, Plaza de Bolívar, elegant mansions adorned with some of South America's most unique artwork and a plethora of standout colonial-era churches.

Tunja was founded by Gonzalo Suárez Rendón in 1539 on the site of Hunza, the pre-Hispanic Muisca settlement. Almost nothing is left of the indigenous legacy, but much colonial architecture remains. Tunja is particularly noted for its colonial churches; several imposing examples dating from the 16th century stand almost untouched by time. With nearly a dozen universities, Tunja is also a center of learning. One in five residents is a student, giving the city a youthful vibrancy.

Tunja is the highest and coldest departmental capital in Colombia. Its mountain climate can be windy or wet any time of year.

◉ Sights

Tunja is a trove of colonial-era churches noted for their Mudejar art, an Islamic-influenced style, developed in Christian Spain between the 12th and 16th centuries. It's particularly visible in the ornamented coffered vaults.

TOP CHOICE Iglesia y Convento de Santa Clara La Real   CHURCH

(Carrera 7 No 19-58; admission COP$3000; ⊙8am-noon & 2-6pm) Founded in 1571, the Iglesia y Convento de Santa Clara La Real is thought to be the first convent in Nueva Granada. In 1863 the nuns were expelled and the convent was used for various purposes, including serving as a hospital. The church, however, continued to provide religious services. The single-naved church interior shelters a wealth of colonial artwork on its walls, most of which comes from the 16th to 18th centuries. Note the golden sun on the ceiling, a Spanish trick to help the *indígenas* convert to Catholicism (the sun was the principal god of the Muisca people). Next to the choir is the cell where Madre Francisca Josefa, a mystic nun looked upon as Colombia's St Teresa, lived for 53 years (1689–1742).

FREE Iglesia de Santo Domingo   CHURCH

(Carrera 11 No 19-55) The nondescript exterior of the mid-16th-century Iglesia de Santo Domingo hides one of the most richly decorated interiors in Colombia. To the left as you enter is the large Capilla del Rosario, dubbed La Capilla Sixtina del Arte Neogranadino (Sistine Chapel of New Granada's Art). Decorated by Fray Pedro Bedón from Quito, the chapel is exuberantly rich in wonderful, gilded woodcarving – a magnificent example of Hispano-American baroque art.

Casa del Fundador Suárez Rendón   MUSEUM

(Carrera 9 No 19-68; admission COP$2000; ⊙8am-noon & 2-6pm) One of the finest historic mansions in town, this place is the original home of the founder of Tunja. Built in the mid-16th century on the eastern side of Plaza de Bolívar, it's a fine example of a magnificent aristocratic residence from the times of the Spanish Conquest. Its most interesting feature is the ceiling, covered with intriguing scenes (the boxed text) that were only recently discovered when a ceiling collapsed. The police will walk you through.

Casa de Don Juan de Vargas   MUSEUM

(Calle 20 No 8-52; admission COP$2000; ⊙9am-noon & 2-5pm Tue-Fri, 10am-4pm Sat & Sun) Once home to scribe Juan de Vargas, Casa de Don Juan de Vargas is another splendid 16th-century residence. It also has been converted into a museum and has a collection of colonial artworks on display. Here again, the most captivating features are the ceilings, covered with eclectic paintings.

FREE Casa Cultural Gustavo Rojas Pinilla   MUSEUM

(Calle 17 No 10-64; ⊙8am-7pm Mon-Fri, 8:30am-3:30pm Sat & Sun) This small but lovely colonial home was the birthplace of Gustavo Rojas Pinilla, who became president of Colombia in a 1953 military coup with promises of reform. Instead, his tenure was marked by corruption and brutality until he too was overthrown three years later. The ground floor contains an art gallery with local and regional exhibits. Upstairs, a small museum explores Pinilla's life through photographs, documents and personal belongings.

Iglesia de San Francisco   CHURCH

(Carrera 10 No 22-23) Built from 1550 to 1572, Iglesia de San Francisco boasts a splendid main retable framed into an elaborate gilded arch at the entrance to the presbytery. Note the impressively realistic sculpture of Christ (carved in 1816), *Cristo de los Mártires*.

🛏 Sleeping

Hotel Casa Real   GUESTHOUSE $$

(📞743 1764; www.hotelcasarealtunja.com; Calle 19 No 7-65; s/d/tr COP$50,000/70,000/90,000; 🌀@🛜) Tunja's most charismatic and friendly option by far, located between the bus station and Plaza de Bolívar, is smartly furnished with tasteful furniture and new armoires and painted in colorful pastel designs. Book rooms 1, 10 or 11 for more natural light.

Hostería San Carlos   GUESTHOUSE $

(📞742 3716; Carrera 11 No 20-12; s/d/tr COP$35,000/60,000/75,000; 🛜) Located in a rambling colonial home and run by a friendly matriarch, the San Carlos is the best downtown budget option. This character-filled hotel has 11 rooms with worn period furnishings. You even get a draft guard to protect the room from gusts of cold under the door.

Hotel American   GUESTHOUSE $

(📞742 2471; Calle 11 No 18-70; s/d COP$25,000/40,000, without bathroom COP$18,000/30,000)

TUNJA'S ENIGMATIC CEILING PAINTINGS

Several colonial mansions in Tunja, including the Casa del Fundador Suárez Rendón and the Casa de Don Juan de Vargas, have their ceilings adorned with unusual paintings featuring a strange mishmash of motifs taken from very different traditions. They include mythological scenes, human figures, animals and plants, coats of arms and architectural details. You can spot Zeus and Jesus amid tropical plants or an elephant under a Renaissance arcade – you probably haven't seen anything like that before. In fact, there's nothing similar anywhere in Latin America.

The source of these bizarre decorations seems to be Juan de Vargas himself. He was a scribe and had a large library with books on European art and architecture, ancient Greece and Rome, religion and natural history. It seems that the illustrations in the books were the source of motifs for the anonymous painters who worked on these ceilings. Since the original illustrations were in black and white, the color schemes are by the design of these unknown artisans.

BOLÍVAR'S BRIDGE

The **Puente de Boyacá** is one of the most important battlefields of Colombia's modern history. On August 7, 1819 and against all odds, the armies of Simón Bolívar defeated Spanish troops led by General José María Barreiro, sealing Colombia's independence.

Several monuments have been erected on the battlefield. The centerpiece is the Monumento a Bolívar, an 18m-high sculpture topped by the statue of Colombia's hero and accompanied by five angels symbolizing the so-called *países bolivarianos*, the countries liberated by Bolívar – Venezuela, Colombia, Ecuador, Peru and Bolivia. An eternal flame for Bolívar burns nearby.

The Puente de Boyacá, the bridge which gives its name to the battlefield and over which Bolívar's troops crossed to fight the Spaniards, is just a small, simple bridge reconstructed in 1939.

The battlefield is on the main Tunja–Bogotá road, 15km south of Tunja. Any bus passing along this road will drop you off.

This basic but clean hotel is the cheapest option downtown. All rooms have lukewarm water and TV.

✖ Eating & Drinking

You'll find a few classier restaurants on the *plazoleta* at the corner of Carrera 8 and Calle 20. Pasaje de Vargas off the central-west side of Plaza de Bolívar is lined with popular cafes.

Pussini CAFE, BAR $
(Carrera 10 No 19-53; coffee COP$2500; beer from COP$2500) Cafe by day, pub by night, Pussini is the pulse of Plaza de Bolívar, an atmospheric two-level bar covered in wood, right up to the bamboo ceilings. Grab the right seat at the bar in the evenings and you have a memorable view across the plaza to the Catedral Santiago de Tunja.

Shalom CAFE, BREAKFAST $
(Calle 19A No 10-64; Pasaje de Vargas; breakfast COP$3000-7000; ⏱7am-5pm) There are many cafes along Pasaje de Vargas, but this is one of the few that actually serves a full breakfast including *huevos pericos* (scrambled eggs with tomato and onion) and warm, gooey *arepas con queso* (corn pancakes with cheese).

El Salon de Onces El Hojaldre CAFE, DESSERTS $
(Carrera 11 No 19-96; items COP$900-3700; ⏱closed Sun) Break sweet bread among nuns, desperate housewives, movers and shakers, and politicians at this classic coffee and snack stop. We simply tore right into those *galletas de arequipe* (milk caramel cookies).

Santo Domingo de Guzmán COLOMBIAN $
(Carrera 11 No 19-66; mains COP$5000-22,000) One of downtown Tunja's most popular eateries, this family-run restaurant serves traditional dishes in a homey atmosphere (hearty set lunches run COP$6800). There's also a bakery and fruit stand on-site.

ℹ Information

Aromatica de Frutas (Carrera 10 No 19-83; per hr COP$600; ⏱9am-7pm) Part cafe, part internet.

Banco BBVA (Carrera 11) Has an ATM.

Bancolombia (Carrera 10 No 22-43) Has an ATM and changes traveler's checks and currency.

Tourist office (☎742 3272; Carrera 9 No 19-68; ⏱8am-noon & 2-6pm) Secretaría de Educación, Cultura y Turismo, inside the Casa del Fundador Suárez Rendón.

ℹ Getting There & Away

The bus terminal is on Av Oriental, a short hilly walk southeast of Plaza de Bolívar. Buses to Bogotá (COP$18,000, 2½ to three hours) depart every 10 to 15 minutes. Northbound buses to San Gil (COP$20,000 to COP$25,000, 4½ hours), Bucaramanga (COP$30,000 to COP$35,000, seven hours) and beyond run at least every hour.

Minibuses to Villa de Leyva (COP$6000, 45 minutes) depart regularly between 5:30am and 7:30pm; and to Sogamoso (COP$6500, 1½ hours) from 5am to 8:30pm.

Villa de Leyva

📱8 / POP 9645 / ELEV 2140M

One of the most beautiful colonial villages in Colombia, Villa de Leyva is a city frozen in time. Declared a national monument in

WORTH A TRIP

THE VALLEY OF THE SUN

Heading some 77km east from Tunja, you'll encounter the largely unexplored region known in the indigenous Muisca language of Chibcha as 'Sugamuxi' – the Valley of the Sun. Ecotourism is starting to blossom here thanks to the Colombian army's ousting of guerrillas in the area about five years ago. Nature rules here, with astonishing treks in and around **Lago de Tota**, Colombia's largest lake, numerous colonial villages around the lake nearly untouched by international tourism, and an out-of-the-blue white-sand Andean beach, the 3015m-high **Playa Blanca** (☎312 522 3003; campsite per person COP$2500), sweetening the deal.

The area's *páramo* ecosystem, a rare glacier-formed tropical ecosystem that exists between 3000m and 5000m in the mountains, characterized by lakes and plains rich with peat bogs and wet grasslands mashed with shrub lands and forest patches, only exists in a few countries in the world, with a large portion in Colombia. Like Parque Nacional Natural (PNN) El Cocuy (p96) to the north, where the *páramo* also thrives, there is naturally excellent trekking opportunities here. Two worthwhile walks in the woods include **Gran Salto de Candelas**, 8km through tropical forest to a beautiful 250m-high waterfall, and **Páramo Ocetá**, also 8km though the *páramo* ecosystem to a spectacular lookout over the Laguna Negra. Get in touch with appropriately named Fernando de la Montaña at **Andino Ecoturismo** (☎312 521 7290; www.ecoturismoboyaca.com) for guided treks in the area.

Surrounding the lake is a series of picturesque colonial villages, highlighted by **Monguí**, once voted the most beautiful village in Boyacá. Founded in 1601, this Christmas-colored village boasts uniform green and white colonial architecture only broken by occasional newer brick constructions that evoke the English countryside. Either way, the beautiful facades are all dripping with colorful red rose-scented geraniums and ivy. It's a truly lovely pueblo, a sort of mini-Villa de Leyva if nobody had ever heard of it. Monguí has a small **tourist office** (☎320 344 2201; culturayturismomongui@gmail.com; Calle 5 No 3-24).

A wonderful place to base yourself in the area is **Finca San Pedro** (☎312 567 7102; www.fincasanpedro.com; dm from COP$20,000, s/d incl breakfast COP$35,000/70,000; @🖥), an excellent, family-run farm-turned-hostel located in the Valle de Iraka, just five minutes' drive from Sogamoso (which is little more than a transit hub, anyway). Wonderfully appointed and dripping in country charm – bougainvillea, Phoenix palms and Araucaria trees dot the landscape – the English-speaking hosts enthusiastically plot your excursions in the area and make you feel right at home, with yoga classes, homespun hospitality and even portable steam rooms!

Alternatively, if you want to bed down in Monguí, **La Casona** (☎778 2498; totoyacaly@hotmail.com; s/d incl breakfast COP$35,000/70,000) is a clean and concise midrange option in a family home, with one of the town's best restaurants attached (mains COP$14,500 to COP$18,500). Check those views!

Regular buses serve Sogamoso from Bogotá (COP$18,000, three to four hours) and Tunja (COP$6500, one hour). From Sogamoso, you can continue on to Iza (COP$2400, 40 minutes) and Monguí (COP$3000, one hour).

1954, the photogenic village has been preserved in its entirety with cobblestone roads and whitewashed buildings.

The city's physical beauty and mild, dry climate have long attracted outsiders. The town was founded in 1572 by Hernán Suárez de Villalobos, who named it for his boss, Andrés Díaz Venero de Leyva, the first president of the New Kingdom of Granada. It was originally a retreat for military officers, clergy and nobility.

In recent years an influx of wealthy visitors and expats has slowly transformed this once-hidden gem. Boutique hotels, gourmet restaurants and tacky tourist shops are replacing many of the old family *hosterías* and cafes. The 2007 *telenovela* (soap opera) *Zorro: La Espada y la Rosa* was filmed here, bringing further publicity to the city. On weekends the narrow alleys can get downright crammed with day-trippers from Bogotá. But thankfully on weekdays the city reverts to a peaceful, bucolic village, one of the loveliest places in Colombia, filled with history, museums, festivals and sightseeing opportunities. Don't miss it.

◉ Sights

Villa de Leyva is a leisurely place made for wandering around charming cobblestone streets, listening to the sound of church bells and enjoying the lazy rhythm of days gone by. Small as it is, the town has six museums, most of which are in old colonial buildings. Villa de Leyva is also famous for its abundance of fossils from the Cretaceous and Mesozoic periods, when this area was underwater. Look closely and you'll notice that fossils have been used as construction materials in floors, walls and pavements. For a marvelous bird's-eye view of the town, hike up one of the many hills surrounding the village (see p86).

TOP CHOICE **Casa Museo de Luis Alberto Acuña**   MUSEUM
(Plaza Mayor; admission COP$4000; ⊗9am-6pm) Featuring works by one of Colombia's most influential painters, sculptors, writers and historians who was inspired by influences ranging from Muisca mythology to contemporary art. This museum has been set up in the mansion where Acuña (1904–93) lived for the last 15 years of his life and is Colombia's most comprehensive collection of his work.

Plaza Mayor   PLAZA
At 120m by 120m, Plaza Mayor is one of the largest town squares in the Americas. It's paved with massive cobblestones and surrounded by magnificent colonial structures and a charmingly simple parish church. Only a small Mudejar fountain in its middle, which provided water to the village inhabitants for almost four centuries, interrupts the vast plaza. Unlike most Colombian cities where the main squares have been named after historic heroes, this one is traditionally and firmly called Plaza Mayor.

As you stroll about, pop into the **Casa de Juan de Castellanos** (Carrera 9 No 13-15), **Casona La Guaca** (Carrera 9 No 13-57) and **Casa Quintero** (cnr Carrera 9 & Calle 12), three meticulously restored colonial mansions just off the plaza that now house quaint cafes, restaurants and shops.

Museo del Carmen   MUSEUM
(Plazuela del Carmen; admission COP$2500; ⊗10am-1pm & 2-5pm Sat & Sun) One of the best museums of religious art in the country, Museo del Carmen is housed in the convent of the same name. It contains valuable paintings, carvings, altarpieces and other religious objects dating from the 16th century onward.

FREE **Casa Museo de Antonio Ricaurte**   MUSEUM
(Calle 15 No 8-17, Parque Ricaurte; ⊗9am-noon & 2-5pm Wed-Sun) Antonio Ricaurte fought under Bolívar and is remembered for his act of self-sacrifice in the battle of San Mateo (near Caracas in Venezuela) in 1814. Defending an armory and closely encircled by the Spaniards, he let them in, then set fire to the gunpowder kegs and blew up everyone, including himself. The battle was won. Casa Museo de Antonio Ricaurte is the house where Ricaurte was born in 1786. It's now a museum, which displays period furniture and weapons as well as some related documents.

FREE **Casa Museo de AntonioNariño**   MUSEUM
(Carrera 9 No 10-25; ⊗9am-12:30pm & 2-6pm Mon-Sat, 8:30am-12:30pm & 2-5pm Sun) Antonio Nariño was known as the forefather of Colombia's independence and Casa Museo de Antonio Nariño is the house where he spent the last two months of his life before succumbing to a lung infection in 1823. Nariño was a fierce defender of human rights and is also revered for translating Thomas Paine's *Rights of Man* into Spanish. The house has been converted into a museum containing colonial objects and memorabilia related to this great man.

FREE **Casa del Primer Congreso de las Provincias Unidas**   MUSEUM
(cnr Carrera 9 & Calle 13; ⊗10am-1pm & 2-5pm Mon-Sat) On October 4, 1812, legislators met here to install the First Congress of the short-lived United Provinces of New Granada and elect its first president, Camilo Torres Tenorio. The 2nd floor of the Casa del Primer Congreso houses a small museum that contains the congressional desk, documents and other artifacts. It was closed for renovation when we visited.

Churches   CHURCHES
Villa de Leyva has four churches, all dating back to the town's early years, two of which are still under religious service. The **Iglesia Parroquial** (Plaza Mayor; ⊗Mass 6pm Mon, Wed,

Villa de Leyva

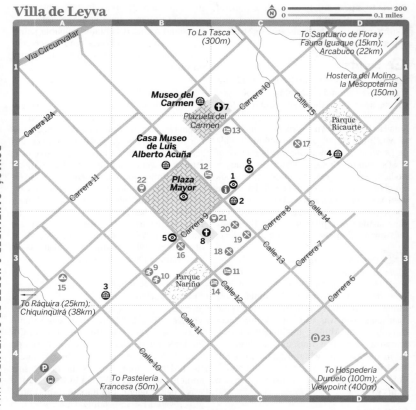

Thu & Fri, noon & 7pm Sat, 7am, 10am, noon & 7pm Sun), the parish church facing the Plaza Mayor, was built in 1608 and has hardly changed since that time. It boasts a marvelous baroque main retable. The only other church currently in religious service, the **Iglesia del Carmen** (Calle 14 No 10-04; ☺Mass 6pm Tue, 6am, 7am, 9am & 11am Sat, 6am, 7am & 11am Sun), has interesting paintings in the chancel and the wooden structure supporting the roof; as well as housing the Museo del Carmen, one of the village's most interesting museums.

🏃 Activities

There are many **hiking** possibilities all around Villa de Leyva, as well as some longer treks in the Santuario de Iguaque (p91). In town, there's a great hike that begins directly behind Renacer Guesthouse (p87), passing two waterfalls to reach a spectacular bird's-eye view of the village; the round-trip hike takes less than two hours.

The alternative to foot power is **cycling** or **horseback riding**; both can be booked from one of the tour operators (see p86). Bikes cost about COP$4000/15,000 per hour/half-day; horses are COP$40,000 for three hours.

Swimming holes can be found beneath many of the nearby waterfalls or just outside town at **Pozos Azules** (admission COP$5000). The two most spectacular falls in the area are La Periquera and El Hayal. In town, you can take the plunge at the freshwater swimming pool at Hostería del Molino La Mesopotamia (p88).

More extreme sporting options in the area include **rappelling**, **canyoning** and **caving**. These activities can be arranged through the following tour operators.

👉 Tours

Taxis at the bus terminal offer round trips to the surrounding sights. The standard routes include El Fósil, El Infiernito and Convento

Villa de Leyva

del Santo Ecce Homo (COP$60,000), and Ráquira and La Candelaria (COP$80,000). Prices are per taxi for up to four people and include stops at the sights.

🚲 Colombian Highlands ADVENTURE SPORTS
(☎732 1379; www.colombianhighlands.com; Carrera 9 No 11-02) Run by biologist and Renacer Guesthouse owner Oscar Gilède, this agency has a variety of off-beat tours including ecotours, nocturnal hikes, bird-watching, rappelling/abseiling, canyoning, caving and hiking, and rents bikes and horses. English spoken.

Guías y Travesías CYCLING
(☎732 0742; guiadevilladeleyva@yahoo.com; Carrera 9 No 11-02) This agency rents bicycles and can provide maps and recommended cycling routes. Regional hikes and tours are also available.

🎉 Festivals & Events

Encuentro de Musica Antigua MUSIC
(Semana Santa) Old-school *Barroco* music festival with concerts inside local churches like Iglesia Parroquial and Iglesia del Carmen.

Ferias y Fiestas Patronales de la Virgen Del Carmen RELIGIOUS
(mid-Jul) This festival and fair honors the patron saint of Villa de Leyva.

Festival de las Cometas KITES
(Aug) Locals and some foreign kite fans compete in this colorful kite festival.

Festival Gastronómico GASTRONOMY
(Sep) A festival for foodies celebrating the region's tasty culinary traditions.

🌳 Festival Nacional del Árbol ENVIRONMENTAL
(mid-Oct) A green celebration aimed at increasing awareness of the environment and conservationism

Festival de Luces FIREWORKS
(Dec) This fireworks festival is usually on the first or second weekend of December.

🛏 Sleeping

Villa de Leyva has a large selection of hotels in all price ranges. Note that prices rise on weekends, when it may be hard to find a room. During high seasons, including Semana Santa and December 20 to January 15, prices can more than double. Plan ahead.

TOP CHOICE Renacer Guesthouse HOSTEL $$
(☎732 1201; www.colombianhighlands.com; campsite per person COP$9000, dm COP$16,000, s/d from COP$50,000/55,000, s without bathroom COP$25,000; @🛜) Located about 1.2km

northeast of Plaza Mayor, this delightful 'boutique hostel' is the creation of biologist and tour guide extraordinaire Oscar Gilède of Colombian Highlands. Everything about this place feels like home – hammocks surrounding an immaculate garden; a communal, open-air kitchen with brick oven; and spotless dorms and rooms. It's a bit tricky to find, but Oscar will credit guests' first taxi ride from the bus terminal (COP$5000). When we came through, he was building a naturally sourced plunge pool and cafe (dinner mains COP$12,000 to COP$16,000) and a sauna was on the cards.

Posada de San Antonio BOUTIQUE HOTEL $$$
(✑7320538; www.hotellaposadadesanantonio.com; Carrera 8 11-80; s/d incl breakfast COP$179,000/210,000; @🛜) Natural light permeates all the nooks and crannies of this antique-packed, charismatic 1860 colonial home, probably Villa's most discerning choice. Rooms feature exposed glimpses of original brick and there's a lovely open kitchen, a character-filled living room, a small portable altar and, of course, a lovely courtyard.

Casa Viena GUESTHOUSE $$
(✑732 0711; www.casaviena.com; Carrera 10 No 19-114; dm COP$15,000, s/d COP$40,000/50,000, without bathroom COP$28,000/35,000; @🛜) Hans and family of Cartagena's Casa Viena fame fled the Caribbean heat and opened this small guesthouse just outside the village on the road to Renacer. There were three simple rooms available at the time of research, with good mattresses and warm bedspreads, the best of which was the room with private bath, which also boasts a nice terrace. Hans cooks up pizzas and Indian cuisine; and his son, Ewald, offers bike tours of the area.

Hostería del Molino La Mesopotamia HISTORIC HOTEL $$$
(✑7321832; Carrera 8 No 15A-265; s/d/tr incl breakfast COP$145,000/180,000/230,000; 🛜🛜) Built in 1568, this old flour mill is one of the oldest and most beautiful buildings in town. It's not gone without complaints from travelers, but it's still worth considering for its colonial architecture, furnishings, artwork and spring-fed, fossil-walled swimming pool (nonguests can plunge in for COP$5000).

Hospedería La Roca GUESTHOUSE $
(✑732 0331; larocahospederia@gmail.com; Plaza Mayor; r per person week/weekend COP$50,000/60,000; 🛜) Located directly on Plaza May-

or, the well-lit La Roca offers 23 pleasant rooms surrounding a gorgeous, plant-filled courtyard. All rooms have high ceilings, new flat-screen TVs and modern bathrooms with hot water. The sassy *bogotana* owner ups the personality on weekends.

Zona de Camping San Jorge CAMPING $
(✑732 0328; campingsanjorge@gmail.com; Vereda Roble; campsite per person high/low season COP$11,000/10,000) Located approximately 2km northeast of town, this huge grassy field has space for 120 tents with lovely views of the surrounding mountains. Amenities include a small restaurant and shop and spotless bathrooms with hot water. It's a 25-minute walk from the plaza: walk north on Carrera 9, passing Museo Paleontológico. At the T-intersection, turn right, then make an immediate left down the well-signed gravel road to the campground.

Hospedaje Sol de La Villa HOTEL $$
(✑732 0224; Carrera 8A No 12-28; r per person high/low season incl breakfast COP$60,000/80,000; 🛜) Located on a quiet side street, this sunny hotel offers clean and well-appointed rooms with private bathroom with hot water and new flat-screen TVs.

Posada de los Ángeles HOTEL $
(✑732 0562; Carrera 10 No 13-94; r per person incl breakfast COP$50,000; 🛜) A pastel-colored affair with modern bathrooms, tile floors and mosquito nets ('just for decoration'). The historic house overlooks Iglesia del Carmen and serves up a great breakfast, though it should be noted we have received reports of in-room theft here.

Zona de Camping CAMPING $
(✑311 550 7687; cnr Carrera 10 & Calle 11; campsite per person high/low season COP$11,000/10,000) This walled, grassy field has campsites and a simple bathhouse, but not much else. Pitch your tent upon arrival and the caretaker will find you later; if the gate is locked, call for the key.

✖ Eating

Villa is the most sophisticated foodie destination in Boyacá. There are a few gourmet food courts in the village, with Casa Quintero and Casona La Guaca offering the best and most diverse options.

TOP CHOICE La Bonita MEXICAN $$$
(Casa Quintero, cnr Carrera 9 & Calle 12; mains COP$19,000-32,000; ⏱10am-5pm) You can get as

good a *cochinita pibil* (anchiote-rubbed pork tacos) here as anywhere in the Yucatán (we know, we've done the research). We're sure the tortilla soup (COP\$15,000) or the baked salmon with mango butter (COP\$29,000) are just as good, but we can't move beyond the *cochinita* (COP\$25,000). You're welcome.

Restaurante Estar de la Villa COLOMBIAN \$

(Calle 13 No 8-85; set meals COP\$7000-10,000; ⏲8:30am-5pm Sun-Fri, to 7pm Sat) Honest to goodness, clean-cut cheapie serving up wholesome daily set meals with just the right amount of motherly love. There's a menu but why bother – just go for the set meal, especially if it's serving *sopa de colí* (green banana soup).

Mercado Municipal COLOMBIAN \$\$\$

(Carrera 8 No 12-25; mains COP\$18,000-44,000; ⏲11am-5pm Tue-Thu, to 10pm Fri-Sun) This chef-driven outdoor restaurant in a 1740 colonial house on the premises of Iglesia Parroquial has resurrected ancient techniques of cooking meats in a 180m-deep underground wood-burning *barbacoa* (barbecue) for ultimate tenderness. The oxtail ragu with spinach gnocchi is superb (COP\$29,000), as are the local oyster mushrooms *(orellanas)* in a *pilpil* (chili-garlic) sauce. The large garden is especially atmospheric at night.

Zarina FUSION \$\$\$

(Casa Quintero, cnr Carrera 9 & Calle 12; mains COP\$25,000-26,000; ⏲noon-11pm Thu-Tue) One of the best eateries in town, though especially notable for its Lebanese slant – the owner's wife is from Lebanon – so you can enjoy a genuine falafel with tahini (order the off-menu version for COP\$15,000). There's also an excellent *lomo* (strip loin) Thai, some

dressed-up Colombian staples and a popular Arab veggie platter.

🌱 Restaurante Savia VEGETARIAN, ORGANIC \$\$

(Casa Quintero, cnr Carrera 9 & Calle 12; mains COP\$12,000-28,000; ⏲noon-10pm Thu-Sun; 🍃) The delightful Savia specializes in inventive vegetarian, vegan and organic fare. Carnivores will love the fresh seafood and poultry dishes such as chicken with apples and caramelized onions. A plaque outside commemorates the last concert performed by former Elvis Presley drummer Bill Lynn before he died in Villa de Leyva in 2006.

Pastelería Francesa BAKERY, FRENCH \$

(cnr Calle 10 & Carrera 6; ⏲8am-7pm Thu-Mon) Ooh la la! An authentic French bakery with croissants, baguettes, tarts, quiches, coffees and hot chocolate. It's great if you can catch it open – the owner likes his vacation time.

Expreso Boyacá FAST FOOD, REGIONAL \$

(Carrera 9 No 11-102; mains COP\$3500-12,000; ⏲from 1pm) From the same owners as Mercado Municipal, this glorified *boyacense* food stall does cheap regional eats that satiate late-night munchies. Try the *mazorcada*: a gooey mess of corn, beef, local sausage, cheese, crunchy potatoes and caramelized onions.

La Waferia CAFE \$

(La Casona del Arroyo, Carrera 9 14-14; waffles COP\$7500-10,900; 🔊) Quaint cafe dishes out a long list of sweet and savory crepes and waffles.

Don Salvador COLOMBIAN \$

(Market; meals COP\$6000; ⏲6am-3pm Sat) Dig into regional *boyacense* cuisine at Villa's bustling Saturday market. Look for this

---

JUST ANOTHER CERAMIC SUNDAY...

Twenty-five kilometers southwest of Villa de Leyva, **Ráquira** is the pottery capital of Colombia where you'll find everything from ceramic bowls, jars and plates to toys and Christmas decorations. Brightly painted facades, a jumble of craft shops and stacks of freshly fired mud and clay pots make a welcoming sight along the main street of this one-horse town. There are many workshops in and around the village where you can watch pottery being made. There are also dozens of craft shops around the main square, all selling pretty much the same stuff, including pottery, hammocks, baskets, bags, ponchos, jewelry and woodcarvings. The best day to visit is Sunday, when the **market** is in full swing.

Ráquira is 5km off the Tunja–Chiquinquirá road, down a side road branching off at Tres Esquinas. Four minibuses run Monday to Friday between Villa de Leyva and Ráquira (COP\$5000, 45 minutes), with a fifth added on weekends. A taxi from Villa de Leyva will set you back about COP\$30,000. A handful of buses from Bogotá also call here daily.

stall, where Don Salvador does the best *mute* (puffed corn soup, served with a side of cow's feet or chicken thigh) and *carne asada* (grilled steak) at the market.

Drinking & Entertainment

The drinking scene in Villa centers around the charming plaza – locals and visitors alike plop down on the steps along Carrera 9, which turns into a full-on street party.

Dortkneipe BAR
(Carrera 9 No 12-88) On Plaza Mayor, folks spill out of this small, unpronounceable bar, which draws hordes for its rare draft beer selection served in COP$5000 1L portions. There's Aguila as well as a local artisanal beer called Donato (it's the thought that counts).

Antique BAR
(Casona La Guaca, Carrera 9 No 13-55; mains COP$13,900-22,900) Locals poo poo the food, but everyone agrees the 2nd-floor terrace of this restaurant is a romantic spot for a drink. Kick back with a glass of wine (COP$6000) or a *canelazo* (COP$5900) – aguardiente (anise-flavored liquor) with *panela* (whole cane sugar) and cinnamon water. There's live music nightly.

La Cava de Don Fernando BAR
(Carrera 10 No 12-03; beers COP$3000-3500) A cozy bar on the corner of Plaza Mayor, with blaring music and candlelit beer bottles as lighting.

La Tasca CLUB, LIVE MUSIC
(Calle 15 No 12A-25; cover COP$5000-15,000; ⊙6pm-late Fri-Sun) The only *discoteca* in town, La Tasca features live music, drinking, dancing and late-night dining.

🛍 Shopping

Check out the colorful market held every Saturday on the square three blocks southeast of Plaza Mayor. It's best and busiest early in the morning.

Villa de Leyva has quite a number of handicraft shops noted for fine basketry and good-quality woven items such as sweaters and *ruanas* (ponchos). There are some artisan shops on Plaza Mayor and more in the side streets, particularly on Carrera 9. A number of weavers have settled in town; their work is of excellent quality and their prices are reasonable. Most craft shops open only on weekends.

ⓘ Information

ATMs (Plaza Mayor, Calle 12) Several ATMs on the south side of the plaza.

Police (320 225 1707; Carrera 10 No 11-10)

Q.inter.net (Carrera 9 No 11-96; per hr COP$1600; ⊙8am-10pm Mon-Fri, 9am-10pm Sun) Internet cafe.

Quinternet (Carrera 9 No 11-75; per hr COP$1600; ⊙9am-9pm) Internet cafe.

Tourist office (Oficina de Turismo; ☑732 0232; cnr Carrera 9 & Calle 13; ⊙8am-12:30pm & 2-6pm Mon-Sat, 9am-1pm & 3-6pm Sun) Provides free maps, brochures and information in Spanish.

ⓘ Getting There & Away

The bus terminal is three blocks southwest of Plaza Mayor, on the road to Tunja. Minibuses run between Tunja and Villa de Leyva every 15 minutes from 5:30am to 7:30pm (COP$6000, 45 minutes). Direct buses travel daily to Bogotá (COP$20,000, four hours, 4:30am, 5am, noon, 12:30pm, 1pm, 2pm, 4pm and 5pm).

Around Villa De Leyva

Don't leave town without exploring some of the many nearby attractions, including archaeological relics, colonial monuments, petroglyphs, caves, lakes and waterfalls.

The area is completely safe. You can walk to some of the nearest sights, or go by bicycle or on horseback (see p86). You can also use local buses, go by taxi or arrange a tour with Villa de Leyva's tour operators (p86). If you choose to go by taxi, make sure you confirm with the driver all the sights you want to see and agree on a price before setting off.

Founded by the Dominican fathers in 1620, the **Convento del Santo Ecce Homo** (admission COP$4000; ⊙9am-5pm) is a large stone-and-adobe construction with a lovely courtyard. The floors are paved with stones quarried in the region, so they contain ammonites and fossils, including petrified corn and flowers. There are also fossils in the base of a statue in the chapel.

The chapel boasts a magnificent gilded main retable with a small image of Ecce Homo, and the original wooden ceiling is full of fascinating details: note the images of pineapples, eagles, suns and moon – used to help convert indigenous peoples; the images of a skull and crossbones with a Bolivian-style winter cap in the Sacristy; and the crucifix in the Capitulary Hall showing Christ alive, a rarity in South America (his eyes are open). Look out for the drawing of Christ in the west cloister – from different angles it appears that the eyes open and close.

The convent is 13km from Villa de Leyva. The morning bus to Santa Sofía will drop you off, from where it's a 15-minute walk to the convent. A round-trip taxi (for up to four people) from Villa de Leyva to El Fósil, El Infiernito and Ecce Homo will cost about COP$60,000, including waiting time.

El Fósil (www.museoelfosil.com; admission COP$4000; ⊙7am-6pm) is an impressive 120-million-year-old baby kronosaurus fossil and the world's most complete specimen of this prehistoric marine reptile. The fossil is 7m long; the creature was about 12m in size but the tail did not survive. The fossil remains in place exactly where it was found in 1977. The fossil is off the road to Santa Sofía, 6km west of Villa de Leyva. You can walk there in a bit more than an hour, or take the Santa Sofía bus, which will drop you off 80m from the fossil.

The **Estación Astronómica Muisca** (El Infiernito; admission COP$4000; ⊙9am-noon & 2-5pm Tue-Sun) dates from the early centuries AD and was used by the Muiscas to determine the seasons. This Stonehenge-like site contains 115-odd cylindrical stone monoliths sunk vertically into the ground about 1m from each other in two parallel lines 9m apart. By measuring the length of shadows cast by the stones, the *indígenas* were able to identify the planting seasons.

The site is 2km north of El Fósil. There's no public transportation, but you can walk there from the fossil in 25 minutes. Bicycle, horse and taxi are other means of transportation.

Santuario de Iguaque

High above the surrounding valley and shrouded in mist is a pristine wilderness that Muiscas consider to be the birthplace of mankind. According to Muisca legend, the beautiful goddess Bachué emerged from Laguna de Iguaque with a baby boy in her arms. When the boy became an adult they married, bore children and populated the earth. In old age, the pair transformed into serpents and dove back into the sacred lake.

Today this Muisca Garden of Eden is a 67.5-sq-km national park called **Santuario de Flora y Fauna de Iguaque** (Colombians/foreigners COP$13,000/35,000). There are eight

SUTAMARCHÁN

While traveling about around Villa de Leyva, it's worth stopping in **Sutamarchán**, the *longaniza* capital of Colombia, 14km west of Villa on the road to Ráquira. *Longaniza* is a regional sausage similar to Portuguese *linguiça*. In town, it's grilled up everywhere – follow your nose. The best spot to try it is **Fabrica de Longaniza, Piqueteadero y Asadero Robertico** (portion COP$5000; ⊙7am-8pm), at the main intersection in town.

small mountain lakes in the northern reserve including Laguna de Iguaque, all sitting at an altitude of between 3550m and 3700m. This unique *páramo* (high-mountain plains), neotropical ecosystem contains hundreds of species of flora and fauna but is most noted for the frailejón, a shrub typical of the highlands.

It can get pretty cold here, with temperatures ranging between 4°C and 13°C. It's also very wet, receiving an average of 1648mm of rain per year. The best months to visit are January, February, July and August. Come prepared.

The **visitors center** (naturariguaque@yahoo.es; dm per person high/low season COP$35,000/28,000, campsite per person COP$8000) has a restaurant and offers simple accommodations in a grubby-looking dorm, or you can pitch a tent outside. Tent rentals are COP$8000. Lodging reservations are required and can be made at Bogotá's Parques Nacionales Naturales (PNN) de Colombia office (p69).

To get to the park from Villa de Leyva, take the Arcabuco-bound bus (departs 6am, 7am, 8am, 10am 1:30pm, 3pm and 4pm) and tell the driver to drop you off at Casa de Piedra (also known as Los Naranjos; COP$3000) at Km12. From here, walk up the rough road to the visitors center (3km). The hike from the visitors center to Laguna de Iguaque takes about three hours. A leisurely round trip takes five to six hours, or longer if you plan to visit some of the other lakes.

La Candelaria

☑8 / POP 300 / ELEV 2255M

This tiny hamlet set amid arid hills, 7km beyond Ráquira, is noted for the **Monasterio de La Candelaria** (admission COP$3000;

BOYACÁ, SANTANDER & NORTE DE SANTANDER SANTUARIO DE IGUAQUE

WORTH A TRIP

IT'S A MIRACLE!

Chiquinquirá is the religious capital of Colombia, attracting flocks of devoted Catholic pilgrims due to a 16th-century miracle involving a painting of the Virgin Mary.

The *Virgin of the Rosary* was painted around 1555 by Spanish artist Alonso de Narváez in Tunja. It depicts Mary cradling baby Jesus and flanked by St Anthony of Padua and St Andrew the Apostle. Soon after it was completed, the image began to fade, the result of shoddy materials and a leaky chapel roof. In 1577 the painting was moved to Chiquinquirá, put into storage and forgotten.

A few years later, Maria Ramos, a pious woman from Seville, rediscovered the painting. Though it was in terrible shape, Ramos loved to sit and pray to the image. On December 26, 1586, before her eyes and prayers, the once faded and torn painting was miraculously restored to its original splendor. From then on its fame swiftly grew and the miracles attributed to the Virgin multiplied.

In 1829 Pope Pius VII declared the Virgen of Chiquinquirá patroness of Colombia. Dubbed 'La Chinita' by locals, the image was canonically crowned in 1919, and in 1927 her sanctuary declared a basilica. Pope John Paul II visited the city in 1986.

Dominating the Plaza de Bolívar, the **Basílica de la Virgen de Chiquinquirá** houses the **Sacred Image**. Construction of the huge neoclassical church began in 1796 and was completed in 1812. The spacious three-naved interior boasts 17 chapels and an elaborate high altar where the painting is displayed. The painting measures 113cm by 126cm and is the oldest documented Colombian painting.

There are eight buses a day between Villa de Leyva and Chiquinquirá (COP$7000, one hour). Buses to Bogotá depart every 15 minutes (COP$14,000, three hours).

⊙9am-noon & 2-5pm). The monastery was founded in 1597 by Augustine monks and completed about 1660. Part of it is open to the public. Monks show you through the chapel (note the 16th-century painting of the Virgen de la Candelaria over the altar), a small museum, a stunning courtyard flanked by the cloister with a collection of 17th-century canvases hanging on its walls, and the cave where the monks originally lived. Some of these artworks were allegedly painted by Gregorio Vásquez de Arce y Ceballos and the Figueroa brothers.

A round-trip taxi from Villa de Leyva to Ráquira and La Candelaria can be arranged for around COP$80,000 (up to four people), allowing some time in both villages.

Another option is to walk along the path from Ráquira (one hour). The path begins in Ráquira's main plaza, winds up a hill to a small shrine at the top and then drops down and joins the road to La Candelaria.

Sierra Nevada del Cocuy

Relatively unknown outside of Colombia, the Sierra Nevada del Cocuy is one of the most spectacular mountain ranges in South America. This gorgeous slice of heaven on Earth has some of Colombia's most dramatic landscapes, from snowcapped mountains and raging waterfalls to icy glaciers and crystal-clear blue lakes.

It is the highest part of the Cordillera Oriental, the eastern part of the Colombian Andes formed by two parallel ranges. A chain of beautiful valleys is sandwiched in between. The Sierra Nevada del Cocuy contains 21 peaks, of which 15 are more than 5000m. The tallest peak, Ritacuba Blanco, reaches 5330m (17,483ft).

Because of its climate and topography, the Sierra Nevada del Cocuy ecosystem has a striking abundance of flora, representing some 700 species. It is especially noted for its frailejóns, many of which are unique to the region. Fauna includes spectacled bears, pumas, white-tailed deer and the famous Andean condor that is a symbol of Colombia. This area is also the ancestral home of the indigenous U'wa people, who still make their home in this harsh terrain.

In 1970 a large swath of this pristine land was set aside for the creation of Parque Nacional Natural (PNN) El Cocuy (p96). With a massive 306,000 hectares, PNN El Cocuy is the fifth-largest national park in Colombia, stretching across the departments of Boyacá, Arauca and Casanare.

Sierra Nevada del Cocuy

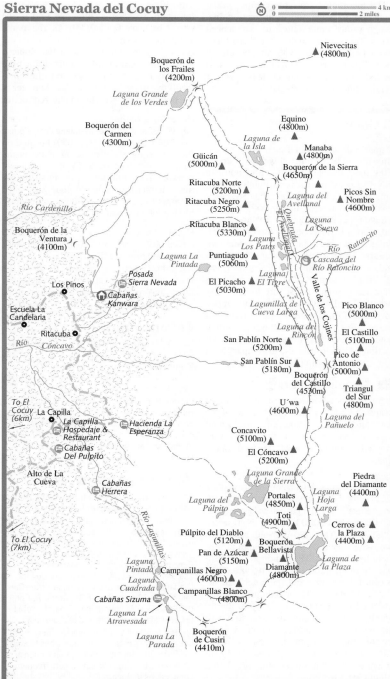

The mountains are quite compact, relatively easy to reach and ideal for trekking, though rather more suited to experienced hikers. The starting points for these hikes are the pretty villages of Güicán (p95) and El Cocuy. The two rival towns have good food and lodging facilities and scenic beauty that even nonhikers will appreciate.

El Cocuy

🏍 8 / POP 5400 / ELEV 2750M

Dramatically surrounded by soaring mountains, the pretty colonial village of El Cocuy is the most traveler-friendly entry point to PNN El Cocuy, with several hotels, restaurants and a few bars. El Cocuy has preserved its colonial character; nearly every building in town is painted white with sea-green trim and topped by red Spanish tiled roofs. The center point of the pueblo is the **Iglesia de Nuestra Señora de la Paz**, the salmon-and-gold church that dominates **Parque Principal**, the town square. After dinner, residents congregate around the square to chat, play basketball and snack on kebabs and *arepas* (corn cakes) from street vendors. The plaza also contains a **diorama** of the surrounding mountain range, but in terms of tourist attractions, there is little else to do apart from enjoy the surrounding natural beauty.

🛏 Sleeping & Eating

There is a good selection of hotels in El Cocuy, all located within three blocks of the town square. Most restaurants are located inside hotels. In the evening, street vendors sell *comida corriente* (fast food) in the square.

TOP CHOICE **La Posada del Molino** HISTORIC HOTEL $
(☑310 494 5076; elcocuycasamuseo.blogspot. com; Carrera 3 No 7-51; r per person high/low season COP$35,000/20,000, cabaña high season COP$180,000) This 220-year-old renovated colonial mansion gives a whole lotta atmosphere for the peso. The building's Swedish-colored (ie blue-and-yellow) interiors evoke its colorful history – and the hotel is reputedly haunted (our TV popped on by itself at 2:49am. No, we weren't sleeping on the remote)! The seven rooms are decorated with fine colonial furnishings and have funky private baths, while simpler, newer cabañas offer five beds each. The gorgeous fossil-strewn courtyard has a babbling brook that will lull you to sleep.

Casa Vieja HISTORIC HOTEL $
(☑313 876 8783; Carrera 6 No 7-78; r per person without bathroom COP$10,000) As the name suggests, this cheapie is located in an old colonial house. Owner and artist Roberto Arango has decorated the courtyard garden with his original paintings and often performs live music for guests. The character of the building makes up for the barren rooms.

Hotel Casa Muñoz HOTEL $
(☑789 0328; www.hotelcasamunoz.com; Carrera 5 No 7-28; r per person COP$20,000) Located on the town square, this newer hotel has clean, comfy rooms with cable TV, firm beds and private baths with hot water, all surrounding a haphazard concrete courtyard filled with geraniums. The 2nd-floor rooms have hidden lofts that can sleep larger groups.

Hotel Villa Real HOTEL $
(☑789 0038; Calle 7 No 4-50; r per person with/without bathroom COP$15,000/12,000) A rambling hotel around the corner from the town square with basic rooms and a popular lunchtime restaurant that serves set meals for COP$5000.

ℹ Information

Banco Agrario de Colombia (cnr Carrera 4 & Calle 8) The only ATM in town.

El Pino.com (Carrera 3 8-53; per hr COP$1500; ⏰8am-noon & 2-8pm) Dreadfully slow internet, a block from La Posada del Molino.

Parque Nacional Natural (PNN) El Cocuy Headquarters (☑789 0359; cocuy@parques nacionales.gov.co; Calle 8 No 4-74, ⏰8am-noon & 1-5:45pm) All park visitors must report here to register their itineraries and pay the admission fee.

ℹ Getting There & Away

All buses arrive and depart from their respective offices on the town square along Carrera 5.

Luxurious Libertadores buses to Bogotá depart from the square's Hotel Casa Muñoz at 8pm daily (COP$40,000, 11 hours); in Bogotá buses depart from the main terminal to El Cocuy at 8:30am. Concorde buses depart the square at 4am and 6pm (COP$40,000, 11 hours) for Bogotá. Fundadores *busetas* to Bogotá depart from Carrera 5 No 5-38 at 4:30am, 5:30pm and 7:30pm (COP$40,000, 11 hours); they depart Bogotá to El Cocuy at 6am, 6:30pm and 8:30pm daily.

Alternatively, if you don't feel like hanging out all day, you can catch a Cootradatil bus to Soatá (COP$15,000, four hours) at 7:30am, noon and 12:30pm, where you can catch more frequent connections to Bogotá.

To Güicán, Cootradatil buses depart at noon, 4pm and 8pm (COP$3000, 30 minutes). You can also catch the Fundadores buses from Bogotá to Güicán, which you can hop on in El Cocuy for the final leg (COP$3000, 30 minutes) at 6:30am and 7:30pm.

To Bucaramanga, take the Concorde bus to Capitanejo and then change buses. The total trip takes about 14 hours along mostly unpaved roads that are prone to landslides and delays. You are normally better off returning to Tunja and catching the frequent northbound buses to Buca and beyond.

For information on getting to and from the park, see p99.

Güicán

⏱8 / POP 7416 / ELEV 2963M

Though not as photogenic or traveler friendly as El Cocuy, the chilly village of Güicán has nevertheless become the main starting point for trekkers heading up to the mountains, mainly because it provides a closer and easier hike to PNN El Cocuy. And for nonhikers, Güicán offers plenty of sights and tourist attractions that don't necessarily involve walking uphill. Most of the city's colonial architecture was destroyed in fires and civil wars. It was replaced with modern, new buildings painted in bold, bright colors. Güicán is the heart of the indigenous U'wa community. Religious tourism is also a major source of revenue, associated with the miracle of the Virgen Morenita de Güicán.

◉ Sights & Activities

Güicán's most famous attraction is the **Virgen Morenita de Güicán**, an image of a dark-skinned Virgin Mary that appeared to the indigenous U'wa people in 1756 (see the boxed text, p95). The shrine to the Morenita is located inside the **Nuestra Señora de la Candelaria** church on the town square, Parque Principal. The brown brick and faux marble church isn't much to look at outside, but inside it's richly decorated and painted in pastel pinks, greens and blues.

East of town is a 300m-high cliff known as **El Peñol de los Muertos**, where U'wa people jumped to their deaths upon the arrival of the conquistadores rather than live under Spanish rule. The trail to the cliff begins at the end of Carrera 4. A hike to the top of the cliff takes about two hours. The **Monumento a la Dignidad de la Raza U'wa** depicting this mass act of suicide is located at the entrance of town.

🛏 Sleeping & Eating

Hotel El Eden　　　　　　　GUESTHOUSE $
(☎311 808 8334; luishernandonc@hotmail.com; Transversal 2 No 9-58; campsites/r per person COP$5000/25,000) More Noah's Ark than El Eden, this family-run guesthouse is a favorite with foreigners. The garden is filled with turkeys, ducks, rabbits, gerbils and a trout pond, and the wood-filled rooms smell of forest. Most have private baths and some have lofts. Eden is a 12-minute walk north of the plaza. To get here, walk north up

BOYACÁ, SANTANDER & NORTE DE SANTANDER GÜICÁN

VIRGEN MORENITA DE GÜICÁN

Güicán is known throughout Colombia for the miracle of the Virgen Morenita de Güicán, which was an apparition of the dark-skinned Virgin Mary that appeared to the indigenous U'wa people. The story begins in the late 17th century when Spanish conquistadores arrived in the area and set about converting the U'wa to Christianity. Rather than bow to Spanish rule, U'wa chief Güicány, for whom the town is named, led his tribe to their deaths by leaping off the cliff now called El Peñol de Los Muertos. Güicány's wife Cuchumba was spared because she was pregnant. Cuchumba and a handful of survivors fled to the mountains and hid in a cave. On February 26, 1756, an apparition of the Virgin Mary mysteriously appeared on a cloth. The image of Mary had a dark complexion and indigenous features, just like the U'wa, who quickly converted to Christianity.

A small chapel was built in Güicán to house the Virgen Morenita. During one of the many civil wars between the rival towns of Güicán and El Cocuy, the Virgen was stolen and hidden in El Cocuy, supposedly behind a wall in what is now La Posada del Molino hotel. The family residing there was haunted until they returned the Virgen to Güicán, where it resides today under lock and key.

The grand Festival of the Virgen Morenita is celebrated yearly on February 2 to 4, attracting faithful religious pilgrims from far and wide.

Carrera 4, turn right onto the dirt road leading past the basketball court, take your first right and then second left.

Brisas del Nevado
HOTEL $

(☑310 629 9001; Carrera 5 No 4-57; r per person with/without bath COP$30,000/25,000) The comfiest hotel in town also houses Güicán's best restaurant. Most rooms have private baths and TV. The best rooms are the two private cabañas located in the garden behind the main building.

Hotel Guaicani
GUESTHOUSE $

(☑312 463 1066; www.hotelguaicani.com; Calle 5 No 6-20; r per person COP$15,000) This is the newest and most acceptable cheapie in town. Rooms are simple and clean and Victor, the owner, can also make your trekking arrangements.

ℹ Information

The nearest ATM is in El Cocuy.

Cafeteria La Principal (Carrera 5 No 3-09; per hr COP$15,000; ⊙8am-pm) One lonely computer for internet on the plaza.

Parque Nacional Natural El Cocuy (☑310 230 3302; Carrera 4 No 3-30; ⊙8am-noon & 1-5pm Mon-Sat) All park visitors must pay the park admission fee here and register their itinerary, but it's often closed outside high season. You are better off handling affairs at the headquarters in El Cocuy.

ℹ Getting There & Away

All buses arrive and depart from their respective offices on the plaza except Libertadores, whose office is just off the plaza on the Carrera 5 side of the Casa Cural.

Luxurious Libertadores buses to Bogotá depart from the plaza at 7pm daily (COP$45,000, 12 hours); buses from Bogotá to Güicán depart Bogotá's main bus terminal at 8:30pm daily (COP$45,000, 12 hours). Less comfortable Concorde buses to Bogotá depart the plaza at 3am and 5pm (COP$45,000, 12 hours) and at 3:30am, 4:30pm and 6pm with Fundadores (COP$43,000, 12 hours); they depart Bogotá to El Cocuy at 7:30am, 6:30pm, 7pm and 8:30pm.

To El Cocuy, local Cootradatil buses depart at 7am, 11am and 2pm (COP$3000, 40 minutes). Alternatively, take one of the Bogotá-bound buses, which all pass through El Cocuy on their way to the capital. To go to Bucaramanga, Cúcuta, Santa Marta or other points northwest, take a Bogotá-bound bus to Capitanejo and change buses there.

For information on getting to and from the park, see p99.

Parque Nacional Natural (PNN) El Cocuy

Parque Nacional Natural (PNN) El Cocuy is the main attraction of the Sierra Nevada del Cocuy region. Established in 1977, the park covers a massive 306,000 hectares, or about 1181 sq miles. The western boundary of the park begins at the 4000m elevation line; the eastern half drops to just 600m elevation to the Colombian *llanos* (plains).

Most of PNN El Cocuy is made up of a diverse ecosystem known as the *páramo*. This glacially formed, neotropical system of valleys, plains and mountain lakes includes the largest glacier zone in South America north of the equator. Sadly, the park's glacier fields are rapidly melting due to climate change. At the present rate, park officials believe the glaciers will be gone within 20 to 30 years.

Despite the harsh environment, PNN El Cocuy is home to diverse species of flora and fauna. Animals you might encounter include the spectacled bear, also called the Andean bear, deer, eagles, condors, mountain tapirs, chinchillas and the beautiful spotted ocelot. The mountaintop plains are covered in a variety of shrubbery, the best known being the yellow-flowered frailejón that is native to the area.

The park has 15 peaks that are at least 5000m. The highest is Ritacuba Blanco at 5330m. The park's most famous landmark is an unusual rock formation called the Púlpito del Diablo (5120m; Devil's Pulpit). This outdoor playground is popular for hiking, trekking, mountaineering, camping, climbing and paragliding, though the latter is not commercially available (that is, only for private flyers).

From 1985 until early this century, PNN El Cocuy was occupied by ELN guerrillas until the Colombian army moved in. Today the park is once again safe for visitors (the little-used eastern plains area of the park in Arauca and Casanare is still questionable). Colombian soldiers have a base in the mountains and regularly patrol the trails. This peace has quickly brought visitors back to the peaks. In 2003 fewer than 100 people climbed PNN Cocuy; that figure jumped to an estimated 9000 in 2010, according to park officials.

Climbing Cocuy

The mountains of PNN El Cocuy are relatively compact and easy to reach. The complete Güicán–El Cocuy Circuit Trek takes six or seven days round trip, but there are many shorter day hikes; the hike to the snowline is only about three hours from the northern park boundary.

There is no special experience required. However, due to the elevation and terrain, park officials recommend that hikers have at least some previous trekking experience and be in good health. Park entry is prohibited to children under 12 years, pregnant women, and people with heart or lung ailments.

The starting points for hiking PNN Cocuy are the archrival villages of Güicán and El Cocuy. By far the most popular option is to hike the circuit clockwise from Güicán. The hike from here is considered easier, and if you hire horses, they are able to climb further up to the snowline before you must continue on foot.

All visitors to the park must first report to the PNN El Cocuy offices in either Güicán or El Cocuy, register their itineraries and pay the park admission fee (foreigners/Colombians COP$35,000/13,000). Don't forget to check back in after your hike; if you don't show up by your return date, park officials will launch search and rescue operations.

Guides, while not required, are highly recommended.

When to Go

The only period of reasonably good weather is from December to February. The rest of the year is rainy and there is snow at high altitudes and on the highest passes. The weather changes frequently. The Sierra Nevada is known for its strong winds.

What to Bring

All park visitors must be completely self-sufficient. There are no residents or services inside the park. That means bringing all your own high-mountain trekking equipment, including a good tent, a sleeping bag rated to below 10°C, warm and waterproof clothing, good hiking boots, flashlights, first-aid kit, gas stove and food. You cannot buy outdoor equipment in El Cocuy or Güicán, but you may be able to find camping gear in Bogotá. The circuit (sadly) no longer traverses a glacier, so you won't need any special equipment.

If you don't have a tent or basic trekking gear, the only way to explore the mountains is in a series of short, one-day walks from a base at one of the cabañas. This, however, will give you just a taste of these magnificent mountains.

 Tours

You can hire guides and horses from any of the cabañas near the mountains or at Ecoturismo Comunitario Sisuma (see below) in El Cocuy. Expect to pay about COP$45,000 a day for a *campesino* (who can merely show you the way) for up to eight people; or COP$80,000 for an actual accredited trekking guide for up to six people. Horses and horse handlers will each cost about COP$35,000 per day. Solo hikers and small groups can be paired up with others to keep costs down.

Veteran climber **Rodrigo Arias** (☑320 339 3839; www.colombiatrek.com) of Coopserguías is an experienced, highly recommended guide and the only English speaker in the mountains. He can arrange personalized tours and all-inclusive packages for individuals or groups. For the complete El Cocuy circuit all things in, expect to pay from COP$1,500,000 per person for two guides and three people, or COP$1,800,000 if there are only two of you, excluding transportation from Bogotá or wherever. He also rents camping gear and equipment.

Ecoturismo Comunitario Sisuma (☑314 348 9718; www.elcocuyboyaca.com) is a community-driven concession of guides and services, who also operates the only cabañas within the park boundaries at Laguna Pintada (p99). They can also give you a ride from El Cocuy to the top of the mountains near La Capilla, Hacienda La Esperanza or Cabañas Herrera for COP$80,000.

GÜICÁN–EL COCUY CIRCUIT TREK

DAYS ONE & TWO: GÜICÁN TO LAGUNA GRANDE DE LOS VERDES

This section can be done in a single day from Güicán, but it would be a hard, rapid ascent to high altitudes. To acclimate yourself, spend a leisurely first day getting to one of the cabañas and stay overnight there.

On day two, hike from Cabañas Kanwara to the top of the Ritacuba Blanco up its gently sloping back face. The ascent takes five hours, but start very early because the top tends to cloud over by noon.

The next leg is to Laguna Grande de los Verdes. Walk to the Río Cardenillo creek along either a rough road or a path, about two hours' walk total. Once you cross the creek, it's a steady two-hour ascent to the Boquerón del Carmen pass (4300m). Keep to the right-hand side of the valley as you descend from the pass. The trail crosses the

WARNING!

The circuit is not easy for those without previous trekking experience. The average altitude is between 4200m and 4600m and there are no people living along the route, so you must be absolutely self-sufficient. There are no short cuts; and phone signals disappear after the first day. Most importantly, the weather is unpredictable so you must be prepared for rain or snow at any time.

valley and continues along the left-hand slope just below the cliffs, finally arriving at the Laguna Grande de los Verdes (4100m). Here you can look for some natural caves close to the lake if you need to pitch a tent for the night.

DAY THREE: LAGUNA GRANDE DE LOS VERDES TO LAGUNA DEL AVELLANAL

The average walking time between these two lakes is about seven hours. The trail skirts around the eastern side of the Laguna Grande de los Verdes and heads up to the Boquerón de los Frailes pass (4200m). From here onwards to Laguna de la Plaza (and even further), you'll be enjoying magnificent views of snowy peaks.

After a short descent the trail divides. Take the right-hand branch, which heads south along the foot of rocky cliffs. After about three hours you will arrive at the Laguna de la Isla, passing high above its western side. Continue up to the Boquerón de la Sierra pass (4650m). It's often covered with snow, especially in the rainy season, but the trail is easy to find. From the pass, if the weather is clear, you will see the Laguna del Avellanal (4398m) below and the long, magnificent Valle de los Cojines beyond, lined on both sides by snowy peaks. The trail drops down to the lake where you can camp, although the lake shore is quite rocky. Alternatively, there is a cave a few hundred meters west of the lake where enormous rocks have formed a tentlike roof.

DAY FOUR: LAGUNA DEL AVELLANAL TO LAGUNA DEL PAÑUELO

This leg will require about seven hours of constant walking, not including stops. From Laguna del Avellanal the trail descends slowly, following the river into the Valle de los Cojines. You will pass a few small water-

falls on your right before reaching the most spectacular of all, the Cascada del Río Ratoncito. Here the main trail turns eastward and follows the river down into Los Llanos. Use this trail down to see the falls only, but then climb back up again to the point where it turns east.

Cross the creek and continue south along the Valle de los Cojines, keeping close to its right-hand (western) side, just above the wide, plain bed of the valley. The trail here is faint and disappears, but don't worry: just head on to the far end of the valley, sticking all the time to the right-hand slope. Once you reach the end of the valley you begin to ascend. From there you will get to the Laguna del Rincón (4350m) in 30 minutes.

From the lake you climb one hour up to what used to be a glacial pass, the Boquerón del Castillo (4530m), now a moraine that boasts breathtaking views. There is no trail, so just head up to the lowest point between the ranges. From the pass, it's a one-hour walk down to the small Laguna del Pañuelo (4300m), where you will camp for the night.

The pass is often hidden in clouds and fog, especially during the rainy/snowy season. If this is the case, don't attempt to cross – it's too dangerous. Camp at the Laguna del Rincón and cross over the pass the following morning.

DAY FIVE: LAGUNA DEL PAÑUELO TO LAGUNA DE LA PLAZA

This bit may be quite difficult as there is no trail. The walking time can be six to eight hours, depending on how well you find your way. The best advice is to keep close to the rocky walls on your right at all times and stay at roughly the same altitude. Do not descend. Pay special attention when passing El Cóncavo where there are several rock terraces; you should follow the upper ones. Previous trekkers have left behind cairns to mark the right trail and you will probably find these helpful signs on the way.

If all goes well, you should reach the Laguna Hoja Larga within five hours. Another hour further, you will arrive at the marvelous, large Laguna de la Plaza (4200m), where you can pitch your tent.

DAY SIX: LAGUNA DE LA PLAZA TO LAGUNILLAS

Take the path from the southern end of the Laguna de la Plaza and you'll soon get to the well-defined trail leading to the Alto de la Cueva. It's a three-hour walk to the last pass, the Boquerón de Cusiri (4410m), then an hour's descent to the lovely chain of lakes, Lagunillas, where you will find lots of charming campsites. If you are here early enough, you continue on to the Alto de la Cueva.

DAY SEVEN: LAGUNILLAS TO ALTO DE LA CUEVA

From Lagunillas you have an easy four-hour walk beside the Río Lagunillas to the Alto de la Cueva, where the Himat meteorological station is located. You are back on the road. Hitch (transportation is scarce) or walk along the road for another four hours to El Cocuy. There are also footpaths to both El Cocuy and Güicán.

🛏 Sleeping

After a visit to El Cocuy or Güicán, most hikers choose to acclimate to the altitude by staying overnight at one of several cabañas located just outside the park boundaries. The most comfortable cabañas are located in the north end of the park near Güicán. The best-known is **Cabañas Kanwara** (✆311 231 6004; r per person COP$35,000). The three A-frame cabins each have 15 beds, a fireplace, kitchen and bath. Another good choice is **Posada Sierra Nevada** (✆311 237 8619; paramoynieve@hotmail.com; r per person COP$25,000), the highest at 3960m.

Halfway between El Cocuy and Güicán you'll find the **Cabañas Del Pulpito** (✆310 628 8854; r per person COP$38,000) and the rustic working farmhouse of **Hacienda La Esperanza** (✆310 209 9812; haciendalaesperanza@gmail.com; r per person incl breakfast COP$35,000). In the tiny hamlet of La Capilla, a good choice with a few basic rooms is **La Capilla Hospedaje & Restaurant** (✆314 249 9395; r per person COP$15,000).

At the southern end of the park, **Cabañas Herrera** (✆310 341 3649; campsite/r per person COP$5000/25,000) offers four rooms with private bath and a camping zone. Beyond Herrera, within the park's boundaries at Laguna Pintada, **Cabañas Sizuma** (✆314 348 9718; www.elcocuyboyaca.com; r per person with/without bathroom COP$35,000/30,000) is run by a local concession of guides.

❶ Getting There & Away

From Güicán, it's a five-hour hike straight up to Cabañas Kanwara, where the northern circuit trails begin. Private car hire to one of the cabañas will set you back about COP$80,000 to COP$100,000. Some cabañas also offer transportation; prices vary depending on destination and group sizes. A cheaper, last resort alternative is to hop a ride on a *lechero* (COP$5000 to COP$10,000), the morning milk trucks that make the rounds to the mountain farms, though this shouldn't be considered comfortable or safe. The *lecheros* leave Güicán plaza at 5:30am, reach El Cocuy plaza at 6am and make a counterclockwise circuit back to Güicán. There are several *lecheros*, so you must ask around to find the one going to your destination. Most *lecheros* do not stop directly at the cabañas; you'll be let off at the nearest intersection where you must hike up the rest of the way.

SANTANDER

The north-central department of Santander is a patchwork of steep craggy mountains, deep canyons, plummeting waterfalls, raging rivers, unexplored caves and a temperate, dry climate. Mix them together and it's easy to see why Santander has become a favorite destination for outdoor lovers. Extreme sports nuts can choose from whitewater rafting, paragliding, caving, rappelling, hiking and mountain biking. Visitors withj more sanity can enjoy exploring the rustic charms of colonial Barichara, shopping in Girón or getting their dance on in the nightclubs in the department capital city of Bucaramanga.

San Gil

✆7 / POP 44,561 / ELEV 1110M

For a small city, San Gil packs a lot of punch. This is the outdoor capital of Colombia and a mecca for extreme sporting enthusiasts. The area is best known for white-water rafting, but other popular pastimes include paragliding, caving, rappelling and trekking. Closer to earth, San Gil has a quaint 300-year-old town square and Parque El Gallineral, a beautiful nature reserve on the banks of the Río Fonce.

San Gil may not be the prettiest town in Colombia, but dig beneath the exterior shell and you'll discover a wonderful city of natural beauty and friendly, welcoming residents. Don't be surprised if you end up extending your stay. San Gil definitely lives up to its motto, 'La Tierra de Aventura' – the land of adventure.

◉ Sights

Cascadas de Juan Curi   WATERFALL
Take a day trip to this spectacular 180m-high waterfall where you can swim in the natural pool at its base or relax on the

BOYACÁ, SANTANDER & NORTE DE SANTANDER SAN GIL

rocks. Adventure junkies can rappel the sheer face of the falls; book this activity with one of the tour companies (see p100). Juan Curi is 22km from San Gil on the road to Charalá. Buses to Charalá (COP$3500, 30 minutes) depart twice hourly from the east side of the bridge on Calle 10. Ask the driver to let you out at *las cascadas* (cascades), where two 20-minute trails lead up to the falls. The property owner may charge you COP$5000.

Parque El Gallineral   PARK
(☏724 4372; cnr Malecón & Calle 6; admission COP$4000; ◷8:15am-5:15pm) San Gil's showpiece is the mystical Parque El Gallineral, a 4-hectare park set on a triangle-shaped island between two arms of the Quebrada Curití and Río Fonce. Nearly all of the 1876 trees are covered with long silvery tendrils of moss called *barbas de viejo* (old man's beard), hanging from branches to form translucent curtains of foliage and filtered sunlight. It's like a scene set in JRR Tolkien's Middle Earth. Several paths and covered bridges snake through the urban forest and over the rapids. After your hike, relax with a swim in the large spring-fed pool or sip a *cerveza* (beer) at one of the pricey restaurants and cafes.

Parque La Libertad   PLAZA
The tree-lined plaza of Parque La Libertad, also called Parque Principal, is San Gil's most visible landmark and the heart of its social life. On weekend nights the plaza is packed with multiple generations of Colombian families enjoying the festive atmosphere while street vendors hawk warm *arepas* and cold *cerveza*. The handsome 18th-century stone **Catedral Santa Cruz** (cnr Carrera 9 & Calle 13) dominates the north end of the plaza.

🦜 Courses

Connect4   LANGUAGE
(☏726 2660; www.idiomassangil.com; Carrera 8 No 12-25, local 201) Offers a 12-hour Spanish-language express course (COP$234,000) and private lessons (from COP$20,000 per hour).

🏃 Activities & Tours

Several tour agencies in San Gil run whitewater rafting on local rivers. A 10km run on Río Fonce (Class 1 to 3) costs COP$30,000 per person and takes 1½ hours; experienced rafters can tackle the extreme rapids of the Río Suárez (COP$125,000, up to Class 5). Most operators also offer paragliding, caving, horseback riding, rappelling/abseiling, mountain biking, quad biking, paintball, bungee jumping and ecowalks.

For most activities, it doesn't matter whom you book with, you will go with whichever company's turn is next, thanks to the **Allianza Deportes Aventura** (☏724 4545; Carrera 11 No 6-32; ◷ticket window 8am-6pm), an association formed between most of the outfitters in San Gil in 2011.

Those listed following opted out due to their specific specializations.

Colombia Rafting Expeditions   RAFTING
(☏311 283 8647; www.colombiarafting.com; Carrera 10 No 7-83) The rafting specialist for the Río Suárez; also offers hydrospeeding and kayaking.

Macondo Adventures   OUTDOOR ADVENTURES
(☏724 8001; www.macondohostel.com; Macondo Guesthouse, Carrera 8 No 10-35)

Colombian Bike Junkies   MOUNTAIN BIKING
(☏316 327 6101; www.colombianbikejunkies.com; Calle 12 No 8-35) Based out of Gringo Mike's and modeled after Gravity in Bolivia, this upstart extreme mountain bike company offers a 50km downhill adrenaline overdose on two wheels through the Chicamocha Canyon.

🛏 Sleeping

San Gil has plenty of downtown budget and moderately priced lodging options. In addition to the options here, there are many basic cheapie hotels on Calle 10. Folks looking for a little more pampering should check out the luxury hotel-resorts on the outskirts of town along Via Charalá or Via Mogotes.

Macondo Guesthouse   HOSTEL $
(☏724 8001; www.macondohostel.com; Carrera 8 No 10-35; dm from COP$15,000, s/d COP$40,000/50,000, without bathroom COP$30,000/40,000; @🛜🏊) Dressed up in new digs, this San Gil classic remains a laid-back and secure (CCTV) hostel that's a bit like crashing at a friend's place. The new space offers a wonderful leafy courtyard with a 10-person Jacuzzi, and there's a variety of dorm and private room options. The Australian owner and staff are a treasure trove of information and can book all of your adventures in the area. Don't miss Tejo Tuesdays or BBQ Thursdays and don't even think about showing up without a booking.

Sam's VIP
HOSTEL $

(☎724 2746; www.samshostel.com; Carrera 10 No 12-33; dm per person COP$15,000, s COP$35,000-50,000, d COP$50,000-70,000; @⊛⊠) An upstart choice on the plaza that is very comfortable and wins accolades for approaching boutique-hostel levels with its furnishings and decor. The staff is very friendly – invite them into the small pool, with wonderful mountain views; or for a drink on the expansive terrace overlooking the plaza. There is also a superb, straight-out-of-suburban-America kitchen for guests.

Santander Alemán TV
GUESTHOUSE $

(☎724 0329; www.hostelsantanderalemantv.com; cnr Carrera 10 & Calle 15; dm COP$18,000, s/d incl breakfast COP$35,000/50,000; @⊛) The newer, more upscale guesthouse from Santander Alemán has a terrific terrace with views (hence the name: Terrace Vista) around the corner from the local bus terminal. The eight double rooms are clean and comfortable and a great choice as a step-up from a hostel but with the same traveler camaraderie.

La Mansión de Sam Gil
BOUTIQUE HOTEL $$

(☎724 6044; Calle 12 No 8-71; s incl breakfast high/low season from COP$30,000/35,000, d from COP$35,000/50,000; ⊛@⊛) Set in a colonial mansion on the corner of Parque Central and just purchased by Sam of Sam's VIP fame, who has given it a modern tweak as well as opening a gastropub. The best room offers dual balconies overlooking the plaza at the corner of Carrera 9 and Calle 12.

Santander Alemán
GUESTHOUSE $

(☎724 2535; www.hostelsantanderaleman.com; Calle 12 No 7-63; dm from COP$15,000, s/d incl breakfast COP$20,000/35,000; @⊛) The more hostel-like guesthouse of Santander Alemán. A good third choice.

Centro Real
HOTEL $

(☎724 0387; Calle 10 No 10-41; s/d from COP$15,000/30,000; ⊜⊛) A friendly, modern hotel with 41 comfy rooms. It's one of the nicest of the many budget hotels along this block. Prices spike on weekends and holidays.

🍴 Eating

San Gil is not the most gastronomic area of Colombia, but it does have some decent restaurants serving home-cooked local cuisine. There are many fast-food joints on Carrera 10 between Calles 11 and 12. For self-catering there is a **Cajasan Supermercado** (Carrera 10 No 10-50) and **Autoservice Vera Cruz** (Calle 13 No 9-24).

⧉ TOP CHOICE Gringo Mike's
AMERICAN, BURGERS $

(www.gringomikes.net; Calle 12 No 8-35; sandwiches COP$9500-13,000; ⊙8am-noon & 5-11pm; ⊛) In a moody, candlelit courtyard, you'll find this US-UK operation thrilling homesick travelers with a surplus of sandwiches categorized by your poison: ham, chicken, roast beef, vegetarian, chorizo and...bacon. Breakfast burritos and brownies round out the fun with highlights including a brie and bacon burger, Green Ranch chicken sandwich and a spicy ground-beef burrito. Great cocktails, too.

El Maná
COLOMBIAN $

(Calle 10 No 9-42; set meals COP$10,000; ⊙11am-2:30pm & 6-8:30pm Mon-Sat, 11am-2:30pm Sun) This popular, word-of-mouth favorite is the best Colombian restaurant in town. Huge set meals feature traditional dishes like chicken in plum sauce, *carne asada* and grilled mountain trout. The bummer is it closes early if you're out all day.

Plaza de Mercado
MARKET $

(Carrera 11 btwn Calles 13 & 14; ⊙6am-3pm Mon-Wed, to 2pm Thu & Sun, to 4pm Fri & Sat) For a true locals' experience, head to this bustling covered market where you can grab plenty of *comida corriente*, tamales and fresh-squeezed juices. Don't miss the stuffed *arepas* at Solo Arepas del Mercado (7am to 12:15pm) – best breakfast in town (COP$1500 to COP$1800).

Green Food
VEGETARIAN $

(Calle 11 No 8-40; set meal COP$7500; ⧉) Vegetarians and vegans will appreciate that Green Food lives up to its name, providing all-natural healthy, delicious set meals and à la carte dishes like veggie meats, sandwiches, salads and more.

🍷 Drinking & Entertainment

If you are looking for espresso, several cafes on the plaza now have proper machines.

Café Con-Verso
LOUNGE

(Calle 12 No 7-81; drinks COP$8000-12,000; ⊙from 5pm) The colorful hand-painted murals, Sinatra, Kafka and Obregón portraits and art deco decor provide a welcome change of atmosphere to San Gil. The friendly artsy lounge keeps punters happy with strong drinks and chilled-out sounds.

Santa Lucia Cafe
CAFE, BAR

(Carrera 9 No 11-68) Sitting in the courtyard of a pretty, colonial-like 'shopping mall,' Santa Lucia is all lattes and cappuccinos by day, beers and live music (on weekends) during the evening. It gets packed, having swept away a lot of the middle-class drinking crowd from La Habana, which is above on the 2nd floor, and now skews a bit more teenager.

Discoteca El Trapiche
CLUB

(Via Charalá; ⊙10pm-dawn Fri & Sat) One of several discos located on the outskirts of San Gil, El Trapiche is a proper nightclub with smoke, lasers and a kicking sound system and wacky DJ churning out salsa and reggaeton. It's located 2km southeast of San Gil on the road to Charalá. Don't waste your time unless it's Saturday night.

❶ Information

There are several ATMs in and around the plaza. The official tourism website is www.sangil. com.co.

4-72 (Carrera 10 No 10-50) Post office; next to Cajasan Supermercado.

Bancolombia (Calle 12 No 10-44) ATM.

Telecom (Calle 13 No 9-63; per hr COP$1200) One of several internet cafes around the plaza.

Tourist office (⏍724 4617; cnr Carrera 10 & Calle 12)

❶ Getting There & Away

San Gil has numerous bus stations, but you'll most likely arrive at the intercity bus terminal located 3km west of downtown on the road to Bogotá. Local buses shuttle regularly between the terminal and the city center, or take a taxi (COP$3000 to COP$3300).

Frequent buses depart to Bogotá (COP$35,000, seven hours), Bucaramanga (COP$15,000, 2½ hours), Santa Marta via Bucaramanga (COP$60,000, 13 hours), Barranquilla (COP$70,000, 15 hours), Medellín (COP$65,000, 11 hours) and Cúcuta (COP$40,000, nine hours).

Buses to Bucaramanga (COP$15,000, two hours) via Parque Nacional del Chicamocha depart from the **Cotrasangil bus terminal** (cnr Carrera 11 & Calle 8) every 20 minutes until 7:30pm.

The **local bus terminal** (cnr Calle 15 & Carrera 10) has frequent buses to Barichara (COP$3800, 45 minutes) from 6:15am to 8:15pm. This terminal also serves Guane, Charalá and Curití.

Barichara

⏍7 / POP 7447 / ELEV 1336M

Barichara is the kind of town that Hollywood filmmakers dream about. A Spanish colonial town of striking beauty, it boasts cobblestone streets and whitewashed buildings with red-tiled roofs that look almost as new as the day they were created some 300 years ago. It's no wonder that many Spanish-language films and *telenovelas* are shot here. Granted, the movie-set appearance owes a debt to considerable reconstruction efforts made since the town was declared a national monument in 1978.

Barichara is located 20km northwest of San Gil high above the Río Suárez. According to legend, in 1702 a farmer discovered an apparition of the Virgin Mary on a rock in his field. The locals built a small chapel here to commemorate this miracle. Three years later Spanish Captain Francisco Pradilla y Ayerbe founded the town of Villa de San Lorenzo de Barichara, after the Guane word *barachalá,* meaning 'place of relaxation.'

The town's natural beauty, temperate climate and bohemian lifestyle have long attracted visitors. In recent years Barichara has become a magnet for affluent Colombians. Compared to Villa de Leyva, Barichara is more upscale but less touristy. Many boutique hotels, spas and gourmet restaurants have opened here in recent years, but the town retains its traditional atmosphere. It is, without a doubt, one of the most beautiful small colonial towns in Colombia. Don't miss it.

◉ Sights

The main attraction of Barichara is its architecture. The 18th-century sandstone **Catedral de la Inmaculada Concepción** (Parque Principal) is the most elaborate structure in town, looking somewhat too big for the town's needs. Its golden stonework (which turns deep orange at sunset) contrasts with the whitewashed houses surrounding it. The building has a clerestory (a second row of windows high up in the nave), which is unusual for a Spanish colonial church. The cathedral faces **Parque Principal**, the main town square dotted with palm trees, tropical plants, a water fountain and benches perfect for people-watching.

The **Iglesia de Santa Bárbara** (cnr Carrera 11 & Calle 6) atop a hill at the north end of town has been carefully reconstructed in

Baricharra

◎ Top Sights

Capilla de Jesús Resucitado
   Cemetery...A2
Capilla de San Antonio........................A4
Catedral de la Inmaculada
   Concepción B3

◎ Sights

1 Capilla de Jesús Resucitado...............A3
2 Casa de la Cultura A3
3 Iglesia de Santa Bárbara................... B1
4 Parque para las Artes......................... B1

🛏 Sleeping

5 Hotel Corotá.......................................A3
6 La Nube Posada..................................B3
7 Tinto Hostel..B5

✦ Eating

8 Filomena...B2
9 Panadería Central...............................B3
10 Plenilunio Café B3
11 Restaurante La Casona.....................B3

⌂ Shopping

12 Fundación Tierra Viva B3

lightning damaged it. Do visit its **cemetery**, next to the chapel, noted for interesting tombs elaborated in stone. Also have a look at the **Capilla de San Antonio** (cnr Carrera 4 & Calle 5), the youngest of the town's churches, dating from 1831.

The **Casa de Cultura** (⌨726 7002; Calle 5 No 6-29; admission COP$1000; ⊙9am-noon & 2-5:30pm Mon-Sat, 9am-1pm Sun), a colonial house laid out around a fine patio and situated on the main square, features a mishmash collection of fossils, Guane pottery, paintings, typewriters, tools and other tchotchkes.

🛏 Sleeping

Barichara is not cheap; budget travelers are better off staying in San Gil. Prices where not noted here can spike 30% or more during *temporada alta* (high season), roughly December 20 to January 15 and Semana Santa. During high season, reservations are a must.

the 1990s (only the facade survived). Continue up the hill behind the church to reach **Parque para las Artes**, a lovely little park decorated with water features and statues carved by local sculptors, and an outdoor **amphitheater** that occasionally hosts live music concerts. From the park, enjoy the breathtaking views of the neighboring valley.

The cemetery chapel, the **Capilla de Jesús Resucitado** (cnr Carrera 7 & Calle 3), unfortunately lost a part of its bell tower when

EL CAMINO REAL TO GUANE

Don't miss the spectacular hike to the tiny hamlet of Guane on the historic **El Camino Real**. This ancient stone-paved road was built by the indigenous Guane people and rebuilt continuously over the centuries. It was declared a national monument in 1988. From Barichara, the 9km easy hike takes about two hours to complete. The trail is mostly downhill, occasionally crossing over the modern highway to Guane. You'll begin the hike by climbing down the rim of a canyon and then traversing a valley filled with cacti and trees, occasionally encountering grazing goats or cows but rarely other humans. Notice the many fossils embedded in the stone road. El Camino Real begins at the north end of Calle 4, where a sign marks the beginning of the trail.

In the sleepy town, the handsome main square features a fine rural church, the **Santa Lucía Iglesia**, built in 1720. Across the square is the unique **Museum of Paleontology & Archaeology** (admission COP$2000; ⊗8am-noon & 1-5pm), with a collection of more than 10,000 fossils, a 700-year-old mummy, a few conehead skulls, Guane artifacts and religious art. The curator locks the front door and gives a personal tour (in Spanish) whenever someone shows up, so just hang tight.

During daylight most travelers opt to hike to Guane and catch a bus back. Buses to Barichara depart from Guane's plaza at 6:30am, 10am, noon, 3pm and 6pm. If you miss the last one or don't want to wait, look for the bile-toned '77 Renault in the plaza – the owner will give you a ride back (COP$18,000 to COP$20,000).

Don't forget your water, sunscreen and proper footwear.

La Nube Posada   BOUTIQUE HOTEL **$$$**
(⊡726 7161; www.lanubeposada.com; Calle 7 No 7-39; r high season from COP$265,000, s/d low season from COP$150,000/225,000; ⊜⊛) Hidden behind the simple exterior, this old colonial home has been transformed into an unassuming boutique hotel with sleek, minimalist decor. The eight simply furnished rooms, with queen-sized beds and vaulted ceilings with exposed wood beams, surround an abstract courtyard. The on-site gourmet restaurant-bar is one of the best in town. The one outright flaw is the bathrooms – they are fine for a Holiday Inn, but you deserve better in Barichara.

Hotel Coratá   HISTORIC HOTEL **$$**
(⊡726 7110; hotelcorata@hotmail.com; Carrera 7 No 4-08; r incl breakfast high season COP$120,000, s/d incl breakfast low season COP$60,000/90,000; ⊛) Aficionados of historical residences will fall in love with Coratá, a 300-year-old building decorated with antiques and wood furnishings. The rooms have vaulted ceilings, TV and private bathroom. Three backpacker rooms with shared bath go for COP$35,000 to COP$40,000.

Tinto Hostel   HOSTEL **$**
(⊡726 7725; tinto-hostel@hotmail.com; Calle 6 No 2-61; dm COP$15,000, s/d/tr COP$40,000/50,000/60,000; @⊛) A hostel finally makes its way to Barichara, tucked away in a welcoming home on a planned residential block that, though only 15 years old, blends right in with the historic town. Dorms are cramped, but there's a nice kitchen and small outdoor terrace.

La Mansión de Virginia   GUESTHOUSE **$$**
(⊡315 625 4017; hostalMV@hotmail.com; Calle 8 No 7-26; s high/low season from COP$75,000/55,000, d high/low season from COP$120,000/80,000; ⊛) A tranquil, friendly establishment with clean, comfy rooms with TV and private bathroom (some with hot water) and requisite courtyard. Rates include breakfast. To get here, head two blocks east from Parque Principal and four blocks north.

✖ Eating & Drinking

Barichara is a foodies' paradise. Many gourmet restaurants have opened in recent years, offering nouveau-Colombian cuisine and traditional regional dishes like *cabrito* (grilled baby goat). The regional specialty is the famous *hormigas culonas* (see the boxed text, p105).

There is practically no nightlife. A few corner shops sell aguardiente, beer and the local specialty, *chicha de maíz,* an alcoholic drink made from maize.

<u>TOP CHOICE</u> Color de Hormiga   COLOMBIAN **$$$**
(Calle 8 No 8-44; mains COP$16,000-25,000; ☺12:30-4:30pm) You will begin hearing about this restaurant the moment you step foot in Santander. Literally named 'The Color of Ants,' Barichara's best chef specializes in dishes made with the region's famous delicacy. The filet mignon drenched in ant sauce and topped with fried ants is a must. There are also many insect-free dishes, like chicken breast with blue cheese, but you've come all this way: dig into the ants! The lovely thatched-roof, open-air restaurant faces a lush garden and fish ponds.

Plenilunio Café   ITALIAN **$$**
(Calle 6 No 7-74; mains COP$6000-17,000; ☺6:30-9pm) There is way too much microwaving going on, but this low-key Italian spot still manages to churn out good housemade raviolis, pastas and crepes in a cozy, lantern-lit room with just five tables.

Filomena   CAFE **$$**
(Calle 6 No 8-7; panini COP$8500-10,000; ☺6-10pm Tue-Fri, 11am-10pm Sat & Sun) Tiny, adorable cafe offer rich paninis, strawberries dipped in chocolate and cappuccinos.

Restaurante La Casona   COLOMBIAN **$**
(Calle 6 No 5-68; set meals COP$8000) This friendly family restaurant serves cheap lunches and typical regional dishes in an artistic courtyard.

Panadería Central   BAKERY **$**
(Calle 6 5-82; items COP$300-1500) Typical Colombian bakery: stuffed donuts, fat ham and cheese croissants, yummy *milhojas* (creamed puff pastry slathered with *arequipe*) and strong espresso.

Shopping

Barichara is well known for its fine stonework. There are several stone-carving shops along Calle 5 where you can buy sculptures and other stone goods. Barichara is also famous for tobacco.

Barichara has many boutique shops and galleries. **Fundación Tierra Viva** (www.fundaciontierraviva.org; Carrera 7 No 6-20; ☺closed Mon) is a fascinating gallery where local art is produced using dirt.

Information

There are a few ATMs in town; the most convenient is on the plaza to the right of the cathedral. The official tourist website is at www.barichara-santander.gov.co.
4-72 (Carrera 6 No 4-90) Post office.
Barichara On Line (cnr Calle 5 & Carrera 7; per hr COP$1800) Internet on the plaza.
Hospital (Carrera 2, btwn Calles 3 & 4)
Telecom (Carrera 7, No 4-67; per hr COP$1500) Internet.

BARICHARA'S BOOTYLICIOUS BUGS

Of Colombia's culinary traditions, perhaps none is so peculiar as Santander's delicacy, *hormigas culonas* – literally, fat-bottom ants. The tradition dates back more than 500 years when indigenous Guane people cultivated and devoured ants for their supposed aphrodisiac and healing properties. The giant dark-brown colored ants are fried or roasted and eaten whole, or ground into a powder. Containers of fried ant snacks are sold in just about any corner shop in Santander, but especially Barichara, San Gil and Bucaramanga. They are normally in season during spring, but can now be found year-round. They taste like, well, crunchy dirt mixed with old coffee grounds. It's definitely an acquired taste.

Tourist office (☑315 630 4696; Carrera 5) Located at the entrance to town from San Gil. Students sometimes run a kiosk in the town plaza but there's no set schedule.

❶ Getting There & Away

Buses shuttle between Barichara and San Gil every 30 minutes from 5am to 6:30pm (COP$3800, 45 minutes). They depart from the **Cotrasangil bus office** (Carrera 6 No 5-74) on the main plaza. Buses to Guane (COP$1700, 15 minutes) depart at 6am, 9:30am, 11:30am, 2:30pm and 5:30pm.

Parque Nacional del Chicamocha

Halfway between San Gil and Bucaramanga is the spectacular canyon of Río Chicamocha and Colombia's newest national park, **Parque Nacional del Chicamocha** (www.parquenacionaldelchicamocha.com; Km54 Via Bucaramanga-San Gil; adult/child COP$13,000/7000; ☺9am-6pm Tue-Thu, to 7pm Fri-Sun), nicknamed 'Panachi.' The windy, cliff-hugging road between the two cities is one of the most scenic drives in Santander.

Opened in 2006, the park houses a **Museum of Guane Culture**, several restaurants, a forgettable **ostrich farm** (admission COP$2000) and the **Monumento a la Santandereanidad** commemorating the revolutionary spirit of Santanderians. But the real attraction here is the majestic canyon itself. The best views on land are from the **mirador**, providing a 360-degree vantage of the area. Or for a real bird's-eye view, the new 6.3km-long, 22-minute **teleférico** (cable-car ticket COP$38,000; ☺ 9am-11am & 1-5:30pm Wed-Thu, 9am-4:30pm Fri-Sun) descends to the base of the canyon then ascends to the top of the opposite rim. The round-trip ticket includes park admission.

Adrenaline junkies can zipline (COP$25,000) – though a word of warning: a young girl died ziplining here in 2009 under hazy circumstances (the park took some reactionary safety steps and there have been no further incidents); or paraglide (COP$170,000), which is an astonishing and peaceful ride.

Any bus between San Gil and Bucaramanga will drop you off at the park. To get back to either city, walk down to the highway and flag a passing bus. For those heading north, a better option is to just go to the parking lot near the park entrance and look for the frequent Cotrasangil buses to Bucaramanga (COP$10,000, one hour), which ply the road and look for passengers every 30 minutes.

Bucaramanga

☑7 / POP 524,000 / ELEV 960M

With a greater metropolitan population of about one million people, Bucaramanga, the capital of Santander, is one of the largest cities in Colombia. Surrounded by mountains and packed with uninspiring skyscrapers, this modern city is filled with an air of vibrancy.

Buca, as it's known to locals, was founded in 1622 and developed around what is today the Parque García Rovira, but most of its colonial architecture is long gone. Over the centuries the city center moved eastwards, and today Parque Santander is the heart of Bucaramanga. Further east are newer, posh neighborhoods peppered with hotels and nightspots.

Dubbed 'The City of Parks,' Buca is filled with lovely green spaces. Unfortunately, most of the city is not particularly attractive, and is made even worse by the horrific traffic and overpopulation.

Buca really comes to life at night. Its nightlife is legendary thanks to dozens of clubs, hundreds of bars and 10 universities. Non-party animals may find it rather boring. Nevertheless, Buca is worth a stopover on the long road between Bogotá and the coast or as a base to visit the nearby colonial town of Girón.

◉ Sights

Museo Casa de Bolívar   MUSEUM
(Calle 37 No 12-15; admission COP$2000; ☺8am-noon & 2-6pm Mon-Fri, 8am-noon Sat) Housed in a colonial mansion where Bolívar stayed for two months in 1828, this museum displays various historic and archaeological exhibits, including weapons, documents, paintings, and mummies and artifacts of the Guane people who inhabited the region before the Spaniards arrived.

Mercado Central   MARKET
(cnr Calle 34 & Carrera 16; ☺4am-6pm Mon-Sat, to 2pm Sun) Buca's colorful, well-organized central market is worth a stroll, especially for its 4th-floor food court, with all manner of local eats and mountain vistas to boot.

Catedral de la Sagrada Familia   CHURCH
(Calle 36 No 19-56) Facing Parque Santander is Buca's most substantial piece of religious

architecture. Constructed over nearly a century (1770–1865), it's a massive, eclectic edifice with fine stained-glass windows and a ceramic cupola brought from Mexico.

FREE **Museo de Arte Moderno de Bucaramanga** MUSEUM
(www.bucaramanga.gov.co; Calle 37 No 26-16; ◷8am–noon & 2-6pm Mon-Fri, 8am–noon Sat) This museum houses rotating exhibits of modern paintings and sculptures.

Capilla de los Dolores CHURCH
(cnr Carrera 10 & Calle 35) In Parque García Rovira, this is Bucaramanga's oldest surviving church. It was erected in stone in 1748–50, but no longer operates as a church.

FREE **Casa de la Cultura** MUSEUM
(Calle 37 No 12-46; ◷8am–noon & 2-6pm Mon-Fri, 8am–noon Sat) Diagonally opposite Museo Casa de Bolívar in an historic building, this museum features a collection of paintings donated by the local artists.

🏃 Activities

Colombia Paragliding PARAGLIDING
(☎312 432 6266; www.colombiaparagliding.com; Ruitoque) Bucaramanga's most popular sport is paragliding. The hub for this high-flying activity is atop the Ruitoque mesa. Colombia Paragliding offers 15-minute tandem rides for COP$50,000, or go all-out and become an internationally licensed paragliding pilot; 10-day courses including lodging begin at COP$1,900,000. Owner/instructor Richi speaks English and also runs Nest hostel and is co-owner of Kasa Guane Bucaramanga (KGB).

🛏 Sleeping

Nest HOSTEL $$
(☎678 2722; www.colombiaparagliding.com; Km2 Via Mesa Ruitoque; dm/s/d per person COP$30,000/45,000/70,000; @🛜🏊) The sister hostel to KGB, this fly-site hostel is located next to Colombia Paragliding's launch pad, 20 minutes' drive from downtown perched on a hilltop with amazing views of the city. The majority of guests are paragliding students, but it's also a good choice for anyone seeking peace and quiet. Rates include breakfast and laundry services, and there's a wonderful kitchen for guests and a small pool.

Kasa Guane Bucaramanga HOSTEL $
(☎657 6960, 312 432 6266; www.kasaguane.com; Calle 49 No 28-21; dm/s/d per person COP$21,000/

35,000/50,000; ◔@🛜) Two young English lads have taken over management of this Buca staple, better known as KGB, and given it a much-needed kick in the pants. Located in one of the nicest neighborhoods in town, it offers dorms and private rooms, huge hot-water bathrooms, kitchen and laundry facilities, hammocks, a satellite TV room and pool-table terrace. The vibe is being worked on and serious renovations were under way during research time – expect price increases accordingly.

Hotel Principe HOTEL $$
(☎630 4317; www.hotel-principe.net; Carrera 17 No 37-69; s/d with air-con COP$70,000/80,000, with fan COP$60,000/78,000; ◔🌀🛜) This moderately priced hotel in the heart of downtown is popular with tourists and business guests alike. The large rooms have cable TV and super-comfy beds. Other amenities include wi-fi, bar and restaurant.

La Mansion del Marquez HOTEL $$
(☎630 4632; hotelmansiondelmarquez@hotmail.com; Calle 35 No 18-83; s/d with fan COP$50,000/60,000, with air-con COP$68,000/80,000; ◔🌀🛜) Just off Parque Santander, this affordable, central hotel has small, clean rooms, some nicer than others – look out for old TVs and tired bedspreads.

Solar Hotel Chicamocha BUSINESS HOTEL $$$
(☎634 3000; Calle 34 No 31-24; s/d COP$263,000/309,000; 🌀@🛜🏊) Standard, 10-story, 192-room business hotel. Amenities include a swimming pool, gym, sauna, Turkish bath, two restaurants, three bars and room service.

🍴 Eating

Buca is packed with restaurants, from fast-food joints to upscale bistros. Typical regional dishes include *mute* (a thick soup of meat and veggies) and *cabro* or *cabrito* (goat). The legendary *hormiga culona* is a snack you can buy in delis and neighborhood shops.

TOP CHOICE **Mercagán** STEAKHOUSE $$
(Carrera 33 No 42-12; steaks COP$15,900-36,400) Often touted as the best steak in the whole of Colombia, this traditional *parrilla* (restaurant where they serve grilled meats) run in four locations by four brothers *is* all it's cracked up to be: perfect slabs of meat from their own farm come in 200g, 300g or 400g sizes (good luck!), served on sizzling iron plates with yucca and an *arepa*.

BOYACÁ, SANTANDER & NORTE DE SANTANDER BUCARAMANGA

Bucaramanga

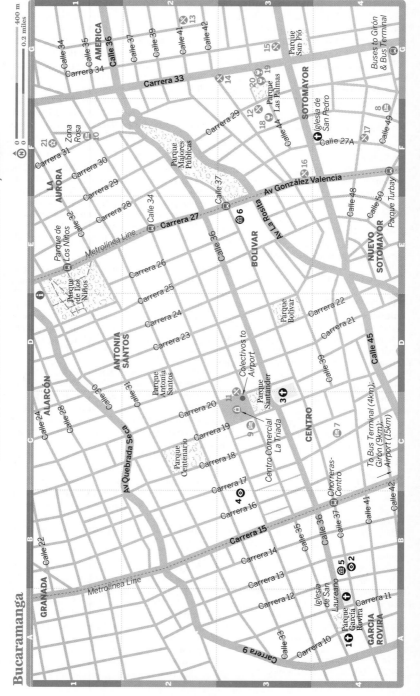

Bucaramanga

Burgers (COP$13,900 to COP$19,500), too, depart the grill here on a regular basis. It may or may not be the best in the country, but it's the best in Bucaramanga! There's a second location nearby on Parque San Pío, which should be open on nights this one is closed.

Restaurante La Carreta   COLOMBIAN $$$
(Carrera 27 No 42-27; mains COP$31,000-43,000; ⊘noon-3:30pm & 6pm-midnight) Housed in a historic mansion, La Carreta has a 40-year-old tradition and a good address for a fine dinner surrounding a lovely courtyard with a gorgeous mango tree. We ordered trout, but the two-story steaks going by caused a fair bit of order envy.

SazonArt   COLOMBIAN $
(cnr Calle 48 & Carrera 27A; set meals COP$7000; ⊘7am-1pm Tue-Sat, 8am-3pm Sun-Mon) One of the better set meal spots you'll come cross in Santander, this very popular, very clean corner restaurant dishes out a few choices daily, conveniently written in Spanish on the board to help those along who can read better than they can *hablan*.

Kebab Spice   MIDDLE EASTERN, ASIAN $
(www.kebab.com.co; Calle 41 No 35-30; mains COP$8000-21,000; ⊘closed Mon; 🕾) A Colombian-Pakistani culinary hybrid dishes up fast-foody grilled kebabs, biryanis, curries and falafel, culling recipes from India, Pakistan and Turkey – not life changing, but not something you see everyday in Colombia and a welcome change of pace.

Guru Food & Drink   CAFE, BAR $$
(www.gurucafebar; Carrera 29 No 42-44; mains COP$14,000-21,000; ⊘2:30pm-late, closed Sun; 🕾) Locals rave about this Parque Las Palmas staple, but we're not convinced: servers seem...confused? And the Tex-Mex meets Colombian-Thai menu yielded a good chicken curry but with no rice? Hmmm. Well, locals know best.

Govinda's   VEGETARIAN $
(Carrera 20 No 51-95; set meals COP$6000; ⊘8am-3pm Mon-Sat; 🖉) Vegetarians will delight in this Hare Krishna restaurant serving hot, healthy cuisine in a relaxing environment.

🍷 Drinking

Many great bars are located in Sotomayor near Parque Las Palmas, though the area has endured a slight infiltration of riffraff, with trendier options congregating on Calle 52 near Carrera 33. Those on foot should head south on Carrera 33 to Calle 52 and walk east.

Café Con-Verso (Calle 44 No 28-63; ⊘from 5pm Mon-Sat) is a beautiful chill-out lounge with great music and drinks. **Santander Beer Club** (Calle 44 No 29A- 06; ⊘from 4pm) touts artisanal beers (COP$7000), though seems to be perpetually out – order a spicy, yummy *michelada* (rock salt and lime juice)/aguardiente mix instead. Asian-atmosphered **Buddha** (Carrera 33 No 44-04; ⊘till 2am) and the Simpson's-themed **Moe's Bar** (Carrera 33 No 44-12; ⊘from 6pm) sit side-by-side on Carrera 33 around the corner, but Moe's was looking to move when

DON'T MISS

GIRÓN

The cobbled streets, horse carts and lazy atmosphere of whitewashed **San Juan de Girón** are a world away in time, but just 9km from bustling Bucaramanga. The pleasant town was founded in 1631 on the banks of the Río de Oro. In 1963 it was declared a national monument. Today it's a magnet for artists and day-trippers, anxious to escape the city but in exchange for an increase in temperature – Girón sits in a breezeless hole in the valley and is baking most of the year.

Take the time to stroll about Girón's narrow cobblestone streets, looking at whitewashed old houses, shaded patios, small stone bridges and the waterfront *malecón* (promenade). The **Catedral del Señor de los Milagros** on Parque Principal (the main plaza) was begun in 1646 but not completed until 1876. Don't miss the pleasant plazas, **Plazuela Peralta** and **Plazuela de las Nieves**, which features a charming village church, the 18th-century **Capilla de las Nieves**.

If you want to bed down for a night, **Giron Chill Out** (☎646 1119; www.gironchillout. com; Carrera 25 No 32-06; s/d COP$98,000/124,000, without bathroom COP$45,000/85,000; @🛜) is a charming option along a quiet street.

For cheap eats, grab a bite at the nice vendor stalls on the waterfront. Of several fine restaurants in town, **Restaurante La Casona** (Calle 28 No 28-09; mains COP$15,000-34,000; ☺till 8pm) is the best, serving up typical hearty food in colonial-style surroundings.

Frequent city buses from Bucaramanga (COP$1550) deposit you on the corner of Carrera 26 and Calle 32, one block from Parque Principal. Buses back to Buca collect passengers on the corner of Calle 29 and Carrera 26.

we came through. **Dash** (Calle 52 No 34-27; ☺closed Sun & Mon), next to Malabar on Calle 52, draws 'Estratas 5 & 6' – Colombia's bold and beautiful.

☆ Entertainment

Bucaramanga comes to life when the sun goes down. *La vida nocturna* (the nightlife scene) attracts clubbers from around the region. Buca's best bars and clubs are located on the east side of town on Carrera 39 between Calles 48 and 49 and Calle 52 between Carreras 34 and 35. Things change here quicker than a baby's diaper, so what was hot when we came through will probably be closed when you arrive, but stick to these addresses and you'll have a good time. **Malabar** (Calle 52 No 34-27; ☺ 9pm-late Thu-Sat) was iron hot when we visited.

For salsa dancing, try old standbys **Cepita** (Hotel Chicamocha, Calle 34 No 31-24) and **Calison** (Calle 33 No 31-35). Most clubs don't get cranking until 11pm and are open until dawn on weekends.

ℹ Information

There is no shortage of ATMs; many are clustered near Parque Santander along Calle 35, and in Sotomayor on Carrera 29.
Bancolombia (Carrera 18 No 35-02)
Click & Play (Calle 34 No 19-46, room 115,

Centro Comercial La Triada; per hr COP$1800; ☺8am-7pm Mon-Fri, 9am-3pm Sun) Internet and international phone calls.
Davivienda (Carrera 20 No 48-72)
HSBC (Centro Comercial, room 121)
Police (☎633 9015; Calle 41 No 11-44)
Tourist information/Tourism police (☎634 5507; www.imct.gov.co; Parque de Los Niños) At the Biblioteca Pública Gabriel Turbay, the tourism police pull double-duty here, surprisingly well. There are maps, brochures and lots of willingness to help. There are also PITs at the airport and bus terminal.

ℹ Getting There & Away
Air

The Palonegro airport is on a *meseta* (plateau) high above the city, off the road to Barrancabermeja. The landing here is quite breathtaking. Local buses marked 'Aeropuerto' link the airport and the city center every hour or so; you catch them on Carrera 15. It's faster to go by **colectivos** (COP$10,000; ☺6am-6pm Mon-Sat), which park off Parque Santander on Carrera 20 across from Govinda's restaurant. A taxi from the city center is a fixed COP$30,000. Avianca, Copa, Lan and Satena all serve Buca.

Bus

Bucaramanga's **bus terminal** (☎637 1000; www.terminalbucaramanga.com) is situated southwest of the city center, midway to

Girón; frequent city buses marked 'Terminal' go there from Carrera 15 (COP$1550) or take a taxi (COP$6000). Buses depart regularly to Bogotá (COP$50,000, 10 hours), Cartagena (COP$80,000, 12 hours), Santa Marta (COP$60,000, nine hours), Pamplona (COP$25,000, four hours) and Cúcuta (COP$30,000, six hours).

ⓘ Getting Around

Metrolínea

To ease congestion, Buca inaugurated a massive public transportation system, **Metrolínea** (www.metrolinea.gov.co), modeled on Bogotá's Trans-Milenio, in 2009. The first phase of the nearly COP$500,000,000 project covers the city of Bucaramanga to Floridablanca, while subsequent phases to Piedecuesta, Girón, Ciudadela Real de Minas and along Carrera 33 remain under construction. Of little interest to tourists at the moment, the main lines run north–south along Carrera 15 and Carrera 27 (along the latter, they remain traditional bus stops rather than stations).

A single ride costs COP$1550.

NORTE DE SANTANDER

Norte de Santander is where the Cordillera Oriental meets the hot, lowland plains that stretch into neighboring Venezuela. The scenic road from Bucaramanga climbs to 3300m at the provincial border town of Berlin before it begins its rapid descent toward Venezuela. The east side of the mountains offers a cool retreat, and colonial-era towns such as Pamplona make a pleasant stopover on the overland trail. Cúcuta is a dry, hot market town better known for contraband than its sights, though you may need to stop here if you're crossing the border.

Pamplona

⏱7 / POP 55,300 / ELEV 2290M

Spectacularly set in the deep Valle del Espíritu Santo in the Cordillera Oriental, colonial-era Pamplona is a delightful town of old churches, narrow streets and bustling commerce. With an average temperature of just 16°C, it's a welcome respite from the heat of nearby Bucaramanga and Cúcuta, and a nice stopover if you're en route to or from Venezuela.

Pamplona was founded by Pedro de Orsúa and Ortún Velasco in 1549, making it the oldest town in the region. Soon after its foundation five convents were established and the town swiftly developed into an important religious and political center. A construction boom saw the rise of churches and noble mansions.

Unfortunately, an earthquake occurring in 1875 wiped out a good part of the town. The inviting plaza is now a mix of reconstructed colonial and modern architecture.

Pamplona was a schooling center from its early days, and the traditions have not been lost; today the town is home to the Universidad de Pamplona, and the large student population is very much in evidence. Pamplona has a distinctly cultured air, and boasts more museums than Cúcuta and Bucaramanga combined.

◉ Sights

Pamplona has quite a collection of museums and almost all are set in restored colonial houses. Check out **Casa de las Cajas Reales** (cnr Carrera 5 & Calle 4), a great colonial mansion, and at **Casa de Mercado** (cnr Carrera 5 & Calle 6), the 19th-century market building, just off the main square. There are some 10 old churches and chapels in town, reflecting Pamplona's religious status in colonial days, though not many have retained their splendor. The **Iglesia del Humilladero**, at the entrance to the cemetery, boasts the famous Cristo del Humilladero, a realistic sculpture of Christ brought from Spain in the 17th century. Pop into the striking cemetery as well.

Museo de Arte Moderno Ramírez Villamizar MUSEUM
(www.mamramirezvillamizar.com; Calle 5 No 5-75; admission COP$3000; ⏱9-11:30am & 2-5:30pm Tue-Sat) In a 450-year-old mansion, this museum has about 40 works by Eduardo Ramírez Villamizar, one of Colombia's most outstanding artists, born in Pamplona in 1923. The collection gives an insight into his artistic development from expressionist painting of the 1940s to geometric abstract sculpture in recent decades.

Museo Arquidiocesano de Arte Religioso MUSEUM
(Carrera 5 No 4-53; admission COP$1000; ⏱10am-noon & 3-5pm Wed-Sat & Mon, 10am-noon Sun) Features religious art, comprising paintings, statues and altarpieces, collected from the region. There is an especially impressive silver collection.

FREE Casa Colonial MUSEUM
(Calle 6 No 2-56; ⏱8am-noon & 2-6pm Mon-Fri, 8am-noon Sat) One of the oldest buildings

Pamplona

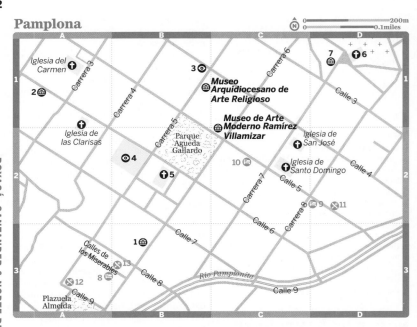

Pamplona

◎ Top Sights

◎ Sights

🛏 Sleeping

✕ Eating

in town, Casa Colonial dates from the early Spanish days. The collection includes some pre-Columbian pottery, colonial sacred art, artifacts of several indigenous communities including the Motilones and Tunebos (the two indigenous groups living in Norte de Santander department), plus antiques. Donations appreciated.

Catedral   CHURCH
(Parque Agueda Gallardo) The 17th-century Catedral was badly damaged during the earthquake of 1875 and altered in the reconstruction. The five-nave interior (two outer aisles were added at the beginning of the 20th century) is rather austere except for the magnificent main retable that survived the disaster. The central figure of San Pedro was made in Spain in 1618.

Casa Anzoátegui   MUSEUM
(Carrera 6 No 7-48; admission COP$1000; ⊙8am-noon & 2-6pm Mon-Sat) A disappointing museum related to the crucial events surrounding General José Antonio Anzoátegui, the Venezuelan hero of the independence campaign who fought under Bolívar. His strategic abilities largely contributed to the victory in the Battle of Boyacá of 1819. He died here, three months after the battle, at age 30.

FREE **Museo Fotográfico**   MUSEUM
(Carrera 7 No 2-44) A curiosity rather than a museum, but do go in to see hundreds of old

photos. The resident painter loves to show off his collection to foreigners.

✦ Festivals & Events

Semana Santa RELIGIOUS
(Holy Week; Easter week) The town is known nationwide for its solemn celebrations.

Fiestas del Grito de Independencia CULTURAL
(Jun–Jul) Also called the Fiestas de Pamplona, the feast is celebrated for two weeks preceding July 4, commemorating the day when Pamplona rebels declared their independence from Spain on July 4, 1810. The festival features concerts, bullfights, parades, bands and the must-see beauty pageant.

🛏 Sleeping

1549 Hostal BOUTIQUE GUESTHOUSE $$$
(2568 0451; www.1549hostal.com; Calle 8B No 5-84; s/d incl breakfast COP$80,000/120,000; @🐾) Pamplona's most discerning option is a seven-room guesthouse in a colonial home on a pleasant side street with a good cafe. Rooms are a tad tiny, but character-driven touches like local art and creative bric-a-brac give it a leg up in both design and intimacy. Two rooms have fireplaces.

El Solar HOTEL $$
(2568 2010; www.elsolarhotel.com; Calle 5 No 8-10; s/d from COP$65,000/110,000; @🐾) Though its website sells it a bit more boutiquey than it actually is, El Solar is still a good choice with a popular bar-restaurant that is warmed by a cozy, hanging firepit at night. Bottom-floor rooms are spacious with new bathrooms while the more expensive 2nd floor has more modern rooms with fantastic windows and big kitchens. But quiet it ain't.

Hotel El Álamo HOTEL $
(2568 2137; Calle 5 No 6-68; s/d/tr COP$30,000/ 40,000/50,000) A friendly choice with rooms with private bathroom that are a bit small but clean and probably the best bet in the budget category. Hot water is 6am to 9am only.

🍴 Eating

TOP CHOICE Paelo's Gourmet COLOMBIAN, FUSION $$
(Calle 5 No 8-77; mains COP$12,000-20,000) The Venezuelan chef here calls his restaurant 'Emotional Gastronomy.' Try not to cry tears of joy when you realize just how good this is for Pamplona. The menu has fine pasta, meat and fish dishes, but outpunches its weight class on more sophisticated recipes

like the namesake *Pamplonas:* chicken breast stuffed with regional vegetables sautéed in white wine and served under a bed of carrots marinated in butter and olive oil.

Piero's PIZZERIA $$
(Carrera 5 No 8B-67; pizza COP$13,000-25,000; 5-10pm) Who knows how an actual Italian ended up here, but he did, and now there is great pizza and pasta to show for it. Oddly, though, the classics are missing (where is the pizza margarita?), but what's here, somewhat curbed for Colombian tastes, is solid, including an enjoyable spaghetti *'rabiata'* (arrabiata).

El Solar COLOMBIAN $
(Calle 5 No 8-10; set meals COP$7000) Inside the El Solar hotel, this is Pamplona's best set meal restaurant as evidenced by the daily turnout for lunch – locals pack into it. Tasty daily specials are chalkboard-advertised outside and an adorable staff insures it's all churned out tastily and swiftly. Our dessert, *rollitos de guava* (crystallized guava stuffed with *arequipe*), was the best *comida corriente* dessert we encountered in Colombia.

Town Cafe CAFE $
(Calle 6 No 8-20; from 3pm; 🐾) The town's best cafe, a trendy little number with good espresso, baked goods, wi-fi and, oddly, an extensive gourmet hot dog menu.

ℹ Information

4-72 (Calle 6 No 6-36) Post office.
Banco de Bogotá (Carrera 6) East of Parque Agueda Gallardo. Has an ATM.
Click (Carrera 6 No 8-12; per hr COP$1500) Internet.
Davivienda (Calle 6 No 6-70) ATM.

ℹ Getting There & Away

Pamplona's new bus terminal is just 600m southwest of the main square. You can walk to town in about 10 minutes, or pay COP$2500 for a cab.

Pamplona is on the Bucaramanga–Cúcuta road, and buses pass by regularly to both Cúcuta (COP$10,000, two hours, 72km) and Bucaramanga (COP$25,000, 4½ hours, 124km). There are several direct buses per day to Bogotá (COP$50,000) as well as the Caribbean coast.

The road from Bucaramanga to Pamplona is in very poor condition, notably near Berlin where most buses stop for a food and toilet break. Passengers prone to motion or altitude sickness should consider taking Dramamine or similar medication. And bring a sweater.

GETTING TO VENEZUELA

For many visitors, the border town of Cúcuta is either their first or last impression of Colombia, and it isn't a good one. Cúcuta is a hot, muggy, filthy, crime-ridden city; its most well-known attraction is the notoriously dodgy bus terminal. Get-in, get-out.

If you're heading to Venezuela, take one of the frequent buses or *colectivos* (shared taxis; around COP$2000 to COP$2500, paid in either pesos or bolívars) that run from Cúcuta's bus terminal to San Antonio del Táchira in Venezuela. A private taxi runs about COP$15,000. You can also catch *colectivos* and buses to San Antonio from the corner of Av Diagonal Santander and Calle 8, in central Cúcuta. Changing transportation at the border isn't necessary. Don't forget to get off just before the bridge to have your passport stamped by immigration. This border is open 24 hours a day, seven days a week.

There's a 30-minute time difference between Colombia and Venezuela, since Venezuelan President Hugo Chávez' 2007 time-switch decree. Move your watch forward 30 minutes when crossing from Colombia into Venezuela. Nationals of the US, Canada, Australia, New Zealand, Japan, the UK and most of Western and Scandinavian Europe don't need a visa to enter Venezuela. Once in Venezuela, pick up a tourist card – it's issued directly by the DIEX office in San Antonio del Táchira, on Carrera 9 between Calles 6 and 7. From San Antonio there are seven departures a day to Caracas (80BsF to 95BsF, 14 hours) all departing late afternoon or early evening for an overnight trip.

If possible, take as many US dollars as possible to Venezuela, which can either be shockingly expensive (at the official exchange rate) or quite a bit more down to earth (on the active black market, called *dólar paralelo*). It isn't difficult to find someone to exchange US dollars at the black market rate – check www.dollar.nu for current *dólar paralelo* rates to avoid getting fleeced.

If you must sleep in the border area, you are better off in San Antonio. **Hotel Don Jorge** (771 1932; hoteldonjorge@hotmail.com; cnr Calle 5 & Carrera 9, San Antonio del Táchira; d/tr/ste 220/240/320BsF;) is a consistently decent choice.

Villa del Rosario

7 / POP 78,611 / ELEV 280M

About 10km southeast of Cúcuta on the road to the Venezuelan border is the sedate suburb of Villa del Rosario. Here, Colombia's founding fathers met in 1821 to draw up the constitution of the new country of Gran Colombia, and inaugurate Simón Bolívar as its first president. History buffs will want to take a look.

The site of this important event in Colombia's history has been converted into a park, the **Parque de la Gran Colombia**. The park's central feature is the ruin of **Templo del Congreso**, the church (built in 1802) where the sessions of the congress were held. The congress debated in the sacristy of the church from May to October, before agreeing on the final version of the bill. Then the inauguration ceremony of Bolívar and Santander as president and vice president of Gran Colombia took place in the church. The original church was almost completely destroyed by the 1875 earthquake and only the dome was rebuilt. A marble statue of Bolívar has been placed in the rebuilt part of the church.

To get to the Parque de la Gran Colombia from Cúcuta, take the bus to San Antonio del Táchira (COP$2000 to COP$2500), which passes the park on the way to the border. Don't take buses marked 'Villa del Rosario' – they won't bring you anywhere near the park.

Caribbean Coast

Best Places to Eat

» Josefina's (p166)

» Ouzo (p143)

» Punta Gallinas (p159)

» Pachamama (p148)

» La Cevicheria (p129)

Best Places to Stay

» Reserva Natural El Matuy (p150)

» Gypsy Residence (p146)

» Barlovento (p151)

» Hotel Casa Lola (p127)

» Punta Gallinas (p159)

Why Go?

Sun-soaked and stewed in culture, Colombia's 1760km of Caribbean coastline has long been its tourism mainstay, drawing more domestic and international visitors than any other part of the country.

The lengthy coast covers a range of ecosystems, from the dense jungles of Darién Gap on the border with Panama in the southwest, to the barren desert of La Guajira near Venezuela in the northeast.

The crown jewel along the coast is Cartagena, a colonial city with a beauty and romance unrivaled anywhere in Colombia. Santa Marta, where legendary liberator Simón Bolívar breathed his last, also offers a sense of history. But the main attraction of this area is the Parque Nacional Natural (PNN) Tayrona, a wonderful stretch of preserved beach and virgin rainforest. If sunbathing and historic sightseeing don't appeal, the arduous Ciudad Perdida (Lost City) trek will satisfy adventurers and adrenaline junkies, and has become a rite of passage for many travelers.

When to Go
Cartagena

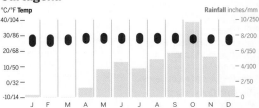

Dec & Jan The beaches are at their best at Christmas as the humidity drops.

Feb Barranquilla Carnaval – four-day Mardi Gras celebrations.

Apr Book early for the Festival de la Leyenda Vallenata, full of accordion-loving whiskey-drinkers.

MAIN POINTS OF ENTRY

» Cartagena: Rafael Nuńez International Airport

» Barranquilla: Ernesto Cortissoz International Airport

» Santa Marta: Símon Bólivar International Airport

» Maicao: Buses from Venezuela terminate here

Fast Facts

» Population: 9,750,000
» Area: 1760km of coast
» Telephone area code: 5

Top Tip

All of the airports on this stretch of coast are tiny – you'll likely be offered a luggage-carrying service for a fee, but you really don't need it.

Resources

» Lonely Planet (www. lonelyplanet.com/colom bia/caribbean-coast) Portal on destination information, traveller forum and more.

» Cartagena Caribe (www. cartagenacaribe.com) News and listings.

» Colombia Reports (www. colombiareports.com/travel -in-colombia/cartagena. html) Regular news updates.

» Turismo Colombiano (www.buritaca2000.com) Information on Cuidad Perdida.

» Parques Nacionales (www.parquesnacionales. gov.co) General information on national parks.

Caribbean Cuisine

Seafood-lovers – your boat just came in. Snapper, grouper, oysters, shrimp, lobster, prawn, ceviche – you'll find it all here, and it's likely to be fresher than you've ever tasted. But there's more to life than mollusks and crustaceans, and Cartagena and Santa Marta both have great, atmospheric restaurants to suit all budgets. Creative cookery abounds, and if pennies are tight there's plenty of simple, delicious street food: the papa rellena – a battered and deep-fried potato ball filled with spiced ground meat – is delicious, and the juice stands will blow your mind. The fruit here is so exotic that most don't even have names in English.

DON'T MISS

Barranquilla, an hour northeast of Cartagena, hosts the continent's biggest Mardi Gras (Carnaval) celebrations after Río. For most of the year, the town is a hardworking, busy port town of over a million inhabitants. But come February, for four days the city descends into a rum-soaked bacchanal of masquerade, massive floats with sound systems, public dancing, carnival floats and musical madness (see p139). It can be chaotic, irreverent and edgy, but it's always massive fun. Wallflowers need not apply.

Best Beaches

» Capurganá and Sapzurro (p164) are ramshackle towns on the border of Panama with a chilled-out Caribbean vibe. Being off the beaten track makes them quieter than other resort towns.

» Islas de San Bernardo (p163) and Tolú (p162) are popular with Colombian families.

» Taganga (p146) is a dive resort and magnet for travelers seeking cheap and cheerful PADI scuba certification by day and parties by night.

» Parque Nacional Natural (PNN) Tayrona (p150) has a collection of wonderful windswept beaches, strewn with giant boulders and fringed with virgin rainforest.

» La Guajira Peninsula (p156) in Colombia's badlands has very few tourist facilities, but the beaches here (eg Playa Taroa) reward the determined traveler with 60m-high sand dunes and gigantic, mind-dwarfing views that will humble even cynics into silence.

» Palomino (p149) is a perfect beach and is the best-kept secret on the coast. Shhh!

CARTAGENA & AROUND

The capital of the Bolívar department, Cartagena has a raw beauty and historical significance. It's also a major port and the gateway to offshore destinations like the northern section of Parque Nacional Natural (PNN) Corales del Rosario y San Bernardo and sleepy down-shore towns like Mompox.

Cartagena

5 / POP 944,000 / ELEV 2M

Cartagena de Indias is the undisputed queen of the Caribbean coast, a fairytale city of romance, legends and superbly preserved beauty lying within an impressive 13km of centuries-old colonial stonewalls. Cartagena's old town is a Unesco World Heritage Site – a maze of cobbled alleys, balconies covered in bougainvillea, and massive churches casting their shadows across plazas.

But then there is the outer town, full of traffic, the working class, and a chaotic nature that can leave you dazed and confused in minutes. It is here that Cartagena becomes a typical workhorse South American city. To the south, the peninsula of Bocagrande – Cartagena's Miami Beach – is where fashionable *cartagenos* sip coffee in trendy cafes, dine in glossy restaurants and live in the upscale luxury condos that line the area like guardians to a New World.

Cartagena is a place to drop all sightseeing routines. Instead, just stroll through the old town day and night. Soak up the sensual atmosphere, pausing to ward off the brutal heat and humidity in one of the city's many open-air cafes.

Holding its own against Brazil's Ouro Preto and Peru's Cuzco for the continent's most enthralling and righteously preserved colonial destination, it's hard to walk away from Cartagena – it seizes you in its aged clutches and refuses to let go.

History

Cartagena was founded in 1533 by Pedro de Heredia on the site of the Carib settlement of Calamari. It quickly grew into a rich town, but in 1552 an extensive fire destroyed a large number of its wooden buildings. Since that time, only stone, brick and tile have been permitted as building materials.

Within a short time the town blossomed into the main Spanish port on the Caribbean coast and the major northern gateway to South America. It came to be the storehouse

for the treasure plundered from the local population until the galleons could ship it back to Spain. As such, it became a tempting target for all sorts of buccaneers operating on the Caribbean Sea.

In the 16th century alone, Cartagena suffered five sieges by pirates, the most famous (or infamous) of which was led by Sir Francis Drake. He sacked the port in 1586 and 'mercifully' agreed not to level the town once he was presented with a huge ransom of 10 million pesos, which he shipped back to England.

It was in response to pirate attacks that the Spaniards built up a series of forts around the town, saving it from subsequent sieges, particularly from the biggest attack of all, led by Edward Vernon in 1741. Blas de Lezo, a Spanish officer who had already lost an arm, a leg and an eye in previous battles, commanded the successful defense. With only 2500 poorly trained and ill-equipped men, don Blas managed to fend off 25,000 English soldiers and their fleet of 186 ships. The Spaniard lost his other leg in the fighting and died soon after, but he is now regarded as the savior of Cartagena. You can see his statue outside the Castillo de San Felipe (p125).

In spite of the high price it had to pay for the pirate attacks, Cartagena continued to flourish. The Canal del Dique, constructed in 1650 to connect Cartagena Bay with the Río Magdalena, made the town the main gateway for ships heading to ports upriver, and a large part of the merchandise shipped inland passed through Cartagena. During the colonial period, Cartagena was the most important bastion of the Spanish overseas empire and influenced much of Colombia's history.

The indomitable spirit of the inhabitants was rekindled again at the time of the independence movement. Cartagena was one of the first towns to proclaim independence from Spain, early in 1810, which prompted Bogotá and other cities to do the same. The declaration was signed on November 11, 1811, but the city paid dearly for it. In 1815, Spanish forces under Pablo Morillo were sent to reconquer and 'pacify' the town and took it after a four-month siege. More than 6000 inhabitants died of starvation and disease.

In August 1819, Simón Bolívar's troops defeated the Spaniards at Boyacá, bringing freedom to Bogotá. However, Cartagena had to wait for liberation until October 1821,

Caribbean Coast Highlights

1 Soak up the history as you stroll the colonial streets of sensual old-town **Cartagena** (p117)

2 Beach-hop through **Parque Nacional Natural (PNN) Tayrona** (p150)

3 Trek through thick Colombian jungle to the mysterious **Ciudad Perdida**

(p153) the former pre-Columbian capital of the Tayrona people

4 Traverse the feral seaside desertscape at **Punta Gallinas**

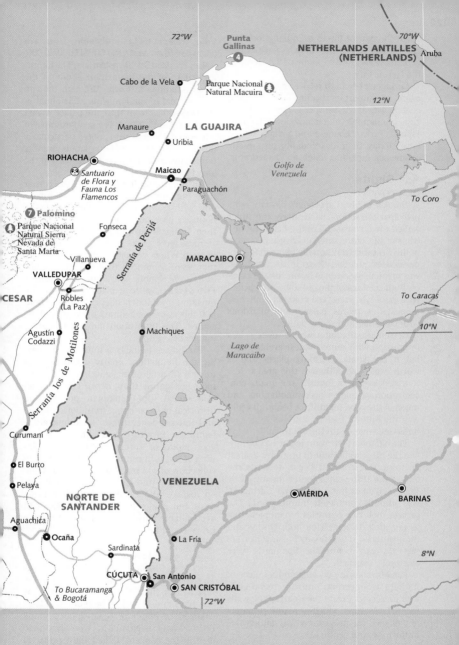

when the patriot forces eventually took the city by sea. It was Bolívar who gave Cartagena its well-deserved name of 'La Heroica,' the Heroic City.

Cartagena began to recover and was once again an important trading and shipping center. The city's prosperity attracted foreign immigrants, and many Jews, Italians, French, Turks, Lebanese and Syrians settled here. Today their descendants own many businesses, including hotels and restaurants.

⊙ Sights

OLD TOWN

Without a doubt, Cartagena's old city is its principal attraction, particularly the inner walled town consisting of the historical districts of El Centro and San Diego. El Centro in the west was traditionally home to the upper classes, and San Diego in the northeast was previously occupied by the middle classes. Both sections of the old town are packed with perfectly preserved colonial churches, monasteries, plazas, palaces and mansions with balconies and shady patios.

Getsemaní, the outer walled town, is less impressive with more modest architecture, but it has some charming places and is worth exploring. Although this area is less tourist-oriented, it houses the main concentration of budget accommodations and much of the good nightlife. A beautiful walkway, the **Muelle Turístico de los Pegasos**, links Getsemaní with the old town.

The old town is surrounded by **Las Murallas**, the thick walls built to protect it against enemies. Construction began towards the end of the 16th century, after the attack by Francis Drake; until that time Cartagena was almost completely unprotected. The project took two centuries to complete due to repeated damage from both storms and pirate attacks. It was finally finished in 1796, just 25 years before the Spaniards were eventually expelled.

Las Murallas are an outstanding piece of military engineering, and are remarkably well preserved, except for a part of the walls facing La Matuna, which were unfortunately demolished by 'progressive' city authorities in the mid-20th century.

The best approach here is to wander about leisurely, savoring the architectural details, street life and street food along the way. Don't just seek out the sights detailed here – there are many other interesting places that you will find while walking around.

TOP CHOICE Palacio de la Inquisición   MUSEUM
(Plaza de Bolívar; adult/child COP$13,000/10,000; ◷9am-6pm Mon-Sat, 10am-4pm Sun) The haunting Palace of the Inquisition is one of the finest buildings in town. Although the site was the seat of the Punishment Tribunal of the Holy Office from 1610, the palace wasn't completed until 1776. It is a good example of late-colonial architecture, noted particularly for its magnificent baroque stone gateway topped by the Spanish coat of arms, and the long balconies on the facade.

On the side wall, just around the corner from the entrance, you'll find a small window with a cross on top. Heretics were denounced here, and the Holy Office would then instigate proceedings. The principal 'crimes' were magic, witchcraft and blasphemy. When culprits were found guilty they were sentenced to death in a public *auto-da-fé* (public execution of heretics). Five *autos-da-fé* took place during the Inquisition until independence in 1821. About 800 folk were condemned to death and executed. The Inquisition did not judge the indigenous people.

The palace is today a museum, displaying the Inquisitors' gnarly instruments of torture (a gruesome sight but by far the most fascinating thing here). The museum also houses pre-Columbian pottery and historical objects dating from both colonial and independence times, including arms, paintings, furniture and church bells. A good model of Cartagena from the beginning of the 19th century and an interesting collection of old maps of the Nuevo Reino de Granada from various periods are also on display. There are no English translations, but guides (COP$35,000 in English) are available. Go in a group if you can: these prices count for up to five people.

TOP CHOICE Convento & Iglesia de San Pedro Claver   MUSEUM, CHURCH
This convent was founded by Jesuits in the first half of the 17th century, originally as San Ignacio de Loyola. The name was later changed in honor of Spanish-born monk Pedro Claver (1580–1654), who lived and died in the convent. Called the 'Apostle of the Blacks' or the 'Slave of the Slaves,' the monk spent all his life ministering to the enslaved people brought from Africa. He was the first person to be canonized in the New World (in 1888).

The convent is a monumental three-story building surrounding a tree-filled courtyard, and part of it is open as a museum (🖉664 4991; Plaza de San Pedro Claver; adult/child COP$6000/4000; ☺8am-5pm Mon-Sat, to 4:30pm Sun). Exhibits include religious art and pre-Columbian ceramics as well as a new section devoted to Afro-Caribbean contemporary pieces like wonderful Haitian paintings and African masks.

You can visit the cell where San Pedro Claver lived and died in the convent, and also climb a narrow staircase to the choir loft of the adjacent church. Should you need one, guides (COP$16,000 in English for a group of up to seven) are generally found by the ticket office. Iglesia de San Pedro Claver was completed in the first half of the 18th century. The church has an imposing stone facade, and inside there are fine stained-glass windows and a high altar made of Italian marble. The remains of San Pedro Claver are kept in a glass coffin in the altar. His skull is visible, making this an altar with a difference.

Iglesia de Santo Domingo   CHURCH
(Plaza de Santo Domingo; adult/child COP$12,000/8000; ☺9am-7pm Tue-Sat, noon-8pm Sun) The Santo Domingo Church, built toward the end of the 16th century, is reputedly the oldest church in the city. It was originally built in 1539 in Plaza de los Coches, but the original building succumbed to fire and was rebuilt in its present location in 1552. Builders gave it a particularly wide central nave and covered it with a heavy roof, but it seems they were not too good at their calculations and the vault began to crack. Massive buttresses had to be added to the walls to support the structure and prevent it from collapsing. The builders also had problems with the bell tower, which is distinctly crooked.

The interior is spacious and lofty. The figure of Christ carved in wood is set in the baroque altar at the head of the right-hand aisle. The floor in front of the high altar and in the two aisles is paved with old tombstones dating mostly from the 19th century.

The church was previously only open during mass, but you can now take a 20-minute self-guided audio tour, offered in most European languages.

Puerta del Reloj   GATE
Originally called the Boca del Puente, this was the main gateway to the inner walled town and was linked to Getsemaní by a drawbridge over the moat. The side arches of the gate, which are now open as walkways, were previously used as a chapel and armory. The republican-style tower, complete with a four-sided clock, was added in 1888.

Plaza de los Coches   SQUARE
Previously known as Plaza de la Yerba, the triangular plaza just behind Puerta del Reloj was once used as a market for enslaved people. It is lined with old balconied houses with colonial arches at ground level. The arcaded walkway, known as El Portal de los Dulces, is today lined with confectionery stands selling local sweets. The statue of the city's founder, Pedro de Heredia, is in the middle of the plaza.

Plaza de la Aduana   SQUARE
This is the largest and oldest square in the old town and was used as a parade ground. In colonial times, all the important governmental and administrative buildings were here. The old Royal Customs House was restored and is now the City Hall. A statue of Christopher Columbus stands in the center of the square.

Museo de Arte Moderno   MUSEUM
(Plaza de San Pedro Claver; adult/child COP$5000/3000; ☺9am-1pm & 3-6pm Mon-Thu, 9am-noon & 3-7pm Fri, 10am-1pm Sat, 9am-1pm Sun) The Museum of Modern Art is a perfectly sized museum (not overwhelmingly huge), housed in a part of the 17th-century former Royal Customs House. It presents temporary exhibitions from its own collection, including works by Alejandro Obregón, one of Colombia's most remarkable painters, who was born in Cartagena. There's also sculpture and abstract art – all well worth a look. The second floor houses temporary exhibitions.

Museo Naval del Caribe   MUSEUM
(Calle San Juan de Dios No 3-62; adult/child COP$7000/4000; ☺10am-5:30pm) Opened in 1992 on the 500th anniversary of Columbus' discovery of the New World, the Naval Museum occupies a great colonial building, which was once a Jesuit college. It features, for the most part, a grand collection of reconstructed cityscapes and boat models from throughout the centuries, but woefully lacks much in the way of actual artifacts (although there are some nice torpedoes).

Plaza de Bolívar   SQUARE
Formerly the Plaza de Inquisición, this leafy and shaded plaza, surrounded by some of

Cartagena Old Town

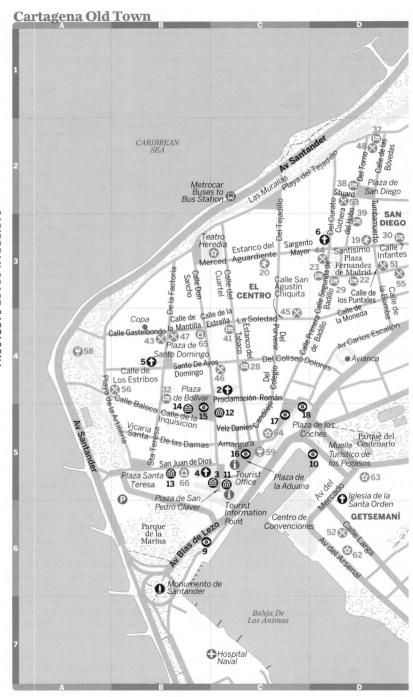

CARIBBEAN COAST CARTAGENA

CARIBBEAN SEA

Av Santander

Las Murallas
Playa del Tejadillo

Metrocar
Buses to
Bus Station

Plaza de
San Diego

Del Torno
Calle de las
Bóvedas

37
48
38
Stuard
53
39
SAN
DIEGO

Del Curato
Cochera
del Hobo

Tumbamuerto

Teatro
Heredia

Estanco del
Aguardiente

Merced

Sargento
Mayor

6

Santisimo
Plaza
Fernandez
de Madrid

19
30

Calle 7
Infantes

Del Tejadillo

20

EL
CENTRO

Calle San
Agustín
Chiquita

44

23

29
45

Calle de
los Puntales

51
55
22

Calle de
la Bomba

Copa

Calle Gastelbondo

43

47

65

41

La Soledad

Estanco del
Tabaco

Del
Porvenir

Calle Primera
de Badillo

Calle Segunda
de Badillo

Calle de
la Moneda

Av Carlos Escallon

Avianca

Calle de
la Mantilla

Calle de la
Estrella

Calle del
Cuartel

Calle Don
Sancho

De la Factoría

Plaza de
Santo Domingo

5

Santo De Ayos
Domingo

46

28

Del Coliseo Dolores

Del
Colegio

58

Calle de
Los Estribos

56

32

Plaza
de Bolívar

14
15

2
12

Proclamación

Román

Velz Danies

17

18

Plaza de los
Coches

Parque del
Centenario

Playa de la Artillería

Calle Baloco

Vicaria
Santa
Teresa

De las Damas

Sta Teresa

Amargura

16
59

64

Muelle
Turístico de
los Pegasos

10

63

Av Santander

San Juan de Dios

Plaza Santa
Teresa

13
66

4
3
11

Tourist
Office

Plaza
de la Aduana

Plaza de San
Pedro Claver

Tourist
Information
Point

Centro de
Convenciones

Iglesia de la
Santa Orden

GETSEMANÍ

Av del Mercado

52

62

Calle Larga

Parque
de la
Marina

Av Blas de Lezo

9

Monumento de
Santander

Av del Arsenal

Bahía De
Las Ánimas

Hospital
Naval

the city's most elegant balconied colonial buildings, offers wonderful respite from the Caribbean heat. A statue of the eponymous Simón Bolívar stands in the middle of the plaza.

FREE **Museo del Oro y Arqueología**   MUSEUM
(Plaza de Bolívar; ☺10am-1pm & 3-7pm Tue-Fri, 10am-1pm & 2-5pm Sat, 11am-4pm Sun) The Cartagena Gold Museum is like a miniature version of Bogotá's world-class gold museum (p48). Though small, it offers a fascinating collection of gold and pottery of the Sinú (also known as Zenú) people, who inhabited the region of the present-day departments of Bolívar, Córdoba, Sucre and northern Antioquia before the Spanish Conquest. Some pieces are exquisitely detailed. Should you be heading to Bogotá, this gold museum offers just a taste of the bigger and grander one there. It's also a superb spot to cool right down as the air-con is set to arctic levels.

Catedral   CATHEDRAL
(adult/child COP$12,000/8000; ☺10:30am-7pm Tue-Sun) Work on the cathedral began in 1575, but in 1586, while still under construction, it was partially destroyed by the cannons of Francis Drake, and was not completed until 1612. Alterations were made between 1912 and 1923 by the first archbishop of Cartagena, who covered the church with stucco and painted it to look like marble. He commissioned the dome on the tower. Restoration work has uncovered the lovely limestone on the building's exterior. Apart from the tower's top, the church has basically preserved its original form. It has a fortlike appearance and a simply decorated interior with three naves and massive semicircular archways supported on high, stone columns. The main retable, worked in gold leaf, dates from the 18th century. You can take a self-guided audio tour that lasts about 25 minutes.

Iglesia de Santo Toribio de Mangrovejo   CHURCH
Compared with the other churches, this one is relatively small. It was erected between 1666 and 1732 and its ceiling is covered with Mudejar paneling. During Vernon's attack on the city in 1741, a cannonball went through a window into the church when it was filled with worshipers, but fortunately there were no casualties. The cannonball is now on display in a glassed niche in the left wall.

Cartagena Old Town

⦿ Sights

1	Casa de Rafael Núñez	F1
2	Catedral	C4
3	Convento de San Pedro Claver	C5
4	Iglesia de San Pedro Claver	B5
5	Iglesia de Santo Domingo	B4
6	Iglesia de Santo Toribio de Mangrovejo	D3
7	Las Bóvedas	E1
8	Monumento a la India Catalina	E3
9	Muelle Turístico de la Bodeguita	B6
10	Muelle Turístico de los Pegasos	D5
11	Museo de Arte Moderno	C5
12	Museo del Oro y Arqueología	C5
13	Museo Naval del Caribe	B5
14	Palacio de la Inquisición	B5
15	Plaza de Bolívar	B5
16	Plaza de la Aduana	C5
17	Plaza de los Coches	C5
18	Puerta del Reloj	C5

⊕ Activities, Courses & Tours

19	Aventure Colombia	D3
20	Diving Planet	C3
21	Nueva Lengua	E6

⊜ Sleeping

22	Bantú	D3
23	Casa La Fe	D3
24	Casa Mara	E5
25	Casa Relax	E6
26	Casa Viena	E5
27	Casa Villa Colonial	F5
28	Centro Hotel	C4
29	Chill House	D3
30	El Viajero Cartagena	D3
31	Hostal La Casona	E4
32	Hostal Santo Domingo	B4
33	Hotel Casa Lola	E5
34	Hotel Familiar	E5
35	Hotel Holiday	E5
36	Hotel Marlin	E5
37	Hotel San Pedro de Majagua	D2
38	Hotel Sofitel Santa Clara	D2
39	Hotel Tres Banderas	D3
40	Hotel Yolanda	E5
41	La Passion	C4
42	Media Luna Hostel	E5

⊗ Eating

43	8-18	B4
44	Bocaditos Madrid	D3
45	BrianZola	C4
46	El Bistro	C4
47	El Rincón de la Mantilla	B4
48	El Santissimo	D2
49	Gato Negro	E5
50	Getsemaní Café	E5
51	Girasoles	D3
	I Balconi	(see 61)
52	La Casa de Socorro	D6
53	La Cevicheria	D2
54	La Guacha	E5
55	La Mulata Cartagena	D3
56	La Vitriola	B4
57	Restaurante Coroncoro	E5

⊙ Drinking

58	Café del Mar	A4
59	Donde Fidel	C5
60	La Casa de la Cerveza	E7

⊛ Entertainment

61	Café Havana	E5
62	Mister Babilla	D6
63	Quiebra Canto	D5
64	Tu Candela	C5

⊜ Shopping

65	Ábaco	B4
66	Upalema	B5

Las Bóvedas HISTORIC BUILDING

These are 23 dungeons, built between 1792 and 1796, hidden within the 15m-thick city walls. These dungeons were the last major construction carried out in colonial times and were destined for military purposes. The vaults were used by the Spaniards as storerooms for munitions and provisions. Later, during the republican era, they were turned into a jail. Today they house craft and souvenir shops.

Casa de Rafael Núñez MUSEUM

(adult/child COP$1000/500; ⊙9am-5:30pm Tue-Fri, 10am-4pm Sun) This mansion, just outside the walls of Las Bóvedas, was the home of the former president, lawyer and poet, Rafael Núñez. He wrote the words of Colombia's national anthem and was one of the authors of the constitution of 1886, which was in use (with some later changes) until 1991. The wooden mansion is now a museum featuring some of Núñez's documents and personal possessions. The chapel opposite the house, known as the Ermita del Cabrero, holds his ashes.

Monumento a la India Catalina STATUE

The monument at the main entrance to the old town from the mainland is a tribute to the Carib people, the group that inhabited this land before the Spanish Conquest. The lovely bronze statue depicts Catalina, a beautiful Carib woman who served as interpreter to Pedro de Heredia upon the arrival of the Spaniards. The statue was forged in 1974 by Eladio Gil, a Spanish sculptor living in Cartagena.

Muelle Turístico de la Bodeguita PORT

Often incorrectly referred to as Pegasos (given the close location of the two sites), this is the old port of Cartagena on the Bahía de las Ánimas. Not much goes on here other than the departure of tourist boats to Playa Blanca and Isla del Rosario (there's also a cruise office here for bookings). The new harbor where big ships dock is on Manga Island.

SPANISH FORTS

The old city is a fortress in itself, yet there are more fortifications built at strategic points outside the city. Some of the more important ones are listed here.

Castillo de San Felipe de Barajas FORTRESS

(Av Arévalo; adult/child COP$16,000/8000; ☺8am-6pm) The castillo is the greatest and strongest fortress ever built by the Spaniards in any of their colonies. The original fort was commissioned in 1630 and was quite small. Construction began in 1657 on top of the 40m-high San Lázaro hill. In 1762 an extensive enlargement was undertaken, which resulted in the entire hill being covered over with this powerful bastion. It was truly impregnable and was never taken, despite numerous attempts to storm it.

A complex system of tunnels connected strategic points of the fortress to distribute provisions and to facilitate evacuation. The tunnels were constructed in such a way that any noise reverberated all the way along them, making it possible to hear the slightest sound of the approaching enemy's feet, and also making it easy for internal communication.

Some of the tunnels are lit and are open to visitors – an eerie walk not to be missed. Take a guide (COP$30,000 in English) if you want to learn more about the curious inventions of Antonio de Arévalo, the military engineer who directed the construction of the fortress.

The fortress is a 20-minute walk from the old town, or take a local bus from the Parque del Centenario. A taxi costs COP$6000. Entrance is free the last Sunday of every month between February and November.

Fuerte de San Sebastián del Pastelillo FORT

This fort, on the western end of Manga Island, was constructed in the middle of the 16th century as one of the town's first defense posts. It's quite small and not particularly inspiring, but it's quite close to the old town – just across the bridge from Getsemaní. Today the fort is home to the Club de Pesca, which has a marina where local and foreign boats anchor.

CONVENTO DE LA POPA

On a 150m-high hill, the highest point in the city, about 2km beyond Castillo de San Felipe de Barajas is this **convent** (adult/child COP$8000/6000; ☺8:30am-5pm). Its name literally means the Convent of the Stern, after the hill's apparent similarity to a ship's back end. Founded by the Augustine fathers in 1607, its official name is actually Convento de Nuestra Señora de la Candelaria. Initially it was just a small wooden chapel, which was replaced by a stouter construction when the hill was fortified two centuries later, just before Pablo Morillo's siege.

A beautiful image of La Virgen de la Candelaria, the patroness of the city, is in the convent's chapel, and there's a charming flower-filled patio. There is also a chilling statue of a speared Padre Alonso García de Paredes, a priest who was murdered along with five Spanish soldiers for trying to spread the good word. The views from here are outstanding and stretch all over the city. The patron saint's day is February 2 (see p126).

There is a zigzagging access road leading up to the convent (no public transportation) and paths cutting the bends of the road. It takes 30 minutes to walk to the top, but it's not recommended for safety and climatic reasons – walking up would be equivalent to a trek in the desert! Take a cab and expect to pay up to COP$45,000. Haggle politely but insistently and you might get it for half that.

MERCADO BAZURTO

For adventurous souls only, Cartagena's labyrinthine central **market** (Av Pedro de Heredia; ☺24hr) is both dirty and enthralling, an all-out assault on your senses. If it's marketable, it's for sale here: endless stalls of fruits and vegetables, meat, fish and plenty of options to grab a quick bite or juice up on a chilled beverage. If you can find it, look for Cecilia's restaurant, which sometimes serves up river turtle, shark and cow's tongue (it's in the area known as Pescado Frito – ask and people can direct you). You won't likely buy anything here, but it's a fascinating glimpse into the daily lives of real *cartagenos*. Don't wear flashy jewelry and pay close attention to your camera and wallet, but otherwise grab a taxi (COP$7000 from the old town) and explore away.

🏃 Activities

Cartagena has grown into an important scuba-diving center, taking advantage of the extensive coral reefs along its coast. La Boquilla, just outside town, is also popular for kitesurfing.

aQuanaútica   KITESURFING
(☑656 8243; www.kitesurfcolombia.com; Hotel Las Americas, Cielo Mar) Kitesurfing school.

Diving Planet   DIVING
(☑664 2171; www.divingplanet.org; Calle Estanco del Aguardiente No 5-94) Two-tank dives including transportation, lunch and certified instructors cost COP$225,000. Also offers PADI-certification courses (COP$990,000).

🐟 Courses

Amaury Martelo   SPANISH
(☑313 526 3910; amartesi@yahoo.com; per hr COP$25,000; ☺1-5pm Mon-Sat) A recommended tutor for private Spanish lessons.

Nueva Lengua   SPANISH
(☑660 1736; www.nuevalengua.com; Calle del Pozo No 25-95, Getsemaní) Language courses at this casual school start at COP$350,000 for 15 hours of instruction over five days.

👉 Tours

City tours in a *chiva* (a colorful, traditional bus) depart daily at 2pm from various hotels in upscale Bocagrande. The four-hour tour includes rides around Bocagrande and Castillo Grande and a walking tour of the walled city, plus visits to the Convento de la Popa and Castillo de San Felipe de Barajas. Any travel agency can book this for you, but you'll need to find your own way to Bocagrande for the pickup point. By taxi, it's COP$7000 from the old town.

You can also take a city tour in a horse-drawn carriage, which gives a glance of Bocagrande and the walled city. The carriages start gathering at the corner of Av San Martín and Calle 4 in Bocagrande around 4pm to 5pm and depart from there up until midnight. A one-hour tour that takes in the waterfront to the old town costs from COP$50,000 to COP$60,000. After a run around the main streets of the walled city they return via either Av San Martín or the waterfront, whichever you prefer. There are also nighttime tours, which are more a party parade than a sightseeing tour.

For tours to Isla del Rosario, see p141; for Volcán de Lodo El Totumo, see p135.

🎭 Festivals & Events

Feria Taurina   BULLFIGHT
The bullfighting season takes place at the bullring on Av Pedro de Heredia during the first week of the year.

Fiesta de Nuestra Señora de la Candelaria   PROCESSION
February 2 is the day of Cartagena's patron saint. A solemn procession is held on that day at the Convento de la Popa during which the faithful carry lit candles. Celebrations begin nine days earlier, the so-called Novenas, when pilgrims flock to the convent.

Reinado Nacional de Belleza   BEAUTY PAGEANT
The national beauty pageant celebrates Cartagena's independence day. Miss Colombia, the beauty queen, is elected on November 11, the high point of the event. The fiesta, which includes street dancing, music and fancy-dress parades, strikes up several days before the pageant and the city goes wild. The event, also known as the Carnaval de Cartagena or Fiestas del 11 de Noviembre, is the city's most important annual bash.

🛏 Sleeping

Cartagena has a reasonable choice of places to sleep and, despite its touristy status, hotel prices remain reasonable compared to other large cities. If you're in a position to splash out, there are a few amazing restored colonial options. The tourist peak is from late December to late January, but even then you'll find a room.

Most travelers stay within the walled city. In this area, Getsemaní is the main place to find budget accommodations, especially on Calle de la Media Luna, while El Centro and San Diego host the old city's top-end hotels.

Hotel Casa Lola
TOP CHOICE
HOTEL $$$

(☑664 1538 Calle del Guerrero, No 29-108, Getsemaní; r COP$279,500) This stylish boutique hotel has an artful interior that contrasts with its plain front door. Inside you'll find thoughtfully designed decor – revolutionary art and cowskin rugs rub up against eclectic bric-a-brac. Filled with light and featuring lots of exposed brickwork, the rooms are super-chic and service is excellent.

Casa Villa Colonial
HOTEL $$

(☑664 5421; www.casavillacolonial.com; Calle de la Media Luna No 10-89, Getsemaní; s/d COP$80,000/120,000; ❈🛜) A complete bargain for the price – you'll get got four-star personal service, beautiful communal areas with comfortable sofas, and silent air-con. The best rooms have small balconies onto the courtyard, and there's a small kitchen for guest use with endless great coffee.

El Viajero Cartagena
HOSTEL $

(☑660 2598; Calle 7 Infantes 9-45 Cartagena de Indias; dm COP$22,000, r per person COP$55,000; ❈🛜) This massive backpacker blockbuster is owned by a brilliantly funny Uruguayan traveler and football fanatic, Federico Lavagna. All rooms have air-con – an absolute dream in this heat and at this price. The beds are firm, the kitchen is well organized and spotless, and there's a very friendly, social vibe in the lovely open courtyard. Breakfast is included.

La Passion
HOTEL $$$

(☑664 8605; www.lapassionhotel.com; Calle Estanco del Tabaco 35-81, El Centro; s/d from COP$250,000/390,000; ❈🛜❄) Perhaps the most discreet hotel entrance in town leads to this hidden gem, which is run by a French movie producer and his Colombian partner. The republican-style home dating to the early 17th century features eight uniquely decorated rooms and a potpourri of international design touches (Fez, Greece, Tlaquepaque) offset by modern indigenous photographs. Some rooms feature Roman baths and outdoor showers, but the pool and rooftop terrace with front-row views of the cathedral clinch it.

Media Luna Hostel
HOSTEL $$

(☑664 3423; Calle de la Media Luna No 10-46, Getsemaní; dm/s/d COP$23,000/50,000/81,000; ❈🛜) A shrewd addition to the sleeping scene in Cartagena, this boutique spot is mercilessly gobbling up the competition thanks to its massive communal spaces, suntrap roof terrace, bar, bike hire, pool, clean and minimal decor, crisp bedlinen and chilled staff.

Bantú
HOTEL $$$

(☑664 3362; www.bantuhotel.com; Calle de la Tablada No 7-62, San Diego; s/d incl breakfast from COP$382,500/440,500; ❈🛜❄) Two wonderfully restored 15th-century homes make up this lovely 23-room, open-air boutique hotel, rife with exposed-brick archways, original stone walls and lush vegetation. Smartly appointed rooms are full of local artistic touches that blend sympathetically with the old building. There's also a rooftop pool, shower and Jacuzzi.

Hotel Sofitel Santa Clara
HOTEL $$$

(☑664 6070; www.hotelsantaclara.com; Plaza de San Diego, San Diego; r from COP$420,000; ❈🛜❄) The original details preserved in this 17th-century convent are exquisite. The entire hotel was built within the walls of a convent and the former cloister now forms massive hallways that surround the gorgeous interior walls and open-air courtyard. There is a crypt you can descend into in the middle of the trendy bar, and little things like original cannonballs (used as doorstops) and oratories throughout elevate this choice to a level not reached elsewhere in the old town.

Casa Mara
HOSTEL $$

(☑664 5480; Calle del Espiritu Santo No 29-129, Getsemaní; s/d COP$70,000/120,000; ❈🛜) Escape the hustle of the main drag and ensconce yourself here down a quiet side street. Rooms are simply decorated and are centered around a neat courtyard with a great pool and fan-cooled communal areas. The owners are kind and considerate and very helpful.

Hotel Yolanda
HOTEL $$

(☑664 8310; Calle del Espiritu Santo No 29-101, Getsemaní; r with fan COP$140,000; ❈🛜) Swaddled in exuberant tropical vegetation, the common areas around the pool are wonderfully relaxing, and the rooms, decked out in wood and yet more jungle plants, are natural and restful.

Centro Hotel
HOTEL $$$

(☑664 0461; www.centrohotelcartagena.com; Calle del Arzobispado No 34-80, El Centro; s/d incl breakfast from COP$160,000/199,000; ❈🛜) The simple but clean Centro Hotel is perfectly located just steps from Plaza de Bolívar.

Well-maintained rooms are arranged around an open courtyard and some offer juliette balconies that open over the street.

Hotel Tres Banderas
HOTEL $$$

(☑660 0160; www.hotel3banderas.com; Calle Cochera del Hobo No 38-66, San Diego; r incl breakfast from COP$188,500; ✳☎) This hotel run by French-Canadians offers pleasant common areas with a fake waterfall and scattered coconut trees. For an extra COP$10,000, higher-floor rooms offer nice balconies but smaller bathrooms. The area is tranquil and picturesque.

Casa La Fe
B&B $$$

(☑664 0306; www.casalafe.com; Calle Segunda de Badillo No 36-125, San Diego; r incl breakfast from COP$243,000; ✳☎) A British-Colombian pair run this boutique B&B decorated with (tasteful) religious art. Eat in the jungly interior courtyard or soak in the rooftop Jacuzzi. Higher-priced rooms have balconies overlooking Plaza Fernandez de Madrid. Free bike hire for the hardcore – you'll sweat your bodyweight in an hour at this latitude.

Chill House
HOSTEL $

(☑662 2386; Calle La Tablada, Parque Fernandez de Madrid, No 7-10; dm from COP$16,000, r without/ with air-con COP$65,000/90,000; ✳☎) If you find Getsemaní a little sketchy (and some travelers will, especially women traveling alone) this is a great newcomer. It's less cramped than Casa Viena, and is on a beautiful square near some good, cheap places to eat. A winner.

Hotel Familiar
HOSTEL $

(☑664 2464; Calle El Guerrero No 29-66, Getsemaní; s/d COP$23,000/40,000) Another no-frills Getsemaní option that offers a little more peace and quiet than other budget spots as it's down a quieter side street and some rooms are set away from the road. Ripe for a makeover as Getsemaní continues to flourish.

Hostal Santo Domingo
HOSTEL $$

(☑664 2268; Calle Santo Domingo No 33-46, El Centro; r without/with air-con COP$66,000/76,700; ✳) Move it to Getsemaní and they could only charge half this – but it is on a beautiful street in the center of town and is steps away from some of the most beautiful buildings in Latin America. Popular with an older, slightly more relaxed crowd than downtown spots.

Casa Relax
HOTEL $$

(☑664 1117; Calle del Pozo No 29B-119, Getsemaní; r incl breakfast from COP$140,000; ✳☎✳) A good place to soak up some restored colonial atmosphere without taking out a second mortgage. Run by an occasionally brusque pipe-smoking French gentleman, it's included here mainly for its large swimming pool and comical parrots.

Casa Viena
HOSTEL $

(☑664 6242; www.casaviena.com; Calle San Andrés No 30-53, Getsemaní; dm with air-con COP$17,000, d without/with bathroom COP$40,000/54,000; ✳☎) Old-school Austrian-run joint on a rowdy street in Getsemaní – earplugs are your friend. The chilly dorm is cramped and needs a lick of paint, but you get free internet, coffee and local calls. You're swapping comfort and cost for camaraderie and convenience, though.

Hotel Holiday
HOSTEL $

(☑664 0948; www.holidayhostelcaribe.com; Calle de la Media Luna No 10-47, Getsemaní; dm/s/d COP$15,000/20,000/40,000; ☎) A sociable, younger crowd gathers at this hostel. It offers plenty of tours – along with a selection of slightly grubby but just-about acceptable rooms.

Hotel Marlin
HOSTEL $

(☑664 3507; www.hotelmarlincartagenacol.com; Calle de la Media Luna No 10-35, Getsemaní; s/d with fan COP$35,000/45,000, with air-con COP$40,000/50,000; ✳☎) Windows? Who needs them? All they do is let in the heat and the noise. Popular with Colombians and tourists alike, this friendly budget choice has a laundry and kitchen facilities. Some rooms are gloomy, and the streetside ones are noisy.

Hostal La Casona
HOSTEL $

(☑664 1301; Calle Tripita y Media No 31-32, Getsemaní; s/d with fan COP$40,000/60,000, with air-con COP$50,000/70,000; ✳) This good-value hotel has a lush courtyard to compensate for its basic but perfectly decent rooms. The gaudy tropical aesthetic may induce a migraine in more sensitive souls.

✖ Eating

Plenty of snack bars all across the old town serve typical local snacks such as *arepas de huevo* (fried maize dough with an egg inside), *dedos de queso* (deep-fried cheese sticks), empanadas (meat and/or cheese pastries) and *buñuelos* (deep-fried maize and cheese balls).

Try typical local sweets at confectionery stands lining El Portal de los Dulces on the Plaza de los Coches (p121).

In restaurants, you'll see the ubiquitous *arroz con coco* (rice sweetened with coconut) as an accompaniment to most fish and meat dishes. Fruit stalls are also everywhere (often with tropical fruit looking so ripe and colorful you'd swear it was Photoshopped).

Part of the charm of eating in Cartagena is just wandering around the various plazas and seeing what takes your fancy. Plaza Santo de Domingo and Plaza de San Diego are both popular options for atmospheric plaza dining and people-watching, though the former is much more touristy – the waitresses practically beg you to chose their cafe over the one next door, promising, *'Es diferente!'* when you know it probably isn't.

TOP CHOICE **La Cevicheria** SEAFOOD $$
(☎664 5255; Calle Stuart No 7-14, San Diego; mains COP$25,000-52,000, ceviche COP$16,000-42,500; ⏱lunch & dinner) This place is tiny and hidden, but its ceviche is the best this side of heaven, and its chilli sauce would scare Lucifer. Each dish is prepared with panache and elegance. The octopus salad, dressed with pesto and sesame, is incredible.

La Vitriola SEAFOOD $$$
(☎664 8243; Calle Balocco No 2-01, El Centro; mains COP$20,000-59,000; ⏱lunch & dinner) Perfectly lit and comfortably furnished, this 400-year-old colonial home converted to a seafood restaurant is famous – and deservedly so. The *mero* (grouper) *Don Román,* with a tamarind, nam pla and chilli sauce, is the standout dish, tasting like a day trip to Bangkok. Do your mouth a favor and hit the teriyaki octopus, too. There's a great wine list and live Cuban music.

El Santíssimo COLOMBIAN FUSION $$$
(☎550 1531; Calle del Torno 39-76, San Diego; mains COP$30,000-60,000; ⏱lunch & dinner) This upscale casual spot is doing some interesting things with the flavors and food of Colombia, and each dish is paired with a suggested wine. Star dish here is the *obatala,* a traditional Caribbean beef stew, thick with dissolved yucca and gorgeously gooey plantain.

La Mulata Cartagena COLOMBIAN $
(☎664 6222; Calle Quero No 9-58, El Centro; set meal COP$7000-8000; ⏱lunch) Stylish *comida corriente* (set lunch) option that's both outstanding and cheap. A daily set menu

offers a handful of excellent choices and fresh juices in an atmosphere entirely too hip for the price. It's arguably the best value in Cartagena. There's no sign outside – it's under the Defensoría del Pueblo.

I Balconi PIZZERIA $$
(☎660 9880; Calle del Guerrero 29-146; Getsemaní; COP$16,000-19,000; ⏱lunch & dinner) Stylishly perched above Havana bar, here you'll find the best pizza in Cartagena, if not Colombia. The Italian owner is so fanatical about quality ingredients that he has commissioned a local cheesemaker and schooled him in the ways of gorgonzola and parmesan. The results are fabulous. Service is impeccable and the room is breezy with cool art on the walls.

La Guacha STEAKHOUSE $$
(☎664 1683; Calle de Espiritu Santo No29-07; Getsemaní; COP$20,000-30,000; ⏱lunch & dinner) Sometimes you just need a large, rare steak and a glass of decent Malbec. When that call comes, answer it here. The breezy, elegant room is all high ceilings and exposed brick, the meat superlative (especially the *punta de anca,* or topside of rump); it's served in stylishly hewn and artfully charred hunks that ooze flavour. A steal at this price.

8-18 COLOMBIAN FUSION $$$
(☎664 2632; Calle Gastelbondo No 2-124, El Centro; mains COP$32,000-50,000; ⏱lunch & dinner Mon-Sat) Very innovative takes on modern *costeña* cuisine at this intimate and trendy boutique restaurant. The oxtail stewed in red wine is the top-seller. One of Cartagena's best, even if service can veer on the snooty.

El Bistro EUROPEAN $$
(☎664 1799; Calle de Ayos No 4-46, El Centro; sandwiches from COP$11,000, mains COP$12,500-22,000; ⏱lunch & dinner Mon-Sat) A casual, German-run restaurant serving up a daily-changing chalkboard menu of Euro bistro fare accompanied by superb home-made German bread and, of course, great beer. It's hip without trying too hard, and the food is rock-solid.

Gato Negro CAFE $
(☎660 0958; Calle San Andrés No 30-39, Getsemaní; mains COP$7000-8000; ⏱breakfast & lunch; ☎) This new German-run option concentrates on a plain and simple breakfast menu – omelettes, Nutella crepes, muesli – but does it really well. There's a set lunch as well. There's also wi-fi, a rarity for whatever reason.

BrianZola ICE CREAM $
(☑664 2564; cnr Calle San Agustín Chiquita & Calle de la Universidad, El Centro; pizza COP$12,000-22,000, ice cream from COP$6500; ⊘breakfast, lunch & dinner) This is the spot to cool off with Italian gelato in a plethora of exotic Colombian flavors like *mora* (blackberry), *arequipe* (milk caramel), *zapote* (a type of red avocado) and *guanábana* (soursop). It also does recommendable pizzas. It's attached to Juan Valdéz cafe.

El Rincón de la Mantilla SEAFOOD $$
(☑660 1436; Calle de la Mantilla No 3-32, El Centro; mains COP$19,000-30,000; ⊘8am-midnight Mon-Sat) Decorated with baskets and seashells that gently wave from the rafters, this atmospheric Colombian place specializes in typical coastal fare.

Several simple restaurants in Getsemaní serve set meals for around COP$6000 to COP$12,000. They include **Restaurante Coronoro** (☑664 2648; Calle Tripita y Media No 31-28, Getsemaní; ⊘breakfast, lunch & dinner) and **Getsemaní Café** (☑317 781 5694; Calle San Andrés No 30-34, Getsemaní; ⊘breakfast, lunch & dinner). In San Diego, **Girasoles** (☑664 5239; Calle de los Puntales 37-01, San Diego; set meals COP$5000; ⊘breakfast & lunch; ☑), a veggie restaurant and healthfood store, does a set menu of meat-free options changing daily.

🍷 Drinking

Cartagena's bar scene is centered on the Plaza de los Coches in El Centro for salsa and vallenato, while along Calle del Arsenal in Getsemaní, the clubs are bigger and the prices higher. Weekends are best and the action doesn't really heat up until after midnight.

Donde Fidel SALSA
(☑664 3127; El Portal de los Dulces No 32-09, El Centro; ⊘11am-2am) The sound system here, when it kicks, has been know to reduce grown men to tears – as does the extraordinary salsa collection of Don Fidel himself. This is music of love, loss and lament. A Cartagena institution, smooching couples dance in alcoves under portraits of the owner and various gurning megastars. The vast seated terrace is perfect for people-watching.

TOP CHOICE **Café del Mar** BAR
(☑664 6513; Baluarte de Santo Domingo, El Centro; cocktails COP$18,000-26,000; ⊘5pm-late) Ocean breezes swoop in off the coast and bring a relaxing freshness to this chic outdoor lounge perching on the western ramparts of the old city. Dress up a notch or two if you want to blend in. DJs might merely fax in their sets of Ibiza-tinged pop-house, but the view to Bocagrande makes it worth it.

La Casa de la Cerveza BAR
(☑664 9261; Baluarte San Lorenzo del Reducto, Getsemaní; ⊘4pm-4am) Another chic spot set high atop the city's walls, similar to Café del Mar, but with stupendous views out toward Castillo de San Felipe. DJs spin tracks nightly and, in case you get hungry, there's grilled meat, empanadas, and decent ceviche all under COP$40,000.

☆ Entertainment

Nightclubs

You can go on a night trip aboard a *chiva* (a typical Colombian bus) with a band playing vallenato and all-you-can-drink aguardiente (easy, now). *Chivas* depart from hotels in Bocagrande around 8pm for a three- to four-hour trip, and leave you at the end of the tour in a club. Most agencies and hostels can book this for you.

TOP CHOICE **Café Havana** BAR
(☑664 7568; cnr Calle del Guerrero y Calle de la Media Luna, Getsemaní; cover COP$5000; ⊘8pm-4am Thu-Sat, 5pm-2am Sun) Café Havana has it all: live salsa from horn-blowing Cubans, strong drinks, wood-panelled walls and a ceiling full of whirring fans. Go with a clued-up Colombian who'll point out the disgraced ex-presidents, their wives and mistresses, the TV presenters and supermodels who all get down around the massive central bar. Still the best bar in town bar none.

Mister Babilla CLUB
(☑664 7005; Av del Arsenal No 8B-137, Getsemaní; cover COP$15,000; ⊘9pm-4am) This massive, multispace club is a curiosity. Is it a rock club? A salsa joint? A pumping house club? A vallenato hot spot? It's all of the above, and is as crowded as it's flirty. Try to ignore the decor and get on the floor instead.

Quiebra-Canto CLUB
(☑664 1372; Camellon de los Martines, Edificio Puente del Sol, Getsemaní; ⊘7pm-4am Tue-Sat) It gets tight with an eclectic crowd of all shapes and sizes at this excellent Getsemaní spot for salsa, son (a kind of slow salsa) and reggae. It's on the second floor overlooking

Pegasos and the clock tower. Purists insist the salsa here is hotter than at Café Havana.

Tu Candela CLUB
(☑664 8787; El Portal de los Dulces No 32-25, El Centro; cover COP$12,000; ☺8pm-4am) Wall-to-wall reggaeton, vallenato, merengue and some decent salsa. Tu Candela is cramped – but the atmosphere is cool and the decor, lighting and service are all good. It's rumored that one night, the management turned off the massive plasma screens that have shown bad music videos at all other times in the bar's history. Convert the cover charge to cocktails at the bar.

Sports

Cartagena's local soccer team, Real Cartagena, plays games at Estadio Olímpico Jaime Merón León, located 5km south of the city in Villa Olímpico. Games run throughout the year. Buy tickets at the stadium. A taxi there will cost around COP$12,000.

 Shopping

Cartagena has a wide range of shops selling crafts and souvenirs, and the quality of the goods is usually high. The biggest tourist shopping center in the walled city is Las Bóvedas (p124), offering handicrafts, clothes, souvenirs and the like. The best wares here are at **Artesanías India Catalina II** (No 6) for homewares and art; **D'Yndias** (No 15) for high-quality hammocks, Juan Valdéz coffee, and handbags; and **La Garita** (No 23) for colorful kitchenware, T-shirts and better-quality general merchandise.

For something a little more unique, the exclusive artisan homewares and handicrafts at **Upalema** (☑664 5032; Calle San Juan de Dios, Edificio Rincon No 3-99, El Centro; ☺9:30am-10pm Mon-Sat, 10am-10pm Sun) aren't reproduced anywhere on the street. It's pricey, but it's top-quality stuff, unrivaled elsewhere.

Ábaco (☑664 8338; cnr Calles de la Iglesia & de la Mantilla No 3-86; ☺9am-8:30pm Mon-Sat, 4-8:30pm Sun) has a good selection of books on Cartagena and a few English-language choices. There's also Italian beer and Spanish wine.

 Information

Dangers & Annoyances

Cartagena is the safest metropolis in Colombia – around 2000 police officers patrol the old city alone. That said, don't flaunt your wealth, and stay alert at night in less populated areas like Getsemaní. You are more likely to be irritated

by peddlers than become a victim of any crime. Aggressive hassling in the streets by unofficial vendors selling tourist tat, women or cocaine is definitely the No 1 nuisance here. A simple 'No quiero nada' ('I want nothing') should shoo them away.

Internet Access

These two places are open seven days a week and offer air-conditioning.
Contact Internet Café (☑664 0681; Calle de la Media Luna No 10-20; per hr COP$1000; ☺8am-9pm) Has a four-meg line – genuinely nippy.
Micronet (☑664 0328; Calle de la Estrella No 4-47; per hr COP$1500; ☺9am-9pm Mon-Fri, to 6pm Sat)

Money

There are many street 'moneychangers' fluttering around Cartagena offering fantastic rates. They are all, without exception, expert swindlers. Casas de cambio (currency exchanges) and banks are ubiquitous in the historic center, especially around Plaza de los Coches and Plaza de la Aduana.
Citibank (Av Venezuela, edificio Citibank, piso 1; ☺8am-noon & 2-4:30pm Mon-Fri)
Davivienda (cnr Av Venezuela & Carrera 9) Has an ATM.
Giros y Finanzas (Av Venezuela No 8A-87; ☺8am-5pm Mon-Fri, to 1pm Sat) This casa de cambio in the old town represents Western Union.

Post

4-72 (Calle 8B, No 173, edificio Villa Anamaria, local 1; ☺8am-5pm Mon-Fri, to noon Sat) Postal services.

Tourist Information

Tourist office (Turismo Cartagena de Indias; ☑660 1583; www.turismocartagenadeindias. com; Plaza de la Aduana; ☺9am-1pm & 2-6pm Mon-Sat, 9am-5pm Sun) The main tourist office is situated in Plaza de la Aduana. There are also small booths in Plaza de San Pedro Claver and Plaza de los Coches as well as the administrative offices at Muelle Turístico.

Travel Agencies

Aventure Colombia (☑314 588 2378; www. aventurecolombia.com; Calle del Santíssimo No 8-55; ☺9am-noon & 2-7pm Mon-Thu, 9am-7pm Fri & Sat) Friendly French-Colombian outfit offering excursions around Cartagena and the coast, including La Guajira and PNN Tayrona.

Visa Information

Ministerio de Relaciones Exteriores (☑666 0172; Carrera 20B No 29-18, Pie de la Popa; ☺8am-noon & 2-5pm) Immigration and visa extensions; about 1km east of the old town. Plan on a half-day minimum to get it sorted.

❶ Getting There & Away

Air

The airport is in Crespo, 3km northeast of the old city, and is serviced by frequent local buses. There are also *colectivos* to Crespo (COP$1500), as well as nicer air-conditioned shuttles called Metrocar (COP$1800), both of which depart from Monumento a la India Catalina. (For Metrocar, look for the green-signed buses.) By taxi, there's a surcharge of COP$4000 on airport trips. It's COP$10,000 to COP$13,000 from the center to the airport. The terminal has four ATMs and a *casa de cambio* (in Domestic Arrivals), which changes cash and traveler's checks.

All major Colombian carriers operate flights to and from Cartagena. There are flights to Bogotá (from COP$353,420 one way), Cali (from COP$288,260 one way), Cúcuta via Bogotá (from COP$463,820), Medellín (from COP$250,380 one way), San Andrés (from COP$273,000 round trip) and other major cities.

Avianca (☑664 7822; www.avianca.com; Av Venezuela, Centro Edificio Citibank, local B1; ☺8am-12:30pm & 2-6pm Mon-Fri, 8am-1pm Sat) flies to Miami via Bogotá, major domestic destinations and San Andrés (Thursday, Saturday and Sunday at 10:15am). **Copa** (☑655 0428; Carrera 3 No 8-116, Bocagrande, ☺8am-12:30pm & 2-6pm Mon-Fri, 9am-1pm Sat) has daily flights to Panama City from COP$442,600. **Copa Airlines Colombia** (☑664 1388; Calle del Cabo, Centro Comercial Invercredito No 18; ☺8am-noon & 2-6pm Mon-Fri, 9am-12:30pm Sat), previously Aerorepública, has flights to Bogotá and from there, connections to Cali, Medellín and San Andrés (Monday, Wednesday, Thursday and Friday at 1pm).

Boat

A pleasant way of getting to Panama is by sailboat. There are various boats, mostly foreign yachts, which take travelers from Cartagena to Colón via San Blas Archipelago (Panama) and vice versa, but there is no set schedule. The trip takes four to six days and normally includes a couple of days at San Blas for snorkeling and spearfishing. Trips hover around the COP$800,000 mark and often include food. Boats with semiregular departures include the German-helmed **Papillon** (☑314 540 5411; sailwithtom@gmail.com), the French-Brazilian **Atoll** (☑301 422 2662; federico_layolle@yahoo.com.br) and **Seeadler** (☑507 448 2426; www.sailseeadler.com), run by a bearded German named Guido.

In 2011, Colombian captains lobbied the government to regulate the trade as many captains are foreign nationals and so require working visas – which many of them do not have. Many boats, both Colombian-owned and foreign-owned, can be overcrowded. Ask for the boat's brand name and model number, and run an internet search on its capacity. As always, it is caveat emptor, and in a crowded, competitive market, always seek impartial advice and the names and email addresses of previous satisfied customers.

Bus

The bus terminal is on the eastern outskirts of the city, far away from the center – give yourself 45 minutes to get there in all but the darkest hours.

Large green-and-red-signed Metrocar buses shuttle between the city and the terminal every 15 to 30 minutes (COP$2000, 40 minutes). In the center, you can catch them on Av Santander. A taxi from the bus station to El Centro is COP$15,000 plus an additional COP$500 after 8pm.

Several bus companies serve Bogotá and Medellín throughout the day. Among them, **Expreso Brasilia** (☑663 2119; www.expreso brasilia.com) heads to Bogotá (COP$128,000, 18 hours, six buses daily) and Medellín (COP$108,000, 13 hours, six buses daily). **Unitransco** (☑663 2067) serves Barranquilla (COP$12,000, 2½ hours) with continuing services to Santa Marta (COP$28,000, four hours, four buses daily), Mompox (COP$40,000, six hours, once daily) and Tolú at 6:30am (COP$23,000, three hours, once daily). There are additional buses to Barranquilla throughout the day, where you can switch to a bus to Santa Marta if they don't continue on. For Montería, Expreso Brasilia leaves every 45 minutes from 6:30am to 3:30pm (COP$40,000, 4½ hours).

If you can't get a seat on the daily bus to Mompox and want to go the alternative route via Mangangue, **Torcoroma** (☑663 2379) leaves at 5:30am and every 30 minutes until noon (COP$35,000, three hours) and Expreso Brasilia goes at 10:30am (COP$30,000). For Riohacha

CRAZY CAPTAINS

Beware of any con men attempting to lure you into 'amazing' Caribbean boat trips. Inquire at Casa Viena (p128), which now has a tourist office attached. It's also a good idea to head down to the yacht club and inspect the boats and meet the captain before getting on board – travelers have reported everything from crack-smoking crazies to incompetent sailors at the helm of some of these boats.

on La Guajira Peninsula, **Rapido Ochoa** (📞663 2119) leaves at 9:30pm daily (COP$30,000, eight hours).

Expreso Brasilia and **Expreso Amerlujo** (📞653 0907) operate buses to Caracas, Venezuela (COP$220,000, 20 hours) via Maracaibo (COP$135,000, 12 hours). Unitransco is a bit cheaper than the other two, but you have to change buses on the border in Paraguachón. Each company has one departure daily at 8:30am. All buses go via Barranquilla, Santa Marta and Maicao. While the service is fast and comfortable, it's not that cheap. You'll save quite a bit if you do the trip to Caracas in stages by local transportation, with a change in Maicao and Maracaibo.

On overland trips to Panama, Unitransco/ Expreso Brasilia head to Montería (COP$50,000, seven hours) where you can switch for buses to Turbo (from COP$25,000, five hours). It's worth noting that if you do not leave Cartagena before 11am, you risk missing the last bus for Turbo and will have to sleep in Montería.

Fuerte de San Fernando & Batería de San José

On the southern tip of the Isla de Tierrabomba, at the entrance to the Bahía de Cartagena through the Bocachica strait, is **Fuerte de San Fernando**. On the opposite side of the strait is another fort, **Batería de San José**, and together they once guarded access to the bay. A heavy chain was strung between them to prevent surprise attacks in the 1700s.

Originally, there were two gateways to Cartagena Bay, Bocachica and Bocagrande. Bocagrande was partially blocked by a sandbank and two ships that sank there. An undersea wall was built after Vernon's attack in order to strengthen the natural barrage and to make the channel impassable to ships. It is still impassable today and all ships and boats have to go through Bocachica.

Around Cartagena

The fort of San Fernando was built between 1753 and 1760 and was designed to withstand any siege. It had its own docks, barracks, sanitary services, kitchen, infirmary, storerooms for provisions and arms, two wells, a chapel and even a jail, much of which can still be seen today.

The fortress can be reached only by water. Water taxis departing from Muelle Turístico de la Bodeguita in Cartagena do the journey for COP$7000. Admission to the fort is COP$7000. If you require a guide, plan on an additional COP$10,000.

Islas del Rosario

This archipelago, about 35km southwest of Cartagena, consists of 27 small coral islands, including some tiny islets. The archipelago is surrounded by coral reefs, where the color of the sea ranges from turquoise to purple. The whole area has been declared a national park, the Parque Nacional Natural (PNN) Corales del Rosario y San Bernardo. Sadly, warm water currents have eroded the reefs around Islas del Rosario, and the diving is not as good as it once was. But water sports are still popular and the two largest islands, Isla Grande and Isla del Rosario, have inland lagoons and some tourist facilities, such as hotels and a resort.

The usual way to visit the park is on a one-day boat tour of the islands. Tours depart year-round from the Muelle Turístico de la Bodeguita (p125) in Cartagena. Boats leave between 8am and 9am daily and return about 4pm to 6pm. The cruise office at the *muelle* (pier) sells tours in big boats (COP$70,000 per person), as well as smaller boats, which can be booked for a private/nonprivate (COP$65,000/50,000) launch. There are also a number of smaller operators offering tours from the pier, often at lower prices. Popular budget hotels in Cartagena sell tours too, and may offer lower prices – COP$40,000 is common. (Tours usually include lunch, but do not include port taxes and the national park entrance fees and aquarium entry; check with your tour operator to confirm.)

Generally the large boats offer a slower pace and extra features. The most popular large boat, the *Alcatraz,* can accommodate 160 people. There is food on board, music and room to move around. On the small boats, you are confined to your seat, but you get around the area more quickly and can see more. However, reports suggest some of the smaller

boats rush around too quickly and safety may be an issue – some small boats have sunk.

The boats all take a similar route to the islands, though it may differ a little between small and large boats. They all go through the Bahía de Cartagena and into the open sea through the Bocachica strait, passing between Batería de San José and, directly opposite, the Fuerte de San Fernando. The boats then cruise among the islands (there is generally Spanish narration along the way) and get as far as the tiny Isla de San Martín de Pajarales, which has an aquarium (COP$25,000) with various marine species. The island has a shady wooded area to chill for those who opt not to visit the aquarium, or you can take a refreshing dip in the sea while you hang around and wait for the trip to continue. The boats then take you to Playa Blanca on the Isla de Barú for lunch and two hours or so of free time.

To visit the far superior Islas de San Bernardo – it's considerably south of the Islas del Rosario section of the park, near Cartagena – see p163.

Sleeping & Eating

The islands have some tourist infrastructure so you can stay longer, go sunbathing, swimming, diving or snorkeling, or just take it easy in a hammock.

Eco Hotel Las Palmeras HOTEL **$$**
(☎314 584 7358; www.culturadelmar.com; Isla Grande; 2-day all-inclusive packages from COP$160,000 per person) This Isla Grande ecotourism option employs only local women and offers hammocks in a thatched-roof dorm as well as singles and doubles. Rates include three meals. Extra days are COP$160,000.

Hotel San Pedro de Majagua HOTEL **$$$**
(☎5 664 6070, ext 4008; www.hotelmajagua.com; Isla Grande; r & bungalows from COP$357,600) This high-end option offers stays on Isla Grande in chic stone bungalows with fiber-woven roofs and minimalist decor. There are two beaches and a restaurant. Bookings can be made via its Cartagena branch (Map p122); hotel guests pay COP$82,000 extra per person for transportation from Cartagena.

Playa Blanca

Playa Blanca lives up to its name – it is indeed a lovely stretch of sugary sand and one of the finest beaches around Cartagena. The government has wised up to this, however, and the whole area is under consideration to be zoned as a massive resort complex.

The beach is located about 20km southwest of Cartagena, on the Isla de Barú. It's the usual stop for boat tours to the Islas del Rosario. When the boat tours arrive, peddlers descend upon tourists, which has the potential to turn an otherwise idyllic beach into a two-hour challenge (the only thing worth buying is *cocada*, a sweet coconut treat that comes in a variety of flavors). To be fair, though, this is how folks here earn their living, as invasive as their hawking of wares may sometimes seem. There are also instant beach massages available (from COP$20,000 to COP$30,000).

This spot is also good for snorkeling as the coral reef begins just off the beach. You can rent gear for COP$5000 on the beach.

Sleeping & Eating

The beach has some rustic places to stay and a few restaurants all serving more or less the same thing – fresh fish and rice – for around COP$15,000.

La Estrella CABINS $$
(✆312 602 9987; hammock COP$8000, d from COP$50,000) If you want to stay close to the water, Jose, a friendly local, offers nice tents under thatched roofs that sleep three to four people, typical hammocks (with mosquito net), and a sand-floored hut or two.

Getting There & Away

As these things go in Cartagena, the easiest way of getting to the beach is on a tour, but you'll find it far more peaceful at other times. Head to Av El Lago, behind Cartagena's main market, Mercado Bazurto, in a taxi (COP$7000), and ask the driver to let you off at the boats to Playa Blanca. Boats depart (when full) between 7:30am and 9:30am daily except Sunday. The trip takes one hour. Expect to pay COP$25,000, but never pay anyone (ie the captain) until you reach the beach.

Alternatively, buses (COP$1500) marked 'Pasocaballos' leave throughout the day from the corner of Av Luis Carlos Lopez and Calle del Concolon in La Matuna. Ask the driver to let you off at the ferry across Canal del Dique (COP$1500). Once on the other side, take a moto-taxi (COP$15,000) to Playa Blanca. This route takes about three hours.

La Boquilla

A small fishing village and kitesurfing haven, La Boquilla is 7km north of Cartagena and sits at the northern tip of a narrow peninsula, bordered by the sea on one side and the Ciénaga de Tesca on the other. If you get up at 4am, you can catch locals at the *ciénaga* (shallow lake or lagoon) working with their famous *atarrayas* (round fishing nets) that are common in Colombia, particularly on the Caribbean coast.

There's a pleasant place known as El Paraíso, a five-minute walk from the bus terminus, where you can enjoy a day on the beach. You can also arrange a boat trip with the locals along the narrow water channels cutting through the mangrove woods to the north of the village. Negotiate the price, and pay upon return.

There is a collection of restaurants in palm-thatched shacks on the beach. These attract people from Cartagena on weekends; most are closed at other times. Fish is usually accompanied by *arroz con coco* (coconut rice) and *patacones* (fried plantains).

Frequent city buses run to La Boquilla from India Catalina in Cartagena (COP$1500, 30 minutes).

Volcán de Lodo El Totumo

No, it's not the world's largest termite mound. About 50km northeast of Cartagena, a few kilometers off the coast, is an intriguing 15m mound, looking like a miniature volcano. It is, indeed, a volcano, but instead of erupting with lava and ashes, it spews forth mud.

Legend has it that the volcano once belched fire but the local priest, seeing it as the work of the devil, frequently sprinkled it with holy water. He not only succeeded in extinguishing the fire, but also in turning the insides into mud to drown the devil.

The crater is filled with lukewarm mud, which has the consistency of cream. You can climb into the crater and frolic around in a refreshing mud bath, containing minerals acclaimed for their therapeutic properties. Once you've finished, go and wash the mud off in the lagoon, just 50m away.

The volcano is open from dawn to dusk and you pay a COP$5000 fee to have a bath. Bring plenty of small bills to tip the various local who will pamper you during your time here – massaging you rather inexpertly, rinsing you off, holding your camera and taking photos. All in all, it's a lot of fun.

Getting There & Away

El Totumo is on the border of the Atlántico and Bolívar departments, roughly equidistant between Barranquilla and Cartagena, but Cartagena is a far more popular jumping-off point for the volcano and has better public transportation and numerous tours.

The volcano is about 50km northeast of Cartagena by the highway, then 1km along a dirt side road that branches off inland. To get to the volcano from Cartagena, grab a taxi to the main bus terminal (COP$1500), and take an hourly bus bound for Galerazamba. Get off before Galerazamba at Lomita Arena (COP$3000, 1½ hours). Ask the driver to let you off by the petrol station and walk along the highway 2.5km toward Barranquilla (30 minutes), then to the right 1km to the volcano (another 15 minutes). Alternatively, you can grab a moto-taxi for COP$5000. The last direct bus from Lomita Arena back to Cartagena departs at around 3pm.

A tour is a far more convenient and faster way of visiting El Totumo, and not much more expensive than doing it on your own. Several tour operators in Cartagena organize minibus trips to the volcano (COP$30,000 transportation only, COP$33,300 with lunch included in Manzanilla del Mar, a small fishing village with an average beach). Tours can easily be purchased through hotels, including Casa Viena (p128) and Hotel Holiday (p128).

NORTHEAST OF CARTAGENA

The departments of Atlántico and Magdalena sit northeast of Cartagena, where the highest coastal mountain range in the world, the Sierra Nevada de Santa Marta, begins to rise from the sea just after Barranquilla. The increasingly more charming Santa Marta, the coast's other colonial city, and the beautiful coastal and mountainous attractions around it – namely Parque Nacional Natural (PNN) Tayrona and Ciudad Perdida – are some of Colombia's most visited attractions.

Barranquilla

📍 5 / POP 1.2 MILLION / ELEV 10M

Barranquilla is a hardworking, industrial port town laid out in a tangled ribbon along mangroves and the Caribbean, sweltering and hustling in the blinding sun, and is mainly dedicated to making money. But once a year the town clocks off, checks in its commonsense at the door, puts on its glad rags and goes wild as it throws the country's biggest street party.

There's little reason to visit outside of Mardi Gras madness. At any other time of the year, you'll likely only visit the bus station on your way to much more agreeable Santa Marta or the village of Taganga, both just an hour north and far more appealing to tourists.

History

Barranquilla was founded in 1629, but didn't gain importance until the middle of the 19th century. Despite its potential as a port on the country's main fluvial artery, navigation problems at the mouth of the Río Magdalena hindered development. Most of the merchandise moving up and down the Magdalena passed through Cartagena, using Canal del Dique, which joins the river about 100km upstream from its mouth.

Only at the end of the 19th century did progress really begin. The opening of Puerto Colombia, Barranquilla's port built on the coastline 15km west of the town, boosted the development of the city.

By the early 20th century, Barranquilla was one of the major ports from which local goods, primarily coffee, were shipped overseas.

Progress attracted both Colombians from other regions and foreigners, mainly from the US, Germany, Italy and the Middle East. This, in turn, gave the city an injection of foreign capital and accelerated its growth. It also brought about the city's cosmopolitan character.

◉ Sights

The city center (where the town was originally settled) is along the Paseo Bolívar, close to the river. Most of this sector, especially the area between the Paseo and the river, is inhabited by wild street commerce – it's actually one vast market stretching to the water like a flattened hillside shantytown.

A few kilometers northwest is El Prado, Barranquilla's new center, and the most pleasant district of the city. El Prado is cleaner, greener and safer than the city center. Calle 72 is the district's principal shopping street, lined with restaurants, shops and supermarkets. Strolling around, you'll find some architectural relics from the late 19th and early 20th centuries, the time when El Prado began to develop. Note the buildings in the Islamic-influenced Moorish style – you'll find some of them on and just off Carrera 54.

Iglesia de San Nicolás   CHURCH
(cnr Paseo Bolívar & Carrera 42) This mock-Gothic church halfway along Paseo Bolívar

DOWN BY THE RIVER – MOMPOX

Mompox hangs suspended in time like the pause between two ticks of a clock, or the space between two heartbeats.

But the endless flow of the Río Magdalena all around the town serves as a constant reminder that really, nothing ever stops – even if, when you walk the quiet streets here, it feels like you've slipped through a wormhole into the 16th century, especially if you arrive during the solemn Easter processions, which are second only to those in Popayán.

Founded in 1540 by Alonso de Heredia (brother of Cartagena's founder, Pedro de Heredia) on the eastern branch of the Río Magdalena, Mompox was an important trading center and active port through which all merchandise from Cartagena passed via the Canal del Dique and the Río Magdalena to the interior of the colony. The town flourished, minted coins for the colony, and became famous for its goldsmiths, traces of which can be found today in the town's superb filigree jewelry. Mompox declared its independence in 1810, the first town in Colombia to do so.

Towards the end of the 19th century, shipping was diverted to the other branch of the river, the Brazo de Loba, bringing the town's prosperity to an end and leaving it isolated.

However, a journey here today is very highly recommended. With a plethora of beautiful colonial churches and buildings, quiet streets, fascinating history and a great place to stay, it's like Cartagena without the hustle or the hassle.

El Kilate (685 5151; Calle 13 No 1-47; ☺7am-8pm) has good filigree, while La Casa del Artesano (Carrera 1 with Calle 20) sells the best rocking chairs in town (the town is famed for its furniture). A real highlight is a macabre wander around the ridiculously atmospheric Cementerio Municipal (Calle 18; ☺8am-noon & 2-5pm).

For a good dinner, try Comedor Costeño (685 5263; Calle de la Albarrada No 18-45; set meal COP$4000-8000; ☺7am-5pm). There's also decent street food in an amazing colonial square, the Plaza Santo Domingo. For a late drink, try Luna de Mompox (311 412 2843; Calle de la Albarrada; ☺6pm-1am Mon-Thu, to 3am Fri-Sun) right on the water's edge.

An outstanding spot to lay your head is La Casa Amarilla (685 6326/301 362 7065; lacasaamarillamompos.com; Carrera 1 No 13-59; dm COP$16,000, r per person from COP$45,000; luxury ste COP$250,000; ❀🛜). The friendly owner, Richard McColl, is both a Mompos resident and a British travel journalist. He can arrange tours of the wetlands and offers helpful information and bike hire.

Most travelers come to Mompox from Cartagena. Unitransco has a direct bus, leaving Cartagena (COP$45,000, eight hours, daily at 7am), but service is unreliable, so call ahead (or check with Richard at La Casa Amarilla, who always has up-to-date travel information). A faster way is to take an Expreso Brasilia bus to Magangué (COP$35,000, four hours, six buses daily). When it arrives in Mangangué, continue walking down the road and around to the right at the river and buy a ticket for a *chalupa* (boat) to Bodega (COP$7000, 20 minutes, frequent departures until about 3pm). The ticket booth is located across from El Punto del Sabor. Once in Bodega, hop in a *colectivo* (shared taxi or minivan) to Mompox (COP$12,000, 45 minutes). There may also be direct *chalupas* from Magangué to Mompox.

Traveling to or from Santa Marta or Taganga, there's a door-to-door service to Mompox (COP$70,000, six to eight hours, daily at 3am and 11am) through Omaira (311 414 8967). You need to call a day or two in advance.

From Bucaramanga to Mompox, take an overnight bus with Cotransmagadalena and Cotaxi to El Banco, Magdalena (12 hours, COP$60,000) Then take a 4WD *colectivo* from El Banco (two hours, COP$35,000). There are many operators and the ride is bumpy.

From Mompox there's a 6am bus to El Banco to catch the 9am bus to Bucaramanga (and connections to San Gil/Barichara). Ask at La Casa Amarilla for up-to-date travel information.

is worth entering for its main altarpiece and pulpit.

Museo de Caribe   MUSEUM
(www.culturacaribe.org, Parque Cultural del Caribe, Calle 36 No 46-66; admission COP$10,000; ☺ 8am-5pm Mon-Fri, 9am-6pm Sat & Sun) A very smart, modernistic, multimedia-heavy permanent exhibition detailing the culture, history, nature and people of Colombia's Carribbean. You're advised by staff to start on the upper floor and work your way down – but there's no real reason to do this. If you want to avoid hordes of schoolkids, do the route in reverse.

Museo Romantico   MUSEUM
(Carrera 54 No 59-199; adult/child COP$5000/free; ☺9-11:30am & 2.30-5:30pm Mon-Fri) The confusingly named Museo Romantico is actually a museum of the city's history, featuring exhibits relating to Barranquilla's past.

FREE Museo de Antropología   MUSEUM
(Calle 68 No 53-45; ☺8am-noon & 2:30-5pm Mon-Fri) On the 1st floor of the building of the Universidad del Atlántico, this musuem displays a small collection of pre-Columbian pottery from different regions, including pieces from the Calima, Tumaco and Nariño cultures.

Museo de Arte Moderno   MUSEUM
(Carrera 56 No 74-22; admission COP$3000; ☺3-7pm Mon, 9am-1pm & 3-7pm Tue-Fri, 9am-1pm Sat) Fills its space with rotating exhibitions from its larger permanent collection, which includes nationally renowned painters like Obregon Alejandro.

Catedral Metropolitana   CHURCH
(cnr Calle 53 & Carrera 46) This modern cathedral was completed in 1982. Don't be put off by its squat, heavy, somewhat bunkerlike exterior – go inside. The beautiful interior features a number of impressive and large stained-glass windows.

🛏 Sleeping

The center of budget accommodations is on and around Paseo Bolívar (Calle 34), but this area is seedy – just check the number of army personnel present even during the day. You can find rooms here for as little as COP$10,000, but there's little telling what went down in them before you checked in. If you would like to be safer and in a more pleasant environment, stay in El Prado; it's a rather upper-class district so you will pay for the privilege. You'll also find the best

food and nightlife around Carrera 53 and between Calles 79 and 80.

Hotel Howard Johnson   HOTEL $$$
(☎368 2183; Carrera 48 No 70-188; s/d incl breakfast COP$136,000/181,000; ✳🔊☱) This modern business-style hotel is an excellent choice, within walking distance from El Prado museums and nightlife, and home to friendly staff.

Hotel Barahona 72   HOTEL $$
(☎358 4600; www.hotelesbarahona.com; Carrera 49 No 72-19; s/d incl breakfast COP$83,000/100,000; ✳🔊) Some of the large rooms in the cheapest El Prado option were recently renovated. Overall, it's pretty good value for money when you consider the location.

Hotel Skal   HOTEL $
(☎351 2069; Calle 41 No 41-35; s/d with fan COP$20,000/25,000, with air-con COP$25,000/35,000; ✳☱) In the event that backpackers do find their way into downtown Barranquilla, they often stay at this musty option, somewhat made up for by the bonus pool. It's on a safe street next to a police station.

Hotel Colonial Inn   HOTEL $
(☎379 0241; Calle 42 No 43-131; s/d with fan COP$35,000/45,000, with air-con COP$45,000/60,000; ✳🔊) A comfortable city-center option, with an air of faded glory about the lobby.

Hotel El Prado   HOTEL $$$
(☎369 7777; www.hotelelpradosa.com, in Spanish; Carrera 54 No 70-10; s/d incl breakfast from COP$175,500/212,500; ✳🔊☱) One of the coast's grand dames, this 1920s republican-style mansion is Barranquilla's most historic and posh hotel. Rooms are nice but basic, so it's more about soaking up the historical atmosphere within its walls and the large, tropical pool area.

🍴 Eating & Drinking

One of Barranquilla's saving graces is food. Most of the good restaurants are in El Prado. In the center around Paseo Bolivar, you can find cheap eats under COP$2000.

El Veradero   CUBAN $$$
(☎356 5638; Carrera 51B No 79-97; mains COP$30,000-50,000; ☺lunch & dinner) OK, it's a chain diner, but it's a very good chain. The seafood here is great, portions are generous and even the *moros y cristianos* (rice and beans) are well made. The live music can be a bit hit and miss, though.

La Casa del Sancochito COLOMBIAN $
(Calle 74 No 47-48; set meal COP$7000; ⏱lunch) A great little spot serving set meals of Colombian specialties like its namesake, a traditional meat stew, and a great curried *carne asada* (grilled meat). The outdoor wooden tables are always full.

Harry's Café BAR
(☑345 6431; Calle 80 No 53-18; mains COP$10,000-28,000; ⏱dinner) Like a TGI Friday drunk on Latin fever, this yankee-themed bar and grill is a little mall-like, but most nights you'll find fun locals and a rock soundtrack.

★★ Festivals & Events

Carnaval de Barranquilla MARDI GRAS
(www.carnavaldebarranquilla.org) This is one of the continent's biggest street parties. It's held in February on the four days before Ash Wednesday, so the date changes each year. Much like the carnival in Rio de Janeiro, there are street bands, masquerade and fancy dress, live performances, and a riotous, slightly unhinged atmosphere as the town drinks and dances itself into the ground. It can be rough and ready, and you need to keep an eye on your possessions and your companions, but let your hair down and it could be a highlight of your trip.

☆ Entertainment

Barranquilla's local soccer team, Junior, plays at **Estadio Olympico Metropolitano Roberto Meléndez** (Vía Circunvalación & Av Murillo), south of Centro. You can buy tickets at the gates.

ℹ Information

Cappucino.com (☑358 4465; Carrera 48 No 72-65; per hr COP$1500; ⏱7:30am-7:30pm Mon-Sat) Internet cafe.

HSBC (Carrera 52 No 72-131; ⏱8-11:30am & 2-4pm Mon-Fri) Has an ATM.

Panamanian consulate (☑360 1870; Carrera 57 No 72-25, Edificio Fincar 207-208; ⏱9:30am-noon & 2-4pm Mon-Fri)

Servientrega (☑356 0527; Calle 70 No 52-63; ⏱8-11:30am & 2-6:30pm Mon-Fri, 8am-12:30pm Sat) Postal services.

Tourist office (Comité Mixto de Promoción Mixta del Atlántico; ☑330 3864; Vía 40 No 36-135; ⏱8am-noon & 2-5pm Mon-Fri) The tourist office is in the Antiguo Edificio de Aduana, a healthy hike southeast of El Prado. It has lots of info, but staff aren't champing at the bit to help.

ℹ Getting There & Away

Air
The airport is about 10km south of the center and is accessible by buses that say 'Aeropuerto' (COP$1300). Taxis will cost COP$15,000. It always takes more than an hour to get there. Almost all main Colombian carriers service Barranquilla. El Prado has airline ticketing offices for most major airlines. **LAN** (☑368 8845; www.lan.com; Carrera 54 No 72-27; ⏱8am-noon & 2-6pm Mon-Fri, 9am-noon Sat) flies to Medellín (from COP$288,000 one way) and Montería (from COP$316,000 one way). **Copa/AeroRepública** (☑368 4040; www.aerorepublica.com; Calle 72 No 54-49; ⏱8am-6pm Mon-Fri, 9am-1pm Sat) goes to Bogotá (from COP$212,000 one way), Medellín (from COP$289,000 one way), Panama City (COP$667,000 one way) and San Andrés (from COP$1,000,000 round trip, on Tuesday, Saturday and Sunday), returning the same days at 11am. **Avianca** (☑353 4691; www.avianca.com; Calle 76 Cra 55, Carrefour Bldg; ⏱8am-6pm Mon-Fri, 9am-1pm Sat) flies to Bogotá (from COP$205,000 one way), Medellín (from COP$339,100 one way), Cali (from COP$317,060 one way) and Miami (from COP$1,250,000 one way). There are constant promotions and prices can be half those listed.

Bus
The bus terminal is located 7km from the city center. It's not convenient, and it may take up to an hour to get to the terminal by urban bus. It's much faster to go by taxi (COP$15,000, 30 minutes).

Expreso Brasilia (☑323 0111; www.expreso brasilia.com) departs for Bogotá (COP$110,000, 18 hours, several times daily from 5:30am) and Medellín (COP$85,000, 12 hours, from 6am). They run services to Santa Marta (COP$8000, two hours, every 30 minutes from 2:30am to 11:30pm) with continuing services to Riohacha on the Guajira Peninsula (COP$32,000, four hours). Expreso Brasilia also has services to Cartagena (COP$12,000, two hours, every 15 to 30 minutes from 4am to 11pm). **Unitransco** (☑323 0030) services Tolú hourly every morning (COP$35,000, five hours) and Mompox (COP$40,000, six hours, once daily at 7:30am). **La Costeña** (☑323 1360) also heads to Santa Marta every 10 minutes from 5am to 8:30pm for slightly less than the competition (COP$7000, two hours).

Expreso Brasilia operates one daily bus at 11pm direct to Maracaibo, Venezuela (COP$85,000, nine hours) and on to Caracas, Venezuela.

Santa Marta
☑5 / POP 448,000 / ELEV 2M
Santa Marta is South America's oldest surviving city and the second most important colonial city on Colombia's Caribbean coast.

It's always been a convenient base to explore the outstanding nearby attractions, including Ciudad Perdida and Parque Nacional Natural (PNN) Tayrona, but a complete overhaul of Parque de los Novios (also known as Parque Santander) and the pedestrianization of a number of neighboring streets has given the city some desperately needed public space. Evenings here are now filled with friends meeting, drinking and enjoying some of the area's great new restaurants.

Santa Marta attracts throngs of holiday-making Colombians in search of the simple pleasures of rum, fun and sun. It's packed with revelers on weekends, sucking down snow cones, burying themselves in sand, and gathering along the rocky piers for glistening sunsets. The climate is hot, but the heat here is drier than Cartagena, and the evening sea breeze cools the city and makes it pleasant to wander about.

History

Rodrigo de Bastidas planted a Spanish flag here in 1525, deliberately choosing a site at the foot of the Sierra Nevada de Santa Marta to serve as a convenient base for the reputedly incalculable gold treasures of the indigenous Tayronas.

As soon as the plundering of the Sierra began, so did the inhabitants' resistance. By the end of the 16th century the Tayronas had been wiped out and many of their extraordinary gold objects (melted down for rough material by the Spaniards) were in the Crown's coffers.

Santa Marta was also one of the early gateways to the interior of the colony. It was from here that Jiménez de Quesada set off in 1536 for his strenuous march up the Magdalena Valley to found Bogotá two years later.

Engaged in the war with the Tayronas and repeatedly ransacked by pirates, Santa Marta didn't have many glorious moments in its colonial history and was soon overshadowed by its younger, more progressive neighbor, Cartagena. An important date remembered nationwide in Santa Marta's history is December 17, 1830, when Simón Bolívar died here, after bringing independence to six Latin American countries.

◉ Sights

The principal tourist seaside boulevard is Av Rodrigo de Bastidas (Carrera 1C), alive until late at night. From here there's a good view over the bay and a small, rocky island, El Morro offshore.

Most tourist activity occurs between the waterfront and Av Campo Serrano (Carrera 5), the main commercial street. The beach resort of El Rodadero, 5km south of the center, is popular with Colombian holiday-makers. Buses shuttle frequently between the center and El Rodadero; the trip takes 15 minutes.

FREE **Museo Del Oro**   MUSEUM
(Calle 14 No 2-07; ⊘8-11:45am & 2-5:45pm Mon-Fri) The Gold Museum is in the fine colonial mansion known as the Casa de la Aduana (Customs House). It has an interesting collection of Tayrona objects, mainly pottery and gold, as well as artifacts of the indigenous Kogi and Arhuaco. Don't miss the impressive model of Ciudad Perdida, especially if you plan on visiting the real thing.

Catedral   CHURCH
(cnr Carrera 4 & Calle 17) This massive white-washed cathedral claims to be Colombia's oldest church, but work wasn't actually completed until the end of the 18th century, and thus reflects the influences of various architectural styles. It holds the ashes of the town's founder, Rodrigo de Bastidas (just to the left as you enter the church). Simón Bolívar was buried here in 1830, but in 1842 his remains were taken to Caracas, his birthplace.

Quinta de San Pedro Alejandrino   HACIENDA
(Av Libertador; adult/child COP$10,000/6000; ⊘9:30am-4:30pm) This hacienda on the outskirts of town is where Simón Bolívar spent his last days and died. The hacienda was established at the beginning of the 17th century and was engaged in cultivating and processing sugarcane. It had its own *trapiche* (sugarcane mill) and a *destilería* (distillery).

During the Bolívar era, the hacienda was owned by a Spaniard, Joaquín de Mier, a devoted supporter of Colombia's independence cause. He invited Bolívar to stay and take a rest at his home before his intended journey to Europe. Since its inauguration, ownership has changed more than 15 times. Highlights among the wares in the hacienda include an absolutely decadent marble bathtub.

Several monuments have been built on the grounds in remembrance of Bolívar, the most imposing of which is a massive central structure called the **Altar de la Patria**. Just to the right of this is the **Museo Bolivariano**, which features works of art donated by Latin American artists, including those from Colombia, Venezuela, Panama, Ecuador, Peru and Bolivia, the countries liberated by Bolívar.

The outstanding grounds, home to Santa Marta's 22-hectare **Jardín Botánico**, are also worth a stroll. Some of the property's trees are worth the trip out here alone. A new convention center and concert hall were under construction at time of research.

The *quinta* is in the far eastern suburb of Mamatoco, about 4km from the city center. To get here, take the Mamatoco bus from the waterfront (Carrera 1C); it's a 20-minute trip (COP$1200) to the hacienda.

Activities

Most dive schools have settled in nearby Taganga, but there are also some operators in the city center, including **Atlantic Divers** (421 4883; Calle 10C No 2-04; 8am-8pm). A four-day PADI-certification course costs COP$800,000.

There's some good **hiking** around Santa Marta, including walks in the Parque Nacional Natural Tayrona (PNN), though if you're after some longer and more adventurous trekking, the hike to Ciudad Perdida is the region's showpiece.

Tours

Santa Marta's tour market revolves around Ciudad Perdida. There are now four main outfits authorized to escort tourists on the five- or six-day trek, three of which are based in Santa Marta (see p153). You'll also find other hiking options available. Speak with **José 'Chelo' Gallego** (316 232 5366; jose087301@hotmail.com) for tailor-made trips to the mountains. He's an expert with many years' experience.

Sleeping

Santa Marta's *centro* is jam-packed with small hotels and family-run residencies, most of them cheap and fairly laid-back. If the following are full, there are more options just a few steps away, though be warned that some streets around 10C are known for prostitution, and all that trade entails.

Casa Verde TOP CHOICE HOTEL $$$
(431 4122; Calle 18 No 4-70; s/d COP$165,000/ 220,000) If you're what the relaxed and attentive live-in owner calls 'a retired backpacker,' this cute five-room spot, with pebble-lined walls and floors, smart bathrooms, crisp bed linen and intelligently designed, pristinely whitewashed rooms is your spot. Lounge in the cooling pool near the lobby to feel more than a little like a Roman emperor.

HIGH SOCIETIES

As you travel up and down the Caribbean coast, you might see Kogi people hopping on local buses with bags full of seashells. But they're not collecting them as ornaments. The indigenous groups of the Sierra Nevada de Santa Marta collect them for a sacred, ritualized method of consuming coca known as the *poporo*.

The active alkaloids in coca leaves, when chemically refined into cocaine and snorted, smoked or injected, are a powerful stimulant. When the leaves are chewed alone, they have little effect. However, when chewed together with an alkaline substance, their active ingredients are multiplied, enabling users to walk many miles without rest or food, even at altitude – handy if you live in the world's highest coastal mountain range.

For the *poporo*, thousands of seashells called *caracucha* are collected, roasted over a fire and then pounded into a fine powder. This powder is then placed into a hollowed-out gourd, known as a *totuma*, which represents femininity. Men receive this as they come of age.

Women of these tribes collect coca leaves and dry them by placing them into *mochilas* (bucket-shaped, woven shoulder bags) packed with hot stones. Men then take a large wad of leaves, put them in their mouths, and dip a small stick into the *totuma* to gather some of the powdered shell, which they suck off the stick. Any excess spittle and powder mix is wiped back on the outside of the gourd, causing it to grow – symbolizing wisdom. They then chew the mixture for up to 30 minutes, as their basified saliva causes the coca leaves to release their active components, giving users a slightly cocaine-like high. It is believed the *poporo* instills knowledge, just as reading a book or going to college increases students' intelligence.

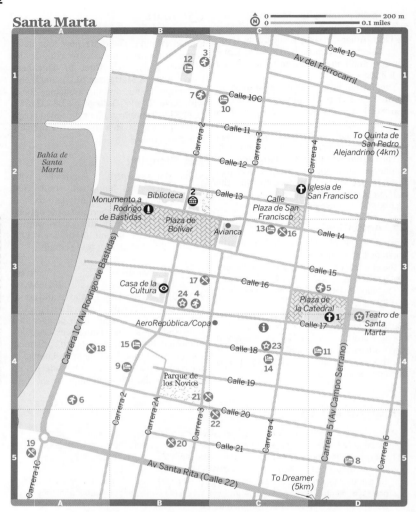

Santa Marta

Aluna   HOSTEL **$$**
(☎432 4916; Calle 21 No 5-72; dm COP$20,000, s/d COP$40,000/60,000, with air-con COP$60,000/80,000; ﹡) A lovely hotel with nicely proportioned dorms, cosy private rooms and spacious, breezy communal areas. The well-equipped kitchen has lockers. The best book exchange on the coast speaks of an intelligent, widely read crowd. Ask owner Patrick about his place up in nearby Paso Del Mango, a bird-watcher's paradise.

La Brisa Loca   HOSTEL **$$**
(☎431 6121; Calle 14 No 3-58; dm with/without air-con from COP$28,000/20,000, r with air-con from COP$70,000; ﹡⊚) This vast, 82-bed capacity hostel has everything its young, festive crowd needs. Beds are firm, and rooms and dorms are cool and large with in-room lockers. The pool, bar and pool table together with weekend costume parties make for a fun time. Ryan and Evan, the sharp American owners, look like surfers but are shrewd businessmen who do it for love as well as money.

Dreamer   HOSTEL **$$**
(☎433 3264; Diagonal 32, Los Trupillos (Mamatoco); dm from COP$15,000, s/d COP$55,000/70,000; ﹡) A very high-end and intelligently designed hostel with rooms clustered around

Santa Marta

⊙ Sights

⊕ Activities, Courses & Tours

🛏 Sleeping

🍴 Eating

✪ Entertainment

one of Santa Marta's best swimming pools. Even the dorms get air-con, a clean shared bathroom and good beds. It's a little way out of town, but it's actually really well located for trips to Ciudad Perdida, Parque Nacional Natural (PNN) Tayrona, Minca, and some of the better beaches in the area. The Italian owners oversee the kitchen, so the food is said to be fantastic, too.

🏠 **La Casa**   HOTEL **$$$**
(☎421 2483; www.lacasasantamarta.com; Calle 18 No 3-53; s/d incl breakfast from COP$168,000/ 237,000; ❋🛜❄) This three-room boutique hotel, full of socially conscious local art, is in a restored 18th-century home run by a lovely young woman who has worked with Afro-Caribbean and Sierra indigenous communities for the past decade. Each room in the house is a tribute to those communities and

features gorgeous original tile flooring and doors. Breakfast includes organic products from the Sierra.

Solymar Hostal   HOTEL **$$**
(☎431 0208; Carerra 2 No 19-06; s/d with fan COP$50,000/60,000, with air-con COP$60,000/ 75,000; ❋🛜) It might feel a little like a motel or a Latin 'love' hotel, but this 33-room hotel is nothing of the sort. Its rooms are small but decent, clean and new, and it's near the beach. Great if you want to avoid the back-packer scene.

Casa De Isabella   HOTEL **$$$**
(☎431 2082; Carerra 2N No19-20; r from COP$287,000, ste COP$430,000) The lobby's an extravaganza in slightly gaudy Latin bling, but rooms are large and stylish. The upper suite – all minimalist chic, antiques and exposed beams – has a a vast, four-poster bed, and a private roof terrace and pool with a sea view. There's another pool downstairs for lesser mortals to pose in.

Casa Familiar   HOTEL **$**
(☎421 1697; www.hospederiacasafamiliar.freeserv ers.com; Calle 10C No 2-14; dm/s/d COP$15,000/ 22,000/35,000) A friendly, popular hotel with private rooms and dorms as well as a high-speed laundry service. Rooms are spartan and beds are bricklike, but it's acceptable for a night or two.

Hotel Miramar   HOTEL **$**
(☎423 3276; elmiramar_santamarta@yahoo.com; Calle 10C No 1C-59; dm COP$10,000, s/d without bathroom COP$12,000/20,000, with bathroom COP$15,000/25,000;🛜) The Miramar attracts a certain type of traveler: shoestringers and rich kids slumming it for kicks. But it has heritage, and is popular and social. There's an in-house tourism agency and restaurant.

✖ Eating

Santa Marta has some of the best food on the coast. An influx of Latin and North American restaurateurs have simplified the menus, focusing on ambience, classic cooking and stylish presentation, rather than replicating the pretentious fusion food that can be found in Cartagena. The best places are on or near the Callejon de Restaurantes (Carrera 3 between 16 and 17) or around the Parque de los Novios.

TOP CHOICE 🏅 Ouzo   MEDITERRANEAN **$$**
(☎423 0658; Carrera 3 No 19-29, Parque de los Novios; mains COP$20,000/45,000; ⊙dinner

Mon-Sat) Ouzo offers a stripped-back, classic Greek/Italian menu with outstanding bruschetta – a fragrant flavour-slap atop a wispy crunch of wheat – with the octopus as star. The octopus is slow-cooked for two hours in a garlicky broth, then slammed on the coals to sear and seal in the flavour. Great service and a superbly designed interior means the heat stays in the kitchen.

Agave Azul　　　　　　　　MEXICAN $$
(☎431 6121; Calle 14 No 3-58; mains COP$18,000-40,000; ☺dinner Mon-Sat) OK. So you're not in Mexico. But close your eyes and bite into a perfect tostada that totters with toppings including the town's most tender meat, the sweetest, most buttery avocados, and a tart, crispy salad, and you might be forgiven for firing a few rounds into the ceiling in joy. Now open your eyes and you'll see the presentation is superbly delicate. Steaks are amazing, too.

TOP CHOICE El Santo　　　　　MEDITERRANEAN $$
(☎423 6170; Calle 21 No 2A-52; mains COP$21,000-$30,000; ☺dinner Wed-Sun) An intimate but relaxed bistro. Try the signature dish, an astonishingly tender red-wine braised lamb with a bold, herby stuffing of garlic, thyme and rosemary. All the ingredients are of the highest quality and are cooked in a dramatic open kitchen. Ask the chef about his new, modern tapas place, too.

Cocteleria Juancho　　　　　　KIOSK $
(Carrera 1 btwn Calle 22 & 23 No 18-67; ceviche COP$5000-13,000; ☺breakfast, lunch & dinner) This ceviche street stall has been packing in loyal locals for 33 years. Here it is all about the prawn ceviche, which comes in four sizes. They can be a bit heavy-handed with the dreaded golf sauce, so ask them to hold off a touch. It's next door to the Gino Passcalli store.

Ben & Josep's　　　　　　STEAKHOUSE $$
(☎317 280 5039; Carrera 1 No 18-53; mains COP$24,000-39,000; ☺dinner Mon-Sat) It's the best of the waterfront options, and meat is the deal. Drinks start at 4pm (call ahead to reserve an outdoor table on weekends). The filet mignon with a pepper sauce is simple and classily executed.

Basilea　　　　　　　　EUROPEAN $$$
(☎431 4138; Calle 16 No 2-58; mains COP$30,000; ☺lunch & dinner Mon-Sat) An intimate Med-French place with punchy air-con and massive artworks, offering brave twists on classic dishes like the fiery red pepper steak. If you can overlook the snooty atmosphere and service, the food makes it worth the trip.

 Entertainment

Santa Marta, until the recent renovation of Parque de los Novios, really lacked a central focus to its nightlife. The parque now serves as an informal gathering place where young and old can crack a cold beer, meet friends, flirt and gossip before heading out to drink and dance till the dawn breaks.

Bars

Son Tapas　　　　　　　　　SALSA
(Calle 21 No 3-10; ☺4pm-1am Tue & Wed, 4pm-3am Thu-Sat) Live salsa, free nibbles and an intimate, late-night vibe, this bar just off the Parque de los Novios serves a slightly older, less wild crowd than some spots in town such as La Puerta, and has a touch of midnight magic to it.

Crabs　　　　　　　　　　ROCK BAR
(Calle 18 No 3-69; ☺8pm-3am Wed-Sat) Santa Marta, are you ready to rock? A great new rock bar with pool table, outdoor smoking terrace, decent-priced beers and spirits, and video screens paying homage to some of the more obscure monsters of rock. I mean, when did you last see an Alice Cooper video?

La Puerta　　　　　　　　　CLUB
(☎Calle 17 No 2-29; ☺6pm-1am Tue & Wed, to 3am Thu-Sat) Here, students and gringos eye each other up and get happily trashed in a beautifully benign Colombian style. Soca, salsa, house, hip hop and reggae warm up the packed dancefloor. The gusting fans surrounding it will make you and other dancers look dramatically windswept and much more attractive – especially after half a bottle of aguardiente.

Sports

El Union Magdalena is Santa Marta's local soccer team. Games are played at **Estadio Eduardo Santos** (cnr Av Liberador & Carrera 19), less than 2km from Centro. Games run throughout the year. Buy tickets at the stadium. A taxi there costs COP$8000.

ℹ Information

4-72 (☎421 0180; Calle 22 3 No 2-08; ☺8am-noon & 2-6pm Mon-Fri, to noon Sat) Post office.

Aviatur (☎421 3848; Calle 15 No 3-20; ☺8am-noon & 2-4pm Mon-Fri) Make reservations here for the concession's camping and higher-end options (Ecohabs) at Parque Nacional Natural (PNN) Tayrona.

Bancolombia (🖃421 0185; Carrera 3 No 14-10; ⊙8-11:30am & 2-4pm Mon-Thu, 8-11:30am & 2-4:30pm Fri) Changes traveler's checks and US dollars only.

Davivienda (cnr Calle 14 & Carrera 4) Bank with an ATM. Highest cash advances in town.

Fondo de Promoción Turística de Santa Marta (🖃422 7548; Calle 10 No 3-10, El Rodadero; ⊙8am-noon & 2-6pm Mon-Fri, 8am-noon Sat) Santa Marta's member-based tourism office can provide loads more info than its government counterpart.

Hospital Centro Julio Mendez Barreneche (🖃421 2226; Carrera 14 No 23-42)

Parques Nacionales Naturales de Colombia (🖃423 0758; www.parquesnacionales.gov.co; Calle 17 No 4-06) Limited national park info.

Policía Nacional (🖃421 4264; Calle 22 No 1C-74)

Tamá Café (🖃431 2289; Carrera 2 No 16-06; per hr COP$1500; ⊙8:30am-6:30pm Mon-Fri, 9am-1pm Sat) Organic coffeehouse and internet cafe.

Tourist office (🖃438 2587; Calle 17 No 3-120; ⊙8am-noon & 2-6pm Mon-Fri) The city tourist office.

Villa Café.Bar (🖃431 0431; Calle 17 No 2-43; per hr COP$1500; ⊙7am-7pm Mon-Sat) Internet cafe.

❶ Getting There & Away
Air
The airport is 16km south of the city on the Barranquilla–Bogotá road. City buses marked 'El Rodadero Aeropuerto' will take you there in 45 minutes from Carrera 1C. Flights include Bogotá (from around COP$200,000 one way) and Medellín (from COP$300,000 one way).

AeroRepública/Copa (🖃421 0120; www.aerorepublica.com; Carrera 3 No 17-27; ⊙8am-6pm Mon-Fri, 9am-1pm Sat)

Avianca (🖃421 4018; www.avianca.com; Carrera 2A No 14-47; ⊙8am-6pm Mon-Fri, 9am-1pm Sat)

Bus
The bus terminal is on the southeastern outskirts of the city. Frequent minibuses go there from Carrera 1C in the center.

Expreso Brasilia (🖃430 6244) offers three buses daily to both Bogotá (COP$80,000, 18 hours) and Medellín (COP$108,000, 15 hours). It has departures every 30 minutes until 7:30pm to Barranquilla (COP$10,000, two hours); and hourly departures until 5:30pm to Cartagena (COP$20,000, four hours). It also heads north to Riohacha (COP$15,000, 2½ hours) every 30 minutes until 5pm, with a continuing service to Maicao (COP$25,000, four hours), the last Colombian town before the border with Venezuela.

Here you can change for buses to Maracaibo (Venezuela). Don't linger much beyond the bus station – safety has improved dramatically in Maicao, but it remains the distribution center for all sorts of contraband from Venezuela. There are also two direct buses to Tolú (COP$40,000, seven hours) and three to Bucaramanga (COP$70,000, nine hours).

Rapido Ochoa (🖃430 1040) offers similar services with expanded operations to Sincelejo (COP$44,000, four times daily – only the 1:30pm service is direct) and Riohacha (COP$15,000, every hour).

For Venezuela, you are better off catching a direct bus from Santa Marta to Maracaibo (COP$95,000, seven hours) with **Expreso Amerlujo** (🖃430 4144), departing daily at noon, with a continuing service to Caracas (COP$185,000, 18 hours). Alternatively, if the times don't work for you, **Cootragua** (🖃430 1650) goes to Paraguachón (COP$30,000, 4½ hours) on the border at 10am daily, where you can change for Maracaibo. All passport formalities are done in Paraguachón. Change money here, expect a bag search and wind your clock forward one hour when crossing from Colombia to Venezuela.

Minca
Perched 600m high up in the Sierra Nevada above Santa Marta sits Minca, a small mountain village famous for organic coffee and, perhaps more importantly, much cooler temperatures. There's not much in town itself, but there are a couple of scenic places to hide away in the fresh mountain air for a few days, and the whole place is a haven for bird-watching with over 300 species nearby.

Sans Souci (🖃310 590 9213; sanssouciminca@yahoo.com; campsite per person COP$10,000, dm COP$15,000, r per person COP$35,000; 🕱) is a simple, German-run *finca* (farm) tucked away above town that offers spectacular views across the Sierra to Santa Marta.

With its prime location practically on top of the Rio Gaira and its well-appointed rooms full of the Italian-Colombian owners' art, **Sierra's Sound** (🖃421 9962; Calle Principal; s/d COP$70,000/140,000) is a stylish little mountain getaway. The restaurant serves Colombian and Italian meals.

For a good bird-watching guide to the area, try **Francisco Troncoso** (🖃316 815 9378; francisco_troncoso@hotmail.com).

Minca is reached easily from Santa Marta by taxi (COP$40,000) or bumpily by mototaxi (COP$6000), the latter departing from

La Y (pronounced *Jay*), an intersection in the suburb of El Yucol 8km west of Santa Marta's *centro* on the way to Riohacha.

Taganga

♫5 / POP 5000

Taganga is an almost obligatory stop on the Gringo Trail. Whether that phrase fills you with dread or delight will determine your response to this once-tiny Colombian fishing village, set in a beautiful, deep, horseshoe-shaped bay 5km northeast of Santa Marta. It's grown quickly and without much concern for locals or the environment but, love it or loathe it, Taganga remains one of the Caribbean coast's most visited destinations.

Taganga has officially arrived on the global tourism map and has something of a reputation as a party zone, and has become a popular destination for Israeli travelers to decompress and kick back after completing their military service.

The beach here isn't particularly nice, but with heaps of fishing boats dotting the bay and the imposing sierras hulking behind them, it is one of the coast's most picturesque spots and many travelers love hanging out here for weeks at a time – and many of them have stayed for life. There's plenty of youthful camaraderie and it's a good place for solo wanderers who want to meet like-minded souls for onward travel.

Most travelers use Taganga as their base for treks to Ciudad Perdida and visits to Parque Nacional Natural (PNN) Tayrona.

Activities

Taganga is a popular scuba-diving center, with plenty of dive schools offering dives and courses. Local services here are among the cheapest you'll find anywhere in the world. Four-day open-water PADI courses range from COP$550,000 to COP$670,000. Beware of the many cowboy operators. The following schools are recommended.

Aquantis Dive Center   DIVING
(☑421 9344; www.aquantisdivecenter.com; Calle 18 No 1-39; ☺6:30am-9pm) Friendly and professional, this Belgian-run company offers PADI-certification for COP$630,000 and two-tank dives for COP$150,000. The best in town

---

> **WORTH A TRIP**

MACONDO: MAGIC & REALITY

Welcome to Macondo. Locals, maps, bus drivers and government officials will tell you it's really named Aracataca, and residents themselves rejected a name change in a 2006 referendum, but anyone who has read Gabriel García Márquez's masterpiece, *One Hundred Years of Solitude*, will feel they have stepped into the birthplace of magic realism as they walk or cycle the streets here.

Dutch artist Tim Buendía, who claims to be the last surviving member of the Buendía family featured in *One Hundred Years of Solitude,* has set up the country's only Márquez tour, which will leave you deliciously lost between dreams and memories.

Buendía – whose real name is Aan't Goor – came here in 2008 and was so charmed by the town he opened a hostel, **Gypsy Residence** (☑321 251 7420; thegypsyresidence. com; Calle 9 No 1-74, Barrio Cataquita; dm COP$20,000, s/d COP$50,000/60,000; ☎). The hotel is named after a key character in *One Hundred Years of Solitude*, Melquíades, a gypsy who astounds the town by showing them ice for the first time, and who prophesizes Macondo's eventual destruction.

On the one-day tour (COP$99,000 per person) you'll visit all of the town's Márquez-themed attractions, and Buendía has such a passion for his subject and such a love for his topic that you'll overlook the fact that some of them are in a poor state of repair – although the excellent museum, a re-creation of the Márquez family home, is very well curated.

You can visit the telegraph office where the author's father worked, and if things go to plan, you'll be able to visit the grave of Melquíades with its headstone, which Buendía (or is it Aan't Goor?) is planning to build in a quiet side street. It's a fabulously fun way to spend a day – even if you're not a literature fan.

There are regular local buses to and from Santa Marta's market (COP$7000 1½ hours). Tell them you want to go to Macondo. It exists, even though everyone denies it.

Taganga

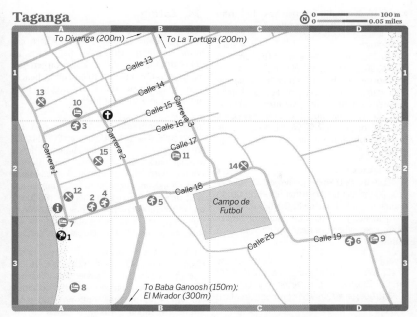

Taganga

Poseidon Dive Center   DIVING
(📞421 9224; www.poseidondivecenter.com; Calle 18 No 1-69; ⏰7am-7pm) Well-equipped dive school, courses cost COP$670,000.

Tayrona Dive Center   DIVING
(📞421 5349; Calle 18 No 1-39) Offers PADI certification for COP$580,000 in low season.

🎓 Courses

Academia Latina (📞421 9390; www.academia-latina.com; Calle 14 No 1B-75) Offers classes starting from COP$150,000 (minimum 10 hours per week). It's inside Casa Holanda.

🛌 Sleeping

Casa de Felipe   HOSTEL $
(📞421 9120/316 318 9158; www.lacasadefelipe.com; Carrera 5A No 19-13; dm COP$16,000-20,000, s/d COP$45,000/60,000, apt 2/4 people COP$100,000/120,000; 📶) This lovely hostel run by a friendly Frenchman is one of the better-equipped budget options you'll stumble across. In a beautiful house on lush grounds above the bay, it's all here: great staff, pleasant rooms, a good bar, kitchen, cable TV, numerous hammocks, excellent breakfast, and friendly folk from around the

world. It's located a few blocks uphill from the beach, past the soccer pitch.

La Tortuga
HOSTEL $

(📞320 258 9677; Calle 9 No 3-116; dm from COP$20,000; s/d COP$60,000/70,000; 📶) A new hostel with beautiful bamboo construction, comfy beds, a great kitchen, and fresh sea breezes high up on the sunset-facing terrace bar. The communal garden area has a large plastic pool to cool your blood, and the friendly Colombian owner can't do enough to help you.

Oso Perezoso
HOSTEL $

(📞421 8041 Calle 17 No 2-36; hammock COP$13,000, r per person incl breakfast from COP$22,000; 📶) Rooms are small but neat, though the stairs to them are perilous, and there's a breezy rooftop bar where you can string your own hammock.

Divanga
HOTEL $$

(📞421 9092; www.divanga.com; Calle 12 No 4-07; dm COP$30,000, r per person incl breakfast COP$40,000; 📶🏊) Another French-run place not short on atmosphere – colorful local artworks don the walls and doors of the rooms, most of which surround a swimming pool. There's a rooftop deck and bar that catches a lovely sea breeze. It's more tranquil than Casa de Felipe, so opt to stay here if that's a priority.

Casa Blanca
HOTEL $$

(📞421 9232; Carrera 1 No 14-61; r per person incl breakfast COP$35,000; 📶) The cheapest beachfront option, but it's a little rundown these days and near to the bass-boom of new nightclub El Mirador after dark. Located at the far southern end of the beach. The higher rooms have better views.

Casa Holanda
HOTEL $$

(📞421 9390; Calle 14 No 1B-75; COP$70,000/ 90,000 🌀📶) Simple, smart and clean rooms, with crisp white cotton sheets and firm beds, right in the center of town. Has a fairly decent restaurant downstairs.

Ballena Azul
HOTEL $$$

(📞421 9009; www.hotelballenaazul.com; cnr Carerra 1 & Calle 18; r without/with air-con COP$80,000/140,000; 🌀📶) Its website would have you think this is South Beach – which is not quite correct – but it is Taganga's fanciest hotel. The whitewashed colonial-like home is right on the beach, and has an annex next door.

Eating

There's a bunch of open-air budget restaurants along the waterfront, where *comida corriente* with fresh fish starts at COP$$10,000. If you're cooking, you can buy fresh fish daily at the north end of the beach. Doña Mera's drinks stand – the first you pass in town – does the best juice.

Pachamama
TOP CHOICE / FRENCH $$

(📞421 9486; Calle 16 No 1C-18; mains COP$14,000-20,000; ⏱dinner) You'll find Pachamama down a quiet backstreet in a small walled compound. With Tiki stylings and a laid-back vibe, it's like an indoor beach bar – but casual as it may be, the French chef has produced one of the most creative menus on the coast. The langoustines in bacon and tarragon are sensational, and the tuna carpaccio is perfect.

La Baguettes de Maria
SANDWICHES $

(Calle 18 No 3-47; mains COP$5000-10,000; ⏱lunch & dinner Sun-Fri, dinner Sat) Massive, overfilled fresh baguettes with delicious chicken, beef or tuna options. And who knew how much you'd miss olives on the road? Upside: everything is made to order. Downside: continents often drift before your sandwich arrives.

Bitácora
ITALIAN $$

(📞421 9121; Carrera 1 No 17-13; mains COP$10,000-20,000; ⏱breakfast, lunch & dinner) Semi-stylish spot serving everything from filet mignon in bacon-and-mushroom sauce to veggie lasagna. At night, it's good for a pre-clubbing drink and to watch the street scenes.

Cafe Bonsai
BAKERY $$

(Calle 13 No 1-07; from COP$12,000; ⏱breakfast, lunch & dinner; 🌀📶) 'Hi, can I have roast chicken, marinated cheese and egg mayo on sourdough rye bread, please?' Not a sentence you hear every day in Colombia. Bonsai is cool and cooled (it has air-con and wi-fi), with a vast menu, delicious homemade bread and amazing chocolate truffles. It's quite overpriced, but still completely fantastic.

Baba Ganoosh
THAI $$

(📞Carrera 1 No 18-22; mains from COP$17,000; ⏱dinner) This new 60-seater is set over two floors, with massive bay views. The carpets and low cushions give it a semi-Asian vibe. And although the paint was drying when we visited, owner-chef Patrick Verdegall used to have a queue 30-long when he cooked at Casa de Felipe. His filet mignon was renowned and his Thai green curries were authentic, and reports made after we left say he's pulled it off again.

 Drinking

El Garaje CLUB
(🖉421 9003; Calle 8 No 2-127; ⊗8:30pm-late Wed-Sat) El Garaje lost its crown as the top spot in Taganga with the arrival of El Mirador. It now serves as an after-party destination for the town's zombies who fear the dawn. The gnarled tree on the dance floor is still cool, though.

El Mirador CLUB
(Carrera 1B No 18-117; ⊗8:30pm-late Wed-Sat) Here they are in their ragged tropi-cool finery; shaking and thumping, boozing and bumping – it's your 100% uncut backpacker disco paradiso. The rum flows, the speakers throb with mainstream pop, and the bayview dance floor hums hot with promise and passion (or maybe that's just your sunburn). If you like discos, drinking and flirting, you'll love it.

❶ **Information**

Being a backpacker hub, Taganga sees its fair share of petty theft. Keep an eye on your things at the beach and don't leave them unattended, and avoid crimes of opportunity elsewhere by not leaving your valuables near an open window, or within reach of anyone.

There's only one ATM in Taganga, and it's always, always broken or empty. The nearest ATM is in Santa Marta. The tourist information point is directly on the beachfront as you arrive from the main road.

Centro de Salud (🖉421 9067; Calle 14 No 3-05)

Litera-Te (🖉317 273 2862; Calle 20 No 3B-24) Foreign book exchange featuring books in 18 different languages.

Mojito Net (🖉421 9149; Calle 14 1B-61; per hr COP$1000-2000; ⊗9am-2am) This is a nice air-conditioned spot for surfing the internet and sipping a cocktail.

Policía Nacional (🖉421 9561; Carrera 2 No 17A-38)

❶ **Getting There & Away**

Taganga is easily accessible; there are frequent minibuses (COP$1200, 15 minutes) from Carrera 1C and Carrera 5 in Santa Marta. A taxi costs COP$10,000. You can also head to Cabo San Juan de la Guía in Parque Nacional Natural (PNN) Tayrona by boat each day at around 10am for COP$40,000. It takes an hour and boats leave from the tourist information point.

This was once illegal, but the park authorities now permit it and charge admission to the park (COP$35,000) right on the beach – a great, and painless, beach-hopping way to arrive.

Palomino

🖉5 / POP 4000

Hiding 500m from the main highway connecting Santa Marta with Riohacha is one of Colombia's most perfect beaches, where there are a number of great places to stay ranging from boutique hotels to simple campsites.

If you're not looking for the party vibe and hedonism of Taganga, Palomino delivers perfect peace, great food and pristine white beaches at affordable prices. Previously riven by paramilitary action and general criminality, Palomino is now safe and many new hotels have opened.

Palomino lies between the San Salvador and Palomino Rivers that flow from the Sierra Nevada de Santa Marta, and along its beaches you'll find Wayuu indigenous fishermen using traditional nets, a backbreaking system of fishing that can often result in no dinner for the struggling workers – or a crazy bonanza that ends in a free-for-all as every man tries to take his share.

It's calm, clean and so peaceful that the highlights of a day at Palomino are sunrise, sunset, and watching a passing flock of pelicans. That's your lot, and it's everything you want from a Caribbean beach, and nothing more. To get here, take the Mamatoco bus from the market in Santa Marta (COP$7000, 1½ hours) and jump out at the gas station, walking down to the beach or grabbing a mototaxi to drive you the 500m to the beach (COP$2000). Buses and bikes run all day and until late at night.

🛏 **Sleeping**

La Casa De Rosa CAMPGROUND $
(🖉315 445 9531; campsite COP$6000, tent COP$8000) If you come traveling to escape the rigors, crowds and stresses of modern urban life, you've just hit the jackpot. This is the simplest campsite on the coast, with bucket showers drawn from a well. The two twinkly-eyed sisters, Milena and Paolina, are sweeter than *panela* and will make you supper if you order in the morning. If Milena *really* likes you she might kill you a cockerel.

Finca Escondida CABIN $
(🖉320 560 8280; dm COP$25,000, r per person COP$50,000) A very chilled-out German

CARIBBEAN COAST PALOMINO

biker runs this well-built set of rooms and wooden cabins set in grounds with dozens of fruit trees. The attached restaurant, with heliconia on each table, does a fabulously fresh red snapper (COP$12,000) served with a sincere smile and ice-cold beers.

TOP CHOICE **Reserva Natural El Matuy**   CABIN $$
(☑315 751 8456; reservas@agroecotur.org; cabañas per person full board COP$150,000) There are six simple and very well-decorated cabañas here, with embroidered bedspreads, outdoor bathrooms and showers, and porches with hammocks. Light is from candles only. You have to reserve, and the cost includes three (amazing) meals.

La Sirena   CABIN $
(☑312 861 4850; ecosirena.com; cabañas from COP$45,000) Airy beachside cabins with lots of space and a healthy, holistic vibe. Your chakras will never be better attended, but if the New Age vibe puts you off, dig into the excellent food and juices and lap up the view or drift away to the sound of waves.

Hukumeizi   HOTEL $$
(☑315 354 7871; hukumeizi@gmail.com; cabañas with full board COP$180,000 per person) Fluttering white curtains lead the way into vast, minimally decorated rooms that look as pristine as a space station. The beds are vast, showers are ultramodern, and even the beachside sofas are shaded. It's popular with families and super-chilled Colombians.

Parque Nacional Natural (PNN) Tayrona

One of Colombia's most popular national parks, Tayrona grips the Caribbean coast in a jungly bear hug at the foot of the Sierra Nevada de Santa Marta. The park stretches along the coast from the Bahía de Taganga near Santa Marta to the mouth of the Río Piedras, 35km to the east, and covers some 12,000 hectares of land and 3000 hectares of sea.

The scenery varies from sandy beaches along the coast in the north to rainforest at an altitude of 900m on the southern limits of the park. The extreme western part is arid, with light-brown hills and xerophytic plant species, such as cacti. The central and eastern parts of the park are wetter and more verdant, largely covered by rainforest. May and June and September to November are the wettest periods. At least 56 endangered species call the park home, but most stay out of sight, deep in the forest.

The region was once the territory of the Tayrona people, and some archeological remains have been found in the park. The most important of these are the ruins of the pre-Hispanic town of Pueblito (called Chairama in the indigenous language), considered to have been one of Tayrona's major settlements. Here the remains of over 500 dwellings were discovered, estimated to have been home to 4000 people at one point in history.

For many travelers (too many in high season), the park's biggest attraction is its beaches, which are set in deep bays and shaded with coconut palms. Vicious currents ensure most are not suitable for swimming, though you can swim and snorkel at a select few. Tayrona beaches are among the most picturesque on Colombia's coast. Some of the beaches are bordered by coral reefs, providing reasonable snorkeling and scuba-diving opportunities. Snorkeling gear is available for rental in the park if you don't bring your own from Santa Marta. Mosquito repellent is essential and be wary of snakes in the area – if you are bitten, Ecohabs (p151) keeps antivenin on hand, though most folks don't know it. Do not let them take you to Santa Marta!

About 95% of Tayrona is privately owned and the park is managed by a concession, Aviatur (p144), which seems to do a very good job of building luxury accommodations, but a poor job of maintaining trails.

One important thing to keep in mind: high season nowadays attracts such an influx of tourists that the park's visitor capacities are often ignored. At Cabo San Juan de la Guía in December 2010, the three flush toilets had to be shared between 400 people that had been admitted. The army was called in to make sure no more people could enter. Many travelers complain of overcrowding, poorly maintained trails, dirty bathrooms, and exhausting waits for food and services. Do consider limiting your visit here to the low season (February to November), or be prepared for the possibility that much of Tayrona's undeniably world-class charms may be lost in the crowds.

⊙ Sights

Tayrona's eastern part features most of the park's attractions and tourist facilities, and is by far the most popular and visited area of the park. Its main gateway is **El Zaíno**, 34km east of Santa Marta on the coastal road to Riohacha, where you pay the COP$35,000 park admission fee (Colombians pay COP$13,000). The military does a very thorough search at the main gate of all who enter, checking for drugs and drinks in glass bottles. Unofficial tour guides gather here; they charge considerably less than Aviatur's official guides (COP$100,000 vs COP$122,000 for Pueblito, for example), though guides really aren't necessary if you plan on keeping to the main tourist routes.

From El Zaíno, a 4km paved side road goes northwest to **Castilletes**, the longest beach in the park and the first place you can turn in for the night. A van plies the route constantly and charges just COP$2000.

A few more kilometers down the road is **Cañaveral**, also on the seaside. Here there is a campground, upscale cabañas and a restaurant. The beaches in Cañaveral are good, but there is no shade, and swimming can be dangerous because of treacherous offshore currents. Each year, four or five tourists drown here. If you don't want to continue walking, horses are available to Arrecifes (COP$16,000 one way).

From Cañaveral, most visitors take a 45-minute walk west along a trail to **Arrecifes**, where there are budget lodging and eating facilities – nowadays these are the best value and best managed in the park. Bear in mind that sea currents here are just as dangerous as those in Cañaveral, although decent, safe beaches are found nearby.

From Arrecifes, a 10-minute walk will take you to **La Aranilla**, a gorgeous, tiny cove framed by massive boulders, with chunky sand and glints of fool's gold dancing in the water. A 20-minute walk northwest along the beach will bring you to **La Piscina**, a deep bay with quiet waters, making it reasonably safe for swimming and snorkeling.

Another 20-minute walk by path will take you to **Cabo San Juan de la Guía**, a beautiful cape with a great beach, and by far the most crowded area of the park.

Not many people know of the two other beaches on the 20-minute walk between La Piscina and Cabo – both **Playa Del Puerto** and **Playa Caiman** are beautiful and offer some respite from the Cabo madness. Wander through the wood towards the sea, dodge the land crabs, and you'll find them yourself.

From the cape, a scenic path goes inland uphill to **Pueblito**, providing some splendid tropical-forest scenery. It will get you to Pueblito in a bit more than an hour, but this path is definitely more challenging than others in the park – the majority of the uphill climb is over stones, some of them massive. It is not an easy trail and you can forget about it when it rains or if you have a large pack.

Not much of Pueblito's urban tissue has survived, apart from small fragments of the stone paths and foundations of houses, but it's worth seeing, especially if you aren't planning a trip to Ciudad Perdida.

From Pueblito, a path continues southwest to Calabazo on the main road. After five minutes, the path splits to the right down to **Playa Brava**.

🛏 Sleeping & Eating

Castilletes is the first point reached after El Zaino, and offers peaceful camping with sea views. Cañaveral is favored by the well-to-do; Arrecifes is mainly popular with families and those wanting peace and quiet and clean bathrooms, while Cabo San Juan de la Guía is the most popular spot with backpackers.

Accommodations in Cabo San Juan de la Guia are not recommended; walk the 20 minutes to Arrecifes instead.

CASTILLETES

Camping Castilletes   CAMPGROUND $
(☑313 653 1830; campsite/tent per person COP$12,000/24,000) This campground sits on 1.5km of beach that is also the park's most popular spot for sea-turtle nesting. The beach is swimmable in September and October (other months are only safe for advanced swimmers). It's a good choice if you want to dump your bags and crash out. Its position, near the main entry to the park, makes it a good choice if you want to avoid the poorly maintained trails, which can be knee-deep in mud in the rainy season.

CAÑAVERAL

Ecohabs   CABIN $$$
(☑344 2748; www.concesionesparquesnaturales. com; cabins COP$550,000;☏) This colony of cabañas is operated by the park's concession and feature small LCD televisions with Directv, L'Occitane bath products and some spectacular views. They are made in the style of Tayrona huts and are peppered about a coastal hill. Cabins sleep two to four

Parque Nacional Natural Tayrona

people. Rates rise in the tourist season by about 20%. Another larger cabin at the foot of the hill houses a restaurant. It's by far the nicest spot to stay, but it's overpriced.

Campsite CAMPGROUND $
(campsite per person COP$14,000) The Eco-habs concession also runs this campground, but it's right next door to the horse stables, so you won't be taking in any tropical sea breezes. Sites here can be booked at Aviatur's offices in Santa Marta (p144). You can also book through the office in Bogotá (p69).

ARRECIFES

Camping Don Pedro CAMPGROUND $
(☑315 320 8001; campingdonpedro@gmail. com; hammocks COP$10,000, campsite per person COP$8000, tent COP$12,000, cabañas COP$80,000) Of the three places to stay and eat in Arrecifes, this is the best. It's reached via a 300m split off the main trail just before Arrecifes. The spacious grounds are well maintained and have an abundance of fruit trees. Cooking facilities are available to guests, while excellent meals, including superb fresh fish, cost an average COP$12,000.

Yuluka CAMPGROUND $
(☑3442748; www.aviatur.com/concesionesparques naturales.com; hammocks COP$20,000, campsite per person COP$11,500, cabañas incl breakfast from COP$351,500) This is by far the best option for campers. The bathrooms here are five-star, right out of a boutique hotel. The cabins, which hold up to five people, are similar in quality to Ecohab's but without the sea views. The restaurant serves gourmet

meals (three courses from COP$20,000) like shrimp brochettes grilled with onions and paprika.

Finca El Paraíso CAMPGROUND $
(☑317 312 1945, in Santa Marta 431 3130; campsites COP$10,000, hammocks COP$13,000, tents 2-/4-/6-people COP$25,300/30,500/50,000, cabins from COP$120,000) The closest campground to the beach, El Paraíso has a fresh juice stand, lockers for personal belongings and a restaurant (mains COP$17,000 to COP$50,000) with a nice beach view. Best to call the Santa Marta office number, as signal can be patchy.

Bucarú CAMPGROUND $
(☑in Santa Marta 431 3130) A 10-minute walk further west along the beach is an offspring of El Paraíso. It offers similar facilities for marginally less money (and comfort). Both Finca El Paraíso and Bucarú can be booked through their Santa Marta office (Carrera 7B No 28A-103), or you could just turn up.

CABO SAN JUAN DE LA GUÍA

Camping Cabo San Juan de la Guía CAMPGROUND $
(campsite COP$15,000, hammocks COP$20,000, tents per person COP$30,000) Most backpackers end up at this campground (note, there is no landline or signal for cell phones), which rivals those of European festivals in high season. There is a decent beach here as well as a restaurant (mains COP$8000 to COP$30,000). For COP$25,000, you can sleep in the hammocks high atop the *mirador* on the rocks above the beach – it beats listening to the thrum of the generator.

There are also two private double rooms on the top floor of the mirador (COP$100,000). You can rent snorkeling gear here (ask around for Leonard).

LOS NARANJOS

Barlovento
HOTEL $$

(☏313 293 6733; www.barloventotayrona.com; r per person incl meals COP$150,000) The single most beautiful spot to hang your hat in the area – perhaps in all of Colombia – is just outside the park at Playa Los Naranjos. In this spectacular setting, where the Río Piedras bursts out of the Sierra Nevada and empties into the Caribbean, sits an architecturally unique home, clinging to a cliff-face. Barlovento features open-air beds that jut out on a deck over the sea, so the waves crash right under your mattress. The food is simply sensational.

Ciudad Perdida

There is rarely anything more mysterious than the discovery of an ancient abandoned town, and Ciudad Perdida (literally 'Lost City') has lived up to its name for four centuries. Known by its indigenous name of Teyuna, it was built by the Tayrona people on the northern slopes of the Sierra Nevada de Santa Marta, and was most probably their biggest urban center. Today, it's one of the largest pre-Columbian towns discovered in the Americas.

The city was built between the 11th and 14th centuries, though its origins are much older, going back to perhaps the 7th century. Spread over an area of about 2 sq km, it is the largest Tayrona city found so far, and it appears it was their major political and economic center. Some 2000 to 4000 people are believed to have lived here.

During the Conquest, the Spaniards wiped out the Tayronas, and their settlements disappeared without a trace under lush tropical vegetation. So did Ciudad Perdida, until its discovery by *guaqueros* (grave robbers) in the early 1970s. It was a local man, Florentino Sepúlveda, and his two sons Julio César and Jacobo, who stumbled upon this city on one of their grave-robbing expeditions.

Word spread like wildfire and soon other *guaqueros* came to Ciudad Perdida. Fighting broke out between rival gangs, and Julio César was one of the casualties. In 1976 the government sent in troops and archeologists to protect the site and learn its secrets, but sporadic fighting and looting continued for several years. During this time, the *guaqueros* dubbed the site the *Infierno Verde* (Green Hell).

Ciudad Perdida lies on the steep slopes of the upper Río Buritaca valley at an altitude of between 950m and 1300m. The central part of the city is set on a ridge from which various stone paths lead down to other sectors on the slopes. Although the wooden houses of the Tayrona are long gone, the stone structures, including terraces and stairways, remain in remarkably good shape.

There are around 170 terraces, most of which once served as foundations for the houses. The largest terraces are set on the central ridge and these were used for ritual ceremonies. Today, the city is quite overgrown, which gives it a somewhat mysterious air.

Archeological digs have uncovered Tayrona objects (fortunately, the *guaqueros* didn't manage to take everything), mainly various kinds of pottery (both ceremonial and utilitarian), goldwork and unique necklaces made of semiprecious stones. Some of these objects are on display in the Museo del Oro in Santa Marta (p140) and in Bogotá (p48). It's a good idea to visit the museum in Santa Marta before going to Ciudad Perdida.

ᗱ Tours

Previously one agency, Turcol, had sole access to Ciudad Perdida. However in 2008 the Colombian military cleared out the paramilitaries in the area, which has effectively opened up the route to Ciudad Perdida to

THE LOST CIVILIZATION

In pre-Columbian times, the Sierra Nevada de Santa Marta on the Caribbean coast was home to various indigenous communities, of which the Tayrona, belonging to the Chibcha linguistic family, was the dominant and most developed group. The Tayrona (also spelt Tairona) are believed to have evolved into a distinctive culture since about the 5th century AD. A millennium later, shortly before the Spaniards came, the Tayrona had developed into an outstanding civilization, based on a complex social and political organization and advanced engineering.

The Tayronas lived on the northern slopes of the Sierra Nevada where they constructed hundreds of settlements, all of a similar pattern. Due to the rugged topography, a large number of stone terraces supported by high walls had to be built as bases for their thatched wooden houses. Groups of terraces were linked by a network of stone-slab paths and stairways.

Recent surveys have pinpointed the location of about 300 Tayrona settlements scattered over the slopes, once linked by stone-paved roads. Of all these, Ciudad Perdida (Lost City), discovered in 1975, is the largest and is thought to have been the Tayrona 'capital.'

Tayrona was the first advanced indigenous culture encountered by the Spaniards in the New World, in 1499. It was here in the Sierra Nevada that the conquerors were for the first time astonished by the local gold, and the myth of El Dorado was born.

The Spaniards crisscrossed the Sierra Nevada, but met with brave resistance from the indigenous people. The Tayronas defended themselves fiercely, but were almost totally decimated in the course of 75 years of uninterrupted war. A handful of survivors abandoned their homes and fled into the upper reaches of the Sierra. Their traces have been lost forever.

healthy competition. There are now four main agencies, based in Santa Marta or Taganga, guiding groups of travelers on the five- or six-day hike to the ancient ruins. You cannot do the trip on your own or hire an independent guide.

Once the market opened in 2008, the race to the bottom began, and prices and quality fell. The government intervened and regulated prices and service, and the official price of the tour is now set at COP$650,000 – pay any less and the money will be taken from your guide's fees, health insurance or life insurance. Or yours.

The price includes transportation, food, accommodation (hammocks with mosquito nets and mattresses on some nights), porters for your food, non-English speaking guides and all necessary permits.

Be wary of snakes, stinging caterpillars, wasps and other things that go bump in the night. Also – this simply cannot be stressed enough – take the strongest mosquito repellent you can find and reapply it every few hours. Local brand Nopikex contains 21% Deet, and you'd be well advised to stock up on brands containing 50% Deet concentration minimum in countries where it is available – ie *not* Colombia. On our trip one poor soul managed to accumulate 175 bites on just one leg.

Tours are in groups of four to 12 people, and depart year-round as soon as a group is assembled. In the high season, expect a tour to set off every day. In the low season, the four agencies pool resources and form a joint group. Other companies are middlemen for these agencies and there's really no reason to use them.

The Hike

In the rainy season, the trip takes 2½ days uphill to Ciudad Perdida, with a half-day at the site on the third day if the weather holds, then two days back downhill, the round trip covering 40km. In the dry season, the schedule differs slightly, and you may climb to the Ciudad Perdida site on the morning of the fourth day before beginning the return journey downhill. You can also choose to do the trip in six days, in either season. Ask your tour company for a more detailed itinerary.

It is a challenging hike (each day covers five to eight kilometers), but not mercilessly so. If you've never hiked before in your life you'll find it tough, but on our tour even unfit first-timers completed the journey. At times, you will be scrambling alongside vertiginous river banks, clutching on to vines, and most people find a stick helps with balance. Rainy season brings its own horrors, such as surging rivers (one tourist was swept to their death in the heavy rains of 2011), heavy, boot-caking mud and collapsed walkways. It's also worth noting that the camp used by all of the tour agencies on day three is poorly maintained; mosquito nets are damaged, and there were reports of bedbugs from some travelers.

There are significant climbs which can be brutal in the scorching jungle heat. When the sun isn't blazing, it's likely to be muddy, so you'll trade sweat for loose traction. (The driest period is from late December to February or early March.) Depending on the season, on day three you might have to cross the Río Buritaca nine times, at times waist-deep, and finally, you will have to slog up Ciudad Perdida's mystical, moss-strewn rock steps – 1260 of them in total – that lead to the site.

Along the way, the food is surprisingly good and the accommodations are better than expected, and often by rivers where you can cool off in natural swimming pools. The scenery is nothing short of astonishing.

Worth it? Most definitely. The site, a high plateau surrounded by blindingly brilliant jungle, is fascinating and you will likely only be sharing it with your group for at least half a day in the low season.

Please be aware that the mountains are sacred to all the indigenous people that live there; your sensitivity to this is appreciated. This means leaving absolutely no litter, and behaving within the Lost City site as if it were

WHAT TO BRING

We asked 20 people of mixed hiking ability to provide us with a list of essential, or nice-to-have items. These were the top-rated choices.

Must have

☐ Flashlight

☐ Water container

☐ Insect repellent

☐ Sunscreen

☐ Long pants

☐ Two pairs of shoes (strap sandals work best for river crossings)

☐ Water-purifying pills

☐ Ciprofloxacin or Loperamide (antibiotics and anti-diarrhea medicine)

Nice to have

☐ Playing cards

☐ Medicine and bandages for blistered feet

☐ Hiking poles

☐ Sweatband

☐ Peaked cap

☐ Waterproof bag cover

☐ Sweatpants or pyjamas for the evenings

☐ Zip-lock bags to keep stuff dry

☐ Knee brace or support bandage

☐ Towel

☐ Small bag with waist strap

☐ Antihistamine pills to soothe mosquito bites, and cream to treat blisters

☐ Five more pairs of socks

☐ A book for the evenings

☐ Earplugs to drown out fellow walkers' snoring

a church, mosque, or synagogue. Beware, too, that competition between the agencies is still fierce, with all that entails.

Tour Operators

Magic Tours HIKING TOURS
(Map p147; ☑317 679 2441; magictour186@yahoo.com; Calle 14 No 1B-50, Taganga; ☺8am-6pm) This well-run agency is the only one that pays pensions, general health insurance and life insurance for their superbly informed and outstandingly professional guides. The food is excellent, coffee is frequently served, and many of the guides are *from* the mountains (not Santa Marta). There's also an office in Santa Marta (☑421 9429).

ExpoTur HIKING TOURS
(Map p142; ☑420 7739; Calle 17 No. 2-59, Santa Marta; ☺8am-noon & 2-6:30pm) Had English-speaking staff when we visited, monitors email constantly and replies promptly. This agency treats its guides well.

Guias y Baquianos Tours HIKING TOURS
(Map p142; ☑431 9667; guiasbaquianostour@yahoo.es; Calle 10C No 1C-59, Santa Marta; ☺8am-noon & 2-6pm Mon-Sat) Located inside Hotel Miramar, this was the original agency to offer treks to Ciudad Perdida.

Turcol HIKING TOURS
(Map p142; ☑421 2256; www.buritaca2000.com; Carrera 1C No 20-15, Santa Marta) This agency has the most experience on the route since the late '90s. It offers new mosquito nets, decent grub, purified water and its own housing on some nights. Although its employees could be more professional, its guides are just as good as any of the other firms. It has a second office at Calle 10C No C1-83 (Map p142) and a satellite office in front of Casa de Felipe in Taganga (Map p147).

🛈 Getting There & Away

Ciudad Perdida lies about 40km southeast of Santa Marta as the crow flies. It's hidden deep in the thick forest amid rugged mountains, far away from any human settlement, and without access roads. The only way to get there is by foot and a round trip takes five or six days. The trail begins in El Mamey.

LA GUAJIRA PENINSULA

English pirates, Dutch weapons smugglers and Spanish pearl-hunters have all tried to conquer the Guajira Peninsula – a vast swath of barren sea and sand that is Colombia's northernmost point – but none were able to overcome the indigenous Wayuu people, who wisely traded with, or waged war upon, the invaders.

The Wayuu's complex and autonomous political and economic structures meant they were ready to mount a staunch defence of their lands - on horseback and, to the surprise of the Spanish, with firearms.

This is a diesel-and-dust landscape with more than a whiff of lawlessness. Smugglers pile everything from refrigerators to cameras to humans onto buses and trucks from Maicao, near the border with Venezuela, to ship to the rest of Colombia and beyond. And then there's the Wayuu, living autonomously on the edge of the continent in small familial villages known as *rancherías*.

The peninsula is split into three sections: Southern Guajira, home to its capital, Riohacha; Middle Guajira, on the border with Venezuela; and Upper Guajira, where you'll find end-of-the-world paradises like Cabo de la Vela and Punta Gallinas, the latter an immaculate collision of desert and sea that is the Caribbean coast's most remarkable setting.

Riohacha

☑5 / POP 213,000
Riohacha, 175km northeast of Santa Marta, is the gateway to the northern, semiarid desert region, and was traditionally the end of the line. But as ecotourism in the peninsula has developed in recent years, you might find yourself spending the night here on the way to or from more isolated and beautiful parts of Colombia. The town isn't teeming with things to do, but there's a 5km-long beach strewn with palm trees, and the long pier, constructed in 1937, makes for a lovely evening stroll.

🔾 Sights & Activities

From the highway from Santa Marta, Carrera 15 is the main commercial thoroughfare through town, turning into the beachfront Carrera 1 as it turns east and parallels the beach across the center of the city. Riohacha's main plaza, Parque José Prudencio Padilla, sits two blocks inland between Carreras 7 and 9.

The 1.2km-long **walking pier**, constructed in 1937, is an impressive piece of maritime architecture. On weekend evenings, the **malecón** (boardwalk) and its parallel street, Carrera 1, fill with revelers taking in the waterfront restaurants and bars. Unless it's raining, you'll find Wayuu women in traditional clothing, selling handicrafts.

The town's leafy main square, **Parque José Prudencio Padilla**, set two blocks back from the beach, brings a welcome escape from the blistering sun. The **Cathedral de Nuestra Señora de los Remedios**, with a venerated image of the Virgin on its high altar since colonial times, is also here.

The main attraction around Riohacha itself is a trip out to the **Santuario de Flora y Fauna Los Flamencos**, a 700-hectare nature preserve 25km from town in Camarones, which you'll pass if you're arriving here from Santa Marta. Pink flamingos inhabit this tranquil area in great numbers: up to 10,000 in the wet season (September through to December), and bunches of up to 2000 can usually be seen in one of the four lagoons within the park.

Admission to the park is free, but if you want to see the flamingos, you'll need to take a canoe (one to three people COP$30,000, per person extra COP$15,000) out on the water. The skippers usually know where the birds are hanging out, but will not take you if they are beyond a reasonable distance. Be warned – if it's not flamingo season, this is a dull, dull day trip.

🛏 Sleeping & Eating

El Castillo del Mar　　　　　HOTEL **$$**
(☎727 5043; hotelcastillodelmar@gmail.com; Calle 9A No 15-352; cabañas with fan per person COP$25,000, s/d with air-con COP$60,000/90,000; ❄🛜) It looks a little fortresslike, but inside, this German-owned hotel is a colorful and curious spot. Whitewashed cabañas are large and comfortable, and there's plenty of bougainvillea scattered about the property. It's the best value in town.

Mi Casona　　　　　　　　　HOTEL **$$**
(☎728 5680; Calle 2 No 10-16; s/d COP$60,000/ 70,000; ❄) This is the cheapest livable option near the beach in *centro* – and it's still massively overpriced. It's a small *residenciales* with well-maintained rooms and nice bathrooms.

La Cascada　　　　　　　COLOMBIAN **$$**
(☎727 4446; Calle 2 No 9-93; mains COP$10,000-29,000; ⊗breakfast, lunch & dinner) A local's joint serving simple *comida corriente* for

COP$9000 and fancier dishes like chicken with mandarin sauce. They do mean – and massive – frappés, too.

Asadero Don Pepe　　　　　　GRILL **$**
(☎727 4446; Calle 1 cnr Carrera 10; mains COP$6000-12,000; ⊗dinner) Pepe serves up hunks of grilled meat over coals with huge sides of potato and salad on the main drag. It's Wayuu-owned, and the goat is particularly good.

Donde Aurora　　　　　COLOMBIAN **$**
(Carrera 8 btwn No 23-24; mains COP$8000; ⊗6:30-9:30pm) If you want to try friche, the Wayuu delicacy of goat stewed in its own blood and guts, take a cab here – but beware, they sell out by 7pm most nights. It's a tin-roofed shack with no sign, no name, no number, and no menus, the tables are plastic and the toilet (for men) is a patch of wall. But the food is fantastic – and you'll eat until you have hiccups.

ℹ Information
4-72 (☎727 3853; Calle 2 No 06-46 ⊗8am-5pm Mon-Fri) Postal services.
Banco AV Villas (Carrera 7 No 03-16) Has an ATM.
Electrocomputer (☎727 3101; Calle 2 No 9-62; per hr COP$1500; ⊗7am-8pm Mon-Sat) Internet cafe with a 4-meg connection.
Hospital (☎727 3312; Av de los Estudiantes)
Kaí Ecotravel (☎311 436 2830; www.kai ecotravel.com) This excellent agency opened La Guajira to ecotourism and has spent years fostering relationships with the Wayuu, allowing access to Punta Gallinas and Parque Nacional Natural (PNN) Macuira, both Wayuu-controlled. They are the best source for tours on the peninsula as well as homestays with indigenous families, and offer transportation-only deals to Cabo de la Vela if they have spare seats.
Policía de la Guajira (☎727 3879; cnr Calle 15 & Carrera 7)
Tourist office (☎727 1015; Carrera 1 No 4-42; ⊗8am-noon & 2-6pm Mon-Fri)

ℹ Getting There & Away
Air
The airport is 3km southwest of town. A taxi costs COP$5000 from town. **Avianca** (☎727 3627; www.avianca.com; Calle 7 No 7-04; ⊗8am-6pm Mon-Fri, 9am-1pm Sat) operates one flight in and out per day to Bogotá, departing at 12:35pm (from COP$323,000 one way). From Bogotá, the flight leaves for Riohacha at 10:30am.

Bus

The bus terminal is at the corner of Av El Progreso and Carrera 11, about 1km from the center. A taxi to the bus station is COP\$5000. **Expreso Brasilia/Unitransco** (✆727 2240) services Santa Marta (COP\$15,000, 2½ hours) and Barranquilla (COP\$25,000, five hours) every 30 minutes; Cartagena (COP\$35,000, seven hours) and Maicao (COP\$5000, one hour), on the border with Venezuela, hourly; and Bogotá (COP\$90,000, 18 hours) once daily at 3pm.

Coopetran (✆313 333 5707) heads to Bucaramanga twice daily at 8am and 3:30pm (COP\$80,000; 12 hours). Buses to Valledupar are at 8am, 3pm and 3:30pm (COP\$20,000, 3½ hours).

To reach Cabo de la Vela, **Cootrauri** (✆728 0000; Calle 15 No 5-39) runs *colectivos* as they fill up every day from 5am to 6pm to Uribia (COP\$12,000, one hour), where you must switch for the final leg to Cabo (COP\$10,000 to COP\$15,000, 2½ hours). Just let the driver know you are heading to Cabo and he will drop you off at the switch point. The last car for Cabo de La Vela leaves Urribia at 1pm. Private rides to Cabo are available and will take you and three friends there and back in a day, rushing through the highlights at break-neck speed, which kind of misses the point (COP\$400,000, haggle and you might get it for less). You can also hitch a lift with **Kaí Ecotravel** (✆311 436 2830), for COP\$50,000 if they have a spare seat; they depart daily.

To visit Santuario de Fauna y Flora Los Flamencos, you must catch a *colectivo* from the Francisco El Hombre traffic circle, next to Almacen 16 de Julio, bound for the town of Camarones. The driver will drop you at the entrance to the park.

Buses bound for Caracas (COP\$175,000, 18 hours) also depart daily from Riohacha, with Expreso Brasilia leaving at 4pm.

Cabo de la Vela

✆5 / POP 1500

The remote Wayuu fishing village of Cabo de la Vela, 180km northwest of Riohacha, juts out from the Guajira Peninsula like the hump of a long-lost camel, wandering in the desert between the cape and Urribia. The village itself is little more than a dusty rural community of Wayuu, living in traditional huts made from cactus that ride right up against the sea. But the surrounding area is a highlight of the Upper Guajira and one of the most starkly beautiful spots in Colombia. The cape for which it's named is full of rocky cliffs above and sandy beaches below, all set against a backdrop of stunning desert ochres and aquamarines.

The village has electricity by generator only and there are few fixed phone lines, internet or any of life's other distractions. In the last couple of years, Cabo has become a hotbed of ecotourism and now boasts a wealth of indigenous-style accommodations.

Cabo de la Vela is not for everyone – you are definitely off the grid here. It's not uncommon to see Wayuu men toting large rifles, or a goat-slaughtering in someone's living room. But for a certain kind of traveler – you know who you are – Cabo is the sort of place in which you can lose yourself indefinitely.

If you're looking for peace, Cabo is best avoided around Easter, December and January, when Colombians arrive to party.

◉ Sights & Activities

Wayuu and tourists alike head to **El Faro**, a small light-tower on the edge of a rocky promontory, for postcard-perfect sunsets. The view is indeed stunning – just watch out for *langosta,* massive flying locust-type insects, the size of model airplanes, which look a bit like lobsters. It's a 45-minute walk from town, or you can wrangle a ride with a local for COP\$30,000 or so for a round trip. Take plenty of water, insect repellent and a hat.

Just beyond El Faro is **Ojo del Agua**, a nicely sized crescent-shaped dark-sand beach bound by 5m-high cliffs. The beach gets its name from a small freshwater pool that was discovered here, a deeply sacred site for Wayuu.

But the jewel of the area is **Playa del Pilón**, far and away the most beautiful beach in Cabo. Here you'll find a startling rust-orange collection of sand backed by craggy cliffs that glow a spectacular shade of greenish-blue, especially at sunrise and sunset. In wet season, add in lush desert flora and fauna to the mix and the whole scene is rather cinematic (though in high season, you must add in 1000 tourists on the small beach and a few kitesurfers). **Pilón de Azucar**, a 100m hillside, looms over the beach and provides the area's most picturesque viewpoint, the whole of Alta Guajira displayed before you with the Serranía del Carpintero mountain range in the distance. Picture a tropical beach on the rocky coast of Ireland and you have an idea of the scene here. A statue of **La Virgen de Fátima**, erected here in 1938 by Spanish pearl-hunters, stands at the top of the viewpoint as the patron saint of Cabo.

🛏 Sleeping & Eating

There are over 60 rustic **Posadas Turísticas de Colombia** (www.posadasturisticasde colombia.com) in Cabo de la Vela, part of a government-sponsored ecotourism project. Lodging is generally in Wayuu huts fashioned from *yotojoro,* the inner core of the *cardon* cactus that grows in the desert here. You can choose between smaller hammocks, larger and warmer traditional Wayuu *chinchorros* (locally crafted hammocks) or beds with private bathrooms (though running water is scarce). Bring your own towel. Nearly all posadas double as restaurants, more or less serving the same thing – fish or goat in the COP$10,000 to COP$15,000 range and market-price lobster.

Pujuru Hostal-Restaurant   GUESTHOUSE $
(📱310 659 4189; www.pujuru.com; hammocks COP$10,000, chinchorros COP$15,000, s/d COP$25,000/50,000) Run by an attentive Wayuu woman named Nena, this *posada ecoturística* offers well-constructed huts for private rooms, and luggage lockers for those in hammocks. The generators run from 6pm to 10pm and the restaurant (mains COP$10,000 to COP$15,000) serves up a tasty *pargo rojo* (red snapper), though the shrimp and rice is greasy and best avoided. Showers are bucket style.

Hostería Jarrinapi   GUESTHOUSE $
(📱311 683 4281; hammocks COP$10,000, r per person COP$30,000) A little fancier on the infrastructure hierarchy, these huts, complete with a front desk and running water, feel almost like an actual hotel. The generators pump all night – meaning your fan whirs and you sleep. The restaurant (mains COP$5000 to COP$35,000) does the usual suspects, but also cheaper fast food, too.

Refugio Pantu   GUESTHOUSE $
(📱313 581 0858; chinchorro per person COP$20,000, r per person COP$30,000) If you want to trade solitude for beach, this posada sits north of town, the last one in a long line that extends toward El Faro. Its restaurant and cabanãs are *yorotoro chic,* a step up in construction with liberal use of stone, and hotel-grade bathrooms. President Uribe even slept here in 2005. It's a hike to town and the beach here isn't pretty or sandy.

ℹ Getting There & Away

Arriving in Cabo de la Vela is not the easiest trip you'll make in Colombia, so most folks come on an organized tour – **Kai Ecotravel** (www. kaiecotravel.com) is a good bet. That said, it's possible to come on your own, and all the more rewarding. From Riohacha, you must catch a *colectivo* at **Cootrauri** (📱728 0976; Calle 15 No 5-39) to Urribia; it will depart as it fills up every day from 5am to 6pm (COP$12,000, one hour). The driver will let you out in front of Panaderia Peter-Pan, from where trucks and 4WDs leave for Cabo (COP$10,000 to COP$15,000, 2½ hours). Non-4WD vehicles are a definite no-go.

Punta Gallinas

Punta Gallinas is a beautiful illustration of one of life's simplest lessons: the greater the effort, the greater the reward. Those who make the (considerable) push to get here will be rewarded with one of the most dazzling landscapes in South America.

Located approximately 75km north of Cabo de la Vela, Punta Gallinas is accessed via Bahía Hondita, where burnt-orange cliffs surround an emerald bay with a wide and wild beach. There is absolutely nothing here except a large colony of pink flamingos. The bay is home to just eight Wayuu families numbering about 60 people. The land they call home is spectacular: a feral desertscape peppered with vibrant green vegetation (in winter). It attracts herds of goat and is buzzing with swarms of massive locusts.

As the continent gives way to the Caribbean, massive sand dunes toppling 60m in height push right up against the shimmering turquoise sea like a five-story sand tsunami in reverse. This is **Playa Taroa**, Colombia's most beautiful and least trampled-upon beach, accessed by sliding down a towering sand dune right into the water. It's startlingly untouched, with a wondrous sense of isolation so all-enveloping you'll either want to whoop and cackle out loud or sit, silently, for a very long time.

As you walk back through the desert at dusk, check out the ancient smashed ceramic pots and the rubbish piles of burnt conches – evidence of simple dinners eaten round campfires thousands of years ago.

There's one accommodation choice, booked through the tour companies named on p160. It does great food, including succulent grilled lobster, and staff can help show you around the desert.

There is virtually no way to reach Punta Gallinas without the help of an organized tour. Although the area only recently became accessible to foreign travelers, annual visitor numbers doubled from 1500 in 2008 to 3000 in 2011.

From September to November, access is by three-hour boat ride from Puerto Bolívar, a short drive from Cabo de la Vela near the El Cerrejón coal mine. The rest of the year, vehicles can reach Bahía Honda, the first of the three side-by-side bays in the area, where a one-hour boat ride lands you in Punta Gallinas. Contact Aventure Colombia (p131) in Cartagena or Kaí Ecotravel (p157) in Riohacha to make the trip; the latter is an ecotourism pioneer in the area.

VALLEDUPAR

Lying in the long, fertile valley formed by the Sierra Nevada de Santa Marta to the east, and Venezuela's Serrania del Perija to the west, is Valledupar. Valledupar has remained off the traveler radar as it's not a hugely touristic town, and was landlocked during the darker days of the Colombia civil conflict, with the town held virtual hostage by the guerrillas that controlled the mountains.

Those days have passed now, and the town has a lot to recommend it, with a small, well-preserved colonial center, some great outdoors activities nearby and a bustling nightlife that punches above its weight.

This is cattle-and-cowboy country, and in some ways it could be claimed to be the cultural heart of Colombia. Valledupar is mythologized and venerated by Colombians as the birthplace and cradle, the nursery and university of vallenato, the coast's ubiquitous, manic, accordion-driven folk music that sings of love, politics, and the pain of losing your woman (or horse) to another man.

The town is not yet swamped by tourists, which can mean that travel arrangements are improvised and can be uncertain – but this is part of the city's charm.

The city's Festival de la Leyenda Vallenata, held each April, is a four-day orgy of vallenato and Old Parr whiskey – the favored tipple here. They love it so much locals call the town Valle De Old Parr. Room prices quadruple – and book out a year in advance.

● Sights & Activities

Valledupar is a place to chill out, relax and recharge. It makes a great stop if you're completing a circuit around Santa Marta, La Guajira Peninsula and onwards to Aracataca.

 **Balneario La Mina**   SWIMMING
The Río Badillo carves a bizarre, brainlike path through the riverbed down from the Sierra Nevada to make this a great swimming hole. Take plenty of strong insect repellent and beware the surging currents in wetter months. Take a colectivo from Carrera 6 in the center of town to Atanquez and jump out at La Mina (45 minutes, COP$6500); service runs from 11am to 2pm. The return is trickier, but can be made on mototaxi for COP$10,000. You must leave before 4pm to ensure your return, locals say.

There's a really worthwhile women's cooperative here, run by Maria Martinez, who everyone calls La Maye. All proceeds benefit local women who lost their husbands and sons in the years of conflict, and the woven bags are of very high quality. She also serves a cheap (COP$10,000) fantastic *sancocho de gallina,* or cockerel stew, cooked over a wooden fire and served in the yard of her simple home.

Balneario Hurtado   SWIMMING
On Sundays and holidays, the vallenatos come here to bathe in the Río Guatapurí, cook and socialise. There are a few simple restaurants and wandering snack vendors, and all in all it's a super-chilled family day out. It lies alongside the Parque Lineal; buses head there from Cinco Esquinas in the centre of town.

🛌 Sleeping & Eating

Provincia Hostel   HOSTEL $
(☑580 0558; Calle 16A No 5-25; dm COP$18,000; s/d with fan COP$40,000/45,000, with air-con COP$45,000/50,000; 🛜) Hands-down the number-one place to stay – whatever your budget. It's social without being rowdy, quiet without being boring, and the owners are so good at giving tourism information that the local town council sends all foreigners here as they know more than the officials. The owners can suggest great day trips. Rooms are better than any hotel in town. Bicycle rental available.

Parrillada El Joe   GRILL $$
(☑574 9787; Calle 16A No 11-40; mains COP$19,500-40,000; ⏱lunch & dinner) A Valledupar institution, with the mixed grill the star attraction. The mixed grill is big enough for two and features a mountain of flesh for the price – though you may want to get them to hold the *ubre,* or udder, which even for fanatical omnivores may be a step too far.

'ROCK STAR? I'D RATHER PLAY THE ACCORDION'

Andres 'Turco' Gil, an accordionist of such virtuosity that he is know as 'El Maestro,' runs an academy for budding players in a suburb of Valledupar, and behind the unassuming exterior you'll find an atmosphere of dedication and devotion as dozens of young hopefuls desperately learn to play the squeezebox. El Maestro invites children from poor backgrounds, often displaced by the civil conflict, to study for free at his school, and encourages them to realize their dreams. The school has no government funding, but that hasn't stopped its students from going on to perform all over the world, including gigs at the White House (Bill Clinton was a huge fan).

While many foreigners find it hard to connect to the music, which combines the scratchy rhythms of the *guacharaca,* the pounding of the *caja vallenata* drum and the bellowed lyrics, dig deeper and you'll find there's more to it than meets the ear: it's a fascinating, even political mode of cultural expression and is loved by nearly all Colombians.

The instruments show the fusion of three cultures: the drum from enslaved Africans, the *guacharaca* from the indigenous Kogi people, and the accordion from the European newcomers. At the start of the century before the postal service was established, vallenatos, as the songs are called, were even used as a way to send messages from one village to another. To witness the passion of El Maestro's students, such as a young blind player named Juan David Atencia, is inspiring. You'll find the school at Calle 31, No 04-265, a COP$7000 cab ride from town, or ask at Provincia Hostel for details on how to offer your services as a volunteer there.

Compae Chipuco COLOMBIAN **$**
(☑311 40 4078; Calle 16 No 6-05; mains COP$7000; ☺lunch) Sit under the massive mango tree and chow down on a seriously good *corriente* (set lunch), including fish, meat and chicken options every day. Whipcracking service, hearty food and simple flavors.

El Varadero CUBAN **$$**
(☑570 6175; Calle 12 No 6-56; mains COP$20,000-32,000, ☺lunch & dinner) Cuban seafood is the fare in this chain restaurant, but it is very good seafood indeed. The lobster salad to start is great, as are the garlic mussels. And just to complete the continent-hopping menu, try the seafood Al Macho, served Peruvian style with yellow peppers. Skip the pasta unless you're an incredibly homesick Italian.

☆ Entertainment

Parque Lineal MUSIC
The biggest party in town is the Parque Lineal, where locals park their cars, throw open the doors ad blast salsa and vallenato from their booming sound systems. Couples dance and smooch, friends hang out and drink and macho dudes compete for the loudest, most ridiculously hardcore system. Some even run laser shows from the boot of their Prados; strobes and smoke machines have been reported on extra-special nights. Strangers are more than welcome (just take a bottle of Old Parr whiskey along) and you don't need a car – any cab can take you there for COP$4000. That's how Valledupar rolls.

La Iguana CLUB
(Carrera 9 No 10-44, Barrio Novalito; admission free; ☺ 9pm-4am Wed-Sat) It's a one-room box with a sound system at one end and air-con set to stun an elephant, full of friendly and very drunk locals who stand in baffled silence until the vallenato starts up. Then they whoop, holler, drink, and grab the nearest single person near them and get down and dirty. Huge fun – even if you do have to wear a shirt to get in. If this doesn't appeal, there's plenty more options a small stagger away.

ⓘ Getting There & Away

The bus station is 30 minutes in a taxi (COP$4000) from the center; there are no buses. **Coopetran** (☑571 6205) serves Villavicencio to and from Riohacha (COP$20,000, three hours), Santa Marta (COP$22,000, two hours), Cartagena (COP$25,000, 5½ hours), Barranquilla (COP$25,000, 4½ hours), Medellín (COP$90,000, 12 hours) and Bucaramanga (COP$60,000, eight hours).

SOUTHWEST OF CARTAGENA

Unspoiled beaches and the road less traveled characterize the Caribbean coast southwest of Cartagena, an area that, due to security concerns, has seen little international tourism in the last two decades. Secure and at the ready these days, areas like Tolú and the Islas de San Bernardo, which previously catered to Colombians only, are now wide open for foreign exploration.

There is quite a notable change in the landscape here from the northern coast through the departments of Sucre, Córdoba, Antioquia and Chocó. Swampy pasturelands dotted with billowing tropical ceiba trees, ground-strangling mangrove trees and crystalline lagoons flank the seaside around the Golfo de Morrosquillo, while the jungle near the Darién Gap rides right up against cerulean waters and beaches where the Golfo de Urabá gives way to Panama near the serene villages of Capurganá and Sapzurro.

Tolú

⏺5 / POP 48,000

You'd never know it, but the tranquil pueblo of Tolú, the capital of the Golfo de Morrosquillo, is one of Colombia's most visited tourist destinations. Colombians flock here throughout the high season for its small-town feel, surrounding beaches and natural playground, but there's rarely a foreigner in sight. The rest of the year, it's a fun spot to get off the gringo trail and holiday like the locals. Tolú is a small town where residents choose bicycles over vehicles, and bicycle taxis, known as *bicitaxis,* are an art form: each one decked out with individual personality and flair – and massive, cranked-up speakers playing salsa and reggaeton.

Tolú's lengthy *malecón,* full of seaside bars, restaurants and small artesan stalls, makes for a fun stroll, but the main draw for foreign tourists is its proximity to Islas de San Bernardo, part of Parque Nacional Natural (PNN) Corales del Rosario y San Bernardo. Here the picturesque beaches on Isla Múcura, wrought with mangroves and postcard-perfect palm trees, are some of the coast's most idyllic.

◉ Sights & Activities

Tolú is the main jumping-off point for day tours to Islas de San Bernardo (p163). In high season, the town swells with Colombian tourists who come to eat and drink along the coast of the Golfo de Morrosquillo, which runs from here to Coveñas. In Coveñas there is less infrastructure but better beaches, many of which are dotted with thatched-roof tables fit for drinking an afternoon away.

For a bit of nature, the wonderful **La Ciénega de Caimanera** sits halfway between Tolú and Coveñas. This 1800-hectare nature preserve is a part-freshwater, part-saltwater bog with five varieties of mangroves. The red mangrove's roots twist and tangle in and out of the water like hyperactive strands of spaghetti. The canoe trip here is a pleasant and beautiful way to live an hour and a half of your life, meandering through artificial mangrove tunnels and sampling oysters right off the roots.

To reach the Ciénega, grab any bus (COP$2000) heading toward Coveñas and ask to be let off at La Boca de la Ciénega. Canoe guides wait for tourists on the bridge, and charge COP$20,000 for one to two people and as little as COP$8000 per person for larger groups.

Tolú's beaches aren't up to much – head 20km south to Coveñas for more agreeable patches of sand. **Playa Blanca** is accessed via moto-taxi from Coveñas. *Colectivos* depart every 10 minutes daily (COP$2500) from near Supermercado Popular at the corner of Carrera 2 and Calle 17 in Tolú. Or go for **Punta Bolivar**, five minutes away from Coveñas by moto-taxi (COP$4000).

🛏 Sleeping

Villa Babilla   HOSTEL $

(📞312 677 1325; www.villababillahostel.com; Calle 20 No 3-40; s/d from COP$30,000/40,000; 🛜) Three blocks from the waterfront, this German-run hostel/hotel offers a gringo-friendly space highlighted by its thatched-roof outdoor TV lounge. There's a kitchen, laundry service and free coffee all day. There's no sign outside but it's the tallest building on the block.

Ibatama del Mar   HOTEL $

(📞288 5110; Carrera 1 No 19-45; s/d with fan COP$20,000/30,000, with air-con COP$40,000/60,000) This decent midrange option on the waterfront offers an interesting courtyard full of old cannons, statues and various mini-gardens.

El Velero   HOSTEL $$

(📞312 658 0129/286 0058; Carrera 1 No 9-26; s/d COP$45,000/70,000; ❄) This second waterfront option is newer, cleaner and much better value than Ibatama del Mar. All rooms have a TV, fridge and sparkling bathroom.

✖ Eating & Drinking

Terraza La 15   SEAFOOD $
(☑288 6226; cnr Carrera 1 & Calle 15; mains
COP$10,000-32,000; ☺breakfast, lunch & dinner)
Simple fried fish served on the seafront,
with other options like a decent *cazuela*,
and service sunnier than a Caribbean dawn.

La Red   SEAFOOD $$
(☑314 501 4631; cnr Calle 20 & Carrera 2; mains
COP$7000-25,000; ☺breakfast, lunch & dinner)
Skip the ceviche, which has seen better
days, and head for the red snapper in gar-
lic and butter – it was swimming offshore a
few hours earlier. Service could most kindly
be described as leisurely, while the decor is
tortoise-shell chic.

The **Casino de Comida** at Calle 20 and
Carrera 1 on the waterfront offer cheap
costeño dishes of meat and fish for around
COP$7000. Around the central **Plaza** there's
a few bakeries for snacks. Do *not* leave Tolú
without eating the country's most sublimely
perfect *arepa*, filled with egg and spiced
meat – from **Doña Mercedes' food stand**
on the southeast corner of the square next to
the Expreso Brasilia office. Crunchy, savory
perfection.

ℹ Information

Bancolombia (☑288 5711; Calle 14 No 2-88;
☺8am-4pm Mon-Thu, to 4:30pm Fri) Has an
ATM. Located on the south side of Plaza Pedro
de Heredia.
Hospital de Tolú (☑288 5256; Calle 16 No
9-61; ☺24hr)
iC@fe (☑286 0118; Calle 17 No 2-20; per hr
COP$2000; ☺9am-10:30pm) Internet access.
Mundo Mar (☑288 4431; www.clubnautico
mundomarina.com; Carrera 1 No 14-40;
☺6:30am-8pm) This well-run agency does
daily tours departing at 8:30am to Islas de
San Bernardo for COP$35,000. You'll be back
by 4pm.
Policía Nacional (☑288 5030; cnr Carrera 5
& Calle 16)
Servientrega (☑286 0630; Carrera 4 No 15-
40; ☺8am-noon & 2-5pm Mon-Fri, 8am-noon
Sat) Postal services.
Tourist office (☑286 0599; Carrera 2 No
15-40; ☺8am-noon & 2-6pm) Located in the
alcadía on the west side of Plaza Pedro Heredia.
Opens when the fancy takes them.

ℹ Getting There & Away

Expreso Brasilia/Unitransco (☑288 5180),
Rapido Ochoa (☑288 5257) and **Caribe Ex-**
press (☑288 5223) share a small bus station on
the southwest side of Plaza Pedro de Heredia.
Buses depart for Cartagena (COP$30,000,
three hours) and Montería (COP$18,000, two
hours) hourly. Other destinations include Bogotá
(COP$120,000, 19 hours) at 8am and 5:30pm;
Medellín (COP$70,000, 10 hours, five depar-
tures daily); and Santa Marta (COP$45,000, six
hours, departures at 7:30am and 5:30pm).

If you are continuing on to Turbo and the
Panamanian border beyond, you must take a
bus to Montería and switch there for Turbo. All of
the Medellín-bound buses stop in Montería, as
does **Transportes Luz** (☑288 6069; Calle 16 No
10-79), a good door-to-door option for groups or
those who need to make it to Montería beyond
standard bus hours. They also offer a private
car/people carrier option to Cartagena – known
as an *aerovan*. Call ahead for reservations.

Islas de San Bernardo

The 10 archipelagoes that make up the Islas
de San Bernardo, set off the coast of Tolú,
are a far more spectacular and interesting
addition to the Parque Nacional Natural
(PNN) Corales del Rosario y San Bernardo
than their neighbors to the north (p134).

Carib *indígenas* (indigenous Caribbeans)
once called the islands home, but they are
more trampled on today by vacationing
Colombians, who have done well to keep
the islands a secret from foreign tourists.
Known for their crystalline waters, man-
grove lagoons and white-sand beaches,
these picturesque islands stand out on the
Caribbean coast as a little oasis of rest and
relaxation.

Day tours (COP$35,000) to the archipela-
go depart daily from the Muelle Turístico in
Tolú at around 8:30am. The full day includes
a fly-by of one of the world's most densely
populated islands, **Santa Cruz del Islote**,
where up to 1000 people, mostly fisherfolk,
live in a tropical aquatic shantytown meas-
uring just 1200 sq meters; and Isla Tintípan,
the largest of the archipelago's islands.

Most of the tourism infrastructure is on
Isla Múcura, where tours stop for three
hours of free time. Here you can rent snor-
keling equipment for COP$5000, kick back
and have lunch and a beer (not included
in the tour), or simply wander around the
mangroves. The best beach and snorkeling
is on **Isla Palma**, where the tour concludes
at the **aquarium** (admission COP$12,000),
which is more of a rustic zoo than a water-
world (though there is a foggy-windowed

aquarium here). You'll also find monkeys, pink flamingos, loads of birds (including many loose macaws) and even a buffalo! It's strange, but sort of interesting.

🛏 Sleeping & Eating

In high season reservations are a must, and expect considerable price hikes from those listed here.

Punta Faro   HOTEL $$$
(☑1 616 3136 in Bogotá; www.puntafaro.com; Isla Múcura; d 3-night all-incl package from COP$1.9 million; ❄☎) The smartest hotel in the archipelago makes liberal use of mangrove wood in its beautiful lobby and bedroom furniture, and caters to (very) wealthy Colombians and business travelers. There's a private beach, three restaurants, two bars and transportation from Cartagena. Equipment such as kayaks and snorkeling gear is included in the price.

Decameron Isla Palma   HOTEL $$$
(☑310 360 9647; www.decameron.com; Isla Palma; d from COP$365,000; ❄☎) This Club Med–like all-inclusive resort on Isla Palma offers all the usual suspects with one additional coup: a thin sliver of sand that takes honors for the best beach in the area.

Donde Wilber   CABINS $$
(☑316 605 5840; Isla Múcura; cabin per person COP$25,000, full board COP$80,000) Ask for Angelo at the dock, and he'll take you through the village (where pigs snuffle through dumps) to a bunch of very ramshackle seaside shacks and a rustic cabin. The mattresses are old but the view is spectacular. It's one-star at best, but it's relaxed and friendly and is owned by locals, meaning your money isn't siphoned off the island. They can arrange fishing trips and snorkeling, too.

Turbo

☑4 / POP 140,000
Part of the department of Antioquia 373km northwest of Medellín, Turbo is a gritty port that you'll have to overnight in if you want to catch a boat to Capurganá or Sapzurro.

🛏 Sleeping & Eating

Residencias Florida   HOTEL $
(☑827 3531/311 327 2569; Carrera 13 No 99A-56; s/d with fan COP$20,000/30,000; ☎) It doesn't look like much, but this simple spot on Turbo's loud Parque Principal is the best choice for foreigners. The extremely friendly and

helpful owner, Jhon, can book your ticket to Capurganá. It's walking distance from the bus terminals and the docks. If you arrive hungry, the restaurant across the road in the park is the town's sole late-food option.

ℹ Information

Banco de Bogotá (Calle101 No 12-131) Has an ATM.

Turbo Internet.com (☑827 5100; Carrera 13; per hr COP$2000; ☺10am-8pm Mon-Fri, to 9pm Sat & Sun) Internet cafe.

ℹ Getting There & Away

From Cartagena, you must catch a bus before 11am to Montería (COP$45,000, 4½ hours) and switch for the bus to Turbo (COP$40,000 to COP$45,000, five hours). **Sotracor** (☑784 9023), **Gomez Hernandez** (☑784 9010) and **Coointur** (☑312 851 4723) depart more or less every half hour to hour from 7am to 5pm between the three companies. In Turbo, there is no central bus station but most of the companies of concern are located on Calle 101. Returns to Montería run from 4:30am to 4pm. **Sotrauraba** (☑827 2039) heads to Medellín hourly from 5am to 10pm (COP$60,000, eight hours) from Turbo.

Boats to Capurganá (COP$55,000, 2½ hours) leave daily from the port from 6am in high season and once at 8:30am in low season. Boats can fill up quickly with locals – arrive at least an hour early. It can be a wet and sometimes bumpy journey, so throw your luggage in a trash bag (vendors sell them for COP$1000). When you return, studiously avoid the clamouring locals who want to 'help' you to your bus. They work on commission and will fleece you. For continuing on to Panama, see the boxed text on p167.

Capurganá & Sapzurro

☑4 / POP 2000
The isolated resort towns of Capurganá and Sapzurro, minutes from the Panamanian border, have done well to stay off the map. These two idyllic, laid-back villages and the surrounding beaches are the most deserted between here and Punta Gallinas on the Guajira Peninsula. But much like Punta Gallinas, access has been both their savior and crutch. Both Capurganá and Sapzurro are only accessible by a lengthy boat trip from Turbo, or by plane, and subsequently remain Colombia's least overrun beaches. The tourism here has been 90% homegrown, due to access and security issues in the past (it is on the border, after all). But that's all changed now, with new foreign-owned hostels and visitor numbers doubling in recent years.

Many travelers say they prefer to spend time here rather than Taganga and the beaches of Parque Nacional Natural (PNN) Tayrona, which can be uncomfortably crowded in high season, and it's easy to let a few days drift into a week exploring the excellent beaches and nature walks in the area. The coral reef here is mainly unexplored and well preserved, and wetsuits aren't required as water temperatures are higher than elsewhere along the coast.

Capurganá sits at the northwest edge of Colombia's Chocó department at the entrance to the Golfo de Urabá and offers the most tourism infrastructure – there is no shortage of accommodations and the town remains supremely relaxed, except during Semana Santa (Holy Week) and in November and December. Sapzurro lies around the corner in a picturesque bay, the last settlement before Panama. It's smaller and offers even more peace and quiet – but neither village has cars.

For those making the overland trek to or from Panama, these two relaxed towns make for an ideal spot to break your journey, with swimming-pool blue beaches and a wealth of nature-related activities in the vicinity.

Keep in mind these are border towns, and no ordinary border at that – it's the gateway between South and Central America. There are many soldiers about.

◉ Sights

Both Capurganá and Sapzurro feel different to the rest of the coast; the painted wooden buildings and tranquil vibe are much more Caribbean. Both towns are perfect places to simply unwind and let time pass, but there are also great beaches and wonderful nature opportunities. **El Cielo**, a one-hour jungle hike into the mountains from Capurganá, passes several natural swimming pools and waterfalls along a trail where you might see howler and squirrel monkeys, toucans and parrots. The pleasant coastal hike to **Aguacate** (one hour) stops at quiet beaches along the way.

The two best beaches in the area are **La Miel** and **Playa Soledad**. La Miel is just across the Panamanian border from Sapzurro (bring your ID – there's a military checkpoint). It's a quick walk up a series of steep steps across the border and back down the other side (turn right at the phone booths and follow the sidewalk). The small beach offers perfect white sand and cerulean waters,

as does **Playa Soledad**, accessed by a three-hour walk east of Capurganá, or on a tour.

Activities

Capurganá has better diving than the coast's main diving destination, Taganga, with a better-preserved reef and visibility up to 25m common from August to October. The sea is rough January to March. At **Dive and Green** (☑316 781 6255; www.diveandgreen.com; ◷8:30am-12:30pm & 2-5:30pm) two-tank dives cost COP$190,000 and PADI certification costs COP$820,000.

🛏 Sleeping & Eating

Restaurants are scarce in Capurganá, so most of the hotels offer all-inclusive packages, though there are a few budget options around the soccer field. Hotel owners often hang around the dock, waiting for passengers. They're a cool bunch, not hustlers.

For a late drink, check out the bars circling the soccer field.

Luz de Oriente   HOSTEL, RESTAURANT $
(☑310 371 4902; Playa Blanca, Capurganá; dm COP$15,000, s/d COP$25,000/40,000) Right on the harbor, the rooms here are clean and tidy and all have sea views. They do a mean mojito in the bar, and a three-course lunch is just COP$10,000.

La Posada   HOSTEL $$
(☑312 662 7599; facebook.com/sapzurrolaposada; Sapzurro; s/d COP$65,000/130,000, camping per person with/without tent COP$10,000/15,000) The most comfortable and well-run spot in town has beautiful gardens with flourishing guava, coconut and mango trees, open-air showers for campers, and beautiful, airy rooms with wooden floors and exposed beams and hammocks on the balconies. If you need to show someone a little romance after months on the road, ask the very friendly owner to set up a candlelit dinner for you on the jetty.

Zingara   HOTEL $$
(☑314 646 8974; Sapzurro; r per person COP$40,000) Owner Clemencia will make you feel instantly welcome in this wooden guesthouse that is also her home. Rooms are simple, clean and airy, and some have ocean views.

Campamento Wittenberg   HOTEL $
(☑311 4366 215; Sapzurró; hammocks COP$10,000, r per person COP$20,000; 🛜) A friendly French-owned joint right on the

border of Panama, where you can find a basic room or two, cheap, healthy breakfasts, fishing trips and sailing courses. The owner has been in Colombia for years and is friendly, professional and very helpful.

Camping El Chileno   HOTEL $
(☑313 685 9862; Sapzurro; hammock COP$10,000, campsite per person COP$12,000) Simple camping and hammock accommodations on the nicest end of Sapzurro's beach. Ask anyone in town for 'El Chileno' – the nickname of the owner – and they will point you in the right direction. Or you may spot his smile at 100m.

Hostal Los Delfines   HOTEL $
(☑310 421 5703; Capurganá; r per person COP$14,000; ❋) This is a great spot for the price – rooms include TVs, private bathrooms and patio hammocks and air-con when the generator's going. The owner, Anibal Palacio, always meets the boat from Turbo.

Cabañas Darius   HOTEL $
(☑314 646 8974; www.darius capurgana.es.tl; Capurganá; dm COP$15,000, r per person COP$20,000) Run by a helpful American, this cozy Capurganá cabin has neat and tidy rooms and bathrooms with freshly tiled floors and a large outdoor kitchen for guests. Ask around for Joey at the dock and his

horse and cart will save you the 20-minute schlep to Playa Roca.

Hotel Almar   HOTEL $$$
(☑01 8000 941 013; www.hotelalmar.com.co; Capurganá; r per person all-incl COP$280,000; ❋ ❋ ➌) This upscale hotel is right on the best beach, Playa Blanca. The log cabin–like structure offers decent-sized rooms and a large sun deck. There's a dive center on the property. The price includes booze.

TOP CHOICE Josefina's   RESTAURANT $$
(☑310 627 1578; Playa Blanca, Capurganá; mains COP$15,000-35,000; ☺lunch & dinner) Scour the entire coast and you won't find better seafood – or a more wonderful welcome – than at Josefina's. Her crab in spicy coconut-cream sauce served in impossibly crispy, wafer-thin plantain cups, is, without exaggerating, of Michelin star quality. Josefina may be moving to a small beach kiosk, so ask around town. It's 100% unmissable.

Hernán Patacón   COLOMBIAN $
(Playa Blanca, Capurganá; mains COP$5000-14,000; ☺11:30am-7:30pm) Gorge on thin, crispy fried plantain heaped up with everything from prawns or chicken and mushrooms to *arequipe* (milk caramel) and cheese for a seafood-jaded palate.

❶ Information

Capurganá Tours (☑824 3173; www.capurga natours.com; ☺8am-noon & 2-6pm Mon-Sat) Friendly English-speaking agency that can book your flights in Panama as well as excursions in the area. There are no banks here, but this agency can do cash advances on credit cards and can arrange transportation from Turbo throughout Colombia.

Coffee Internet (per hr COP$2500; ☺8am-4pm Mon-Sat) There are no street names in this town, but it's close to the tool shop.

Minsterio de Relaciones Exteriores (☑311 746 6234; ☺8am-5pm Mon-Fri, 9am-4pm Sat) Immigration services for those heading to Panama – on the main drag. Opening hours are, let's say, flexible.

Panamanian consulate (☑314 653 4081; ☺8am-4pm Mon-Fri) Near the soccer field.

❶ Getting There & Away

There are only two ways to reach Capurganá and Sapzurro. The most economical route is to catch a boat from Turbo (COP$55,000, 2½ hours), which departs daily from 6am in high season and once at 8:30am the rest of the year. In low season, the boats depart for Turbo at 7:30am.

WORTH A TRIP

THE GOLFO DE URABA

The Golfo de Uraba has a few tiny towns nestled on the fringes of the Darién Gap with decent, affordable accommodations, quiet beaches and amazing hiking. The towns of **Acandí**, **Triganá** and **San Francisco** are all accessible via the boat from Turbo. In tiny San Francisco, try **Ralle's Hostel** (☑314 70 35 151; dm COP$25,000, cabin per person COP$50,000). In Triganá, try **Hosteria Triganá** (☑314 615 6917) or the **Anayansi Cabañas** (☑320 697 9025). Both have rooms and cabins for less than COP$40,000 per person, depending on the season. In Acandí, in March, April and May, hundreds of leatherback turtles, measuring up to 2m in length and weighing up to 750kg, come ashore and lay their eggs. Passionate conservationist **Giuseppe Thaler** (☑313 746 2725; giutha2009@ hotmail.com) can arrange turtle-watching trips in season.

GETTING TO PANAMA

It is not possible to drive from Colombia to Panama – the Pan-American Hwy does not extend through the Darién Gap. Various maniacs have ignored the dangers of crossing the 87km distance in all-terrain vehicles and even on foot, risking encounters with guerrillas, paramiliaries or narcotraffickers.

It is possible and fairly safe, however, to reach Panama (mostly) overland, with just a few sea trips and a short flight. At the time of research the following route was secure and calm, but always check ahead for security updates before setting out, and stick to the coast.

1. Make your way to Turbo. The Medellín–Turbo route (COP$51,000, eight hours) is safe now – but daytime travel is still advised. From Cartagena, you have to go to Montería (COP$35,000, 4½ hours) and change there for Turbo (COP$25,000, five hours). Buses run regularly from 7am to 5pm, and you have leave Cartagena before 11am to avoid getting stuck overnight in Montería. You have to spend the night in Turbo.

2. Catch a boat from Turbo to to Capurganá. One boat departs daily from the hectic docks in Turbo at 8:30am in low season, and several throughout the day (when full) from 6am in high season (COP$55,000, 2½ hours). Arrive at least an hour early to secure a ticket. Hang on to your hat – this can be a bumpy ride. There is a 10kg baggage limit – COP$500/kg overcharge applies.

3. Take a boat from Capurganá to Puerto Obaldia in Panama (COP$30,000, 45 minutes). But first, get your Colombian exit stamp at **Ministerio De Relaciones Exteriores** (☑311 746 6234; ⊘8am-5pm Mon-Fri, 9am-4pm Sat), near Carpuganá's harbor, one day before departure as the office will not be open on the morning you leave. Boats depart Capurganá every day, at 7:30am, so be at the docks for 7am. This is another dicey journey depending on sea conditions.

4. Obtain your Panama entry stamp at Panamanian immigration in Puerto Olbaldía. Then fly to Panama City's domestic Albrook terminal with **Air Panama** (☑+507 316 9000 in Panama; www.flyairpanama.com). There are three departures daily (US$80) from Monday to Friday at 7am, 9:15 am and 4:20pm; on Saturday and Sunday flights depart at 9:15am and 4.20pm. Puerto Olbaldía has very little to offer tourists. Avoid spending any more time than necessary there, and head straight to Panama.

ADA (☑01-8000 514 232; www.ada-aero.com) also operates flights from Medellín (COP$400,000 one way) on Monday, Tuesday, Thursday, Friday and Saturday at noon in low season, and up to three flights daily in high season.

The Darien Gapster (thedariengapster.com) is a motorboat that offers tours to the Kuna Yala in Panama, departing from Sapzurro, or border crossings if you're headed that way. You'll need to get your exit stamp in Capurganá.

San Andrés & Providencia

Includes »

Best Places to Eat

» Restaurante La Regatta (p174)

» Caribbean Place (p179)

» Gourmet Shop Assho (p175)

» Mahi Mahi (p175)

» Café Studio (p180)

Best Places to Stay

» El Viajero San Andrés (p173)

» Sol Caribe Providencia (p179)

» Decameron Los Delfines (p173)

» Casa Harb (p174)

» Sirius Hotel (p180)

Why Go?

The archipelago of San Andrés and Providencia is near Nicaragua, historically tied to England and politically part of Colombia, but while these pristine islands may lack an untainted pedigree, their diverse history and picture-postcard setting make them Colombia's most interesting paradise.

Here you'll find isolated beaches, unspoiled coral reefs and an alluring island flavor, and with just a little digging the 300-year-old English/Creole-speaking Raizal culture emerges.

San Andrés, the largest island in the archipelago and its commercial and administrative hub, attracts many tourists seeking duty-free shopping sprees. The crowds, however, are not difficult to escape.

Providencia offers the same turquoise sea and extensive coral reefs – the second-largest barrier reef in the northern hemisphere is here – but it's much less commercialized. Much of Providencia's colonial heritage is still alive and thriving in small hamlets of colorful wooden homes peppered about the island.

When to Go
San Andrés

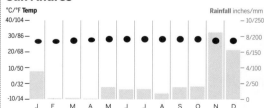

Jan-Jun The dry season means you avoid the Caribbean's hurricanes.

May-Jun Crab migration season – roads are closed to protect them!

Jun-Dec 15 Prices are much lower outside the Christmas peak on both islands.

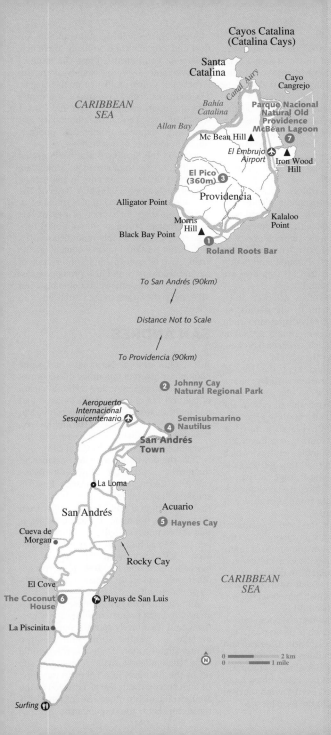

Cayos Catalina
(Catalina Cays)

Santa
Catalina

CARIBBEAN
SEA

Bahía
Catalina

Allan Bay

Canal Aury

Cayo
Cangrejo

Parque Nacional
Natural Old
Providence
McBean Lagoon

Mc Bean Hill ▲

El Embrujo ✈
Airport

Iron Wood
Hill ▲

El Pico
(360m) ③

Providencia

Alligator Point

Morris
Hill ▲

Kalaloo
Point

Black Bay Point

① Roland Roots Bar

To San Andrés (90km)

Distance Not to Scale

To Providencia (90km)

② Johnny Cay
Natural Regional Park

Aeropuerto
Internacional
Sesquicentenario ✈

② Semisubmarino
Nautilus

San Andrés
Town

La Loma

San Andrés

Cueva de
Morgan

Acuario
⑤ Haynes Cay

Rocky Cay

CARIBBEAN
SEA

El Cove

The Coconut ⑥
House

⑦ Playas de San Luis

La Piscinita

Surfing ⑪

Ⓝ 0   2 km
    0   1 mile

San Andrés & Providencia Highlights

① Groove to reggae rhythms over Old Milwaukee's at **Roland Roots Bar** (p181)

② Dig your toes into the pristine sands of beautiful **Johnny Cay** (p171), part of the 4-hectare Johnny Cay Natural Regional Park

③ Trek through iguana country to **El Pico** (p177) for stunning views of Providencia

④ Go into the blue on a **scuba dive** (p180) or in a semisubmarino such as **Semisubmarino Nautilus** (p172) and gawk at Colombia's prettiest coral reefs and marine life

⑤ Swim with the stingrays at sunset off **Haynes Cay** (p172)

⑥ Marvel at the **Coconut House** and nature garden at West View (p175)

⑦ Visit beautiful **Parque Nacional Natural Old Providence McBean Lagoon** (p177)

History

The first inhabitants of the islands were probably a group of Dutch colonists who made their home on Providencia toward the end of the 16th century. In 1631 they were expelled by the English who effectively colonized the islands, home to the Raizal people, an Afro-Caribbean ethnic group. The English brought in black enslaved people from Jamaica and began to cultivate tobacco and cotton. The Spanish, irate at the English success on the islands, unsuccessfully invaded the archipelago in 1635.

Because of their strategic location, the islands provided convenient shelter for pirates waiting to sack Spanish galleons bound for home laden with gold and riches. In 1670 legendary pirate Henry Morgan established his base on Providencia and from here he raided both Panama and Santa Marta. Legend has it that his treasures are still hidden on the island.

Shortly after Colombia achieved independence, it laid claim to the islands, although Nicaragua fiercely disputed its right to do so. The issue was eventually settled by a treaty in 1928, which confirmed Colombia's sovereignty over the islands.

Geographic isolation kept the islands' unique English character virtually intact, though things started to change when a flight service connected the islands to the mainland in the 1950s. In 1954 a government plan to make the islands a duty-free zone brought with it tourism, commerce, entrepreneurs and Colombian culture, which slowly began to uproot the 300-year-old Raizal identity, pushing it aside in favor of big tourism bucks. Unprepared and unqualified to make a living from tourism, locals were caught off-guard.

In the early 1990s the local government introduced restrictions on migration to the islands in order to slow the rampant influx of people and preserve the local culture and identity. Yet Colombian mainlanders account for two-thirds of San Andrés' population. English and Spanish have been the two official languages since 1991.

The tourist and commercial boom caused San Andrés to lose much of its original character; it's now a blend of Latin American and English-Caribbean culture, though there is a movement to restore Raizal roots in San Andrés. Providencia has preserved much more of its colonial culture, even though tourism is making inroads into the local lifestyle.

Although the political status of San Andrés and Providencia is unlikely to change, Nicaragua continues to press the issue of its sovereignty over the islands at the International Court of Justice in the Hague. The court reaffirmed Colombia's sovereignty over the main islands in 2007, but said it would rule on the maritime boundary and secondary islands at a later date undetermined at the time of research.

In 2005 the Seaflower Marine Protected Area (MPA) was established to strengthen protection of key ecosystems in the marine area of the Seaflower Biosphere Reserve. The MPA includes 65,000 sq km of crystalline waters that are zoned for a variety of uses ranging from complete protection to controlled fishing. The objective of this multiple-use MPA is to foster sustainable development in the archipelago by strengthening conservation of marine biodiversity and also promoting sustainable use. The Seaflower is Colombia's first MPA and is the largest in the Caribbean.

SAN ANDRÉS

8 / POP 68,000

Just 150km east of Nicaragua and some 800km northwest of Colombia, the seahorse-shaped island of San Andrés counts 27 sq km of cultural tug-of-war as both its asset and its handicap. Covered in coconut palms, San Andrés, the largest island in the archipelago, is indeed paradisiacal Caribbean, but not everything here is quite so crystal clear.

Take the downtown area, for instance, at the northern end of the island. Colombians call it El Centro, but the island's English-speaking Raizal people refer to it as North End. The cultural elbowing escalates from there. What's not up for debate, however, is that the commercialized area of town won't be splashed across any postcards anytime soon – it's a monstrosity of ferro-concrete blocks housing one duty-free shop after another, only broken up by the occasional hotel or restaurant.

All is not lost on San Andrés, however. A charming brick promenade lines the waterfront, and it's a lovely spot to enjoy a drink or take an evening stroll. And paradise is just slightly more than a canoe paddle away: the endlessly idyllic Johnny Cay sits off in the distance, just 1.5km from shore. In high season it can feel as crowded as the Mediterranean, but otherwise Johnny Cay is the archipelago's finest moment.

San Andrés is best appreciated outside of the downtown hubbub. A 30km scenic paved road circles the island, and several minor roads cross inland. There are two other small towns: La Loma (The Hill) in the central hilly region and San Luis on the eastern coast, both far less tourist-oriented than San Andrés Town and boasting some fine English-Caribbean wooden architecture. Excellent scuba-diving and snorkeling opportunities abound all around the island – visibility and temperature here are nearly unrivaled in the Caribbean.

It only takes a day or two to suss out the Raizal from the Colombians. At just one-third of the island's population, Raizals are now an ethnic minority, but their fading Creole culture – descended from English settlers, African slaves and West Indians from other islands – is what gives San Andrés its unique character, different from that of mainland Colombia.

◉ Sights

Johnny Cay Natural Regional Park   BEACH
(Map p171) This protected 4-hectare coral islet sits about 1.5km north of San Andrés Town. It's covered with coconut groves and surrounded by a lovely, white-sand beach. The sunbathing is good, but be careful swimming here as there are dangerous currents. The cay can fill up far beyond capacity, as tourists fight for space with an estimated 500 iguanas that call it home. Food is available. Boats to Johnny Cay leave from the main San Andrés Town beach (round trip COP$15,000). The last boat back is at 5pm.

La Piscinita   BEACH
(Map p171; admission COP$2000) Also known as West View, just south of El Cove, La Piscinita is a good site for snorkeling, usually with calm water, plenty of fish (which will eat out of your hand) and some facilities, including a restaurant with traditional local food and snorkel rental. When the sea is rough, you can only feed the fish from land.

La Loma   VILLAGE
(Map p171) This small town in the inner part of the island, also known as The Hill, is one of the most traditional places here. It's noted for its Baptist church, the first established on the island (in 1847). In 1896 the church was largely rebuilt in pine brought from Alabama. Definitely take a stroll through here – it's the least Colombian-influenced part of the island.

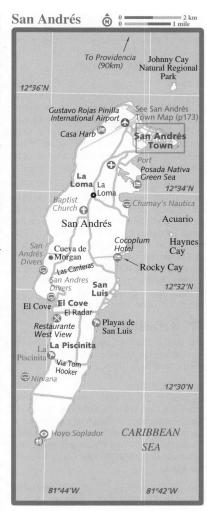

San Andrés

Hoyo Soplador   GEOGRAPHICAL FEATURE
(Map p171) At the southern tip of the island, the Hoyo Soplador is a small geyser where sea water spouts into the air (up to 20m at times) through a natural hole in the coral rock. This phenomenon occurs only at certain times, when the winds and tide are right. An international surf contest is held nearby in January.

San Luis   VILLAGE
(Map p171) Located on the island's east coast, San Luis still boasts white-sand beaches and some fine traditional wooden houses. The sea here is good for snorkeling, though con-

ditions can be a little rough. San Luis has no center as such, and is really just a 3km string of mostly ramshackle houses along the coast, but it's a tranquil alternative to San Andrés Town.

Acuario   BEACH

(Map p171) Next to Haynes Cay, off the east coast of San Andrés, Acuario is frequently visited by tourists by boat (round trip COP$10,000). The surrounding sea is shallow and calm and good for snorkeling. If you forget to bring your snorkeling gear, you can rent some on the beach in Acuario.

Cueva de Morgan   CAVE

(Map p171; admission COP$5000) This is the cave where Welsh pirate Henry Morgan is said to have buried some of his treasure. The cave is 120m long, but it's filled with water, so you see only its mouth. You can't enter the cave and there's not much to see here anyway, yet the magic of alleged riches draws in plenty of tourists. Additional distractions include traditional *mento* dancers shaking it to calypso and *Schottische*, a sort of island polka.

☆ Activities

Due to the beautiful coral reefs all around, San Andrés has become an important diving center, with more than 35 dive spots.

Banda Dive Shop   DIVING

(Map p173; ☑513 1080; www.bandadiveshop. com; Hotel Lord Pierre, Av Colombia, San Andrés Town; ⊙8am-noon & 2-6pm Mon-Sat) Extra-friendly dive shop offering two-tank dives for COP$150,000 and PADI open-water certification for COP$750,000. Best choice on the island.

Chamay's Nautica   WATER SPORTS

(Map p171; ☑513 2077; Via San Luis Km4, San Luis) The go-to shop for water sports. DIY rental possibilities per hour include kayaking (COP$25,000), windsurfing (COP$70,000) and kitesurfing (COP$100,000).

Karibik Diver   DIVING

(Map p173; ☑512 0101; www.karibikdiver.com; Av Newball No 1-248, San Andrés Town; ⊙8am-4pm) This small school provides quality equipment, personalized service and long dives.

San Andrés Divers   DIVING

(Map p171; ☑312 448 7230; www.sanandresdiv ers.com; Av Circunvalar Km9) Though not as centrally located as the others, this large shop and school has a great reputation

and offers PADI certification for a little less (COP$700,000).

Tours

Coonative Brothers   BEACH TRIPS

(Map p173; ☑512 1923) On the town's beach, this boating co-op provides trips to Johnny Cay (COP$10,000) and Acuario (COP$10,000), plus a combined tour to both cays (COP$15,000). It's run by Raizal people and is also a good spot for an excellent local morning pick-me-up, *panela* (raw sugarcane juice) and crab patties.

Snorkeling, Sting Rays, Sunset & Beer   WILDLIFE TOURS

(Map p173; ☑316 240 2182; 3hr tour COP$55,000) The name says it all, really. Jaime Restrepo runs a slightly flexible tour to swim with the stingrays at Haynes Cay, and throws in some deep-water snorkeling and brews on top of the package. It's somewhat casual and limited to groups of 10. The tour leaves at 3pm from Tonino's Marina.

Mundo Marino   BOAT TRIPS

(Map p173; ☑512 1749; www.mundomarino.com; Centro Comercial New Point Plaza, local 234, San Andrés Town; ⊙8am-noon & 2:30-6:30pm Mon-Sat, 8:30am-noon Sun) Operates the Captain Morgan party boat, a two-hour evening boat ride (departing at 8:30pm Tuesday, Thursday and Saturday) with live music and all-you-can-drink national spirits (per person COP$58,000), as well as the Semisubmarino Nautilus.

Semisubmarino Nautilus   WILDLIFE TOURS

(Map p173; 2hr tour COP$45,000) If you're not planning on scuba diving or snorkeling, this trip is probably the next best option for viewing the rich marine wildlife. The Nautilus is a specially designed boat with large windows in its hull, roomy enough for everyone to comfortably sit while it plies the coral beds northeast of the island. Tickets are sold at Mundo Marino.

🛏 Sleeping

The overwhelming majority of the island's accommodations can be found in San Andrés Town. There are some hotels in San Luis, but elsewhere there are very few places to stay. For the most part, accommodation on the island is more expensive than on the mainland, although in 2011 a new hostel, the island's first, opened, and has made a trip here more affordable for those on tighter budgets. Rates rise during high season.

San Andrés Town

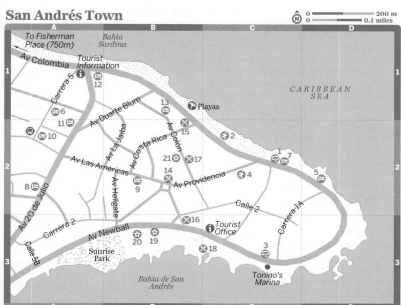

San Andrés Town

SAN ANDRÉS TOWN

TOP CHOICE **El Viajero San Andrés** HOSTEL $
(Map p173; 512 7497; Avenida 20 de Julio 3A-12; dm COP$30,000, s/d COP$75,000/114,000; ❄️🛜) The first hostel on the island is also the very best place to stay, with a great bar, a lively social scene, attentive staff full of informed advice, and a convenient location near the beach. All dorms have air-con and the clean, simple rooms have plasma TVs and five-star mattresses. Highly recommended.

Decameron Los Delfines BOUTIQUE HOTEL $$$
(Map p173; 512 4083; www.decameron.com; Av Colombia No 16-86; r per person COP$324,000; ❄️🛜) The first boutique hotel on the island as well as within the Decameron chain, this stylish, 36-room hotel is quiet and discreet. It features an over-water restaurant, a small pool and smart furniture, housed in a design-forward hotel that wouldn't be out of place in Los Angeles.

Casa Harb
HOTEL $$$

(Map p171; ☏512 6348; www.casaharb.com; Calle 11 No 10-83; d from COP$850,000; ❄️🛜🏊) Located in an impressive republican-style mansion behind the airport, this is a step above anything in the archipelago. The five exquisite suites are individually designed with Asian aesthetics and feature deep soaking tubs. It caters to an exclusive market.

Apartahotel Tres Casitas
HOTEL $$

(Map p173; ☏512 5813; www.apartahoteltres casitas.com; Av Colombia No 1-60; r per person COP$100,000; ❄️🛜🏊) A cute yellow-and-blue clapboard hotel with extra-large rooms, all with kitchenettes and separate living areas. Rates include breakfast and dinner and some rooms have balconies over the sea.

🍃 Cli's Place
GUESTHOUSE $

(Map p173; ☏512 6957; luciamhj@hotmail.com; Av 20 de Julio; r per person from COP$40,000) This Raizal-run place is part of the island's *posada nativa* program, where you bed down with locals. Cli has four simple rooms, some with kitchenettes. It's reached via the alley next to the park across from Pollo Kikiriki.

Hotel Mary May Inn
HOTEL $$

(Map p173; ☏512 5669; jfgallardo@gmail.com; Av 20 de Julio No 3-74; s/d COP$60,000/90,000; ❄️) This small and friendly place offers nine simple but cozy rooms in a nice location two blocks from the beach. The interior design offers a trip back to the 1950s.

Hotel Hernando Henry
HOTEL $$

(Map p173; ☏512 3416; Av Las Américas No 4-84; s/d with fan COP$50,000/80,000, with air-con COP$60,000/100,000;❄️) You won't send postcards home about this place, but most rooms have a balcony and all come with private bath.

Freeport Hotel
HOTEL $$

(Map p173; ☏513 1212; Av Las Américas No 2A-101; s/d COP$75,000/140,000;❄️) Gloomy from the outside but nice and bright inside, this functional option offers good value in a clean and friendly environment. Prices include breakfast and dinner.

Hotel Portobelo
HOTEL $$

(Map p173; ☏512 7008; www.portobelohotel. com; Av Colombia No 5A-69; s/d incl breakfast COP$124,000/152,000; ❄️🛜) This unassuming beachside property is nothing fancy, but offers simple rooms, some with sea views, a small book exchange, cable TV and new air conditioners.

Noblehouse Hotel
HOTEL $$$

(Map p173; ☏512 8264; www.sanandresnoble house.com; Av Colón No 3-80; s/d incl breakfast COP$144,000/179,000; ❄️🛜) This Italian-run operation likes to mix its decors: New England Leaf Peeping one moment, Moorish Seaside the next. The 15 large and kitschy rooms are a comfortable option in town and the staff are super helpful. It's one block from the beach.

SAN LUIS

This hamlet is a 10-minute drive south of San Andrés Town; bus connections are frequent. It offers a little more peace and quiet than El Centro.

Posada Nativa Green Sea

(Map p171; ☏512 6313/317 7514 314; http:// posadags.blogspot.com; Harmony Hall Hill; r per person COP$30,000; ❄️) Run by the fabulous Flory Perez, who has never left the island in her life, these small, simple self-catering cottages offer privacy and peace rather than luxury. But you do get a small terrace and a kitchen, and the pleasure of Flory's wonderful welcome. You'll find it on the San Luis highway around the corner from the massively disturbing crab sculpture.

Cocoplum Hotel
HOTEL $$$

(Map p171; ☏513 2121; www.cocoplumho tel.com; Carretera a San Luis No 43-39; s/d COP$160,000/218,000; ❄️🛜🏊) On a private beach shaded with palm trees, this recently renovated low-key beach resort sports Caribbean architecture and its 44 rooms offer a good midrange alternative to the higher-end options in San Andrés Town. There's a restaurant that serves fresh meals all day, and is open to nonguests. Rocky Cay, a good spot for snorkeling, is nearby.

🍴 Eating

The Creole-Caribbean influence means staples include breadfruit, which takes the place of *patacones* (fried plantains) as the starch of choice, and ubiquitous conch. Be sure to try the most traditional dish, rundown (or 'rondon' in the local creole), a soupy dish of lightly battered fish, plantains, yucca and other gooey starches, all slow-cooked in a healthy dose of coconut milk.

Restaurante La Regatta
SEAFOOD $$$

(Map p173; ☏512 0437; Av Newball, San Andrés Town; mains COP$20,000-90,000; ⏰lunch & dinner Mon-Sat) The islands' best restaurant: the coconut-curry *marinera* is nothing short of perfection. The room itself is fabulous – it's like eating on board a pirate ship.

Gourmet Shop Assho
EUROPEAN $$

(Map p173; ☑512 9843; Av Newball, San Andrés Town; mains COP$24,000-40,000; ⊙dinner) Supressing schoolboy titters over its name may challenge diners, but the food here is not to be scoffed at. It's a wine shop by day and a great diner by night, with a lovely interior, steaks to kill for, and seafood cooked with care and class. It has a fine range of aperitifs and digestifs, too, and the best coffee on the island.

Mahi Mahi
THAI $$

(Map p173; ☑512 4115; Hotel Casablanca, Av Colombia, San Andrés Town; mains COP$24,000-45,000; ⊙lunch & dinner) After lengthy travel in Colombia, this chic Thai spot on the waterfront, part of Hotel Casablanca, will send your palate dancing with its glorious and perfectly seasoned curries and island-tinged dishes.

Miss Celia O'Neill Taste
SEAFOOD $$

(Map p173; ☑513 1062; Av Colombia, San Andrés Town; mains COP$20,000-35,000; ⊙lunch & dinner) A good choice for native food like rondon, stewed crab and stewed fish, served within a colorful home with a large garden and patio. It's across from the Club Nautico.

Mr Panino
ITALIAN, DELI $$

(Map p173; ☑512 0549; Edifico Breadfruit, local 106-107, San Andrés Town; mains COP$20,000-70,000; ⊙lunch & dinner) Parma ham, real cheese, and an Italian specialty deli with numerous sandwiches, pasta, risotto and a beautiful octopus carpaccio. It's nicer than most others in town, though not pricier.

Fisherman Place
SEAFOOD $

(Map p173; ☑512 2774; Av Colombia, San Andrés Town; mains COP$13,000-45,000; ⊙noon-4pm) This open-air, beachside restaurant is a great way to support local fisherfolk and eat well. Rondon and fried fish are the most popular dishes, but the lobster is the clear winner for the price.

Restaurante West View
SEAFOOD $$

(Map p171; ☑513 0341; Circunvalor Km11, West View; mains COP$20,000-60,000; ⊙breakfast, lunch & dinner) This West View option looks ordinary but the food stands out. Try the filet of fish – and do not miss the attached flourishing nature garden, which has an example of every fruit tree that grows on the island.

☆ Entertainment

There are several nightspots in San Andrés Town along the eastern end of Av Colombia. Head here and see what's hot.

Banzai
BAR

(Map p173; Av Newball, local 119, San Andrés Town; ⊙7pm-2am) If you want a late-night drink without going to a club, Banzai is a great cocktail bar and popular with locals. The well-mixed drinks are served expertly to a reggae backbeat, and it's chic without being over-fancy.

THE HOUSE OF COCONUT

Behind the restaurant at West View (where you can get a mean rondon for COP$25,000) you'll find a curious house and ecopark project run by the courtly and welcoming Mr Forbes. The house, every single part of it, including all of its decorations, are made of coconut. The floor, the walls, the ceilings, the beds, the desk, the chairs, the lamps, the fan blades, the curtains, the curtain poles, the door handles, the coat hooks, the false flowers in the vases, the vases themselves: all are made of a coconut-derived product. Even the light switches are crafted from the wood of the coconut tree, which Mr Forbes (it felt unseemly to ask his Christian name) says is the most useful tree on earth.

Over a glass of delicious coconut wine, he tells us that every part of the tree can be used from the minute it is planted until it dies 50 years later. He has yearned to build this dream coconut house for his entire life, ever since he was punished by his father as a boy for stealing two coconuts. His punishment? To stand holding two coconuts at head height, arms outstretched to his left and right, for the entire day.

He is the architect, designer, carpenter and builder of the house. It stands in a peaceful garden surrounded by the trees and fruit bushes of the islands, with coconuts, of course, very strongly represented. Guests can stay there, he says, but it was impossible, even after several more glasses of coconut wine, to get him to agree a price. Though he did climb a coconut tree and toss a few down.

Blue Deep · CLUB
(Map p173; Sunrise Beach Hotel, Av Newball, San Andrés Town; cover after 11pm COP$10,000; ☺9:30pm-3am Thu-Sat) The biggest disco in town holds 700 sweaty bodies. There is live music (salsa and reggaeton), which provides the soundtrack for a decent mix of locals and tourists, stumbling about after too many frothy rum punches.

Éxtasis · CLUB
(Map p173; ☑512 3043; Hotel Sol Caribe San Andrés, Av Colón, San Andrés Town; cover COP$20,000; ☺9:30pm-3am Mon-Thu, to 4am Fri & Sat) A good disco, with TV screens (soccer, of course) and three rows of lounge chairs for those that prefer voyeurism. You can recoup COP$12,000 of the cover in cocktails.

❶ Information
4-72 (☑Av Newball, Edificio Cámara de Comercio, local 101, San Andrés Town; ☺ 8am-noon & 2-6pm Mon-Fri, 8am-noon Sat) Post office.

Banco de Bogotá (Map p173; ☑512 4195; Av Colón No 2-86, San Andrés Town) ATM.

Cafe Internet Platinium (Av 20 de Julio, San Andrés Town; per hr COP$2500; ☺8am-10pm) In front of Supertodo Supermarket.

Tourist office (Secretaría de Turismo; Map p173; ☑513 0801; Av Newball, San Andrés Town; ☺8am-noon & 2-6pm Mon-Fri) Across from Restaurante La Regatta. It has a tourist information booth at the corner of Avs Colombia and 20 de Julio.

❶ Getting There & Away
Air
San Andrés airport, Gustavo Rojas Pinilla International Airport (also known as Aeropuerto Internacional Sesquicentenario), is northwest of the town center. You must buy a tourist card (COP$44,000) on the mainland before checking in for your San Andrés–bound flight. Airlines that service San Andrés include **Avianca** (☑512 3349; Av Colón, edificio Onaissi, San Andrés Town; ☺8am-noon & 2-6pm Mon-Fri, 8am-1pm Sat) and **Copa Airlines Colombia** (☑512 7619; Sucursal Centro Comercial San Andrés, San Andrés Town; ☺8am-noon & 2-6pm Mon-Fri, 9am-1pm Sat). There are direct connections to Bogotá (from COP$388,000), Cali (from COP$388,700), Cartagena (from COP$334,000), Medellín (from COP$365,000) and Barranquilla (from COP$294,500). **Copa** (☑512 6248) flies direct to Panama City (from COP$494,186).

Satena (☑512 3139; Gustavo Rojas Pinilla International Airport) operates two flights per day between San Andrés and Providencia in low season (round trip from COP$398,200) and up to six in high season. Decameron's affiliated airline **Searca** (☑512 2237) also flies the route.

Boat
Cargo boats travel to Providencia from San Andrés and often take passengers, but prepare to stomach a rough, five-hour sea journey. The trip costs COP$40,000 to COP$45,000.

❶ Getting Around
San Andrés' airport is in San Andrés Town, a 10-minute walk northwest of the town center, or COP$10,000/5000 by taxi/moto-taxi.

Local buses circle a large part of the island; they also ply the inland road to El Cove. They are the cheapest way to get around (per ride COP$1200) unless you want to walk. They can drop you off close to all the major attractions.

A bus marked 'San Luis' travels along the east-coast road to the southern tip of the island; take this bus to San Luis and the Hoyo Soplador. The bus marked 'El Cove' runs along the inner road to El Cove, passing through La Loma. It'll drop you in front of the Baptist church, within easy walking distance of Cueva de Morgan and La Piscinita. You can catch both buses near the Hotel Hernando Henry.

You can travel more comfortably by taxi, which can take you for a trip around the island (COP$50,000). Otherwise, hire a bicycle (per half-/full day COP$10,000/$20,000). Cycling around San Andrés is a great way to get a feel for the island. Roads are paved and there is little traffic to contend with. You can also hire scooters (COP$40,000 per day) and golf carts (around COP$80,000 per day) in addition to the usual suspects – many of the rental businesses are on Av Newball. Shop around as prices and conditions vary.

PROVIDENCIA

☑8 / POP 5000
Around 90km north of San Andrés, the much smaller and quainter island of Providencia feels not only like a world away, but like a different country entirely. Tourism has not been spliced into the gene pool here, so the quiet, laid-back hamlets that nestle against white-sand beaches feel much more authentic than San Andrés'. And without a direct connection to the Colombian mainland, the island hasn't seen nearly the same levels of cultural invasion, leaving the original traditions and customs more or less intact. All this combined with gorgeous topography standing sentinel over swaths of turquoise-

blue sea gives Providencia no small claim to being paradise.

Traditionally known as Old Providence, the island covers an area of 17 sq km. It is the second-largest island of the archipelago. A mountainous island of volcanic origin, it is much older than San Andrés and is home to the second-largest barrier reef in the Americas.

Santa Isabel, a village at the island's northern tip, is the local administrative headquarters. Santa Catalina, a small island facing Santa Isabel, is separated from Providencia by the shallow Canal Aury, spanned by a pedestrian bridge.

Strict zoning laws have held large-scale development at bay, and, unlike in San Andrés, English is still widely spoken. There's much English-Caribbean–style architecture, with each homeowner trying to outdo their neighbor by the stroke of a paintbrush.

What tourist industry does exist can be found in the tiny hamlets of **Aguadulce** and **Bahía Suroeste** on the west coast, a 15-minute ride by *colectivo* from the airport. Here you'll find small cottages, hotels and cabañas strung along the road, and a handful of restaurants. While you can see virtually the whole island in a day, travelers end up staying longer than they expected, scuba diving, hiking or just lying in a hammock with a Club Colombia in hand.

Friendly locals, warm seas and impressive mountainous topography all help make Providencia Colombia's Eden.

Planes to and from Providencia are sometimes cancelled due to high winds; this happened to our author, who was forced to do remote research from San Andrés.

⊙ Sights & Activities

Providencia's beaches are pleasant, but relatively small and narrow. The main ones are at Bahía Aguadulce, Bahía Suroeste and (the best) at Bahía Manzanillo at the southern end of the island.

Parque Nacional Natural (PNN) Old Providence McBean Lagoon   NATIONAL PARK
(admission COP$12,000) To protect the habitat, a 10-sq-km area in the island's northeast was established in 1995. About 10% of the park's area covers a coastal mangrove system east of the airport; the remaining 905 hectares cover an offshore belt including the islets of Cayo Cangrejo and Cayo Tres Hermanos. An 800m-long ecopath helps you identify differ-

ent species of mangroves and the fauna that inhabit them.

Santa Catalina   ISLAND
Some tiny, deserted beaches exist on the island of Santa Catalina, worth a look if only to see Morgan's Head, a rocky cliff in the shape of a human face, best seen from the water. An underwater cave is at the base of the cliff. The shoreline changes considerably with the tides; during high-tide beaches get very narrow and some totally disappear.

Hiking
The mountainous interior of the island, with its vegetation and small animal life, is attractive and provides pleasant walks. Probably nowhere else in Colombia can you see so many colorful lizards scampering through bushes. Beware of a common shrub with spectacular hornlike thorns; ants living inside have a painful bite. Mosquitoes also abound on the island.

Don't miss a trip to **El Pico Natural Regional Park** for outstanding 360-degree views of the Caribbean from El Pico (360m). The most popular trail begins in Casabaja. Ask for directions as several paths crisscross on the lower part (further up there are no problems), or ask in Casabaja for a guide. Some locals will take you up for a small fee. It is a steady 1½-hour walk to the top. Carry drinking water – there is none along the way.

Snorkeling & Diving
Snorkeling and diving are the island's other big attractions. You can rent snorkeling gear in Aguadulce (COP$10,000). Diving trips and courses can be arranged with recommended local operators **Felipe Diving Shop** (✆514 8775; www.felipediving.com), run by a native Raizal, and **Sonny Dive Shop** (✆514 8231), both in Aguadulce; and **Sirius Dive Shop** (✆514 8213; www.siriusdivecenter.com) in Bahía Suroeste. Each offers an open-water or advanced course for around COP$750,000.

☞ Tours

Paradise Tour Contact   TOURS
(✆514 8283; www.oldprovidence.com.co; Aguadulce; ⏲8am-noon & 2-6pm Mon-Sat) This small agency offers tours (to El Pico per person COP$60,000) and other services including bicycle rental (per day COP$20,000), horseback riding (COP$50,000), kayaking trips (COP$50,000) and boat excursions around the island (per person COP$75,000).

Providencia

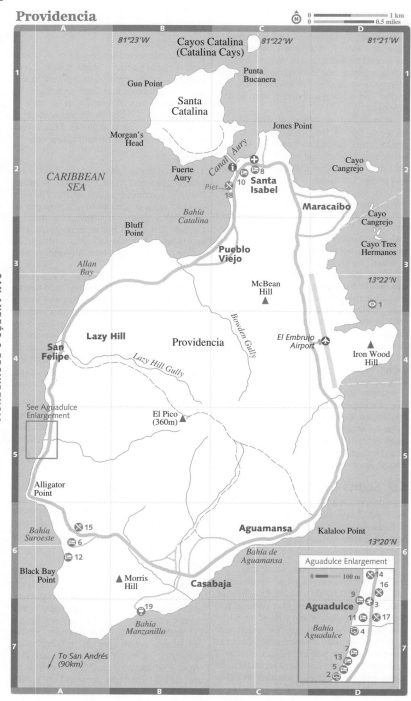

Cayos Catalina
(Catalina Cays)

81°23'W

81°22'W

81°21'W

Gun Point

Punta
Bucanera

Santa
Catalina

Jones Point

Morgan's
Head

CARIBBEAN
SEA

Fuerte
Aury

Canal Aury

Cayo
Cangrejo

Pier

Santa
Isabel

Cayo
Cangrejo

*Bahía
Catalina*

Maracaibo

Cayo Tres
Hermanos

Bluff
Point

Pueblo
Viejo

13°22'N

*Allan
Bay*

McBean
Hill

Lazy Hill

Providencia

Bowden Gully

El Embrujo
Airport

Iron Wood
Hill

San
Felipe

Lazy Hill Gully

El Pico
(360m)

See Aguadulce
Enlargement

Alligator
Point

*Bahía
Suroeste*

Aguamansa

Kalaloo Point

13°20'N

Black Bay
Point

Morris
Hill

*Bahía de
Aguamansa*

Casabaja

*Bahía
Manzanillo*

To San Andrés
(90km)

Aguadulce Enlargement

0   100 m

Aguadulce

*Bahía
Aguadulce*

0   1 km
0   0.5 miles

Providencia

Boats normally call at the Canal Aury, Morgan's Head, Cayo Cangrejo and Roland Roots Bar.

✵ Festivals & Events

Crab Migration   WILDLIFE
This annual event lasts for a week or two in May to June. There may be many crabs on the move then, particularly in Aguadulce and Bahía Suroeste, and roads can be closed to provide safe crossing for them. They aren't absent the rest of the year, either. Keep a look out!

Cultural Festival   LOCAL CELEBRATION
Providencia's major event is in the last week of June. It includes music and dance, a parade of motorcycles and, just for kicks, an iguana beauty pageant.

⌂ Sleeping & Eating

Generally speaking, accommodations and food are expensive on Providencia, even more so than on San Andrés.

AGUADULCE
This 20-house hamlet offers peace, quiet and little else. There are more than a dozen places to stay; some have their own restaurants and offer a bed-and-board package. For better or worse, the Decameron chain has taken over most of the best places to stay, so independent travelers can be shut out in high season.

Sol Caribe Providencia   HOTEL **$$**
(☑514 8036; www.solarhoteles.com; r per person COP$180,000; ❀⊛🛌) Following the island's kaleidoscopic color scheme, this bright yellow hotel is the most upmarket in Aguadulce. There's a pleasant seaside restaurant, rooms with nice hardwood furniture and colorful Caribbean art, and very expensive internet (COP$10,000 per hour). Rates include breakfast and dinner (without them, knock off COP$50,000).

Hotel El Pirata Morgan   HOTEL **$$**
(☑514 8232; www.elpiratamorgan.org; s/d incl breakfast COP$144,000/216,000; ❀⊛🛌) A solid option in the town center, with a handy minimarket downstairs. It lacks the Caribbean flair of the other options, but is also a little cheaper, and offers more lush surroundings than elsewhere on the beach. It's the only hotel, though, without English-speaking front-desk staff.

Mr Mac   HOTEL **$**
(☑514 8283; s/d COP$30,000/50,000) Mr Mac is the cheapest option in town and it's not a bad option at all. Rooms are large, with kitchenettes, and are right on the water.

Cabañas Miss Elma   HOTEL **$$$**
(☑315 303 4208; r per person COP$180,000;❀) With colorful common areas and a wonderfully casual seaside restaurant, rates include three meals.

Caribbean Place   SEAFOOD **$$**
(☑514 8698; mains COP$18,000-53,000;⊙lunch & dinner) Though this wonderful island seafooder isn't cheap, Bogotá-trained chef Martin Quintero is doing serious food in a casual atmosphere. Highlights include mountainous black crab.

Arts & Crafts Café   CAFE **$**
(☑514 8297; ⊙1:30-9pm) This French-run shop-cafe is a good place for espresso and its famous *paleta* popsicles made from island fruits. It's also a great spot for artisanal products like honey, marmalade and tamarind wine. There's a book exchange as well.

Pizza's Place
PIZZERIA $

(☑514 8224; mains COP$6000-55,000; ☺dinner) A cheaper option, doing sandwiches (COP$6000) and pizza (from COP$13,000) in addition to a handful of island staples.

SANTA ISABEL
Strangely, Santa Isabel, despite its gorgeous location in a picturesque bay attached to Santa Catalina, doesn't see much tourism. A touch of work making it over and this place would be much more appealing to travelers.

Old Providence Hotel
HOTEL $

(☑514 8691; s/d COP$50,000/90,000;❋) This hotel offers bland but big rooms, with cable TV, in the town center.

Hotel Flaming Trees
HOTEL $$

(☑514 8049; s/d COP$600,000/100,000;❋) The best choice in this part of the island; offers nine spacious rooms with fridge, TV and local art.

Restaurante Eneidy
SEAFOOD $

(☑514 8758; mains COP$8000-40,000; ☺noon-3pm & 6-10pm) This open-air restaurant is certainly the best place to eat in town, though don't expect any James Beard–nominated dishes.

BAHÍA SUROESTE
This is the second tourist destination after Aguadulce, but there aren't as many facilities. Still, it's the nicest beach and more convenient for hiking, horseback riding and beach drinking.

Sirius Hotel
HOTEL $$$

(☑514 8213; www.siriushotel.net; s/d cabañas from COP$105,000/170,000, s/d from COP$130,000/230,000; ❋☎) You'll find a little more character than in most spots on the island, as well as a dive shop on premises. The suites are large and comfortable (the cabañas less so) but both are on the beach.

Cabañas Miss Mary
HOTEL $$$

(☑514 8454; s/d incl breakfast COP$120,000/ 180,000; ❋☎) Miss Mary provides nicely dressed-up rooms right on the beach, each with large patios and hammocks. There's cable TV and ever-elusive hot water.

TOP CHOICE Café Studio
SEAFOOD $$

(☑514 9076; mains COP$15,000-40,000; ☺11am-10pm Mon-Sat) The island's best restaurant is run by a Canadian woman and her Raizal husband, Wellington, who cooks the island dishes 'she can't get right.' The results are

---

DIVING ON SAN ANDRÉS & PROVIDENCIA

Divers will delight over the underwater viewing opportunities off both San Andrés and Providencia. While the courses may be cheaper at Taganga (p146), the richness of the corals and variety of the marine life rivals almost any place in the Caribbean.

Both San Andrés and Providencia have extensive coral reefs – 15km and 35km respectively. The reefs on both islands are notable for their sponges, which appear in an amazing variety of forms, sizes and colors. Other aquatic inhabitants include barracudas, turtles, lobsters, rays and red snappers. Wreck divers will want to check out the two sunken ships, the *Blue Diamond* and *Nicaraguense*, off the coast of San Andrés.

The top five dive spots:

» **Palacio de la Cherna** A wall dive southeast of San Andrés that begins at 12m and drops off some 300m more. Midnight parrot fish, tiger fish, king crab, lobster and even nurse and reef sharks are common sightings.

» **Cantil de Villa Erika** Southwest of San Andrés. Depths range from 12m to 45m along this colorful reef full of sponges, soft and hard corals, sea turtles, manta and eagle rays, and sea horses.

» **Piramide** A shallow dive inside the reef on San Andrés' north side, this is a haven for stingrays. The quantity of fish, octopus and moray eels make it one of the most active spots on the island.

» **Tete's Place** Large schools of midsized goat fish, grunt fish, schoolmasters and squirrel fish frequent this aquarium-like site 1km offshore at Bahía Suroeste in Providencia.

» **Manta's Place** Despite its name, there are no manta rays at this Providencia site but rather southern stingrays with wingspans of up to 5m. As you survey the sands between coral mounds, you pass over fields of ghost feather dusters, where brown garden eels withdraw into the sand for protection as you pass.

ROLAND ROOTS BAR

Don't leave Providencia without visiting the ridiculously atmospheric **Roland Roots Bar** (☑514 8417; Bahía Manzanillo), which has booths fashioned from bamboo under ramshackle thatched roofs spread among the sands, all set to a booming reggae soundtrack. Roland is famous for his late-night parties and his *coco locos* – jazzed-up piña coladas served in coconuts.

both memorable and reasonably priced. Try Wellington's conch, cooked in his own Creole sauce made with wild basil from their garden, or anything in garlic sauce. Save room for the cappuccino pie!

ℹ Information

Banco de Bogotá (Santa Isabel; ⊘8-11:30am & 2-4pm Mon-Thu, 8-11:30am & 2-4:30pm Fri) ATM.

Communication Center (☑514 8871; Santa Isabel; per hr COP$2500; ⊘9am-12:30pm & 4-9pm Mon-Sat, 2:30-9pm Sun) Aside from the exorbitant hotel option, this is the island's only internet.

Tourist office (☑514 8054; Santa Isabel) Located in the Hotel Aury building next to the pier.

ℹ Getting There & Away

Satena and Searca both fly between San Andrés and Providencia (round trip from COP$366,200) twice daily in low season, several more in high season. You are most likely to buy a round-trip ticket in San Andrés before arriving, but buy your ticket in advance in the high season and be sure to reconfirm your return flight at Providencia's airport.

ℹ Getting Around

Getting around the island isn't the easiest thing to do without your own transportation. *Colectivos* and pickup trucks run along the road in both directions; it's COP$2000 for a ride of any distance. There may be only one or two per hour, but locals will often stop and offer you a ride.

Pickup trucks congregate at the airport waiting for incoming flights and ask as much as COP$20,000 for any distance. To avoid overpaying, walk a bit further from the airport and wave down a *colectivo* or pickup truck passing along the road for the usual COP$2000 fare, though this might not be the best solution if you are carrying lots of bags.

Taxis are hard to come by and quite expensive compared to on the mainland. From the airport, count on COP$20,000 to Santa Isabel or Aguadulce. The bottom line is that if you call, you'll pay for it; if you can spare the time to wait for a ride, you'll get off much cheaper.

A pleasant way to get around is by bicycle, which can be rented from Paradise Tour Contact (p177). You can also rent a scooter (per day COP$40,000 to COP$50,000) from a few small operators in Aguadulce and Santa Isabel.

SAN ANDRÉS & PROVIDENCIA PROVIDENCIA

Medellín & Zona Cafetera

Includes »

Why Go?

Welcome to *país paisa* – *paisa* country – a vibrant region made up of coffee plantations and flower farms, lush cloud forest, dynamic student towns and the busy metropolis of Medellín. It is one of Colombia's most enchanting regions, and is not to be missed.

In Medellín, the country's second-largest city, towers soar skyward, with ambition matched only by its inferiority complex – Chicago to Bogotá's New York. It is an attractive city that seduces most travelers instantly, with its just-perfect climate, green spaces, great restaurants, museums and public artwork, and thumping discos.

Further south is the Zona Cafetera, a rich tapestry of historic villages, charming coffee farms, fantastic nature reserves and grand mountain peaks. Coffee is more than a cash crop here – it is a way of life. You'll never look at your morning cup the same way again.

Best Places to Eat

» Carmen (p192)
» El Mirador (p208)
» Mondongos (p192)
» La Fogata (p212)
» Bahía Mar (p192)

Best Places to Stay

» El Delirio (p213)
» Hacienda Bambusa (p213)
» 61 Prado (p189)
» Casa Kiwi (p189)
» Hacienda Venecia (p204)

When to Go

Medellín

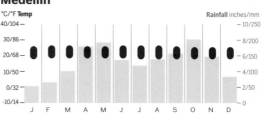

°C/°F **Temp**   Rainfall inches/mm

Jan-Mar Clear conditions expose the peaks of Parque National Natural (PNN) Los Nevados.

Aug The streets of Medellín explode with the vibrant colors of the Feria de las Flores.

Oct-Dec Coffee pickers mass on farms throughout the Zona Cafetera for the main harvest.

National, State & Regional Parks

The big daddy of national parks here is Parque Nacional Natural (PNN) Los Nevados, which soars above 5000m. Recinto del Pensamiento, Los Yarumos and Reserva Ecológica Río Blanco, near Manizales, boast beautiful species of orchids and butterflies. East of Pereira are Santuario Otún Quimbaya and Parque Ucumarí. Armenia's botanical gardens are well worth a visit, as is the stunning Valle de Cocora with its soaring wax palms, near Salento.

ⓘ Getting There & Around

Medellín and Armenia airports both receive international flights. The region is well serviced by buses to Bogotá, Cali and the Caribbean coast.

You should have no problem getting around using the region's frequent, cheap bus services. Avoid long-distance travel during flash heavy rains (most likely during April/May and September/October) as landslides are common.

MEDELLÍN

📍4 / POP 3 MILLION / ELEV 1494M

Medellín packs the punch of a city twice its size. Situated in a narrow valley, the city's skyline reaches for the heavens, setting high-rise apartment and office buildings against a backdrop of jagged peaks in every direction. Its pleasant climate gives the city its nickname – the City of Eternal Spring – and the moderate temperatures put a spring in the locals' step, at work and at play. It's a bustling city of industry and commerce, especially textile manufacturing and exported cut flowers. On the weekends Medellín lets its hair down, and the city's many discos attract the beautiful people.

The city sprawls north and south along the valley floor. Slums hug the upper reaches of the hills. True to its *paisa* (person from Antioquia) roots, Medellín affects an indifference to the rest of Colombia, and puts on metropolitan airs – the traffic officers wear Italian-style round boxy hats, many discos prefer techno to salsa or vallenato, and the city looks overseas for inspiration for its next great public works project.

History

Spaniards first arrived in the Aburrá Valley in the 1540s, but Medellín was not founded until 1616. Historians believe that many early settlers were Spanish Jews fleeing the Inquisition. They divided the land into small haciendas, which they farmed themselves – very

different from the slave-based plantation culture that dominated much of Colombia. With their focus on self-reliance, these early *paisas* came to be known as hard workers with a fierce independent streak – traits they've exported throughout the Zona Cafetera.

Medellín became the capital of Antioquia in 1826 but long remained a provincial backwater, which explains why its colonial buildings are neither sumptuous nor numerous. The city's rapid growth began only at the start of the 20th century, when the arrival of the railroad, together with a highly profitable boom in coffee production, quickly transformed the city. Mine owners and coffee barons invested their profits in a nascent textile industry, and their gamble paid off. Within a few decades, Medellín had become a large metropolitan city.

By the 1980s the city's entrepreneurial spirit was showing its dark side. Under the violent leadership of Pablo Escobar (see p284), Medellín became the capital of the world's cocaine business. Gun battles were common, and the city's homicide rate was among the highest on the planet. The beginning of the end of the violence came with Escobar's death in 1993, and today Medellín is one of the most secure and accessible destinations in the country.

◉ Sights

Museo de Antioquia   MUSEUM
(Map p188; 📞2513636; www.museodeantioquia. co; Carrera 52 No 52-43; adult/student COP$8000/4000; ⊙10am-5:30pm Mon-Sat, to 4pm Sun) In the grand art deco Palacio Municipal, Colombia's second-oldest museum is one of its finest (Museo Nacional in Bogotá is the oldest). The collection includes pre-Columbian, colonial and modern art collections, as well as many works donated by native son Fernando Botero.

Plazoleta de las Esculturas   PLAZA
(Map p188) Also known as Plaza Botero, this public space in front of the Museo de Antioquia is home to 23 of the artist's large bronze sculptures. For more Botero, check out the iconic **La Gorda** (Map p188), in front of the Banco de la República in Parque Berrío. There are three more Botero sculptures in Parque San Antonio, including the **Pájaro de Paz** (Bird of Peace; Map p186).

Cerro Nutibara   HILL
(Map p186) On top of this 80m-tall hill 2km southwest of the city center, sits the kitschy

Medellín & Zona Cafetera Highlights

1 Crane your neck to see the tops of the majestic wax palms in the cloud forest of the **Valle de Cocora** (p216)

2 Head out into the plantation and pick your own coffee in the **Zona Cafetera** (p200)

3 Explore the nature parks around Manizales – **Reserva Ecológica Río Blanco** (p203), **Recinto del Pensamiento** (p203) and **Los Yarumos** (p203) – brimming with orchids, hummingbirds and butterflies

4 Bathe in piping-hot thermal springs high in the mountains at **Termales San Vicente** (p210)

5 Sample the many fine restaurants and bars in **Medellín** (p191)

6 Spend the night in **Río Claro** (p199), your hotel room open to the jungle, the river roaring below

7 Hike among the mighty glaciers of **Parque Nacional Natural (PNN) Los Nevados** (p205)

8 Scale the **Piedra del Peñol** (p197) for amazing views over the Embalse Guatapé

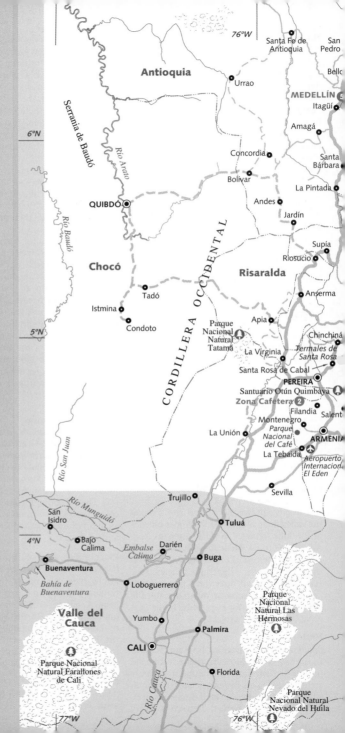

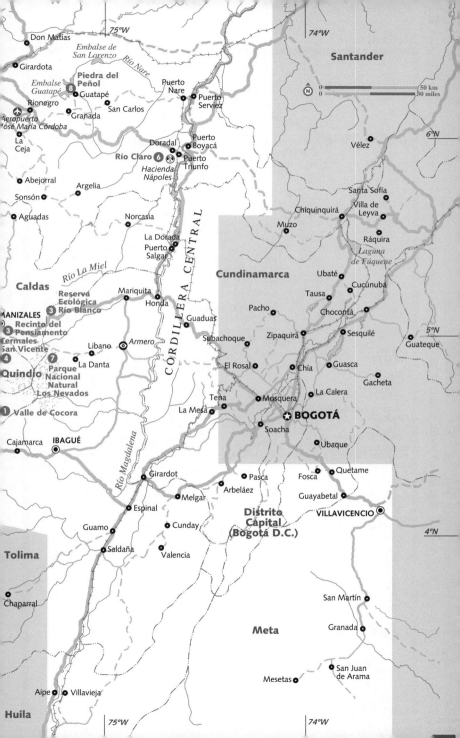

Medellín

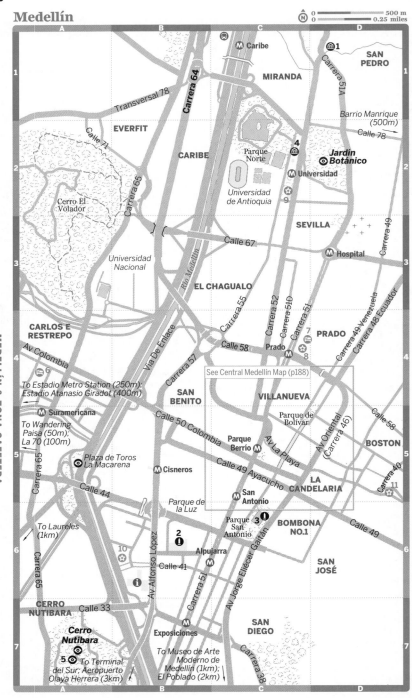

0   500 m
0   0.25 miles

SAN PEDRO

MIRANDA

Carrera 51A

Barrio Manrique
(500m)

EVERFIT

Transversal 78

Calle 71

Carrera 64

Calle 78

Parque
Norte

Jardín
Botánico

4

CARIBE

Carrera 65

Cerro El
Volador

Universidad
de Antioquia

Universidad

9

SEVILLA

Carrera 49

Universidad
Nacional

Calle 67

Hospital

Carrera 49 Venezuela

Carrera 48 Ecuador

EL CHAGUALO

Río Medellín

Carrera 55

Carrera 52

Carrera 51D

Carrera 51

PRADO

7

CARLOS E
RESTREPO

Av Colombia

6

Via De Enlace

Carrera 57

Calle 58

Prado

8

Carrera 49

To Estadio Metro Station (250m);
Estadio Atanasio Girardot (400m)

Suramericana

To Wandering
Paisa (50m);
La 70 (100m)

SAN
BENITO

Calle 50 Colombia

See Central Medellín Map (p188)

VILLANUEVA

Parque de
Bolívar

Calle 58

BOSTON

Carrera 65

Plaza de Toros
La Macarena

Cisneros

Calle 44

Parque
Berrío

Av La Playa

Carrera 40

Calle 49 Ayacucho

LA
CANDELARIA

11

Parque de
la Luz

San
Antonio

Av Oriental
(Carrera 46)

To Laureles
(1km)

2

Parque
San
Antonio

3

BOMBONA
NO.1

Calle 49

10

Alpujarra

SAN
JOSÉ

Carrera 65

Av Alfonso López

Calle 41

Carrera 51

Av Jorge Eliécer Gaitán

CERRO
NUTIBARA

Calle 33

Cerro
Nutíbara

5

Exposiciones

SAN
DIEGO

To Terminal
del Sur; Aeropuerto
Olaya Herrera (3km)

To Museo de Arte
Moderno de
Medellín (1km);
El Poblado (2km)

Carrera 38

Caribe

1

Universidad

Hospital

San
Diego

Medellín

Pueblito Paisa, a miniature version of a typical Antioquian township. Views across the city from the adjacent platform are stunning. Take a taxi to the top and walk back down to check out the **Parque de las Esculturas** (Sculpture Park), which contains modern abstract sculptures by South American artists.

FREE **Jardín Botánico**　　　GARDENS
(Map p186; www.botanicomedellin.org; Calle 73 No 51D-14; ⊗9am-5pm) Medellín's fabulous botanic gardens cover 14 hectares and showcase 600 species of trees and plants, a lake, herbarium, auditorium and a butterfly enclosure. The gardens are easily accessed from the nearby metro stop Universidad.

FREE **Casa Museo Pedro Nel Gómez**　　　MUSEUM
(Map p186; ☎233 2633; Carrera 51B No 85-24; ⊗9am-5pm Mon-Sat, 10am-4pm Sun) Located in the house where the artist lived and worked, this museum has an extensive collection of pieces by prolific local painter Pedro Nel Gómez (1899–1984), as well as changing exhibitions by local artists, and workshops.

Parque Arví　　　PARK
(www.parquearvi.org; Veredas Mazo & Piedras Blancas, Santa Elena) Accessible by the fantastic new Cable Arví Metrocable (Linea L) from the Santo Domingo interchange (COP$3500

one way, 15 minutes), Parque Arví is a big chunk of mountain wilderness in Santa Elena that makes a great escape from the city. Inside the boundaries of the 17.61-sq-km reserve are hiking trails, canopy lines, lakes, and a *mariposario* (butterfly enclosure). Attractions are spread out so it's best to arrive early. The cable car is closed for maintenance on Mondays.

Parque Explora　　　MUSEUM
(Map p186; ☎516 8300; www.parqueexplora.org; Carrera 52 No 73-75; admission COP$15,000-30,000; ⊗8:30am-4pm Tue-Fri, 10am-5pm Sat & Sun) With exhibits on physics, biology and technology as well as a 3D cinema and an excellent aquarium full of species from the Amazon and other Colombian waterways, this is a science museum kids will love, and it may tickle the adult's inner child as well.

Monumento a la Raza　　　MONUMENT
(Map p186; Centro Administrativo La Alpujarra, Calle 44) Rodrigo Arenas Betancur's most impressive work in Medellín tells the story of Antioquia in dramatically twisting metal.

Basílica de la Candelaria　　　CHURCH
(Map p188; cnr Carrera 50 & Calle 51 Boyacá) Medellín's most important church stands guard over Parque Berrío and was constructed in the 1770s on the site of an earlier wooden structure. It features a German-made pipe organ brought to the city by boat up the Río Magdalena and then on horseback.

Catedral Metropolitana　　　CHURCH
(Map p188; btwn Carreras 48 & 49) Overlooking Parque de Bolívar, Medellín's neo-Romanesque cathedral was completed in 1931. Its spacious but dim interior has Spanish stained-glass windows.

Ermita de la Veracruz　　　CHURCH
(Map p188; cnr Calle 51 Boyacá & Carrera 52 Carabobo) Constructed with funds from European immigrants, this fine colonial church was inaugurated in 1803 and has a stone facade and a white-and-gold interior.

Museo de Arte Moderno de Medellín　　　GALLERY
(off Map p186; ☎444 2622; www.elmamm.org; Carrera 44 No 19a-100; admission COP$7000; ⊗9am-5:30pm Mon-Fri, 10am-5pm Sat & Sun) In a refurbished industrial building in Ciudad del Río, 'El MAMM' showcases changing exhibitions of contemporary Colombian art.

Central Medellín

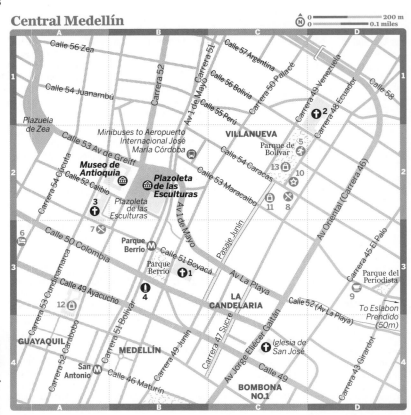

Activities

There are strong thermal winds around Medellín, making it a fine paragliding spot. All the paragliding companies operate out of San Felix in Bello. Take a bus (COP$2800, 45 minutes) from Terminal del Norte.

Zona de Vuelo PARAGLIDING
(☎388 1556, 312 832 5891; www.zonadevueloparap entemedellin.com; Km5.6 Via San Pedro de los Milagros) This experienced operator offers tandem flights (COP$80,000 to COP$100,000) and 10-day-long courses (COP$1,100,000). It can also organize trips to the surrounding region.

Psiconautica ADVENTURE SPORTS
(☎388 1992, 312 795 6321; Km5.6 Via San Pedro de los Milagros) In the same complex as Zona de Vuelo is this one-stop adventure shop with similarly priced paragliding flights, as well as rock climbing, canyoning and abseiling activities. There is a small hostel on-site with amazing views.

Courses

Universidad EAFIT LANGUAGE COURSE
(off Map p191; ☎261 9399; www.eafit.edu.co; Carrera 49 No 7 Sur-50) Private university offering intensive short-term and longer-term Spanish study in a group setting. See its website for the latest schedule and prices.

Baila Latino DANCE COURSE
(☎448 1338; www.academiabailalatino.com; Carrera 43 No 25A-233; individual classes per hr COP$30,000) Learn salsa and other tropical rhythms with friendly and enthusiastic instructors.

Tours

Turibus BUS TOURS
(Map p188; ☎371 5054; www.turibuscolombia.com; tours COP$17,000; ⏰9am & 1pm) Offers budget tours of the city's most iconic attractions. English-speaking guides are sometimes available. Pick up the bus in Parque Poblado or Parque de Bolívar.

Central Medellín

✦ Festivals & Events

Feria Taurina de La Macarena   BULLFIGHTING
(Jan & Feb) The bullfighting season takes place at the Plaza de Toros La Macarena, the 11,000-seat, Moorish-style bullring built between 1927 and 1944.

Festival Internacional de Tango   DANCE
(Jun; www.festivaldetangomedellin.com) The city celebrates its love for tango with competitions, concerts and workshops.

Festival de Poesía de Medellín   LITERATURE
(Jul; www.festivaldepoesiademedellin.org) This fine international festival attracts poets from all corners of the globe.

Feria de las Flores   CULTURAL
(Aug; www.feriadelasfloresmedellin.gov.co) Medellín's most spectacular event is this weeklong festival. The highlight is the Desfile de Silleteros, when up to 400 *campesinos* (peasants) come from the mountains to parade along the streets with flowers on their backs.

Festival Internacional de Jazz y Músicas del Mundo   MUSIC
(Sep; www.medejazz.com) Many North American bands come for this festival. There are usually a couple of free concerts.

Alumbrado Navideño   RELIGIOUS
(Dec & Jan) A colorful Christmas illumination of the city, with thousands of lights strung across the streets and parks. The lights stay on from December 7 to January 7.

🛌 Sleeping

El Poblado has quickly become the place to stay for most travelers. It is close to the bars and restaurants, and is usually safe, even late at night. Those not interested in partying, or who want a less-sanitized experience of Medellín, may like to stay in the more rough-and-tumble center.

61 Prado   GUESTHOUSE $$
(Map p186; ☎254 9743; www.61prado.com; Calle 61 No 50A-60; s/d/ste COP$45,000/70,000/80,000; @📶) This elegant place in the historic Prado neighborhood is a great base from which to explore the sights around the center. The recently renovated rooms are spacious with high ceilings and touches of art throughout, while the candlelit courtyard is a fine place to enjoy a meal prepared in the well-equipped guest kitchen. There is no sign – look for the black gate.

Casa Kiwi   HOSTEL $$
(Map p191; ☎268 2668; www.casakiwi.net; Carrera 36 No 7-10, El Poblado; dm COP$20,000, s/d COP$60,000/70,000, s/d without bathroom COP$40,000/50,000; @📶) Blurring the boundary between hostel and boutique hotel, Casa Kiwi has just had a major facelift and looks fantastic. The bright rooms are decked out with trendy furniture and there are stylish bamboo features throughout. There is a small dipping pool on the rooftop and a great deck overlooking the street downstairs. Its location in the heart of the *zona rosa* (nightlife zone) is a double-edged sword – it is extremely popular with the hard-partying crowd.

Black Sheep   HOSTEL $$
(Map p191; ☎311 1589, 311 341 3048; www.black sheepmedellin.com; Transversal 5A No 45-133; dm COP$20,000-22,000, s/d COP$60,000/75,000, s/d without bathroom COP$45,000/60,000; @📶) This popular hostel close to the Poblado metro has a social but not overly raucous

vibe, pleasant common room, comfortable large beds and piping hot showers. The friendly staff are particularly knowledgeable and on Sundays the owner does a hangover-busting barbecue for COP$11,000. The on-site Spanish classes are recommended.

Hotel Dann Carlton
HOTEL $$$

(Map p191; ☑1 800 094 5525; www.danncarlton. com; Carrera 43A No 7-50; s/d COP$189,000/ 248,000, ste COP$389,000-448,000; ❄@☎) This professionally run hotel is a cut above the rest with quality accommodations and plenty of extras like fresh tropical fruits and elegant flower displays. The suites in particular are huge, with attached sitting room, walk-in closet and massive bathroom. There's a revolving restaurant on the 19th floor with great views of the city. The only drawback is the lack of wi-fi in the rooms.

Hotel Victoria
HOTEL $$$

(www.hotelcasavictoria.com; Carrera 32 No 1 Sur-13; s/d/ste COP$220,000/269,000/390,000; ❄@☎) Located on a hillside below El Tesoro, this fine hotel offers spacious rooms with wooden floors and huge windows offering great views over the city. The suites open onto private terraces. Rates include breakfast. Offers big discounts on weekends.

In House Hotel
HOTEL $$

(Map p191; ☑444 1786; www.inhousethehotel.com; Carrera 34 No 7-109; s/d/tr COP$138,000/ 155,000/212,000; @☎) This new entry into the crowded Poblado boutique hotel market has stylish, bright rooms with pine furniture, work desks and big bathrooms; some have small private patios. A continental breakfast is included.

Wandering Paisa
HOSTEL $$

(off Map p186; ☑436 6759; www.wanderingpaisa hostel.com; Calle 44A 68A-76; dm COP$19,000,

---

PROFITING FROM PABLO

Even after his death, Pablo Escobar Gaviria keeps on making money. When backpackers started flowing back into Medellín – something only made possible by the cartel boss' fall – a couple of young entrepreneurs sensed an opportunity. They began running Escobar-themed tours visiting the pivotal places from his bloody reign over the city: his luxurious homes and offices, the suburban house where he was shot and his grave. More mainstream tour operators soon latched on and even members of Escobar's family have begun running tours where you can discuss the *capo's* (boss's) favorite things with his brother. Needless to say, plenty of Colombians are not impressed with what they see as the glorification of a bloodthirsty terrorist who blew up planes and once paid his henchmen more than US$2000 for every policeman they killed. Others accept that Escobar is an important historical figure and compare the tours to those dedicated to mobsters in Chicago.

Typical tours cost from COP$55,000 to COP$110,000 and usually last half a day. If you do decide to go, **Paisa Road** (☑317 489 2629; www.paisaroad.com) gets positive reviews for its informative and impartial tours.

You can get an even better idea of the sheer scale of Escobar's wealth, ambition and questionable taste at **Hacienda Nápoles** – site of a huge farm four hours from Medellín that he turned into a private kingdom complete with several mansions, a bullring and exotic pets, including giraffes, zebras and several hippopotamuses.

When the government turned up the heat on Escobar the place was abandoned. The hippos went feral and somehow survived and now take center stage at a new dinosaur-themed **adventure park** (☑1800 510 344; www.haciendanapoles.com; admission COP$27,000-50,000) that has opened on the site. It is a truly bizarre place where you can walk through Escobar's abandoned mansion and look over his bombed-out vehicles while a concrete Tyrannosaurus Rex bellows out in the distance. There are also rides for the kids, a butterfly enclosure and some graphic displays on the violence that accompanied Escobar's reign. It's well worth the trip for weirdness factor alone.

The turnoff to Hacienda Nápoles is 1km from Doradal on the Medellín-Bogotá highway. From here to the park gate is a further 2km down an unpaved road. A taxi from town costs COP$10,000. Ask for the driver's number for the round-trip journey. The park can easily be visited on a day trip from Río Claro.

El Poblado

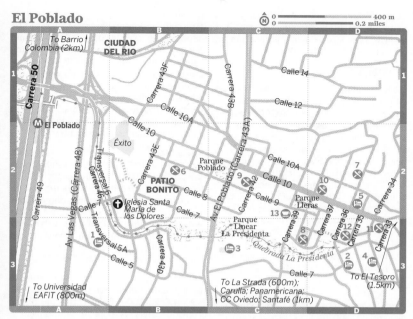

s/d COP$55,000/70,000, s/d without bathroom COP$45,000/55,000; @🛜) Conveniently located near the bars and restaurants of La 70, this comfortable new hostel is a great choice for those wanting to avoid the Poblado circus. There is a small bar and the enthusiastic management are constantly arranging social events and group outings. Bikes are available to explore the neighborhood.

Hotel Conquistadores HOTEL **$**
(Map p188; 📞512 3232; hotelconquistadores@gmail.com; Carrera 54 Cúcuta No 49-31; s/d COP$28,000/34,000; 🛜) On a noisy, unattractive street downtown, this clean family-owned hotel offers real value for those on a tight budget. All rooms have private bath, hot water and cable TV.

Samán Hostel HOSTEL **$$**
(Map p191; 📞581 8908; www.samanhostel.co; Calle 10 No 36-24; dm/s/d/tr without bathroom COP$21,000/65,000/75,000/85,000; 🛜) This small, homely hostel has friendly staff and comfortable accommodations right by the *zona rosa*. It's on a busy road – go for the rooms at the rear.

Palm Tree Hostal HOSTEL **$**
(Map p186; 📞260 2805; www.palmtreemedellin.com; Carrera 67 No 48D-63; dm/s/d without bath-

El Poblado

🛏 Sleeping
1 Black Sheep	A3
2 Casa Kiwi	D3
3 Hotel Dann Carlton	C3
4 In House Hotel	D3
5 Samán Hostel	D2

🍴 Eating
6 Bahía Mar	B2
7 Carmen	D2
8 Il Forno	C3
9 La Casa de Beto	C2
10 Mondongos	D2
11 Tabun	D3
12 Verdeo	D3

🍸 Drinking
13 Café Le Bon	C2

room COP$18,000/28,000/40,000; @🛜) Close to the metro and plenty of cheap eateries, Medellín's original backpacker hostel offers added value with free basic breakfasts, internet access and barbecues.

🍴 Eating

El Poblado is full of upscale restaurants. Southwest of the center, the Laureles neighborhood around Av Nutibara has many unpretentious popular eateries. For a cheap bite, stroll down Pasaje Junín, in central Medellín, during the day.

EL POBLADO

TOP CHOICE **Carmen** INTERNATIONAL $$$
(Map p191; ☎311 9625; www.carmenmedellin.com; Carrera 36 No 10A-27; mains COP$70,000-96,000) Fine dining has finally arrived in Medellín, and leading the charge is Carmen. Run by an American-Colombian couple, both of whom are cordon bleu chefs, Carmen prepares sophisticated international cuisine with a heavy Californian influence. The restaurant itself is made up of distinct dining zones – an intimate dining room overlooking the open kitchen, a conservatory and charming rear patio. The English-speaking waiters can offer recommendations to accompany your meal from the extensive wine list. Reservations are essential.

Verdeo VEGETARIAN $
(Map p191; www.ricoverdeo.com; Carrera 35 No 8A-3; mains COP$12,000-16,000; ⊙closed Mon; ✍) You don't have to be a vegetarian to enjoy the creative dishes on offer at this groovy Poblado co-operative. Take your pick from delicious vegetarian shawarma, burgers, ravioli and salads. The attached grocers is a great place to pick up organic veggies, tofu and other products not found in local supermarkets.

COUNTING CALORIES: BANDEJA PAISA

The artery-busting *bandeja paisa* (*paisa* tray) is famed across Colombia as the most typical plate of Antioquia and the Zona Cafetera. What is harder to get consensus on is what it actually consists of. The dish has its origins among poor farmers who would eat one high-calorie meal a day to give them energy to work in the cool mountain climates. These days there are many variations of the dish served in restaurants all over the country. However among purists, for a plate to be worthy of the name it must include white rice, red beans, ground meat, pork rinds, avocado, fried eggs, plantains, sausage, *arepas* (corn cakes), h*ogao* (warm tomato chutney) and black pudding. It must also all be squeezed onto one oval-shaped plate.

Mondongos COLOMBIAN $$
(Map p191; www.mondongos.com.co; Calle 10 No 38-38; mains COP$18,000-26,000) Medellín families flock to this unremarkable-looking eatery to fill up on delicious *Sopa de Mondongo* (tripe soup). It is served with avocado, banana, lemon and *arepas* (corn cakes), which are added/dunked in the bowl according to each diner's personal ritual. For the full experience, come for Sunday lunch. There is another branch on La 70.

Bahía Mar SEAFOOD $$$
(Map p191; ☎352 0938; Calle 9 No 43B-127; mains COP$20,000-40,000; ⊙lunch & dinner Mon-Sat, lunch Sun) This top-notch seafood place offers *mariscos* (seafood) in an unpretentious Caribbean setting. The signature dish is *langostino Providencia* (Providencia-style king prawns) but it also does enormous shrimp cocktails and light platters of seafood crepes. A top choice for seafood in Medellín.

Tabun MIDDLE EASTERN $$
(Map p191; www.eltabun.com; Carrera 33 No 7-99; mains COP$18,000-25,000) This atmospheric Poblado eatery is popular with Medellín foodies for its generous portions of flavorful Middle Eastern classics. The grilled meats are superb as is the platter of salads served with flatbread baked fresh right in the dining area. On weekends there are sometimes belly-dancing performances.

Il Forno ITALIAN $
(Map p191; Carrera 37A No 8-9; mains COP$7000-18,000) Set in the middle of the *zona rosa*, this open-air Italian restaurant doesn't do gimmicks or discounts, just hearty food at a fair price. It serves pizza and sandwiches, lasagna and ravioli, and even steak. It may not be gourmet, but at this price, who cares?

La Casa de Beto COLOMBIAN $
(Map p191; Carrera 42 No 9-53; mains COP$8000-11,000) More than a little out of place in chic Poblado, Beto's is a no-nonsense diner that serves up hearty plates of simple *paisa* food at budget prices. The set lunch menu (COP$7500) includes soup, meat, sides, salad and a drink. Also prepares filling breakfasts.

Carulla SUPERMARKET $
(off Map p191; ⊙24hr) This supermarket is right next to CC Oviedo. It has a great salad bar (including fruit salad) with selections sold by weight. A convenient place to sample Colombia's many wonderful tropical fruits. It has sandwiches and hot food, too.

CENTRAL MEDELLÍN

Los Toldos　　　　　　　　COLOMBIAN $$
(Map p188; Calle 54 Caracas No 47-11; mains COP$15,000-18,000; ☺lunch & dinner) Elderly waiters wear traditional costumes and old-style Colombian folk music plays on the stereo at this typical *paisa* place. Go for the daily special, about COP$15,000, or indulge in a hearty *bandeja paisa* (*paisa* tray).

Govinda's　　　　　　　　VEGETARIAN $
(Map p188; Calle 51 Boyacá No 52-17; meals COP$6500-7500; ☺lunch Mon-Sat; ✍) Part restaurant, part cultural center, Govinda's has a great-value vegetarian buffet. Choose from a wide range of soups, soy-based mains, salads and vegetable sides. If you arrive late you will probably be limited to the fast-food menu.

Drinking

The city's *zona rosa* is around Parque Lleras in El Poblado, a Disneyland of upscale restaurants and bars. Many late-night options cluster around the former industrial neighborhood of Barrio Colombia, while the biggest discos can be found on the Autopista Sur, the southern highway out of town. Medellín's most exclusive bars and clubs are located on a stretch of Av El Poblado known as the Milla de Oro (Golden Mile). For a more bohemian experience, check out the bars around Parque del Periodista.

Café Le Bon　　　　　　　　CAFE
(Map p191; Calle 9 No 39-09; ☺9am-1am Mon-Sat, to 11pm Sun) One of Medellín's few real coffee shops, Le Bon would not be out of place in a funky arts neighborhood in any North American city. Choose from 14 types of espresso and 10 of cappuccino. In the evening the stereo stays leashed, making it a quiet spot for a cocktail or a beer.

El Acontista　　　　　　　　BAR, CAFE
(Map p188; www.elacontista.com; Calle 53 Maracaibo No 43-81; ☺closed Sun) Attracting a laid-back, intellectual crowd, this chilled bar-cafe near the Parque del Periodista is a great place for drinks and conversation. There is live jazz on Mondays and a bookstore upstairs.

La Strada　　　　　　　　BAR, CLUB
(off Map p191; www.lastrada.com.co; Carrera 43 No 1 Sur-155) Many of Medellín's most exclusive (and expensive) bars and clubs can be found in this multilevel 'entertainment mall' in Poblado. This is where the rich and famous come to see and be seen – dress up or you will be hanging around outside.

☆ Entertainment

Cinema

Teatro Lido　　　　　　　　CINEMA, THEATER
(Map p188; ☎251 5334; www.medellincultura.gov.co/teatrolido; Carrera 48 No 54-20) On Parque de Bolívar, this refurbished theater has regular free screenings of documentaries and alternative films as well as concerts and other events.

Parque de los Deseos　　　　　　　　CINEMA
(Map p186; ☎516 6404; www.fundacionepm.org.co; Carrera 52 No 71-11) Bring something soft to sit on for the free open-air cinema at this sleek, all-concrete space across from the Jardín Botánico. Films are usually shown on weekends; call for the schedule.

Nightclubs

El Tibiri　　　　　　　　SALSA CLUB
(cnr Carrera 70 & Calle 44B; ☺8pm-2am Thu-Sat) Hidden in an unsigned sweaty basement on La 70, this intimate salsa club is one of the best places in town to perfect your moves. There is no cover and the cheap drinks and friendly crowd will get even non-dancers onto the floor.

Luxury　　　　　　　　CLUB
(Carrera 43G No 24-15) The hottest club in Barrio Colombia, Luxury is full of young, hip *paisas* grinding to reggaeton and hip-hop. Avoid the upstairs VIP area – the ground floor is where the fun is at. Turn up somewhere beyond tipsy and you'll fit right in.

Eslabon Prendido　　　　　　　　SALSA CLUB
(Papayera; off Map p188; Calle 53 No 42-55) Hugely popular with backpackers and Medellín's expat community, this unpretentious salsa bar packs a crowd on Tuesdays for its live-band performances. The vibe is very sociable; you don't need to bring a dance partner.

Forum　　　　　　　　CLUB
(www.forumcolombia.com; Carrera 45 No 72-115) Located out of town in Itagüí, Forum is a large techno club that features regular shows by major international DJs. It is usually open until well after sunrise, making it a popular final port of call for the hardcore party set.

Tango

Once the preferred dance of the we're-not-really-Colombian *paisas,* it now lingers on

WHAT'S ON IN MEDELLÍN

» **El Colombiano** (www.quericomedel lin.com) – comprehensive event listings

» **Opción Hoy** (www.opcionhoy.com) – entertainment listings with a cultural focus

» **www.guiaturisticademedellin. com** – a bilingual guide to the city; bookstores sell hard copies

» **www.medellinenescena.org** – for theater event listings

» **www.medellinzonarosa.com** – cinema schedules and nightlife

» **www.tangomedellin.co** – for list-ings on tango-related events

in the memories of the older generation, and those with a taste for nostalgia.

Casa Gardeliana　　　　　　　DANCE
(212 0968; Carrera 45 No 76-50; admission free) Located in Barrio Manrique, the Casa Garde-liana was the main tango venue for years, hosting tango bands and dance shows. It still has them from time to time, though now it's basically a small tango museum and dance academy offering group classes (COP$20,000 per course) and personalized instruction (COP$40,000 per hour).

El Patio del Tango　　　　　　DANCE
(351 2856; www.patiodeltango.com; Calle 23 No 58-38; mains COP$20,000-26,000; ⊙dinner Wed-Sun) Now the tango's major stage in Medellín, this steak restaurant is decorated like a typical Buenos Aires tango dive. Make reservations in advance for the live shows from Thursday to Saturday. It's located south of the center, a couple of blocks northwest of the zoo.

Sports

Medellín has two soccer teams, **Indepen-diente Medellín** (DIM; www.dim.com.co) and **Atlético Nacional** (www.atlnacional.com.co). Both play at **Estadio Atanasio Giradot** (off Map p186) near the aptly named Estadio metro station.

Theater

Medellín has the liveliest theater scene out-side of Bogotá.

Teatro Metropolitano　　　　THEATER
(Map p186; 232 4597; www.teatrometropolitano. com; Calle 41 No 57-30) Medellín's largest and

most modern theater hosts concerts, opera and ballet and is home to Medellín's Philhar-monic Orchestra.

Teatro Pablo Tobón Uribe　　　　THEATER
(Map p186; 239 7500; www.teatropablotobon. com; Carrera 40 No 51-24) This is Medellín's major mainstream theater.

Casa del Teatro Medellín　　　　THEATER
(Map p186; 254 0397; www.casadelteatro.org. co; Calle 59 No 50A-25) Hosts different local theater groups year-round. The theater li-brary has a large collection specializing in Colombian theater.

Shopping

**Centro Comercial Palacio
Nacional**　　　　　　　SHOPPING CENTER
(Map p188; cnr Carrera 52 Carabobo & Calle 48) A palatial building from 1925 in the center, it has been transformed into a shopping mall with more than 200 budget shops (most sell-ing clothing and footwear). The area around the Palacio, nicknamed El Hueco (The Hole) by the locals, features plenty of bargain stores.

**Centro Artesanal Mi
Viejo Pueblo**　　　　　　HANDICRAFTS
(Map p188; Carrera 49 No 53-20) This tourist-orientated handicraft market has a wide se-lection of souvenirs, including hammocks, bags and traditional clothing.

Mercado de San Alejo　　　　MARKET
(Map p188; Parque de Bolívar; ⊙1st Sun each month) This colorful craft market is great for cheap buys or simply to stroll around.

Panamericana　　　　　　BOOKS
(off map p191; www.panamericana.com.co; Car-rera 43A No 6S-150) This huge bookstore has a limited selection of English titles. It also sells maps of Medellín, plus laptops and accessories.

For high-end shopping, head to the malls of El Poblado, including **El Tesoro** (off Map p191; Carrera 25A No 1AS-45), **Santafé** (off Map p191; Carrera 43A No 7 Sur-170) and **CC Oviedo** (off Map p191; Carrera 43A No 6S-15).

 Information

For more information, head to Lonely Planet (www.lonelyplanet.com/colombia/medellin) for planning advice, author recommendations, traveler reviews and insider tips.

Internet Access

There are plenty of internet cafes in El Poblado and the center. Most charge around COP$2000 per hour.

Internet Center (Calle 53 No 47-44; ⊘9am-9pm) International calls and fax service.

Movil Shock (Carrera 43A No 9-70; ⊘7:30am-7:30pm) Near Parque Poblado.

Medical Services

Staff at both these private clinics speak some English.

Clínica Las Vegas (✆315 9000; www.clinica lasvegas.com; Calle 2 Sur No 46-55)

Clínica Medellín (✆311 2800; www.clinica medellin.com; Calle 7 No 39-290)

Money

Banco de Bogota (Calle 50 No 51-37)

CC Oviedo (Carrera 43A No 6 Sur-15) There are lots of moneychangers, ATMs and bank branches in Centro Comercial (CC) Oviedo.

Citibank (Carrera 43A No 1A Sur-49)

Tourist Information

Tourist office (Subsecretaría de Turismo; Map p186; ✆385 6966, 261 6060; www.medellin.travel; Calle 41 No 55-35) In the Palacio de Exposiciones.

Visa Information

Ministerio de Relaciones Exteriores (✆238 9252; www.cancilleria.gov.co; Calle 19 No 80A-40, Barrio Belén) For visa extensions. From El Poblado take the Circular Sur 302/303 bus heading south along Av Las Vegas (Carrera 48).

Getting There & Away

Air

Medellín has two airports. All international flights depart from **Aeropuerto Internacional José María Córdoba**, 35km southeast of the city near the town of Ríonegro. Avianca domestic flights depart from here, including its frequent shuttle service to Bogotá. Buses shuttle between the city center (behind the Hotel Nutibara) and the airport every 15 minutes (COP$7000, one hour, 5am to 9pm), or take a taxi (COP$54,000).

The smaller **Aeropuerto Olaya Herrera** is next door to the Terminal del Sur. Many domestic flights leave from here, including Satena's service from Medellín to the Pacific coast.

Bus

Medellín has two bus terminals. The **Terminal del Norte** (Northern Terminal), 3km north of the city center, handles buses to the north, east and southeast, including Santa Fe de Antioquia (COP$10,000, two hours), Cartagena (COP$130,000, 13 hours), Santa Marta (COP$130,000, 16 hours) and Bogotá

(COP$60,000, nine hours). It is easily reached from the center by metro (alight at Caribe) or by taxi (COP$8000).

The **Terminal del Sur** (Southern Terminal), 4km southwest of the center, handles all traffic to the west and south, including Manizales (COP$35,000, five hours), Pereira (COP$33,000, five hours), Armenia (COP$37,000, six hours) and Cali (COP$50,000, nine hours). From El Poblado it's a quick taxi ride (COP$5000).

❶ Getting Around

Bus

Medellín is well-serviced by buses, although most travelers will find the metro and taxis sufficient for their needs. The majority of routes originate on Av Oriental and Parque Berrío. Buses stop running around 10pm or 11pm.

Metro

Medellín's **Metro** (www.metrodemedellin.gov.co; single ticket COP$1525; ⊘4:30am-11pm Mon-Sat, 5am-10pm Sun) is Colombia's only commuter rail line. It opened in 1995 and consists of a 23km-long north–south line and a 6km-long east–west line. Trains run at ground level except for 5km through the central area where they go on elevated tracks. The metro company also operates three cable car lines, called Metrocable, built to service the impoverished barrios in the surrounding hills and Park Arví in Santa Elena. The rides themselves afford magnificent views and make for a lovely way to check out the town.

Taxi

Taxis are plentiful in Medellín and all are equipped with meters. Minimum charge is COP$4200. A taxi from the center to El Poblado will cost around COP$10,000.

AROUND MEDELLÍN

Long off-limits to Colombian tourists who remained trapped in their cities by the civil war, the countryside around Medellín is now secure and bustling with crowds. To the east lies the artificial reservoir Embalse Guatapé, a popular weekend getaway spot. Nearby is Piedra del Peñol, a 200m-high granite monolith you can climb. From the top you'll find great views over the lake.

To the north of the city lies Santa Fe de Antioquia, a sleepy colonial town that was once the capital of the department. These days it attracts weekenders from Medellín looking to warm up – set at a mere 550m, many hotels and restaurants have pools you can splash around in.

Three hours east of Medellín is Río Claro, a fantastic nature reserve with a peaceful river where you can go rafting or visit cathedral-sized caves full of bats.

Guatapé

📍 4 / POP 4229 / ELEV 1925M

A two-hour bus ride from Medellín takes you to the pleasant holiday town of Guatapé, founded in 1811. A ghost town for many years, tourism has returned to Guatapé with a vengeance. There's an ample selection of hotels catering to weekend visitors – prices almost halve during the week – and restaurants serving hearty *paisa* food. It makes a great day trip, especially on the weekend, when the town is packed with Colombian tourists, and a festival atmosphere reigns. There are boats that can take you out onto the lake – including several with bars and dance floors – and a canopy line that zooms along the shorefront.

Guatapé is also well known for the frescolike adornment of its traditional houses. Brightly painted bas-relief depictions of people, animals and shapes cover the lower half of many houses.

◎ Sights

A block south from the main square is **Calle de los Recuerdos**, a cobblestone street that angles uphill and showcases the best example of the local frescoes.

La Casa del Arriero, the oldest and biggest house in Guatapé, is still occupied by descendents of the original owners. They leave their front door open so you can wander into the central courtyard. Take note of the ornate, painted folding doors as you enter. Very typical of Guatapé.

The **Iglesia del Calma** features a Greco-Roman exterior and a polished wood interior. It was built in 1811 as a form of penance, or so the story goes, by a man who killed an orange thief.

🏃 Activities

A number of boating companies on the *malecón* (promenade) take turns running trips out onto the water. The standard tours include visits to La Cruz (part of the church of old Peñol – now covered by the lake), an impressive sight from the water, and Isla de las Fantasias. Most boats have big sound systems and a dance floor. All charge around COP$10,000 per person and sell cheap drinks. It is also possible to charter smaller boats seating up to 10 (COP$100,000) to see the sights on a private tour. Lakeview Hostel offers budget sightseeing boating trips (COP$20,000 per person) that include a visit to all the regular sights plus Pablo Escobar's abandoned old holiday home on the far side of the lake.

A **canopy ride** (📞861 1083; per ride COP$10,000; ⊗Fri-Sun) at the lake shore runs tourists in a bucket seat across to a large hill on the opposite side.

🛏 Sleeping & Eating

There are plenty of comfortable accommodations options around town, and you can often negotiate a hefty discount during the week. There's also no shortage of quality eats in Guatapé, centered mainly around the plaza.

🥗 El Encuentro   HOSTEL $
(📞861 1374; www.hostelelencuentro.com; Vereda Quebrada Arriba; dm COP$20,000, r COP$55,000-75,000; 🐾) Combining a peaceful ambience, spectacular views and gardens sloping down to a private swimming area, this place feels more like an expensive retreat than a hostel. Some of the elegant rooms have private balconies overlooking the lake. There is a massage room, outdoor yoga area, small kitchen and a groovy bar constructed out of wood and bottles. It is a 10-minute walk from town – take a moto-taxi if you have bags.

Lakeview Hostel   HOSTEL $
(📞861 0097; www.lakeviewhostel.com; dm COP$20,000, r COP$50,000-60,000; 🐾) Across the main bridge, this compact hostel has a fine view over the lake to the town and the Piedra del Peñol from its communal balcony. The sociable owners organize all kinds of activities including kayaking, hikes to local waterfalls and fishing trips.

Guatatur   HOTEL $$
(📞861 1212; www.hotelguatatur.com; s/d COP$115,000/140,000, ste COP$232,000-326,000; 🐾) This modestly priced resort a block from the plaza specializes in weekend package deals for Medellín couples. Several of the rooms have views of the lake, and the suites have Jacuzzis and even better views.

La Fogata   COLOMBIAN $$
(Av El Malecón; mains COP$15,000-18,000) Right opposite the lake with a view of the water and the boats, this place does amazing *paisa* food, including breakfast (COP$6500). Go

for the *trucha* (trout), or if you're really hungry, a *bandeja paisa*.

ℹ Information

There is no ATM in town – the closest machine is in the town of Peñol, a 20-minute bus ride away.

Tourist office (✆861 0555) In the *alcaldía* (town hall) on the main square; it dispenses advice during the week. On weekends, a small shack on the waterfront takes over the role.

ℹ Getting There & Away

If you're coming on a day trip, it makes sense to climb Piedra del Peñol before venturing onward to Guatapé, as it can get cloudy and rain in the afternoon. Buses to and from Medellín (COP$10,000, two hours) run about once an hour. Colectivos shuttle frequently between the turnoff to Piedra del Peñol and Guatapé (COP$1500, 10 minutes) or take a moto-taxi all the way to the entrance (COP$8000).

Returning from Guatapé on the weekend be sure to buy your round-trip ticket immediately upon arrival, as buses fill up fast. The ticket office is on the uphill side of the main plaza.

Piedra del Peñol

ELEV 2100M

Known as **El Peñol** (La Piedra, 'The Rock'; per climb COP$8000), this 200m-high granite monolith is set near the edge of a lake (Embalse Guatapé). A brick staircase of 649 steps rises up through a broad fissure in the side of the rock. From the top there are magnificent views of the region, the fingers of the lake sprawling amid a vast expanse of green mountain.

Coming from Medellín, don't get off the bus in the town of Peñol – ask the driver to let you off at 'La Piedra,' which is another 10 minutes down the road. Take the cobblestone road that curves up and past the gas station (1km) to reach the parking lot at the base of the rock. Here there are a host of restaurants, tourist shacks selling knickknacks, and a bronze statue of the first man to climb the rock. Numerous restaurants serve lunch (COP$7000 to COP$12,000). At the top, shops sell fruit juice, ice cream and *salpicón* (fruit salad punch in watermelon juice).

Santa Fe de Antioquia

✆4 / POP 23,600 / ELEV 550M

This sleepy colonial town is the region's oldest settlement and was once the capital of Antioquia. Founded in 1541 by Jorge Robledo, the clock stands still at 1826, the year the government moved to Medellín. Because it was eclipsed for so long by its neighbor 80km to the southeast, its colonial center never fell to the wrecking ball and today it looks very much like it did in the 19th century. The narrow streets are lined with whitewashed houses, all single-story construction and many arranged around beautiful courtyards. You'll also see elaborately carved – and typically Antioquian – woodwork around windows and doorways.

Set on the low-lying banks of the Río Cauca, these days Santa Fe de Antioquia attracts tourists from Medellín looking to warm up in its steamy climate. It makes a great day trip from Medellín, especially on the weekend, when city folk come to splash around in the many swimming pools around town. Don't miss sampling *pulpa de tamarindo,* the beloved sour-sweet candy made with tamarind from the surrounding valley.

◎ Sights

Of the town's four churches, the **Iglesia de Santa Bárbara** (cnr Calle 11 & Carrera 8; ◷5-6:30pm, plus Sun morning mass) is the most interesting. Built by Jesuits in the second half of the 18th century, the church has a fine, baroque facade. The interior has an interesting, if time-worn, retable over the high altar. Next door, the **Museo de Arte Religioso** (✆853 2345; Calle 11 No 8-12) was closed for renovations at the time of research, but it has an extensive collection of religious objects, including paintings by Gregorio Vásquez de Arce y Ceballos. Some of the works are temporarily on display at the **Museo Juan del Corral** (✆853 4605; museojuandelcorral@mincultura.gov.co; Calle 11 No 9-77; admission COP$1000; ◷10am-5pm, closed Wed), an interesting museum dedicated to the history of the region set in a perfectly preserved colonial mansion.

The **Catedral** (Plaza Mayor; ◷morning & evening mass, plus 11am Sun service) is sometimes referred to as the Catedral Madre, as it was the first church built in the region. However, the original church was destroyed by fire, and the large building you see today was not completed until 1837. Once inside have a look at the *Last Supper* in the right transept, and at an image of San Francisco de Borja with a skull in the transept opposite.

About 5km east of Santa Fe on the road to Sopetrán, the **Puente de Occidente**

Santa Fe de Antioquia

Santa Fe de Antioquia

◉ Top Sights
Iglesia de Santa Bárbara.....................C2
Museo Juan del Corral B1

◉ Sights
1 Catedral...B2
2 Museo de Arte Religioso.....................C2

🛏 Sleeping
3 Hostal Plaza Mayor.............................B2
4 Hotel Caserón Plaza...........................B2

🍴 Eating
5 Restaurante Portón del Parque..........A2

🍷 Drinking
6 La Comedia...C2

(Western Bridge) is an impressive 291m-long bridge over the Río Cauca. Completed in 1895, it was one of the first suspension bridges in the Americas. A small fleet of tricycle moto-taxis now usher tourists to and from the bridge (COP$12,000 round trip). Take care when walking across – the wood is rotten in places and visitors have fallen through and drowned in the river below.

🎊 Festivals & Events

Semana Santa RELIGIOUS
(Holy Week; Easter) Like most traditional towns dating from the early days of the Spanish Conquest, Santa Fe celebrates this with pomp and solemnity. Book accommodations in advance.

Fiesta de los Diablitos CULTURAL
(Dec) The town's most popular festival is held annually over the last four days of the year. It includes music, dance, a craft fair, and – like almost every feast in the country – a beauty contest and bullfights.

🛏 Sleeping

Most people come to Santa Fe as a day trip, but the town has about a dozen hotels catering to all budgets. Prices during the week are much lower than on the weekend.

TOP CHOICE **Hostal Plaza Mayor** HOSTEL $
(☑853 3448; Plaza Mayor; r per person COP$20,000; ❄︎☎︎🏊︎) Set in an old colonial building on the main square, this backpacker-oriented hotel is superb value. It has neat renovated rooms inside the house and bamboo huts by the pool. There are fantastic views of the surrounding mountains from the back deck and bikes are available.

Hotel Caserón Plaza   HOTEL **$$**
(☎853 2040; halcaraz@edatel.net.co; Plaza Mayor;
s/d/tr/q   COP$52,000/97,000/142,000/178,000;
❄☎☷) On the town's main square, this inn
was once home to a member of the local gen-
try. Rooms are arranged around an attrac-
tive courtyard, and there is a nice pool and
garden in the back, plus a decent restaurant.
Air-con is COP$10,00 extra. Day-trippers can
get a meal and pool access for COP$30,000.

✗ Eating & Drinking

There are plenty of decent budget restau-
rants on the main plaza. Most bars are
clumped around the tiny *zona rosa* by the
Plazoleta de la Chinca.

Restaurante Portón del Parque   COLOMBIAN **$$**
(☎853 3207; Calle 10 No 11-03; mains COP$18,000-
30,000; ☺lunch & dinner) Occupying an elegant
colonial house with high ceilings and a
flowery courtyard, this restaurant is widely
considered the best in town. The kitchen
prepares top-quality traditional food and
international favorites. The menu is meat
heavy but mains include a great self-service
salad bar.

La Comedia   CAFE, BAR **$$**
(Calle 11 No 8-03) With a chilled vibe and a low-
volume jazz soundtrack, this arty place in
front of the Iglesia de Santa Bárbara serves a
full range of hot and cold beverages as well
as delicious light meals (mains COP$15,000
to COP$20,000). In the evening, it is the best
place for a low-key drink if the loud bars of
the *zona rosa* don't appeal.

❶ Information

Banco Agraria (Calle 9 No 10-51) This ATM
accepts all cards (Visa, MasterCard, American
Express etc).

Listo Comunicaciones (☎853 3357; per hr
COP$1000; ☺7am-10pm) On the main square;
this interent place also has telephone cabins.
Sign outside says 'Telecom.'

Tourist office (Oficina de Fomento y Turismo;
☎853 4139; Plaza Mayor; ☺8am-noon &
2-6pm) The tourist office is in the Palacio
Municipal on the main plaza and has useful
information on where to stay. It can also direct
you to local craftspeople and jewelry makers.

❶ Getting There & Away

There are hourly buses (COP$10,000, two hours)
to/from Medellín's Terminal de Norte. The last
bus back to Medellín leaves around 8pm.

Río Claro

📷 4 / ELEV 350M

Three hours east of Medellín and five
hours west of Bogotá is the **Reserva Natu-
ral Cañon de Río Claro** (☎268 8855; www.
rioclaroelrefugio.com; Autopista Medellín-Bogotá
Km152; campsite per person COP$5000, r per per-
son incl 3 meals COP$75,000-90,000). A river has
carved a stunning canyon from its marble
bed. Here you can visit a spectacular cave,
go white-water rafting, canopying, or just
swim and hike along its banks. It's also a
favorite spot for bird-watchers who come to
see everything from hummingbirds to her-
ons to vultures.

Set 2km south of the Medellín-Bogotá
highway, the reserve offers a variety of ac-
commodation options. The most impres-
sive are a 15-minute walk upriver from
the restaurant – the rooms face the open
jungle, and you fall asleep to the roar of
the river beside you and the loud thrum
of crickets in the night. You'll wake to see
mist rising up through the jungle-clad can-
yon. Book in advance to make sure you
get a river view. There is also a motel-style
property at the edge of the highway, but
it suffers from the constant highway road
noise.

Be sure to visit the **Caverna de los Guá-
charos** (COP$12,000), a spectacular nearby
cave. Cavern after cavern soar high and
hollow like great cathedrals. A stream runs
through the cave, about 1km long. The en-
trances are guarded by shrill, shrieking
flocks of *guácharos,* a batlike nocturnal
bird. You'll be given a life vest and be ex-
pected to swim part of the way.

The river is a fine place to go rafting
(COP$20,000). The rapids are Class I – hard-
core rafters may be disappointed. Canopy
cables crisscross the river, and make for a
diverting afternoon zipping through the
jungle (COP$20,000).

Bring a swimsuit, towel and flashlight. On
weekends the reserve is often full of Colom-
bian high school students – you may prefer
to come during the week. The food served is
second-rate, with fruit and vegetables making
only cameo appearances. Cooking is only per-
mitted in the camping area. Beer is for sale in
the restaurant but hard liquor is forbidden.

❶ Information

The reserve is 24km west of Doradal, where you
will find a couple of budget hotels and internet

cafes near the main plaza. The closest ATM is in Puerto Triunfo, a further 15 minutes east by taxi/bus.

ℹ️ Getting There & Away

Most Medellín-Bogotá buses will drop you at the reserve's entrance. From any other direction, look for transportation to Doradal, from where you can pick up a bus to the main gate (COP$5000, 20 minutes).

ZONA CAFETERA

Welcome to coffee country. Colombia is famous for its coffee, but nowhere is the prized bean more important than in the departments of Caldas, Risaralda and Quindío, which together make up the heart of the Zona Cafetera, also called the Eje Cafetero. Here you will find jeeps packed with mustachioed coffee-pickers, poncho-wearing senior citizens gossiping in cafes and, of course, endless cups of piping hot arabica. Many working *fincas* (coffee farms) have embraced tourism and welcome visitors onto their plantations to learn all about the coffee-growing process. It is particularly interesting to visit during the harvests (April to May, October to December) when the farms are a hive of activity.

The region was colonized by *paisas* in the 19th century during the *colonización antioqueña* (colonization of the coffee region), and to this day remains culturally closer to Medellín than either Cali or Bogotá, in everything from its traditional architecture to its cuisine. It is an area of spectacular natural beauty. There are stunning vistas everywhere – Salento, in particular, and the adjacent Valle de Cocora, are jaw-dropping. Parque Nacional Natural (PNN) Los Nevados soars above 5000m and offers trekking opportunities through the striking *páramo* (high-mountain plains).

Manizales

📞 6 / POP 388,525 / ELEV 2150M

The northern wheel of the Coffee Axle, Manizales is a pleasantly cool, midsized university town, surrounded on all sides by green mountain scenery. There is a strong student vibe, and many excellent restaurants and nightclubs cater to their tastes and budgetary requirements. Manizales is also the gateway to PNN Los Nevados and three nearby nature reserves – Recinto del Pensamiento, Reserva Ecológica Río Blanco

and Los Yarumos. Several coffee farms offer popular tours.

Manizales is the capital of the Caldas department, and was founded in 1849 by a group of Antioquian colonists looking to escape the civil wars of that time. According to local legend, the original settlement consisted of 20 families, including the family of Manuel Grisales, after whom the new city was named. Manizales' early development was hindered by two earthquakes in 1875 and 1878, and a fire in 1925. For this reason there's not a lot of historical interest left – the real attractions are the surrounding nature activities and the town's popping nightlife.

⊙ Sights

The **Plaza de Bolívar** is the city's main square, with the mandatory statue of Bolívar by Rodrigo Arenas Betancur. It is known as Bolívar-Cóndor, since the sculptor endows Colombia's founder with distinctly birdlike features. The **Palacio de Gobierno**, a pretty neoclassical confection built in 1927, stands on the northern side of the plaza.

The square's south side is dominated by the odd but impressive **Catedral de Manizales** (tower climb COP$7000; ⊙tower 9am-noon & 2-6pm Thu-Mon). Begun in 1929 and built of reinforced concrete, it is among the first churches of its kind in Latin America, and its main tower is 106m high, making it the highest church tower in the country. You can climb to the top for great views of the city.

A short walk east of Plaza de Bolívar is the **Iglesia de la Inmaculada Concepción**. Built at the beginning of the 20th century, it has a beautiful, carved-wood interior reminiscent of a ship's hull.

At Chipre, 2km north and uphill of the center you will find the **Torre al Cielo** (📞880 2345; www.torrealcielo.com; admission COP$3000; ⊙11am-10pm Mon-Wed, 11am-2am Thu-Sat, 10am-10pm Sun), a 45m-high lookout with phenomenal views over town to PNN Los Nevados. Buses run along Av Santander from Cable Plaza to Chipre (COP$1100, 15 minutes) every 30 seconds (yes, that frequently!).

☞ Tours

Along with the following, the Mountain House hostel also offers tours to Parque Nacional Natural (PNN) Los Nevados.

Kumanday Adventures ADVENTURE TOURS
(📞885 4980, 315 590 7294; www.kumanday.com; Av Santander No 60-13) This full-service adven-

ture tour company, next door to the Universidad Católica, offers mountaineering and mountain-biking tours nationwide. It rents a few dorm beds on-site. Also rents and sells tents, sleeping bags and mountaineering equipment.

Ecosistemas TOURS
(☑880 8300; ecosistemas2000@yahoo.com; Carrera 21 No 23-41) Offers excursions and multiday tours to PNN Los Nevados (see p207).

Comfamiliares TOURS
(☑886 0737; cnr Carrera 25 & Calle 50) Another outfit offering tours to PNN Los Nevados (see p207).

✦ Festivals & Events

Feria de Manizales BULLFIGHTING
(Jan) The highlight of Manizales' annual festivals is the bullfights – the feria attracts some of the world's best bullfighters, and Colombia's feistiest bulls. You'll also find the usual assortment of parades and crafts fairs, and of course a beauty pageant.

Festival Internacional de Teatro THEATER
(Sep & Oct) Held annually since 1968, this is one of two important theater festivals in Colombia (the other is in Bogotá). The festival lasts about a week and includes free concerts in Plaza de Bolívar.

🛏 Sleeping

Most accommodations are located in the Cable Plaza area where you will find a large shopping mall and most of the city's best restaurants. Prices more than double during the high season (ie January for the feria).

Mountain House HOSTEL $
(☑887 4736; www.mountainhousemanizales.com; Calle 66 No 23B-137; dm COP$20,000, s/d COP$50,000/55,000, s/d without bathroom COP$40,000/45,000; @🛜) A short walk from the *zona rosa,* this fine choice attracts a relaxed crowd and is one of the few hostels where backpackers and Colombian travelers mix. A small tour office on-site offers a variety of interesting treks in and around Parque Nacional Natural (PNN) Los Nevados. At the time of research, a second, more upmarket hostel with mostly private rooms was being constructed a couple of doors down.

Estelar Las Colinas HOTEL $$$
(☑884 2009, 1 800 097 8000; www.hoteleses telar.com; Carrera 22 No 20-20; s/d COP$161,200/202,484; @🛜) The poshest place in the center, this modern glass-and-concrete hotel isn't pretty to look at, but it has large, comfortable rooms, plus a fine restaurant. Prices include a generous buffet breakfast. Rooms on the upper levels have better views and more natural light.

Varuna Hotel HOTEL $$$
(☑881 1122; www.varunahotel.com; Calle 62 No 23C-18; s/d COP$189,500/229,500; @🛜) A popular business traveler option, this modern hotel offers minimalist rooms with polished wood floors a short walk from Cable Plaza. It has a restaurant serving breakfast, lunch and dinner. Ask for an upstairs room with a view.

Hostal Palogrande HOSTEL $
(☑886 3984; www.hostalpalogrande.com; Calle 62 No 23-36; dm/s/d COP$25,000/30,000/60,000; 🛜) This new hostel right in the *zona rosa* is cheap and super clean with big bathrooms and a nice lounge area. The drawback – thin mattresses and the paper-thin walls make it feel like you are in bed with your neighbors.

Pit Stop Hostel HOSTEL $
(☑887 3797; www.pitstopmanizales.com; Calle 65 No 23B-19; dm COP$21,000, r with/without bathroom COP$40,000/30,000; @🛜) This sociable hostel has a great location near Cable Plaza, free breakfast, a big hot tub and a rocking bar downstairs popular with local metalheads.

🍴 Eating

There is a Carulla supermarket in Cable Plaza and plenty of cheap fast-food outlets on Carrera 23 in the *zona rosa.*

La Suiza BAKERY $
(Carrera 23B No 26-57; mains COP$10,000-14,000; ⏱9am-8:30pm Mon-Sat, 10am-7:30pm Sun) This scrumptious bakery does great pastries and even homemade chocolate. It also does tasty budget breakfasts, plus light lunches, such as mushroom crepes and chicken sandwiches. Also has a branch near Cable Plaza.

Los Geranios COLOMBIAN $$
(☑886 8738; Carrera 23 No 71-67, Milan; mains COP$16,000-18,500) Famous for its large portions of traditional Colombian food, this place is great if you're hungry or just fueling up for a late night. The menu includes *bandeja paisa,* five kinds of *sancocho* (soup), *ajiaco* (a thicker soup made of chicken, corn, many different types of potatoes, avocado, and a local herb known as *guasca*), steak, chicken and even a few fish

dishes. Meals come with five different kinds of sauce.

Spago
ITALIAN $$

(☎885 3328; Calle 59 No 24a-10; mains COP$16,000-33,000; ☺lunch & dinner Mon-Sat, lunch Sun) Manizales is a bit limited when it comes to international dining, but this modern bistro delivers with great home-style Italian food. The flavors here are subtle, the ingredients fresh and the staff professional. Has a fair selection of wines.

Don Juaco
COLOMBIAN $

(☎885 0610; Calle 65 No 23A-44; mains COP$12,000-17,000) Right in the heart of the *zona rosa,* this popular restaurant does great burgers, and the lunch special is excellent value – *cazuela de pollo* (think chicken pot pie without the pastry), with bread, salad, dessert and coffee for COP$14,000.

Drinking & Entertainment

The main *zona rosa* is along Av Santander near Cable Plaza. There are several *viejo-tecas* (nightclubs for patrons 30 and over) near the bullring, 1km southwest of the center. For a drink with a view there are a few *estancos* (small liquor shop with outdoor tables) in Chipre near the *mirador* (lookout). Note that some clubs do not serve beer, only bottles of liquor.

Valentino's Gourmet
CAFE

(Carrera 23 No 63-128; ☺10am-10pm) This small cafe, popular with students, does the best hot chocolate in town. Choose from 20 different espresso and cappuccino styles, and gourmet chocolates, too.

Bar C
CLUB

(Via Acueducto Niza; ☺Thu-Sat) When all the bars in Manizales close at 2am, anyone left standing comes here. Set up on a mountain-top about 3km east of Cable Plaza, there are great views of the city and the stars. A kiosk in the car park serves food until late. DJs play mostly Colombian crossover to please the late-night student crowd. Wide selection of top-shelf liquor.

Bar La Plaza
CAFE, BAR

(Carrera 23B No 64-80; ☺11am-11pm Mon-Wed, to 2am Thu-Sat) This is the place to start your evening. A delicatessen by day, at night it fills up fast, and by 9pm you'll have to wait for a table. The music isn't too loud, so you can converse. There's a young student vibe, and it offers gourmet sandwiches

(COP$11,000) and snack platters of quality salami and cheese to help line your stomach. Does good cocktails.

Chaney
BAR

(Carrera 23 No 63-104; ☺9pm-2am Thu-Sat) Unlike many local clubs, this basement salsa venue actually has a sizable dance floor that is not cluttered with tables, so there is plenty of space to cut loose without knocking over bottles of aguardiente (anise-flavored liqor). This is where the city's serious dancers come to show off.

There are also a couple of old-style tango bars on the so-called Calle de Tango (Calle 24). Check out **Los Nuevos Faroles** (Calle 24 No 22-46; ☺8pm-2am Thu-Sat) and **Reminiscencias** (Calle 24 No 22-42; ☺7pm-2am Thu-Sat), just next door. Wear dress shoes or you ain't getting in.

The **Teatro Los Fundadores** (☎878 2530; www.ccclosfundadores.com; cnr Carrera 22 & Calle 27) is Manizales' leading theater; it also has a cinema.

ℹ Information

The area around the central market is a favored hangout for thieves and is best avoided. Mind the unpainted sidewalk traffic pylons; you are likely to bang your shins at least once.

4-72 (Carrera 23, No 62-65) Post office.

BBVA (Casa Luker, next door to Cable Plaza) All-card ATM.

Ciber Rosales (Carrera 23 No 57-25; per hr COP$1800; ☺8am-8pm) Plenty of computers, plus phone cabins.

Citibank (Carrera 23 No 53B-20) Reliable ATM.

Concesión Los Nevados (☎881 2065; www.concesionnevados.com; Calle 19B No 52-54; ☺7:30am-2:30pm) For accommodations bookings at Parque Nacional Natural (PNN) Los Nevados (see p205).

Tourist office (☎873 2901; www.ctm.gov.co; cnr Carrera 22 & Calle 31; ☺7am-7pm) Enthusiastic staff and plenty of maps and brochures.

Getting There & Away

Air

Aeropuerto La Nubia (☎874 5451) is 8km southeast of the city center, off the road to Bogotá. Take the urban bus to La Enea, then walk for five minutes to the terminal, or grab a cab (COP$10,000). Avianca, ADA and LAN offer frequent services to Bogotá, Medellín and Armenia.

Work on a new international airport near Palestina is seriously behind schedule and is unlikely to be finished by the time you read this.

Bus

Manizales brand-spanking new **bus terminal** ([📞]878 7858; www.terminaldemanizales.com; Carrera 43 No 65-100) is located south of the city and is linked to the downtown area by an efficient cable car (COP$1400) that offers great views of the city. Work on a second line to Villa María was underway at the time of research. If you are staying by Cable Plaza, it is easier to take a taxi direct from the terminal (COP$6000).

Buses depart regularly to Cali (COP$30,000, five hours), Bogotá (COP$50,000, eight hours) and Medellín (COP$35,000, five hours). Minibuses to Pereira (COP$11,000, 1¼ hours) and Armenia (COP$17,000, 2¼ hours) run every 15 minutes or so.

Around Manizales

RECINTO DEL PENSAMIENTO
ELEV 2100M

Set in the cloud forest 11km from Manizales, this **nature park** ([📞]874 4157; www.recintodelpensamiento.com; Km11 Via al Magdalena; admission COP$11,000-15,000; ⏰9am-4pm Tue-Sun) has a fine *mariposario,* several short walks through an impressive orchid-populated forest, and a medicinal herb garden. You'll also see big plantations of *guadua* and *chusqué* (two kinds of Colombian bamboo); note the enormous convention center in the shape of a shitake mushroom built of *guadua.* There's even a *telesilla* – a ski lift-style cable car that can take you to the top of the mountain slope on which the park sits.

Admission includes 2½ hours of mandatory guide service; a couple of the guides speak some English. There's impressive birdlife here – book in advance for bird-watching tours (COP$8000) from 6am to 9am. Wear brown or green clothes; they will lend you binoculars.

To get here, take the bus marked Sera Maltería from Cable Plaza in Manizales (COP$1400, 30 minutes, every 10 minutes), or take a taxi (COP$8000).

RESERVA ECOLÓGICA RÍO BLANCO
ELEV 2100-3800M

Three kilometers northeast of Manizales lies this undeveloped nature reserve. It is an area of high biodiversity and protects numerous endangered species, including the *oso andino* (spectacled bear). There are 362 species of bird present in the park, including 13 of Colombia's 80 endemics. It attracts bird-watchers from around the world, but even the amateur will be delighted by the quantities of hummingbirds, butterflies and orchids you'll see in the peaceful calm of this cloud forest. It makes a great half-day excursion – best in the morning, as it often rains in the afternoon.

Before you can visit you must request permission (free) from **Fundación Ecológica Gabriel Arango Restrepo** ([📞]6-886 6660; www.fundegar.com; Av Kevin Ángel No 59-181). It will organize the services of a local guide (COP$20,000 per day, up to 15 people), who will meet you at the entrance and take you into the reserve. Ask at the office for a copy of the bird list. A taxi to the main gate from Manizales will cost around COP$20,000. Get the number of your driver for the round trip; there is next to no traffic up here.

LOS YARUMOS

Set on a hill with great views over Manizales, this 53-hectare municipal **adventure park** ([📞]875 5621; Calle 61B No 15A-01; base admission COP$2500; ⏰9am-5pm Tue-Sun) has panoramic views of the city. A museum has an impressive collection of preserved butterflies, insects and birds, and a food court offers budget meals and serves beer. A half-dome concert shell sometimes hosts free concerts and cultural events on weekend afternoons. There are numerous short walks you can do through mature secondary forest, plus canopy zip-line tours (short/long COP$8500/17,000) and a challenging adventure course (COP$14,000) with various bridges and obstacles. Tour guides can show you around for free, and several speak some English.

Yarumos is a great place to come on a clear afternoon, when you can see the three peaks of El Ruiz, Santa Isabel and El Cisne. Sunsets are likewise spectacular. A new cable car linking the park directly with Cable Plaza was under construction at the time of research and should be open by the time you read this. Otherwise it's a 40-minute walk from the *zona rosa* or COP$4000 in a taxi.

TERMALES EL OTOÑO

This high-end resort and **thermal spa complex** ([📞]874 0280; www.termaleselotono.com; Km5 Antigua Via al Nevado; admission COP$15,000-25,000; r COP$220,000-452,000) has a number of large thermal pools with views of impressive mountain peaks. The on-site hotel has rooms ranging from generic hotel-type offerings to luxurious cottages with wooden ceilings, open fireplaces and private thermal spas. You don't need to be a hotel guest to use the pools, you can come just for the day. It is a little too busy and developed to be a real nature experience but it is still a relaxing day away from the city. Another cheaper but equally nice set of pools on the other side of the car park opens on weekends. There is no public transportation here. A taxi from Cable Plaza will set you back around COP$15,000.

TERMALES TIERRA VIVA

These small **thermal baths** (☑874 3089; www.termalestierraviva.com; Km2 Vía Enea-Gallinazo; admission COP$12,000-14,000; ⊙9am-10pm Mon-Thu, to 11pm Fri-Sun) are located on the edge of Río Chinchiná just outside town. There are three thermal baths made of rocks set among a pretty garden that attracts hummingbirds and butterflies. There is an excellent elevated restaurant overlooking the river or you can eat by the pools. There is also a small spa offering massages, walking trails, horseback riding and a model farm for the kids. It is quiet during the week, but on the weekends it can feel a little overcrowded. To get here take the Enea-Gallinazo bus (COP$1500) from downtown Manizales. By taxi it is around COP$10,000.

HACIENDA VENECIA

This **hacienda** (☑320 636 5719; www.hacienda venecia.com; budget r per person with/without bath-

room COP$40,000/30,000, s/d COP$220,000/300,000, s/d without bathroom COP$180,000/220,000; ☀) has won numerous awards for its coffee. The well-preserved *paisa* farmhouse is set on a hill with majestic views and has been converted to a lovely boutique hotel. The gardens are well-kept, and there's a pond with lily pads and a round blue pool. The rooms are full of books and old photographs, while the wraparound verandah has hammocks and rocking chairs to rock away the evening.

There are also less atmospheric but clean and comfortable budget accommodations in a new building across the river from the main house also with its own swimming pool.

The hacienda offers a **coffee tour** (COP$20,000) in English or Spanish that includes an informative presentation about Colombian coffee, an introduction to coffee cupping, a class in coffee preparation and a walking tour through the plantation. You can use the pool afterwards and a typical lunch is available for COP$10,000. The outfit will pick you up and drop you off at your hotel in Manizales for an additional COP$10,000 (round trip).

HACIENDA GUAYABAL

A working **coffee farm** (☑850 7831; www. haciendaguayabal.com; Km3 Vía Peaje Tarapacá,

COLOMBIAN COFFEE

Colombia is the third-largest coffee exporter in the world and the only big producer that grows exclusively arabica beans. The coffee bean was brought to Colombia from Venezuela in the early 18th century by Jesuit priests. It was first cultivated in the area that is now Norte de Santander before spreading throughout the country.

Local conditions proved ideal for growing arabica coffee. Colombia's location near the equator means that coffee can be grown high in the mountains, where the beans mature more slowly. This results in a harder, more dense bean that provides consistent flavor when roasted. Frequent rainfall in the region sees bushes that are almost always flowering, which enables two harvests a year. And the plants thrive in the region's volcanic soils, which contain a high amount of organic material.

The main varieties of arabica coffee grown in Colombia are Tipica, Bourbon, Maragogipe, Tabi, Caturra and Colombia. As the beans on a single plant mature at different times, all Colombian coffee needs to be handpicked. This job is performed by small armies of *recolectores* (coffee pickers) that travel from region to region according to the harvests.

The heavy rainfall means that beans cannot be dried in the open like in other coffee-producing regions. Colombian beans are wet-processed or 'washed,' with the fruit surrounding the bean being removed prior to drying. This process takes much of the acidity out of the bean and gives the end product a richer aroma.

While the country is a major coffee producer, outside the Zona Cafetera Colombians are not huge coffee drinkers and almost all the best beans are picked for export. If you want to purchase coffee to take home, it's best to visit some farms yourself and buy single-origin beans direct from the growers.

Chinchiná; r per person incl breakfast, lunch & dinner COP$85,000; [☎]) near Chinchiná, Guayabal offers simple, functional accommodations in a modern house set up on a hill with great views over the surrounding plantations. It runs coffee tours that follow the coffee process from the plant to the cup. The tour here is a little less polished but the guides are very friendly and keen to share their knowledge. It also runs a *guadua* tour where you learn all about this bamboo species native to the area. Each tour costs COP$20,000/$25,000 in Spanish/English and you can hang around afterwards to use the pool. Make sure to stay for lunch – the traditional farm-style food here is absolutely delicious.

To get here, take any bus from Manizales to Chinchiná (COP$2300, 30 minutes), then from the main plaza in Chinchiná take the bus marked 'Guayabal Peaje' (COP$1000, 10 minutes, every 15 to 30 minutes). Ask the driver to let you off before the toll booth at the small village of Guayabal; from here it's a 2km walk down the small road between the houses.

Parque Nacional Natural (PNN) Los Nevados

ELEV 2600M-5325M

Following a spine of snow-covered volcanic peaks, this 583-sq-km national park provides access to some of the most stunning stretches of the Colombian Andes. Its varied altitude range encompasses everything from humid cloud forests and *páramo* to glaciers on the highest peaks. The main peaks, from north to south, are El Ruiz (5325m), El Cisne (4750m), Santa Isabel (4950m), El Quindío (4750m) and El Tolima (5215m).

Thirty-seven rivers are born here providing water to 3.5 million people in four departments. The glaciers in the park are receding, and research is underway to measure the impact on the environment.

The best months to see snow in Los Nevados are October and November and from March to May. Outside of those times you're more likely to get the dry windy conditions favorable to trekking and clear views.

At the time of research, most of the northern section of the park – including the camping ground at Chalet Arenales – was off limits because of volcanic activity around Nevado del Ruiz. Hiking was only permitted in the vicinity of El Cisne – and only with an official guide. The information provided here includes destinations that were restricted – check on the situation in Manizales before heading out.

The southern part of the park is accessible only by foot. From Refugio La Pastora in the Parque Ucumarí a 15km trail goes uphill to the Laguna del Otún. Another access route begins from Valle de Cocora, from where a path heads uphill to the *páramo* and on to the extinct Nevado del Quindío (4750m). This area is fast becoming the preferred access point to Los Nevados for serious hikers. Security in this zone has improved dramatically, but it's still worth checking the latest before setting out.

NEVADO DEL RUIZ

This is the highest volcano of the chain. Its eruption on November 13, 1985, killed more than 20,000 people and swept away the town of Armero, a town on the Río Lagunillas. El Ruiz had previously erupted in 1845, but the results were far less catastrophic; today, the volcano continues to grumble, resulting in restrictions on activities in this part of the park.

The principal access road into the park is from the north. It branches off from the Manizales-Bogotá road in La Esperanza, 31km east of Manizales, and winds its way 33km through the unique landscape of the *páramo* to the snowline at about 4800m at the foot of Nevado del Ruiz.

The volcano actually has three craters: Arenas, La Olleta and Piraña. It is possible to summit the main one, Arenas (5321m), but you will need to request permission from **Parques Nacionales** (☑886 4703, 885 4581; nevados@parquesnacionales.gov.co) in Manizales in advance. It is a technical climb but is not considered difficult mountaineering.

The entrance to the park is at Las Brisas (4050m), but you need to pay admission to the park in advance at **Concesión Los Nevados** (☑881 2065; www.concesionnevados.com; park admission Colombians/foreigners COP$26,000/40,000; ☺7:30am-2:30pm).

About 7km uphill from Las Brisas is Chalet Arenales (4150m), where there is a campground (COP$10,000 per person), and 10km further up the road there is a shelter known as El Refugio (4800m), which sells coffee and snacks. From here it's a half-hour walk to the flag pole (4900m); if conditions permit you can walk 1½ hours further to the beginning of the glacier at 5100m, then 30 minutes back down. The snow glare can be ferocious; wear sunglasses and sunscreen.

The extinct Olleta crater (4850m), on the opposite side of the road from El Refugio, is covered with multicolored layers of sandy soil and normally has no snow. The walk to the top will take about 1¼ hours from the road, and it's possible to descend into the crater.

CENTRO DE VISITANTES EL CISNE

Twenty-four spectacular kilometers from Las Brisas is this **hotel** (campsite per person COP$10,000, s/d COP$145,000/165,000), set at a gasping 4180m. The cabins at El Cisne offer comfortable, heated lodging surrounded by the striking landscapes of high mountain

Parque Nacional Natural Los Nevados

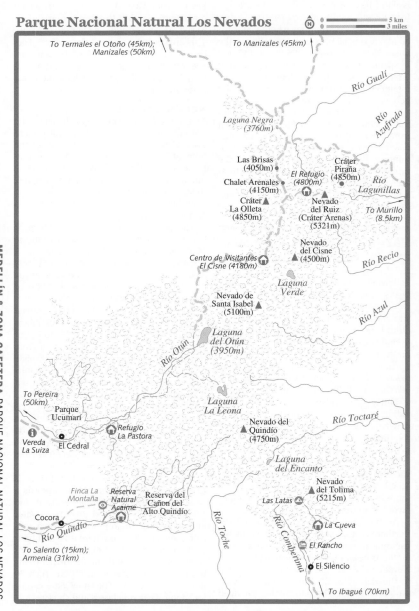

páramo. There is a mixture of accommodations for 30 people, plus a camping area and restaurant. It's a romantic getaway that will leave you breathless (literally). Advance reservations from the Concesión Los Nevados are essential.

From Las Brisas, transportation (COP$30,000 per person round trip) to El Cisne is sometimes available in the park pickup – call Concesión Los Nevados to check availability. If you have your 4WD vehicle you can drive all the way – a park guide will jump in at Las Brisas to show you the road.

NEVADO DEL TOLIMA

The Nevado del Tolima (5215m), the second-highest volcano in the chain, is the most handsome of all with its classic symmetrical cone. On a clear day it can be seen from as far away as Bogotá. Its last eruption took place in 1943.

It is best reached via Ibagué, the ugly capital of the Tolima department; however security is still an issue in this part of the park, so be sure to check conditions before attempting the climb. Landslides are also common in this area and an experienced guide is essential. A recommended guide is 'Truman' David Bejarano (☑273 4433, 315 292 7395).

It's a challenging multiday climb, requiring ice axe and crampons, though you can rejuvenate afterwards in the natural hot springs at El Rancho (2650m).

☞ Tours

Public transportation to the concession area of the park is nonexistent. Most tourists visit Los Nevados as part of an all-day group excursion to Nevado del Ruiz from Manizales. While convenient, the tours involve a lot of time on buses and very little hiking and are often a disappointment for those looking for a real mountain experience. Both Ecosistemas (☑880 8300; ecosistemas2000@ yahoo.com; Carrera 21 No 23-41, Manizales) and Comfamiliares (☑886 0737; cnr Carrera 25 & Calle 50, Manizales) offer tours (Colombians/ foreigners COP$105,000/125,000) from Manizales including transportation, breakfast and lunch, admission to the park and a visit to Termales El Otoño (p203), near Manizales, on the way back to town. If you want to spend some time in the park, you can pay COP$30,000 extra and use your return leg on another day.

For a longer stay in the park, Ecosistemas, Kumanday Adventures and Mountain House in Manizales all offer multiday excursions to less-visited areas of the park, including trips to the summits of Nevado de Santa Isabel and Nevado del Tolima.

Pereira

☑6 / POP 457,000 / ELEV 1410M

Hardworking Pereira is not your typical tourist destination. In fact it's not really a tourist destination at all. Almost all visitors to Pereira come for one thing – to do business. Founded in 1863, Pereira is the capital of Risaralda and the economic powerhouse of the Zona Cafetera – a hot industrial center most noted for its traffic and throbbing nightlife. While it doesn't offer much in the way of attractions, if you want to experience a fast-paced Colombian city away from the gringo trail, Pereira certainly fits the bill. It is also the gateway to Parque Ucumarí and Santuario Otún Quimbaya, a pair of top nature reserves, and the enchanting thermal springs of Santa Rosa and San Vicente.

◉ Sights

The downtown area is notably thin on attractions, perhaps because earthquakes have repeatedly damaged the center, most recently in 1995 and 1999. In the middle of the main square, presiding over the city's commerce and interaction, sits Rodrigo Arenas Betancur's **Bolívar Desnudo**, an 8.5m-high, 11-tonne bronze statue of the Liberator, naked on horseback, urging his stallion forward with a manic passion, buttocks clenched to his plunging mount. The **jardín botánico** (☑321 2523; www.utp.edu.co/jardin; admission COP$5000) at the Universidad Tecnológia de Pereira has orchids, exotic bamboos and medicinal plants and is a welcome respite from the hustle and bustle of the city.

🎊 Festivals & Events

Fiestas de Pereira CULTURAL
(Aug) In August the town switches into super-party-mode to celebrate the city's founding, with live music, dance shows, art exhibits and the obligatory beauty pageant.

🛏 Sleeping

Hotel Abadia Plaza HOTEL $$$
(☑335 8398; www.hotelabadiaplaza.com; Carrera 8 No 21-67; s/d incl breakfast COP$203,000/ 208,000; ❄@☎) This stylish place is as close

as Pereira comes to a boutique hotel, with original art on the walls, plush rooms with marble bathrooms and noise-resistant windows. There's a quality gym and sauna.

Hostel Sweet Home HOSTEL $
(☑345 4453; www.sweethomehostel.com; Carrera 11 No 44-30; dm/s/d incl breakfast COP$20,000/35,000/55,000; @⊕) A new alternative to the grubby downtown budget hotels, this homely hostel is not in the most convenient location, but it's clean, comfortable and a short taxi ride from anywhere you need to go.

Hotel Cumanday HOTEL $
(☑324 0416; Carrera 5 No 22-54; s/d COP$25,000/50,000) A step up from the rest of the downtown budget options, this small hotel has hot water, cable TV and laundry service. If you ask the friendly staff you can use the hotel kitchen. Rooms at the back are quieter.

Hotel Mi Casita HOTEL $$
(☑333 9995; Calle 25 No 6-20; s/d COP$49,000/69,000; @⊕) Not far from the Parque El Lago, this place is popular with travelers and has all the necessary amenities, but the rooms are pretty ordinary with low ceilings and clashing color schemes.

Eating

TOP CHOICE El Mirador ARGENTINE $$$
(☑331 2141; www.elmiradorparrillashow.com; Entrada Av Circunvalar Calle 4; mains COP$24,000-38,000; ⊙noon-2am Mon-Sat) Outside the city on top of a mountain with fantastic views of the twinkling lights of Pereira is this gem. The food is for the most part Argentine – with quality cuts of beef the specialty. Wash it down with a bottle from the extensive wine list. There is often live music here – call to find out what's coming up. Taxis add a COP$2000 surcharge for the trip.

Grajales Autoservicios CAFETERIA $
(Carrera 8 No 21-60; mains COP$8000-15,000; ⊙24hr) At this large, self-service 24-hour restaurant-cum-bakery you can put together your own lunch or dinner. It's also a top choice for breakfast.

Mama Flor COLOMBIAN $$$
(Calle 11 No 15-12, Los Alpes; mains COP$18,000-34,000; ⊙noon-11pm Mon-Sat, to 5pm Sun) Set up on a hill in a quiet residential neighborhood, this old-time restaurant is famous for its down-home Colombian food. Eat out on the large covered verandah with a decent bottle of wine. Grill is a specialty here; try the *parrilla de carnes* (mixed grill; COP$55,000), which is big enough for two.

Plaza Minorista SELF-CATERING $
(cnr Carrera 10 & Calle 41) Self-caterers should head here, where you can stock up on fruit and vegetables and also get a cheap lunch.

Drinking & Entertainment

The Sector Circunvalar is full of bars and small discos, but the late-night action is a little way outside of the city in La Badea, where all the big clubs are located. Downtown there are a number of bars popular with a bohemian crowd.

El Parnaso BAR
(Carrera 6 No 23-35; ⊙closed Sun) Walk down the long corridor through the unmarked doorway to emerge in this arty garden bar with funky wood carvings and an open fireplace. It serves tasty pizzas and burgers and the hip indie-rock soundtrack is restrained enough to enjoy a conversation.

Bar Celona BAR
(Av Circunvalar No 8-136) Owned by an FC Barcelona soccer fan (club posters decorate the walls) this unpretentious drinkery plays good ol' fashioned Colombian music; don't be surprised if the crowd joins in the chorus to a favorite song. It's spread over two floors; the smaller second level has views of the bustling street. A lively place to start your evening.

Leña Verde SALSA CLUB
(☑330 6162; La Badea) Great for people-watching, this popular *salsateca* (salsa dance club) attracts all types from baggy-trousered homeboys to smooth romantics with tight shirts and perfectly manicured mustaches. But everyone has one goal – to get blind drunk and dance all night. Bring a dance partner – it's not the safest place to be hitting on strangers as it can be a rough crowd.

Paradise CLUB
(www.discotecaparadise.com; Transversal 7, detras de Makro) Set apart from the main *zona rosa*, this massive club has a neat retractable roof and an enormous dance floor with enormous speakers to match that pump out reggaeton at ear-splitting volume. It also hosts techno nights – check the website.

❶ Information

There are numerous ATMs across the street from the Pereira bus station in the LA14 shopping center.

MEDELLÍN & ZONA CAFETERA PEREIRA

4-72 (Carrera 9 No 21-33) Post Office.

BBVA (Carrera 7 No 19-64) On Plaza de Bolívar.

Booking office (☑333 6157; Av Circunvalar No 15-62; ☺8am-5pm Mon-Fri, to 3pm Sat) Oversees bookings for the thermal pools in Termales San Vicente (p210).

Ciber La 24 (Calle 24 No 4-09; per hr COP$1800; ☺6am-10pm Mon-Fri, to 8pm Sat) Internet and calls.

Hospital San Jorge (☑335 6333; Carrera 4 No 24-88)

Tourist office (☑325 4157; www.risaralda. com.co; cnr Carrera 10 & Calle 17; ☺Mon-Fri) In the Centro Cultural.

❶ Getting There & Away

Air

Pereira's international **Aeropuerto Matecaña** (☑326 0021) is 5km west of the city center, 20 minutes by urban bus, or around COP$10,000 by taxi. Airlines Avianca, LAN, Copa and Satena serve domestic destinations. Copa also has direct flights to Panama.

Bus

The **bus terminal** (☑321 5834; Calle 17 No 23-157) is 1.5km south of the city center. Many urban buses will take you there in less than 10 minutes. There are regular departures to Bogotá (COP$50,000, nine hours). A number of buses go to Medellín (COP$33,000, six hours) and Cali (COP$29,000, four hours). Minibuses run every 15 minutes to Armenia (COP$7200, one hour) and Manizales (COP$11,000, 1¼ hours). There is also service to Santa Rosa de Cabal (COP$5000, 45 minutes).

❶ Getting Around

Pereira's new **Megabus** (www.megabus.gov.co) system runs crosstown and out to Dosquebradas. It's similar to Bogotá's TransMilenio and Cali's Mio, but on a smaller scale. The taxi minimum is COP$3700 with a COP$700 surcharge after 7pm.

Finca Villa Martha

One of the very first *fincas* in the area to open up to tourists, this small **property** (☑332 9385, 310 421 5920; www.fincavillamartha. com; vía Marsella Km9; s/d incl breakfast & dinner COP$75,000/150,000, ❏❄) on the road to Marsella still has a very personal touch. Owners Martha and Rafael will show you the entire process of getting the coffee from the bushes into your cup. Tourism is the main business here, but you can still purchase bags of beans from their small harvest

to take with you. The brick rooms feature elegant touches of bamboo and there is a large pool surrounded by plantain trees. Call before you leave to arrange a pickup at 'La Bodega' where the Pereira-Marsella bus (COP$2000, 25 minutes) will drop you.

Termales de Santa Rosa

 6 / ELEV 1950M

These spectacular **thermal springs** (☑363 4959; www.termales.com.co; admission COP$35,000; ☺9am-10pm) are located at the foot of three adjacent waterfalls, the largest 170m high. Opened in 1945 and built in the style of a Swiss chalet, the hotel and tourist complex have the air of another place and time. There is one large pool open to the general public, while hotel guests have exclusive access to a medium-sized pool under the original water source and two pothole-sized baths. There is also a full spa service, bar and cafeteria.

The on-site **Hotel Termales** (☑363 4966; r per person incl meals COP$197,000-247,000) seems overpriced considering the worn condition of the original house where guests have to go outside to use the shared bathrooms. The accommodations are better in the new wing and there are discounts available during low season. Some may prefer to base themselves nearby and come for the day.

Owned and managed by the hotel, the adjacent **Balneario de Santa Rosa thermals** (☑314 701 9361; www.termales.com.co; admission COP$30,000; ☺9am-midnight) are cheaper and only slightly less impressive, with a 25m-waterfall crashing down next to four nearby thermal pools. There is more green space and less concrete here. Colombian music blasts from the speakers and a bar/cafeteria serves food, beer and liquor to crowds of local visitors. There's also a spa offering massage and a shaded lounge area for when you've had too much sun.

There are no accommodations on-site for these springs, but three small hotels cluster 500m from the entrance to the *balneario* (swimming hole). The cheapest is friendly **Cabaña el Portal** (☑320 623 5315; r per person COP$20,000). It has hot water and satellite TV, and also serves hearty budget meals.

Further down the road just outside Santa Rosa de Cabal is **Mamatina** (☑363 4899; mamatina.src@hotmail.com; La Leona Km1 vía Termales; s/d incl breakfast COP$35,000/70,000, ste COP$150,000), which offers modern, comfortable accommodations with views over the surrounding farms. The popular grill restaurant here is a great place to try *chorizos santarosanos* – regarded as the best sausage in Colombia.

❶ Getting There & Away

The thermals are 9km east of Santa Rosa de Cabal, off the Pereira-Manizales road. *Chivas* leave *la galería* (market area) in Santa Rosa at 7am, 10am, noon, 3pm and 5pm (COP$2500, 45 minutes). The *chivas* turn around and go back to Santa Rosa soon after their arrival at the springs. There are sometimes additional departures on weekends. Jeeps from *la galería* in Santa Rosa can take you out here for around COP$20,000.

There is frequent daytime Santa Rosa–Pereira bus service (COP$2000, 40 minutes). Buses to Manizales (COP$7000, one hour) stop at the gas station on the Pereria-Chinchiná road, four blocks from the park.

Termales San Vicente

📶 6 / ELEV 2250M

Set at the head of a steep, forested valley and straddling a cold creek, these newer **thermal pools** (📞333 6157; www.sanvicente.com.co; admission COP$25,000, r per person COP$80,000-180,000, campsite per person COP$55,000) are 18km east of Santa Rosa de Cabal but feel a world away. There are five thermal pools (37°C), two of which are reserved for hotel guests. Most visitors hang around in the concrete main pool, but the natural Piscina de las Burbujas near the entrance is far nicer. A short walk further down the valley lie the spectacular Pozos del Amor, where the thermal waters mix with the rushing stream to create amazing natural spas surrounded by thick forest – it is hard to imagine a more romantic setting.

The complex also has three natural saunas, built over 80°C to 90°C hot springs below and a full range of spa treatments, including mud therapy, algae facials, peels and, a rarity in Colombia, excellent massage. A 300m-long canopy line zips across the narrow valley to a 30m-waterfall you can rappel down.

There is a wide range of accommodations on offer. Cabins range from split-log rustic to modern minimalist with working fireplace and private thermal pool. Most have electric shower heads. There are also less appealing hotel-style accommodations and some budget rooms above the reception. Rates include admission and breakfast.

The baths are operated from the **booking office** (📞333 6157; Av Circunvalar No 15-62,

Pereira; ⊙8am-5pm Mon-Fri, to 3pm Sat) in Pereira, where you can make inquiries. It offers an excellent value package for day visitors (COP$55,000), which includes round-trip transportation from Pereira, admission, lunch and a snack. The bus leaves from the office at 8am and returns at 5pm. Transportation only is COP$20,000 each way. You can also hire a jeep from *la galería* in Santa Rosa de Cabal (COP$50,000/80,000 one way/round trip). Be sure to book a day or two in advance, especially for weekends and holidays.

Santuario Otún Quimbaya

This nature reserve 18km southeast of Pereira protects a 489-hectare area of high biodiversity between 1800m and 2400m. Set on the Río Otún, it boasts more than 200 species of birds and butterflies and two rare species of monkey, among other wildlife. The reserve has several short hiking trails along the river and through the forest and Spanish-speaking guides are available (COP$35,000 per group). The best time to come is August and September, and December and January, when the persistent drizzle eases somewhat.

The **visitor center** (Map p206; 📞313 695 4305; www.fecomar.com.co; Vereda La Suiza; admission COP$5000) provides accommodations (dorm beds/singles/doubles COP$25,000/30,000/60,000) and budget meals. There are electric showers (24-hour electricity) but no central heating, and fires are not allowed. Alcohol is also prohibited. Ask for a room on the 2nd floor – the rooms here have small balconies facing the forest and birdsong.

The visitor center is located in Vereda La Suiza, a small municipality. **Transporte Florida** (📞334 2721; Calle 12 No 9-40, La Galería, Pereira) in Pereira offers daily *chiva* services (COP$3000, 1½ hours) at 7am, 9am and 3pm, with an extra service at noon on weekends. The 9am and 3pm services continue past the visitors center to El Cedral, where they immediately turn around and head back. The *chiva* terminal is in a dangerous part of town; ask your taxi driver to take you all the way into the parking area.

Parque Ucumarí

Established in 1984 just outside the western boundaries of the Parque Nacional Natural (PNN) Los Nevados, this 42-sq-km reserve protects a rugged, forested land around the middle course of the Río Otún, about 30km southeast of Pereira. More than 185 species of bird have been recorded here.

From here you can hike up Río Otún, leading through a gorge to PNN Los Nevados. You can even get to Laguna del Otún (3950m) but it's a steady, six- to eight-hour walk uphill. It's possible to do the round trip within a day, though it's a strenuous hike. If you have camping gear, it's better to split the trek and do some side excursions up in the *páramo*.

The cabins at **Refugio La Pastora** (Map p206; ✆313 695 4305; dm/campsite per person COP$18,000/5000), at an elevation of 2500m, offer accommodations and budget meals. It has ecological paths traced through verdant hills and you can see the lush vegetation and spot some of the park's rich wildlife. The ambience here is far more laid-back than in La Suiza; ask the guy who runs the place to build a bonfire – BYO wine and marshmallows. There is no phone reception here but leave a message and the manager will get back to you or call **Fecomar** (✆313 695 4305; www.fecomar.com.co; Vereda La Suiza) to make a reservation.

To get here from Pereira, take the *chiva* to El Cedral (COP$4900). From El Cedral it's a 5km, 2½-hour walk, or rent a horse (COP$20,000/30,000 one way/round trip).

Armenia

✆6 / POP 290,000 / ELEV 1640

Far more slow-paced than its rivals, Armenia is the most traditional of the cities in the Zona Cafetera and feels more like a big town than a departmental capital. Its residents are proud of their coffee culture – and are never too busy to enjoy a cup in one of the city's many small cafes.

Like its neighbors, there is not much in the way of attractions here for visitors. Devastated by an earthquake in 1999 that flattened much of the city center, Armenia has never fully recovered. The center of the city is makeshift – check out the hastily reconstructed cathedral, made of prefab concrete slabs – and the de facto center has moved north of downtown, along Av Bolívar.

Most travelers will pass through Armenia only long enough to change buses for Salento. Still, the city is interesting enough for a day trip – the new pedestrian mall that stretches along Carrera 14 makes for a pleasant stroll, and Parque de la Vida is worth a visit.

◉ Sights

FREE **Museo del Oro Quimbaya**　　MUSEUM
(✆749 8433; museoquimbaya@banrep.gov.co; Av Bolívar No 40N-80; ☉10am-5pm Tue-Sun) Check out the bling-bling of the pre-Columbian Quimbaya culture at this excellent gold museum that also houses a fine ceramics collection. There are English translations of the informative wall panels on printed cards by the door. For Spanish speakers, free guided tours are also available. It's in the Centro Cultural, 5km northeast of the center. Grab bus 8 or 12 northbound on Av Bolívar (COP$1500).

Parque de la Vida　　PARK
(✆746 2302; cnr Av Bolívar & Calle 7N; admission COP$1000) If all the concrete is getting too much, stop by this tranquil park located in a valley in the middle of the city. It features both gardens and forested areas, as well as several small lakes and a fast-flowing stream. Keep an eye out for the *guatin* (a kind of large rodent) or they may nick your picnic lunch.

✖ Festivals & Events

Desfile de Yipao　　CULTURE
(Oct) Charge your batteries – this is one photo op you don't want to miss. An important part of Armenia's annual birthday party celebration, the Yipao is a fantastic parade in which local working jeeps are loaded down with literally tonnes of plantain, coffee and household goods and paraded through town (see the boxed text, p213).

▭ Sleeping

Casa Quimbaya　　HOSTEL $
(✆732 3086; www.casaquimbaya.com; Calle 16N No 14-92; dm/s/d COP$20,000/45,000/60,000; ☎) With a handy location near the university, bars and restaurants, this relaxed place has comfortable rooms and spotless bathrooms. Throw in enthusiastic young management and cozy common areas and you have a great budget choice.

Armenia Hotel　　HOTEL $$$
(✆746 0099, 1 800 097 8080; www.armeniahotelsa.com; Av Bolívar No 8N-67; s/d/tr COP$198,000/241,000/343,000; ❖@☎) The best hotel in town, the Armenia has nine floors built around a vaulted interior atrium with a glass ceiling. The rooms are spacious and are decked out with stylish *guadua* furniture and many offer great views of the

Cordillera Central or the city. There is a heated outdoor pool and a full-service restaurant downstairs.

Hotel Bolívar Plaza
HOTEL $$

(☑741 0083; www.bolivarplaza.com; Calle 21 No 14-17; s/d/tr COP$113,000/145,000/180,000; @ ☎) This friendly boutique hotel has a sleek, almost nautical facade that rises just across from Plaza de Bolívar. Rooms are smallish but well equipped and have soundproof windows that keep out the cacophony below. Some also have small balconies that look out onto the plaza.

Hotel Casa Real
HOTEL $

(☑741 4550; Carrera 18 No 18-36; s/d COP$24,000/ 30,000; ☎) Located above some shops in a busy commercial street, this basic hotel is nothing fancy, but it offers amenities not usually found at this price, including hot water, cable TV and wi-fi. The rooms at the back are quieter, while those at the front have more natural light.

✗ Eating

There are plenty of cheap eats in the center during the day and also around the Universidad de Quindío, where numerous bars and small eateries pursue the student market.

La Fogata
COLOMBIAN $$

(Carrera 13 No 14N-47; mains COP$25,000-30,000) This fine restaurant is one of Armenia's most famous eateries and with good reason. It does excellent steaks and seafood as well as *vuelve a la vida,* a fish soup rumored to be an aphrodisiac. The restaurant sits on a triangular property not far from CC Portal del Quindío – look for the manicured bushes outside.

La Fonda Antioqueña
COLOMBIAN $

(Carrera 13 No 18-59; mains COP$10,000; ☉8am-7pm) A block from Plaza de Bolívar is this fine *paisa* restaurant. It serves lovingly prepared traditional fare, including *bandeja paisa,* and, on weekends, *sancocho.* The *almuerzo ejecutivo* (executive lunch; COP$7000) changes every day and is a great deal. Be sure to try *mazamorra,* a typical Zona Cafetera drink made of cooked corn served with a splash of milk.

Natural Food Plaza
VEGETARIAN $

(Carrera 14 No 18N-40; meals COP$8000-10,000; ☑) An oasis in a city of slim pickings for herbivores, this delicious vegetarian cafe prepares an excellent set lunch (COP$7000) as well as great burgers, crepes and even a vegetarian *bandeja paisa.* Many of the ingredients come from the owner's organic farm.

🍷 Drinking & Entertainment

Armenia has a lively bar scene, although not as good as Manizales or Pereira. The area around the Universidad de Quindío northeast of the center on the road to Pereira has several cheap bars. In the area around Bambusa Plaza there are numerous popular dance bars playing mostly reggaeton that attract a young crowd. Most of the bigger clubs are in the *zona rosa* up on a hill outside town. A taxi up here will cost around COP$10,000, but coming home the charge is COP$20,000.

Bar Boston
BAR

(Calle 12N No 14-39) This is a mild-mannered restaurant by day and rocking bar at night that showcases talented local bands.

Guitarra y Rumba
CLUB

(Km2 vía Circasia; ☉Thu-Sat) This place is one of the longest-running clubs in the *zona rosa* and has a big disco space and cover band every night.

Mirador de la Plaza Taberna
BAR

(main plaza) For a quiet beer on the main plaza; the bar also serves espresso and has photos of Armenia before the 1999 earthquake.

ⓘ Information

4-72 (Carrera 15 No 22-38) Post office.

Banco de Bogota (Calle 21 16-30) ATM runs Visa and Cirrus/Maestro networks.

CC Portal del Quindío (Av Bolívar No 19N-46) This big mall has numerous ATMs.

Hospital San Juan de Diós (☑749 3500; cnr Av Bolívar & Calle 17N)

Facilcom Comunicaciones (Calle 21 No 15-53; per hr COP$1500; ☉8am-9pm Mon-Sat, 8am-7pm Sun) Internet access and cheap international calls.

Tourist office (Corporación de Cultura y Turismo; ☑741 1519; Plaza de Bolívar) On the ground floor of the Gobernación del Quindío building. Very helpful staff; lots of information.

ⓘ Getting There & Around

Air

Aeropuerto Internacional El Edén (☑747 9400) is 18km southwest of Armenia (COP$20,000 by taxi), near the town of La Tebaida on the road to Cali. Avianca, EasyFly and Lan offer services to Bogotá and ADA flies to Medellín. Spirit has direct flights to Fort Lauderdale, Florida.

Bus

The **bus terminal** (☑747 3355; Calle 35 No 20-68) is 1.5km southwest of the center and can be reached by frequent city buses that run along Carrera 19 (COP$1500).

There are plenty of buses to Bogotá (COP$40,000, eight hours), Medellín (COP$30,000) and Cali (COP$22,000, 3½ hours). There are regular minibuses to Pereira (COP$7800, one hour), Manizales (COP$17,000, 2½ hours) and Salento (COP$3200, 30 minutes). There are also direct buses to Popayán (COP$31,000, six hours).

Taxi

During the day the downtown area is full of merchants and shoppers but after dark robberies are not uncommon; taxis are a cheap and secure way to get to your destination.

Around Armenia

Tiny Quindío packs plenty into its modest boundaries with fantastic rural accommodation options, one of Colombia's best botanical gardens and fun theme parks that appeal to visitors of all ages. Coffee-farm tourism began here, and there are hundreds of *fincas* catering to a variety of tastes, mostly Colombian. Numerous publications catalog and rate them. The Armenia tourist office has a lengthy list of options. Also check out **Haciendas del Café** (www.clubhaciendasdel cafe.com) and **Quindio Turismo** (www.quindio turismo.com).

JARDÍN BOTÁNICO DEL QUINDÍO

Armenia's excellent 15-hectare **botanical garden** (☑742 7254; www.jardinbotanicoquindio.

org; Km3 Vía al Valle, Calarcá; admission COP$14,000; ☺9am-4pm) has the best *mariposario* in the Zona Cafetera. The 680-sq-meter butterfly house is in the shape of a giant butterfly and houses up to 3000 butterflies (up to 50 different species). There's also a 22m-tall lookout tower, ferns, orchids, a *guadua* forest and an extensive collection of palm species. More than 110 species of birds have been recorded here. Admission includes the services of a guide – they are all volunteers so tips are appreciated – and the best time to visit is in the morning when the butterflies are most active.

To get here, take a bus from Plaza de la Constitución in Armenia or pick up the yellow/green bus marked 'Calarcá' along Av Bolívar (COP$1500, 40 minutes).

HACIENDA BAMBUSA

Once a bustling **coffee farm** (☑740 4935, 311 506 9912; www.haciendabambusa.com; s/d/tr COP$252,000/306,000/396,000; ☎☒), Bambusa is now an exclusive country retreat with beautiful lush gardens and plantain, mandarin and cacao plantations. There is a river and plenty of bush on the property and more than 200 species of birds have been recorded here. The rooms are bright and spacious – and some have private balconies overlooking the excellent pool. Reservations are essential.

EL DELIRIO

Just outside Montenegro, the elegant **El Delirio** (☑741 5106; casadelirio@hotmail.com; Km1, Vía Montenegro; s/d/tr incl breakfast COP$130,000/170,000/245,000; @☎☒) strikes

---

AN ICONIC RIDE

If you spend any time at all in the Zona Cafetera it is highly probable that you will take at least a couple of rides in a classic WWII Willys jeep.

These veterans don't just look great parked in formation around the town plaza – they are still the main form of transportation in rural parts of the Zona Cafetera. Willys are used to transport everything from passengers to pigs, *platano* (plantain), furniture and, of course, coffee. And unlike buses, a Willys jeep is never really full – don't be surprised if your driver packs in 16 passengers or more.

The first jeeps to arrive were army surplus models sent from the USA in 1950. In order to sell the vehicles to farmers in the Zona Cafetera, a kind of traveling jeep show was created with expert drivers maneuvering the vehicles up and down the stairs in front of the town churches and moving loads through obstacle courses in the plazas. The locals were sold instantly – and so began a love affair that lasts to this day.

Willys jeeps are such an integral part of rural Colombian culture that a 'yipao' is a legitimate measure of agricultural products in Colombia (it's about 20 to 25 sacks of oranges). To see these majestic vehicles in all their glory check out Armenia's fabulous Yipao parade (p211), where pimped-out jeeps are loaded up with agricultural products and furniture and driven around town on two wheels, or check out www.willyscolombia.com.

WORTH A TRIP

RECUCA

This innovative **coffee farm** (☎749 8528; www.recuca.com; Vereda Callelarga, Calarcá; tours COP$15,000) offers tours that provide an insight into life on a *finca*. Visitors get to throw on traditional clothes, strap on a basket and hit the plantation to pick their own beans before heading back to the hacienda to learn all about the coffee-making process. You can also learn some of the traditional dances popular with *campesinos* (peasants) seeking to warm up on cold mountain nights. It's more than a little cheesy but is also great fun. If you want lunch you will need to reserve a day in advance. From Armenia take any bus (COP$1600) from the terminal to Río Verde and ask to be let off at the entrance. From here it is a 2km walk through some plantain farms or ask the watchman to call for a jeep (COP$5000 per vehicle).

a perfect balance between old-fashioned farmhouse and modern comfort. The owner is an interior designer and the place is decked out with antiques from throughout the region. The comfortable rooms have flat-screen TVs and spotless modern bathrooms. It is surrounded by a small coffee plantation and pretty manicured gardens full of birds.

FINCA VILLA NORA

Located between Armenia and Pereira this coffee, avocado and guava **farm** (☎741 5472, 310 422 6335; www.quindiofincavillanora.com; s/d incl breakfast & dinner COP$150,000/260,000;) offers accommodations in its traditional white-and-red-trimmed house with a wide wraparound verandah. It's simpler in style than many other rural hotels, and the owners run both the lodging and the farm. There's a small pool and a barbecue. Many rooms have shared baths, and there's only one TV. Staff can pick you up from Armenia airport (COP$60,000) or Quimbaya (free).

HACIENDA COMBIA

Close to the botanic gardens, this large, professionally run place on a working **coffee farm** (☎746 8472; www.combia.com.co; s/d incl breakfast COP$120,000/150,000; @) has great mountain views and top-notch facilities, including an infinity pool and spa, but lacks a little character compared to some of the smaller *fincas*.

PARQUE NACIONAL DEL CAFÉ

☎6 / ELEV 1300M

This **theme park** (☎741 7417; www.parquenacionaldelcafe.com; Km6 Vía Montenegro; admission COP$18,000-50,000; ⊙9am-4pm Wed-Sun) has a rollercoaster and a waterslide, a small coffee museum, bumper cars and a horseback-riding trail. At the entrance is an 18m-high lookout tower that has great views over Armenia. A cable car offers bird's-eye views of the park, and links the museum with a re-creation of a typical Quindian town. Don't go if it's raining, as most attractions are outdoors.

Buses depart Armenia bus terminal every 15 minutes (COP$1400, 30 minutes, 7am to 7pm).

PANACA

This **farm-themed park** (☎1 800 012 3999, 310 404 2238; www.panaca.com.co; admission COP$22,000-53,000; ⊙9am-6pm Tue-Sun) caters to city Colombians nostalgic for their rural past. Located just near Quimbaya, a short bus ride from Armenia, it has more than 4500 domestic animals, including many rare domestic breeds. The real highlight of any visit are the animal shows, especially pig races in the *cerdodromo* (pig-o-drome!).

Salento

☎6 / POP 4000 / ELEV 1900M

Set amid gorgeous green mountains 24km northeast of Armenia, this small town survives on coffee production, trout farming and, increasingly, tourists, who are drawn by its quaint streets, typical *paisa* architecture, and proximity to the spectacular Valle de Cocora. It was founded in 1850, and is one of the oldest towns in Quindío.

The main drag is Calle Real (Carrera 6), full of *artesanías* (local craft stalls), restaurants and internet cafes. At the end of the street are stairs leading up to Alto de la Cruz, a hill topped with a cross. From here you'll see the verdant Valle de Cocora and the mountains that surround it. If the skies are clear (usually only early in the morning), you can spot the snowcapped tops of the volcanoes on the horizon.

Activities

Horseback riding is a popular activity in Salento, however, there have been a number of recent incidents (including a couple of deaths) involving tourists riding horses around Salento. Make sure to take a guide and get comfortable with your mount before hitting the mountains.

There are a number of exhilarating mountain-bike trips in the area, including a recommended run from El Rocio on the edge of Parque Nacional Natural (PNN) Los Nevados back to town. You can rent bikes at Plantation House.

If you are in the mood to throw rocks at gunpowder, check out **Los Amigos** (Carrera 4 No 3-32; ⊙6pm-midnight Mon-Fri, noon-2am Sat, noon-midnight Sun), a small tejo (a traditional game where 2kg weights are tossed into a pit to hit and explode gunpowder-filled pieces of paper called *mechas*) club.

☞ Tours

Álvaro Gomez offers **horseback-riding trips** (☑096 759 3343, 311 375 8293) to several nearby waterfalls, along an old, unfinished railway track, plus a longer day trip up into Cocora. He charges COP$40,000 per person for a half-day trip, more for night tours or trips to Valle de Cocora.

Charismatic coffee grower Don Elías offers a tour of his **organic farm** (COP$5000; Spanish only). The farm is about a 45-minute walk from town – from the central park walk north for a block, then west across the yellow bridge. Keep going straight, it is about 200m after the turnoff to El Ocaso.

Plantation House owns a small coffee *finca* a short walk from its hostel and offers **tours** (guests/nonguests COP$5000/10,000) of the property in English several times a week. Check its website for schedules.

🛏 Sleeping

Tralala   HOSTEL $
(☑314 850 5543; www.hosteltralalasalento.com; Carrera 7 No 6-45; dm COP$20,000, s/d COP$45,000/60,000; 🛜) In a brightly renovated colonial house only half a block from the town's central park, this small, well-run hostel was clearly created by someone who knows exactly what travelers want. It has all the facilities you could possibly need, including comfortable mattresses, piping-hot showers, two kitchens, a fully stocked DVD library and lightning-fast wi-fi, all set around a lush garden with a peaceful elevated terrace.

Plantation House   HOSTEL $
(☑316 285 2603; www.theplantationhousesalento. com; Calle 7 No 1-04; dm COP$18,000-21,000, s

& d COP$45,000-50,000; @🛜) The original Salento hostel is an old-school backpackers experience. While it is not luxurious, it has amazing views, a great atmosphere and a bright new kitchen/social area with an open fireplace. It is possible to stay on the owner's nearby coffee farm and there are quality mountain bikes for rent. It can also facilitate multiday hikes into PNN Los Nevados through the Valle de Cocora.

Ciudad de Segorbe   HOTEL $$
(☑759 3794; www.hostalciudaddesegorbe.com; Calle 5 No 4-06; dm/s/d COP$22,000/45,000/65,000; @) While the elegant rooms with wooden floors and tiny balconies overlooking the mountains in this two-story house are an excellent deal, it is the wonderfully warm Spanish-Colombian hosts that make this peaceful hotel really stand out from the pack. An excellent breakfast is served in the interior courtyard.

🍴 Eating & Drinking

On weekends the plaza explodes with food stalls that prepare local specialties, including delicious trout and crispy *patacones* (fried plantains) smothered in *hogao* (warm tomato chutney).

La Eliania   INTERNATIONAL $
(Carrera 2 No 6-65; mains COP$5000-12,000; ⊙8am-1pm & 4-9pm) Prepares quality breakfasts as well as gourmet pizzas, sandwiches and if you're in the mood for something different, real Indian curries. The portions are generous and prices are very reasonable for the quality involved.

Rincón del Lucy   COLOMBIAN $
(Carrera 6 No 4-02; meals COP$6000; ⊙breakfast & lunch) Sit on great tree trunk slabs of tables to eat the best-value meal in town: fish, beef or chicken served with rice, beans, a banana and soup.

Alegra   INTERNATIONAL $$
(cnr Calle 4 & Carrera 7; mains COP$12,000-24,000; ⊙11:45am-7:45pm Thu-Mon) A cozy little restaurant offering an interesting selection of freshly prepared home-cooked meals, including veggie burgers, pastas and salads accompanied by an excellent selection of hot drinks and juices.

Café Jesús Martín   CAFE
(www.cafejesusmartin.com; Carrera 6A No 6-14; ⊙8am-9pm) This groovy cafe serves top-quality espresso coffee roasted and prepared

in the owner's Salento factory. It's got a distinctly upper-crust feel to it; don't expect to see too many local farmers drinking here. Also serves wine, beer and light meals. Ask about the coffee-tasting tours.

Donde Mi Apá BAR
(Carrera 6 No 5-24) This is the place where hardworking mountain folk come to get seriously smashed after a tough day at the office. The cozy interior is full of assorted antiques/junk from all over the Zona Cafetera, and behind the bar there is an extraordinary collection of 18,000 pieces of worn vinyl covering all genres of *musica vieja* (old music) that are dusted off sporadically to launch passionate group singalongs.

ℹ Information

Banco Agrario de Colombia (main square) The only ATM in town. Often out of cash on weekends.

El Sitio (Carrera 7 No 5-07; per hr COP$1500; ☉9:30am-10pm Mon-Sat, 1-10pm Sun) Internet and international calls by the park.

ℹ Getting There & Away

Minibuses run to/from Armenia every 20 minutes (COP$3200, 40 minutes, 6am to 9pm). You can also take a taxi direct from Armenia (30 minutes, COP$50,000).

There is direct bus service from Pereira (COP$5000, 1½ hours) at 6:30am, 1:30pm and 4:30pm during the week. Buses leave Salento for Pereira at 7:50am, 2:50pm and 5:50pm. On the weekends buses ply this route every hour. Coming from Pereira, you can also take an Armenia-bound bus to Los Flores and cross the road to grab a Salento-bound bus from Armenia.

Valle de Cocora

In a country full of beautiful landscapes, Cocora is one of the most striking. The valley stretches east of Salento into the lower reaches of PNN Los Nevados, with a broad, green valley framed by sharp peaks. Everywhere you'll see *palma de cera* (wax palm), the largest palm in the world (up to 60m tall). It's Colombia's national tree. Set amid the misty green hills, they are breathtaking to behold.

The most popular walk is the 2½-hour walk from the small hamlet Cocora to the **Reserva Natural Acaime** (Map p206; admission COP$3000 incl refreshment). As you arrive in Cocora the trail is on the right-hand side as you walk into the valley and away from Salento. It starts in Cocora by a blue gate and a shop and goes down past the trout farm. The first part of the trail is through grassland, the second through dense cloud

---

WORTH A TRIP

FILANDIA

A short distance from Salento, slow-paced Filandia is a traditional coffee town that is every bit as charming as its popular neighbor, but gets a fraction of the visitors. It has some of the best-preserved architecture in the region, as well as the **Colina Iluminada** (Km 1 Vía Quimbaya; admission COP$3000; ☉2-7pm Mon-Fri, 10am-7pm Sat & Sun) *mirador* (lookout), an impressive 19m-tall wooden structure that offers breathtaking views over three departments and, on a clear day, PNN Los Nevados.

Numerous small coffee farms, many of which welcome visitors, surround the town. You can arrange visits and accommodations at the excellent **tourist office** (☎758 2172; Casa de la Cultura) by the central park in Filandia. It can also organize guides for treks to Cañon del Río Barbas and Reserva Natural Bremen – La Popa, undeveloped forested areas full of birdlife that offer the chance to spot howler monkeys.

There are several great-value accommodations in town, the best of which is **La Posada del Compadre** (☎313 335 9771; www.laposadadelcompadre.com; Carrera 6 No 8-06; r incl breakfast COP$60,000), which has charming rooms and amazing views. **Hostal Tibouchina** (☎758 2646; Calle 6 No 5-05; r per person incl breakfast COP$30,000) by the park is another comfortable option.

Filandia is famous for its woven baskets. You can stop by the workshops and buy direct from the *artesanos* (craftspeople) or visit the cooperative by the park.

Buses run to/from Armenia (COP$3500, 45 minutes) every 20 minutes until 9pm. Coming from Salento, you can pick up this service at Las Flores where the Salento road joins the main highway.

forest. At Acaime there are basic **accommodations** (dm COP$15,000), and you can get a hot chocolate (with cheese). You'll also see plenty of hummingbirds feeding.

About 1km before you reach Acaime there's a turnoff to Finca La Montaña, an energy-sapping one-hour hike up a fairly steep moutainside, from where you can take an easy downhill trail back to Cocora (1½ hours). It is worth the extra effort to complete the loop, rather than tracking back the way you came, as the trail offers spectacular views of the valley from above and takes you right among the wax palms. It is possible to rent horses in Cocora to go to Acaime (COP$40,000 per person), though a guide is recommended – horses without a guide have been known to refuse to cross the rivers!

Longer walks into the national park are possible, including the option to stay overnight with local farmers. Inquire at Plantation House (p215), in Salento, for more information.

Jeeps leave Salento's main square for Cocora (COP$3000, 30 minutes) at 6:10am, 7:30am, 9:30am, 11:30am, 3pm and 4pm, coming back an hour later. There are additional services on weekends. Or if these times don't suit, you can also contract a jeep privately for COP$24,000.

Cali & Southwest Colombia

Why Go?

Southwest Colombia, often overlooked by visitors, is one of the most diverse and interesting regions in the country. It is Andean and African, modern and pre-Columbian – a land of contrasts that stimulates the senses at every opportunity.

Here you will find the best archaeological sites in the country and some of its finest colonial architecture. It's a place of immense biodiversity where you can pass through desert, jungle and *páramo* (high-mountain plain) eco-systems in just one day. Nature lovers will find active volcanoes, thermal springs and spectacular mountain ranges all easily accessible from thriving metropolitan centers with fashionable accommodations.

Cali is the biggest city in the region and is famous for its vibrant salsa clubs, but it also has plenty to offer non-dancers including charming old neighborhoods, fine restaurants and hip bars all served up with a big portion of *caleño* attitude.

Best Places to Eat

» Hotel Camino Real (p233)

» El Zaguán de San Antonio (p224)

» Bahareque (p224)

» Asadero de Cuyes Pinzón (p244)

Best Places to Stay

» Posada San Antonio (p223)

» Now Hotel (p223)

» Hotel Los Balcones (p231)

When to Go

Cali

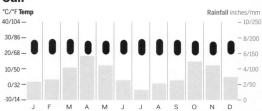

Sep Head to Cali's Festival Mundial de Salsa and Popayán's Congreso Nacional Gastronómico.

Jul-Sep Local thermal winds pack an extra punch for the best kitesurfing on Lago Calima.

Dec & Jan Clear skies make for pleasant hiking in Parque Nacional Natural (PNN) Puracé.

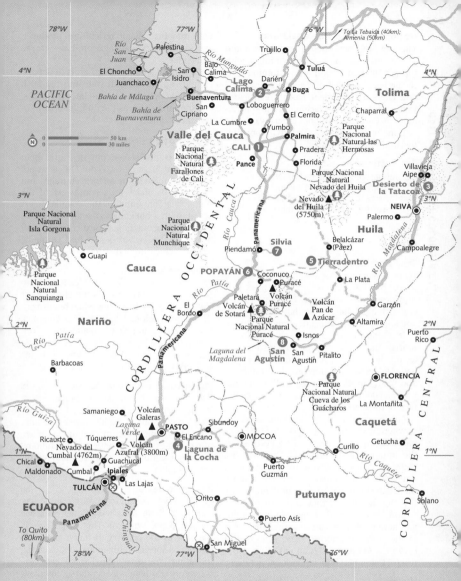

Cali & Southwest Colombia Highlights

1 Learn to swivel your hips and boogie in the sweaty salsa joints of **Cali** (p225)

2 Soar above the waves amid green mountain scenery while kitesurfing **Lago Calima** (p228)

3 Spend the night stargazing in Colombia's tiniest desert, the **Desierto de la Tatacoa** (p241)

4 Take a boat ride on **Laguna de la Cocha** (p245) and visit cloud forest–clad Isla Carota in the middle

5 Hike the spectacular hills of **Tierradentro** (p239) to visit ancient underground tombs

6 Wander through the elegant streets of **Popayán** (p229) for its excellent

museums and imposing colonial mansions

7 Get up close to the indigenous Guambiano culture at the market in **Silvia** (p232)

8 Gawk at giant pre-Columbian sculptures in phenomenal natural settings at **San Agustín** (p235)

National, State & Regional Parks

The archaeological sites of San Agustín and Tierradentro are both protected areas, with topography that is even more stunning than the archaeological stuff. Laguna de la Cocha and Laguna Verde near Pasto are worth a visit, and the Parque Nacional Natural Farallones de Cali, while still not officially open to visitors, offers numerous hiking opportunities in the periphery.

❶ Getting There & Away

Cali's airport receives flights from North and South America and Europe. Efficient buses connect the area to the rest of the country. See p314 for more on travel to/from Colombia.

CALI

📞 2 / POP 2.5 MILLION / ELEV 969M

While it may not have the looks to front the tourist brochure, Cali is the kind of place that provides all the substance. It is a hot, gritty city with a passion for life that draws you in and stays with you long after you leave town.

It is not an easy place to get to know – tourism doesn't seem to be high on anyone's agenda here – but if you make the effort you will find great nightlife, good restaurants, and plenty to do, especially in the evening, when a cool mountain breeze dissipates the heat of the day.

Cali is rich in Afro-Colombian heritage; nowhere is the nation's racial diversity and harmony more apparent than here. From the impoverished barrios to the slick big clubs, everyone is moving to one beat, and that beat is salsa. Music here is much more than entertainment, it is a unifying factor that ties the city together.

Caleños are proud of their vibrant culture and have a rebellious attitude that's reflected in the city's catchphrase: *'Cali es Cali y lo demás es loma, ¿oís?'* (Cali is Cali, and the rest [of Colombia] is just mountain, ya hear?).

History

After helping Francisco Pizarro conquer the Incas, Sebastián de Belalcázar (also known in Latin America as Benalcázar) quarreled with his former boss and moved north to strike out on his own. After founding Quito and Popayán, he arrived in the Valle del Cauca in 1536, where he dubbed his new settlement Santiago de Cali.

Over the centuries Spaniards shipped in thousands of African slaves to work the valley's sugarcane and cotton plantations. The Valle remains a major agricultural producer, and in higher regions also produces grapes and coffee.

Cali was a small town in orbit to departmental capital Popayán well into the 20th century, when railroads, and later highways, overtook the rivers as the dominant form of transportation.

◉ Sights

The city center is laid out in a grid plan around the Plaza de Caycedo. This is where you'll find most of the historic churches and museums. A short walk southwest of the center lies San Antonio, the colonial heart of Cali with a bohemian vibe and hip cafes. North lies the bustling Av Sexta (Av 6N), and nearby Av 9N, where you'll find Granada, the city's chic dining district.

Iglesia de la Merced   CHURCH
(cnr Carrera 4 & Calle 7; ⊙6:30-10am & 4-7pm) Begun around 1545, this is the city's oldest church. It's a lovely whitewashed building in the Spanish colonial style, with a long, narrow nave, and humble wood and stucco construction. Inside, a heavily gilded baroque high altar is topped by the Virgen de las Mercedes, the patron saint of the city.

Museo Arqueológico la Merced   MUSEUM
(Carrera 4 No 6-59; admission COP$4000; ⊙9am-1pm & 2-6pm Mon-Sat) Housed in the former La Merced convent, Cali's oldest building, this interesting museum contains a collection of pre-Columbian pottery left behind by the major cultures from central and southern Colombia.

Zoológico de Cali   ZOO
(📞892 7474; www.zoologicodecali.com.co; cnr Carrera 2A Oeste & Calle 14 Oeste; admission COP$10,000; ⊙9am-5pm) This large zoo is the best in the country. It has a good collection of species indigenous to Colombia, including *chiguiros* (capybaras), *oso hormigueros* (anteaters), condors, monkeys and a *mariposario* (butterfly enclosure). It's 2km southwest of the center in Barrio Santa Teresita and is most easily accessed by taxi.

Iglesia de San Antonio   CHURCH
Constructed in 1747, this small church is set atop a hill, the Colina de San Antonio, west of the old center. It shelters valuable *tallas quiteñas,* 17th-century carved-wood statues of the saints, representing the style known as the Quito School. The park surrounding the church offers great views of the city.

Museo de Arte Moderno
La Tertulia GALLERY
(www.museolatertulia.com; Av Colombia No 5 Oeste-105; admission COP4000; ⊙10am-6pm, closed Mon) Presents temporary exhibitions of contemporary painting, sculpture and photography. It's a 15-minute walk from the city center along the Río Cali.

FREE **Museo del Oro** MUSEUM
(Calle 7 No 4-69; ⊙10am-5pm Mon-Sat) One block east from Iglesia de la Merced, this museum has a small but fine collection of gold and pottery of the Calima culture.

Iglesia de San Francisco CHURCH
(cnr Carrera 6 & Calle 10) This neoclassical construction dating from the 18th century is most renowned for the adjacent **Torre Mudéjar** (cnr Carrera 6 & Calle 9), an unusual brick bell-tower, one of the best examples of Mudejar art in Colombia.

Iglesia de la Ermita CHURCH
(cnr Av Colombia & Calle 13) Overlooking the Río Cali, this neo-Gothic church houses the 18th-century painting of *El Señor de la Caña* (Lord of the Sugarcane); many miracles are attributed to the image.

🏃 Activities

Tren Turístico Café y Azucar TOURS
(☎6202326; www.trenturisticocafeyazucar.com.co; Vásquez Cobo No 23N-47) Colombia's long-neglected railway network now offers scenic excursions from Cali to La Cumbre (COP$25,000), on the road to Buenaventura, and La Tebaida (COP$56,000), near Armenia. There's also a nighttime party train and occasional trips to San Cipriano and Buga. All tours include live music and bar service. Check the website for schedules.

Club Social Los Amigos TEJO
(☎442 1258; Calle 49 No 8A-23) This large, working-class bar east of the center has three *canchas de tejo* (areas where you can play a round of this unique, traditional Colombian game where 2kg weights are tossed into a pit to hit and explode gunpowder-filled pieces of paper called *mechas*), as well as *canchas de sapo* (throwing metal discs into holes in a wooden target box) and billiards. A taxi here will cost around COP$10,000.

Hiking
No trip to Cali is complete without visiting **Cerro de las Tres Cruces**, three crosses that tower over the city. The views of the city are spectacular. It's a hefty two- to three-hour walk round trip from Granada heading northwest – bring plenty of water – or take a taxi (COP$35,000).

Eighteen kilometers west of the city lies marker **Km18**. There are numerous bars and restaurants here. At 1800m it's pleasantly cool, and the nearby cloud forest is an Important Bird Area (see www.mapalina.com) with high biodiversity. The walk from here to the small town of Dapa (four hours) – off the Cali–Yumbo road – is a pleasant stroll. There are numerous crossroads – always take the left-hand fork.

There are regular bus services to Km18 (COP$2000, one hour). Buses and jeeps service Dapa every half hour (COP$4000, 30 minutes).

🍴 Courses

There are many professional salsa schools in Cali. Expect to pay around COP$35,000 per hour for private lessons. Recommended schools include **Compañía Artística Rucafé** (☎557 8833; Carrera 36 No 8-49, El Templete), **Son de Luz** (☎315 4224; www.sondeluz.com; Carrera 80 No 43-34) and **Swing Latino** (☎374 2226; www.elmulatoysuswinglatino.com; Carrera 31 No 7-25). Those on a budget should check out the popular group classes at **Manicero** (☎513 0231; faimball@hotmail.com; Carrera 39 No 9-56).

For language courses, head to **Universidad Santiago de Cali** (☎518 3000, ext 421; www.usc.edu.co/idiomas; cnr Calle 5 & Carrera 62), which runs a respected Spanish program for foreigners. See the website for more details.

🎉 Festivals & Events

Festival de Música del Pacífico
Petronio Álvarez MUSIC
(Aug; www.festivalpetronioalvarez.com) A festival of Pacific music, heavily influenced by the African rhythms brought by the many slaves that originally populated the Pacific coast.

Festival Mundial de Salsa SALSA
(Sep; www.mundialdesalsa.com) Don't miss this one, which features amazing dancers.

Calle del Arte CULTURE
(Sep) San Antonio hosts this street-closing festival with live music, *artesanías* (local craft stalls), theater, dance and food.

Feria de Cali CULTURE
(Dec; www.feriadecali.com) Cali's big bash is from Christmas to New Year, with parades,

Cali

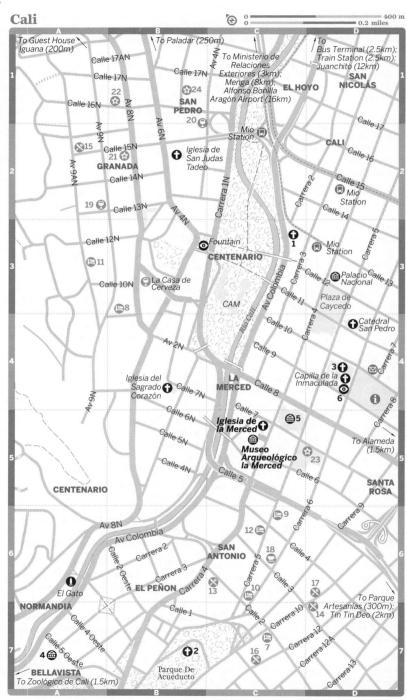

0   400 m
0   0.2 miles

To Guest House
Iguana (200m)

To Paladar (250m)

To Ministerio de
Relaciones
Exteriores (3km);
Menga (8km);
Alfonso Bonilla
Aragón Airport (16km)

To
Bus Terminal (2.5km);
Train Station (2.5km);
Juanchito (12km)

Calle 17AN

Calle 17N

Calle 17N

EL HOYO

SAN
NICOLÁS

Calle 16N

22

24

SAN
PEDRO

20

Calle 17

CALI

Av 8N

Calle 16

15

Calle 15N

Mio
Station

Carrera 2

Calle 15

Av 9N

21

GRANADA

Iglesia de
San Judas
Tadeo

Mio
Station

Av 9AN

Calle 14N

Carrera 1N

Calle 14

19

Calle 13N

Av 4N

Carrera 5

Calle 12N

Fountain

CENTENARIO

1

Mio
Station

11

Carrera 3

Calle 12

Palacio
Nacional

Calle 13

Calle 10N

La Casa de
Cerveza

Av Colombia

Calle 11

Plaza de
Caycedo

Carrera 6

8

CAM

Río Cali

Calle 10

Catedral
San Pedro

Carrera 7

Av 2N

Calle 9

Av 6N

Iglesia del
Sagrado
Corazón

Calle 7N

LA
MERCED

Calle 8

3

Capilla de la
Inmaculada

6

Calle 6N

Calle 7

Iglesia de
la Merced

5

Carrera 8

Calle 5N

Museo
Arqueológico
la Merced

23

To Alameda
(1.5km)

CENTENARIO

Calle 4N

Calle 5

Calle 6

SANTA
ROSA

Av 8N

Carrera 6

Carrera 9

Av Colombia

9

Carrera 2

12

SAN
ANTONIO

Calle 4

Carrera 3

18

Calle 3

El Gato

Calle 2 Oeste

EL PEÑON

Carrera 4

13

10

Carrera 5

17

NORMANDIA

Calle 1

Carrera 10

14

To Parque
Artesanías (300m);
Tin Tin Deo (2km)

Calle 4 Oeste

Calle 2

Carrera 12

7

4

Calle 5 Oeste

16

Carrera 12A

BELLAVISTA
To Zoológico de Cali (1.5km)

2

Parque De
Acueducto

Carrera 13

Cali

music, theater, a beauty pageant and general citywide revelry.

🛏 Sleeping

For a taste of Cali's colonial origins, lay your head in laid-back San Antonio; if you are after nightlife head for Granada.

Posada San Antonio　　　　HOTEL $$
(☎893 7413; www.posadadesanantonio.com; Carrera 5 No 3-37; s/d/tr COP$100,000/120,000/150,000;@⑤) Right in the heart of San Antonio, this old colonial building surrounds a pleasant courtyard. All rooms have private bath and cable TV, and breakfast is included in the price. There's no air-con, but the up-

per third of the doors open separately, letting the air circulate while you sleep. There are also some cheaper, less atmospheric rooms around the rear patio.

Now Hotel　　　　BOUTIQUE HOTEL $$$
(☎488 9797; www.nowhotel.com.co; Av 9AN No 10N-74, Granada; r COP$450,000; ❄@⑤⬚) This arty boutique hotel has an industrial-chic theme with plenty of metal, mesh, polished concrete and colored glass. The rooms have all the comforts, including remote-control lights and hi-tech showers with eight different water flows. There are full-wall black-and-white images printed behind each bed and fantastic private balconies with views over the city. The rooftop pool and bar area is a great place for a cocktail in the early evening. You can sometimes get special deals on weekends.

Jovita's Hostel　　　　HOSTEL $
(☎893 8342; www.jovitashostel.com; Carrera 5 No 4-56, San Antonio; dm COP$18,000, s/d COP$35,000/50,000, without bathroom COP$30,000/40,000; @⑤) In a freshly renovated colonial house with a plant-filled internal courtyard, Jovita's is a hostel, salsa school and yoga center rolled into one. Many of the rooms don't have windows but the high roof keeps them cool and there are lovely common areas with hammocks. There are free daily dance classes.

Guest House Iguana　　　　HOSTEL $
(☎660 8937; www.iguana.com.co; Av 9N No 22N-46; dm COP$18,000, s/d COP$40,000/50,000, without bathroom COP$32,000/40,000; @⑤) This laid-back Swiss-owned hostel has a variety of comfortable accommodations spread over two adjoining houses. There is a pleasant garden area and free salsa classes several times a week. It's north of the center, within walking distance of the restaurants in Granada and Chipichape.

Jardin Azul　　　　GUESTHOUSE $$
(☎556 8380; www.jardinazul.com; Carrera 24A No 2A-59; r COP$100,000-120,000, tr COP$150,000-180,000; ⑤⬚) Set in a converted house on a hill near the colonial sector east of the center, this spotless small hotel has huge, bright rooms with big beds and imported cotton sheets. Some rooms have private balconies and views of the city. There is a small pool set in an appealing garden that attracts plenty of birds.

Café Tostaky   HOSTEL $

(☎893 0651; www.cafetostaky.blogspot.com;
Carrera 10 No 1-76; dm/s/d without bathroom
COP$17,000/25,000/40,000, apt COP$50,000-
80,000;@🛜) Right in the heart of San Antonio, this French-owned hostel has a kitchen
you can use, free internet and cable TV.
Downstairs it runs a chilled cafe (open 3pm
to 11pm) that serves crepes and good coffee. Worth visiting even if you're not staying
here.

Pelican Larry   HOSTEL $

(☎392 1407; www.pelicanlarrycali.com; Calle 20N
No 6AN-44, Granada; s/d COP$50,000/60,000,
dm/s/d without bathroom COP$18,000/40,000/
50,000; @🛜) With a great central location
and a lively ambience, this new hostel is a
great base from which to explore the city's
nightlife. It has big spacious rooms with
solid beds and a pleasant rear patio where
the owner prepares his famous barbecues
(COP$12,000).

Casa de Alférez   HOTEL $$$

(☎661 8111; reservas@mercurecasadelalferez.com.
co; Av 9N No 9-24; s COP$390,000-673,000, d
COP$405,000-688,000; ❄@) This ultraluxuri-
ous five-star hotel offers rooms with king-
sized feather beds. Huge French windows
open onto small balconies on a lovely, tree-
lined street. The excellent restaurant down-
stairs is open to the public. Rates include a
buffet breakfast.

La Casa Café   HOSTEL $

(☎893 7011; lacasacafecali.blogspot.com; Carrera
6 No 2-13, San Antonio; dm/s/d without bathroom
COP$15,000/25,000/30,000;@🛜) This groovy
cafe-bar rents great-value dorm beds and
private rooms on the 2nd floor of its colo-
nial building. Two have quiet street views of
San Antonio and there is a small communal
kitchen. The cafe area downstairs has Jenga
sets, card games and dominoes you can bor-
row while lingering over coffee, juice, des-
serts and beer.

✖️ Eating

The best cheap eats in town are at *la galeria*
(food market) in Alameda, a colorful local
market with plenty of small lunch counters
serving seafood and *comidas tipicas* (typi-
cal food).

El Zaguán de San Antonio   COLOMBIAN $$

(Carrera 12 No 1-29; mains COP$20,000-24,000)
This San Antonio institution serves high-
quality traditional *vallecaucana* food –

which means plenty of meat. The fresh
juices are sensational and on Sunday it
prepares *sancocho de gallina* (free-range
chicken soup) cooked the traditional way
over a wood fire. The food is fantastic but
the real reason to come here is for the
amazing view from the rooftop, which is
also a great place for a drink.

Bahareque   COLOMBIAN $

(Calle 2 No 4-52; mains COP$6000-18,000; ⏰lunch
daily, dinner Thu-Sat) You might have to fight
for a table at this popular San Antonio
restaurant, which serves a great set meal
(COP$6500). Sample amazing salads gar-
nished with tropical fruit, plus good steaks
and chicken for carnivores. On Saturday it
offers a menu of traditional regional dishes.

El Solar   ITALIAN $$$

(Calle 15N No 9-62; mains COP$18,000-34,000)
This hugely popular restaurant serves con-
sistently excellent Italian food in a large
covered courtyard. On the menu are fresh
homemade pastas, risottos, gourmet pizzas
and salads. There is also a fine selection of
seafood with sauces made from local sea-
sonal fruits.

Dona Francia   ICE CREAM $

(Carrera 27 No 3-100; snacks COP$5000) Sit on
benches outside this Cali institution and en-
joy sensational juices, sorbets and possibly
the best fruit salad in all of Colombia. It's
one block east from Parque del Perro.

El Buen Alimento   VEGETARIAN $

(☎375 5738; Carrera 10 No 3-02; mains
COP$10,000-14,000; 🖊) This hip vegetarian
cafe serves excellent meat-free versions of
Colombian classics, as well as creative fu-
sion dishes such as Mexican lasagna. There
are several different varieties of veggie
burgers and great fresh juices. It also offers
delivery service and frozen meals to go.

Paladar   COLOMBIAN $$$

(Av 6AN No 23-27; meals COP$24,000-30,000;
⏰9:30am-8:30pm Mon-Sat) It looks like an
average cafeteria, but wait till you see what
it serves – homemade lasagna, casseroles of
every sort, even the occasional stewed rab-
bit. The dessert selection is divine – cakes,
pies, mousses; it makes us drool just thinking about it. The house specialty, *pastel
Paladar* (a multilayered chocolate and mo-
cha cake), is orgasmic, and if you like lemon
meringue pie, get in before noon – it goes
quickly.

Zahavi
BAKERY $

(Carrera 10 No 3-81; pastries COP$2000-6000, sandwiches COP$12,000) This posh bakery in San Antonio serves excellent coffee, rich gooey brownies and delicious gourmet sandwiches.

Drinking

Macondo
CAFE

(www.macondocafe.blogspot.com; Carrera 6 No 3-03) This San Antonio institution does great coffee, a wide range of desserts, light sandwiches and salads, and serves beer and wine till late. Try the scrumptious cocktails, like the Melquiades (mango, chocolate, coffee, Baileys, whiskey and blackberry sauce) or the Macondo de Lulo (coffee ice cream with fresh *lulo* fruit and whiskey).

Saloon
BAR

(Av 9N No 13-01) This edgy, arty bar has a student vibe. Foreign DJs occasionally spin here, and there's sometimes live music. You can get sandwiches, salads and light meals (COP$10,000 to COP$12,000). It also hosts art installations.

Xixaola
BAR

(www.xixaola.com; Calle 8 No 38-90, Callejón Inducon, Menga; ⏰7pm-6am) Located about a kilometer from the main strip in Menga, down a country road past several small farms, this bar boasts large concrete Pharaohs, a small lake, bonfires and a restaurant (mains COP$16,000 to COP$20,000) specializing in grilled meat. Don't come if it's raining.

Tertuliadero La Fuente
BAR

(Av 4N No 15-39; ⏰Fri & Sat) This humble, matchbox-sized bar with a couple of wooden tables and a battered sound system is a much loved hang-out among the local university set – perhaps as a result of its cheap drinks. It is a great place to dance salsa if you don't fancy fighting for space in the fashionable clubs.

☆ Entertainment

Cali is famous for its bar-hopping weekend *chiva* (a colorful, traditional bus) tours. Board the bus and dance your way through gridlock as you visit six or so discos. Check out **Chiva Rumbo de Lujo** (☎684 2127) or **Chivas Rumbahabana** (☎372 8617; www.chivasrumbahabana.com). Expect to pay around COP$20,000 per person, or COP$300,000 to COP$400,000 per bus. You may enjoy yourself more if you put together your own group and contract the *chiva* privately. For

---

the latest on what's on around town, check the entertainment columns of Cali's broadsheet, *El País* (www.elpais.com.co), or online at Rumbas Cali (www.rumbascali.com).

Nightclubs

Av Sexta (Av 6N) is full of bars and clubs. Most are pretty ordinary but there are a couple of gems in the side streets. The hippest new spot in town is Parque del Perro, where bars and restaurants surround the park. Just north of the Cali municipal boundary is Menga, where numerous discos (not constrained by the *ley zanahoria;* see boxed text above) are open till dawn. Further afield is Juanchito, where several big *salsatecas* (salsa dance clubs) cluster.

Zaperoco
SALSA CLUB

(www.zaperocobar.com; Av 5N No 16-46; ⏰Tue, Fri & Sat) If you only visit one salsa bar in Cali, make sure it's Zaperoco. Here the veteran DJ spins pure *salsa con golpe* (salsa with punch) from old vinyl while rows of industrial fans try in vain to keep the place cool. Somewhere under the mass of moving limbs there is a dance floor – but we've never worked out exactly where it is. It is a high-energy place – a night out here will burn more calories than a half-marathon in the tropics. Tuesday night there are live bands.

Tin Tin Deo
SALSA CLUB

(www.tintindeocali.com; Calle 5 No 38-71, San Fernando; cover COP$5000-10,000; ⏰7pm-2am Thu, to 3am Fri & Sat) This atmospheric salsa joint attracts some of the best dancers in Cali. Posters of famous salsa singers look down on you from the wall. Drinks are moderately priced, and the cover charge is *consumible;* that is, you get it back in drinks at the bar.

Changó
SALSA CLUB

(www.chango.com.co; Via Cavasa, Juanchito) The most famous *salsateca* in Juanchito, this huge, sophisticated club has plush booths and a big, smoking-hot dance floor. There's no cover charge, but it's a COP$15,000, 20-minute taxi ride from town. Sometimes there are dance shows. If you can't make it you can listen in on the live internet radio feed.

Kukaramakara   CLUB
(www.kukaramakara.com; Calle 28N No 2bis-97) This big disco is famous for its live music. Come early if you want a table, or hang out on the 2nd-floor interior balcony, looking down at the band below. The grill serves food until 1:30am.

Lulu   CLUB
(www.luludisco.com; Calle 16N No 8-42) The open bar at this popular gay-friendly disco keeps everyone on the dance floor – which is convenient as there are virtually no chairs or tables. There is usually a group of hardcore drinkers lining up outside before it opens.

Lolas   CLUB
(www.lolasclubcali.com; Antiguo via Yumbo) Cali's most prestigious and expensive club is set in a huge white dome in Menga. Inside is like something out of a big-budget Euro house video with glamorous young *caleñas* dancing on tables while high-tech lasers slash through clouds of smoke. Groups of unaccompanied men won't get in.

Tienda Vieja   LIVE MUSIC
(☑513 4444; www.tiendavieja.com; cnr Autopista Sur & Carrera 43; ☺4pm-1am Thu, 4pm-3am Fri & Sat, 2pm-2am Sun) This happy, well-worn but well-loved Cali institution has live bands that play salsa and Colombian crossover. Seating is in small, colorful wooden chairs – they're not comfortable, but then you came here to dance, right?

Cinema
Cali's many shopping malls all have cinemas, including Chipichape (www.chipichape. com; Av Sexta No 39N-25), Cosmocentro (Calle 5 No 50-00), Palmetto Plaza (www.palmet toplaza.com; Calle 9 No 48-51) and Unicentro (www.unicentro.com; Carrera 100 No 5-169).

For more thought-provoking fare, check the program of the Cinemateca La Tertulia (☑893 2939; www.museolatertulia.com; Av Colombia No 5 Oeste-105), which generally has two shows daily from Tuesday to Sunday. Attracting large crowds for its art-house screenings is Lugar a Dudas (☑668 2335; www.lugaradudas.org; Calle 15N No 8N-41; admission free; ☺11am-8pm Tue-Fri, 4:30-8pm Sat). It serves coffee and snacks.

Soccer
Cali has two *fútbol* (soccer) teams. Deportivo Cali (www.deporcali.com) plays in the new Estadio Deportivo Cali near the airport in Palmira. America de Cali (www. america.com.co) plays in the city at Estadio Pascual Guerrero (cnr Calle 5 & Carrera 34). Any Palmira-bound bus can take you to the former; the Mio passes outside the latter.

Theater
The city's oldest existing theater, Teatro Municipal (☑684 0593; Carrera 5 No 6-64), was completed in 1918. Today it's used for various artistic forms, including musical concerts, theater and ballet. If there is nothing going on, you can ask the security officer to show you around. Frequent free concerts are held at Teatro al Aire Libre Los Cristales (☑558 2009; Carrera 14A No 6-00), an open-air amphitheater.

🛍 Shopping
There are several cheap outlets selling hammocks, clothes, necklaces and earrings from throughout the region near *la galeria* in the Alameda neighborhood.

Chipichape   MALL
(www.chipichape.com; Av Sexta No 39N-25) On the northern edge of town, this indoor-outdoor mall is one of the largest malls in Colombia.

⸢TOP CHOICE⸥ Parque Artesanías   MARKET
(☺10am-8pm) On Loma de la Cruz, this is one of Colombia's best *artesanía* markets. You'll find authentic, handmade goods from the Amazon, Pacific coast, southern Andes and even Los Llanos.

ℹ Information
Dangers & Annoyances
During the day, the city center is alive with street vendors and crowds. After dark and on Sunday it can get dodgy. Also avoid the area east of Calle 5 and along the Río Cali at night. Take a taxi and take extra care with your belongings.

Internet Access
There is free wi-fi at most of Cali's big malls.
Redes Sociales (Av 9AN No 16N-17; per hr COP$1400; ☺9am-10pm Mon-Sat, noon-7pm Sun) Fast internet access.

Medical Services
Centro Medico Imbanaco (☑682 1000; www. imbanaco.com; Carrera 38A No 5A-100) Best private medical facility in town.

Money
Most of the major banks have offices on Av Sexta (Av 6N).

Banco de Bogota Central (Carrera 5a No 10-39); Granada (Av 6N No 25N-47)
Citibank (Av 5N No 23AN-49, Parque Versalles)

Post
4-72 (Calle 10 No 6-25) Post office.

Tourist Information
Tourist office (Secretaría de Cultura y Turismo; ☑886 0000, ext 2400; Carrera 7 btwn Calle 9 & Calle 10) On the 1st floor of the Gobernación building.

Travel Agencies
Comfenalco Valle (☑886 2727; Calle 5 No 6-63, torre C) Comfenalco's travel agency is one of the best in town. Organizes trips nationwide.

Visa Information
Ministerio de Relaciones Exteriores (☑664 3808; www.cancilleria.gov.co; Av 3N 50N-20, La Flora) For visa extensions.

❶ Getting There & Away

Alfonso Bonilla Aragón Airport (Aeropuerto Palmaseca; ☑666 3200) is 16km northeast of the city, off the road to Palmira. Minibuses between the airport and the bus terminal run every 10 minutes until about 8pm (COP$4000, 30 minutes), or take a taxi (around COP$55,000).

Avianca offers frequent shuttle services to Bogotá as well as a number of direct flights to Medellín. Satena flies to Medellín, Ipiales on the border, and to Guapi on the coast. LAN flies nonstop to Lima, Copa direct to Panama and Tame flies to Esmeraldas, Ecuador. There are also regular flights to Miami and Madrid with American Airlines and Avianca respectively.

Buses run regularly to Bogotá (COP$65,000, 12 hours), Medellín (COP$50,000, nine hours) and Pasto (COP$40,000, nine hours). Pasto buses will drop you off in Popayán (COP$12,000, three hours) or you can take the hourly minibuses there (COP$14,000, 2½ hours). There are regular departures to Armenia (COP$22,000, four hours), Pereira (COP$29,000, four hours) and Manizales (COP$30,000, five hours).

❶ Getting Around

Cali's air-conditioned electric bus network, the **Mio** (www.metrocali.gov.co), will remind many of Bogotá's TransMilenio. The main route runs from north of the bus terminal along the river, through the center and down the entire length of Av Quinta (Av 5). Other routes spread out across the city. It costs COP$1500 per ride.

The **bus terminal** (☑668 3655) is 2km north of the center. It's a sweaty walk in Cali's heat – take the Mio, or a taxi (COP$5000).

AROUND CALI

Parque Nacional Natural (PNN) Farallones de Cali

This 1500-sq-km national park protects the headlands around Cali. During the height of the civil war it was closed and has yet to be officially reopened. At the time of research, security was still an issue in some areas, and parts of the park remained off limits to travelers. However, with an experienced guide there are a number of hikes you can do leaving out from the communities of Pance or Peñas Blancas. Be sure to check the situation on the ground before heading out.

Arawata (☑395 3833; www.arawatacali.com; Carrera 65 No 12-86) in Cali organizes a variety of trips into the park and has mountaineering gear for rent. Also check out **Conserveden Tours** (☑371 9279; conserveden@gmail.com) or **Ecoaventura** (☑300 774 5353; www.ecoaventuravalle.blogspot.com). Alternatively ask around for local guides in Pance.

Pance

☑2 / POP 2000 / ELEV 1550M
This small holiday town in the mountains on the eastern edge of PNN Farallones is full of holiday *fincas* (farms). The weather is a pleasantly cool change from the heat of Cali. On the weekend its one street opens and all the bars and restaurants are in full flower. During the week it's empty and you can't even get a meal. Come on the weekend, preferably Sunday, to eat and drink your way down the hill. You can also do a day hike to some nearby waterfalls, or organize the longer treks to into PNN Farallones de Cali.

Pico de Loro is a seven-hour round-trip hike west from Pance. Expect to pay around COP$70,000 per group for a local guide to show you the way. Pico Pance, PNN Farallones' iconic peak, is a three- to four-day trek.

To visit the nearby waterfalls, walk 1km downhill from town to the bridge and turn right. Walk 3km uphill to El Topacio, where you will find a visitor center. From here it's a 20-minute walk to the waterfalls. You don't need a guide.

Anahuac (☑331 4828; campsite per person COP$7000, r per person incl meals COP$37,000) is a small private nature reserve, which sits next to Río Pance amid secondary forest and a small farm growing fruit and flowers.

There's a four-room brick cabin and a four-room wood cabin, but the small two-story *bohíos* (tiny huts with windows facing forest) will appeal most to travelers. There's a wood-fired stove in a basic kitchen where you can cook. You can camp with your tent or theirs, or just come out for the day (admission COP$3000). Serves budget meals all week long.

❶ Getting There & Away

Minibuses leave from the bus terminal in Cali heading to Pance roughly every hour (COP$2000, 1½ hours). They are marked 'Recreativo' and 'Pueblo Pance.' For Anahuac take the bus marked 'Recreativo 1A.'

Lago Calima

This artificial reservoir attracts kitesurfers and windsurfers from around the world for its year-round winds. The lake covers the flooded Darién valley of Río Calima, and was built in 1965. Some 86km north from Cali, its temperate climate also attracts *caleños* looking to cool off on weekends. The green hills that surround the lake are populated with holiday *fincas*.

Every afternoon, around lunchtime, a brisk mountain thermal picks up, bringing wisps of cloud and a steady 18-knot wind down from the mountains. From July to September this can increase to 25 knots. Kitesurfing and windsurfing competitions are held in these months, when world champions in the two sports come to compete. Water temperature is a steady 18°C.

Most tourist activity stretches along the northern bank of the lake, from the small town of Darién at the eastern end to the dam to the west. There's no beach; launching points are from grassy slopes that lead down to the water.

Because transportation is infrequent in the area, Lago Calima makes a difficult day trip. You're better off coming for a day or two, especially on the weekend, when the many holidaymakers give the place a party atmosphere.

Darién

☏2 / POP 7000 / ELEV 1800M

This small town has a few budget hotels, a couple of supermarkets, two ATMs, a couple of internet cafes and, on the weekends, several lively discos. Most everything clusters within two or three blocks of Parque Los Fundadores, the main plaza. Of interest is the **Museo Arqueológico Calima** (Calle 10 No 12-50; admission COP$2500; ⏰8am-5pm Mon-Fri, 10am-6pm Sat & Sun), where you'll find a collection of almost 2000 pieces of pre-Columbian pottery. It's a perfectly pleasant little town, but a trip to Lago Calima is the drawcard.

🏃 Activities

Kitesurfing & Windsurfing

There are numerous schools offering classes and rentals. Most also offer accommodations. Expect to pay roughly COP$60,000 per hour for windsurfing instruction and COP$80,000 to COP$100,000 per hour for kitesurfing instruction. Rentals go for around COP$60,000 per hour.

Cogua Kite School   KITESURFING
(☏253 3282, 318 608 3932; www.coguacustom. com; Carrera 12 No 10-28) This is a laid-back outfit that offers personalized classes with English-speaking instructors. The owner also runs a small kiteboard factory, where he makes custom boards from coconut fiber and *guadua* (a type of bamboo). He'll even let you design and custom-make your own board. There are budget accommodations available on the lake shore and at its hostel in town.

Escuela Pescao Windsurf y Kitesurf   WINDSURFING, KITESURFING
(☏311 352 3293, 316 401 6373; www.pescaowind surfing.com) In a big warehouse, this outfit sits on the edge of the lake. The wheelchair-bound former champion kitesurfer shouts instructions through a megaphone. It offers accommodations (campsite per person COP$20,000, cabins for six to 10 people COP$180,000) in the warehouse in tents with mattresses and sleeping bags.

Calima Xtremo   ADVENTURE SPORTS
(☏321 638 9218; calimaxtremo@gmail.com) Next to the Comfandi complex, Calima Xtremo offers the usual classes and rentals as well as kite-buggies – a land-based option where the kite pulls you around in a small vehicle – and jet-ski hire. It has accommodations (dorm beds COP$20,000, rooms COP$50,000 to COP$70,000) on a nearby *finca* and in Darién.

Boating

Numerous captains offer excursions on the lake. Try **El Arriero Paisa** (☏253 3597; restau rantearrieropaisa@yahoo.es; entrada 5), a small resort just outside town that also organizes boat trips. Expect to pay around COP$10,000 per person, minimum six people.

🛏 Sleeping & Eating

Hostería Los Veleros　　　　　HOTEL **$$$**
(📞684 1000; www.comfandi.com.co; s/tw/d/tr/q COP$167,200/193,400/203,400/246,600/281,800; ☒) The best hotel on the lake, Los Veleros is part of the Comfandi complex, and prices include two meals and admission to the recreation center, with three pools, Jacuzzi and sauna, and activities for the kids. Some of the rooms have balconies with spectacular views of the lake. Packed on the weekend; during the week you'll have the place to yourself. An on-site disco on Saturday night sometimes goes till dawn.

Hostal Cogua　　　　　　　　HOSTEL **$**
(📞318 608 3932; www.coguacustom.com; Carrera 7 No 15-10; dm COP$20,000) Run by the local kiteboard manufacturers, this small, cozy hostel has basic dormitory accommodations, a shared kitchen and Direct TV. If there is no-one around, swing by its kiteschool office.

Meson llama　　　　　　　COLOMBIAN **$$**
(📞667 9703; www.mesonilama.com; mains COP$18,000-22,000) About 10km from Darién is this large, exposed-timber restaurant with great views of the lake. It does all the basics very well – *sancocho* (a typical Colombian stew), *churrasco* (grilled meat) baby beef and trout. It also offera boat trips (COP$10,000 per person), horseback riding (COP$20,000, around two hours) and comfortable accommodations.

El Fogón de la Abuela　　　COLOMBIAN **$**
(Carrera 6A No 8-61; mains COP$5000-10,000) This cheap restaurant does a filling set meal. It's on a noisy street two blocks from the main square.

❶ Getting There & Away

There is a direct bus service every hour to/from Cali (COP$12,000, 2½ hours) during the day. Coming from the north, get off in Buga and grab the half-hourly service to Darién (COP$6500, 1½ hours).

Note that there are two bus routes that come out here to Lago Calima and Darién. They cost the same. If you're going direct to Darién, ask for the bus via Jiguales; for the kitesurfing/windsurfing schools, ask for the bus that goes *'por el lago'* ('along the lakeshore').

❶ Getting Around

There are no taxis in Darién. Jeeps sometimes hang out on the main square, and can take you around town and along the lakeshore, but these are expensive (around COP$20,000 to Comfandi).

Minibuses shuttle between Darién and the dam at Lago Calima (COP$1500), past the kite schools, from 7am to 7pm on the hour. You can also jump on buses heading to Buga/Cali – but make sure they are taking the lake exit.

CAUCA & HUILA

These two departments are home to Popayán, one of Colombia's loveliest colonial cities, plus the country's two most important archaeological sites – San Agustín and Tierradentro. Here you'll also find the peculiar Desierto de la Tatacoa, a striking anomaly near Neiva, halfway between Bogotá and San Agustín.

In the days of river travel in Colombia, both Cauca and Huila were major hubs of commerce. The introduction of the railroad and highways in the early 20th century stunted their growth, and these days a sleepy languor envelops the region.

Popayán

📞2 / POP 266,000 / ELEV 1760M

This small colonial town is famous for its chalk-white facades (its nickname is La Ciudad Blanca, or 'the White City'), and is second only to Cartagena as Colombia's most impressive colonial settlement. It sits at the southern end of the Valle del Cauca, and for hundreds of years was the capital of southern Colombia, before Cali overtook it.

The town was founded in 1537 by Sebastián de Belalcázar, and Popayán became the most important stopping point on the road between Cartagena and Quito. Its mild climate attracted wealthy families from the sugar haciendas of the hot Cali region. In the 17th century they began building mansions, schools and several imposing churches and monasteries.

In March 1983, moments before the much-celebrated Maundy Thursday religious procession was set to depart, a violent earthquake shook the town, caving in the cathedral's roof and killing hundreds. Little damage is visible today. The city has numerous universities, and there's a lively cafe and bar culture catering to local students.

◉ Sights

Iglesia de San Francisco CHURCH
(cnr Carrera 9 & Calle 4) The city's largest colonial church is also its most beautiful. Inside are a fine high altar and a collection of seven unique side altars. The 1983 earthquake cracked open the ossuary, revealing six unidentified mummies. Two are left, and you can visit them on a one-hour **guided tour**

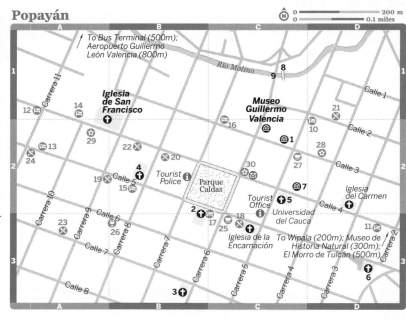

Popayán

(admission COP$2000; ☾8am-noon & 4-6pm) of the church that includes the five-story bell tower and the outdoor cupolas. Look for the tourist policeman outside the church doors who conducts the tours.

FREE **Museo Guillermo Valencia** MUSEUM (Carrera 6 No 2-69; ☾10am-noon & 2-5pm) This late-18th-century building is full of period furniture, paintings, old photos and documents that once belonged to the Popayán-born poet who lived here. It has been left more or less as it was when Valencia died in one of the upstairs bedrooms.

Museo de Historia Natural MUSEUM (museo.unicauca.edu.co; Carrera 2 No 1A-25; admission COP$3000; ☾9am-noon & 2-5pm) One of the best of its kind in the country, this museum on the grounds of the university is noted for its extensive collection of insects, butterflies and, in particular, stuffed birds.

Casa Museo Mosquera MUSEUM (Calle 3 No 5-38; admission COP$2000; ☾8am-noon & 2-5pm) This interesting museum is housed in an 18th-century mansion that was once home to General Tomás Cipriano de Mosquera, a politician and historian who was Colombia's president on four occasions between 1845 and 1867. Note the urn in the wall; it contains Mosquera's heart.

Museo Arquidiocesano de Arte Religioso MUSEUM (Calle 4 No 4-56; admission COP$5000; ☾9am-12:30pm & 2-6pm Mon-Fri, 9am-2pm Sat) You don't have to be an expert on religious art to be impressed by this collection of paintings, statues, altar pieces, silverware and liturgical vessels, most of which date from the 17th to 19th centuries.

Puente de la Custodia BRIDGE (Carrera 6) Also frequently called Puente Chiquita (Little Bridge), this stone bridge just north of the old center was constructed in 1713 to allow priests to cross the Río Molino to bring the holy orders to the sick of this poor northern suburb. About 160 years later, the solid 240m-long 11-arch **Puente del Humilladero** was built alongside the old bridge, and is still in use.

Iglesia La Ermita CHURCH (cnr Calle 5 & Carrera 2) Constructed in 1546, Popayán's oldest church is worth seeing for its fine main retable and the fragments of

old frescoes, which were only discovered after the earthquake.

There are a number of other colonial churches in town including, the **Iglesia de Santo Domingo** (cnr Carrera 5 & Calle 4), **Iglesia de San José** (cnr Calle 5 & Carrera 8) and the **Iglesia de San Agustín** (cnr Calle 7 & Carrera 6). The neoclassical **catedral** (Parque Caldas) is the youngest church in the center, built between 1859 and 1906 on the site of a previous cathedral, which had been completely destroyed by an earthquake.

The **Capilla de Belén**, a chapel set on a hill just east of the city center, offers nice views over the town. **El Morro de Tulcán**, a hill topped with an equestrian statue of the town's founder, provides even better vistas. It's said to be the site of a pre-Columbian pyramid and is a good place to watch the sunset. Both destinations are isolated and robberies are quite common – don't carry any valuables. It is possible to organize an escort from the tourist police.

★ Festivals & Events

Semana Santa PROCESSION (Holy Week; Easter) Popayán's Easter celebrations are world-famous, especially the nighttime processions on Maundy Thursday and Good Friday. Thousands of the faithful and tourists from all over come to take part in this religious ceremony and the accompanying festival of religious music. Hotel prices quadruple at this time; book well in advance.

Congreso Nacional Gastronómico FOOD (Sep; www.gastronomicopopayan.org) Top chefs from a different country each year are invited to come and cook up a storm in the first week of September. Admission to all of the week's events costs COP$300,000.

🛏 Sleeping

Hotel Los Balcones HOTEL $$ (☑824 2030; www.hotellosbalconespopayan.com; Carrera 7 No 2-75; s/d/apt COP$61,600/115,000/170,100;@🛜) Climb 200-year-old stone stairs to your room in this regal 18th-century abode. The place has an almost medieval feel with old wooden furniture, stuffed eagles and a maze of corridors. In the lobby, MC Escher sketches hang next to a case of ancient pottery and plush leather furniture. Rooms are spacious and have a TV. It also has an apartment with a small kitchen for rent.

WORTH A TRIP

SILVIA

A picturesque mountain town 53km northeast of Popayán, Silvia is the center of the Guambiano region. The Guambiano people don't live in Silvia itself, but in the small mountain villages of Pueblito, La Campana, Guambia and Caciques. The whole community numbers about 12,000.

The Guambiano are considered one of the most traditional indigenous groups in Colombia. They speak their own language, dress traditionally and still use rudimentary farming techniques. They're also excellent weavers.

On Tuesday, market day, they come to Silvia to sell fruit, vegetables and handicrafts. This is the best time to visit the town. Almost all the Guambiano come in traditional dress; men in blue skirts with a pink fringe and bowler hats, women in hand-woven garments and beaded necklaces, busily spinning wool. They come in *chivas* (colorful buses) and congregate around the main plaza. They don't like cameras, and may get aggressive if you take their picture; respect their culture and keep your gear in your bag.

The market begins at dawn and goes until the early afternoon. It is not a tourist market – fruit and vegetables, raw meat, discount clothing and shoes dominate – but you may find a poncho or sweater that takes your fancy.

From the main plaza, walk uphill to the church for 360-degree views of the surrounding countryside. Down by the river you can rent horses (COP$6000 per hour) to ride around a small lake.

Silvia attracts weekend tourists from Cali looking to cool off, and there are numerous good-value hotels in town if you decide to stay.

Buses depart Popayán roughly every hour (COP$6000, 1½ hours), with extra early-morning services on Tuesday. From Cali, take a Popayán-bound bus as far as Piendamó (COP$12,000, two hours) from where you can pick up an onward bus to Silvia (COP$3000, 30 minutes).

Hotel Dann Monasterio HOTEL $$$
(☎824 2191; www.hotelesdann.com; Calle 4 No 10-14; s/d COP$275,000/345,000, ste COP$520,000; ❄@≋) This Franciscan monastery-turned-hotel offers large, elegantly appointed rooms around a vast arcaded courtyard. The wi-fi signal can't penetrate the thick adobe walls, but there are ethernet cables in each room. There's a pool in the back garden. Prices include a round of golf at the local *club campestre* (country club).

Hosteltrail HOSTEL $
(☎831 7871; www.hosteltrail.com; Carrera 11 No 4-16; dm COP$17,000, s/d COP$40,000/50,000, without bathroom COP$32,000/42,000; @📶) Popayán's most popular budget choice, Hosteltrail is a modern, friendly place on the edge of the colonial center with everything weary travelers need. There is fast internet, express laundry, fully equipped kitchen and eager staff with a wealth of local know-how. It organizes visits to a nearby coffee farm and downhill mountain biking from Coconuco.

Parklife Hostel HOSTEL $
(☎300 249 6240; www.parklifehostel.com; Calle 5 No 6-19; dm COP$17,000, s/d COP$40,000/50,000, without bathroom COP$32,000/42,000; @📶) You'd be hard pressed to find a hostel with a better location than Parklife – it's attached to the cathedral wall. The house has plenty of its original style; there are wood floors, chandeliers and antique furniture. It's an atmospheric place – you can hear the church choir from the communal atrium. The front rooms have superb views over Parque Caldas.

Hotel Colonial HOTEL $$
(☎831 7848; Calle 5 No 10-94; s/d/tr COP$50,000/65,000/80,000; @📶) Recently renovated, this efficient small hotel in a colonial house in the center is excellent value. The rooms have comfortable beds, flat-screen TVs and spotless bathrooms. Rooms upstairs get more natural light.

Casa Familiar Turística HOSTEL $
(☎824 4853; Carrera 5 No 2-07; dm/s/d COP$14,000/20,000/30,000; 📶) Popayán's original budget digs are a great option for those looking to immerse themselves in local culture – you are basically sharing the colonial house with the friendly Colombian owners. There's hot water and laundry facilities, and you can use the kitchen.

Hostel Caracol HOSTEL $
(📞820 7335; www.hostelcaracol.com; Calle 4 No 2-21; dm COP$17,000, s without bathroom COP$28,000-32,000, d without bathroom COP$45,000; @📶) In a renovated colonial house, this new laid-back option from the owners of the Hosteltrail is popular with slightly older independent travelers. It has comfortable rooms set around a courtyard common area and plenty of information about attractions and entertainment in town.

Hotel La Plazuela HOTEL $$$
(📞824 1084; www.hotellaplazuela.com.co; Calle 5 No 8-13; s/d/tr/q incl breakfast COP$130,000 /180,000/231,000/280,000; 📶) In a beautiful, whitewashed mansion complete with a lovely courtyard, this classy hotel has been fully refurbished but still has much of the original, antique furniture. The front rooms have effective soundproof windows and provide views of Iglesia San José.

✖ Eating

A local specialty is *empanadas de pipián,* fried snacks served with a spicy satay-style peanut sauce.

Hotel Camino Real FRENCH, COLOMBIAN $$$
(📞824 3595; Calle 5 No 5-59; mains COP$25,000-35,000) The owners of this hotel are key players in the Congreso Nacional Gastronómico and their passion for food is evident in the interesting menu, which combines both French and Colombian elements. Every plate here is of the highest quality. Go for one of the excellent set menus (COP$40,000), which include two appetizers, a main, cheeses and a fruit mousse. Reservations are recommended.

Mora Castilla CAFE $
(Calle 2 No 4-44; snacks COP$2500-4000; ⏱10am-7pm) This humble cafe prepares excellent *salpicón* (fruit salad), juices and traditional snacks including *tamales* (steamed cornmeal dough) and *carantantas* (a kind of toasted corn chip). If you're still hungry, pop next door to sample some of Doña Chepa's famous *aplanchados* (flat pastries).

Lonchería La Viña COLOMBIAN $$
(Calle 4 No 7-79; mains COP$14,000-24,000; ⏱24hr) You will sit elbow-to-elbow with your fellow diners in this popular grill restaurant that prepares big portions on a large barbecue inside the dining room. There are 10 different cuts of beef, as well as fish, chicken and a couple of token salads. At lunch it offers a fine set meal (COP$8000).

La Fresa CAFETERIA $
(Calle 5 No 8-89; snacks COP$400-2000; ⏱8am-8pm) A grimy corner store with a couple of plastic tables, La Fresa is famed throughout Popayán for its outrageously delicious *empanadas de pipián*. Most locals wash them down with a *malta* (a wheat-based soda) or *gaseosa* (regular soda).

Restaurante Italiano ITALIAN $$
(Calle 4 No 8-83; mains COP$15,000-26,000) Swing open the saloon doors of this Swiss-owned Italian joint and you'll find great pizza and pasta, and a decent wine list. The set meal (COP$7500) is one of the best we've had in Colombia.

Sabores del Mar SEAFOOD $
(Calle 5 No 10-97; lunch COP$6000) Run by an energetic family from Guapi, this tiny nautical-themed place serves a great-value seafood lunch. Try the fillets of *toyo* (a kind of shark).

El Quijote COLOMBIAN $$
(Calle 10N No 8-14; mains COP$15,000-25,000) On the highway outside of town, Quijote does great grilled meat and fantastic salads, and sometimes has live guitar music. Well worth the short taxi ride.

Restaurante Vegetariano Maná VEGETARIAN $
(Calle 7 No 9-56; meals COP$4000; 📷) The best of several cheap vegetarian diners in Popayán, Maná has a set meal with plenty of options to choose from and serves a tasty hot breakfast with real orange juice and fruit.

♟ Drinking

There are numerous cafes in the center that are popular with local students. Be sure to try a *champú* or *lulada,* fruit drinks typical of this region.

Check out **Capriccio Café** (Calle 5 No 5-63; ⏱8:30am-12:30pm & 2-8:30pm Mon-Sat), which roasts its own coffee and does great iced-coffee drinks. **Madeira** (cnr Calle 3 & Carrera 5; ⏱9am-8:30pm Mon-Fri, 12:30-7:30pm Sat) sometimes hosts live music and serves excellent coffee in tiny earthenware cups.

Near the university, **Wipala** (Carrera 2 No 2-38; ⏱2pm-1am Mon-Sat, 3-10pm Sun; 📶) is a groovy cafe-bar (with wi-fi) with an internal garden that has live music and specializes in *hervidos* – hot citrus drinks with a kick. It also prepares vegetarian foods and snacks.

El **Sotareño** (Carrera 6 No 8-05) is a 40-year-old classic bar, and plays tango, bolero and ranchera on scratched old vinyl.

Be sure to check out **CC Campanario** (www.campanariopopayan.com; Carrera 9 No 24AN-21; ☺9am-1am). This monster shopping mall has a huge drinking hall and is a popular meeting spot in the early evening. There's also a gourmet food court nearby.

☆ Entertainment

Most of Popayán's big clubs cluster outside of town on the highway to Cali.

For salsa, try **Bar La Iguana** (Calle 4 No 9-67), which cranks the volume on weekends and shows videos on a large projection screen. **Acapella** (Calle 3 No 4-52) is a rowdy karaoke bar popular with the university crowd.

Late at night, head to **Corona** (Calle 4 No 5-78), a pumping disco inside a hotel in the old center with three zones each playing different styles of music. Out on the highway, **Millenio** (www.millenio.com.co; Autopista Norte; ☺9pm-3am Fri & Sat) plays salsa, electronica and reggaeton in a warehouse-like space.

❶ Information

4-72 (Calle 4 No 5-74) Post office.

Banco de Bogota (Parque Caldas) ATM that takes all cards, including Visa and Cirrus/Maestro networks.

Banco de Occidente (Parque Caldas) Another reliable ATM.

Hospital San José (☑820 0975; www.hospitalsanjose.gov.co; Carrera 6 No 10N-142)

La Red (Calle 5 No 7-15; per hr COP$1400) Fast internet by the park.

Ministerio de Relaciones Exteriores (☑823 1027; Calle 4N No 10B-66) Visa extensions.

Tourist office (Oficina de Turismo de Popayán; ☑824 2251; Carrera 5 No 4-68)

Tourist police (☑822 0916; Carrera 7 No 4-36) More helpful than the regular tourist office. In the Gobernación building.

❶ Getting There & Away

Air

Aeropuerto Guillermo León Valencia is right behind the bus terminal, 1km north of the city center. Avianca flies three times a day direct to Bogotá.

Bus

The bus terminal is 1km north of the city center. There are frequent services to Cali by both bus (COP$12,000, three hours) and minibus (COP$14,000, two hours). There are several daily buses direct to Armenia (COP$40,000, seven hours). Buses to Medellín (COP$60,000, 11 hours) depart at 7pm, 8pm and 1am.

There are six buses daily to San Agustín (COP$28,000, five hours). Buses to Tierradentro (COP$18,000, five hours) leave at 5am, 8am, 10:30am, 1pm and 3pm. The 10:30am service takes you all the way to the Museo Arqueológico entrance.

There are hourly buses to Pasto (COP$25,000, six hours). The road from Popayán to the Ecuadorean border is one of the few major routes in Colombia you should not travel after dark, not because of guerrilla activity but rather due to late-night bandits.

Coconuco

There are two thermal springs near the town of Coconuco, south of Popayán on the road to San Agustín. On weekends they are elbow-to-elbow kids and rum-soaked parents; during the week they are empty, and you'll likely be the only guest.

On weekends and evenings people come to party while loud music blares at 24-hour **Agua Hirviendo** (☑314 618 4178; admission COP$5000; ☺24hr). You read that right, a 24-hour thermal spring. Several cabins rent rooms nearby (ahem, both by the hour and overnight), and an adjacent restaurant serves meals until late. There are two large thermal pools and several small baths.

The water is not nearly as piping hot as Agua Hirviendo, but **Termales Aguatibia** (☑824 1161, 315 578 6111; termaguatibia@yahoo.es; admission COP$8000; ☺8am-6pm) is a more family-oriented spa and has a lot less concrete. Set at an altitude of 2560m amid spectacular green scenery, its restaurant has great views of the countryside and serves budget meals. There are five thermal pools, a thermal mud spring and a 53m-long 'toboggan' – a butt-bruising concrete slide. There is also a small thermal lake where you can rent inflatable rafts (COP$3000 per 30 minutes). There are several short walks nearby, including a 300m path up the hill to the water source.

During the week there is hourly transportation from Popayán to Coconuco (COP$3000, one hour, 31km), more on the weekends. From here you can grab a jeep (COP$7000 per vehicle) – if you can convince one of the drivers to put down their drink for a while. You will probably end up taking a moto-taxi (COP$2000).

San Agustín

📱8 / POP 31,300 / ELEV 1695M

Five thousand years ago, two primitive cultures lived in the adjacent river valleys of the Magdalena and the Cauca. Divided by uncrossable peaks, the rivers were their highways, and here, near San Agustín, within several days' march of each other, lie the headwaters of both rivers. It is here that those two civilizations met to trade, to worship, and to bury their dead.

The volcanic rocks thrown great distances by the now-extinct nearby volcanoes proved irresistible to the local sculptors, who set about working them into grand monuments. The result is more than 500 life-sized statues (the largest is 7m high) scattered over a wide area in the lush green hills surrounding San Agustín. Many of them are anthropomorphic figures, some realistic, others resembling masked monsters. There are also sculptures depicting sacred animals such as the eagle, jaguar and frog. Archaeologists have also uncovered a great deal of pottery, but very little in the way of gold – unlike the Tayrona on the Caribbean coast, these people had no gold to mine.

Little else is known about the peoples of San Agustín. They didn't have a written language and had disappeared many centuries before the Europeans arrived. But their legacy is one of the most important archaeological sights on the continent – a mystical place in a spectacular landscape that is well worth making a detour for.

The area around town offers plenty of attractions to keep visitors for a while after they have seen the archaeological sites. There is great hiking and some of the best horseback riding and whitewater-rafting trips in southern Colombia.

◉ Sights

You'll need three days to see all the archaeological sites – with one day for the

WORTH A TRIP

PARQUE NACIONAL NATURAL (PNN) PURACÉ

Forty-five kilometers east of Popayán along the unpaved road to La Plata lies this 830-sq-km **national park** (📱in Popayán 823 1212; admission Colombians/foreigners COP$8000/19,000; ☺8am-6pm). It's the only place in Colombia you can see condors. Nearly a dozen of the great vultures were reintroduced to the park – three remain. The park wardens will tempt them down with food so you can see them up close.

The visitor center (3350m) rents unheated **cabins** (campsite per person COP$8000, r per person COP$33,000) and serves budget meals; there's no hot water, but some cabins have working fireplaces.

In good weather you can summit **Volcán Puracé** (4750m), the highest of the seven volcanoes in the Coconuco range. It's about five hours up and three hours down along a well-signposted trail, although because of the difficulty of the climb a guide is recommended – ask at the visitor center. The best time to climb is December and January; the weather from June to August can be foul. Consider spending the night before in a cabin to get an early start to the day.

To get here, take any La Plata–bound bus to the **Cruce de la Mina** (COP$10,000, 1¼ hours). On the way you may be asked to pay a small entrance fee at Puracé (an indigenous community). If you are coming for the day, it's best to take the first bus at 4:30am. From Cruce de la Mina it's a 1.5km walk uphill to the **Cruce de Pilimbalá**. Turn left for the visitor center (1km) or go straight for 1.5km to visit the **sulfur mine** (📱318 780 6690; emicauca@hotmail.com). The mine is run by the local indigenous community who took over when the mining company closed. You can go 200m into the mine tunnel to a shrine to the Virgin Mary. The community leaders are keen to get into ecotourism and you can find guides here to take you along an alternate route to the summit.

About 8km past the Cruce de la Mina are the **Termales de San Juan** (3200m), which bubble up amid an otherworldly *páramo* (high-mountain plain) setting – spectacular. Unlike Coconuco, these thermals aren't for bathing. It's a 1.1km-walk from the highway along a well-marked path. There you'll find a ranger station (often unoccupied) with bathrooms.

The last bus back to Popayán passes the Cruce de la Mina at around 5pm. Bring food, water and a copy of your passport for the military checkpoint in Puracé.

San Agustín

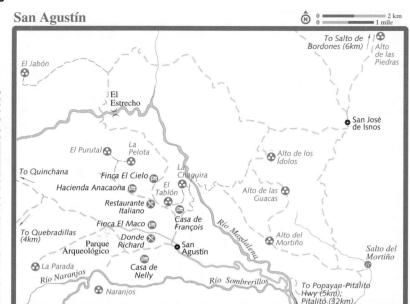

archaeological park; one day on horseback to El Tablón, La Chaquira, La Pelota and El Purutal (four hours round trip); and one day for a jeep tour to El Estrecho, Alto de los Ídolos, Alto de las Piedras, Salto de Bordones and Salto de Mortiño (six hours). If you are visiting both the park and Alto de los Ídolos, purchase a combined entrance ticket (COP$16,000) at either location.

It is highly recommended to visit the more remote sites with a local guide – there is little in the way of signs or explanations outside the Parque Arqueológico. The going rate for a guide is around COP$30,000 per day; COP$40,000 for an English-speaking guide. You can rent horses for around COP$30,000 per half-day, plus you'll be expected to pay for the guide's horse (thus making it cheaper to go in a group). Jeep tours to the sites go for around COP$150,000 to COP$180,000 per day (maximum five people).

Parque Arqueológico ARCHAEOLOGICAL SITE
(admission adult/child COP$10,000/5000; ⊗8am-4pm) The 78-hectare archaeological park is 2.5km west of the town of San Agustín. There are in total about 130 statues in the park, either found in situ or collected from other areas, including some of the best examples of San Agustín statuary. Plan on spending around three hours in the park. Reputable guides congregate in the museum's outdoor cafe, but you don't really need one.

At the entrance to the park is the **Museo Arqueológico** (⊗8am-5pm), which features smaller statues, pottery, utensils, jewelry and other objects, along with interesting background information about the San Agustín culture.

Besides the various clusters of statues (called *mesitas*) is the **Fuente de Lavapatas**. Carved in the rocky bed of the stream, it is a complex labyrinth of ducts and small, terraced pools decorated with images of serpents, lizards and human figures. Archaeologists believe the baths were used for ritual ablutions and the worship of aquatic deities.

From here, the path winds uphill to the **Alto de Lavapatas**, the oldest archaeological site in San Agustín. You'll find a few tombs guarded by statues, and get a panoramic view over the surrounding countryside.

Alto de los Ídolos ARCHAEOLOGICAL SITE
(admission COP$10,000; ⊗8am-4pm) Located across the Río Magdalena 4km southwest of San José de Isnos (a clutch of houses 26km northeast from the town of San Agustín), this is the second-most important archaeological park in the region. It's home to the largest statue (7m) in the San Agustín area.

Alto de las Piedras
ARCHAELOGICAL SITE

This site is 7km north of Isnos and has tombs lined with stone slabs painted red, black and yellow. One of the most famous statues, known as Doble Yo, is here; look carefully as there are actually four figures carved in this statue. You'll also find an intriguing statue of a female figure in an advanced state of pregnancy.

El Tablón, La Chaquira, La Pelota & El Purutal
ARCHAELOGICAL SITES

These four sites are relatively close to each other; most people visit as part of a horse-riding tour. Don't miss La Chaquira, with divinities carved into the mountain face and overlooking the stunning gorge of the Río Magdalena.

Other Archaeological Sites
ARCHAELOGICAL SITES

There are several more archaeological sites to see if you are not in a hurry, including **La Parada**, **Quinchana**, **El Jabón**, **Naranjos** and **Quebradillas**. Apart from its archaeological wealth, the region is also noted for its natural beauty, and features two spectacular waterfalls, **Salto de Bordones** and **Salto de Mortiño**. It's also worth a walk or ride to **El Estrecho**, where the Río Magdalena passes through 2.2m narrows. All these sights are accessible by road or on horseback.

⚡ Activities

One of the best ways to explore the mountains surrounding San Agustín is on horseback. Unlike in some parts of the country, the horses available to tourists here are more often than not in excellent condition. You can travel by horseback to some of the archaeological sites around town or head out on some epic multiday adventures.

Laguna del Magdalena
HORSEBACK RIDING

An interesting horseback-riding trip is the three-day journey to Laguna del Magdalena, the birthplace of the Río Magdalena (3327m), 60km from San Agustín. The region was historically infested with guerrillas but is now considered safe. Expect to pay around COP$150,000 per person for the trek. A recommended tour leader is **Francisco 'Pacho' Muñoz** (☑311 8277 972) – you can usually find him hanging around at Finca El Maco. Pacho can also take you to Tierradentro or, if you are willing to purchase horses, will even lead you all the way to Ecuador.

Magdalena Rafting
RAFTING

(☑311 271 5333; www.magdalenarafting.com; Calle 5 No 16-04) The Río Magdalena offers challenging whitewater rafting through some phenomenal landscapes. Magdalena Rafting offers 1½-hour tours (COP$45,000 per person) with Classes II to III rapids for novices, and full-day, Class V tours (COP$120,000) for experienced pros. Minimum four people per group. It also offers kayaking classes.

🛏 Sleeping

You'll enjoy your time in San Agustín more if you stay outside the center of town.

🏕 Casa de François
HOSTEL $

(☑837 3847; www.lacasadefrancois.com; campsite per person COP$8000, dm/s/d COP$17,000/30,000/40,000; @) Set in a garden just above town overlooking the hills, this creative, ecological hostel is constructed of glass bottles embedded in rammed-mud walls. The breezy, elevated dormitory has fantastic views and the spacious shared kitchen is one of the best around. There is free internet and the hostel will pay your taxi from town upon arrival.

Finca El Maco
HOSTEL $

(☑837 3437, 311 271 4802; www.elmaco.ch; campsite per person COP$8000, hammock COP$8000, dm COP$16,000, s/d COP$40,000/60,000, without bathroom COP$33,000/50,000; @) This Swiss-owned hostel has a variety of cabins set amid a pretty garden. The restaurant serves homemade organic yoghurt and cheese, wholemeal bread, green salads and an excellent curry. The owner can organize trips throughout the region. Take the road to the Parque Arqueológico and turn right at the Hotel Yalconia. From here it's a 400m walk uphill. Take a taxi (COP$7000) if you have luggage.

Hacienda Anacaona
HOTEL $$

(☑311 231 7128; www.anacaona-colombia.com; Via al Estrecho; s/d/tr COP$60,000/100,000/135,000; @) This peaceful colonial-style hotel is one of the most comfortable options in the area. It is set amid a well-maintained garden and has good views. Prices include breakfast. Frequent *colectivos* from town can drop you here (COP$2000).

Finca El Cielo
HOTEL $$

(☑313 493 7446; www.fincaelcielo.com; Via al Estrecho; r per person COP$40,000) A few hundred meters after the Anacaona is this pretty posada built of *guadua* and with tremendous views out over the surrounding, misty green hills. The friendly owners live on the ground floor and prepare good home-cooked meals with advance notice.

Casa de Nelly   HOSTEL **$**
(📞310 215 9067; www.hotelcasadenelly.co; Vereda La Estrella; dm COP$18,000, s/d COP$35,000/70,000, without bathroom COP$25,000/50,000) The original San Agustín hostel has a range of comfortable accommodations set around one of the prettiest gardens in town and a spacious social area with an open fireplace.

There are numerous budget hotels in the center of town. Your best bet is **Residencias El Jardín** (📞837 3455; Carrera 11 No 4-10; r per person COP$12,000-15,000), or try the **Hotel Colonial** (📞837 3159; Calle 3 No 11-25; r per person $10,000-15,000).

Eating

In the market (La Galería) you will find cheap meals and plenty of crisp fresh produce for self-caterers.

TOP
CHOICE **Donde Richard**   COLOMBIAN **$$**
(📞312 432 6399; Via al Parque Arqueológico; mains COP$15,000-22,000; ⏱noon-7pm, closed Wed) This grill restaurant on the road to the Parque Archaeológico does the best food in town. On Sunday it prepares *asado huilense,* the local specialty of slow-cooked, marinated pork. A great spot for lunch on the way back from the park.

Restaurante Italiano   ITALIAN **$$**
(📞837 9650; Vereda el Tablón; mains COP$15,000-20,000) A little way out of town, this unpretentious restaurant serves authentic traditional Italian plates, including a selection of homemade pastas. A taxi here will cost around COP$4000.

El Fogón   COLOMBIAN **$$**
(📞837 3431; Calle 5 No 14-30; mains COP$18,000) A local institution, El Fogón serves up big portions of Colombian favorites and an excellent-value set lunch (COP$7000). There is another branch close to the Parque Arqueológico.

Drinking

A number of lively bars are clustered in town near the police station. Also worth a look is **El Faro** (Carrera 13 No 6-50; ⏱closed Tue), a groovy small bar that sometimes hosts live music and has a great menu of light meals; it's four blocks up the hill from the plaza. **Territorio Libre** (Calle 5 No 14-27) is a rocking disco opposite El Fogón – in the chilly wee hours it lights a small bonfire out back.

Shopping

Farmers come to buy and sell at San Agustín's Monday **market**. It's a raucous scene with few tourists. Besides fruit, vegetables and *panela* (dried sugarcane juice) you'll find clothing, shoes and bags at budget prices. If you miss the Monday market, head for **La Galería** (cnr Calle 3 & Carrera 11; ⏱5am-4pm); it's open the rest of the week, but is more subdued.

Information

Local touts pushing hotels and 'cheap' tours hang around in the center and often hustle passengers of arriving intercity buses. A proposed new bus terminal should reduce the problem but until then contract professional guides and jeeps through your hotel, at the archaeological park or at the tourist office.

Banagrario (cnr Carrera 13 & Calle 4) ATM providing services for Visa and Cirrus/Maestro networks.

Banco de Bogota (Calle 3 No 10-61) ATM only.

Enter.net (Carrera 10 No 3-46; per hr COP$1500; ⏱7am-11pm) A dozen computers.

Hospital Arsenio Repizo Vanegas (📞837 3565; Calle 3 No 2-51)

Tourist office (📞837 3062, ext 15; cnr Calle 3 & Carrera 12; ⏱8am-noon & 2-5pm Mon-Fri) There are numerous tour agencies masquerading as the 'official tourist office.' The real tourist office is this one, which is in the *alcaldía* (town hall).

Tourist police (📞837 3606; Carrera 3 No 11-56)

Getting There & Away

Bus company offices are on the corner of Calle 3 and Carrera 11 (known as Cuatro Vientos). There are regular minibuses to Neiva (COP$23,000, four hours) and several buses in the afternoon and evening to Bogotá (COP$54,000, 12 hours). Not all Pitalito–Popayán buses (COP$28,000, five hours) stop in San Agustín. If you're in a hurry, take a shared taxi 5km to the crossroads, or *el cruce* in Spanish (COP$2000, 10 minutes). Arriving from Popayán, buses with few passengers will drop you here and pay your taxi fare to San Agustín. The taxi drivers often take you direct to a hotel they work with – be firm about where you want to go.

For Tierradentro, go to Pitalito (COP$5000, 45 minutes) and change for La Plata (COP$20,000,

MOCOA: JUNGLE ROUTE TO ECUADOR

If you are planning to travel from San Agustín to Ecuador, you don't need to return to Popayán. Just four hours from Pitalito by bus, the department of Putumayo is a land of rushing rivers, dense jungle and amazing wildlife. If you are not going to get to Leticia this trip, it is well worth making a detour to this accessible corner of the Amazon. The departmental capital is Mocoa. The town itself is an unremarkable agricultural center, but there is great nature right on its doorstop, including dozens of waterfalls and excellent trekking.

Next to one of Mocoa's best swimming holes to the southeast of the center, **Casa del Río** (📞420 4004; www.casadelriomocoa.com; Vereda Caliyaco, via Mocoa-Villagarzón; dm/s/d COP$17,000/32,000/38,000; @📶) has new comfortable rooms in a lush garden full of birds.

From Mocoa you can head to Pasto (COP$24,000, six hours) on the Trampolin de la Muerte (Trampoline of Death) – one of the most dangerous and spectacular roads on the continent. It is an unpaved, single-carriage road with sheer 400m drops into rocky ravines the entire way. When you meet oncoming traffic you often have to navigate this treacherous track in reverse! It is considered safer to travel in a pickup than by bus. It's just two hours to the border from Pasto. Alternatively, you can take a bus to the border at San Miguel (COP$30,000, six hours) and cross into Ecuador near the town of Nueva Loja (Lago Agrio), from where there are bus services and flights to Quito.

At the time of research the San Miguel border crossing was beginning to get some use, but security in the area remains sketchy. Check the situation with the authorities in Mocoa and only travel during the day.

2½ hours), where you can get a bus to San Andrés (COP$10,000, 2½ hours). Some buses may drop you at the crossroads; from here it's a 20-minute walk uphill to the Tierradentro museums and hotels.

ℹ️ Getting Around

A bus runs the 2km to the park every 15 minutes (COP$1200) from the corner of Calle 5 and Carrera 14. *Chivas* and vans ply the nearby country roads, especially from Saturday to Monday. They can take you to and from your hotel for around COP$2000.

Half a dozen new taxis now service San Agustín. They can take you around town and, more importantly, to your lodging outside of town. The fixed rates are posted inside the cab.

Tierradentro

🔁2 / ELEV 1750M

Tierradentro is the second-most important archaeological site in Colombia (after San Agustín) but gets surprisingly few visitors. Located well off the beaten track down some rough dirt roads, it is a peaceful place with friendly locals and awe-inspiring archaeological wonders. Where San Agustín is noted for its statuary, Tierradentro is remarkable for its elaborate underground tombs. So far, archaeologists have discovered about 100 of these unusual funeral temples, the only examples of their kind in the Americas. There is a fabulous walk you can do that takes in all the major tomb sites amid gorgeous mountain scenery.

👁️ Sights

Scattered across the hills around the town of San Andrés de Pisimbalá, Tierradentro consists of five separate sites, four with tombs and one with above-ground statuary, plus two adjacent museums.

Measuring from 2m to 7m in diameter, the tombs are scooped out of the soft volcanic rock that forms the region's undulating hillsides. They vary widely in depth; some are just below ground level, while others are as deep as 9m. The domed ceilings of the largest tombs are supported by massive pillars. Many are painted with red and black geometric motifs on white backgrounds. In addition, figures are carved into the columns and walls of many chambers.

Little is known about the people who built the tombs and the statues – the Páez (or Nasa) indigenous group that lives in the area today is not thought to be connected to the ruins. Most likely they were of different cultures, and the people who scooped out the tombs preceded those who carved the statues. Some researchers place the 'tomb'

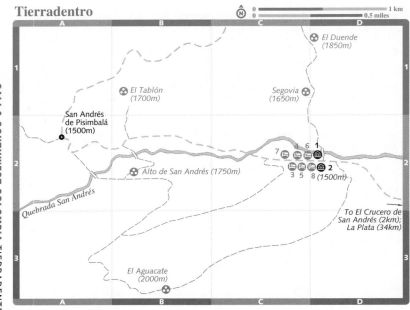

Tierradentro

civilization somewhere between the 7th and 9th centuries AD, while the 'statue' culture appears to be related to the later phase of San Agustín development, which is estimated to have taken place some 500 years later.

The ticket office for the **archaeological park** (☏313 829 3066; adult/child or senior COP$10,000/5000; ⊙8am-4pm) is inside the museum complex. You will be given a bracelet that enables access to both museums and the tombs. It is valid for two days. It is worth visiting the museums before heading out to the tombs as there is not much in the way of explanation at the sites themselves.

A 25-minute walk uphill from the museums is the little town of **San Andrés de Pisimbalá**. The town is mildly famous for its beautiful thatched adobe **church**. A small *artesanías* shop sells miniature replicas of the church.

Burial Sites & Statues

You can visit all the burial sites in Tierradentro on a full-day, 14km walk. The walk takes you through some spectacular scenery, and it's well worth doing the entire loop. You can follow the loop in either direction, but it is recommended to head out counterclockwise, otherwise you will have a tough uphill climb at the beginning of the hike. Some of the tombs have electric lighting, but it isn't always functioning; bring a flashlight (torch). The tombs are open from 8am to 4pm.

Going counterclockwise, a 20-minute walk uphill from the museums is **Segovia**, the most important burial site. There are 28 tombs here, some with well-preserved decorations. Twelve of the tombs have electric lighting, which works only sporadically.

A 15-minute walk uphill from Segovia brings you to **El Duende**, where there are four tombs, though their decoration hasn't been preserved. From here it's a 25-minute walk along the highway to **El Tablón**, which has nine weather-worn stone statues, similar to those of San Agustín, excavated in the area and now thrown together under a single roof. The better preserved statues can be seen in the Museo Arqueológico. If you're walking, be aware the site is poorly signposted; look up and to the left until you see the faded blue sign. You can also get to El Tablón from the main San Andrés road, which is well signposted but muddy.

Continue into town. Next to the restaurant La Portada you'll find the path to **Alto de San Andrés**, with six large tombs; two have remarkably well-preserved paintings. Two of the tombs are closed because of structural instability and humidity, and another has caved in completely.

El Aguacate is the most remote burial site, but has the best views. From Alto de San Andrés it's a 1½-hour walk, then downhill another 1½ hours to the museums. There are a few dozen tombs, but most have been destroyed by *guaqueros* (tomb raiders). Only a few vaults still bear the remains of the original decoration.

Museums

The **Museo Arqueológico** contains pottery urns used to keep the ashes of the tribal elders. Some of the urns are decorated with dotted patterns and, in some cases, with representations of animals. There are also miniature models of what the tombs may have looked like when they were freshly painted.

The **Museo Etnográfico** has utensils and artifacts of the Páez people, and exhibits from colonial times, including a *trapiche* (sugarcane grinder), *bodoqueras* (blow-dart guns) and traditional indigenous clothing.

🛏 Sleeping & Eating

There are half a dozen basic lodgings clustered within the 500m stretch uphill of the museum. Many are run by endearing senior citizens – there's not much going on for young folk around here. All the budget options charge COP$10,000 to COP$15,000 per person.

One of the best budget options is **Residencias y Restaurante Pisimbalá** (☑311 612 4145), which has five rooms with hot-water private bathrooms. It serves cheap meals, including options for vegetarians. The on-site *tienda* sells locally made coca-flavored wine. Other good options include **Hospedaje La María** (☑312 752 7860), **Residencias Lucerna**, which has a kitchen you can use, **Residencias Ricabet** (☑312 795 4636), further uphill with a park bench outside where you can wait for the morning bus, and **Mi Casita** (☑312 764 1333).

Close by is the recently refurbished **Hotel El Refugio** (☑321 811 2395; s/d/tr COP$40,000/52,000/74,000; 🏊), the most luxurious option in the area. It has comfortable rooms with mountain views, cable TV and a big pool.

If you are going to be here for a while, you may prefer to stay in San Andrés de Pisimbalá. Right by where the bus arrives, **La Portada** (☑311 601 7884; s/d COP$20,000/30,000) has large, clean rooms with hot water in a wooden lodge, and serves the best food in town in its breezy restaurant. Try the homemade ice cream. The friendly owners will give you a map and plenty of advice on visiting the tombs and onward transportation. They can also organize horse rental. A block away, near the football field, **Residencia El Viajero** (☑312 746 5991; Calle 6 No 4-09; r per person COP$10,000) offers basic rooms with shared bathroom in the sweet elderly owner's home.

The town also has a couple of *tiendas* (shops) selling snacks and drinks.

ℹ Information

There is no tourist office, bank or internet service near Tierradentro. Several of the hotels offer Comcel cell-phone minutes. There is a small community health center in San Andrés de Pisimbalá.

ℹ Getting There & Away

A direct bus to Popayán (COP$18,000, four hours) leaves San Andrés de Pisimbalá at 6am and passes in front of the museums. There are other buses to Popayán (9am, 11am, 1pm and 4pm) from El Crucero de San Andrés (a 20-minute walk downhill from the museums). There are sometimes *colectivos* (COP$1000) and moto-taxis (COP$3000) to take you to/from the crossroads but it is often faster to walk.

Buses and pickups leave San Andrés de Pisimbalá at 6:30am, 8am, noon and 4pm for La Plata (COP$10,000, two hours), where you can pick up connections to Bogotá, San Agustín and Neiva for the Desierto de la Tatacoa.

Desierto de la Tatacoa

Halfway between Bogotá and San Agustín lies the Tatacoa Desert. It is a striking landscape of eroded cliffs and gullies, sculpted by the infrequent rain. Because of the dry, clear conditions, lack of light pollution, and location at the equator, Tatacoa is a great spot for stargazing – the skies above both the northern and southern hemispheres are spread out for all to see.

Tatacoa isn't really a desert, although the thermometer says otherwise – it can hit 50°C at times. It's technically semi-arid dry tropical forest, averaging 1070mm of rain per year. Surrounded by mountains in every direction, the peaks around Nevado de Huila (5750m) grab most of the incoming precipitation, leaving 330-sq-km Tatacoa arid. The result is an ecosystem unlike anywhere else in Colombia – there are scorpions and weasels, fruit-bearing cacti, and 72 bird species have been recorded here.

To get here, you'll have to pass through Neiva, the hot, sleepy capital of the Huíla department and a port on the Río Magdalena. There's nothing in Neiva of interest. Take a bus to Villavieja, an hour's ride northwest. You can spend the night in Villavieja or, better yet, spend the night in the desert (see below).

Be sure to bring sturdy shoes (there are cactus spines on the ground) and a flashlight (torch).

Villavieja

☑8 / POP 7338 / ELEV 440M

This small desert town was founded in 1550 and has largely been forgotten about since. A few families continue to eke out a living herding goats and raising cattle, but most have turned to tourism – hordes of *bogotano* (inhabitants of Bogotá) tourists come on weekends and holidays to warm up.

◉ Sights & Activities

The region used to be a sea bed and contains numerous important fossils from the Miocene era; paleontologists continue to work in La Venta, a remote region of the desert. You can see some of their findings, including the bones of an armadillo the size of a tractor, at the **Museo Paleontológico** (☑313 804 9580; admission COP$2000; ☺8:30am-noon & 2-5pm) on the main square.

Be sure to visit **Conservas del Desierto** (☑311 883 1570; conservasdeldesierto@yahoo.es; Carrera 5 No 5-78; ☺8am-10pm), which sells various products made from the locally grown nopal cactus, including cactus sweets, pickled cactus heart, and cactus wine (8.7% alcohol). The cactus is reputed to have medicinal properties, and is quite tasty.

As you leave town you'll pass through **Bosque del Cardón**, a small cactus forest.

Four kilometers from Villavieja is **El Cusco**, where you'll find the **Observatorio Astronómico de la Tatacoa** (☑879 7584; www.tatacoa-astronomia.com; viewings COP$10,000; ☺7pm-9pm). Here you'll find a visitor center, which can arrange bike and horse rentals. In the evenings, local astronomer **Javier Fernando Rua Restrepo** (☑310 465 6765) shows visitors around the sky using two tripod telescopes. Call ahead to check conditions. Every July at the new moon, university groups and Colombian stargazing enthusiasts congregate here for a four-day, three-night **Fiesta de Estrellas** (Star Party).

A lookout point across the road from the observatory has impressive views, and is a fine place to watch the sunset. Below the lookout are the **Laberintos del Cusco** (Cusco Labyrinths), a striking maze-like landscape of undulating red rock formations that seem totally out of place in tropical Colombia. As you stand on the front porch of the visitor center, walk down to the main road and turn left. At the red-roofed bar (100m) look for the trail that heads downhill. Follow the trail for 45 minutes until you return to the main road.

Four kilometers past the observatory is **Ventanas**, a lookout point so named for its commanding views out over the desert. Another 5km takes you to **Los Hoyos**, where there is a swimming pool fed by a natural spring deep in a barren gray valley.

🛏 Sleeping & Eating

There are several basic hotels in town but most travelers prefer to spend the night in the desert itself. In the desert, most accommodations are basically four concrete walls with a corrugated tin roof; all serve meals.

Villa Paraiso   HOTEL $
(☑879 7727; hotelvillaparaisovillavieja@yahoo.es; Calle 4 No 7-69; s/d COP$20,000/50,000) The best choice in town, Villa Paraiso has neat rooms with private bathrooms, real beds and cable TV set around a pleasant patio area.

Campground   CAMPGROUND $
(campsite per person COP$5000; El Cusco) Behind the observatory is a large campsite with room for 40 tents. You can also rent a hammock for COP$10,000 and string it up side on the Greek pillars on the front porch. The building is powered by solar panels.

Estadero Doña Lilia   GUESTHOUSE $
(☑313 311 8828; r per person with/without bathroom COP$25,000/20,000; Desierto) About

400m past the observatory, Estadero Doña Lilia has comfortable rooms with impressive views and serves delicious meals.

Noches de Saturno GUESTHOUSE $
(✆313 305 5898; r per person COP$30,000; ≋) Next-door to Estadero Doña Lilia, this place has a nice shady garden full of birds and a pool. Price includes breakfast. Visitors can use the pool for COP$3000.

Doña Elbira GUESTHOUSE $
(✆312 559 8576; s/d COP$15,000/30,000) A short walk down the road from Noches de Saturno, this option has a couple of cabins scattered across the desert scrub, about 1km after the observatory.

Estadero la Tranquilidad del Desierto GUESTHOUSE $
(✆310 287 9474; r per person COP$20,000) About 2km past the observatory, this option has one room with three beds. You can use the kitchen and the owners live in town so it is completely silent in the evenings.

Sol y Sombra COLOMBIAN $
(✆879 7582; Carrera 4A No 5-86; meals COP$4000-5000; ☺breakfast, lunch & dinner) For a tasty meal in the center of town. It prepares simple breakfasts and a variety of Colombian favorites.

About 1km from the observatory heading away from town, **Rincón de Cabrito** is a food stand selling goat's milk, cheese, *arequipe* (a sweet dessert of milk and sugar) and other goat milk–based desserts.

ℹ Information

Banco Agrario (✆879 7503, 879 7513; Calle 4 No 4-30; ☺8am-1pm Mon-Fri) There's no ATM in town, but Banco Agrario will let you withdraw cash with a credit card and passport.
Internet cafe (Carrera 3 No 4-13; per hr COP$1500)
Tourist office (✆311 829 5651) Located by the park.

ℹ Getting There & Away

Vans hop the 37km between Neiva and Villavieja (COP$5000, one hour) from 5am to 7:30pm. They leave with a minimum of five passengers; there are frequent services in the early morning and late afternoon, but during the day you could wait an hour or two.

There are frequent services between Bogotá and Neiva (COP$35,000, five hours). There are several buses a day direct to San Agustín (COP$23,000, four hours). For Tierradentro, change at La Plata (COP$18,000, four hours).

ℹ Getting Around

There is a handful of moto-taxis in town that charge a stiff COP$15,000 to COP$20,000 to take up to three people to the observatory. You could walk the 4km, but there's no shade, shelter or water on the way.

NARIÑO

Welcome to Ecuador – almost. Nariño is Colombia's most southwesterly department, and the Ecuadorean influence here is strong.

The Andes here loom high and forbidding on their southerly march. The 'volcano alley' that runs the length of Ecuador begins here – pleasant Pasto, the departmental capital, sits a mere 8km from an active volcano covered in patchwork farmland.

Most people visit the region only to cross the border, but it's worth spending a few days here. Pasto has a compact center that's worth a stroll, Laguna de la Cocha is unmissable, and the towering Santuario de Las Lajas near Ipiales is an astonishing sight to behold.

Pasto
✆2 / POP 411,706 / ELEV 2551M

Just two hours from Ecuador, Pasto is the capital of the department and the logical jumping-off point for the border. It's also a good base for visiting Laguna de la Cocha, Laguna Verde and, if it ever stops grumbling, Volcán Galeras.

It is a pleasant enough city with several fine colonial buildings as well as a bustling downtown area, but there is little here to hold most travelers' attention for more than an overnight stop.

The weather here is cool – so cool, in fact, you'll see *helado de paíla* advertised; it's ice cream made fresh in a copper tub sitting on a platform of ice.

◉ Sights

On Pasto's main square, **Iglesia de San Juan Bautista** dates from the city's first days; it was rebuilt in the mid-17th century. Grand outside and gold-encrusted inside, it is a fine example of colonial baroque architecture.

For insight into the pre-Columbian cultures of Nariño, check out the **Museo del**

Oro (Calle 19 No 21-27; admission free; ⊙10am-5pm Tue-Sat), which has a small but interesting collection of indigenous gold and pottery.

The **Museo Taminango de Artes y Tradiciones** (Calle 13 No 27-67; adult COP$2000; ⊙8am-noon & 2-6pm Mon-Fri, 9am-1pm Sat) has a hodgepodge of antiques but is worth seeing since it's housed in a meticulously restored *casona* (large house) from 1623, reputedly the oldest surviving house in town.

🛏 Sleeping

TOP CHOICE **Hotel Casa Lopez** HOTEL $$
(☏720 8172; hcasalopez@yahoo.com; Calle 18 No 21b-07; s/d COP$100,000/130,000; 🛜) In a perfectly restored colonial home in the center, this family-run hotel is in a league of its own in terms of comfort, service and attention to detail. Set around a pretty courtyard, the charming rooms have polished wooden floors and antique furnishings. The affable

owners are some of the most accommodating hosts around – don't be surprised if they pop around with a hot-water bottle or a cup of hot chocolate in the evening.

Koala Inn HOSTEL $
(☏722 1101; Calle 18 No 22-37; s/d COP$20,000/30,000, without bathroom COP$14,000/25,000) Pasto's only backpacker hostel could do with a makeover, but it's cheap, centrally located, and has all the facilities you are likely to need. The rooms by the street can be noisy.

Hotel San Sebastian HOTEL $
(☏721 8851; Carrera 22 No 15-78; s/d/tr COP$33,000/53,000/73,000; 🛜) Of the many cheap hotels that cluster in the center, this is the best value. It doesn't have a lot of character but the rooms are clean and have hot water and cable TV.

🍴 Eating

Asadero de Cuyes Pinzón COLOMBIAN $$
(☏731 3228; Carrera 40 No 19B-76, Palermo; cuy COP$29,000) *Pastusos* (locals, ie people from Pasto) get dressed up to eat at this place about 1.5km from the center of town. There's only one thing on the menu: *asado de cuy* (grilled guinea pig). You'll be given plastic gloves so you can rip the grilled rodents apart and share them. One *cuy* is big enough for two. Pasto is the only place in Colombia where *cuy* is mainstream and popular.

Caffeto CAFE $$
(☏729 2720; www.krkcaffeto.com; Calle 19 No 25-62; mains COP$8000-18,000; ⊙8am-8pm Mon-Sat) This fancy bakery-cafe does gourmet sandwiches, omelettes and salads served on unusual crockery. The cakes are stupendous,

Pasto

and it does enormous ice-cream sundaes and serves real espresso coffee. Enough to satisfy even the most jaded traveler's inner yuppie.

Salón Guadalquivir   CAFE $
(Plaza de Nariño; snacks COP$2000-6000; ☺8am-12:30pm & 2:30-7:30pm Mon-Sat) This cozy cafe serves classic *pastuso* treats, including *quimbilito* (a sweet pastry of raisin, vanilla and sweet corn) and *tamales de añejo* (the Pasto version of *tamales*). The walls are lined with posters from the annual Carnaval de Blancos y Negros.

 Drinking

Pasto has some cozy bars and a couple of decent discos. Numerous drinkeries are located a few blocks north of Plaza de Nariño. Av de Estudiantes has a number of budget restaurants and bars, including **Absalon** (🕿731 0695; Calle 20 No 31C-23; ☺6pm-1am Mon-Sat), a mellow spot that plays Colombian crossover music.

For a shot of culture, head to **Mestizo Peña Bar** (🕿722 7881; Calle 18 No 27-67), an Andean bar that has live amplified panpipe music and serves *guayusa*, a type of medicinal tea from the Amazon, and *hervidos*, piping hot fruit drinks laced with cane spirit.

 Shopping

The city is known for *barniz de Pasto*, a processed vegetable resin used to decorate wooden objects in colorful patterns. It can be bought at **Casa del Barniz de Pasto** (cnr Carrera 25 & Calle 13). **Plaza de Bomboná** (Calle 14 btwn Carreras 28 & 30; ☺7am-7pm Mon-Sat, to 1pm Sun) is a covered market with craft shops that sell bargain leather goods, plus *lechona* (stuffed pig) if you get the munchies for some roast pork.

ℹ Information

Most of the major banks are around Plaza de Nariño.
4-72 (Calle 15 No 22-05) Post office.
Banco de Bogota (Calle 19 No 24-68) Reliable ATM.
Ciber C@fe PC Rent (🕿723 8298; Calle 18A No 25-36; per hr COP$1600; ☺8am-9pm Mon-Fri, 9am-8pm Sat, 2-6pm Sun) Fast internet near Plaza de Nariño.
Tourist office (Oficina Departamental de Turismo de Nariño; 🕿723 4962; www.turismonarino.gov.co; Calle 18 No 25-25) Looks flash but is a bit short on practical information. Ask here

CARNAVAL DE BLANCOS Y NEGROS

Pasto's major event is **Carnaval de Blancos y Negros** (www.carnavaldepasto.org) held on January 5 and 6. Its origins go back to the times of Spanish rule, when slaves were allowed to celebrate on January 5 and their masters showed approval by painting their faces black. On the following day, the slaves painted their faces white.

On these two days the city goes wild, with everybody painting or dusting one another with grease, chalk, talc, flour and any other available substance even vaguely black or white in tone. It's a serious affair – wear the worst clothes you have and buy an *antifaz*, a sort of mask to protect the face, widely sold for this occasion. Asthmatics should not attend – you'll be coughing up talcum powder for days afterwards.

about the latest update on the trail for Volcán Galeras and security issues at Laguna Verde.

 Getting There & Away

Air

The airport is 33km north of the city on the road to Cali. *Colectivos* (COP$8500, 45 minutes) for the airport leave from the corner of Calle 18 and Carrera 25. A taxi will cost around COP$30,000.

Avianca and Satena service Pasto, with daily flights to Bogotá and Cali and connections to other cities.

Bus

The bus terminal is 2km south of the city center. Frequent buses, minibuses and *colectivos* go to Ipiales (COP$8000, two hours); sit on the left for better views. Plenty of buses ply the spectacular road to Cali (COP$39,000, nine hours). These buses will drop you off in Popayán (COP$28,000, six hours). More than a dozen direct buses depart daily to Bogotá (COP$90,000, 22 hours).

Laguna de la Cocha

2 / ELEV 2760M

Set amid rolling green hills, and often shrouded in mist, this spectacular lake is a must-do day trip on your visit to Pasto. You can take a boat ride around the lake, stopping at **Isla Corota** (admission COP$1000) along the way. The island is a national park,

VOLCÁN GALERAS

Just 8km from the center of Pasto, Volcán Galeras (4267m) continues to grumble and threaten. Its lower slopes are a patchwork of farms and bright-green pastureland. There's a lookout tower at the top, and on a clear day you can see as far as Tumaco and the Pacific coast.

Galeras is one of Colombia's most active volcanoes. The trail was officially closed to the public in 2006 due to seismic activity, although you may still be able to climb. Contact the tourist office (p245) in Pasto for the latest update.

and at an altitude of 2830m offers a rare glimpse of a well-preserved, evergreen cloud forest. There's a small chapel and a biological research station on the island; a 550m-long boardwalk takes you the length of the island to a *mirador* (lookout). Boats to the island cost COP$25,000 for up to 10 people. The boat will wait for you and take you on a circle of the island on the way back.

🛏 Sleeping & Eating

At the mouth of the Río Encano, where it empties into the lake, you will find numerous hotels and restaurants serving roast chicken, grilled *cuy, sancocho* and of course trout, which is farmed along the shores of the lake.

Many hotels cater to couples looking for a weekend away. The most spectacular is **Hotel Sindamanoy** (📞721 8222; www.hotelsin damanoy.com; s/d/tr/ste COP$110,000/145,000/ 193,000/180,000; 🅿), which is on the lake-shore a short boat ride from Río Ecano; you'll see its faux-Swiss chalet facade from Isla Corota. It has impressive views of the island and lake. The overall decor is a flash-back to the '70s – rooms have yellow carpet, stucco walls and fake wood paneling – but many also have working fireplaces. The res-taurant (mains COP$14,000 to COP$22,000) is the best place to eat in the area. If you're coming just for lunch, a boat from the res-taurants at the edge of the lake near the Río Encano costs around COP$20,000 round trip; from Pasto direct in a private taxi you'll pay around COP$15,000.

By the Río Encano, **Encanto de la Cocha** and **Restaurante Rafa** are popular lunch options.

❶ Getting There & Away

Shared taxis to the lake (COP$3800, 45 minutes) leave from the Iglesia de San Sebastián in central Pasto during the week, and behind the Hospital Departmental (corner Calle 22 and Carrera 7) on weekends and holidays. Shared taxis seat four people; if you're in a hurry, pay for all four seats.

Laguna Verde

You'll see photos of this emerald-green lake all over Pasto. It sits in the crater of the ex-tinct Volcán Azufral (3800m), near Túquerres (3700m), a two-hour journey west of Pasto. It is possible to visit the lake on a day trip. Upon arrival in Túquerres, transfer to one of the old jeeps that will take you to the base of the volcano (around COP$15,000), from where it's a two-hour hike to the crater. Bring plenty of water and snacks – once you leave Túquerres there are no shops.

Security in this area can be an issue – con-tact the tourist office in Pasto for the latest before setting out. You may be able to join an existing tour.

Ipiales

📞 2 / POP 123,341 / ELEV 2900M

Only 7km from the Ecuador border, Ipiales is an uninspiring commercial town driven by trade across the frontier. There is little to see or do here, except for the colorful Saturday **market**, where the *campesinos* (peasants) from surrounding villages come to buy and sell goods. A short side trip to the Santuario de Las Lajas is the real drawcard, though the Panamericana from Pasto is also thrilling.

🛏 Sleeping & Eating

There are few good reasons to spend the night in Ipiales. Pasto is a far nicer city, and those wanting to visit Las Lajas will find cheap, decent accommodations right next to the sanctuary. Budget restaurants in Ipiales cluster around Plaza de la Independencia. For some typical grub head to Barrio El Charco, where there are almost a dozen places selling barbecue *cuy*. They are flat-tened out and cooked over an open fire on a mechanical spit that resembles a rodent Ferris wheel.

Hotel Belmonte　　　　　　HOTEL $
(📞773 2771; Carrera 4 No 12-111; s/d COP$12,000/ 19,000) For a long time the backpackers' choice in Ipiales, but there aren't a lot of

other options. Think genteel, grandmotherly poverty but with electric shower heads and cable TV.

Hotel Los Andes HOTEL $$
(☏773 4338; Carrera 5 No 14-44; s/d/tr COP$48,000/68,000/98,000;@☏) The largest place in town, Los Andes has 33 rooms around an interior courtyard. A loud TV in the lobby echoes up to all the rooms. Some of the rooms have street views – not necessarily an improvement.

ℹ Information

Banco de Bogota (Carrera 6 No 13-55) ATM (with services for Visa and Cirrus/Maestro networks); on main plaza.

Interactive.Net (Plaza la Pola; per hr COP$1400; ☉7am-11pm) Internet and calls; on main plaza.

ℹ Getting There & Away

Air

The airport is 7km northwest of Ipiales, on the road to Cumbal, and is accessible by taxi (COP$10,000). Satena has flights to Cali, with onward connections to other cities.

Bus

Ipiales has a new, large bus terminal, about 1km northeast of the center. Urban buses can take you into the center of town (COP$900), or grab a taxi (COP$3000).

There are frequent buses to Bogotá (COP$100,000, 25 hours). Several companies run regular buses to Cali (COP$45,000, 10 hours). All these buses will drop you in Popayán (eight hours). Don't travel at night on this route.

There are plenty of buses, minibuses and colectivos to Pasto (COP$6000 to COP$8000, 1½ to two hours). They all depart from the bus terminal. Sit on the right for better views.

For information on crossing into Equador, see the boxed text below.

Santuario de Las Lajas

ELEV 2600M

Built on a stone bridge spanning a deep gorge at the village of Las Lajas, the neo-Gothic Santuario de Las Lajas is a strange but spectacular sight. On Sunday the place is full of pilgrims and vendors selling ice cream and souvenirs; during the week it gets hardly any visitors. The pilgrims place their faith in the Virgin Mary, whose image is believed to have emerged from an enormous vertical rock 45m above the river sometime in the mid-18th century. Plaques of thanksgiving line the walls of the canyon, many from prominent Colombian politicians.

The church is directly against the rocky wall of the gorge where the image appeared. A gilded painting of the Virgin, accompanied by Santo Domingo and San Francisco, has been painted directly on the rocks just to be sure there is no confusion. The first chapel was built in 1803; today's church, designed by Nariño architect Lucindo Espinoza, was built between 1926 and 1944.

In the lower floors of the church a **museum** (admission COP$1500; ☉8:30am-5pm) has exhibits on the history of the church, plus some religious and pre-Columbian art.

🛏 Sleeping & Eating

Casa Pastoral HOTEL $
(☏775 4463; s/d/tr/q COP$12,000/18,000/36,000/48,000) Run by nuns for a long time, this large, basic hotel caters to the faithful and heathen alike. Some rooms have views of the church. All rooms come with private

GETTING TO EQUADOR

Passport formalities are processed in Rumichaca, not in Ipiales or Tulcán (on the Ecuadorean side of the border). The border is open from 5am to 10pm.

Frequent colectivos travel the 2.5km from Ipiales to the border at Rumichaca (COP$1500), leaving from the bus terminal and the market area near the corner of Calle 14 and Carrera 10. Minibuses (COP$1400) leave when full half a block north of the market on Calle 14. After crossing the border on foot, take another colectivo to Tulcán (6km). On both routes, Colombian and Ecuadorean currency is accepted.

There are no direct flights from Ipiales to Ecuador, but you can easily get to Tulcán, from where Tame has daily flights to Quito. Heading to Tulcán from the border, you pass the airport 2km before reaching town.

For information on getting to Colombia from Ecuador, head to shop.lonelyplanet.com to purchase a downloadable PDF of the Northern Highlands chapter from Lonely Planet's Ecuador & the Galapagos Islands guide (8th edition).

bathrooms with hot water, and a large cafeteria serves simple budget meals. Take the first set of stairs on your left as you walk downhill toward the church. Bookings are recommended. Two other hotels next door offer a similar style of accommodations.

Restaurante El Santuario COLOMBIAN $
(mains COP$6000-7000; ⊙6am-3pm Sun) Crossing the bridge heading away from the church, walk along the opposite side to get to this small restaurant, which has great views. It serves breakfast, lunch, snacks and coffee. The waterfalls a bit further along offer the best views of the church.

🛈 Getting There & Around

The sanctuary is located 7km southeast of Ipiales. Shared taxis and vans run regularly from the corner of Carrera 6 and Calle 4 in Ipiales (COP$2500, 20 minutes) and from the town's bus station (COP$2500, 15 minutes). You can also pay for all four seats. On Sundays there are direct shared taxis from Pasto if you prefer the greater creature comforts that city offers.

Pacific Coast

Why Go?

There are few destinations as ruggedly spectacular as the Pacific region of Colombia. This is where the jungle not so much meets the sea as comes crashing headlong into it. It is a place where waterfalls pour out of forest-covered bluffs onto spectacular gray-sand beaches, thermal pools lie hidden in dense jungle and tiny indigenous villages cling to the edge of wild rivers. It's a place where whales and dolphins frolic so close to shore you can admire them from your hammock and majestic sea turtles come even closer. There are plenty of comfortable ecoresorts throughout the region and you will find budget guesthouses in the many friendly Afro-descendant communities whose residents eke out a living from fishing and agriculture.

Security has, for the most part, been sorted out but the crowds have yet to arrive. Make sure you visit before they do.

Best Places to Stay

» Morromico (p256)

» El Almejal (p254)

» El Cantil (p257)

Best Places to Spot Whales

» Parque Nacional Natural (PNN) Ensenada de Utría (p254)

» Parque Nacional Natural (PNN) Isla Gorgona (p260)

» El Valle (p253)

When to Go
Buenaventura

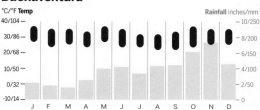

Jan-Mar Lighter rains make for better hiking and other outdoor activities.

Jul-Oct Humpback whales arrive in the region after an epic journey from Antarctica.

Sep-Dec Watch giant marine turtles scramble up beaches where they were born to lay their eggs.

Pacific Coast Highlights

1 Scuba dive with whales off **Parque Nacional Natural (PNN) Isla Gorgona** (p260) or join a whale-watching tour at **Parque Nacional Natural (PNN) Ensenada de Utría** (p254)

2 Surf the Pacific's 2m waves at **Ladrilleros** (p258)

3 Swim with hundreds of hammerhead sharks at **Isla Malpelo** (p261), Colombia's most difficult scuba dive destination

4 Linger amid tropical gardens on the black-sand beaches of **Guachalito** (p256)

5 Go catch-and-release sportfishing for blue marlin and sailfish near **Bahía Solano** (p251)

6 Travel up the Río Juribidá in dugout canoes from **Jobí** (p256) to remote waterfalls

7 Relax in thermal pools deep in the jungle near **Jurubidá** (p256)

8 Fly along ziplines above virgin forest at **Playa Mecana** (p253)

National, State & Regional Parks

Parque Nacional Natural (PNN) Isla Gorgona (p260) and Parque Nacional Natural (PNN) Isla Malpelo (p261) are both protected marine parks boasting excellent diving. Parque Nacional Natural (PNN) Ensenada de Utría (p254), halfway between El Valle and Nuquí, attracts whales in season, which play in a narrow bay, just a few hundred meters offshore.

Dangers & Annoyances

Security in this region has improved dramatically, but guerrilla groups remain active in remote areas, especially around Tumaco and in the northern reaches of Chocó.

When we visited things were calm, but you may like to confirm it's still safe before planning a visit.

ⓘ Getting There & Around

Only the Cali–Buenaventura highway links the Pacific coast to the rest of Colombia. Most travelers arrive by light plane from Cali or Medellín. For details on air travel to the Pacific coast, see p252. It's also possible to travel from Panama by boat; for more details, see p252.

There are no roads along the Pacific coast. Boat travel is your only option for traveling in the region.

CHOCÓ

The Chocó is one of the wettest places on earth. On average, it receives 16m to 18m of rain per year. This defines the region, the people and its culture. When the sun shines, it's too hot to move too fast, and when it rains – almost every day – no one wants to go out and get wet. No wonder people joke about *hora chocoana* (Chocó time). Life here is slow.

The region is sparsely populated and remains covered in dense jungle. Pre-2001 it was a popular tourist destination but then the civil war arrived, destabilizing the area, and tourist arrivals plummeted.

There is now a sizable Colombian military presence in the area and the situation has improved dramatically. You will see the occasional military patrol on the beach, but it's all fairly unobtrusive. At the time of research all of the main tourist areas listed here were secure but check the latest before heading out.

Bahía Solano

☑ 4 / POP 9200

Bahía Solano is the largest settlement on the Chocó coast. It is famous for its deepsea sportfishing – some of the best in the

world – and as a base to go whale-watching (see p31). It sits at the mouth of the Río Jella and faces north into the ocean. There is no beach in or near town.

◉ Sights & Activities

Near the south end of town flows the **Quebrada Chocolatal**. You can hike upriver for about half an hour to the **Cascada Chocolatal** that empties into an icy-cold swimming hole. The jungle towers over you on both sides of the riverbank in a cascade of flowers and birdsong. On the same road a narrow, overgrown path leads upward to a small shrine to the Virgin Mary that offers great views over the town and the beach.

There is good **scuba diving** in 500ft-deep Bahía Solano. The warship *Sebastián de Belalcázar,* which survived the attack on Pearl Harbor, was sunk near Playa Huína to create an artificial reef (Buqué Hundido). Cave divers may like to explore the caves near Cabo Marzo. There are two dive operators in town: **Posada del Mar** (☑682 7415, 314 630 6723; rfajardo@bis.com.co) has more experience and offers packages with dives and accommodations; and by the bridge over the river, **Cabo Marzo** (☑314 861 8742; blackmarlin19@hotmail.com) is more expensive but has better gear. Expect to pay around COP$185,000 to COP$220,000 for two dives.

Colombia's Pacific coast is one of the only places in South America where you can pull in record-breaking blue marlin and sailfish. Expect to pay around COP$1,600,000 per day for four to five anglers. A recommended skipper is **Vicente Gonzalez** (☑311 302 3513).

🛏 Sleeping & Eating

All the hotels in the town itself are down by the waterfront in Barrio El Carmen. If you're after a cheap, local meal, head to the no-name shacks near the hospital where you can get fried fish and *patacones* (fried plantains).

Rocas de Cabo Marzo　　　　HOTEL $$$
(☑682 7525; r per person incl meals COP$110,000; @) One of the few people who speaks English in the zone, the attentive owner of this small, comfortable hotel organizes sportfishing trips and offers guide services in the surrounding area. The food here is excellent.

Posada del Mar　　　　GUESTHOUSE $$
(☑682 7415, 314 630 6723; posadadelmarbahia solano@yahoo.es; r per person COP$35,000; ☎) The best budget option in town has a

number of brightly painted wooden huts dotted around a pleasant garden.

Hotel Balboa Plaza
HOTEL **$$**

(☑682 7075; Carrera 2A No 6-73; s/d/ste COP$66,000/110,000/275,000; ❄) Built by Pablo Escobar, the Balboa remains the largest hotel in town. It's a bit ragged around the edges but offers spacious rooms and a large pool.

Hotel Bahía
HOTEL **$**

(☑682 7048; s/d COP$30,000/40,000; ❄) Basic rooms with satellite TV for when the rains kick in. You'll pay COP$10,000 more for air-con.

Cabalonga Restaurant
COLOMBIAN **$$**

(cnr Carrera 3 & Calle 3; mains COP$16,000-20,000) One of the few proper restaurants in town, this open-air establishment serves a curious mix of gourmet plates and fast food. On weekends it turns into a bar.

Shopping

You'll find a good variety of locally made *artesanías* (handicrafts) at rock-bottom prices, some made by the local indigenous peoples. Worth a look are the carvings of *tagua,* a hard resin sometimes called 'vegetable ivory' (the hard nut of a species of palm). There are two good no-name *artesanía* shops at the airport and two more in town.

Information

There is no tourist information office in town. Pick up a copy of the magazine *La Guía de Bahía* for a map, tourist info and tide tables.

Emergency
Police (☑112) On the waterfront.

Internet Access
Bahia.com (per hr COP$2400; ⊙7am-9pm) Fastest internet in town. Opposite the hospital.

Medical Services
Drogas Bahía (☑682 7064) Pharmacy that stocks the basics. Opposite Hotel Bahía.
Hospital Julio Figueroa Villa (☑emergency 112, 682 7884)

Money
Banco Agrario de Colombia (☑682 7522; ⊙8am-2pm Mon-Fri) The only bank in town with the only ATM on the Chocó coast. It's sometimes empty – don't rely on it.
Super Giros (☑682 7044) You can receive domestic wire transfers here. Opposite the hospital.

Post
Servientrega (☑682 7835) Opposite Banco Agrario.

Visa Information
Capitanía de Puerto (☑682 7064) Register with the harbormaster if arriving under your own sail. On the waterfront.
Ministerio de Relaciones Exteriores (☑682 6984, 314 470 8229; www.cancilleria.gov. co; ⊙8am-noon & 2-6pm Mon-Fri, 8am-noon Sat) Processes entry/exit stamps. In Barrio El Carmen.

Getting There & Away

Air
Aeropuerto José Celestino Mutis is serviced by Satena, Aexpa and ADA. The airport's nickname is 'Sal Si Puedes' (Get Out If You Can). Because of heavy rain, planes are sometimes unable to leave. It would be unwise to book international connections for the same day you leave Bahía Solano.

A moto-taxi to/from the airport costs around COP$10,000.

Boat
It's possible to travel to Buenaventura on the many cargo boats that bring in supplies. The journey takes about 24 hours, generally leaving in the afternoon (both ways), depending on the tides. One recommended supply boat is the **Renacer El Pacífico** (☑2 242 4785; Muelle El Piñal, Buenaventura). It charges COP$120,000 for a *camarote* (bunk bed) in an air-con cabin. Call several days in advance, as service is infrequent.

You can travel onward to Panama (six to eight hours). Boats usually run at least once a week to Jaqué, Panama. Expect to pay around US$100 per person. Among the captains regularly making the trip are **'Profesor' Justino** (☑313 789 0635) and **Walter Gonzalez** (☑312 816 4906).

Be sure to stamp out of Colombia at the Ministerio de Relaciones Exteriores office in Bahía Solano before leaving town. To enter Panama you'll need a yellow fever vaccination and enough cash to prove you can travel onward (a minimum of US$500). Once you reach Jaqué and stamp in to Panama, there are flights for around US$85 to Panama City. There is also a boat service once a week for around US$15.

Road
For travel to/from El Valle, *chivas* and Jeeps leave opposite the school when full, usually late morning (COP$5000 to COP$10,000, one hour). Express moto-taxis cost around COP$40,000.

Around Bahía Solano

PUNTA HUÍNA
A 20-minute boat ride takes you to this pretty beach with a mixture of gold and black

sand. It's lined with coconut palms and several modest resorts. A small indigenous community lives here, along with descendants of African slaves. Punta Huína has no phone signal, but a small **Compartel** (☑8 522 4621) office offers satellite phone calls.

There are several short jungle walks you can do in the vicinity, including to **Playa de los Deseos**, **Cascada El Tigre** and **Playa Cocalito**.

There is no public transportation here, but all the hotels we've listed offer transportation. Otherwise, if you hang around the wharf around lunchtime, you should be able to grab a ride with local villagers (COP$10,000) or you can rent an express boat (COP$100,000). It's also possible to walk here from Bahía Solano (four hours). A guide (COP$50,000) is recommended.

🛏 Sleeping

Los Guásimos HOUSE RENTAL **$**
(☑312 833 0760; r per person COP$25,000) Probably the best deal on the entire Pacific coast, this recently constructed house sits alone on a hill across the river at the end of the beach. It sleeps up to 10, but if you have six or more you get the entire place. It has a large deck and barbecue area with magnificent views. Bring your food and Pambelé, the owner, will organize a local cook to prepare meals (COP$25,000 per day). He also rents tent space behind his bar by the river and runs cheap diving trips.

Choibana LODGE **$$$**
(☑310 878 1214; www.choibana.com; r per person incl meals COP$120,000) On a private beach backed by thick jungle, this atmospheric wooden lodge is a great place to take it easy. The pick of the rooms is the romantic hut set on stilts over a rocky outcrop away from the main house – the views from the bed are phenomenal.

Cabañas Brisas Del Mar HOTEL **$$**
(☑313 649 2041; r per person incl meals COP$70,000) This full-service budget choice has five rooms with 1m-high gaps between the walls and the ceiling (expect to hear your neighbor snoring at night, or worse). There are great views of the ocean from the top-floor balcony. The owner runs tours with his boat.

Playa de Oro Lodge HOTEL **$$$**
(☑in Medellín 4361 7809; www.hotelesdecostaa costa.com; r per person incl meals COP$130,000) This family-oriented resort is right on the beach and surrounds a small garden and

---

WARDING OFF THE EVIL EYE

Cabalonga, a hard nut grown in the Chocó, is worn on a necklace by indigenous children to ward off the *mal de ojo* (evil eye) that some elderly women are thought to possess.

---

playground for the kids. Each room has a small wooden balcony with a hammock, and 2nd-floor rooms have good views of the sea. The big bar area also boasts excellent views and is a great place for an evening drink.

PLAYA MECANA
A 25-minute boat ride from Bahia Solano lies **Playa Mecana**, a 5km-long beach strewn with coconut palms. It is also possible to walk here – you must leave at or before low tide *(mareada baja)*. It's 1½ hours' walk each way.

Here you can visit the nonprofit **Jardín Botánico del Pacífico** (☑321 759 9012; www.jardinbotanicodelpacifico.org; admission COP$10,000), a 200-hectare nature reserve running alongside the Río Mecana made up of mangroves, virgin tropical forest, and a botanical garden of native plants and trees. It's staffed by members of the local Emberá indigenous tribe who can take you on fantastic treks or boat rides up the river into their traditional lands. There is also great bird-watching and a number of canopy lines. If you want to stick around a while, there are elegant accommodations on the beach (COP$150,000 per person including transportation and meals). A backpacker lodge was under construction at the time of research.

El Valle

☑4 / POP 3500

On the southern side of the peninsula from Bahía Solano sits its smaller neighbor, El Valle. At the west end of town is the pleasant Playa Almejal, with fine surf and an excellent resort. El Valle is a good jumping-off point to visit Ensenada de Utría. It's also a good place to spot turtles during nesting season (September to December) at Estación Septiembre, and to spot whales just off the coast (in season).

👁 Sights & Activities

🏞 **Estación Septiembre** WILDLIFE RESERVE
(☑3115 356 504; Colombians/foreigners COP$8000/10,000) On Playa Cuevita, 4.8km

PACIFIC COAST EL VALLE

south of El Valle along the coast, is the turtle-nesting sanctuary of Estación Septiembre (also a research station). From June to December sea turtles arrive to lay eggs. The best time to see them is at night. The conservation project is run by the community – visitors are essential to keep it running. There are cabins you can stay in (per person COP$40,000). You can walk here from El Valle (two hours) either along a bush track or along the beach. If you take the beach, you will wade across a couple of waist-deep rivers, while a guide is recommended for the bush route. The staff can also organize night-time turtle-watching tours departing from El Valle.

Cascade del Tigre WATERFALL
A two-hour walk north of El Valle through the jungle and along the shore takes you to Cascade del Tigre, an impressive waterfall with a swimming hole where you can bathe. Local guides charge around COP$30,000 per person. It's a full-day excursion.

🛏 Sleeping & Eating

TOP CHOICE **El Almejal** HOTEL $$$
(🗗in Medellín 4230 6060; www.almejal.com.co; cabañas per person COP$170,000) The most luxurious resort in the Bahía Solano area, El Almejal also has the most ingenious cabin design – the walls of the lounge area open completely, allowing a breeze to pass through. A small creek spills into an artificial swimming hole near the back of the cabins; select a nearby cabin for the soothing sound. Concrete stairs behind the hotel lead uphill to a lookout point – during whale-watching season you can sometimes spot whales playing just off the coast.

Humpback Turtle HOSTEL $$
(🗗312 756 3439; thehumpbackturtle@gmail.com; camping COP$10,000, dm/s/d COP$20,000/35,000/60,000) One of the most remote hostels in Colombia, this hip place at the end of Playa Almejal is right on the beach by a towering waterfall. There is a thatched-roof bar area and a kitchen you can use. The managers rent boards and offer multiday surfing tours in the surrounding area.

Hotel Valle HOTEL $
(🗗682 7907; hotelvalle@gmail.com; r with/without bathroom COP$30,000/20,000, apt COP$40,000) This budget home-style posada (hotel) is your best option in town. The smaller rooms share an interior shower block, and there's a breezy terrace with hammocks upstairs.

Rosa del Mar COLOMBIAN $
(mains COP$8000-10,000) In the street in front of the church, Doña Rosalia cooks up the best meals in town. Sit down and enjoy fresh seafood in her living room in front of the deafening TV.

🍷 Drinking

El Mirador BAR
(🕙Fri & Sat) About 200m past El Almejal on the main beach, built on top of a rocky out-cropping, is El Mirador, one of Colombia's most spectacular bars. You can sit at the makeshift tables and suck down rum while the stereo blasts reggaeton at the crashing waves.

❶ Information

El Valle businesses offer tourist information through the **Tío Tigre Asociación** (🗗682 7907). It can help you with information about the region and organize tours. It's located just before the bridge to Playa Almejal. There are a couple of no-name internet places in town charging COP$2400 per hour.

Hospital El Valle (🕙24hr) There's one doctor and one nurse in this rudimentary facility.

Police (🗗682 7952)

Servientrega (🗗682 7835) Expensive postal services.

Supergiros (🗗682 7960; 🕙8am-noon & 2-8pm) Receive domestic wire transfers here.

❶ Getting There & Away

Most *chivas* and Jeeps to Bahía Solano (COP$5000 to COP$10,000, one hour) leave in the morning. There are usually services at 7am and 8am. There is sometimes a service at 4pm.

Boats leave for Nuquí (COP$60,000, 1½ hours) on Monday afternoons. The departure time depends on the tides.

Parque Nacional Natural (PNN) Ensenada de Utría

This narrow inlet of water is one of the best places to see whales close-up from land. During the calving season they enter the *ensenada* (inlet) and play just a few hundred meters from shore. Long closed due to security concerns, the **Centro de Visitantes Jaibaná** (Colombians/foreigners COP$13,000/35,000), on the eastern shore of the *ensenada,* has now reopened and is fully functioning with refurbished cabins for up to 30 people. There are a number of short walks you can do in the nearby mangroves, and at night you may see glow-in-the-dark mushrooms.

Mano Cambiada in Nuquí has the concession to manage the park and runs the **cabins** (r per person with/without bathroom COP$150,000/120,000). Prices include all meals. With advance notice it can organize diving in and around the park.

The public boats from Nuquí to El Valle/Bahía Solano can drop you at the park for COP$60,000. If you have a group, a private transfer costs around COP$300,000 from Nuquí or El Valle.

The park can organize a guide (COP$50,000, four hours) to take you on foot from El Valle to Lachunga at the mouth of the Río Tundo at the northwestern corner of the *ensenada*. From here you can be picked up in a boat (COP$10,000 per person) and taken to the visitors center.

Nuquí

📞 4 / POP 8000

Further south along the coast is the small town of Nuquí. It boasts a fine beach free of flotsam and driftwood, and the secluded nearby beach of Guachalito has some of the best resorts along this coast. A number of indigenous communities live up the river.

The town itself is paved in a mixture of concrete and gravel, but has no car traffic. It isn't a particularly attractive place but it's a convenient base from which to explore the surrounding area. There is no bank or ATM here.

An Olympic-sized beach, **Playa Olímpica** (5km long), sits just south of the mouth of the Río Nuquí and stretches as far as the eye can see. A local named Señor Pastrana can paddle you across the river in his dugout canoe (COP$5000). To find him, walk south along the main beach road, past the church; he lives a block from the river.

With an office near the park, **Transporte Ecce Homo** offers tours to Playa Olímpica and then up the Río Nuquí into the jungle (COP$10,000 to COP$30,000 per person), and also to Guachalito, including Cascada de Amor and Las Termales (COP$50,000 per person), and to Morromico, Jurbidá and Utría (COP$55,000 per person). These prices vary depending on group size and the cost of gasoline.

🛏 Sleeping & Eating

Most hotels cluster at the northern end of town, near the beach. There are a number of simple posadas in town.

Donde Jesusita   GUESTHOUSE $
(📞683 6489; r per person COP$30,000) This simple guesthouse close to the dock is run by the grandmother of tourism in the Nuquí area. She is getting on a bit now but is a real character and a warm host. The breezy rooms are upstairs and have fine views.

Hotel Nuquí Mar   HOTEL $$
(📞311 306 2852; nuquimar@hotmail.com; r per person COP$45,000, ste COP$150,000) Right on the beach next to the military base, this new hotel has appealing wooden rooms with screens on the windows and sparkling tiled bathrooms. The suite on the top floor has a large private balcony.

Vientos de Yubarta   HOTEL $$
(📞312 217 8080; ameli_06@hotmail.com; r per person incl 2 meals COP$85,000) This attractive hotel 1km north of town along the beach has bamboo-and-wood rooms with good box-spring mattresses.

Unless you're traveling in a group, hotels in Nuquí do not serve food. A number of local women cook for tourists in their home. The best is **Doña Pola** (📞683 6254; Barrio La Union; meals COP$8000), down a side street between the hospital and the military base. At the airport local women sell *mecocadas* (COP$1000), a tasty confection of coconut and guava paste.

Shopping

Artesanías Margot   HANDICRAFTS
(📞683 6058) Next to the airport, this small *artesanías* shop has a great selection of wooden carvings and other local arts and crafts. It even sells authentic blow-dart guns.

ⓘ Information

Ciber Alfredo (📞314 611 1520; per hr COP$3000) The only internet access in town.
Droguería Nuquí (📞683 6105) Basic pharmacy.
Hospital San Pedro Claver (📞683 6003)
Mano Cambiada (📞683 6550, 311 872 7887; www.manocambiada.org) Tourist information center across from the airport.
Police (📞112) On the waterfront.
Super Giros (📞683 6067) Receive domestic wire transfers here.

Getting There & Away

Aeropuerto Reyes Murillo (📞683 6001) is serviced by **Satena** (📞683 6057, 311 876 8957; nuqui@satena.com) and ADA, with flights to

Medellín and Quibdó. **Aexpa** (☏1800 011 6288; www.aexpa.com.co) flies several times a week to Quibdó and Buenaventura.

Transporte Maritimo (☏314 764 9308) offers services to El Valle (COP$60,000, 1½ hours) on Monday and Bahía Solano (COP$70,000, two hours) on Friday. Boats usually leave early in the morning.

Several cargo boats service Nuquí from Buenaventura. The recommended *Nuquí Mar* departs Nuquí weekly. Ask around town for **Gigo** (☏312 747 8374), the owner. It's a 16-hour trip and costs COP$100,000 including meals. In Buenaventura the *Nuquí Mar* leaves from **Muelle Pizarro** (☏243 4851) in El Piñal.

Around Nuquí

JURUBIDÁ

This colorful community of brightly painted houses, 45 minutes by boat from Nuquí, has plenty of attractions but doesn't receive many visitors. The bay in front of the village is dominated by the Archipelago de Jurubidá – dozens of spectacular rock formations covered in forest. When the tide drops you can walk out to a number of natural pools that form in the rocks.

Grupo Los Termales (☏313 709 8707; frente Centro de Salud), a local co-operative, can organize guides to the Termales de Jurbidá (COP$5000 per person), a pair of thermal pools surrounded by dense jungle. The trip involves a short canoe ride and a beautiful walk alongside a crystal-clear river. The co-operative can also organize canoe trips through the mangroves (COP$15,000 per person) and boat trips to the indigenous communities a couple of hours upriver (COP$100,000 to COP$150,000).

If you want to spend the night, **Restaurante Artesenal Jessica** (☏311 753 4110; r per person COP$12,000) has simple rooms and a breezy porch. The owner makes interesting handicrafts.

There is usually transportation to/from Nuquí (COP$15,000, 45 minutes) on Monday, Wednesday and Friday. You can also hire a boat for around COP$150,000.

MORROMICO

Situated on a magnificent private beach protected by forested headlands, **Morromico** (☏8521 4172, 8522 4653; www.morromico.com; r per person COP$180,000) is a beautiful small ecoresort surrounded by thick jungle, 10 minutes by boat from Jurubidá. The hotel is set in lush gardens framed by a pair of waterfalls where you can bathe in crystal-clear mountain waters. The stylish semi-open rooms let in the sounds of the jungle and are powered by a small hydroelectric plant. The charismatic owner organizes boat trips and some pretty hardcore treks through the mountains to local indigenous communities. Rates includes three filling meals. Reservations are essential.

GUACHALITO

A half-hour boat ride west of Nuquí is Guachalito. It's a long beach, clear of flotsam and debris. There are orchids and heliconias everywhere, the jungle encroaches on the beach, platter-sized mushrooms grow on the trees and coconut palms sway over the gray sand.

The Gonzalez family inhabits the beach's east end. Several hotels are scattered along 8km of the beach to Las Termales. On the way you'll pass El Terquito and El Terco, two almost-islands that serve as landmarks. You can walk the length of the beach (1½ hours).

A 1km (20-minute) walk from the Gonzalez settlement, 200m inland from the beach, is **Cascada de Amor** – a natural, 2m-deep swimming hole where a pretty waterfall empties into a natural rock pool. Another 15-minute walk uphill takes you to an even bigger and more beautiful waterfall.

🛏 Sleeping

Originally Guachalito referred only to the Gonzalez family settlement at the eastern end of the beach. Four generations live here,

---

WORTH A TRIP

COQUÍ & JOBÍ

This pair of friendly villages, 25 minutes by boat from Nuquí, both have community tourism organizations. In Jobí, **Grupo de Guias Pichinde** (☏310 824 4269, 312 250 4159) can take you up the Río Jobí in dugout canoes to the waterfalls of Chontadura and Antaral. Chontadura is closer, while Antaral has a greater quantity of water and a bigger swimming hole. It can also arrange visits to the indigenous villages along the river. In Coquí the **Grupo de Guias** can arrange boat trips through the mangroves.

There are simple posadas in both villages offering accommodations for around COP$20,000 to COP$30,000 per person.

and their five posadas – run by competing siblings – all offer a similar level of comfort at a price of COP$100,000 to COP$160,000 per person including all meals.

La Joviseña (☑314 683 8856) offers the most luxury with four detached cabins spread throughout a large garden. At **Mar y Río** (☑314 656 9688, 311 3436 448), you'll stay with the family and eat at their kitchen table. **Luna de Miel** (☑314 431 2125, 311 602 3742; clunademiel@hotmail.com) has two rustic rooms and a pleasant balcony with great views. **Peñas de Guachalito** (☑313 7743 552) has simple concrete rooms by a tropical garden full of coconut palms.

To the west of the Guachalito settlement there are a number of ecohotels and resorts. Most offer packages including transportation from the airport, accommodations and food.

El Cantil　　　　　　　　　　HOTEL **$$$**
(☑in Medellín 252 0707, 352 0729; www.elcantil.com; s/d/tr incl meals COP$277,000/454,000/561,000) The most luxurious hotel on this beach, El Cantil has six duplex cabins and is surrounded by papaya plants and coconut palms. A small hydroelectric plant produces power for the restaurant and bar; the cabins are lit by candles. The restaurant (famous for its food) is a short walk up the hill; it's a great place from which to spot whales in season. Diving expeditions can be organized and surfing guides can show you the best spots.

La Cabaña de Beto y Marta　　HOTEL **$$$**
(☑311 775 9912; r per person incl meals COP$200,000) This delightful hotel owned by two *paisas* (inhabitants of Antioquia Panamericana) has four secluded cabins with hammocks and chairs on the deck from which to watch the sunset. The whole thing is set amid a spectacular garden, including lots of fruits and vegetables you'll find on your plate come dinnertime. It's located just past Cascada de Amor.

Pijibá Lodge　　　　　　　　HOTEL **$$$**
(☑in Medellín 474 5221; www.pijibalodge.com; s/d/tr incl meals COP$248,000/473,000/612,000) The three duplex cabins of Pijibá are constructed entirely of natural materials and let in plenty of fresh air. The food here has an excellent reputation.

Piedra Piedra　　　　　　　　HOTEL **$$$**
(☑315 596 3386; www.piedrapiedra.com; s/d/tr incl meals COP$200,000/360,000/510,000) Set on a hill, this intimate place feels less resort-like than its neighbors. It has a freshwater pool on a rocky outcrop with views of El Terco. Kayaks can be rented.

TERMALES

The small village of Termales has a wide gray-sand beach and a couple of places to stay for those who want to get a bit closer to the local culture. A gravel path leads 500m inland from the village's one road to **Las Termales** (admission COP$5000), a pair of thermal pools by a pleasant river. At the time of research the community was constructing concrete accommodations and a restaurant here that, when complete, are likely to detract significantly from the atmosphere.

With a large balcony overlooking the beach, **Refugio Salomon** (☑313 756 7970; r per person incl meals COP$70,000) has simple rooms with private bathrooms and serves delicious home-style meals.

There is no phone coverage in Termales but you can make calls via a homemade antenna at one of the local stores.

❶ Getting There & Away

The fast boat (COP$22,000, 45 minutes) from Nuquí to Arusí, west of Termales, can drop you anywhere along the way. It leaves Arusí on Monday, Wednesday and Friday mornings and returns about 1pm. There is a slower boat (COP$18,000, one hour) on Tuesday, Thursday and Saturday.

SOUTH COAST

Buenaventura
☑2 / POP 327,000

The largest (and only) city on this coast, Buenaventura is Colombia's busiest port. More than 60% of Colombia's legal exports pass through these docks; much of her illegal exports pass through here too. The city has two parts. The main docks and city center are on an island in the bay with slums stretching east on the continental side. A bridge connects the two.

The only reason to come here is transportation. Most tourist traffic runs through the *muelle turístico* (tourist wharf). This part of town is quite safe, and many restaurants and hotels cluster nearby. Cargo boats depart from El Piñal, just under the bridge.

🛏 Sleeping & Eating

There are several comfortable hotels, including some with water views, in the area around the *muelle turístico*.

Buenaventura's market, *la galería,* is famous for its food. A dozen stalls surround the 2nd floor of the market. Many are owned by *costeña* grandmothers, preparing *sancocho de pescado* (fish in coconut milk) as their foremothers have for centuries. The market is a bustling, crowded chaos of butchers, fishmongers, greengrocers and vendors selling *pescado ahumado* (smoked fish). The usual assortment of cutpurses haunt the market, so take care with your belongings. A taxi here from the tourist wharf will cost around COP$3000. Specify that you want to go to *la galería* in Pueblo Nuevo.

Hotel Titanic HOTEL **$$**
(📞241 2046; Calle 1A No 2A-55; r/tr/ste COP$57,000/73,000/96,000; ❄️@) One block from the entrance to the tourist wharf is this five-story hotel. All rooms have cable TV, air-con and ethernet wall outlets. The rooftop bar-restaurant has good views over the water. Many rooms lack windows; suites accommodate up to five people.

Hotel Tequendama Estación HOTEL **$$$**
(📞243 4070; www.sht.com.co; Calle 2 No 1A-08; s/d COP$303,300/341,200, ste COP$374,000; @🛜🏊) The best hotel in town is a flashback to Colombia's flapper days. Built in the 1920s and since refurbished, this white neoclassical confection boasts deluxe rooms and verandahs all the way around. The pool (open 9am to 6pm) is open to the public for COP$18,000.

ℹ️ Information

Banco de Bogota (Calle 2 No 2A-40) One block from the tourist wharf.

Ciber P@cífico (per hr COP$2000; ⏰8am-8:30pm Mon-Sat, 1-8pm Sun) Internet and phone calls, just outside the tourist wharf.

ℹ️ Getting There & Away

There are frequent bus services between Cali and Buenaventura (COP$18,000, three to four hours). From Cali sit on the left side of the bus for the best views.

Tourist speedboat services heading north and south depart from the tourist wharf. Cargo boats leave from El Piñal.

Around Buenaventura

JUANCHACO & LADRILLEROS
📞2 / POP 3500

An hour's boat ride north of Buenaventura are Juanchaco and neighboring Ladrilleros. Juanchaco faces Bahía Malaga and accumulates a fine collection of Buenaventura's garbage on its beaches. Ladrilleros, on the other side of the peninsula, faces the roaring open waves of the Pacific Ocean. During the rainy season (or rather, rainier season, August to November) the ocean comes crashing in 2m-to 3m-high waves. The best beach in the area is north of Ladrilleros at La Barra, where there is a small fishing community and some very basic accommodations.

Ladrilleros is a popular weekend getaway spot for people from Cali; during the week you will likely have the place to yourself.

The best time for surfing is the wet(ter) season (August to November). **Pedro Romero** (📞320 666 2491; Cabaña Villa Malaty, Sector Villa Paz, hacia La Barra) rents surfboards (per hour COP$20,000, with instructor COP$30,000) and runs kayaking tours in the mangroves (COP$50,000). On weekends and holidays you'll find him on the beach (from 6:30am to sunset). Otherwise find him at the address indicated.

🛏️ Sleeping & Eating

There are a dozen or more hotels in Ladrilleros. Most are pretty basic.

Half a dozen basic eateries serve budget meals of fish and rice. La Zarca and Doña Francia are considered the two best in town. For a tasty snack try the shrimp empanadas (savory pastries) at Restaurante Delfin.

Aguamarina Cabañas HOTEL **$$**
(📞246 0285, 311 728 3213; www.reservaaguamarina.com; r/cabañas per person incl 2 meals COP$85,000/65,000; ❄️) This friendly place on the ocean bluff has attractive two-story cabins and more modern hotel accommodations. There are picnic benches where you can sit and admire the views. The owner offers guide services in the surrounding region and budget whale-watching tours (COP$30,000).

Hotel Palma Real HOTEL **$$$**
(📞317 502 5931; www.hotelpalmarealcolombia.com; r per person incl 2 meals COP$90,000; ❄️🏊) This upscale hotel is popular with *caleños* (residents of Cali) on romantic getaways. There's a Jacuzzi and a pretty pool, and a poolside bar serves drinks and plays loud music. There are only ocean glimpses through the dense jungle.

🍸 Drinking

Templo del Ritmo BAR
(📞246 0104; ⏰Thu-Sat) On a bluff overlooking the sea, Templo del Ritmo cranks up the volume on weekends, when *caleños* come to party.

ℹ️ Information

There is an internet cafe in Juanchaco with intermittent connection. There are no ATMs here, and few people accept credit cards. You'll find the nearest ATM just outside the *muelle turístico* in Buenaventura.

ℹ️ Getting There & Away

The most reliable boat operator on the *muelle turístico* is **Asturias** (☎242 4048, 313 767 2864; barcoasturias@yahoo.com). It offers daily services to Juanchaco (round trip COP$54,000, 1¼ hours) at 10am, 1pm and 4pm, returning at 8am, 1pm and 4pm. The round-trip fare is good for 15 days.

From Juanchaco it's 2.5km to Ladrilleros. The road loops around a naval airbase that divides the two towns. You can walk (30 minutes) or hop on a motorcycle (COP$2000, five minutes). Large groups can haggle with the jeep drivers who hang out at the end of the Juanchaco beach (COP$20,000-ish). To get to La Barra you can either take a moto-taxi or a small boat along the river – both charge COP$15,000 per person.

San Cipriano

☑️2 / POP 500

This tiny town is as famous for its mode of arrival as for the town itself. Situated on the little-used Cali–Buenaventura railroad and 15km from the nearest road, residents have come up with ingenious homemade rail trolleys powered by motorcycles, the front wheel fixed in the air, the back wheel in contact with one of the rails. They fly through the jungle at ridiculous speed. There is only one track and many trolleys are lacking in the brakes department. While not common, crashes have been reported. Hold on tight and wear shoes so you can jump off in an emergency.

The town is in the middle of the jungle on the Pacific side of the mountain range. A nearby river with crystal-clear water makes for a relaxing swim. You can go inner-tubing along much of its length – many places rent tubes for around COP$1500/8000 per hour/day. There is also a butterfly enclosure and several waterfalls you can walk to. Guides for treks charge around COP$20,000. The Fundación San Cipriano charges COP$1500 admission to the area.

🛏️ Sleeping & Eating

Half a dozen hotels offer extremely basic lodging. Most offer budget meals. On weekends a couple of bars blast out the music for partying *caleños*.

Hotel David   GUESTHOUSE $

(☑️312 815 4051; r without bathroom per person COP$10,000) Several hundred meters after you pay your admission fee you'll find this friendly place, with rooms with hard mattresses and shared bathrooms. It serves some of the best food in town. Most of the rooms are doubles but there are also a few quads and twins.

Hotel Río Bello   GUESTHOUSE $

(☑️241 0094; r per person COP$15,000) One block before the entrance you will find the 'best' hotel in town. It has dark concrete rooms with little natural light and even less ventilation. But it's one of the only places with private bathrooms.

ℹ️ Getting There & Away

From Cali, take any bus heading to Buenaventura and get off at the junction to Córdoba (COP$18,000, three hours). From here it's a 1km walk downhill to the railway line. The official round-trip fare for a rail trolley to San Cipriano is COP$8000.

From Buenaventura, take the Ruta 5 bus marked Córdoba from the terminal (COP$2000, one hour). The bus runs every half-hour or so. If you don't want to walk back uphill, you can grab this bus back to the junction.

Buenaventura taxis can also deliver you to Córdoba for COP$25,000 to COP$40,000.

Guapi

☑️2 / POP 5000

This small fishing town is the main launching point for Isla Gorgona. It is famous for *ceviche guapense* (cooked seafood with mayonnaise and ketchup), and also for its *artesanías* – you'll find handmade musical instruments and intricately wrought gold jewelry, plus the usual assortment of hand-woven goods.

The town itself holds little of interest. The main drag is Calle Segunda, paved in brick, where the locals go about their business. Those looking for boats headed north or south should go down to the waterfront where the various companies have open-air kiosks that sell tickets.

🛏️ Sleeping & Eating

Hotel Río Guapi   HOTEL $

(☑️8400983; s/d/tr COP$40,000/58,000/84,000) A block from where the Aviatur boat leaves for Isla Gorgona, the Río Guapi's 40 rooms are the best in town. The floors are tile, the walls concrete, and there's a fan and cable TV. The downstairs restaurant is one of the best places to try *ceviche guapense.*

❶ Getting There & Away

Aeropuerto Juan Casino Solis (☑840 0188) is serviced by Satena with flights to Cali. Aexpa also offers a charter service. The coconut and guava sweets on sale at the airport are worth trying.

Pacífico Express (☑313 761 7571, 313 715 3335) offers daily services from Buenaventura in a covered speedboat (COP$90,000, three to four hours). There are also regular cargo boats (COP$60,000, 12 hours) running the same route. Information and reservations are available from **Bodega Liscano** (☑244 6089, 244 6106).

Parque Nacional Natural (PNN) Isla Gorgona

Todo está prohibido, goes the joke on this island – everything is forbidden. Somehow this seems rather appropriate; it was the site of a prison from 1960 to 1984. Now it's a **national park** (Colombians/foreigners COP$13,000/35,000) with a resort on the grounds of the former prison. And everything is forbidden – park guards will search your bags for liquor, fishing gear and aerosol cans, and confiscate them.

The two main reasons to come here are for scuba diving and whale-watching, preferably at the same time. Gorgona is not on any of the main shipping channels, so whales continue to come here every year to calve and raise their young. Several boats offer live-aboard diving trips to Gorgona, if you prefer not to stay on the island.

The island is 38km off the coast, 11km long by 2.3km wide. It is covered in young, secondary rainforest (the convicts chopped down most of the trees for cooking fuel), which harbors an abundance of poisonous snakes. Gorgona is also noted for a large number of endemic species, including monkeys, lizards, bats and birds. Sea turtles come during breeding season and lay eggs on the beaches.

In darker times, Gorgona was one of the few safe places tourists could visit on the Pacific coast. Now that conditions have improved, you'll find there are better beaches and wilder jungle elsewhere.

The concession to the island is owned by **Aviatur** (☑607 1500; www.parquegorgona.com.co; per person incl meals COP$253,000; @). Most people visit as part of a three-day package tour from Guapi (around COP$1,000,000 per person) including boat transportation, accommodations, meals and a couple of hikes on the island. Diving packages (COP$1,330,000 per person) are also available.

☞ Tours

For divers who don't want to stay on the island, two boats out of Buenaventura offer weekend live-aboard diving trips, departing the *muelle turístico* on Friday night and returning Monday morning. The *Maria Patricia* (owned by Asturias) and the **Doña Mariela** (☑681 2724) both charge around COP$1,100,000 per diver, including six or seven dives, meals, transportation and a visit to the island. They can also provide transportation to the island (bunk below deck COP$240,000, 10 hours), including dinner and breakfast.

MELODIES FROM THE FOREST

The Pacific region, like many parts of Colombia, is all about music and dance. But here the soundtrack for letting one's hair down is not booming reggaeton or salsa – many villages don't have electricity – it's the sweet acoustic tones of the *marimba de chonta.* Made from the wood of a spiny palm tree native to the zone and tubes of *guadua,* the *marimba de chonta* has a distinct sound famous throughout the country. The instrument has its origins in Africa and is part of the cultural heritage of that continent brought to the Pacific region by freed slaves. It is still made the traditional way in artisanal workshops throughout the region, but especially around Guapi and Tumaco.

The *marimba de chonta* is traditionally played hanging from the ceiling, although these days you often see it supported by a stand, and accompanied by percussion instruments including the *bombos, cununos* and *guasas.* It is the main musical protagonist in *El Currulao* – the typical dance of the area.

The best place to hear the *marimba de chonta* in all its glory is during the Festival Petronio Álvarez in Cali. Or for a taste of the traditional sounds mixed with the modern, look for recordings by the fantastic Chocquibtown.

ISLA MALPELO

This tiny, remote Colombian island has some of the best diving in the world. It's a mere 1643m long and 727m wide, and is 378km from the mainland. It is the center of the vast **Santuario de Flora y Fauna Malpelo** (ecoturismo@parquesnacionales.gov.co; admission per day on Colombian/foreign boat COP$153,000/82,000), the largest no-fishing zone in the eastern Tropical Pacific, which provides a critical habitat for threatened marine species.

The diversity and, above all, the size of the marine life is said to be eye-popping, including over 200 hammerhead sharks and 1000 silky sharks. It is also one of the few places where sightings of the short-nosed ragged-tooth shark, a deepwater shark, have been confirmed. The volcanic island has steep walls and impressive caves. The best time to see the sharks is January to March, when colder weather drives them to the surface to feed. A small contingent of Colombian soldiers guard Malpelo, and it's forbidden to set foot on the island.

The quality of the diving is matched only by the difficulty of getting there, and the difficulty of the diving itself. The island can only be visited as part of a live-aboard dive cruise, usually lasting eight days. Travel time is 30 to 36 hours each way from Buenaventura, and there is no decompression chamber on the island. There are strong currents that pull you up, down and sideways – you may well surface kilometers from where you entered the water.

Only advanced divers with experience and confidence should attempt this trip. You'll need your own wetsuit (minimum 5mm), with hood, gloves, diving computer, dive horn and decompression buoy.

Boats from two countries offer this trip. Your cheapest options are the Colombian-flagged *Doña Mariela* or *Maria Patricia* (see p260). Both charge around COP$3,800,000 per diver for eight days. The **Inula** (☑in Germany 49 5130 790326, in Panama 507 6672 9091; www.inula-diving.de), out of Puerto David, Panama, offers 11-day trips including six days diving around the island for US$2700 to US$4455 per diver.

Only one dive boat at a time is permitted near Malpelo. There are only a handful of cruises each year, and they fill up fast.

ℹ Information

Gorgona got its Greek mythology–derived name for a reason: it's an island full of poisonous snakes. You'll be given gumboots for protection. Yellow fever vaccinations are essential – park guides may demand to see your certificate on arrival.

ℹ Getting There & Away

Aviatur runs a speedboat to the island from Guapi (round trip COP$150,000, 1¼ hours) when there is demand; it's essential to book in advance. Cargo boats running from Buenaventura to Guapi can occasionally drop you off on the island.

Amazon Basin

Includes »

Best Places to Stay

» Reserva Natural Palmarí (p272)

» Malokas Napü (p271)

» Cabañas del Friar (p271)

» Amazon B&B (p266)

» Mahatu Jungle Hostel (p266)

Best Places to Eat

» Tierras Amazónicas (p267)

» Las Margaritas (p271)

» La Cava Tropical (p267)

» São Jorge (p269)

» Várzea (p267)

Why Go?

Amazon. The very word evokes images of pristine jungle, incredible wildlife and one famous river. The Amazon basin, which Colombians call Amazonia, is a 643,000-sq-km region accounting for a third of Colombia's total area – about the size of California. Visitors can never quite account for the strange exhilaration they feel when they come face to face with the rainforest for the first time.

With transportation limited to rivers that crisscross the jungle, indigenous groups deep in the jungle have managed to keep their cultures intact. But in the cities, many indigenous and mestizo (mixed race) people now live modern lifestyles, driving Yamahas and only breaking out their traditional garb and customs for the benefit of tourists. A visit here remains a transcendent experience, from thrilling rainforest treks to simple hammock siestas soundtracked by the otherworldly sounds of the jungle.

When to Go
Leticia

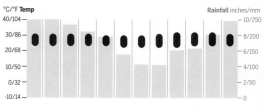

Sep-Nov Lower water levels afford excellent hiking and reveal white-sand beaches on the Río Yavarí.

Mar-May Get closer to the canopy in wet season, the climax of bird-watching and wildlife season.

Jul & Aug Loathe mosquitoes? The *terra firme* forest sees most retreat to the canopy.

Leticia

🎵 8 / POP 39,667 / ELEV 95M

As the capital city of the Amazonas province, Leticia is the largest city for hundreds of kilometers yet still looks and feels very much like a small frontier town. It's located on the Amazon River at the crossroads – or more accurately, the cross river – point where Colombia, Brazil and Peru meet. Leticia is located about 800km from the nearest Colombian highway.

Leticia was founded in 1867 as San Antonio. The origin of its current name has been lost to history. In any case, it was part of Peru until 1922 when both countries signed

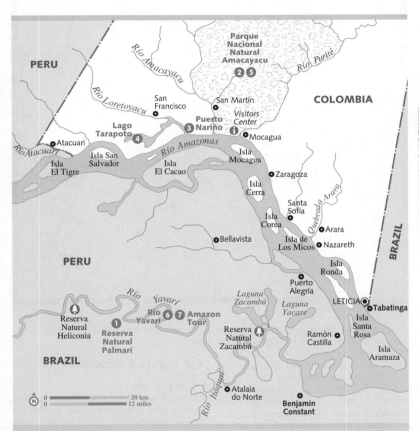

Amazon Basin Highlights

1 Spend a few days observing abundant wildlife at the excellent **Reserva Natural Palmarí** (p272) on the Río Yavarí.

2 Monkey around with numerous species of ornery rehabilitating primates at **Fundación Maikuchiga** (p270)

3 Unwind in the car-free, sustainable and funky remote village of **Puerto Nariño** (p270)

4 Spot pink and gray dolphins on the warm waters of the mighty **Lago Tarapoto** (p271)

5 Be serenaded by parrots in the rainforest of **Parque**

Nacional Natural (PNN) Amacayacu (p270)

6 Slip silently into the jungle by canoe up the tributaries of the **Río Yavarí** (p272)

7 Go beyond the lodges on a deep, multiday **Amazon tour** (p265), where you'll really be welcomed to the jungle!

Leticia

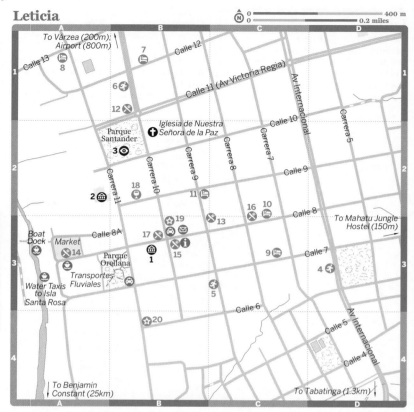

AMAZON BASIN LETICIA

a controversial agreement that ceded the land to Colombia. In 1932 a war broke out between Colombia and Peru, finally ending in 1933 after the League of Nations negotiated a cease-fire, ultimately awarding Leticia to Colombia. In the 1970s Leticia became a lawless hub of narcotics trafficking until the Colombian army moved in and cleaned things up.

Leticia is on the banks of the Amazon on the Colombia–Brazil border. Just across the frontier sits Tabatinga, a Brazilian town much the same size as Leticia, with its own airport and port – the main gateway for boats downstream to Manaus. Visitors can freely move between the two cities as well as the Brazilian city of Benjamin Constant, 25km downstream, and the Peruvian island of Santa Rosa opposite Leticia/Tabatinga. Travelers wishing to venture further into either country must meet immigration requirements.

Despite oppressive heat, humidity and man-eating mosquitoes, Leticia makes a pleasant base for exploring the rest of the Amazon.

Sights & Activities

Mundo Amazónico GARDENS
(☎592 6087; www.mundoamazonico.com; Km7.7 Via Tarapacá; tours COP$20,000; ☺7am-2pm Mon-Sat) Opened in 2009, this interesting 29-hectare reserve was designed to preserve endangered flora and fauna of the Amazon. The extensive botanical gardens boast some 700 species of flora divided into five sections. A visit here will enhance your knowledge of what you see in the wild, and friendly owner Rafael Clavijo can give the hourly tours in English.

FREE Museo Etnografico Amazónico MUSEUM
(Carrera 11 No 9-43; ☺8:30-11:30am & 1:30-5pm Mon-Fri, 9-11am Sat) This small museum located inside the dolphin pink–colored Biblio-

Leticia

teca del Banco de la República building has a small collection of indigenous artifacts including musical instruments, textiles, tools, pottery and weapons, and lots of freaky ceremonial masks.

Galería Arte Uirapuru   HANDICRAFTS, MUSEUM
(Calle 8 No 10-35; ⊘9am-12:30pm & 3-7pm Mon-Sat, 9am-12:30pm Sun) Leticia's largest craft shop, selling artifacts from local indigenous groups as well as a natural Amazonian 'pharmacy.' At the back of the shop is Museo Uirapuru, featuring a tiny exhibition of historic crafts (not for sale).

Parque Santander   PARK
A visit to this park just before sunset makes for an impressive spectacle as you witness thousands of small screeching *pericos* (parrots) arriving for their nightly rest.

Reserva Tanimboca   ADVENTURE SPORTS, KAYAKING
(☎310 791 7570; Km11 Via Tarapacá; ⊘8am-4pm) Visitors can monkey around atop 35m-high

trees, then slide 80m along zip lines from one tree to another through the beautiful forest canopy (COP$60,000); and visit the small serpentario (COP$7000). There's also kayaking (COP$35,000). Or splurge for an overnight stay in a treehouse (per person including breakfast COP$99,000), which includes a nocturnal jungle hike.

☞ Tours

The real jungle begins well off the Amazon proper, along its small tributaries. The deeper you go, the more chance you have to observe wildlife in relatively undamaged habitats and to visit indigenous settlements. This involves time and money, but the experience can be rewarding. A three- to four-day tour is perhaps the best way to balance the cost of the trip with the insight it will give you into the workings of the jungle, but it's also important to mention that expectations must be managed. Significant wildlife spotting is exceedingly rare in the Amazon: the animals aren't exactly social with people, they are hidden in the canopy, and encroachment by both tourism and local customs and industry have driven populations of various animals to frighteningly low numbers. You have a reasonable chance of spotting macaws, monkeys and a pink or gray dolphin in addition to numerous birds and the occasional odd fauna, but keep in mind the jungle is also about the sights, sounds and allure of one of the world's most fascinating and mysterious places.

Several companies organize multiday tours to the small nature reserves along the Río Yavarí (p272) on the Brazil–Peru border. Always agree on price, activities and duration before embarking on your trip. Avoid any unsolicited tour guides who approach you in the airport or streets.

The mudslinging between Leticia tour operators is as thick as the riverbank – allegations of incompetence, theft, sexual assault, drug use and drug-running, killing of animals and otherwise environmentally unsound practices are rampant among them. Choose carefully and go with your gut – there are very few angels in the jungle.

One highly experienced guide we recommend is **Elaise Cuao** (☎311 828 7430; aguilaharpia@hotmail.es), who speaks English, Portuguese and a little French.

Also recommended:

Amazon Jungle Trips   JUNGLE TOURS
(☎592 7377; www.amazonjungletrips.com.co; Av Internacional No 6-25) With more than 25 years

AMAZON BASIN LETICIA

of experience catering to backpackers, Amazon Jungle is one of the oldest and most reliable tour companies in Leticia. Owner Antonio Cruz Pérez speaks English and can arrange individually tailored tours, including trips to the Reserva Natural Zacambú in Río Yavarí and the newer Tupana Arü Ü lodge located 60km upriver on the Amazon and deeper into the jungle.

Selvaventura   JUNGLE TOURS
(☑592 3977; www.selvaventura.com; Carrera 9 No 6-85) Owner Felipe Ulloa speaks English, Spanish and Portuguese and can arrange a variety of trips into the jungle. The office is inside a small and simple guesthouse they have opened up, where dorm beds go for COP$15,000 to COP$20,000 and you can camp or sleep in a hammock for COP$10,000.

Tanimboca Tours   JUNGLE TOURS
(☑592 7679; www.tanimboca.org; Carrera 10 No 11-68) In addition to the activities at Reserva Tanimboca, the friendly folks here can organize boat or hiking trips into the jungle outside Leticia, including trips to indigenous villages. The owner speaks Serbian, German and English and several of the guides speak English.

🛏 Sleeping

Note that prices can skyrocket during high season, especially around Christmas and Easter.

TOP CHOICE> Amazon B&B   B&B $$$
(☑592 4981; www.amazonbb.com; Calle 12 No 9-30; r incl breakfast COP$125,500, cabañas COP$176,000; ❄🅰🛜) Leticia's newest and most charming option, this small hotel opened in 2010 with six cabañas and four rooms surrounding a well-manicured garden. The cabañas come with small, enclosed terraces with hammocks and all decor follows a minimalist-chic aesthetic previously unseen in town. The Amazon Spanish College is also on the property.

Mahatu Jungle Hostel   HOSTEL $
(☑311 539 1265; www.mahatu.com; Calle 7A No 1-40; dm per person COP$20,000-25,000, s/d without bathroom COP$40,000/50,000; @🛜🖥) An urban jungle in the heart of Leticia, this hostel sits on five hectares, complete with duck- and geese-filled ponds, throngs of *pericos* and loads of exotic fruit trees – cashew, *asaí, cananguche* and *copasú*

among them. Rooms are dead simple – and somewhat overpriced – with shared bath and the occasional crooked mattress, but you're paying for the lush environs. Owner/philosopher Gustavo Rene is multilingual.

La Jangada   GUESTHOUSE $$
(☑312 361 6506; lajangadaamazonas.com; Carrera 9 No 8-106; dm per person COP$25,000, s/d COP$45,000/65,000;@🛜) An excellent guesthouse run by a young Swiss-Colombian couple; the Swiss half has traversed 45,000km of Amazon rivers in his ecologically sound bicycle-powered boat, on which you can now do day tours (from COP$60,000). There's a five-bed dorm with a breezy balcony and hammock and a few private rooms with fan.

Hotel de la Selva   HOTEL $$
(☑314 803 4661; hoteldelaselvaleticia@hotmail.com; Calle 7 No 7-28; s/d COP$45,000/80,000, with air-con COP$60,000/100,000;❄🛜) Our favorite budget atmosphere; the jungly, plant-filled entrance corridor and common areas make this friendly place even more welcoming. There are 14 rooms, all with private bath, some even shaken up a bit with local handicrafts and *costilla* wood bedframes. There's no doubt you're in the jungle here, baby. Breakfast is COP$7000.

Hospedaje Los Delfines   GUESTHOUSE $$
(☑592 7488; losdelfinesleticia@hotmail.com; Carrera 11 No 12-81; s/d COP$40,000/70,000; 🛜) A 10-minute walk from the town center, this small, family-run place has 10 spacious if basic rooms with beds and hammocks, surrounding a gorgeously landscaped courtyard filled with flowers and fruit. Good value here (if you get a toilet seat).

Hotel Yurupary   HOTEL $$
(☑592 4741; www.hotelyurupary.com; Calle 8 No 7-26; s/d incl breakfast COP$69,000/98,000; ❄🛜🖥) This moderately priced favorite has large, recently refurbished rooms with private bathroom and TV. The outside courtyard features a refreshing swimming pool, garden, bar and restaurant.

🍴 Eating

Leticia's local specialty is fish, including the delicious *gamitana* and the overfished *pirarucú*, which is best avoided out of season as locals routinely ignore regulations preventing fishing for this species when it's spawning.

Prices tend to be a bit higher than in 'mainland' Colombia, but many restaurants serve cheap set meals. You can also find cheap eats at the **local market** (cnr Calle 8 & waterfront; ⊙5am-7pm). For a classier meal, try the Decalodge Ticuna.

TOP CHOICE **Tierras**
Amazónicas   SEAFOOD, AMAZONIAN **$$**
(Calle 8 No 7-50; mains COP$10,000-18,000; ⊙closed Mon) At first glance, this looks like an unapologetic tourist trap with walls covered in kitschy Amazonia knickknacks. Nonetheless, it's a fantastic place for a fun dinner. The specialty is fish. The *gamitana pupeca* (wrapped in plantain leaves) is delicious after you wade through the bones. There's a full bar and occasional live music. This is the *real* rainforest cafe.

Várzea   COLOMBIAN, PIZZERIA
(Carrera 10 No 14-12; pizza COP$13,500-18,000; ⊙from 5pm, closed Sun) Off the beaten track on the road to the airport, this trendy little neighborhood bar-restaurant is one of Leticia's best-kept secrets. For starters, the unconventional music is a welcome respite – think REM and reggae, not Shakira and reggaeton – and the pizzas, made with a tapioca crust (cassava), are excellent, along with upscale *patacones* (fried plantains) and crepes.

La Cava Tropical   COLOMBIAN **$**
(Carrera 9 No 8-22; set meals COP$6500; ❋) This open-air restaurant is the locals' lunchtime favorite. The set meals include a soup (often a tasty *sancocho*), small salad, a meat dish with a side of beans or veggies, and bottomless fruit juice, all for just COP$6500. It can get quite crowded during the weekday lunch rush and there's an air-con section!

La Casa del Pan   CAFE **$**
(Calle 11 No 10-20) Facing Parque Santander, the rickety outdoor tables at this bright, bustling bakery are sensitive – sneeze and you'll spill your coffee. But it's an atmospheric spot for breakfast (eggs, bread and coffee for COP$4500).

Viejo Tolima   BREAKFAST, COLOMBIAN **$**
(Calle 8 No 10-20; mains COP$2500-15,000; ⊙Mon-Fri) Great, clean spot for excellent breakfast (yummy *caldos* – soups), fruit juices and other local bites.

Supermercado Hiper   SUPERMARKET **$**
(Calle 8 No 9-29) For self-caterers.

🍷 Drinking & Entertainment

TOP CHOICE **Várzea**   BAR
(Carrera 10 No 14-12; ⊙from 5pm, closed Sun) This neighborhood bar is hands-down Leticia's best spot for a tipple, starting with the *chuchuhuasca*, an Amazonian herbal concoction whose bark, roots and leaves are a famous ethnomedicine and reportedly aphrodisiacal. Excellent cocktails, good grub (including pizza, COP$13,500–18,000) and cool music complete the package.

Titíco   BAR
(Calle 9 No 10-40; ⊙Wed-Sat) Adjoining Discoteca Kahlua, this nice chill-out bar is much more inviting than its neighbor, with a terrace overlooking the city.

Barbacoas   BAR, POOL HALL
(Carrera 10 No 8-28) Unlike most Colombian billiards clubs that only cater to men, ladies are warmly welcomed at Barbacoas – probably because the pool tables are hidden in a separate back room. The sidewalk cafe is a pleasant place to people-watch over a beer or Leticia's best *tinto* (black coffee).

Boa   CLUB
(Calle 11 No 6-19; ⊙from 7pm Thu-Sat) Leticia's more upscale nightclub, which hosts a funny live-music mix on Thursday and Friday with Brazilian *pagoda* (a type of samba) and live reggaeton. On Saturdays DJs take over. It caters to a mix of well-to-do locals and tourists alike.

ℹ Information

Dangers & Annoyances
A longstanding military presence in the region tries to keep Leticia/Tabatinga and surrounding region safe, but there are issues. Former narcotraffickers, guerrillas, paramilitaries and *raspachines* (coca-plant harvesters) who have been re-inserted into mainstream society and now live in the outskirts of Leticia and Puerto Nariño run poker houses, dubious bars and the like around the city. Don't wander outside these urban areas on your own at night, especially Leticia's infamous 'Los Kilometros' road. In Peru, narcotraffickers remain in business in this wayward corner of the country and have harassed tourists who have wandered off the beaten track. Tour operators and lodges in the region have been issued warnings about where they can and cannot bring tourists, so don't stray on your own beyond areas where local tourism guides normally operate.

Emergency
Police (☏592 5060; Carrera 11 No 12-32)

Internet Access

Sluggish internet runs around COP$2000 per hour. **Papelería Internacional** (Av Internacional No 6-40) and **Centro de Negocios** (Carrera 10 No 8-96) have a good selection of terminals in air-conditioned premises.

Medical Services

San Rafael de Leticia Hospital (☑592 7075; Av Vásquez Cobo No 13-78) You'll also find many pharmacies along Carrera 10 and elsewhere.

Money

There are many ATMs, but it's next to impossible to change traveler's checks here. To exchange currency, look for the *casas de cambio* on Calle 8 between Carrera 11 and the market. They change US dollars, Colombian pesos, Brazilian reais and Peruvian soles. Shop around as rates vary. Businesses in both Tabatinga and Leticia generally accept both reais and pesos.

Banco BBVA (cnr Carrera 10 & Calle 7) ATM.

Banco de Bogotá (cnr Carrera 10 & Calle 7) ATM.

Cambios El Opita (cnr Carrera 11 & Calle 8) Currency exchange.

Post

4-72 (Calle 8 No 9-56) Post office.

Tourist Information

Tourist office (Secretaría de Turismo y Fronteras; ☑592 7569; Calle 8 No 9-75; ☺7am-noon & 2-5pm Mon-Sat, 7am-noon Sun) Friendly, English-speaking. There is also a small booth at the airport during scheduled flights.

Visa Information

Locals and foreigners are allowed to come and go between Leticia, Tabatinga and Benjamin Constant without visas or passport control, but if you plan on heading further afield, you must get your passport stamped at the Ministry of Foreign Relations office at Leticia's airport and/or at **Policía Federal** (☑97 3412 2180 in Brazil; Av da Amizade 650, Tatabinga; ☺8am-noon & 2-6pm), near the hospital in Tabatinga. Due to the recent dissolution of Departamento Administrativo de Seguridad (DAS), Colombia's former security arm, visa information is particularly subject to change. For additional info, see p312.

Citizens of some countries, including the USA, Canada, Australia and New Zealand, need a visa to enter Brazil and it may be costly. To avoid a lot of stress and heartache, it's strongly recommended to arrange your visa before arriving in the Amazon. But if you must, bring a passport photo and yellow-fever vaccination certificate to the **Brazilian consulate** (☑592 7530; Calle 9 No 9-73; ☺8am-noon & 1-3pm Mon-Fri). Processing time is one to three days, depending on volume. If you're coming from or going to Iquitos, get your entry or exit stamp at the **Policía Internacional Peruviano (PIP) office** (Isla Santa Rosa). Travelers coming here from Brazil may need to visit the **Colombian consulate** (☑412 2104; Rua General Sampaio 623, Tabatinga; ☺8am-2pm Mon-Fri) to get the necessary visa.

If you need a Colombian visa extension, there is no need to pay an extension fee. Simply stamp out and head to Brazil or Peru for one day and return for a fresh 60 days up to the allocable time per year.

ℹ Getting There & Away

There are no overland crossings to Leticia. (For further information, head to shop.lonelyplanet.com to purchase a downloadable PDF of the Amazon Basin chapter from Lonely Planet's *Peru* guide (7th edition) and the Amazon chapter in *Brazil* (8th edition).

GETTING TO PERU

High-speed passenger boats between Tabatinga and Iquitos (Peru) are operated by **Transtur** (☑3412 2945; www.transtursa.com; Rua Marechal Mallet 248, Tabatinga) and **Transportes Golfinho** (☑97 3412 3186; www.transportegolfinho.com; Rua Marechal Mallet 306, Tabatinga). Boats leave from Isla Santa Rosa daily around 4am except Monday, arriving in Iquitos about 10 hours later. Don't forget to get your Colombian exit stamp at the Leticia airport Ministry of Foreign Relations office the day before departure.

The journey costs USD$70 in either direction, including breakfast and lunch (mint-condition banknotes only; or COL$140,000). During dry season you can sometimes only access Isla Santa Rosa from Tabatinga's Porta da Feira, where water levels are always high. Check ahead. In fact, it's always easier in the middle of the night to go from Tabatinga, but taxi prices from Leticia can skyrocket to COP$30,000 for the ride.

Be warned: there are slower, cheaper boats to Iquitos, but they are not comfortable and barely seaworthy.

Note there are no roads out of Iquitos into Peru. You have to fly or continue by river to Pucallpa (five to seven days), from where you can go overland to Lima.

DON'T MISS YOUR BOAT!

Tabatinga is one hour ahead of Leticia. Don't miss your boat!

Air

All foreigners must pay COP$18,500 tourist tax upon arrival at Leticia's airport, Aeropuerto Internacional Alfredo Vásquez Cobo, to the north of the town.

AeroRepública (www.aerorepublica.com.co) and **Lan** (www.lan.com) have daily flights to Bogotá. Book early for the best rates.

Trip (www.voetrip.com.br) and **Tam** (www.tam.com.br) fly from Tabatinga International Airport to Manaus daily (R$389 to R$886). The airport is 4km south of Tabatinga; *colectivos* marked 'Comara' from Leticia will drop you nearby. Don't forget to get your Colombian exit stamp at Leticia's airport and, if needed, a Brazilian visa before departure.

When departing Letica's airport, all foreigners must check-in at the Ministry of Foreign Relations before proceeding through airport security, regardless if you've left Colombia or not.

ⓘ Getting Around

The main mode of public transportation is by moto-taxi, the folks on motorcycles that zip around town with an extra helmet. The base rate is COP$2000. Frequent *colectivos* (COP$2000 to COP$6000) link Leticia with Tabatinga and the 'Kilometer' villages north of Leticia's airport. Standard taxis are pricier than in the rest of Colombia; a short ride from the airport to town runs COP$7000, to Tabatinga's airport COP$15,000 and to the Porto Bras in Tabatinga COP$10,000.

Tabatinga (Brazil)

☑ 97 / POP 52,272 / ELEV 95M

This gritty, unattractive border town doesn't have much to offer in terms of tourist attractions. Most visitors are only here to catch a boat to Manaus or Iquitos, or they're on a quick border hop just to say they've been to Brazil. While it's distinctly less pleasant than Leticia, you might consider staying here if you're taking an early-morning boat to Iquitos. For visa information see p268; for information on getting there and away, see the boxed text, right. Prices listed in this section are in Brazilian reais, though Colombian pesos are accepted. Brazil's telephone country code is +55.

Tabatinga has a helpful, English-speaking **tourist information center** (Centro de Infor-

mação Turística; Av da Amizade s/n; ⊙8am-6pm Mon-Fri, to noon Sun), where you can pick up maps of the city and other helpful info.

🛏 Sleeping

Avoid the hotels near the border; some of them double as brothels.

Novo Hotel   HOTEL **$$**
(☑3412 3846; novohoteltbt@hotmail.com; Rue Pedro Texeira No 9; s/d/tr/q incl breakfast R$50/70/80/100; ❄@) Conveniently located just three blocks from Porta da Feira, this friendly, clean option is perfect if you're catching an early boat.

🍴 Eating & Drinking

TOP CHOICE São Jorge   PERUVIAN **$$**
(Av da Amizade 1941; mains R$20-38) Locals on both sides of the border rave about the authentic ceviche at this simple Peruvian-run spot: the mountainous pile of excellent citrus-cooked fish and onions served on a bed of sweet potatoes and chunky corn serve two. It seems strange to walk from Colombia to Brazil for Peruvian ceviche, but that's the beauty of the tri-border!

Restaurante Tres Fronteiras do Amazonas   BRAZILIAN, AMAZONIAN **$$**
(Rua Rui Barbosa s/n; mains R$20-45) This attractive palm-thatched open-air restaurant offers a wide choice of fish and meat dishes, plus a selection of drinks, including cheap *caipirinhas* (the national cocktail of Brazil

AMAZON BASIN TABATINGA (BRAZIL)

GETTING TO BRAZIL

Boats to Manaus (Brazil) leave from Tabatinga's port on Wednesday and Saturday around 2pm, with a stop in Benjamin Constant. The journey to Manaus takes three days and four nights and costs around R$170 if you bring your own hammock, or about R$800 to R$1000 for two people in a double cabin.

Traveling upstream from Manaus to Tabatinga, the trip usually takes six days, and costs about R$220 in your hammock or R$900 to R$1200 for a double cabin.

Lancha Rápida Puma (☑97 9154 2597 in Brazil; Tabatinga) runs high-speed boats to Manaus that depart Porto Bras on Friday at 8am (R$430, 30 hours).

made with limes, sugar and *cachaça*, a rum-like distilled spirit; R$5). The food is an odd Brazilian-Peruvian-Colombian hodgepodge and the menu is in Portunol.

Bella Epoca BRAZILIAN **$$**
(Rua Pedro Texeira 589; per kg R$21; ⊘11am-3pm) A passable Brazilian *por kilo* (pay-by-weight) restaurant, where you'll find various salads, mains and *churrasco* (grilled meats, including Brazil's tastiest cut, *picanha*).

Bar Mirador BAR
(Rua T-11; ⊘till 9pm) A dead-simple Brazilian drinking den that is a spectacular spot for a cold sunset beer overlooking the Amazon. It's located about 50m up the hill from the Posto Policial (Police Post) in Barrio Dom Pedro, just south of the floating dock. You have to walk through somebody's ramshackle backyard to enter!

☆ Entertainment

Scandalos CLUB
(cnr Av da Amizade & Rua Pedro Texeira; cover Fri-Sun R$5) Some people in Tabatinga told us this club was 'un-Christian, immoral and homosexual,' which means, of course, it's awesome! Located about five blocks from the border, it attracts a young, sexy crowd dancing till dawn.

Isla Santa Rosa (Peru)

Five minutes by boat from Leticia, this tiny island village on the Amazon River has a few rustic *hospedajes* (hostels) and some bars and restaurants, but not much else other than a sketchy reputation. About the only tourist attraction is the giant 'Welcome to Peru' sign. If you're traveling from or going to Iquitos, you'll need to come here and visit the **Policía Internacional Peruviano (PIP)** office to get an exit/entry stamp in your passport. Everything is located along the foot-path through town. Water taxis (COP$3000) ply the Leticia–Isla Santa Rosa route from dawn to dusk in high-water season.

Parque Nacional Natural (PNN) Amacayacu

Sprawling across almost 300,000 hectares, **Parque Nacional Natural (PNN) Amacayacu** (☎8 520 8654; foreigners/Colombians COP$35,000/13,000) is an ideal spot from which to observe the Amazonian rainforest up close. About 75km upriver from Leticia, the park is home to 500 species of birds, 150 mammals and dozens of reptiles, including crocs, boas and anacondas. And millions of mosquitoes. Activities include kayaking, bird-watching and multiday hikes.

Visitor amenities include dorm lodges with shared baths, seven luxury cabins with private baths, and a good restaurant. The luxury hotel chain Decameron runs the park's tourist facilities, and with it comes sky-high prices. Simple dorm bunks cost COP$104,000 to COP$195,000 depending on the season; rooms start at COP$360,000 for a double.

High-speed boats to Puerto Nariño (see p272) will drop you off at the visitor center (COP$24,000, 1½ hours from Leticia). Boats often fill up; buy your tickets in advance. Getting back to Leticia can be a bit trickier. The best option is to flag down a high-speed boat returning from Puerto Nariño; they pass by the visitor center at around 11:30am and 4:30pm, but won't stop if they're full. As a last resort, try flagging down one of the slow cargo ships or *peque-peques* (small motorized boats) back to Leticia.

Puerto Nariño

☎8 / POP 7574 / ELEV 110M
The tiny Amazonian village of Puerto Nariño, 75km upriver from Leticia, is living

---

HEY, HEY, IT'S THE MONKEYS...

Monkey lovers will want to make a beeline deeper into the jungle inside Parque Nacional Natural (PNN) Amacayacu to visit **Fundación Maikuchiga** (☎313 309 2866; www.maikuchiga.org), where Brit Sara Bennett runs a rustic rehabilitation center that, on our visit, featured 21 monkeys spread among seven species roaming free on the grounds. Visits are very expensive (COP$120,000 for up to six people, COP$20,000 for each additional person plus park admission fees) but it's easily a highlight: the friendly monkeys will likely climb all over you, and try to steal your lipstick/wallet/iPhone/whatever.

Note: the center works under stringent regulations in terms of visitor numbers, so it's recommended you contact the center in advance for permission to visit.

proof that man and nature can peacefully coexist.

Puerto Nariño has elevated the concept of green living to an art form. Motorized vehicles are banned. The spotless city is laid out on a grid of landscaped, pedestrian-only sidewalks. Every morning, citizen brigades fan out to tidy up the town.

The little town's ambitious recycling and organic waste management programs would put most world cities to shame. Trash and recycling bins are located on practically every corner. Rainwater is collected in cisterns for washing and gardening. Electricity comes from the town's energy-efficient generator, but only runs until midnight. Fall asleep to the sounds of jungle chit-chat and the pitter-patter of raindrops on tin roofs.

The majority of Puerto Nariño's residents are indigenous Tikuna, Cocoma and Yagua peoples. Their community experiment in ecological living has led to an important source of income: ecotourism. This tranquil town is a great base from which to visit beautiful Lago Tarapoto and the Amazon in general.

Sights & Activities

Fundación Omacha (www.omacha.org), located on the riverfront just east of the docks, is a conservation and research center working to save the Amazon's freshwater mammals, mostly notably pink dolphins, manatees and otters. Next door, the **Centro de Interpretación Natütama** (admission by donation; ⊗closed Tue) has a fascinating museum with nearly 100 life-sized wood carvings of Amazonian flora and fauna.

For a bird's-eye view of the village, climb the **mirador** (foreigner/Colombian COP$7000/5000) tower, located at the top of Calle 4.

Lago Tarapoto, 10km west of Puerto Nariño, is a beautiful jungle lake that was once home to many of the Amazon's famous pink dolphins (*botos*) and gray dolphins. Though many have begun to move elsewhere due to tourism encroachment, sightings are still possible. Varied flora, including the Victoria Regia, the world's largest water lily, flourish here. A half-day trip to the lake in a *peque-peque* can be organized from Puerto Nariño (COP$50,000 for up to three people). Locals can take you on boat excursions to many other places, including the Parque Nacional Natural Amacayacu.

An excellent local guide is jovial **Willinton Carvajal** (☑313 375 5788), who only speaks Spanish but gets the job done.

Sleeping

There are about a dozen hotel options in town.

Malokas Napü   GUESTHOUSE $
(☑310 488 0998; olgabeco@yahoo.com; Calle 4 No 5-72; r per person with/without balcony COP$30,000/25,000; @) Our favorite hotel has the look and feel of a treehouse fort. The rooms are simple but comfortable, with basic furnishings, fan and shared baths with super-refreshing rain-style showers, and everyone who works here is above and beyond friendly. Try for rooms 7 and 8 of the back building, which share a balcony with hammocks overlooking the courtyard garden and jungle.

Cabañas del Friar   CABAÑAS $
(☑311 502 8592; altodelaguila@hotmail.com; r per person COP$20,000) About 20 minutes west of town, famous friar Hector José Rivera and his crazy monkeys run this hilltop jungle oasis overlooking the Amazon. The complex includes several simple huts, shared facilities and a lookout tower. The true joy of staying here is the playful interaction between the monkeys, dogs and macaws – endless entertainment! To get here, take Carrera 6 west out of town across the big bridge to the well-maintained sidewalk, keep left at the cemetery and walk through the high school campus (fascinating in itself) and hang a right at the football pitch.

Hotel Lomas del Paiyü   HOTEL $
(☑313 268 4400; hotellomasdelpaiyu@yahoo.com; Calle 7 No 2-26; s/d COP$30,000/50,000, r per person without bathroom COP$20,000) This tin-roofed, just-renovated 22-room hotel is a reliable choice and ownership is now in the hands of friendly *bogotanos*. Some bathrooms are almost as big as the rooms and cheaper rooms come in the form of rustic cabañas with communal hammocks.

Eating & Drinking

Puerto Nariño is sorely lacking worthy restaurant options with one exception. There are a few fast-food joints and grocery stores on the main road facing the river. 'Nightlife' involves drinking at one of the hole-in-the-wall bars fronting the basketball courts.

Las Margaritas   COLOMBIAN, AMAZONIAN $
(Calle 6 No 6-80; set meals COP$6000-12,000) Hidden behind a picket fence under a huge

palapa (thatched roof), Las Margaritas is the best restaurant in town. Excellent home-cooked meals are served buffet-style from traditional clay cookware. Breakfast doesn't stand out as much as lunch and dinner, but it's all shockingly tasty.

Café Omague COLOMBIAN, AMAZONIAN **$**
(Carrera 2 No 5-65; ☺from 3pm) This small cafe runs by friendly locals offers a chalkboard menu of cassava crepes and other small bites, with candlelit tables that are nearly romantic. Serves during power outages, which are frequent.

ⓘ Information

There are no banks or ATMs in Puerto Nariño, and credit cards are not accepted anywhere. Bring plenty of cash from Leticia.

Compartel (cnr Carrera 6 & Calle 5; per hr COP$2000; ☺closed Sun) Provides internet access plus local and international telephone service.

Hospital (cnr Carrera 4 & Calle 5)

Tourist office (☎313 235 3687; cnr Carrera 7 & Calle 5; ☺closed Sun) Located inside the *alcaldía* (municipal town hall building), but there's a kiosk just outside on the riverfront.

ⓘ Getting There & Away

High-speed boats to Puerto Nariño depart from Leticia's dock at 8am, 10am and 2pm daily (COP$29,000, two hours); round-trip boats to Leticia depart at 7:30am, 11am and 4pm.

You can purchase tickets at **Transportes Fluviales** (☎592 6752; Calle 8 No 11) near the riverfront in Leticia. Boats can get very full, so buy your tickets early or the day before.

Río Yavarí

Within reach of large stretches of virgin forest, the meandering Río Yavarí offers some of the best opportunities to see the Amazon up close and undisturbed. A few privately owned reserves provide simple accommodations plus guided tours and activities, including kayaking, bird-watching, dolphin watching, jungle treks and visits to indigenous settlements. The lodges provide accommodations and food.

Costs take into account the number of people in the party, length of the stay, season and number of guided tours; count on COP$150,000 to COP$250,000 per person per day. There are no regularly scheduled boats, so you will have to arrange transpor-

tation with the reserves. Hiring a private boat from Leticia is also an option – an extraordinarily expensive one. Expect to pay COP$150,000 one way plus fuel (from COP$250,000).

Note that visitors to Río Yavarí must get a Brazilian entry stamp and, if necessary, a visa in Tabatinga or Leticia (see p268).

RESERVA NATURAL PALMARÍ

About 105km by river from Leticia, ecofierce Palmarí's rambling lodge and research center sits on the high, south (Brazilian) bank of the river, overlooking a wide bend where pink and gray dolphins often gather. It's the only lodge with access to all three Amazonian ecosystems: *terra firme* (dry), *várzea* (semiflooded) and *igapó* (flooded).

The lodge itself is rustic, much of it recently rebuilt after arsonists set fire to it in 2010. It has helpful guides employed from the surrounding community (so no English, but *mucho* authenticity and expertise), and offers a wide choice of walking trips and night treks, boat excursions and kayaking trips, and excellent food served up by Brazilian kitchen staff. You'll find Palmarí offers the best walking options around the region, is the only option to encounter *terra firme* forest and is the best spot in the region to see animals. In fact, when a tapir strolled into the dining room during dinner on our first night, we knew we'd come to the right place!

Independent traveler rates include room and board (per night COP$250,000 for a bed or hammock) as well as all excursions and activities except the excellent, high-adrenaline canopying (COP$60,000). Nicer private cabañas with private bathrooms are reserved for guests on multiday packages that include transportation, but they are not a big enough step up to justify upgrading from the backpacker rate unless you just love pretty sinks.

The reserve is managed from Bogotá by owner **Axel Antoine-Feill** (☎310 786 2770; www.palmari.org; Carrera 10 No 93-72, Bogotá), who can speak several languages including English. His representative in Leticia is **Victoria Gomez** (☎310 793 2881), though Victoria only speaks Spanish.

To get here, either arrange transportation from Leticia with the lodge, or travel the cheap and adventurous way: from the floating dock in Tabatinga, take a '*Taxi do Río – Catraya*' boat, which leave when full to Benjamin Constant (R$15, 30 minutes).

From there, if you are traveling light, grab a moto-taxi (R$25, 30 minutes) or take one of the small vans that leave when full (R$15, 45 minutes) to the village of Atalaia do Norte. There you can make arrangements with Palmarí for boat transportation to the lodge (COP$60,000); or, if you're lucky, negotiate a local boatsman to take you for R$60 to R$80, though they aren't exactly hanging out ready to roll.

RESERVA NATURAL ZACAMBÚ

Zacambú is one of the reserves nearest to Leticia, about 70km by boat. Its lodge is on Laguna Zacambú, just off Río Yavarí, on the Peruvian side of the river. The lodge is simple, with small rooms with shared bathrooms, and a total capacity of about 30 guests. Plan on COP$160,000 per person per night including food and transportation.

Zacambú sits on a flooded forest that is a habitat for many species of butterflies, but unfortunately is also a popular hangout for mosquitoes. Its proximity to Peruvian communities also means it's not the best spot for wildlife. You are better off at its newer lodge on the Amazon (see p265).

Both the lodge and tours are run from Leticia by **Amazon Jungle Trips** (☑8 592 7377; www.amazonjungletrips.com.co; Av Internacional No 6-25).

Understand Colombia

population per sq km

COLOMBIA   US   UK

≈ 32 people

Colombia Today

A Country on the Rise

Colombia makes evangelists of all who visit it and few visitors leave with anything but a positive impression. And while the global economy sputters, Colombia is powering ahead full throttle as foreign investment and tourists pour in. The economy has been growing steadily for several years, and Colombia's finance minister projected a further 5% growth in 2012. While it's undeniable that for many rural poor life has yet to improve, Colombia today is racing ahead to become one of the hottest, most exciting destinations on the continent.

It wasn't always so. Until 2002 the country was riven by a war that saw the FARC (the leftist guerrilla insurgency) controlling much of the country while locked in combat with the government and right-wing paramilitary groups, such as the AUC (formed to tackle FARC ascendancy). There followed eight years of the hardline, but scandal-tainted presidency of Álvaro Uribe, who drove the FARC back into the mountains and jungles with a US-funded military offensive. The guerrillas' numbers plunged from 17,000 to 9000 as many deserted or were killed. Kidnappings and extortion also dropped markedly. In 2006, the 26,000 members of the AUC disarmed, albeit in a process condemned as too lenient by Amnesty International.

The Pragmatic President

Harvard-educated Juan Manuel Santos took power in 2010, winning a landslide victory over an eccentric former mayor of Bogotá, Antanas Mockus. His presidency has been marked by a more pragmatic political style, but one underpinned by a continuation of his predecessor's intransigence toward the guerrilla. He has adopted a twin strategy against the FARC: by calling for a ceasefire ahead of talks, and simultaneously crushing the insurgents.

Fast Facts

» Population: 44,725,500

» GDP growth (2010): 5.2%

» Exports: coffee, coal, oil, gold, bananas, cut flowers, chemicals, emeralds

» US foreign aid to Colombia (2009): US$838 million

» Unemployment: 11.8%

» Life expectancy: 71 years (men), 78 years (women)

» Internet country code: .co

Top Books

» *One Hundred Years of Solitude* (Gabriel García Márquez) Magic realist masterpiece.

» *Calamari* (Emilio Ruiz Barrachina) Cartagena-set historical romance.

» *Beyond Bogota – Diary of a Drug War Journalist in Colombia* (Garry Leech) Essential reading for news that's not in the papers.

» *Delirium* (Laura Restrepo) Explores personal and political madness in mid-80s Bogotá.

» *Six Months on Minimum Wage* (Andrés Felipe Solano) Life in a Medellín factory.

Top Films

» *Todos Sus Muertos* (2011) Devastating critique of corruption and apathy in Colombia.

» *Apaporis* (2010) Incisive documentary into indigenous Amazonian life.

» *Perro Come Perro* (2008) Tarantino-esque gangster flick.

belief systems
(% of population)

90
Roman Catholic

8.1
Protestant

1.9
No religious beliefs

if Colombia were 100 people

58 would be White & Amerindian
20 would be White
14 would be White & black
3 would be Black & Amerindian
4 would be Black
1 would be Amerindian

In September 2010, Colombian government forces raided FARC commander Mono Jojoy's camp, killing him. They discovered that the FARC, who have long funded their efforts through narco-trafficking and taxation of the coca trade, had turned to illegal gold mining to finance their operations. Soon after, the government launched a clampdown on illegal mines, which also affected *campesino* (peasant) artisanal miners.

Then on November 4, 2011, Colombian soldiers bombed the camp of FARC leader Alfonso Cano, killing him. Santos said Cano's death was 'the most resounding blow to this organization in its entire history' and that 'the last phase of this almost 50-year-old conflict is nearing.' Instantly, a new, militaristic FARC leader was elected, Rodrigo Londoño Echeverry, alias Timochenko. In a surprise move, the FARC leader called for peace talks. Santos refused, saying the offer was unacceptable until the insurgents disarmed. The future of the conflict remains uncertain.

Cocaine, Coffee & Commerce

Santos has called for a major rethink on the drug war, arguing that as long as demand remains high in the USA and Europe, production and supply will remain profitable. Even though the trade has been affected by costly drives to eradicate crops and take out cartels, Colombia still produces an estimated 410 tonnes of cocaine annually. Several drug kingpins were killed or arrested in 2011, chief among them Juan de Dios Usuga, who controlled the powerful northern cartel, the Urabeños.

Colombia's other, legal, major export, coffee, also took a major hit that year – but it was precipitation rather than politics that caused it. Throughout 2011, farmers all over Colombia – the world's second-largest exporter of arabica beans – were hit by torrential rains, with production down 14%.

Explosive Fun

Play tejo – a traditional game where 2kg weights are tossed into a pit to hit and explode gunpowder-filled pieces of paper called *mechas*. It's a rural game that's been taken to most big cities. Drinking and hollering are compulsory.

Dos & Don'ts

» *Maria Eres Llena de Gracia* (2008) Moving tale of teen pregnancy and drug-trafficking.

» *Soñar No Cuesta Nada* (2006) Colombian soldiers find millions of FARC dollars – and keep it.

» *Rosario Tijeras* (2004) Vengeful hit-woman's thrilling tale.

» Do haggle gently on almost all intercity bus fares – you can often get a discount of up to 20%.

» Don't feel obliged to buy the small trinkets vendors will hand you on bus journeys.

» Do wait for a top-up when you buy a juice in the street; it's called a *ñapa* and is customary.

» Don't take cocaine. There's much more fun to be had in Colombia, and the drug trade fuels the ongoing armed conflict.

Later that year, the US Congress ratified a free-trade agreement with Colombia that had been stalled for years by Democrat concerns over human rights violations, particularly the assassinations of trade unionists, as documented by Amnesty International. This could lead to possible losses for Colombian farmers unable to compete against subsidized US crops.

Only in Colombia

Perhaps the most emblematic event of recent years came in October 2011, when Gustavo Petro, ex-leader of the M-19 leftist guerrilla movement that stormed Bogotá's Palace of Justice in 1985, became mayor of Bogotá. If traveling in Colombia for pleasure was once unthinkable, to have a notorious former guerrilla in a position of high office is, to seasoned Colombia-watchers, equally unthinkable.

Another surreal drama unfolded in March 2011 when fans at the soccer stadium in Cúcuta decided to redefine the word 'fanatic' at a match between their team, Cúcuta Deportivo, and Envigado. Friends of Christopher Jacome, a 17-year-old fan who was murdered while playing soccer near his home, brought their friend's dead body, in a coffin, on to the terraces at the game for one last match.

Colombian Salsa

» *El Preso* (Fruko Y Sus Tesos)

» *Pantera Mambo* (LA 33)

» *Rebelion* (Joe Arroyo)

» *Oiga, Mira Vea* (Orquesta Guayacan)

» *Gotas De Lluvia* (Grupo Niche)

Food Tips

» If you don't want soup with your lunch or dinner, order it 'seco' (dry).

» The squeamish might want to avoid *ubre* (udder) and *mondongo* (tripe).

» Street coffee in Colombia is awful – sadly, the best is exported.

Full or Half?

When you order a rum in Colombia, unlike in Europe and the USA, you won't get a mixed drink. Instead, you'll, *hic,* be given a full or half-bottle, with cola, ice and limes.

History

Colombia's history is, inescapably, one of war and bloodshed. Whether that's the cruelty of the Spanish colonial conquests, the fight with Spain for independence, the ongoing 50-year civil war between the FARC guerrillas and the paramilitaries or the narco-chaos of the 1980 and '90s, Colombia has always been synonymous with violence.

Violence has receded in recent years, and Colombia today is a safer place for its residents and for travelers. While the conflict has diminished, however, FARC still controls much of the jungle, and paramilitaries and drug cartels are still active.

Pre-Columbus Colombia

Set where South America meets Central America, present-day Colombia saw the continent's first inhabitants arrive between 12,500 and 70,000 years ago, having migrated from the north. Most – such as the ancestors of the Inca – just passed through. Little is known of the groups who did stick around (eg the Calima, Muisca, Nariño, Quimbaya, Tayrona, Tolima and Tumaco). By the time the Spaniards arrived, the first inhabitants were living in small, scattered communities, subsisting on agriculture or trade. They hardly rivaled the bigger civilizations flourishing in Mexico and Peru.

The area's biggest pre-Columbian sites (San Agustín, Tierradentro and Ciudad Perdida) were already long abandoned when the Spaniards arrived in the 1500s. Ciudad Perdida, the Tayrona jungle city, was built around 700 AD, with hundreds of stone terraces linked with stairways. The Muisca, one of the country's larger indigenous groups, occupied present-day Boyacá and Cundinamarca, near Bogotá (itself named from a Muisca word), and numbered 600,000 when the Spanish arrived.

Spanish Conquest

Colombia is named after Christopher Columbus, even though he never set foot on Colombian soil. One of Columbus' companions on his second

The largest indigenous group between the Maya and Inca at the time of the Spanish Conquest, the Muiscas inspired El Dorado myths with their gold *tujos* (offerings), while their *chicha* (fermented-corn beer) still intoxicates Colombians today.

EXPLORERS

The Explorers of South America (1972), by Edward J Goodman, brings to life some of the more incredible explorations of the continent, from those of Columbus to Humboldt, some of which refer to Colombia.

voyage, Alonso de Ojeda, was the first recorded European to arrive in 1499. He briefly explored the Sierra Nevada de Santa Marta and was astonished by the wealth of the local indigenous people. The shores of present-day Colombia became the target of numerous expeditions by the Spaniards. Several short-lived settlements were founded along the coast, but it was not until 1525 that Rodrigo de Bastidas laid the first stones of Santa Marta, which is today the earliest surviving town. In 1533 Pedro de Heredia founded Cartagena; with a better harbor it quickly became the principal center of trade.

In 1536 an advance toward the interior began independently from three directions: under Gonzalo Jiménez de Quesada (from Santa Marta), Sebastián de Belalcázar (aka Benalcázar; from present-day Ecuador) and Nikolaus Federmann (from Venezuela). All three managed to conquer much of the colony and establish a series of towns, before meeting in the Muisca territory in 1539.

Of the three, Quesada got there first, crossing the Valle del Magdalena and Cordillera Oriental in 1537. At the time, the Muisca were divided into two rival clans – one ruled by the Zipa from Bacatá (present-day Bogotá), the other by Zaque in Hunza (present-day Tunja) – whose rivalry helped Quesada conquer both clans with only 200 men.

Belalcázar, a deserter from Francisco Pizarro's Inca-conquering army, subdued the southern part of Colombia, founding Popayán and Cali. After crossing Los Llanos and the Andes, Federmann arrived in Bogotá shortly after Belalcázar. The three groups squabbled for supremacy until King Carlos V of Spain finally established a court of justice in Bogotá in 1550 and brought the colony under the control of the viceroyalty of Peru.

The Colonial Era

In 1564 the Crown established a new authority, the Real Audiencia del Nuevo Reino de Granada, which had dual military and civil power and greater autonomy. The authority was run by a governor, appointed by the King of Spain. The Nuevo Reino at that time comprised present-day Panama, Venezuela (other than Caracas) and all of Colombia, except what is today Nariño, Cauca and Valle del Cauca, which were under the jurisdiction of the Presidencia de Quito (present-day Ecuador).

The population of the colony, initially consisting of indigenous communities and the Spanish invaders, diversified with the arrival of African slaves to Cartagena, South America's principal slave-trading port. During the 16th and 17th centuries the Spaniards shipped in so many Africans that they eventually surpassed the indigenous population in number. The emergence of *criollos* (locally born whites) added to the mix.

With the growth of the Spanish empire in the New World, a new territorial division was created in 1717, and Bogotá became the capital of its

1499	1537-38	1564	1717
On his second journey to the New World, Alonso de Ojeda lands at Cabo de la Vela – and a scientist onboard surprises the crew by discovering the place isn't actually Asia.	Conquistador Gonzalo Jiménez de Quesada twice founds a new settlement, Santa Fe de Bogotá. First, without permission from the Crown, in 1537, then with approval in 1538.	The Spanish Crown establishes the Real Audiencia del Nuevo Reino de Granada in Bogotá, subject to the viceroyalty of Peru in Lima.	Bogotá becomes capital of the viceroyalty of Virreinato de la Nueva Granada, an area that encompasses present-day Colombia, Ecuador, Venezuela and Panama.

GOLD!

From day one of their arrival, tales of gold overwhelmed the conquistador mind-set. Eventually glimpses of gold artifacts – and stories of much more inland – gave birth to the myth of El Dorado, a mysterious jungle kingdom abundant in gold and, in some versions, surrounded by mountains of gold and emeralds. Long into the colonial period, the struggling Nueva Granada viceroyalty was based on a one-export economy: gold.

Eventually the legend became linked with the Muisca and their famous Laguna de Guatavita (p74), which has suffered endless efforts to dig up enough wealth to change the world. Not much was ever found, alas. Read more in John Hemming's fascinating book, *The Search for El Dorado* (2001).

In 2012, with the global economy still in choppy waters and investors seeking a safe haven for funds, the price of gold has rocketed. The New York Times has reported that the FARC are now turning away from white gold – cocaine – to the more traditional yellow variety as it is more lucrative.

own viceroyalty, the Virreinato de la Nueva Granada. It comprised the territories of what are today Colombia, Panama, Ecuador and Venezuela.

Independence from Spain

As Spanish domination of the continent increased, so too did the discontent of the inhabitants – particularly over monopolies of commerce and new taxes. The first open rebellion against colonial rule was the Revolución Comunera in Socorro (Santander) in 1781, which broke out against tax rises levied by the Crown. It began taking on more pro-independence overtones (and nearly taking over Bogotá) before its leaders were caught and executed. When Napoleon Bonaparte put his own brother on the Spanish throne in 1808, the colonies refused to recognize the new monarch. One by one, Colombian towns declared their independence.

In 1812 Simón Bolívar, who was to become the hero of the independence struggle, appeared on the scene. He won six battles against Spanish troops, but was defeated the following year. Spain recovered its throne from Napoleon and then set about reconquering the colonies, finally succeeding in 1817. Meanwhile, in 1815 Bolívar had retreated to Jamaica and taken up arms again. He went back to Venezuela, but Spanish forces were too strong in Caracas, so Bolívar headed south, with an army, and marched over the Andes into Colombia, claiming victory after victory.

The most decisive battle took place at Boyacá on August 7, 1819. Three days later Bolívar arrived triumphantly in Bogotá. Though some lesser battles were yet to come (including a victory at Cartagena in 1821), a congress met shortly after the Boyacá battle and pronounced

1808	1819		1830
Napoleon defeats Spanish King Ferdinand VII and installs his brother on the Spanish throne, sending a glimmer of possibility for independence-minded thinkers across South America.	Simón Bolívar – crossing Los Llanos with an army of Venezuelans and Nueva Granadans from present-day Colombia – defeats the Spanish army at Boyacá and the Republic of Gran Colombia is founded.		Gran Colombia splits into Colombia (including modern-day Panama), Ecuador and Venezuela; Bolívar sends himself into exile; he dies in Santa Marta.

» Statue of Simón Bolívar

the independent Republic of Colombia – comprising today's Venezuela, Colombia and Panama.

The Formation of Political Parties

Although the conquistador Sebastián de Belalcázar was rewarded for killing thousands of indigenous people, the Spanish Crown sentenced him to death for ordering the assassination of rival conquistador Jorge Robledo in 1846.

With Colombia independent, a revolutionary congress was held in Angostura (modern-day Ciudad Bolívar, in Venezuela) in 1819. Still euphoric with victory, the delegates proclaimed a new state, Gran Colombia, uniting Venezuela, Colombia, Panama and Ecuador (although Ecuador and parts of Venezuela were still technically under Spanish rule).

The Angostura congress was followed by another, held in Villa del Rosario, near Cúcuta, in 1821. It was there that the two opposing tendencies, centralist and federalist, first came to the fore. The two currents persisted throughout Bolívar's administration, which lasted to 1830. What followed after Bolívar's departure was a new (but not the last) inglorious page of Colombia's history. The split was formalized in 1849 when two political parties were established: the Conservatives (with centralist tendencies) and the Liberals (with federalist leanings). Fierce rivalry between these two forces resulted in a sequence of insurrections and civil wars, and throughout the 19th century Colombia experienced no fewer than eight civil wars. Between 1863 and 1885 alone there were more than 50 antigovernment insurrections.

In 1899 a Liberal revolt turned into the Thousand Days War, which resulted in a Conservative victory and left 100,000 dead. In 1903 the US took advantage of the country's internal strife and fomented a secession-

THE FALL OF SIMÓN BOLÍVAR

Known as 'El Libertador,' Simón Bolívar led armies to battle the Spanish across northern South America, won the Colombian presidency, and ranks as one of the nation's great heroes. It's therefore surprising how it ended for him: humiliated, jobless, penniless and alone. He said, shortly before his death from tuberculosis in 1830, 'There have been three great fools in history: Jesus, Don Quixote and I.'

How did it happen? A proponent of a centralized republic, Bolívar was absent – off fighting back the Spanish in Peru and Bolivia – during much of his administration, leaving the running of the government to his vice president, and rival, the young federalist Francisco de Paula Santander, who smeared Bolívar and his ideas of being a lifetime president with the 'm' word: monarchist.

In 1828 Bolívar finally assumed dictatorship of a republic out of control, and restored a (hugely unpopular) colonial sales tax. Soon after, he narrowly escaped an assassination attempt (some believe Santander planned it) and a long-feisty Venezuela finally split from the republic. By 1830 Bolívar had had enough, abandoning the presidency – and then his savings, through gambling. He died a few months later.

1880	1899	1903	1948
Colombia elects Dr Rafael Núñez, who helps ease tension between state and church with new 'regeneration' policies outlined in a constitution that will stay in place for over a century.	The three-year Thousand Days War between Liberals and Conservatives erupts around the country, providing a key backdrop for Gabriel García Márquez' One Hundred Years of Solitude.	Long cut off from the rest of Colombia, Panama secedes from the country.	Likely Liberal presidential candidate, populist leader Jorge Eliécer Gaitán, is murdered leaving his office, setting off Bogotá and the country into bloody riots – the culprits are never identified.

ist movement in Panama, then a Colombian province. By creating an independent republic there, the US was able to build and control a canal across the Central American isthmus. It wasn't until 1921 that Colombia eventually recognized the sovereignty of Panama and settled its dispute with the US.

The 20th Century: Sowing the Seeds

The turn of the 20th century saw Panama ceded from Gran Colombia, but there was a welcome period of peace, as the economy started to boom (particularly due to coffee) and the country's infrastructure expanded under the defused partisan politics of leader General Rafael Reyes. The brief lapse into a gentler world didn't last long, however. Labor tensions rose (following a 1928 banana strike) and the struggle between Liberals and Conservatives finally exploded in 1946 with La Violencia, the most destructive of Colombia's many civil wars to that point (with a death toll of some 200,000). Following the assassination of Jorge Eliécer Gaitán, a charismatic, self-made populist Liberal leader, more widespread riots broke out around the country (which came to be known as El Bogotazo in Bogotá – where Gaitán was killed – and El Nueve de Abril elsewhere). Liberals soon took up arms throughout the country.

Generations of Colombians remained divided into the two political camps and each held a deep mistrust of the opposition. It's believed that 'hereditary hatreds' helped fuel revenge attacks and were the cause of countless atrocities (including rapes and murders) committed over the course of the next decade, particularly in rural areas.

The 1953 coup of General Gustavo Rojas Pinilla was the only military intervention the country experienced in the 20th century, but the coup was not to last. In 1957 the leaders of the two parties signed a pact to share power for the next 16 years. The agreement, later approved by plebiscite (in which women were allowed to vote for the first time), became known as the Frente Nacional (National Front). During the life of the accord, the two parties alternated in the presidency every four years. In effect, despite the enormous loss of lives, the same people were returned to power. Importantly, the agreement also disallowed political parties beyond the Liberals and the Conservatives, forcing any opposition outside of the normal political system and sowing the seeds for guerrilla insurrection.

The Birth of the FARC & Paramilitaries

While the new National Front helped ease partisan tensions between Conservatives and Liberals, new conflicts were widening between wealthy landowners and the rural mestizo and indigenous underclass, two-thirds of whom lived in poverty by the end of La Violencia. Splinter leftist groups

During the colonial period, the local demographic picture became increasingly complex, as the country's three racial groups – mestizos (people of mixed European-indigenous blood), mulattos (people with European-African ancestry) and zambos (African-indigenous people) – mixed.

In his magic-realism novel, *One Hundred Years of Solitude,* Gabriel García Márquez depicts the back-and-forth brutality of Liberal and Conservative rivalries and vendettas in ongoing conflicts from 1885 to 1902 in the fictional village of Macondo.

1964	1974	1982	1982
The Colombian military drops napalm on a guerrilla-held area, giving rise to the Fuerzas Armadas Revolucionarias de Colombia (FARC); the Ejército de Liberación Nacional (ELN) and M-19 follow.	The National Front ends, and newly elected president Alfonso López Michelsen launches the first major counterinsurgency against all three main guerrilla groups.	Gabriel García Márquez wins the Nobel Prize in Literature. In his acceptance speech he remarks that while Europeans value the continent's art, they have no respect for its political movements.	Pablo Escobar is elected to the Colombian Congress; President Belisario Betancur grants amnesty to guerrilla groups and frees hundreds of prisoners; Colombia drops out of the contest to hold the World Cup.

COLOMBIAN COFFEE

Colombia's coffee boom began in the early 20th century, and found its exclamation point when Juan Valdéz and his mule became the Colombian Coffee Federation's icon in 1959. (It was voted the world's top ad icon as recently as 2005.) In 2004 Valdéz opened more than 60 cafes in Colombia, the US and Spain – helping locals shift from a cup of weak coffee to espresso.

Despite competition from low-cost, lower-quality beans from Vietnam, Colombia's high-quality arabica-bean industry still employs around 570,000 and earned the country US$2.6 billion in 2011 as prices surged on short global supplies.

FARC

For accounts from FARC and paramilitary leaders, Steven Dudley's engaging *Walking Ghosts: Murder & Guerrilla Politics in Colombia* (2004) follows the rise and fall of FARC's Unión Patriótica party. Mario A Murillo's *Colombia & the United States: War, Unrest & Destabilization* (2004) is another left-leaning take.

began emerging, calling for land reform. Colombian politics hasn't been the same since. Much of what happened has been documented by international human rights groups such as Human Rights Watch.

New communist enclaves in the Sumapáz area, south of Bogotá, worried the Colombian government so much that its military bombed the area in May 1964. The attack led to the creation of the Fuerzas Armadas Revolucionarias de Colombia (FARC; Revolutionary Armed Forces of Colombia, led by Manuel Marulanda) and the more military-minded Jacobo Arenas. They vowed to overthrow the state and to redistribute land and wealth among the whole country, seizing it from Colombia's elites.

Other armed guerrilla groups included a fellow Marxist rival, the Ejército de Liberación Nacional (ELN; National Liberation Army), which built its popularity from a radical priest, Father Camilo Torres, who was killed in his first combat experience. The urban M-19 (Movimiento 19 de Abril, named for the contested 1970 presidential election) favored dramatic statements, such as the robbery of a Simón Bolívar sword and seizing the Palace of Justice in Bogotá in 1985. When the military's recapture of the court led to 115 deaths, the M-19 group gradually disintegrated.

FARC's fortunes continued to rise, though, particularly when President Belisario Betancur negotiated peace with the rebels in the 1980s. Wealthy landowners formed the AUC (Autodefensas Unidas de Colombia; United Self-Defense Forces of Colombia) or paramilitary groups, to defend their land in response to the FARC's advance. The roots of these groups – all generally offshoots of the military – began in the 1960s, but grew in the '80s.

Cocaine & Cartels

Colombia is the world's biggest supplier of cocaine, despite exhaustive efforts to track down cartel leaders, drop de-vegetation chemicals on coca farms, and step up military efforts. All for that little *erythroxylum coca*

1984	1990	1993	1995
Justice Minister Rodrigo Lara Bonilla is assassinated for supporting an extradition treaty with the US.	The M-19 demilitarizes; the cartels declare war on the government and the extradition treaty, and a government building near the Paloquemao market in Bogotá is destroyed by a bomb.	One-time Congress member – and a more famous cocaine warlord – Pablo Escobar is killed a day after his 44th birthday on a Medellín rooftop by Colombian police aided by the US.	The towns of San Agustín and Tierradentro in Colombia's southwest, with their many mysterious statues, carvings and burial tombs, are added to the Unesco World Heritage Sites list.

leaf – which you can buy in its unprocessed form in some Colombia markets. When the first Europeans arrived, they at first shook their heads over locals chewing coca leaves, but when (forced) work output started to decline, they allowed its usage. Eventually the Europeans (and the world) joined in, and in the centuries to follow, Andean cocaine eventually found its way worldwide for medicinal and recreational use.

The cocaine industry boomed in the early 1980s, when the Medellín Cartel, led by former car thief (and future politician) Pablo Escobar, became the principal mafia. Its bosses eventually founded their own political party, established two newspapers and financed massive public works and public housing projects. At one point, Escobar even stirred up secession sentiments for the Medellín region. By 1983 Escobar's personal wealth was estimated to be over US$20 billion, making him one of the world's richest people (number seven according to *Forbes* magazine).

When the government launched a campaign against the drug trade, cartel bosses disappeared from public life and even proposed an unusual 'peace treaty' to President Betancur. The *New York Times* reported in 1988 that the cartels had offered to invest their capital in national development programs and pay off Colombia's entire foreign debt (some US$13 billion). The government declined the offer, and the violence escalated.

The cartel-government conflict heated up in August 1989, when Liberal presidential candidate Luis Carlos Galán was gunned down by drug lords. The government's response was to confiscate nearly 1000 cartel-owned properties and sign a new extradition treaty with the US, which

Read personalized accounts of the poverty the displaced face in Alfred Molano's *The Dispossessed: Chronicles of the Desterrados of Colombia* (2005).

HISTORY COCAINE & CARTELS

THE DISPLACED

Caught in the crossfire between paramilitaries and guerrilla forces, and sometimes outright targets in what the UN says is a 'strategy of war,' one in 20 Colombians (about 4 million, says the Internal Displacement Monitoring Centre) have become internally displaced since the 1980s, making Colombia home to more displaced persons than any country except Sudan.

Hundreds of people become displaced daily, forced out of their homes at gunpoint – usually stolen for the land, livestock or its location on drug transportation routes – but sometimes not until after a loved one is murdered. Most of the dispossessed are left to fend for themselves, living in tarp-covered huts outside the main cities. Those who are able to obtain new land frequently find it in areas with no infrastructure, schools or hospitals. Often, displaced children fall into a world of drugs and crime.

But there has been some improvement of late with the introduction in 2011 of the Victims' Law, which aims to compensate and return land to those who had it stolen. Observers are monitoring its impact with interest.

KRZYSZTOF DYDYNSKI/LONELY PLANET IMAGES ©

2000
Colombia and the USA agree on the expansive Plan Colombia to cut coca cultivation by 2005; the US eventually spends over US$6 billion with no drop in cocaine production over its first decade.

2002
President Álvaro Uribe is elected on an uncompromising anti-FARC ticket; he launches an immediate and effective clampdown.

2004
Carlos 'El Pibe' Valderrama, the flamboyantly coiffured midfielder, is included in Pelé's FIFA 100 list of greatest living footballers chosen by the soccer legend to celebrate the 100th anniversary of FIFA.

» Statue, San Agustín (p 235)

led to a cartel-led campaign of terror resulting in bombed banks, homes and newspaper offices, and, in November 1989, the downing of an Avianca flight from Bogotá to Cali, which killed all 107 onboard.

After the 1990 election of Liberal César Gaviria as president, things calmed briefly, when extradition laws were sliced and Escobar led a surrender of many cartel bosses. However, Escobar soon escaped from his luxurious house arrest and it took an elite, US-funded 1500-strong special unit 499 days to track him down, shooting him dead atop a Medellín rooftop in 1993.

Amid the violence, the drug trade never slowed. New cartels have learned to forsake the limelight; by the mid-1990s, guerrillas and paramilitaries chipped in to help Colombia keep pace with the world's rising demand.

The War Heats Up

As communism collapsed around the globe, the political landscape for the guerrillas shifted increasingly to drugs and kidnapping (kidnapping alone, by one account, brought FARC some US$200 million annually), and paramilitary groups aligned themselves with drug cartels and pursued the guerrillas with the cartels' blessing.

After September 11, 'terrorism' became the new buzzword applied to guerrillas, and even some paramilitaries. One group that made the US list of international terrorists, and which notoriously had been paid US$1.7 million by the Chiquita fruit company, was the infamous AUC. The firm paid a $25 million dollar fine in US courts in 2007 for its repeated funding of the AUC.

Linked with cocaine since 1997, the AUC was inspired by paramilitary groups previously under the watch of the slain Medellín Cartel leader Rodríguez Gacha. The AUC was later run by brothers Fidel and Carlos Castaño, who set out to avenge their father, who was slain by guerrillas. The AUC, with a force of up to 10,000 troops, attacked *campesinos* (peasants) it alleged were guerrilla sympathizers. The guerrillas attacked any *campesinos* they said were AUC supporters.

When the Álvaro Uribe administration offered lenient sentences for paramilitaries or guerrillas who demobilized, AUC handed over their guns in 2006. But the violence is not over. In 2008 there was a rise in the number of deaths of union leaders, paramilitary groups formed under new names (such as the Black Eagles) and FARC continued its fight even while lacking popular support. By 2012, FARC had been driven to the jungles and hinterlands of Colombia.

Uribe's Reign

Fed up with violence, kidnappings and highways deemed too dangerous to use, the nation turned to right-wing hardliner Álvaro Uribe – a politi-

One of the best books on Colombia's history is David Bushnell's *The Making of Modern Colombia: A Nation in Spite of Itself* (1993), which follows colonization, partisan conflicts throughout independence, and the emergence of cocaine politics in the 1980s.

Killing Pablo: The Hunt for the World's Greatest Outlaw (2002), by Mark Bowden, is an in-depth exploration of the life and times of Pablo Escobar and the operation that brought him down. While the book has some reputed small inaccuracies, it is a thrilling crime read.

2006	2006	2006	2008
Uribe is swept to power once more as his 'Democratic Security' policy brings stability and prosperity for many.	Up to 20,000 AUC paramilitaries disarm in return for lenient sentences for their massacres and human rights abuses.	Shakira's 'Hips Don't Lie' breaks the 10-million mark in global sales and hits the number one spot in 25 countries – becoming the most successful song worldwide that year.	FARC is duped into handing over its highest-value hostage, French-Colombian presidential candidate, Ingrid Betancourt, to the Colombian army.

PLAN COLOMBIA

In 2000 the US entered the war against the drug cartels, with the controversial 'Plan Colombia,' concocted by the Bill Clinton and Andrés Pastrana administrations to curb coca cultivation by 50% within five years. As the decade closed, and with US$6 billion spent, even the normally rah-rah US International Trade Commission called the program's effectiveness 'small and mostly direct.' The worldwide street price for Colombian cocaine hadn't changed – indicating no lack of supply – and, after a few years of dipping coca cultivation, by 2007, a UN report concluded that cocaine production rose by 27% in 2007 alone, rebounding to its 1998 level.

Originally the money was supposedly to be split half-and-half between efforts to equip/train the Colombian military and developmental projects to offer *campesinos* (peasants) attractive alternatives to coca farming. It didn't turn out that way. Nearly 80% of the money ended up with the military (as well as helicopter-drop devegetation chemicals that infamously killed food crops, along with elusive coca crops). In 2007 a Pentagon official told *Rolling Stone* that Plan Colombia ended up being less about 'counternarcotics' than 'political stabilization,' in particular the ongoing fight with FARC.

Emerging in the first decade of the century, new harder-to-track *cartelitos* (smaller sized mafia groups) replaced the extinguished mega cartels (capped with the 2008 extradition to the US of Medellín narco-king Don Berna). The *cartelitos* relocated to harder-to-reach valleys (particularly near the Pacific coast). Many are linked to FARC, who tax coca farmers (earning FARC between US$200 to US$300 million annually, according to the *New York Times*); other *cartelitos*, however, are linked with paramilitary groups.

As a result, Colombia still supplies about 90% of the USA's cocaine – often getting it there overland via Mexican cartels.

In Barack Obama's 2011 budget proposal, Plan Colombia was not specifically mentioned. Colombia continued to receive military aid, albeit 20% less than the previous year, at US$228 million.

cian from Medellín who had studied at Oxford and Harvard, and whose father had been killed by FARC. Uribe ran on a full-on antiguerrilla ticket during the testy 2002 presidential election. While his predecessor Andrés Pastrana had tried negotiating with FARC and ELN, Uribe didn't bother, quickly unleashing two simultaneous programs: a military pushback of groups such as FARC, and a demobilization offer for both sides.

Even Uribe's harshest critics acknowledge much overdue progress was made under his watch. From 2002 to 2008, notably, murder rates fell 40% overall and highways cleared of FARC roadblocks became safe to use.

In March 2008, Uribe approved a tricky bombing mission across Ecuador's border, resulting in the successful killing of FARC leader Raúl Reyes. The bombing mission, however, nearly set the region into broader

The official site of the US Colombian embassy can be found at www. colombiaemb.org. It has good up-to-date information on the country.

2008	2009	2009	2010
The FARC announces that its founder, Manuel 'Sureshot' Marulanda dies, aged 78, of a heart attack in the jungle.	The country's secret service is accused by the public prosecutor of tapping the phones of thousands of journalists, politicians, activists and NGO workers, and using the information to harass and threaten them.	The UN calls false positives 'systemic,' and confirms thousands of cases, vindicating claims made for years by NGOs dubbed as terrorist sympathizers by the Uribe government.	Colombia receives 1.4 million foreign visitors, according to official statistics, shaking off its decades-long reputation as a danger zone as President Uribe's security measures hit home.

conflict, with Venezuelan president Hugo Chávez immediately moving tanks to the Colombian border, but things soon settled – and Uribe's approval levels hit 90%.

However, his presidency was ultimately tainted by scandal and by 2008, following his public feuds with the Colombian Supreme Court, 60 congressmen had been arrested or questioned for alleged 'parapolitics' links with paramilitaries.

The *falso positivos* (false positives) scandal, as documented by the UN in an in-depth 2010 report, showed how the Colombian military was incentivized to increase bodycount. From 2004, incidences of false positives - where army units killed innocent young men and claimed them as guerrillas killed in combat - soared. As the scandal grew, Uribe fired 27 officers in November 2008, and leading commander General Mario Montoya resigned.

During Uribe's presidency the Colombian army killed 3000 young, uneducated, innocent so-called 'false positive' *campesinos* in a strategy described by UN special rapporteur on extrajudicial executions, Phillip Alston, as 'systemic.'

FARC on the Defensive

After the constitutional court in 2010 refused to allow a referendum to allow Uribe to run for a third term, his defense minister Juan Manuel Santos was voted in on a landslide, and almost immediately claimed the single greatest victory ever won against the FARC: the killing of its new leader, Alfonso Cano.

Whether this will bring FARC to the negotiating table and heed the country's call for peace will become apparent in the next decade. But within days, a new, bellicose leader, Rodrigo Londoño Echeverri, alias Timochenko, on whose head the US has placed a US$5 million bounty, took control of the guerrilla organization.

'Peace in Colombia will not be born from any guerrilla demobilization, but from the abolition of the causes that give rise to the uprising,' said the FARC in a statement following Cano's death.

There's little overt, official censorship in Colombia. But journalists, fearful of being targeted by bipartisan violence in the nation's ongoing civil conflict, routinely self-censor, says monitoring group Reporters Without Borders. It ranked Columbia 145th out of 178 countries in the NGO's 2010 survey of press freedom.

The CIA World Factbook website (www.cia.gov) has a breakdown of Colombian government, economy and population issues to keep you in the know.

2010	2010	2011	2011
The Colombian Constitutional Court rules against a referendum that would have allowed President Uribe to run for a third term.	Juan Manuel Santos, former defense minister under Uribe and son of an influential family, is elected as president in a landslide victory.	Alfonso Canos, leader of the FARC and its chief ideologue, is killed in a bombing raid, raising hopes of an end to the conflict.	A US-Colombia free trade deal is agreed to by US congress after years of deliberation and delay over Democrats' concerns over human rights.

Life in Colombia

Colombians are some of the warmest, most genuinely friendly and un-cannily helpful people you'll encounter in South America. They handle life with good humor and a light-heartedness that is infectious. Many Colombians will prefer to shrug and crack a joke instead of grumble.

The country's geographical diversity – mountains and sea – has left discreet influences on the national psyche. Colombia is principally an Andean nation, and the majority live in the mountains in Bogotá, Medel-lín and Cali. The way of life here is industrious, and the Spanish is crisp and formal. The Caribbean coast has looked outwards to the Caribbean basin for centuries, and the pace of life is slower, and *costeños* (people from the coast) are more laid-back, and speak a heavier-accented, more drawling Spanish.

Lifestyle & Attitude

Wealthy urban Colombians live a very different life to their poorer counterparts. Their children go to private schools, they treat intercity planes like taxis and whizz through city streets updating their Face-book status on their smartphones. They play golf in country clubs at weekends, and, more than likely, they own a small private *finca* (farm) where they occasionally indulge their rural fantasies.

Poorer Colombians buy their phone calls by the minute in the street, wait in interminable intercity and urban traffic jams, and dream of send-ing their children to any school at all. Indigenous people, and those in isolated rural communities in areas where the civil conflict still grinds on, are often focused on ensuring they have enough food to survive.

Between these extremes, Colombia boasts one of the largest middle-class populations in Latin America, where many of its neighbors suffer great disparity in wealth. The country's free-market policies and rela-tively low level of corruption have helped the middle class to flourish.

All Colombians, though, are bound by strong family ties, not just to im-mediate blood relatives but also to their extended family, and childless visi-tors over 21 years of age will be quizzed endlessly on their plans to start a family. And though the dominant faith is Catholicism, very few attend Mass.

Women are the heart of a Colombian household. Machismo may be alive and well outside the home, where men are unquestionably in charge, but inside the Colombian home, women rule the roost. That's not the only place they rule. Women make up a significant number of the country's high-ranking politicians and diplomats, including cabinet ministers and ambassadors. In fact, a quota law passed in 2000 requires that at least 30% of appointed positions in the executive branch be filled by women.

Try not to get uptight if a Colombian is late – anything up to 45 min-utes – and don't take it personally; instead, perhaps go with the flow and enjoy a culture that truly believes that most things aren't worth rushing for! Bus timetables, in particular, are a laughable fiction.

Same-sex couples who have been living together for two years are recognized under Colombian law. In July 2011, the Colombian Congress ruled that if the Con-stitutional Court does not legislate on same-sex marriages by June 2013, they will be automati-cally granted all marriage rights.

NO ROAD? NO SEX!

Three hundred women in the town of Barbacoas in the Nariño department in the southwest of the country became so enraged at the decades-long delay in completing a 35km road linking the town with the outside world that they launched a sex strike in 2011.

The strike, known as the *huelga de piernas cruzadas* (cross-legged strike) came to an end in October 2011, after several long, hard months for the town's menfolk. Their demand for a road was driven by a desire to reach neighboring towns and markets more easily, and they felt that they had a better chance of success if their husbands, who have more power in this macho area, were sex-starved. Even the mayor of the town, whose wife moved to a separate room during the strike, offered to take a lie detector test to prove that he'd been unwillingly celibate when quizzed by journalists.

It's unclear whether the women were inspired by the ancient Greek play *Lysistrata* by Aristophenes, but their tactics were identical.

The road-building has begun, with a tentative completion date of 2013. Male Barbacoans are said to have their *fingers* tightly crossed.

Most Colombians don't use drugs, except perhaps students in major cities, though it's undeniable that many do love to drink – and how. The Carnaval de Barranquilla is a riot of licentiousness and rum-doused ribaldry.

People & Place: A Cultural Sancocho

The population is around 45 million, making it the third most populous country in Latin America after Brazil and Mexico. Each city has its unique cultural mix, making traveling here as satisfyingly varied as a rich *sancocho* (soup).

Many European immigrants populated Medellín, while much of the population of Cali is descended from former enslaved people. Bogotá and the surrounding areas saw much intermarriage between European colonists and indigenous people, while Cali and the Caribbean and Pacific coasts have a high proportion of African-Colombians.

Slavery was abolished in 1821, and the country has the largest black population in South America after Brazil. The last four centuries have seen plenty of intermarriage, meaning a great number of Colombians are mixed race.

The main areas where indigenous groups continue to live traditional lifestyles are in the southern mountains near Ecuador, the Sierra Nevada de Santa Marta, and the Amazon. In San Andrés you can also find indigenous Raizal people, whose culture has modernized with the advent of tourism.

Balls & Bulls

Colombians love soccer. The national league has 18 teams across the country, and attracts rowdy and boisterous crowds during the two seasons (February to June and August to December). The standard of play is often poor, making for comical, error-prone matches.

Animal-lovers will be disappointed to witness the popularity of bullfighting in Colombia, whether at formal events or at *correlejas*, the wild-side variant that sees amateurs pitting their addled wits against a charging *toro* with predictably gory consequences. The formal bullfighting season peaks during the holiday period between mid-December and mid-January, and attracts some of the world's best matadors. The January Feria de Manizales is of great appeal to aficionados. Cock-fighting is also wildly popular in rural areas.

After soccer, baseball is the second most popular team sport in Colombia. Cycling is also hugely popular, with Bogotá's Ciclovía (p50) each Sunday bringing in thousands of cyclists and skaters to the city's roads, many of which are closed for the day.

In 2011, Luis Moreno of football team Pereira outraged local animal-lovers when he killed Barranquilla team Junior's good-luck charm, an owl, by kicking it in the head after it landed on the pitch. 'I did it to see if the owl could fly,' he told local media. The bird later died. He later admitted he kicked the bird because he was frustrated with the match, and apologized for his avian outrage.

The Arts

Ask most people to name three famous Colombian artists, and you'll get Gabriel García Márquez, sculptor Fernando Botero, and Shakira. But Colombia's artists have a lot more to offer than magic realism, fat-bottomed statues and hip-swinging pop.

Music

Colombia is famous for its music, and silence is a very rare commodity, whether on the country's two coasts, in the highlands, in the capital, or on the vast plains that sweep towards Venezuela.

Vallenato, born a century ago on the Caribbean coast, is based on the German accordion. Carlos Vives, one of the best-known modern Latin musical artists, modernized the form and became a poster boy for the music. Vallenato's spiritual homeland is Valledupar (see Parque Lineal, p161). The style is not to everyone's taste, but if you leave Colombia without having danced to it a dozen times, you haven't really been here.

Cumbia, a lively 4/4 style with guitars, accordion, bass, drums and the occasional horn, is the most popular of the Colombian musical styles overseas. Groups such as Pernett and The Caribbean Ravers have modernized the sound, as have Bomba Estereo, who also spiked the party with a dose of acid rock. The funkiest group of recent years has been Choc Quib Town, a Pacific coast hip-hop band, who mix incisive social commentary with tough beats.

Salsa spread throughout the Caribbean and in the late 1960s it hit Colombia, where it's been adopted and made its own. Cali and Barranquilla are its heartland, but it's loved everywhere. The country went into mourning when Joe Arroyo, known locally as El Joe, died in 2011. The modern, tough urban salsa style is best typified by LA 33 of Bogotá.

Joropo, the music of Los Llanos, is accompanied by a harp, a *cuatro* (a type of four-string guitar) and maracas. It has much in common with the music of the Venezuelan Llanos. Chief proponents Grupo Cimarrón will dazzle you with their virtuosity and rapid footwork.

Colombia has also generated many unique rhythms from the fusion of Afro-Caribbean and Spanish influences, including *porro, currulao, merecumbe, mapalé* and *gaita*. The Cartagena-born sound of *champeta*, meanwhile, mixes African rhythms with a bumping, rough-cut, block-party attitude. Reggaeton, with its thumping bass-snare loops, is popular as well, along with the rhythmically driven and heavy on the downbeat merengue.

Colombian Andean music is strongly influenced by Spanish rhythms and instruments, and differs noticeably from the indigenous music of the Peruvian and Bolivian highlands. Among typical old genres are the *bambuco, pasillo* and *torbellino*, instrumental styles featuring predominantly string instruments.

In the cities, especially Bogotá and Medellín, many clubs play techno and house; big-name international DJs sometimes play both cities.

Bogotá is Colombia's cultural capital. For a taste of what's on, check out www.culturarec reacionydeporte. gov.co.

Colombian Literature

Colombia's long (if modest) literary tradition began to form shortly after independence from Spain in 1819 and gravitated towards European romanticism. Rafael Pombo (1833–1912) is generally acclaimed as the father of Colombian romantic poetry and Jorge Isaacs (1837–95), another notable author of the period, is particularly remembered for his romantic novel *María,* which can still be spotted in cafes and classrooms around the country.

José Asunción Silva (1865–96), one of Colombia's most remarkable poets, is considered the precursor of modernism in Latin America. He planted the seeds that were later developed by Nicaraguan poet Rubén Darío. Another literary talent, Porfirio Barba Jacob (1883–1942), known as 'the poet of death,' introduced the ideas of irrationalism and the language of the avant-garde.

Talented contemporaries of literary Nobel Laureate García Márquez (see below) include poet, novelist and painter Héctor Rojas Herazo, and Álvaro Mutis, a close friend. Of the younger generation, seek out the works of Fernando Vallejo, a highly respected iconoclast who has claimed in interviews that García Márquez lacks originality and is a poor writer. Popular young expat Santiago Gamboa has written travel books and novels; Mario Mendoza writes gritty, modern urban fiction; and Laura Restrepo focuses on how violence affects the individual and society. They are prolific writers who have each cranked out major works in recent years.

Telenovelas (soap operas) are Colombia's cultural barometer. Although they aren't high art, they reflect the country's concerns and passions as faithfully as any documentary. A popular show in 2011 was Chepe Fortuna (Fishing For Fortune), a gloriously improbable tale of love, politics, environmentalism and, er, mermaids.

Art & Abstraction

Fernando Botero is to Colombian painting what García Márquéz is to the country's literature – the heavyweight name that overshadows all others. Two other famous Colombian painters, often overlooked, are Omar Rayo

GABRIEL GARCÍA MÁRQUEZ, COLOMBIA'S NOBEL LAUREATE

Gabriel García Márquez is the titan of Colombian literature. Born in 1928 in Aracataca (p146) in the department of Magdalena, he has written primarily about Colombia, but lived most of his life in Mexico and Europe.

García Márquez began as a journalist in the 1950s and worked as a foreign correspondent, from where he criticized the Colombian government and forced himself into exile. His breakthrough came in 1967, with *One Hundred Years of Solitude*. It mixed myths, dreams and reality, and single-handedly invented the magic realism genre.

In 1982 García Márquez won the Nobel Prize in Literature. Since then, he has created a wealth of fascinating work. *Love in the Time of Cholera* (1985) is a story based loosely on the courtship of his parents. *The General in his Labyrinth* (1989) recounts the tragic final months of Simón Bolívar's life. *Strange Pilgrims* (1992) is a collection of 12 stories written by the author over the previous 18 years. *Of Love and Other Demons* (1994) is the story of a young girl raised by her parents' slaves, set amid the backdrop of Cartagena's inquisition. In 1996 García Márquez returned to his journalistic roots with the literary nonfiction novel *News of a Kidnapping*. The book relates a series of kidnappings ordered by Medellín Cartel boss, Pablo Escobar.

García Márquez seemed to be tying up his career when he published the first volume of his memoirs, *Living to Tell the Tale*, in 2002, but came back in 2004, aged 76, with yet another novel, *Memories of My Melancholy Whores*, the story of a dying old man who falls in love with an adolescent girl who sells her virginity to support her family.

In May 2008 he announced that he had finished a new 'novel of love.' Then in 2009, his agent announced the author's retirement. However, in 2010 his editor confirmed the title of his final novel, *En Agosto Nos Vemos* (*We'll Meet In August*) but did not announce a publication date.

FERNANDO BOTERO: LARGER THAN LIFE

Fernando Botero (b 1932) is the most widely recognized Colombian painter and sculptor. Born in Medellín, he had his first individual painting exhibition in Bogotá at the age of 19 and gradually developed his easily recognizable style – characterized by his figures' massive, almost obscene curvaceousness. In 1972 he settled in Paris and began experimenting with sculpture, which resulted in a collection of *gordas* and *gordos* (fat women and men), as Colombians call these creations.

Today, his paintings hang on the walls of world-class museums and his monumental public sculptures adorn squares and parks in cities around the globe, including Paris, Madrid, Lisbon, Florence and New York.

Moving from his typically safe subject matter in 2004, he shocked Colombia with a collection of works examining the country's civil war; and in 2005, he produced a controversial series of images that split critical opinion, featuring scenes from Iraq's Abu Ghraib prison, where US forces tortured and humiliated detainees. While some lauded Botero's move into more political matters, others regarded it as too little, too late, and still others thought this out-of-character development was inappropriate.

(1928–2010), known for his geometric drawings, and Alejandro Obregón (1920–1992), a Cartagena painter famous for his abstract paintings.

Colombia is also home to a good deal of colonial religious art. Gregorio Vásquez de Arce y Ceballos (1638–1711) was the most remarkable painter of the colonial era. He lived and worked in Bogotá and left behind a collection of more than 500 works, now distributed among churches and museums across the country.

Since the end of WWII, the most distinguished painters are Pedro Nel Gómez, known for his murals, watercolors, oils and sculptures; Luis Alberto Acuña, a painter and sculptor who used motifs from pre-Columbian art; Guillermo Wiedemann, a German painter who spent most of his creative period in Colombia and drew inspiration from local themes, though he later turned to abstract art; Edgar Negret, an abstract sculptor; Eduardo Ramírez Villamizar, who expressed himself mostly in geometric forms; and Rodrigo Arenas Betancur, Colombia's most famous monument-maker.

These masters were followed by a slightly younger generation, born mainly in the 1930s, including artists such as Armando Villegas, a Peruvian living in Colombia, whose influences ranged from pre-Columbian motifs to surrealism; Leonel Góngora, noted for his erotic drawings; and the most internationally renowned Colombian artist, Fernando Botero (see above).

The recent period has been characterized by a proliferation of schools, trends and techniques. Artists to watch out for include Bernardo Salcedo (conceptual sculpture and photography), Miguel Ángel Rojas (painting and installations), Lorenzo Jaramillo (expressionist painting), María de la Paz Jaramillo (painting), María Fernanda Cardozo (installations), Catalina Mejía (abstract painting) and the talented Doris Salcedo (sculpture and installations).

THEATER

The Bogotá Festival Ibero-americano de Teatro, the world's largest such event, was set up in 1976 by Colombia's most influential actress, Fanny Mikey (1930–2008). In 2012, 65 international companies performed. See www.festival deteatro.com.co for more.

The Natural World

From snowcapped, craggy Andean mountains and the vast plains of Los Llanos, to the lush tropical forests of the Amazon basin and rolling green valleys, Colombia is a mind-blowingly beautiful and varied country. And despite its modest size, Colombia is the second most biodiverse country on earth, after Brazil.

The Land

Colombia covers 1,141,748 sq km, roughly equivalent to the combined area of California and Texas (or France, Spain and Portugal). It is the 26th-largest country in the world, and the fourth-largest in South America, after Brazil, Argentina and Peru.

While most people assume that Colombia is just a tropical land, the country's physical geography is amazingly varied. The country's environment is generally divided into five habitat categories: wet tropical forests, dry tropical forests, tropical grasslands, mountain grasslands, and deserts and scrublands.

The western part, almost half of the total territory, is mountainous, with three Andean chains – Cordillera Occidental, Cordillera Central and Cordillera Oriental – running roughly parallel north–south across most of the country. A number of the peaks are over 5000m, making them higher than anything in the USA. Two valleys, the Valle del Cauca and Valle del Magdalena, are sandwiched between the three cordilleras. Both valleys have their own eponymous rivers, which flow north, unite and eventually empty into the Caribbean near Barranquilla.

Apart from the three Andean chains, Colombia features an independent and relatively small range, the Sierra Nevada de Santa Marta, which rises from the Caribbean coastline to soaring, snowcapped peaks. It is the world's highest coastal mountain range, and its twin summits of Simón Bolívar and Cristóbal Colón (both 5775m) are the country's highest.

More than half of the territory east of the Andes is vast lowland, which is generally divided into two regions: Los Llanos to the north and the Amazon River basin to the south. Los Llanos, roughly 250,000 sq km in area, is a huge open swath of grassland that constitutes the Orinoco River basin. Colombians say it is like an internal, green sea. The Amazon, stretching over some 400,000 sq km, occupies Colombia's entire southeast and lies in the Amazon basin. Most of this land is covered by a thick rainforest crisscrossed by rivers.

Colombia also has a number of islands. The major ones are the archipelago of San Andrés and Providencia (in the Caribbean Sea, 750km northwest of mainland Colombia), the Islas del Rosario and San Bernardo (near the Caribbean coast), and Gorgona and Malpelo (along the Pacific coast).

Gaviotas: A Village to Reinvent the World (1998), by Alan Weisman, tells the story of Colombian villagers who transformed their barren hamlet in Los Llanos into a global model for a sustainable community.

Colombia is the only South American nation to have coastlines on both the Pacific Ocean and Caribbean Sea.

Wildlife

This huge variety of climatic and geographic zones and microclimates has spawned diverse ecosystems and allowed wildlife to evolve independently. And how. Colombia claims to have more plant and animal species per square kilometer than any other country in the world. Its variety of flora and fauna is second only to Brazil's, even though Colombia is seven times smaller than its neighbor.

Animals

From pink dolphins to colorful parrots, tiny cats to giant rats, Colombia has some of the most diverse animal life on the planet. It has nearly 1700 recorded species of birds – 74 of which are native to the country – representing about 19% of all the birds on the planet. Colombia also has about 450 species of mammal (including 15% of the world's primates), 600 species of amphibian, 500 species of reptile and 3200 species of fish.

Some of the most interesting mammals include sleek cats such as the jaguar and the ocelot, red howler monkeys, spider monkeys, the three-toed sloth, giant anteaters, the goofy piglike peccary and tapir, and the hideous-looking capybara, or *chiguiro,* the world's largest living rodent that can grow to 48cm tall and weigh 55kg.

The waters of Colombia's Amazon are home to the famous rose-colored *boto* (Amazon River dolphin), the Amazonian manatee, and one of the most feared snakes, the anaconda *(Eunectes murinus)* that can grow to 6m (20ft).

Colombia's famous aviary includes 132 species of hummingbirds, 24 species of toucans, 57 types of colorful parrots and macaws, plus kingfishers, trogons, warblers and six of the world's seven vultures, including the Andean Condor – a national symbol of Colombia.

There is also abundant marine life in the country's extensive river systems and along its two coastlines. The islands of San Andrés and Providencia boast some of the largest and most productive coral reefs in the Americas. In 2000 Unesco declared this area the Seaflower Biosphere Reserve in order to protect the ecosystem. The reefs are considered among the most intact in the Caribbean and play an important ecological role in the health of the sea. They provide feeding and nesting grounds for four species of endangered sea turtles and numerous types of fish and lobster. It has been determined that the health of certain fish stocks in the Florida Keys hinges directly on their ability to spawn in the Colombian reefs.

The famous German geographer and botanist Alexander von Humboldt explored and studied regions of Colombia and described it all in *Personal Narrative of Travels to the Equinoctial Regions of America, During the Year 1799-1804.*

Bird-watching enthusiasts should pick up *A Guide to the Birds of Colombia* (1986) by Stephen L Hilty and William L Brown. Two great online resources for bird-watchers are www.colombiabirding.com and www.proaves.org.

THE NATURAL WORLD WILDLIFE

IT'S RAINING, IT'S POURING...

Macondo, the fictional town in Gabriel García Márquez' *One Hundred Years of Solitude*, is destroyed by a deluge lasting almost five years. In 2010 and 2011, Colombians – especially those in the northern areas – must have felt like residents of Macondo, as the country experienced rain levels six times higher than ever recorded. President Juan Manuel Santos called it the worst natural disaster in the country's history, with 3 million people affected, 422 dead, and US$5.1 billion of damage.

The impact of this on Colombians has been devastating, with more than 10,000 sq km of land inundated. Mudslides and road collapses left many areas isolated for months, though floodwaters are now receding. Climate change, the seasonal La Niña phenomenon, and environmental destruction by loggers, cattle breeders and mining companies have all been blamed for the devastation. Simple trips that should take an hour often spiraled into 12-hour-long epic journeys during research for this book. While forecasters hope the worst is over, it's best to avoid the rainy season and travel in December and March or in July and August if you're on a tight schedule.

Endangered Species

The vast savannah of Los Llanos is home to some of the most endangered species in Colombia. Among them is the Orinoco crocodile, which can reach 7m in length. According to the Nature Conservancy, only 1800 of these crocs remain in the wild, making it one of the most critically endangered reptiles in the world. Other endangered creatures from Los Llanos include the Orinoco turtle, giant armadillo, giant otter and black-and-chestnut eagle.

The cottontop tamarin, a tiny monkey weighing just 500g, and its larger cousin, the brown spider monkey, are two of the most critically endangered primates in the world, according to the 2008 International Union for Conservation of Nature (IUCN) Red List of Threatened Species. Other critically endangered or endangered animals on the IUCN list include Handley's slender mouse opossum, mountain grackle and the mountain tapir. And two of the Amazon River's most famous residents, the pink river dolphin and the Amazonian manatee, are considered vulnerable.

Note that some remote restaurants and bars offer turtle eggs, iguanas and other endangered species on their menus. It's also worth noting that the *pirarucú* (a fish popular in the Amazon Basin region around Leticia) has been subject to overfishing; locals routinely ignore regulations preventing fishing for this species when it's spawning. These animals are endangered and eating them may hasten their extinction.

Colombia is the world's second-largest exporter of cut flowers, after the Netherlands. About US$1 billion worth of flowers are exported every year, mostly to the US. Americans buy 300 million Colombian roses on Valentine's Day. But the country cultivates more than 1500 different varieties of flower.

Plants

Colombia's flora is equally as impressive as its fauna and includes more than 130,000 types of plant, a third of which are endemic species. This richness does not convey the whole picture: large areas of the country, such as the inaccessible parts of the Amazon, have undiscovered species. It is estimated that, at a minimum, 2000 plant species have yet to be identified and an even greater number have yet to be analyzed for potential medicinal purposes.

GREEN FEVER

Colombia produces the largest percentage of the world's emeralds (50%; compared to Zambia's 20% and Brazil's 15%). Some estimate that the mines inside Colombia may actually contain up to 90% of the world's emerald deposits. This is good news for emerald prospectors but may not bode so well for the local environment – and perhaps Colombia as a whole. The fighting and destruction related to the production of these glamorous gems has had an impact on the country not so different from cocaine and heroin.

The main emerald-mining areas in Colombia include Muzo, Coscuez, La Pita and Chivor, all in the Boyacá department. Although the Muisca people mined emeralds in pre-Columbian times, the Spanish colonialists went crazy for the shiny green stones and greatly expanded the operations. They enslaved the indigenous locals to mine the gems and eventually replaced those workers with slave labor from Africa. Many of today's miners are the direct descendants of those slaves and live in only slightly better conditions.

The rich deposits in these areas have led to several environmental and social problems. Rampant digging has torn up the countryside and, in an attempt to find new digging sites or to improve their squalid living conditions, miners have continuously pushed further into the forest. Fierce battles have repeatedly been fought between rival gangs of miners, claiming lives and ravaging the mines. Between 1984 and 1990 alone, in one of the bloodiest 'emerald wars' in recent history, 3500 people were killed in Muzo. Yet 'green fever' continues to burn among fortune hunters and adventurers from all corners of the country and it may not stop until the last bewitching green gem is mined.

Colombia has some 3500 species of orchids, more than any other country. Many of them are unique to the country, including *Cattleya trianae*, the national flower of Colombia. Orchids grow in virtually all regions and climate zones of the country, but are mostly found in altitudes between 1000m and 2000m, particularly in the northwest department of Antioquia.

Further up into the clouds you will find the *frailejón*, a unique, yellow-flowering, perennial shrub that only grows at altitudes above 3000m. There are some 88 species of *frailejón*, most native to Colombia. You'll find them in protected places like Sierra Nevada de Santa Marta, Sierra Nevada del Cocuy and Santuario de Iguaque.

National Parks

Colombia has 55 national parks, flora and fauna sanctuaries and other natural reserve areas, all administered by the government's **Parques Nacionales Naturales (PNN) de Colombia** (www.parquesnacionales. gov.co).

Unfortunately, simply declaring an area a national park has not stopped guerrilla activity, drug cultivation, illegal ranching, logging, mining or poaching. Most parks in the Amazon Basin (except Amacayacu) and along the Ecuadorian border should also be considered off-limits. Other parks, such as Los Katios, a Unesco World Heritage Site near Darién Gap, are open but remain dodgy and access is limited; check the current security situation before proceeding.

On the bright side, many parks that were off-limits just a few years ago are now open for tourists and are included in this book. With the recent growth in tourism and ecotourism, the government is finally pumping pesos into its long-underfunded national parks system. New parks have recently opened and more are in the planning stages. Established parks are finally getting much-needed visitor amenities such as lodging and dining facilities, a rarity in Colombia.

This has not been without controversy. PNN has begun contracting with private companies to develop and operate tourist facilities inside some national parks, a move that some environmentalists fear will lead to overdevelopment. Some fear that prices will also increase and make the parks inaccessible to average Colombians. However, environmentalists have had some success checking such development. In 2011, plans for a gaudy seven-star hotel complex in Parque Nacional Natural (PNN) Tayrona were abandoned after pressure from environmental groups.

Colombia's most popular parks are situated along the country's pristine beaches. PNN Tayrona is by far Colombia's most popular national park, followed by Parque Nacional Natural (PNN) Corales del Rosario y San Bernardo and Parque Nacional Natural (PNN) Isla Gorgona.

Many other national parks offer just simple accommodations including basic cabins, dorms or camping. Travelers wishing to stay overnight must book ahead with the PNN central office in Bogotá (p69). There are also PNN regional offices in most large cities and at the parks. Most parks have an admission fee, payable at the entry or at a regional PNN office.

It is always a good idea to check ahead of time with tour agencies and the parks department for up-to-date security and weather conditions of any park before visiting.

Private Parks & Reserves

In recent years the number of privately owned and operated nature reserves has increased. These are run by individual proprietors, rural communities, foundations and nongovernmental organizations. Many are just small, family reserves, sometimes offering accommodations and food.

Conservación Internacional is one of Colombia's most influential environmental advocacy groups. To learn more about its positive work, check out http://conservation.org.co.

About 230 of these private parks are affiliated with the **Asociación Red Colombiana de Reservas Naturales de la Sociedad Civil** (http://res natur.org.co).

Yet another new player in the park scene is the corporation. Future parks might look a lot more like the new **Parque Nacional del Chicamocha** (www.parquenacionaldelchicamocha.com), near Bucaramanga. This for-profit, corporate-run resort opened in December 2006, at a reported cost of US$20 million. In addition to hiking and trekking opportunities, this commercial theme park features dozens of restaurants, cafes, thrill-rides, a zoo, cable cars and, coming soon, a luxury hotel complex.

Environmental Issues

Many challenges remain, not least of which are the problems of climate change, habitat loss, and a loss of biodiversity through giant agribusiness mega-plantations. The rapid push to develop a market-based economy and compete globally has put pressure on Colombia to build on its land and exploit its natural resources; these include farming, legal and illegal logging, and mining (see also Green Fever, p296) and oil exploration. Such deforestation has increased the rate of extinction for many plant and animal species and destabilized soils, leading to the silting of rivers and devastation of marine species.

Colombia is the world's third-largest exporter of coffee (after Brazil and Vietnam). In 2010, 8 million 60kg bags reaped the country $2.8 billion – but the relentless rains of 2011 hit the 2012 production hard.

Even more troubling is the environmental impact of the illegal drug trade (see the boxed text, p302). Other illegal cash crops include marijuana and opium poppies. Attempts to stop farmers cultivating coca simply cause the producers to relocate. They move higher up the slopes and to the more remote, virgin forests of the Andes (aided by an increase in opium cultivation, which favors higher altitudes) and deeper into parks and the Amazon basin. In addition, anti-drug efforts by the Colombian government (and, in large part, funded by the US war on drugs) have also taken some toll: the most common method of eradication has been aerial fumigation of coca fields; these hazardous herbicides destroy not just the coca plants, but surrounding vegetation as well, and no doubt seep into the watershed.

However, environmentalists now wield more clout in government policy. In 2006 President Álvaro Uribe signed the controversial General Forestry Law that opened up the country's forests to logging. Colombian and international environmental groups sued the government – and won. The Colombia Constitutional Court in 2009 ruled that the Forestry Law was unconstitutional because indigenous communities were never consulted. Score one for the greens.

Survival Guide

Safe Travel

Meet the Comeback Kid. Few countries in Latin America or elsewhere have done more to turn around their own image than Colombia, which spent most of the 1980s and '90s as a woefully feared tourism black hole as an intertwined civil military conflict and international drug war wreaked havoc on daily life. But ex-president Álvaro Uribe cracked down hard on violence during his two terms in office, helping Colombia to suddenly find itself an off-the-beaten-path paradise for those in the know. Today, most travelers will find Colombia safer on average than all of the country's immediate neighbors – an astonishing turnaround. Problems remain, however. Street crime remains an issue, and is on the rise in Bogotá, so vigilance and common sense are always required; and guerrillas, paramilitaries and narco-traffickers still linger in many Colombian departments (though they are being pushed further into hiding all the time). Keep your wits about you, avoid travel to dodgy parts of town (and far-flung countryside), and Colombia should offer you nothing but a good time.

Safe & Unsafe Areas

All the areas covered in this guide have been vetted for security issues and providing you do not wander astray from what's included, you aren't likely to run into any problems. If you're curious about an area/region that has been omitted, it's likely due to security issues.

The Fuerzas Armadas Revolucionarias de Colombia (FARC) and/or paramilitaries maintain a presence in the Chocó, Cauca, parts of Nariño, Putumayo, Meta, the jungle area east of the Andes (except for the area around Leticia) and parts of the northeast, (especially Arauca) so avoid these areas where not covered in this guide.

Guerrilla & Paramilitary Activity

There are still isolated pockets of guerrilla activity in remote parts of Colombia, particularly the high mountains and the deep jungle. Going off the beaten track should be done with great caution, if at all. Your worst-case scenario is kidnapping, for financial or political ends. If you run into a situation where you are unsure if the troops you are about to encounter are legit Colombian army or rebels, look at their boots. The guerrillas and paramilitaries will not have military-issued combat boots, but rather rubber galoshes or some version thereof.

Theft & Robbery

Theft is the most common travelers' danger. In general, the problem is more serious in the largest cities. The most common methods of theft are snatching your day pack, cell phone (mobile) or camera, pickpocketing, or taking advantage of a moment's inattention to pick up your gear and run away.

Distraction can often be part of the thieves' strategy. Thieves tend to work in pairs or groups, often on motorcycles; one or more will distract you while an accomplice does the deed. They may begin by making friends with you, or pretend to be the police and demand to check your possessions. Inside banks, pay special attention when withdrawing money from ATMs and be wary of criminals posing as bank employees and offering help – a common robbery tactic.

If you can, leave your money and valuables somewhere safe before walking the streets. In practice, it's good to carry a decoy bundle of small notes, maximum COP$50,000 to COP$100,000, ready to hand over in case of an assault; if you really don't have a peso, robbers can become frustrated and, as a consequence, unpredictable.

Armed hold-ups in the cities can occur even in some more upmarket suburbs. If you are accosted by robbers, it is best to give them what they are after, but try to play it cool and don't rush to hand them all your valuables at once – they may well be satisfied with just your decoy wad. Don't try to escape or struggle – your chances are slim, and people have been murdered for pocket change. Don't count on any help from passersby.

Drugs

Cocaine and marijuana are cheap and widely available in Colombia's major cities. Purchasing and consuming drugs, however, is not a good idea. Most Colombians find Colombian drug tourism very offensive, especially in smaller towns. It's important to note the majority of Colombians don't consume drugs and many believe the foreign drug trade is responsible for the ongoing civil war. So, asking after drugs, or openly using drugs, could land you in a lot of trouble (note, it's illegal to buy, sell or consume drugs in any quantity – see Legal Matters, p307).

Sometimes you may be offered drugs on the street, in a bar or at a disco, but never accept these offers. The vendors may well be setting you up for the police, or their accomplices will follow you and stop you later, show you false police documents and

threaten you with jail unless you pay them off. Never travel with drugs (strip searches are not uncommon). Some police aren't interested in busting you, but have been known to shake folks down for a bribe.

There have been reports of drugs being planted on travelers, so keep your eyes open. Always refuse if a stranger at an airport asks you to take their luggage on board as part of your luggage allowance. Needless to say, smuggling dope across borders is a crazy idea. Have you ever seen the inside of a Colombian prison?

Spiked Drinks

Burundanga is a drug obtained from a species of tree widespread in Colombia and is used by thieves to render a victim unconscious. It can be put into sweets, cigarettes, chewing gum, spirits, beer – virtually any kind of food or drink – and it doesn't have any noticeable taste or odor.

The main effect after a 'normal' dose is the loss of will, even though you remain conscious. The thief can then ask you to hand over your valuables and you will obey without resistance. Cases of rape under the effect of burundanga are known. Other effects are loss of memory and sleepiness, which can last from a few hours to several days. An overdose can be fatal.

GOVERNMENT TRAVEL ADVICE

Government websites with useful travel advisories:

» **Australian Department of Foreign Affairs** (300 555 135; www.smarttraveller.gov.au)

» **British Foreign Office** (0845 850 2829; www.fco.gov.uk)

» **Canadian Department of Foreign Affairs** (800 267 6788; www.dfait-maeci.gc.ca)

» **US State Department** (888 407 4747; http://travel.state.gov)

Interacting with the Police & Military

While the Colombian military is highly trustworthy and the federal police have a reputation as untouchables, local cops have more of a mixed reputation. They don't get paid a lot of money, and incidents of bribery and bullying of tourists have been reported.

Always carry a photocopy of your passport with you, including your entry stamp (you're more likely to avoid trouble if you keep your papers in order), and never carry drugs of any kind, either on the street or when traveling.

In tourist areas, there are an increasing number of tourist police; many speak some English. They are uniformed and easily recognizable by the Policía de Turismo labels on their arm bands. At the first hint of trouble, go to them first if you can.

If your passport, valuables or other belongings

PRACTICAL TIPS

» Avoid wandering off the grid, especially without checking the security situation on the ground

» Avoid ATM use at night

» Carry a quickly accessible, rolled bundle of small notes in case of robbery

» Avoid drug tourism

» Be very wary of drinks or cigarettes offered by strangers or new 'friends'

» Beware of criminals masquerading as plainclothes police

» Think twice about night buses between Popayán–Pasto (and on to Ecuador) and Bucaramanga–Santa Marta

COCAINE HOLIDAY? CONSIDER THE CONSEQUENCES

Drug tourism is an unfortunate reality in Colombia. And why not? Cocaine is cheap, right? *Not exactly.*

What may appear a harmless diversion directly contributes to the violence and mayhem that play out in the Colombian countryside every day. People fight and die for control of the cocaine trade. Purchasing and consuming cocaine helps finance that conflict. It's estimated that FARC alone collects between US$200 and US$300 million per year from cocaine production.

Worse still, the byproducts from the production of cocaine are extremely damaging to the environment. The production process requires toxic chemicals such as kerosene, sulfuric acid, acetone and carbide, which are simply dumped afterward on the ground or into streams and rivers. Further, it's estimated that between 500 and 3000 sq km of virgin rainforest are cut down every year for coca production.

Colombia is one of the most beautiful countries in the world. The people, the music, the dancing, the food – there is already enough stimulation to overwhelm the senses. It is best enjoyed with an ice-cold *cerveza michelada* (beer with rock salt and lime juice), not with cocaine.

are stolen, go to the police station and make a *denuncia* (report). The officer on duty will write a statement according to what you tell them. It should include the description of the events and the list of stolen articles. Pay attention to the wording you use, include every stolen item and document, and carefully check the statement before signing it. Your copy of the statement serves as a temporary identity document and you'll need to present it to your insurer to make a claim.

If you happen to get involved with the police, keep calm and be polite, and always use the formal '*usted*' (the word for 'you,' instead of '*tu*'). Keep a sharp eye out when they check your gear.

Scams

Under no circumstances should you agree to a search by plainclothes police officers asking to inspect your passport and money. Criminals masquerading as plainclothes police may stop you on the street, identify themselves with a fake ID, and then ask to inspect your passport and money. A common scam finds these 'officers' claiming your money is counterfeit, preceded by, of course, its confiscation (a variation on this scam involves jewelry as well). Legitimate Colombian police will never make such a request. Call out for uniformed police officers or decent-looking passersby to witness the incident, and insist on phoning a bona fide police station. By that time, the 'officers' will probably have discreetly walked away.

Overland Travel

Traveling overland in most parts of Colombia, especially during the day, should present no issues other than which iPod playlist you choose to drown out the bus driver's loud and questionable musical taste. In the past, taking night buses was not a good idea – FARC used to control many of the major highways – but this is no longer the case. Night buses to most destinations are a comfortable way to avoid wasting a day in transit, plus you save the cost of a night's accommodation.

The only major routes on which you should avoid night travel are the road from Popayán to Pasto and the border with Ecuador; and to a lesser extent (though still troublesome) the route from Bucaramanga to Santa Marta. There is no longer guerrilla activity, but attacks and armed thieves stopping buses and robbing everyone on board have been reported.

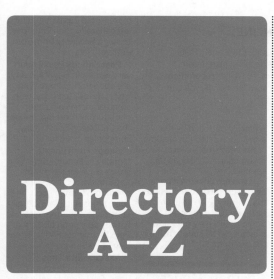

Directory A–Z

Accommodations

There are three main kinds of accommodations in Colombia: backpacker hostels, budget hotels (frequented by Colombians) and top-end hotels. The few midrange hotels on offer tend to cater to Colombian business travelers.

Technically, foreigners are exempt from the 10% IVA tax, but there seems to be universal confusion as to how that law is applied. For all intents and purposes, the posted price will be the price you pay, as the IVA is usually built into the posted price already, and only travelers who have booked and paid for a top-end hotel from abroad really have a shot at not paying IVA – even then the tax will have already been deducted from the posted price.

Camping

For ages camping was out of bounds in Colombia. While the civil conflict continues to rage in remote regions of the country, more and more Colombians are strapping on a pack and getting reacquainted with their beautiful country. In many cases sleeping in a tent is considered a novelty, and many campgrounds charge more to pitch a tent than you would spend for a night in a hotel.

Hostels

Backpacker tourism is booming in Colombia, and new hostels are opening every month. All have dorm beds for around COP$15,000 to COP$30,000, and most have a few private rooms for COP$35,000 to COP$80,000.

Many of the most established hostels are members of the **Colombian Hostels Association** (www.colombian hostels.com). The most comprehensive listing of hostels is at www.hosteltrail.com.

PRACTICALITIES

» Colombians use the metric system for weights and measures, except for petrol, which is measured in US gallons. Food is often sold in *libras* (pounds), which is equivalent to 500g.

» All major cities have daily newspapers. Bogotá's leading newspaper, *El Tiempo* (www.eltiempo.com), has reasonable coverage of national and international news, culture, sports and economics. The leading newspapers in other large cities include *El Espectador* (www.elespectador.com) and *El Colombiano* (www.elcolombiano.com) in Medellín, and *El País* (www.elpais.com.co) and *El Occidente* (www.occidente.co) in Cali. *Semana* (www.semana.com) is the biggest national weekly magazine. Another major weekly, *Cambio* (www.cambio.com.co), is an important opinion-forming magazine.

» Colombia has plenty of national and local TV stations. Each region has its own TV station; Bogotá TV is dominated by **City TV** (www.citytv.com.co). Nationwide channels include **Caracol TV** (www.canalcaracol.com.co) and **RCN TV** (www.canalrcn.com), **Noticias Uno** (www.noticiasuno.com) and **Señal Colombia** (www.senalcolombia.tv).

» Radio stations are likewise plentiful. Try Radionica (99.1) for alternative/modern rock, Universidad Nacional's UN Radio (98.5 FM) for college radio/cultural, and La Zeta (92.9) for Latin/salsa.

» Anti-tobacco laws, passed in 2009, prevent smoking in enclosed spaces, including bars and restaurants. You can even sue a roommate for smoking indoors!

Hotels

Also sometimes called *residencias, hospedajes* or posadas, a hotel generally suggests a place of a higher standard, or at least a higher price. Cheaper accommodations are usually clustered around markets, bus terminals and in the backstreets of the city center. If you speak Spanish and wish to avoid the gringo trail, a budget private room with hot water, air-con and cable TV goes between COP$20,000 and COP$25,000 - cheaper than a hostel.

Midrange hotels are rare in Colombia. Prices tend to jump rapidly from budget cheapies to three- and four-star hotels, with little in between. Nevertheless, there are often a handful of hotels in the COP$65,000 to COP$160,000 range, usually in the city center, which cater primarily to Colombian business travelers.

All the major cities have top-end hotels charging COP$160,000 to COP$1,000,000 per night. Prices vary greatly and don't always reflect quality. The best choice of top-end hotels is in Bogotá, Medellín and Cartagena.

Resorts

There are a handful of package-style resorts on the Caribbean coast and on San Andrés. Most are frequented by Colombians, rather than foreign package tourists, and are usually excellent value. The Pacific coast also has several good all-inclusives, but they are definitely for the more adventurous type as the area is quite remote and

is heavily patrolled by the army. For a selection of some of the best small resorts, see www.posadasturisticasdecolombia.com.

If you are booking a package resort deal from outside the country, you are exempt from the 10% IVA hotel tax. Some hotels may not know this rule, so be sure to ask for the discount.

Business Hours

The office working day is typically eight hours long, usually from 8am to noon and 2pm to 6pm weekdays, but in practice offices tend to open later and close earlier. Most tourist offices are closed on Saturday and Sunday, and travel agencies usually only work to noon on Saturday.

In this guide, specific opening hours are only listed if they differ markedly from the following:

» **Banks** 9am to 4pm Monday through Friday, 9am to noon on Saturday, with variation by cities and rural areas, where banks sometimes close during lunch.

» **Bars and Nightclubs** Bars usually open around 6pm until the law dictates they

close (often 3am); nightclubs are generally open Thursday through Saturday from 9pm until very late.

» **Post Offices** Postal hours vary widely. In Bogotá, many are open from 9am to 5pm from Monday to Friday, with some branches also open on Saturday morning, but on the Caribbean coast many companies close for lunch.

» **Shops** From 9am to 5pm Monday to Friday; some shops close for lunch. On Saturday most shops are open from 9am to noon, or sometimes until 5pm. Large stores and supermarkets usually stay open till 8pm or 9pm Monday to Friday; some also open Sunday.

» **Restaurants** Those opening for lunch open at noon. Restaurants serving breakfast open by 8am. Most of the better restaurants in larger cities, particularly in Bogotá, tend to stay open until 10pm or longer; restaurants in smaller towns often close by 9pm or earlier. Many don't open at all on Sunday. Most cafes are open from 8am until 10pm.

Customs Regulations

Colombian customs are looking for large sums of cash (inbound) and drugs (outbound). If they have the slightest suspicion you are carrying either you can expect an exhaustive search of your belongings and your person. Expect to be questioned in Spanish or English

SLEEPING PRICES

Price indicators for sleeping options in this book denote the cost of a standard double room before discounts.

PRICE INDICATOR	COP$
$	<65,000
$$	65,000–160,000
$$$	>160,000

by a well-trained police officer. The latest method is x-raying your intestines: if you look in any way out of the ordinary, or fail to give a convincing response to the officer's questions, they will x-ray you to see if you are a drug mule.

You can bring in personal belongings and presents you intend to give to Colombian residents. The quantity, kind and value of these items shouldn't arouse suspicion that they may have been imported for commercial purposes. You can bring in items for personal use such as cameras, camping equipment, sports accessories or laptops without any problems.

Be sure to hang onto your receipts for any big-ticket items. Foreigners may request a refund of the 16% IVA (sales tax) on all goods purchased with a foreign credit card above COP$176,000 during their stay in Colombia. Get to the airport with plenty of time to submit your receipts to DIAN (Dirección de Impuestos y Aduanas Nacionales; the customs bureau).

Electricity

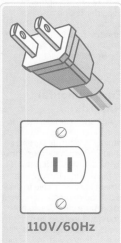

110V/60Hz

110V/60Hz

Embassies & Consulates

Most of the countries that maintain diplomatic relations with Colombia have their embassies and consulates in Bogotá. Some countries also have consulates in other Colombian cities.

Argentina (☑1 288 0900; Av 40A No 13-09, piso 16, Bogotá)

Australia (☑1 694 6320; www.chile.embassy.gov.au/scle castellano/home.html; Calle 69 No 7-51, Apt 302, Bogotá)

Brazil Bogotá (☑1 218 0800; www.bogota.itamaraty.gov. br; Calle 93 No 14-20, piso 8); Leticia (☑8 592 7530; Calle 9 No 9-73); Medellín (☑4 372 0022; Carrera 42 No 54A-155, Autopista Sur)

Canada (☑1 657 9914; www. colombia.gc.ca; Carrera 7 No 115-33, piso 14, Bogotá)

Ecuador Bogotá (☑1 317 5329; Calle 67 No 7-35, oficina 11-02, piso 11); Cali (☑2 661 2264; Edificio Torre de Cali, Calle 19N No 2N-29, oficina 23-02C); Ipiales (☑2 773 2292; Carrera 7 No 14-10); Medellín (☑4 250 8656; Calle 47 No 80-27)

France Bogotá (☑1 638 1400; www.ambafrance-co.org; Car-

rera 11 No 93-12); Bucaramanga (☑7 645 9393; Calle 42 No 37-19)

Germany (☑1 423 2600; www.bogota.diplo.de; Carrera 69 No 25B-44, piso 7, Bogotá)

Israel (☑1 327 7500; www. bogota.mfa.gov.il; Calle 35 No 7-25, piso 14, Bogotá)

Italy (☑1 218 7206; www. ambbogota.esteri.it; Calle 93B No 9-92, Bogotá)

Japan (☑1 317 5001; www. colombia.emb-japan.go.jp; Carrera 7 No 71-21, torre B, piso 11, Bogotá)

Netherlands (☑1 638 4200; www.colombia.nlambassade. org; Carrera 13 No 93-40, oficina 201, Bogotá)

Panama Barranquilla (☑5 360 1870; Carrera 57 No 72-25, Edificio Fincar 207-208); Bogotá (☑1 257 5067; www. empacol.org; Calle 92 No 7A-40); Cali (☑2 486 1116; Av 6 No 25-58); Cartagena (☑5 655 1055; Carrera 1 No 10-10, Bocagrande; ☉8am-noon Mon-Sat); Medellín (☑4 312 4590; Calle 10 No 42-45, oficina 266)

Peru Bogotá (☑1 257 0505; www.embajadadelperu.org. co; Calle 80A No 6-50); Leticia (☑8 592 7755, 8 592 7204; Calle 11 No 5-32)

Spain (☑1 628 3910, ext 340; www.maec.es/subwebs/con sulados/bogota; Calle 94A No 11A-70, Bogotá)

UK Bogotá (☑1 326 8300; www.ukincolombia.fco.gov.uk; Carrera 9 No 76-49, piso 9); Cali (☑2 661 7745; Calle 22N No 6-42, oficina 401).

USA (☑1 315 0811; http:// bogota.usembassy.gov; Calle 24 Bis No 48-50, Bogotá)

Venezuela Barranquilla (☑5 360 6285; Carrera 52 No 69-96; ☉8am-noon Mon-Fri); Bogotá (☑1 636 4011; www.em baven.org.co; Av 13 No 103-16); Cartagena (☑5 665 0382; Carrera 3 No 8-129, Edificio Centro Executivo, piso 14; ☉9-11:30am & 1:30-4pm Mon-Fri); Cúcuta (☑7 579 1954; Av Camilo Daza); Medellín (☑4 351 1614; www.consulvenemedellin.org; Calle 32B No 69-59)

Food

Colombia is not a safe haven for gourmands (how many Colombian restaurants do you normally see around the world?). But that doesn't mean you won't be eating well – Colombia offers high-standard, stomach-filling food at great prices.

Colombians are blessed with a fertile country: fish and plantain on the coast; an eye-popping array of tropical fruit; coffee, chocolate and dairy in the mountains; and cheap, fresh vegetables and meat on all corners. The collective cuisine is known as *comida criolla* (Creole food).

There are plenty of budget places serving meals for less than COP$15,000. Lunch is the easiest: known as *comida corriente* (literally 'fast food'), a two-course meal will consists of soup followed by rice, beans, choice of meat, a token salad, and a glass of tropical fruit juice. Midrange restaurants (COP$15,000 to COP$25,000) tend to be a step up in quality and service and top-end restaurants generally cost more than COP$25,000.

Don't miss uniquely Colombian specialties *ajiaco* (an Andean chicken stew with corn, many different types of potatoes, avocado, and a local herb known as *guasca*) and *bandeja paisa* (the '*paisa* platter'), a gut-busting mound of sausage, beans, rice, egg and *arepa* (corn cakes) – Colombia's de facto national dish despite controversy that its prevalence rarely strays from Antioquia.

In terms of fruit: *zapote, nispero, lulo, uchuwa, borojo, curuba, mamoncillo*. Confused? You will be. Don't try and translate these fruits – they're native to Colombia and you won't find them in many other places in the world.

Gay & Lesbian Travelers

Compared to some Latin American countries, homosexuality is well tolerated in Colombia (it was declared legal by the government in Bogotá in 1981). There is a substantial gay undercurrent in the major cities and as long as you don't broadcast the fact in public (holding hands, kissing etc) you are unlikely to be harassed.

In 2011 Colombia's Constitutional Court ordered Congress to legislate same-sex marriage; if they do not, the ruling dictates same-sex couples will automatically receive all marital rights by June 2013. A loophole not specifying gender in the de facto marriage law had been previously exploited by same-sex couples to register their civil unions with the government. Check the website www.guiagaycolombia. com for more information.

Health

Most visitors travel to Colombia without incident, but there are certain medical conditions to be aware of and several things you can

> **CAFE COUNTRY**
>
> Colombia is *mucho famoso* for coffee, but much of the good stuff is exported. The average everyday swill, called tinto, won't please connoisseurs (or anyone else). Stick to espresso where you can find it.

do to prevent sickness. Most illnesses are the result of Colombia's tropical-zone location. If traveling anywhere along the coast or jungle, you can bank on little tropical nuisances - infected bug bites, rashes or heat exhaustion. Other, more dangerous afflictions, including malaria and yellow fever, can strike travelers who get further off the beaten track or spend a lot of time trekking through national parks. Dengue fever is a risk in lowland population centers. Other problems can occur in the mountains, including *soroche* (altitude sickness). The good news is that Colombia has some of the best medical care in South America.

If you plan to travel in remote areas, you might consider taking a health guide such as Lonely Planet's *Healthy Travel Central & South America* or *Staying Healthy in Asia, Africa & Latin America* by Dirk Schroeder.

Environmental Hazards

» Altitude sickness may develop in travelers who ascend rapidly to altitudes greater than 2500m, including those flying directly to Bogotá.

» Tap water in Bogotá and other big cities is safe to drink, but if you're pregnant or want to be more careful, use bottled water instead. In remote areas, water should be boiled or disinfected with iodine pills; or stick to bottled water.

EATING PRICES

Price indicators for eating options in this book denote the range of the cost of main dishes for lunch and dinner.

PRICE INDICATOR	COP$
$	<15,000
$$	15,000–25,000
$$$	> 25,000

Health Care

Adequate medical care is available in major cities, but may be difficult to find in rural areas. For an online guide to physicians, dentists, hospitals and pharmacies in Colombia, go to the US embassy website at http://bogota.usembassy.gov/root/pdfs/medservices.pdf. If you develop a life-threatening medical problem, you'll probably want to be evacuated to a country with state-of-the-art medical care. For air ambulance service in Colombia, call **Aerosanidades** (☎1 266 2247; www.aerosanidadsas.com; Bogotá), which operates out of 13 airports in Colombia.

Infectious Diseases

» Dengue fever, a mosquito-born viral infection (transmitted by Aedes mosquitoes most commonly during the day and usually close to human habitations, often indoors) which is most often found in the departments of Santander, Tolima, Valle del Cauca, Norte de Santander, Meta and Huila.

» Malaria, also transmitted by mosquito bites, is prevalent in rural areas below 800m in Amazonas, Chocó, Córdoba, Guainía, Guaviare, Putumayo and Vichada.

» Yellow fever is a life-threatening viral infection transmitted by mosquitoes in forested areas, most notably Parque Nacional Natural (PNN) Tayrona and Ciudad Perdida. A yellow fever vaccine is required for visitors to the national parks along the coastal regions. Travelers limiting their visit to the main cities and mountainous regions may not need to be immunized for yellow fever, but be aware that some countries, such as Australia, will not let you into the country if you're flying direct from Colombia without a yellow-fever vaccine. Brazil requires the certificate if you have visited Colombia within 90 days of entering the country. Check your country's government health information for specifics.

Insurance

Ideally, all travelers should have a travel-insurance policy, which will provide some security in the case of a medical emergency, or the loss or theft of money or belongings. It may seem an expensive luxury, but if you can't afford a travel health insurance policy, you also probably can't afford medical emergency charges abroad if something goes wrong.

If need to make a claim on your travel insurance, you must produce a police report detailing loss or theft (see p301). You also need proof of the value of any items lost or stolen. Receipts are the best bet, so if you buy a camera for your trip, for example, hang on to the receipt.

Colombian law stipulates that hospitals must treat you, whether or not you can pay. If you don't have the Spanish to insist on this right, you may have difficulty getting treatment.

Worldwide travel insurance is available at www.lonelyplanet.com/travel_services. You can buy, extend and claim online anytime – even if you're already on the road.

Internet Access

Colombia is a wired country. Internet is everywhere and cheap – rarely more than COP$2000 per hour. In smaller towns and more remote destinations there may not be *banda ancha* (broadband), but rather dial-up or a satellite link. Most internet cafes are open long hours, from 7am to 10pm, but with more limited hours on the weekends. Most cafes provide a range of related services such as printing, scanning and faxing, and some offer cheap international calls.

Almost all hostels and hotels offer wi-fi. Shopping centers often have free wi-fi, major airports offer wi-fi, and so do many restaurants and cafes.

For internet resources, see p17. Where the internet icon (@) appears in reviews, it indicates desktop internet service is available; 🛜 indicates wi-fi.

Language Courses

Universities and language schools in the larger cities run Spanish-language courses. It is generally cheaper and better value to arrange a private one-on-one tutor. Popular backpacker hotels are the best places to ask about independent teachers. Enrolling in a university course is useful if you want to extend your stay beyond the six months a tourist visa permits you.

Legal Matters

If arrested you have the right to an attorney. If you don't have one, one will be appointed to you (and paid for by the government). There is a presumption of innocence and you can expect a speedy trial.

The most common situation that most travelers find themselves in involves drugs. It is illegal to buy, sell or consume drugs in any quantity. In 2009 a new law was passed, *El Artículo 49 de la Constitución,* stating that you cannot carry or consume any type of drugs without medical prescription. Although you will not face legal charges for carrying the old legal limits of marijuana (20g), hashish (5g) and cocaine (1g), you may face deportation for not complying with Colombian law. This law is currently under review and is subject to change.

Maps

It's difficult to find detailed maps of Colombia outside

the country itself. In the USA, **Maps.com** (☑800 430 7532; www.maps.com) has an excellent supply of Colombian maps. A similarly extensive selection is available in the UK from **Stanfords** (☑020 7836 0189; www.stanfords. co.uk).

Within Colombia, folded road maps of the country are produced by various publishers and are distributed through bookstores. Of special note is the Movistar *Guía de Rutas*, a Spanish-language guidebook to Colombia with excellent maps. You can buy it at any tollbooth (ask the bus driver beforehand to buy it for you), or from a handful of better bookstores.

The widest selection of maps of Colombia is produced and sold by the **Instituto Geográfico Agustín Codazzi** (IGAC; ☑1 368 3443; www.igac.gov.co; Carrera 30 No 48-51, Bogotá), the government mapping body, which has its head office in Bogotá and branch offices in departmental capitals.

Money

The Colombian peso (COP$) is the unit of currency in Colombia. For exchange rates at the time of publication, see p17.

ATMs

Almost all major banks have ATMs, and they usually work fine with cards issued outside Colombia (Bancolombia being the ornery exception). Cash machines affiliated with Banco de Bogotá, BBVA and ATH are best. Most banks have a maximum cash withdrawal limit of COP$300,000 per transaction, but it varies. Davivienda allows a maximum of COP$720,000 from most branches, but oftentimes it's denied with foreign cards or those without accounts there. If you need more, just pull out twice.

If you must use an ATM after dark, always use one inside a gas station.

Cash

There are paper notes of COP$1000, $2000, $5000, $10,000, $20,000 and $50,000. The coins you will use are primarily the $100, $200 and $500; the $20 and $50 are rarely seen outside of supermarkets, and some people may refuse to accept them. There used to be a $1000 coin but it was widely counterfeited and has been withdrawn from circulation; Colombians will refuse to accept $1000 coins, and you should do the same.

Credit Cards

Credit cards are common in Colombia and used extensively in the major cities and larger towns. When paying with a credit card, you will be asked, '¿a cuantas cuotas?' (how many payments?). Colombian customers can choose to divide the payment over one to 24 months. Foreign cardholders should just say 'one.'

The most useful card for cash advances is Visa, as it's accepted by most banks. MasterCard is honored by a few banks. Other cards are of limited use.

You can get advance payments on cards from the cashier in the bank or from the bank's ATM. In either case you'll need your PIN number.

International Transfers

If you need money sent to you quickly, **MoneyGram** (www.moneygram.com) and

---

ORIENTATION

Colombian cities, towns and villages have traditionally been laid out on a grid plan. The streets running north–south are called Carreras, often abbreviated on maps to Cra, Cr or K, whereas those running east–west are called Calles, often labeled on local maps as Cll, Cl or C. This simple pattern may be complicated by diagonal streets, called either Diagonales (more east–west and thus like Calles), or Transversales (more like Carreras).

All streets are numbered and the numerical system of addresses is used. Each address consists of a series of numbers, eg Calle 6 No 12-35 (which means that it's the building on Calle 6, 35m from the corner of Carrera 12 toward Carrera 13), or Carrera 11A No 7-17 (the house on Carrera 11A, 17m from the corner of Calle 7 toward Calle 8). Refer to the Orientation map for examples.

The system is very practical and you will soon become familiar with it. It is usually easy to find an address. It's actually one of the most precise address systems in the world; if you have an address you can determine the location of the place with pinpoint accuracy.

In the larger cities the main streets are called Avenidas or Autopistas. They each have their own names and numbers, but are commonly known just by their numbers.

Cartagena's old town is the only Colombian city where centuries-old street names have withstood the modern numbering system. Streets in some other cities (eg Medellín) have both names and numbers, but elsewhere only numbers are used.

Western Union (www.west ernunion.com) are your two principal options. Money-Gram is much cheaper, and is what most overseas Colombians use to send remittances home to their families.

Your sender pays the money, along with a fee, at their nearest MoneyGram or Western Union branch, and gives the details on who is to receive it and where. You can have the money within 15 minutes. When you pick it up, take along photo identification and the numbered password they'll give the sender.

Both services have offices in all the major cities and most smaller towns.

Moneychangers

You are better off using your ATM card in Colombia, as you will get a much better exchange rate. The US dollar is the only foreign currency worth trying to change in Colombia; expect dismal rates for euros, pounds sterling, Australian dollars etc.

Many but not all banks change money; in major cities and border regions there are usually several *casas de cambio* (currency exchanges). Avoid changing money on the street. Most

unofficial moneychangers are laundering drug money; the ones on the street have fast fingers and often dodgy calculators, making it highly unlikely you'll get a fair deal. Colombia produces more than 25% of the world's counterfeit US notes, which is yet another reason to avoid changing money on the street.

Your passport is required for any banking transaction. You'll also have to provide a thumbprint. There's a fair amount of paperwork involved in changing money (to prevent money laundering).

Tipping & Bargaining

A new government regulation dictates that in midrange and top-end restaurants (anywhere there is a service charge), your waiter must ask you if they can add the 10% service charge to the bill. In midrange restaurants it's acceptable to decline to pay the service charge with a polite '*sin servicio, por favor*' if you are dissatisfied. In top-end restaurants refusing the pay the service charge is likely to bring a manager to your table to inquire what was wrong with your meal.

Bargaining is limited to informal trade and services, such as markets and street stalls. In areas where taxis are not metered, especially the Caribbean coast, haggling is essential. If you don't like the price make a point of going to the next taxi in the queue.

Traveler's Checks

Traveler's checks are neither well known nor understood in Colombia. You're better off bringing your bank card and getting cash from the ATM. If you must travel with traveler's checks, make sure they are in US dollars, as you will get the best exchange rate. Do not bring checks in euros, pounds sterling etc. Banks in major cities change US dollar traveler's checks at rates 2% to 5% *higher* than the cash rate (though still not as good as just using your ATM card). Exchange rates vary from bank to bank, so shop around. Some banks charge a commission for changing checks.

Post

Colombia's official postal service is the spiffy new (though terribly named) **4-72** (www.4-72.com.co), which has turned the debilitating pension liabilities and inefficiency of Colombia's former government postal service, Adpostal (shut down in 2006), into a profitable and efficient business. There are also numerous private companies, including **Avianca** (www.aviancaexpress.com), **Deprisa** (www.deprisa.com) and **Servientrega** (www.servientrega.com).

If you want to receive a package in Colombia, you have a choice. The sender can ship via a courier like DHL, which guarantees fast, dependable delivery, but also guarantees Colombian customs will open the box and charge exorbitant duty. If you're not hurried, have

ORIENTATION
1 Calle 6 No 12-35   3 Diagonal 7 No 13-68
2 Carrera 11A No 7-17   4 Transversal 13 No 6-50

the package sent via regular airmail (four to eight weeks).

Identification is required to ship packages or letters from Colombia, so head to the post office with your passport.

Public Holidays

The following days are observed as public holidays in Colombia.

Año Nuevo (New Year's Day) January 1

Los Reyes Magos (Epiphany) January 6*

San José (St Joseph) March 19*

Jueves Santo & Viernes Santo (Maundy Thursday and Good Friday) March/April (Easter). The following Monday is also a holiday.

Día del Trabajo (Labor Day) May 1

La Ascensión del Señor (Ascension) May*

Corpus Cristi (Corpus Christi) May/June*

Sagrado Corazón de Jesús (Sacred Heart) June*

San Pedro y San Pablo (St Peter and St Paul) June 29*

Día de la Independencia (Independence Day) July 20

Batalla de Boyacá (Battle of Boyacá) August 7

La Asunción de Nuestra Señora (Assumption) August 15*

Día de la Raza (Discovery of America) October 12*

Todos los Santos (All Saints' Day) November 1*

Independencia de Cartagena (Independence of Cartagena) November 11*

Inmaculada Concepción (Immaculate Conception) December 8

Navidad (Christmas Day) December 25

* When the dates marked with an asterisk do not fall on a Monday, the holiday is moved to the following Monday to make a three-day long weekend, referred to as the *puente* (bridge).

In general, any holiday falling on a Tuesday (or Thursday) also turns the preceding Monday (or following Friday) into a holiday as well.

Solo Travelers

Travelers on their own are unlikely to have any problems traveling in Colombia. There are hostels in all major cities and many smaller locales, and you'll often find yourself traveling with other foreigners you meet en route.

If you are going to remote regions unfrequented by or unused to foreign visitors, or if you're concerned about security in general, traveling with a friend will certainly ease your mind, and may lessen the likelihood of street crime. See p300 for more information.

SHOP TILL YOU DROP

Colombia is famous for everything from fat emeralds to massive hammocks. Here's a shopping list:

» **Emeralds** Mined chiefly from the Muzo area, emeralds are sold in the flourishing emerald street market at the southwestern corner of Av Jiménez and Carrera 7 and nearby Plaza Rosario in Bogotá, where dozens of *negociantes* (traders) buy and sell stones – sometimes on the sidewalks. See p67.

» **Handicrafts** Boyacá is the country's largest handicraft manufacturer, with excellent handwoven items, basketry and pottery. The Pacific coast also has an interesting selection of basketwork, plus the occasional blow-dart gun. Guapi is famous for its musical instruments, especially handmade drums. You may also find some good handwrought gold jewelry here. If you don't make it to the Pacific coast, the Parque Artesanías (p226) in Cali is a good place to shop.

» **Woodwork** Pasto is known for its woodwork – decorative items covered with *barniz de Pasto*, a kind of vegetable resin. Ceramic miniatures of *chivas* (traditional buses) have become a popular souvenir.

» **Hammocks** These come in plenty of regional variations, from the simple, practical hammocks made in Los Llanos to the elaborate Way'uu-crafted *chinchorros*.

» **Ruanas** Colombian woolen ponchos, known as *ruanas*, are found in the colder parts of the Andean zone. In many villages they are still made by hand with simple patterns and natural colors. Bogotá and Villa de Leyva are good places to buy them.

» **Mochilas** The best and most fashionable *mochilas* (a kind of woven handbag) are those of the Arhuaco from the Sierra Nevada de Santa Marta. They are not cheap, but are beautiful and usually of good quality.

If you make any purchases above COP$176,000, use a foreign credit card and save your receipt. Foreigners can request the 16% sales tax back. See p304.

Telephone

The telephone system in Colombia is modern and works well for both domestic and international calls. Telecom is the national provider; ETB and Orbitel offer competing services. Public telephones exist in cities and large towns, but they are few and far between, and many are out of order. For directory assistance or information call ☑113.

Email cafes almost always have a few *cabinas* (telephone booths) where you can make local calls for around a few hundred pesos a minute. Most generally offer a fax service as well.

Cell Phones

Colombians love their cell phones, and in urban areas almost everyone has at least one. The three major providers are Movistar, Comcel and Tigo. Comcel has the best nationwide coverage, and is the most useful to the traveler. Cell phones are cheap, and many travelers end up purchasing one – a basic, no-frills handset will set you back around COP$45,000 to COP$50,000, or you could bring your own cell phone from home and buy a Colombian SIM card. A Comcel SIM card costs around COP$11,600, which includes COP$5000 worth of prepaid calling minutes, though SIM costs vary by provider. Because it is expensive to call between networks you could, at least in theory, buy a SIM card for each of the three providers and swap them out to change networks.

Colombian cell-phone companies do not charge you to receive calls, only to make them. Street vendors selling *minutos* (minutes) are seen almost everywhere. Many corner stores also have cell phones you can use. These vendors purchase prepaid minutes in bulk, and it is always cheaper to make calls with them than to use credit on your own handset. For this reason many Colombians use their handsets to receive calls only and use street vendors when they need to make calls.

Vendors generally have at least three cell phones – one for each network. The first three digits of the 10-digit number indicate the cell- phone provider, so state the prefix you're calling to and they'll give you the right phone. Expect to pay between COP$200 and COP$400 per minute for a call, depending on the network and provider.

To purchase a phone you'll need to show identification. This is supposedly for security but in fact it's to prevent the street vendors from purchasing phones in bulk and competing with the cell-phone provider's own call centers. There have been cases of identity theft (they will photocopy your documents) so only purchase a cell phone from a provider's official retail outlet.

Phone Codes

It is possible to call direct to just about anywhere in Colombia, but to call a cell phone from a landline, you will need to dial a prefix of 03 before the number (some landlines are blocked from calling cell phones); conversely, to dial a landline from a cell phone, you'll need to prefix the number with 03 + city code. Landline phone numbers are seven digits countrywide, while cell-phone numbers are 10 digits. Area codes are single digits, and you'll find them included immediately under the headings of the relevant destinations throughout this book.

All calls by default go through Telecom (☑09). However, you can specify Orbitel (☑05) or ETB (☑07) by dialing that prefix immediately before the number. There's no need to worry much about this unless you're in Colombia long enough to own and operate your own landline.

Colombia's country code is ☑57. If you are dialing a Colombian number from abroad, drop the prefix of the provider (05, 07 or 09) and dial only the area code and the local number.

Time

All of Colombia lies within the same time zone, five hours behind Greenwich Mean Time. There is no daylight-saving time.

Toilets

There are a handful of public toilets in Colombia. In their absence use a restaurant's toilet. Museums and large shopping malls usually have public toilets, as do bus and airport terminals.

You'll often (but not always) find toilet paper in toilets, so it's wise to carry some with you. Never flush toilet paper. The pipes are narrow and the water pressure is weak, so toilets can't cope with toilet paper. A wastebasket is normally provided.

The most common word for toilet is *baño*. Men's toilets will usually bear a label saying *señores, hombres* or *caballeros*, while the women's toilets will be marked *señoras, mujeres* or *damas*.

Bus-station restrooms will usually charge COP$500 to COP$800 plus COP$200 for toilet paper. If you're a guy wanting to do some stand-up business, ask a bus-company employee where the driver's urinal (*orinario*) is, usually outside along a back wall, which they will sometimes let you use for free.

Traveling with Children

Like most Latin Americans, Colombians adore children.

Due to a high rate of population growth, children make up a significant proportion of the population, and they are omnipresent. Few foreigners travel with children in Colombia, but if you do plan on taking along your offspring, they will find plenty of local companions.

Basic supplies are usually no problem in the cities. There are quite a few shops devoted to kids' clothes, shoes and toys; **Pepeganga** (www.pepeganga.com) in particular is recommended. You can also buy disposable diapers and baby food in supermarkets and pharmacies. Pick up a copy of Lonely Planet's *Traveling with Children* for general tips.

Visas

Nationals of some countries, including most of Western Europe, the Americas, Japan, Australia, New Zealand and South Africa, don't need a visa to enter Colombia; otherwise, the fee is between US$23 and US$50.

All visitors get an entry stamp in their passport upon arrival. Most travelers receive 60 days. It's worth asking for 90, but we only know of a handful of people who've had this granted. Double-check your stamp immediately; errors are sometimes made.

If traveling overland, make sure you get an entry stamp or you'll have troubles later. Overstaying your welcome can result in heavy fines, and in some cases can result in being barred entry in the future. Similarly, make sure you get your departure stamp or there will be trouble the next time around.

Visa Extensions

The former Colombian intelligence agency, DAS (Departamento Administrativo de Seguridad), which was also traditionally responsible for visa extensions, was dissolved in 2011 by President Juan Manuel Santos after years of allegations of corruption, abuse of power and interaction with guerrillas and paramilitaries. At the time of writing, visa extensions were being carried out as usual in former DAS offices by the **Ministerio de Relaciones Exteriores** (MRE; www.cancilleria.gov.co) until a more permanent solution was implemented, rendering the visa information in this edition particularly subject to change.

That said, visa extensions for tourists are doled out in 30-, 60- or 90-day increments up to a total of six months and at the discretion of the officer. To apply for an extension, known as a '*Prórroga de Permanencia*,' you'll be asked to submit your passport, two photocopies of your passport (picture page and arrival stamp) and two passport-sized photos, along with an air ticket out of the country in most cases. The fee of COP$72,350 must be deposited into the government bank account, which was Davivienda at the time of writing but often changes. Show up first to fill out forms, then they'll direct you to a nearby bank to pay the fee.

Expect the process to take an entire morning or afternoon. It can be done at any MRE office in Colombia, which are present in all the

main cities and some smaller towns. You'll usually (but not always) get the extension on the spot; sometimes they'll take your fingerprints, send them to Bogotá for a background check and tell you to come back in a week.

All other visas, including student, work and marriage visas, are processed exclusively in the **MRE** (Av 19 No 98-03, torre 100, Bogotá; ⊙7:30am-noon) office in Bogotá.

Volunteering

Volunteering is a practice that is still in its infancy in Colombia.

Globalteer (☏+44 117 230 9998; www.globalteer.org; 54 Woodchester, Yate, Bristol, BS37 8TX, UK) Offers 'voluntourism' positions of one to 12 weeks in Medellín working with street kids and orphans. Expect to pay around US$2145 for 12 weeks.

Fellowship of Reconciliation (☏1 512 542 1769; www.forusa.org; PO Box 72492, Oakland, CA 94612, USA) Employs volunteers for its two field teams in Bogotá and the Peace Community of San José de Apartadó in the northwestern Urabá region. The international team provides protective accompaniment for the leaders and residents of the Peace Community and supports Colombian conscientious objectors and others seeking to demilitarize life and land. Suitable applicants serve for 12 months and work on raising funds to support the project.

Let's Go Volunteer (☏321 235 0846; www.letsgovol unteer.info; Carrera 5 sur No 22-40, Ibague) A small, Colombian-based NGO that offers opportunities working with children, women, the environment and the elderly. Prices range from one week (US$250) to one month (US$500) to nine months (US$3500).

Women Travelers

Women traveling in Colombia are unlikely to encounter any problems.

The usual caveats apply: bring your street smarts, don't wander alone in dodgy neighborhoods after dark, and keep an eye on your drink. Female travelers are also more likely to be victims of a bag-snatching or mugging attempt, as you will be perceived as less likely to fight back. You should also be careful taking taxis alone after dark – while rare, there have been reports of taxi drivers raping single female passengers.

Dressing conservatively and/or wearing a cheap wedding band may reduce unwanted attention from local men.

Work

There is a growing demand for qualified English-language teachers in Colombia. Some schools may be willing to pay cash-in-hand for a short period of time, but for longer-term employment you will have to find a school willing to organize a work visa. As a general rule, the more popular the city is among travelers, the harder it will be to find employment; for example, Medellín is crammed with English teachers, while Cali is lacking. Don't expect to get rich teaching English: you're unlikely to make more than a few million pesos a month, and usually much less.

Transportation

GETTING THERE & AWAY

Entering the Country

Most travelers will arrive in Colombia by plane, or overland from Ecuador, Venezuela or Brazil. There are also numerous sailboats that bring travelers from Panama via the San Blas Islands.

You'll need a valid passport (with at least six more months of validity) and some nationalities will need a visa. Most travelers will get a 60-day tourist visa, which can be extended up to six months per calendar year. When arriving by plane (but not overland), you'll be given a customs form. You're supposed to keep this and return it at the time of your departure (or face a stiff fine), but no one we know has ever been asked for this form when they left the country. Keep it with your passport just in case, though.

For information on visas, see p312.

Flights and tours can be booked online at www.lonely planet.com/bookings.

Air

Airports & Airlines

Colombia's biggest international airport is Bogotá's **Aeropuerto Internacional El Dorado** (BOG; www.el nuevodorado.com), which will debut a slick renovated terminal by the end of 2014. See p70.

Other major airports servicing international flights:

Aeropuerto Internacional El Edén (AXM) In Armenia (p212).

Alfonso Bonilla Aragón Airport (Aeropuerto Palmaseca; CLO; www.aerocali.com.co) In Cali (p227).

Ernesto Cortissoz airport (BAQ; www.baq.aero) In Barranquilla (p139).

Gustavo Rojas Pinilla International Airport (ADZ; Aeropuerto Internacional Sesquicentenario) In San Andrés (p176).

Aeropuerto Internacional José María Córdoba (MDE) In Medellín (p195).

Matecaña International Airport (PEI) In Pereira (p209).

Aeropuerto Internacional Rafael Núñez (CTG; www.sacsa.com.co) In Cartagena (p132).

Tickets

Colombia requires, technically at least, that visitors have an onward ticket before they're allowed into the country. Airlines and travel agents quite strictly enforce this, and no one will sell you a one-way ticket unless you already have an onward ticket. Upon arrival in Colombia, however, hardly any immigration officials will ask you to present your onward ticket.

The trick is to buy a fully refundable ticket with your credit card and request a refund upon arrival in Colombia. If arriving overland, a printout of an unpaid reservation may also be sufficient to get past the border guards. Scruffy-looking travelers are more likely to be asked to show an onward ticket than those who are neatly attired.

Onward Travel within South America

Airline tickets in South America are expensive. If you are traveling to Ecuador, Venezuela or Brazil, you will find it cheaper to fly domestically

---

THINGS CHANGE...

The information in this chapter is particularly vulnerable to change. Check directly with the airline or a travel agent to make sure you understand how a fare (and ticket you may buy) works and be aware of the security requirements for international travel. Shop carefully. The details given in this chapter should be regarded as pointers and are not a substitute for your own careful, up-to-date research.

to the land border (Ipiales, Cúcuta or Leticia, respectively), cross the land border and take another domestic flight to your final destination.

That said, there are plenty of intercontinental flights out of Bogotá, plus a few out of Cali and Medellín. You can fly Bogotá–Quito (from US$250) and Cali–Quito (from US$300), for example. Plenty of flights also connect Bogotá and Caracas (US$500).

Further afield, a flight to Santiago, Chile, will set you back around US$700, and to Buenos Aires US$800. Expect to pay around US$1100 for São Paulo or Rio de Janeiro in Brazil.

Border Crossings

Colombia borders Panama, Venezuela, Brazil, Peru and Ecuador, but has road connections with Venezuela and Ecuador only. These are the easiest and the most popular border crossings.

You can also cross the border to Peru and Brazil at the three corners near Leticia, and there is boat service to and from Panama and Ecuador.

Brazil & Peru

The only viable border crossing from these two countries into Colombia is via Leticia in the far southeastern corner of the Colombian Amazon. Leticia is reached from Iquitos (Peru) and Manaus (Brazil) by riverboat. See p268 and p269 for details.

Ecuador

Virtually all travelers use the Carretera Panamericana border crossing through Tulcán (Ecuador) and Ipiales (Colombia). See p247 for information. Parts of the Panamericana (particularly the section between Pasto and Popayán) continue to be plagued by late-night bandits; you're advised to travel this leg only during the daytime.

It is theoretically possible to cross the border via cargo boat along the Pacific coast

INTERNATIONAL AIRLINES

The following is a selection of the most popular international airlines serving Colombia. Charter airlines also fly package tourists into Cartagena and San Andrés.

AIRLINE	WEBSITE	TO/FROM
Aerogal	www.aerogal.com.ec	Bogotá/Quito (Ecuador)
Aerolíneas Argentinas	www.aerolineas.com.ar	Bogotá/Sydney (Australia) & Auckland (New Zealand) via Buenos Aires (Argentina)
Air Canada	www.aircanada.com	Bogotá/Toronto (Canada)
Air France/ KLM	www.airfrance.com	Bogotá/Paris (France)
American Airlines	www.aa.com	Bogotá/Miami (US); Cali/ Miami; Medellín/Miami & Tampa (US)
Avianca/ Aviancataca	www.avianca.com	Bogotá, Cali & Medellín/ North America, Central America, South America; & Cuba
British Airways	www.britishairways.com	Bogotá/London (UK)
Copa	www.copaair.com	Bogotá/Panama City (Panama)
Conviasa	www.conviasa.aero	Bogotá/Caracas (Venezuela)
Cubana de Aviación	www.cubana.cu	Bogotá/Havana (Cuba)
Delta	www.delta.com	Bogotá/Atlanta, Chicago & New York/New Jersey (US)
Iberia	www.iberia.com	Bogotá/Barcelona & Madrid (Spain)
Jet Blue	www.jetblue.com	Bogotá/Fort Lauderdale & Orlando (US)
Lan	www.lan.com	Bogotá/Miami (US) & Santiago (Chile); Cali/ Lima (Peru) & Quito (Ecuador); Medellín/Lima & Quito
Lufthansa	www.lufthansa.com	Bogotá/Frankfurt (Germany)
Spirit Air	www.spiritair.com	Armenia, Bogotá, Cali & Medellín/Fort Lauderdale (US)
Tam	www.tam.com.br	Bogotá/São Paulo (Brazil)

DEPARTURE TAX

The international departure tax for a stay in Colombia for 60 days or less is US$34, which is often included in your airline ticket price. For stays longer than 60 days, the tax jumps to $68. Payment is accepted in both dollars and pesos.

near Tumaco, but this crossing in this manner was considered too dangerous for travelers at time of research.

More iffy than off limits, there is also a crossing at Putomayo (p239) that backpackers have begun to safely use, but check the situation on the ground with your hotel before proceeding as this area fluctuates often between acceptable and sketchy.

Panama

Sailboats operate between Colón in Panama and Cartagena in Colombia; see p132. This is a popular form of intercontinental travel, and generally passes through (and stops in) the beautiful San Blas Islands along the way. You can also take small coastal boats from Sapzurro (see p166) across the border to Puerto Olbadia, Panama, from where you can fly to Panama City, and beyond.

It is also possible to arrange transportation from Bahía Solano to Jaqué in Panama (see p252). From here you can continue along Panama's Pacific coast to Panama City or fly.

Venezuela

There are four border crossings between Colombia and Venezuela. By far the most popular with travelers (and probably the safest) is the route via San Antonio del Táchira (Venezuela) and Cúcuta (Colombia), on the main Caracas–Bogotá road. See p114 for details.

There is another reasonably popular border crossing at Paraguachón, on the Maracaibo (Venezuela) to Maicao (Colombia) road. Take this if you plan to head from

Venezuela straight to Colombia's Caribbean coast. Buses and shared taxis run between Maracaibo and Maicao, and direct buses between Caracas/Maracaibo and Santa Marta/Cartagena. Both Colombian and Venezuelan officials at the border will stamp your passport. See p145 and p132 for details.

Not so popular is the crossing from Colombia's Puerto Carreño and either Puerto Páez or Puerto Ayacucho (both in Venezuela). Still less useful is the crossing from El Amparo de Apure (Venezuela) to Arauca (Colombia), a guerrilla-ridden region.

Tours

Some overland South American companies do visit Colombia, but not many. They are often constrained by their insurance coverage, which is void in any area deemed unsafe by the overly cautious US State Department or UK Foreign Office. You might try:
Dragoman (www.dragoman.co.uk)
Exodus Travels (www.exodus.co.uk)
Intrepid Travel (www.intrepidtravel.com)
Last Frontiers (www.lastfrontiers.co.uk)
Wild Frontiers (www.wildfrontiers.co.uk)

GETTING AROUND

Air

Prices are often fixed between the airlines, but it can be worthwhile checking out

their websites just in case. Ticket prices to some destinations drop the last week or two before the date; for some other destinations, they may rise significantly.

You can reserve and pay for domestic flights online with a foreign credit card, but fares often increase, with Avianca, at least, once the price is converted to US$ (you cannot pay in pesos with a foreign credit card). It is often better to reserve online and pay at an Avianca office.

Some airlines offer packages to major tourist destinations (for example, Cartagena and San Andrés), which can cost not much more than you'd pay for air tickets only. If purchasing these package deals from overseas you are exempt from the 10% IVA (sales tax) – be sure to ask for this discount, as many Colombians are unaware of it.

Airlines in Colombia

Colombia has more than half a dozen main passenger airlines and another dozen smaller carriers. Charter airlines also compete on some of the more popular routes. As flight time is usually not much longer than an hour, don't expect any gastronomic treats; on most flights you get no more than a snack. The following fly a variety of routes:
ADA (☎2 444 4232; www.ada-aero.com) This Medellín-based carrier offers regional flights.
Aexpa (☎1 800 011 6288; www.aexpa.com.co) Offers charter services to the Pacific coast.
Avianca (☎1 401 3434; www.avianca.com) Longtime principal domestic airline (in partnership with Taca, often referred to as Aviancataca), with the widest network of both domestic and international routes.
Copa/Aerorepública (☎1 320 9090; www.copaair.com) The second-biggest airline covers much the same domestic territory as Avianca.

EasyFly (☑1 414 8111; www.easyfly.com.co) A budget carrier offering regional flights.

Lan (☑1 800 094 9490; www.lan.com) Lan purchased Colombia's main budget carrier, Aires, and now flies to smaller regional localities in addition to department capitals.

Satena (☑1 800 091 2034; www.satena.com) This is the commercial carrier of the FAC (Colombian Air Force) and services flights to the vast areas of the Amazon,

Los Llanos and the Pacific coast; it lands at 50 small towns and villages that would be otherwise virtually inaccessible.

Bicycle

Colombia is not the easiest of countries for cyclists. Road rules favor drivers and you'll end up fighting traffic on main roadways. Never assume that a driver will give you right of way. On the plus side, most roads are paved

and security is improving. Even the smallest towns will have a repair shop and you can get your bike fixed cheaply and easily. Bike rentals are uncommon but you can buy a bike almost anywhere. However, if you want something really reliable, bring your own bike and all your own kit.

It is also worth noting that cities are becoming more bike-friendly, with new bike tracks and Ciclovia (the weekend closure of selected streets to cars and buses,

Main Domestic Flights

COOL COLOMBIA TRIPS

A number of domestic agencies offer interesting specialty tours nationwide. For a comprehensive listing of tour operators in Colombia, see the Latin American Travel Association's website at www.lata.org. Favorites include the following:

Aventure Colombia Bogotá (☑1 702 7069; www.aventurecolombia.com; Av Jimenez No 4-49, oficina 204); Cartagena (☑314 588 2378; Calle del Santíssimo No 8-55) Excellent French-owned agency offering high adventure from Punta Gallinas to El Cocuy to Caño Cristales.

Colombia 57 (☑6 886 8050; www.colombia57.com) This British-owned, Manizales-based tour operator specializes in custom-tailored tours.

Colombian Journeys (☑1 618 0027; www.colombianjourneys.com; Calle 81 No 11-68, oficina 208, Bogotá) Bogotá-based company offering multilingual tours countrywide.

De Una Tours (☑1 368 1915; www.deunacolombia.com; Carrera 26A No 40-18 Ap 202, La Soledad, Bogotá) This Dutch-owned company focuses on many far-flung destinations.

Ecoguías (☑347 5736; www.ecoguias.com) A long-standing British-owned adventure travel company, Ecoguías focuses on ecotourism trips to various regions of the country, such as Ciudad Perdida, the Zona Cafetera and the Pacific coast.

Mambe Travel (☑1 629 8880; www.mambe.org; Carrera 5 No 117-25, Bogotá) Bogotá-based sustainable tourism that digs deeper into six off-the-beaten-track destinations: the Amazon, the Chocó, La Guajira peninsula, Golfo de Uraba, Sierra Nevada de Santa Marta and Vichada.

---

making them tracks for bikers and skaters instead).

Some bike shops and hostels rent bikes.

Boat

Cargo boats ply the Pacific coast, with the port of Buenaventura as their hub. Travelers with sufficient time can get a bunk bed for the journey northbound to the Chocó or southbound to Guapi, the main jumping-off point for Isla Gorgona.

Before railroads and highways were built, river transportation was the principal means of transportation in mountainous Colombia. The only safe river journey you're likely to take is on the Amazon from Leticia, upriver to Iquitos, Peru or downriver to Manaus, Brazil; see p269 for details.

The Río Atrato and Río San Juan in the Chocó should both be avoided due to guerrilla activity in the region.

Bus

Buses are the principal means of intercity travel, and go just about everywhere. Most long-distance intercity buses are more comfortable than your average coach-class airplane seat, and the overnight buses sometimes have business class–sized seats. A word of warning: Colombian bus drivers turn the air-con down to arctic temperatures. Wear a sweater, a beanie, and gloves, or better yet, bring a blanket. Bus drivers also tend to crank up the music and/or action movie (dubbed in Spanish) on the bus's television, even in the middle of the night. You may like to travel with earplugs.

It is common for buses to stop at *requisas* (military checkpoints), even in the middle of the night. The soldiers manning the checkpoint will ask everyone to get off the bus, check everyone's identification, and then pat you down. They may look through your bags or, more rarely, do a strip search.

Long-distance buses stop for meals, but not necessarily at mealtimes; it depends on when the driver is hungry or when the bus gets to a restaurant that has an arrangement with the bus company. Buses are locked during the stops, and everyone must get off, even in the middle of the night.

All intercity buses depart from and arrive at a *terminal de pasajeros* (passenger terminal). Every city has such a terminal, usually outside the city center, but always linked to it by local transportation. Bogotá is the most important bus transportation hub in Colombia, handling buses to just about every area of the country.

The highway speed limit in Colombia is 80km per hour, and bus companies are obliged to put a large speedometer at the front of the cabin, so passengers can see how fast the bus is going (although in practice they are often broken or disabled). Bus company offices are also obliged by law to post their accident/fatality statistics at the ticket counter, which can give you a good idea of their safety record.

Classes

Most intercity buses are air-conditioned and have good

legroom. On shorter routes (less than four hours), smaller *busetas* ply their trade. There are sometimes also vans, which cost more but are faster. In remote country areas, where the roads are bad, ancient *chivas* (many former US school buses) service smaller towns, picking up and dropping off passengers along the way.

Costs

Bus travel is reasonably cheap in Colombia. Depending on who you ask, bus prices can be negotiable outside of peak holiday times. Try your luck with a polite, '*hay discuento?*' (Is there a discount?), then work your way down the counters, indicating what the previously quoted fare was. You want to take the second-to-cheapest offer; there's usually something wrong with the cheapest bus.

When you get on a bus out on the road, you pay the fare to the *ayudante* (driver's sidekick) and rarely get a ticket. *Ayudantes* have been known to charge gringos more than the actual fare or at least to round the price up. Ask other passengers beforehand to be sure of the correct fare.

Reservations

Outside of peak holiday periods (like Christmas and Easter), reservations are not needed. Just rock up to the bus station an hour before you want to leave and grab the first bus going. On some minor routes, where there are only a few departures a day, it's worth considering buying your ticket several hours before the scheduled departure.

A common trick, especially with smaller buses, is to say they only need one passenger to leave, then they lock your bag in the back and you end up waiting an hour for the bus to leave, watching other buses leave before you do. Don't get into the bus or pay until you see the driver

start the engine and prepare to leave.

Car & Motorcycle

Considering how cheap and extensive bus transportation is in Colombia, there is little reason to bring your own vehicle. What's more, the security situation remains dodgy in remote and rural parts of the country, substantially increasing the risk of vehicle theft and/or assault in isolated parts of the country. Check government websites for warnings before setting out anywhere remote.

In the cities, on the other hand, traffic is heavy, chaotic and mad. Driving 'manners' are wild and unpredictable. It takes some time to get used to the local style of driving, but even if you master it, the risk of an accident remains high. This goes without saying for motorcycle travel as well.

Colombians drive on the right-hand side of the road and there are seat-belt requirements, so buckle up or risk a fine. The speed limit is 60km per hour in the city and 80km per hour on the highway. The nationwide highway police telephone number is ✆767.

If you do plan to drive in Colombia, bring your driver's license. The driver's license from your country will normally do, but if you want to be 100% sure, bring along an International Driving Permit as well.

Bring Your Own Vehicle

There's no way of bringing your vehicle to South America other than by sea or air, involving time, substantial cost and a lot of paperwork. You'll spend less (and be safer) traveling in Colombia by bus.

Rental

Several international rental car companies, such as **Avis** (www.aviscolombia.com) and

Hertz (www.hertzcolombia.com.co) are two reliable companies operating in Colombia. But why bother? Taxis are a cheap, stress-free way to get around the cities, and intercity bus transportation is frequent, cheap and comfortable. Expect to pay around COP$140,000 to COP$170,000 per day, plus gasoline. You'll get better deals, as always, by booking online. Carefully check clauses pertaining to insurance and liability before you sign a rental contract. Pay close attention to any theft clause as it may load a large percentage of any loss onto the hirer.

Hitchhiking

Hitchhiking in Colombia is uncommon and difficult. Given the complex internal situation, drivers don't want to take risks and simply don't stop on the road. As intercity buses are fast, efficient and relatively cheap, it's not worth wasting time on hitching and taking a potentially serious risk.

Local Transportation

Bus

Almost every urban centre of more than 100,000 inhabitants has a bus service, as do many smaller towns. The standard, speed and efficiency of local buses vary from place to place, but on the whole they are slow and crowded. City buses have a flat fare, so the distance of the ride makes no difference. You get on by the front door and pay the driver or his assistant. You never get a ticket.

In some cities or on some streets there are bus stops (*paraderos* or *paradas*), while in most others you just wave down the bus. To let the driver know that you intend to get off you simply say, or shout, '*por aquí, por favor*' (here, please), '*en la esquina, por favor'* (at the corner, please) or *'el paradero, por favor'* (at the coming bus stop, please).

There are lots of different types of local buses, ranging from old wrecks to modern air-conditioned vehicles. One common type is the *buseta* (small bus), a dominant means of urban transportation in cities such as Bogotá and Cartagena. The bus fare is somewhere between COP$600 and COP$1500, depending on the city and type of bus.

A bus or *buseta* trip, particularly in large cities such as Bogotá or Barranquilla, is not a smooth and silent ride but rather a sort of breathtaking adventure with a taste of local folklore thrown in. You'll have an opportunity to be saturated with loud tropical music, learn about the Colombian meaning of road rules, and observe your driver desperately trying to make his way through an ocean of vehicles.

Colectivo

Colectivo in Colombia can mean a midsized bus, a shared taxi, an overloaded jeep, and everything in between. They are most popular in short intercity hops of less than four hours. Because they are smaller than regular buses, they can travel quicker, and charge around 30% more as a result. They often depart only when full.

In some cities they depart from and arrive at the bus terminal, but in smaller towns they are usually found in the main square. The frequency of service varies largely from place to place. At some places there may be a *colectivo* every five minutes, but elsewhere you can wait an hour or longer until the necessary number of passengers has been collected. If you're in a hurry you can pay for all the seats and the driver will depart immediately.

Mass Transit

Mass transit is growing increasingly popular in Colombia. Bogotá boasts the TransMilenio, and Cali and Bucaramanga have similar projects, called the Mio and Metrolínea, respectively. Medellín has its famous Metro, the only commuter rail line in the country. Pereira, too, offers the MegaBús system, another electric bus line.

Motorcycles

Some cities, especially in the north, use motorcycle-taxis, which are a quick way of getting around if you're on your own. These, however, are not the safest method of transportation and are even illegal in some places, including Cartagena (though no one seems to stop them). There may be options of renting a motorcycle, especially in resort-type areas such as San Andrés (p170).

Helmet laws are enforced.

Taxi

Taxis are cheap, convenient and ubiquitous in the major cities and most midsized towns. In the interior of the country all taxis have meters; on the Caribbean coast, it's haggle or pay extra, and many drivers are eager (especially in Cartagena) to see just how much they can take advantage of your naïveté. That said, a surprising proportion of taxi drivers are honest individuals; the better you speak Spanish, the more bargaining power you'll have, and the less likely you'll be to pay hyperinflated prices.

BUSSING ABOUT, CHIVA-STYLE

The *chiva* is a Disneyland-style vehicle that was Colombia's principal means of road transportation several decades ago. Also called *bus de escalera* (which roughly translated means 'bus of stairs,' referring to the stairs along the side) in some regions, the *chiva* is a piece of popular art on wheels. The body is made almost entirely of wood and has wooden benches rather than seats, with each bench accessible from the outside. The body of the bus is painted with colorful decorative patterns, each different, with a main painting on the back. There are homebred artists who specialize in painting *chivas*. Ceramic miniatures of *chivas* are found in just about every Colombian handicraft shop.

Today, *chivas* have almost disappeared from main roads, but they still play an important role on back roads between small towns and villages. There are still a few thousand of them and they are most common in Antioquia, Huila, Nariño and on the Caribbean coast. *Chivas* take both passengers and any kind of cargo, animals included. If the interior is already completely packed, the roof is used for everything and everybody that doesn't fit inside. *Chivas* usually gather around markets, from where they depart for their journeys along bumpy roads. They are rare guests at bus terminals.

Night city tours in *chivas* are organized by travel agents in most large cities and have become a popular form of entertainment. There is normally a band on board playing local music, and a large stock of aguardiente (anise-flavored liquor) to create the proper atmosphere. The tour usually includes some popular nightspots and can be great fun.

There are occasionally deceptive, untrustworthy individuals masquerading in fake taxis. This is rare, but if you are concerned, it is always safer to call for a taxi, which costs a mere few hundred pesos extra. Major bus terminals also offer predictive fares – indicate your destination at the counter and show the printed slip to the driver, who is obliged to charge you no more than whatever the computer spits out. Taxi fares are always per taxi, never per number of passengers. Many taxis have somewhat flimsy doors – be kind, do not slam doors when getting into or out of the vehicle.

Don't use taxis with a driver and somebody else inside. While taxi drivers sometimes have a friend along for company or for security reasons, such a situation may be unsafe for you; this is a common robbery tactic.

A taxi may also be chartered for longer distances. This is convenient if you want to visit places near major cities that are outside local transportation areas but too near to be covered by long-distance bus networks. You can also rent a taxi by the hour in the major cities – a good way to make your own impromptu tour. Expect to pay around COP$25,000 per hour for this service.

Tricycle Moto-Taxi

Chinese-made *tuk-tuks* are becoming increasingly popular in smaller tourist towns. Moto-taxis seat three and have a covered roof, plus a tarp that can be lowered around the sides in case of rain. You'll see these in Santa Fe de Antioquia, the Desierto de la Tatacoa and many of the small towns on the Pacific coast.

Train

Colombia has a nationwide network of train track that is largely unused. The Tren Turístico Café y Azucar (coffee and sugar tourist train) out of Cali now offers occasional excursions into the mountains, and can also serve as infrequent transportation between La Tebaida, near Armenia, and Cali, and also El Cumbre, on the road to Buenaventura, and Cali.

Those visiting San Cipriano, just off the Cali–Buenaventura highway, can enjoy the novel sensation of traveling on a railroad handcart (trolley) powered by a motorcycle.

Language

WANT MORE?
For in-depth language information and handy phrases, check out Lonely Planet's *Latin American Spanish Phrasebook*. You'll find it at **shop.lonelyplanet.com**, or you can buy Lonely Planet's iPhone phrasebooks at the Apple App Store.

Latin American Spanish pronunciation is easy, as most sounds have equivalents in English. Also, Spanish spelling is phonetically consistent, meaning that there's a clear and consistent relationship between what you see in writing and how it's pronounced. Read our coloured pronunciation guides as if they were English, and you'll be understood. Note that kh is a throaty sound (like the 'ch' in the Scottish *loch*), v and b are like a soft English 'v' (between a 'v' and a 'b'), and r is strongly rolled.

There are some variations in spoken Spanish across Latin America, the most notable being the pronunciation of the letters *ll* and *y* – depending on where you are on the continent, you'll hear them pronounced like the 'y' in 'yes', the 'lli' in 'million', the 's' in 'measure' or the 'sh' in 'shut', and in Colombia you'll also hear them pronounced like the 'dg' in 'judge'. In our pronunciation guides they are represented with y because you're most likely to hear them pronounced like the 'y' in 'yes'.

The stressed syllables are indicated with an acute accent in written Spanish (eg *días*) and with italics in our pronunciation guides.

The polite form is used in this chapter; where both polite and informal options are given, they are indicated by the abbreviations 'pol' and 'inf'. Where necessary, both masculine and feminine forms of words are included, separated by a slash and with the masculine form first, eg *perdido/a* (m/f).

BASICS

Hello.	*Hola.*	o·la
Goodbye.	*Adiós.*	a·*dyos*
How are you?	*¿Qué tal?*	ke tal
Fine, thanks.	*Bien, gracias.*	byen *gra*·syas

Excuse me.	*Perdón.*	per·*don*
Sorry.	*Lo siento.*	lo *syen*·to
Please.	*Por favor.*	por fa·*vor*
Thank you.	*Gracias.*	*gra*·syas
You're welcome.	*De nada.*	de *na*·da
Yes.	*Sí.*	see
No.	*No.*	no

My name is ...
Me llamo ...   me *ya*·mo ...

What's your name?
¿Cómo se llama Usted?   *ko*·mo se *ya*·ma oo·*ste* (pol)
¿Cómo te llamas?   *ko*·mo te *ya*·mas (inf)

Do you speak English?
¿Habla inglés?   *a*·bla een·*gles* (pol)
¿Hablas inglés?   *a*·blas een·*gles* (inf)

I don't understand.
Yo no entiendo.   yo no en·*tyen*·do

ACCOMMODATIONS

I'd like a ... room.	*Quisiera una habitación ...*	kee·*sye*·ra oo·na a·bee·ta·*syon* ...
single	*individual*	een·dee·vee·*dwal*
double	*doble*	*do*·ble

How much is it per night/person?
¿Cuánto cuesta por noche/persona?   *kwan*·to *kwes*·ta por *no*·che/per·*so*·na

Does it include breakfast?
¿Incluye el desayuno?   een·*kloo*·ye el de·sa·*yoo*·no

KEY PATTERNS

To get by in Spanish, mix and match these simple patterns with words of your choice:

When's (the next flight)?
¿Cuándo sale *kwan*-do sa-le
(el próximo vuelo)? (el *prok*-see-mo vwe-lo)

Where's (the station)?
¿Dónde está *don*-de es-ta
(la estación)? (la es-ta-*syon*)

Where can I (buy a ticket)?
¿Dónde puedo *don*-de pwe-do
(comprar un billete)? (kom-*prar* oon bee-ye-te)

Do you have (a map)?
¿Tiene (un mapa)? *tye*-ne (oon *ma*-pa)

Is there (a toilet)?
¿Hay (servicios)? ai (ser-*vee*-syos)

I'd like (a coffee).
Quisiera (un café). kee-*sye*-ra (oon ka-*fe*)

I'd like (to hire a car).
Quisiera (alquilar kee-*sye*-ra (al-kee-*lar*
un coche). oon *ko*-che)

Can I (enter)?
¿Se puede (entrar)? se pwe-de (en-*trar*)

Could you please (help me)?
¿Puede (ayudarme), pwe-de (a-yoo-*dar*-me)
por favor? por fa-*vor*

campsite	terreno de cámping	te-*re*-no de *kam*-peeng
cabin	cabaña	ka-*ba*-nya
hotel	hotel	o-*tel*
guesthouse	pensión	pen-*syon*
lodging/hostel	hospedaje	os-pe-*da*-khe
shelter	refugio	re-*foo*-khyo
youth hostel	albergue juvenil	al-*ber*-ge khoo-ve-*neel*
air-con	aire acondicionado	*ai*-re a-kon-dee-syo-*na*-do
bathroom	baño	*ba*-nyo
bed	cama	*ka*-ma
window	ventana	ven-*ta*-na

DIRECTIONS

Where's ...?
¿Dónde está ...? *don*-de es-ta ...

What's the address?
¿Cuál es la dirección? kwal es la dee-rek-*syon*

Could you please write it down?
¿Puede escribirlo, pwe-de es-kree-*beer*-lo
por favor? por fa-*vor*

Can you show me (on the map)?
¿Me lo puede indicar me lo *pwe*-de een-dee-*kar*
(en el mapa)? (en el *ma*-pa)

at the corner	en la esquina	en la es-*kee*-na
at the traffic lights	en el semáforo	en el se-*ma*-fo-ro
behind ...	detrás de ...	de-*tras* de ...
far	lejos	*le*-khos
in front of ...	enfrente de ...	en-*fren*-te de ...
left	izquierda	ees-*kyer*-da
near	cerca	*ser*-ka
next to ...	al lado de ...	al *la*-do de ...
opposite ...	frente a ...	*fren*-te a ...
right	derecha	de-*re*-cha
straight ahead	todo recto	*to*-do *rek*-to

EATING & DRINKING

Can I see the menu, please?
¿Puedo ver el menú, pwe-do ver el me-*noo*
por favor? por fa-*vor*

What would you recommend?
¿Qué recomienda? ke re-ko-*myen*-da

Do you have vegetarian food?
¿Tienen comida *tye*-nen ko-*mee*-da
vegetariana? ve-khe-ta-*rya*-na

I don't eat (red meat).
No como (carne roja). no *ko*-mo (*kar*-ne *ro*-kha)

That was delicious!
¡Estaba buenísimo! es-*ta*-ba bwe-*nee*-see-mo

Cheers!
¡Salud! sa-*loo*

The bill, please.
La cuenta, por favor. la *kwen*-ta por fa-*vor*

I'd like a table for ...	Quisiera una mesa para ...	kee-*sye*-ra oo-na *me*-sa *pa*-ra ...
(eight) o'clock	las (ocho)	las (*o*-cho)
(two) people	(dos) personas	(dos) per-*so*-nas

Key Words

appetisers	aperitivos	a-pe-ree-*tee*-vos
bottle	botella	bo-*te*-ya
bowl	bol	bol
breakfast	desayuno	de-sa-*yoo*-no
children's menu	menú infantil	me-*noo* een-fan-*teel*
(too) cold	(muy) frío	(mooy) *free*-o
dinner	cena	*se*-na
food	comida	ko-*mee*-da

fork	tenedor	te·ne·dor
glass	vaso	va·so
highchair	trona	tro·na
hot (warm)	caliente	kal·yen·te
knife	cuchillo	koo·chee·yo
lunch	almuerzo	al·mwer·so
main course	plato principal	pla·to preen·see·pal
plate	plato	pla·to
restaurant	restaurante	res·tow·ran·te
spoon	cuchara	koo·cha·ra
with	con	kon
without	sin	seen

Meat & Fish

beef	carne de vaca	kar·ne de va·ka
chicken	pollo	po·yo
duck	pato	pa·to
fish	pescado	pes·ka·do
lamb	cordero	kor·de·ro
pork	cerdo	ser·do
turkey	pavo	pa·vo
veal	ternera	ter·ne·ra

Fruit & Vegetables

apple	manzana	man·sa·na
apricot	damasco	da·mas·ko
artichoke	alcaucil	al·kow·seel
asparagus	espárragos	es·pa·ra·gos
banana	banana	ba·na·na
beans	chauchas	chow·chas
beetroot	remolacha	re·mo·la·cha
cabbage	repollo	re·po·yo
carrot	zanahoria	sa·na·o·rya
celery	apio	a·pyo
cherry	cereza	se·re·sa

Signs

Abierto	Open
Cerrado	Closed
Entrada	Entrance
Hombres/Varones	Men
Mujeres/Damas	Women
Prohibido	Prohibited
Salida	Exit
Servicios/Baños	Toilets

corn	choclo	cho·klo
cucumber	pepino	pe·pee·no
fruit	fruta	froo·ta
grape	uvas	oo·vas
lemon	limón	lee·mon
lentils	lentejas	len·te·khas
lettuce	lechuga	le·choo·ga
mushroom	champiñón	cham·pee·nyon
nuts	nueces	nwe·ses
onion	cebolla	se·bo·ya
orange	naranja	na·ran·kha
peach	melocotón	me·lo·ko·ton
peas	arvejas	ar·ve·khas
(red/green) pepper	pimiento (rojo/verde)	pee·myen·to (ro·kho/ver·de)
pineapple	ananá	a·na·na
plum	ciruela	seer·we·la
potato	papa	pa·pa
pumpkin	zapallo	sa·pa·yo
spinach	espinacas	es·pee·na·kas
strawberry	frutilla	froo·tee·ya
tomato	tomate	to·ma·te
vegetable	verdura	ver·doo·ra
watermelon	sandía	san·dee·a

Other

bread	pan	pan
butter	manteca	man·te·ka
cheese	queso	ke·so
egg	huevo	we·vo
honey	miel	myel
jam	mermelada	mer·me·la·da
oil	aceite	a·sey·te
pasta	pasta	pas·ta
pepper	pimienta	pee·myen·ta
rice	arroz	a·ros
salt	sal	sal
sugar	azúcar	a·soo·kar
vinegar	vinagre	vee·na·gre

Drinks

beer	cerveza	ser·ve·sa
coffee	café	ka·fe
(orange) juice	jugo (de naranja)	khoo·go (de na·ran·kha)
milk	leche	le·che
tea	té	te

| (mineral) water | agua (mineral) | a·gwa (mee·ne·ral) |
| (red/white) wine | vino (tinto/ blanco) | vee·no (teen·to/ blan·ko) |

EMERGENCIES

| Help! | ¡Socorro! | so·ko·ro |
| Go away! | ¡Vete! | ve·te |

Call ...!	¡Llame a ...!	ya·me a ...
a doctor	un médico	oon me·dee·ko
the police	la policía	la po·lee·see·a

I'm lost.
Estoy perdido/a. es·toy per·dee·do/a (m/f)

I'm ill.
Estoy enfermo/a. es·toy en·fer·mo/a (m/f)

It hurts here.
Me duele aquí. me dwe·le a·kee

I'm allergic to (antibiotics).
Soy alérgico/a a soy a·ler·khee·ko/a a
(los antibióticos). (los an·tee·byo·tee·kos) (m/f)

Where are the toilets?
¿Dónde están los don·de es·tan los
baños? ba·nyos

SHOPPING & SERVICES

I'd like to buy ...
Quisiera comprar ... kee·sye·ra kom·prar ...

I'm just looking.
Sólo estoy mirando. so·lo es·toy mee·ran·do

Can I look at it?
¿Puedo verlo? pwe·do ver·lo

I don't like it.
No me gusta. no me goos·ta

How much is it?
¿Cuánto cuesta? kwan·to kwes·ta

That's too expensive.
Es muy caro. es mooy ka·ro

Can you lower the price?
¿Podría bajar un po·dree·a ba·khar oon
poco el precio? po·ko el pre·syo

There's a mistake in the bill.
Hay un error ai oon e·ror
en la cuenta. en la kwen·ta

Question Words		
How?	¿Cómo?	ko·mo
What?	¿Qué?	ke
When?	¿Cuándo?	kwan·do
Where?	¿Dónde?	don·de
Who?	¿Quién?	kyen
Why?	¿Por qué?	por ke

ATM	cajero automático	ka·khe·ro ow·to·ma·tee·ko
credit card	tarjeta de crédito	tar·khe·ta de kre·dee·to
internet cafe	cibercafé	see·ber·ka·fe
market	mercado	mer·ka·do
post office	correos	ko·re·os
tourist office	oficina de turismo	o·fee·see·na de too·rees·mo

TIME & DATES

| What time is it? | ¿Qué hora es? | ke o·ra es |
| It's (10) o'clock. | Son (las diez). | son (las dyes) |

morning	mañana	ma·nya·na
afternoon	tarde	tar·de
evening	noche	no·che
yesterday	ayer	a·yer
today	hoy	oy
tomorrow	mañana	ma·nya·na

Monday	lunes	loo·nes
Tuesday	martes	mar·tes
Wednesday	miércoles	myer·ko·les
Thursday	jueves	khwe·ves
Friday	viernes	vyer·nes
Saturday	sábado	sa·ba·do
Sunday	domingo	do·meen·go

January	enero	e·ne·ro
February	febrero	fe·bre·ro
March	marzo	mar·so
April	abril	a·breel
May	mayo	ma·yo
June	junio	khoon·yo
July	julio	khool·yo
August	agosto	a·gos·to
September	septiembre	sep·tyem·bre
October	octubre	ok·too·bre
November	noviembre	no·vyem·bre
December	diciembre	dee·syem·bre

TRANSPORTATION

boat	barco	bar·ko
bus	autobús	ow·to·boos
(small) bus/van	buseta	boo·se·ta
(traditional) bus	chiva	chee·va
plane	avión	a·vyon
(shared) taxi	colectivo	ko·lek·tee·vo
train	tren	tren

LANGUAGE TRANSPORTATION

first	*primero*	pree·*me*·ro
last	*último*	*ool*·tee·mo
next	*próximo*	*prok*·see·mo
A ... ticket, please.	*Un boleto de ..., por favor.*	oon bo·*le*·to de ... por fa·*vor*
1st-class	*primera clase*	pree·*me*·ra *kla*·se
2nd-class	*segunda clase*	se·*goon*·da *kla*·se
one-way	*ida*	*ee*·da
return	*ida y vuelta*	*ee*·da ee *vwel*·ta

I want to go to ...
Quisiera ir a ...   kee·*sye*·ra eer a ...

Does it stop at ...?
¿Para en ...?   *pa*·ra en ...

What stop is this?
¿Cuál es esta parada?   kwal es *es*·ta pa·*ra*·da

What time does it arrive/leave?
¿A qué hora llega/ sale?   a ke o·ra ye·ga/ *sa*·le

Please tell me when we get to ...
¿Puede avisarme cuando lleguemos a ...?   pwe·de a·vee·*sar*·me *kwan*·do ye·*ge*·mos a ...

I want to get off here.
Quiero bajarme aquí.   kye·ro ba·*khar*·me a·*kee*

airport	*aeropuerto*	a·e·ro·*pwer*·to
aisle seat	*asiento de pasillo*	a·*syen*·to de pa·*see*·yo
bus station	*terminal terrestre*	ter·mee·*nal*/ te·*res*·tre
bus stop	*paradero/ parada*	pa·ra·*de*·ro/ pa·*ra*·da
cancelled	*cancelado*	kan·se·*la*·do
delayed	*retrasado*	re·tra·*sa*·do
platform	*plataforma*	pla·ta·*for*·ma
ticket office	*taquilla*	ta·*kee*·ya
timetable	*horario*	o·*ra*·ryo
train station	*estación de trenes*	es·ta·*syon* de *tre*·nes
window seat	*asiento junto a la ventana*	a·*syen*·to *khoon*·to a la ven·*ta*·na

I'd like to hire a ...	*Quisiera alquilar ...*	kee·*sye*·ra al·kee·*lar* ...
4WD	*un todo-terreno*	oon to·do·te·*re*·no
bicycle	*una bicicleta*	*oo*·na bee·see·*kle*·ta
car	*un coche*	oon *ko*·che
motorcycle	*una moto*	*oo*·na *mo*·to

Numbers

1	*uno*	*oo*·no
2	*dos*	dos
3	*tres*	tres
4	*cuatro*	*kwa*·tro
5	*cinco*	*seen*·ko
6	*seis*	seys
7	*siete*	*sye*·te
8	*ocho*	*o*·cho
9	*nueve*	*nwe*·ve
10	*diez*	dyes
20	*veinte*	*veyn*·te
30	*treinta*	*treyn*·ta
40	*cuarenta*	kwa·*ren*·ta
50	*cincuenta*	seen·*kwen*·ta
60	*sesenta*	se·*sen*·ta
70	*setenta*	se·*ten*·ta
80	*ochenta*	o·*chen*·ta
90	*noventa*	no·*ven*·ta
100	*cien*	syen
1000	*mil*	meel

child seat	*asiento de seguridad para niños*	a·*syen*·to de se·goo·ree·*da* pa·ra nee·nyos
diesel	*petróleo*	pet·*ro*·le·o
helmet	*casco*	*kas*·ko
hitchhike	*hacer botella*	a·*ser* bo·*te*·ya
mechanic	*mecánico*	me·*ka*·nee·ko
petrol/gas	*gasolina*	ga·so·*lee*·na
service station	*gasolinera*	ga·so·lee·*ne*·ra
truck	*camion*	ka·*myon*

Is this the road to ...?
¿Se va a ... por esta carretera?   se va a ... por *es*·ta ka·re·*te*·ra

(How long) Can I park here?
¿(Cuánto tiempo) Puedo aparcar aquí?   (*kwan*·to tyem·po) pwe·do a·par·*kar* a·*kee*

The car has broken down (at ...).
El coche se ha averiado (en ...).   el *ko*·che se a a·ve·*rya*·do (en ...)

I had an accident.
He tenido un accidente.   e te·*nee*·do oon ak·see·*den*·te

I've run out of petrol.
Me he quedado sin gasolina.   me e ke·*da*·do seen ga·so·*lee*·na

I have a flat tyre.
Se me pincho une rueda.   se me peen·*cho* *oo*·na *rwe*·da

GLOSSARY

Spanish speakers wanting a complete reference to Colombian slang should pick up a copy of the *Diccionario de Colombiano Actual* (2005) by Francisco Celis Albán.

asadero – place serving roasted or grilled meats

AUC – Autodefensas Unidas de Colombia (United Self-Defense Forces of Colombia); a loose alliance of paramilitary squads known as *autodefensas*

autodefensas – right-wing squads created to defend large landowners against guerrillas, also called *paramilitares* or just *paras;* see also *AUC*

bogotano/a – person from Bogotá

buseta – small bus/van that is a popular means of city transport

cabaña – cabin, or simple shelter; usually found on beaches or up in the mountains

caleño/a – person from Cali

campesino/a – rural dweller, usually of modest economic means; peasant

casa de cambio – currency-exchange office

chalupa – small passenger boat powered by an outboard motor

chinchorro – hammock woven of cotton threads or palm fiber like a fishing net, typical of many indigenous groups; the best known are the decorative cotton hammocks of the Guajiros

chiva – traditional bus with its body made of timber and painted with colorful patterns; still widely used in the countryside

colectivo – shared taxi or minibus; a popular means of public transport

comida corriente – fast food; set lunch

costeño/a – inhabitant of the Caribbean coast

DAS – Departamento Administrativo de Seguridad; the security police, responsible for immigration (dissolved in 2011)

ELN – Ejército de Liberación Nacional (National Liberation Army); the second-largest guerrilla group after the FARC

FARC – Fuerzas Armadas Revolucionarias de Colombia; the largest guerrilla group in the country

finca – farm; anything from a country house with a small garden to a huge country estate

frailejón – *espeletia*, a species of plant; a yellow-flowering, perennial shrub that only grows at altitudes above 3000m, typical of the *páramo*

gringo/a – any white male/female foreigner; sometimes, (but not always) used in a derogatory sense

guadua – the largest variety of the bamboo family, common in many regions of moderate climate

hacienda – country estate

hospedaje – lodging (in general); sometimes, a cheap hotel or hostel

indígena – indigenous; also indigenous person

IVA – *impuesto de valor agregado*, a value-added tax (VAT)

merengue – musical rhythm originating in the Dominican Republic, today widespread throughout the Caribbean and beyond

meseta – plateau

mestizo/a – person of mixed European-indigenous blood

mirador – lookout, viewpoint

muelle – pier, wharf

mulato/a – mulatto; a person of mixed European-African blood

nevado – snowcapped mountain peak

paisa – a person from Antioquia

paradero – bus stop; in some areas called *parada*

páramo – high-mountain plains, at an elevation of between 3500m and 4500m, typical of Colombia, Venezuela and Ecuador

piso – story, floor

poporo – a vessel made from a small gourd, used by the Arhuacos and other indigenous groups to carry lime; while chewing coca leaves, *indígenas* add lime to help release the alkaloid from the leaves; a sacred ritual of the indigenous people of the Caribbean coast

puente – literally 'bridge'; also means a three-day-long weekend (including Monday)

refugio – rustic shelter in a remote area, mostly in the mountains

reggaeton – a mix of hip-hop and Latin rhythms, it has a distinctly urban flavor with fast-paced danceable beats

salsa – type of Caribbean dance music of Cuban origin, very popular in Colombia

salsateca – disco playing salsa music

Semana Santa – Holy Week, the week before Easter Sunday

tagua – hard ivory-colored nut of a species of palm; used in handicrafts, mainly on the Pacific coast

tejo – traditional game, popular mainly in the Andean region; played with a heavy metal disk, which is thrown to make a *mecha* (a sort of petard) explode

Telecom – the state telephone company

vallenato – music typical of the Caribbean region, based on the accordion; it's now widespread in Colombia

behind the scenes

SEND US YOUR FEEDBACK

We love to hear from travelers – your comments keep us on our toes and help make our books better. Our well-traveled team reads every word on what you loved or loathed about this book. Although we cannot reply individually to postal submissions, we always guarantee that your feedback goes straight to the appropriate authors, in time for the next edition. Each person who sends us information is thanked in the next edition – the most useful submissions are rewarded with a selection of digital PDF chapters.

Visit **lonelyplanet.com/contact** to submit your updates and suggestions or to ask for help. Our award-winning website also features inspirational travel stories, news and discussions.

Note: We may edit, reproduce and incorporate your comments in Lonely Planet products such as guidebooks, websites and digital products, so let us know if you don't want your comments reproduced or your name acknowledged. For a copy of our privacy policy visit lonelyplanet.com/privacy.

OUR READERS

Many thanks to the travelers who used the last edition and wrote to us with helpful hints, useful advice and interesting anecdotes:

A Talia Aguayo, Florian Albrecht, Brian Andrews, Pascal Andrey, Anna Asplund **B** Ethan Baron, Ruth Bath, Sina Bauer, Huib Beets, Montserrat Beorlegui, Jana Bergfeld, Carly Bishop, Roxanne Bowman **C** Juan Camilo De Los Rios, Colleen Carroll, Adriana Cepeda, Justin Cohen, Sarah Cohen **D** Edward Davey, Anthony De Lannoy, Jonas De Jong, Tom De Bock, Luis Diaz, Maynard Dodson, Graeme Duke **E** Alan Ereira, Sebastián Espinar **F** June Fujimoto **G** Benedetta Galasso, David Garland, Emily Gipple, Ed Given, Matthew Gnagey, Uli Greiner, Eric Groenen, Monica Groeneveld, Thomas Groß, Danie Grunberg, Francoise Guernier **H** Barry Hamiltoni, Liz Harwood, Brent Helmkamp, Vicky Henriksen-Delaney, Dominic Herr, James Hsu **J** Ariel Jacob, Lloyd Jones, William Joyce, Dimitri Junker **K** Jan Kaper, Kevin Keller, Alexander Klein, Greg Kondrak, David Kramer, Emile Kruger, Justin Kruger **L** Sébastien Lévêque, Belinda Lopez **M** Dominic Maher, Masa Marolt Pecjak, Meryl Marr, Laura Martorell Guaita, Marnie McGregor, Patrick Mathews, Thomas Mayes, Michaelangelo Mazzeo, Ana Milena Moreno, Dan Morris, Jacques Moeschler **N** Nik Nelberg, Noella Nincevic, Dr Adam Norten **O** Annica Ohling, Ted Olander, Karl Olson, Michel Orlhac, Juan Osorio **P** Ulrike Peter, Mary-Louise Phillips, Piotr Piechocki, Rafael Pizarro, Nova Pleman, Johan Poels, Corinne Poulsen **R** Helene Raynaud, Helge Reemtsma, Daniel Richter, Marion Rochegude, Guillermo E Rodriguez-Navarro, Paola Rubio, Michal Rudziecki **S** Diego Salgado, Per Samuelson, Chris Sawka, Ines Schihab, Annett Schlenker, Jonathan Schwartz, Sabrina Schwarz, Rose Shapiro, Paulo Silva, Martin Skjöldebrand, Jennifer Slupianek, Warwick Sprawson, Aznar Sylvie **T** Alysanne Taylor, Rick Tjeerds, Chantal Travers, Andrew Tzembelicos **V** Lotte Van Ekert, Matt Van Der Peet, Arnaud Verstraete **W** David Wang, Gerd Wiss **Y** Farah Yamin, Tany Yao **Z** Eric S Zhou.

AUTHOR THANKS

Kevin Raub

Special thanks to Adriana Schmidt Raub, who wasn't a big fan of my requiring a 'kidnapping briefing' for this gig. Ximena Renjifo, Maria Claudia Renjifo and Laura Cahnspeyer all helped beyond anything resembling reasonable. On the road: Carolina Delgado, Mathieu Perrot-Bohringer, Germán Escobar, Tony Lloyd, Lina María López, Andy Farrington, Alina Cardenas, Oscar Gilede, Mike Ceaser, Laura Jaramillo, Rodrigo Arias, Shaun Clohesy, Mike Anderson, Kat Hiby, Felipe Andrés Velasco, Juan Ananda, Johana de la Selva, Axel Antoine-Feill and Rafael Clavijo.

Alex Egerton

Thanks to everyone at Lonely Planet, especially to Kathleen, Bruce, Alison, Mike and Señor Raub for answering the emails so rapidly. On the ground in Colombia big shouts go out to Laura Cahnspeyer, Carolina Libertad, Urs, Tony and Kim, Jose Ivan, Melissa Montoya, A Ximena Garcia, Ingrid Ruiz, Lina Marcela, Oscar y Carito, Andrea, Dahyana Vargas, Olga Lucia Mosquera and all the wonderful Colombians who contributed along the way. Also thanks to KC and Blue Energy and Nicholas Kazu.

Mike Power

Thanks to everyone at Lonely Planet, especially Kathleen, Alex and Kevin for the support and insights. Colombian crew: Johan for the beers and late-night chats; The One And Only Fredy

Builes, Germán Escobar, Thibaud Perdrix, Miguel at Provincia, Federico Lavagna, Marcela Manrique, José Gallego and his magical motorbike, Tim Buendía and his pregnant cat; and in the UK, Sasha Carolyn Dunn for the sparkling conversations, and for making me laugh, and for being there every time I needed you.

ACKNOWLEDGMENTS

Climate map data adapted from Peel MC, Finlayson BL & McMahon TA (2007) 'Updated World Map of the Köppen-Geiger Climate Classification', *Hydrology and Earth System Sciences*, 11, 163344.

Cover photograph: The beach at Cabo San Juan de la Guía, Parque Nacional Natural (PNN) Tayrona. Jane Sweeney/Lonely Planet Images. Many of the images in this guide are available for licensing from Lonely Planet Images: www.lonelyplanetimages.com.

BEHIND THE SCENES

THIS BOOK

This 6th edition of Lonely Planet's *Colombia* guidebook was researched and written by Kevin Raub, Alex Egerton and Mike Power. The 5th edition was researched and written by Jens Porup, Kevin Raub, Robert Reid and César Soriano. The 4th edition was researched and written by Michael Kohn and Robert Landon. This guidebook was commissioned in Lonely Planet's Oakland office, and produced by the following:

Commissioning Editor Kathleen Munnelly

Coordinating Editors Luna Soo, Gina Tsarouhas
Coordinating Cartographer Andrew Smith
Coordinating Layout Designer Sandra Helou
Managing Editors Annelies Mertens, Angela Tinson
Managing Cartographer Alison Lyall
Managing Layout Designer Chris Girdler
Assisting Editors Beth Hall, Evan Jones, Shawn Low, Kristin Odijk, Charlotte Orr

Assisting Cartographer Sophie Reed
Assisting Layout Designer Wibowo Rusli
Cover Research Naomi Parker
Internal Image Research Nicholas Colicchia
Language Content Branislava Vladisavljevic

Thanks to Brigitte Ellemor, Bruce Evans, Ryan Evans, Yvonne Kirk, Trent Paton, Gerard Walker

NOTES

index

INDEX P-T

000 Map pages
000 Photo pages

how to use this book

These symbols will help you find the listings you want:

👁 Sights   👉 Tours   🍷 Drinking

🐚 Beaches   🎎 Festivals & Events   ⭐ Entertainment

🏃 Activities   🛏 Sleeping   🔒 Shopping

🤿 Courses   🍴 Eating   ℹ Information/Transport

These symbols give you the vital information for each listing:

- ☎ Telephone Numbers
- ⊙ Opening Hours
- Ⓟ Parking
- ⊝ Nonsmoking
- ❄ Air-Conditioning
- @ Internet Access
- 📶 Wi-Fi Access
- 🏊 Swimming Pool
- 🥗 Vegetarian Selection
- 📖 English-Language Menu
- 👪 Family-Friendly
- 🐾 Pet-Friendly
- 🚍 Bus
- ⛴ Ferry
- Ⓜ Metro
- Ⓢ Subway
- 🚊 Tram
- 🚆 Train

Reviews are organised by author preference.

Look out for these icons:

TOP CHOICE Our author's recommendation

FREE No payment required

🌿 A green or sustainable option

Our authors have nominated these places as demonstrating a strong commitment to sustainability – for example by supporting local communities and producers, operating in an environmentally friendly way, or supporting conservation projects.

Map Legend

Sights
- 🏖 Beach
- Buddhist
- Castle
- Christian
- Hindu
- Islamic
- Jewish
- Monument
- Museum/Gallery
- Ruin
- Winery/Vineyard
- Zoo
- Other Sight

Activities, Courses & Tours
- Diving/Snorkelling
- Canoeing/Kayaking
- Skiing
- Surfing
- Swimming/Pool
- Walking
- Windsurfing
- Other Activity/Course/Tour

Sleeping
- Sleeping
- Camping

Eating
- Eating

Drinking
- Drinking
- Cafe

Entertainment
- Entertainment

Shopping
- Shopping

Information
- Post Office
- Tourist Information

Transport
- Airport
- Border Crossing
- Bus
- Cable Car/Funicular
- Cycling
- Ferry
- Metro
- Monorail
- Parking
- S-Bahn
- Taxi
- Train/Railway
- Tram
- Tube Station
- U-Bahn
- Other Transport

Routes
- Tollway
- Freeway
- Primary
- Secondary
- Tertiary
- Lane
- Unsealed Road
- Plaza/Mall
- Steps
- Tunnel
- Pedestrian Overpass
- Walking Tour
- Walking Tour Detour
- Path

Boundaries
- International
- State/Province
- Disputed
- Regional/Suburb
- Marine Park
- Cliff
- Wall

Population
- Capital (National)
- Capital (State/Province)
- City/Large Town
- Town/Village

Geographic
- Hut/Shelter
- Lighthouse
- Lookout
- Mountain/Volcano
- Oasis
- Park
- Pass
- Picnic Area
- Waterfall

Hydrography
- River/Creek
- Intermittent River
- Swamp/Mangrove
- Reef
- Canal
- Water
- Dry/Salt/Intermittent Lake
- Glacier

Areas
- Beach/Desert
- Cemetery (Christian)
- Cemetery (Other)
- Park/Forest
- Sportsground
- Sight (Building)
- Top Sight (Building)

OUR STORY

A beat-up old car, a few dollars in the pocket and a sense of adventure. In 1972 that's all Tony and Maureen Wheeler needed for the trip of a lifetime – across Europe and Asia overland to Australia. It took several months, and at the end – broke but inspired – they sat at their kitchen table writing and stapling together their first travel guide, *Across Asia on the Cheap*. Within a week they'd sold 1500 copies. Lonely Planet was born.

Today, Lonely Planet has offices in Melbourne, London and Oakland, with more than 600 staff and writers. We share Tony's belief that 'a great guidebook should do three things: inform, educate and amuse'.

OUR WRITERS

Kevin Raub

Coordinating Author; Bogotá; Boyacá, Santander & Norte de Santander; Amazon Basin Kevin Raub started his career as a music journalist in New York, working for *Men's Journal* and *Rolling Stone* magazines. The rock 'n' roll lifestyle took its toll, so he took up travel writing while ditching the States for Brazil. While researching Colombia, he forced down ants with *filet mignon*, experienced the most frightening plane ride of his life in an aged 1940s-era DC-3, was nearly assaulted in the Amazon by an opossum and was detained by the Policía Nacional for over an hour at the Israeli embassy – and still loves the place! This is Kevin's 18th Lonely Planet guide. You can find him at www.kevinraub.net.

Read more about Kevin at:
lonelyplanet.com/members/kraub

Alex Egerton

Medellín & Zona Cafetera; Pacific Coast; Cali & Southwest Colombia A journalist by trade, Alex has been coming to Colombia for 15 years, since discovering the beauty of the country while on a mad six-week dash from Venezuela to Mexico. During that time he has learned to love *aguardiente*, climbed several of the country's majestic peaks and become a big fan of *tejo*, but still can't dance salsa. While researching this book, Alex learned to pull wheelies in classic WWII jeeps from one of the best drivers in the Zona Cafetera – something he is now trying to reproduce on the streets in front of his house in rural Nicaragua.

Mike Power

Caribbean Coast; San Andrés & Providencia; Colombia Today; History; Life in Colombia; The Arts; The Natural World Mike, a freelance journalist, has been coming to Colombia repeatedly since 2007, when he lived in Cartagena writing features on Colombia's coca industry and the civil conflict. Before that, he made his Latin bones on an overland trip from Guatemala to Panama City. He then worked as a freelance correspondent for Reuters in Panama, which resulted in atrociously accented Spanish. On this trip, Mike scrambled up the Sierra Nevada de Santa Marta to the Lost City, and wished he could spend a year in the ghostly deserts of La Guajira.

Published by Lonely Planet Publications Pty Ltd
ABN 36 005 607 983
6th edition – August 2012
ISBN 978 1 74179 798 5
© Lonely Planet 2012   Photographs © as indicated 2012
10 9 8 7 6 5 4
Printed in China

Bestselling guide to Colombia – source: Nielsen BookScan, Australia, UK and USA, May 2011 to April 2012